PRAISE FOR *ALL UNDER HEAVEN*

'JEANNE-MARIE GESCHER IS ONE OF THE most respected of the foreign advisors on China. Her argument that history, geography and human nature are essential to understanding the country and its future is one that any China expert would wholeheartedly endorse.'

Peter Batey, OBE, co-founder, European Chamber of Commerce in China, former chairman, Great Britain-China Centre and British Chamber of Commerce in China

'FOR THE FIRST TIME, A HISTORY of China that tells you why it thinks and acts the way it does. Jeanne-Marie Gescher has lived for 25 years in China with open eyes and an inquiring mind, and shows how its history, politics and culture are far more exciting and revealing than most of us steeped in its various clichés understand. China's image of itself and its relations with the outside world derive neither from mysterious aphorisms nor 60 years of eccentric communism, but from a rich and diverse history, including that of the last 100 years. It is a story which has been largely overlooked in the rush to preach to it or make money from it. In truth, you can achieve little in China today without some understanding of its extraordinary past.

Gescher's recommendations for the way forward should be read by everyone who cares about the fundamental questions raised by China's re-emergence as a global power.'

Richard Spencer, former China bureau chief, *Daily Telegraph*

'THERE ARE TWO BOOKS ON CHINA that are 'must reads' this year–
Hank Paulson's and Gescher's…All Under Heaven could not be more
different, but it is no less important … there's nothing quite like this
out there.'

Peter Wheeler, former Goldman Sachs partner
(and first Chief Representative in Beijing)

'IN 1997 I WROTE THAT THE future would be determined by the ability
of business and governments to perform against a triple bottom line of
people, planet and profit. Jeanne-Marie's powerful new book reminds
us that in China, with its vast population, people are pivotal. Their
future is ours. Required reading for all true business leaders.'

John Elkington, co-founder of SustainAbility, executive chairman
and co-founder of Volans, author of the best-selling
Cannibals with Forks, co-author (with Pamela Hartigan)
of The Power of Unreasonable People and (with Jochen Zeitz)
of The Breakthrough Challenge

'IF CHINA IS THE HEAVENLY EMPIRE, then Jeanne-Marie Gescher is an
enlightened prophet who transports us from an ancient splendour to
the tumultuous realities of China today, offering deep knowledge and
sparkling insights every step of the way.'

James L. McGregor, author of the best-selling One Billion
Customers: Lessons from the Front Lines of Doing Business in
China, former CEO of Dow Jones & Company in China and
Wall Street Journal Bureau Chief in China and Taiwan

'THIS IS A MAGISTERIAL BOOK: ABOUT China but also about what it is
to be human on a planet approaching 9 billion people. Jeanne-Marie
brings to her subject the gifts of empathy, integrity and knowledge,
which she so powerfully discusses. She also brings the energy and
enthusiasm which those of us privileged to have heard her speak,
know that she has for understanding China and the world.'

Professor David Grayson CBE, director,
Doughty Centre for Corporate Responsibility,
Cranfield University School of Management

'FAR TOO MUCH COMMENT ABOUT CHINA starts with the prior thesis that China is either saviour of the world economic system or a disaster waiting to happen. Far too many books assume that modern China's story begins with Deng Xiaoping in 1978 or perhaps as far back as liberation in 1949. In contrast, in *All Under Heaven*, Jeanne Marie Gescher has written a book which explores China through the stories Chinese people tell of themselves; looks at the key questions about China's future and its impact on the rest of us from the perspective of those people and thinks about China, as many Chinese themselves do, across the span of 5000 years not 50. The result is a profoundly optimistic book about China and one which talks about China in very different, very human terms. This book is critically important in helping business and political leaders think about China, its future and how it will affect us in technicolour not in the black and white we are used to.'

Sir Martin Davidson, formerly, Chief Executive,
The British Council

'*ALL UNDER HEAVEN* IS A TOUR de force that succeeds brilliantly in opening up this most complex of countries.'

Paul Fletcher, Chairman, Actis

'JEANNE MARIE GESCHER HAS WRITTEN AN extraordinary, lyrical and profoundly human book. *All Under Heaven* is immensely ambitious, yet hits its mark. Spanning history, nature and the big existential questions that bind humankind together, this is a book for anyone interested in understanding 'another' point of view. It is about China and more than China. Gescher's book contains powerful messages for leaders of all stripes. Above all it is an invitation to business leaders to embrace the opportunity to think differently about why and how we engage with China, a metaphor for the big global questions facing business today. How do we learn from other narratives? Why are we relevant, and what do we have to give as well as gain?

Insightful and provocative, *All Under Heaven* is a beautiful mix of compassion, wisdom and enquiry. It is essential reading for anyone venturing to build a global company.'

Lindsay Levin, founder, Leaders Quest

'FOR THIRTY YEARS, JEANNE-MARIE GESCHER HAS observed how societies change, above all the social and economic and political revolutions through which China has passed. Her experience of founding a business in China, helping identify risks unimaginable to even sophisticated investors, and helping cope with crisis confirms her credibility as an expert on today's China. But what makes this book remarkable is its extraordinary sweeping coverage of history – she puts today's China perfectly in historical context: what happened 1000 years ago is not at all remote from today's political event. This book based on decades of practical experience, supplemented by profound perceptions of China's history, is also a delight to read.'

Professor Ian S. Forrester, Q.C.

'JEANNE-MARIE PROVIDES FASCINATING AND WELL INFORMED insights into a Chinese view of the world. This is an important and stimulating book.'

Roderick Wye, Associate Fellow, Asia Programme, Chatham House

'FINALLY! A BOOK THAT LOOKS BENEATH the surface and weaves together all the hidden strands of belief and historical stories that create the visible but often incomprehensible China we see today. Jeanne-Marie Gescher has written a masterpiece like no other book on China. In the past 13 years of intensive and extensive visits to China, I have always turned to Jeanne-Marie to understand the China narrative – to fill in the gaps between what appears to be obvious to business on the surface, and the invisible connections between business, the larger political picture and society – current and past.

Jeanne-Marie's ability to go both deep into the Chinese psyche, and broad across time, sectors, diverse realities and perceptions, in an engaging story-telling style, makes this book a compelling read. At over 600 pages, it is not for the faint-hearted looking for a 'beginner's' guide'. But for those of us who want to understand better what it means to be Chinese, how China sees itself and the world and what are the invisible, unspoken strands that make up the Chinese DNA of today, it is essential reading. As important for business as for policy or even the arts, if you are truly serious about China, this is a must read.'

Fields Wicker-Miurin, OBE, FKC

'*ALL UNDER HEAVEN* IS A BIG and important book whose scale reflects the ambition and range of its author. Defying the conventions of mainstream publishing to span history, politics, culture, business, literature and philosophy, and written in an almost lyrical style, it's a work that is difficult to categorise. It is not surprising that Gescher, with twenty-five years of questioning Western models, has looked at the publishing industry and decided to create her own publisher, Kaduba House. A riveting read, *All Under Heaven* is a truly remarkable and ground-breaking achievement.'

Victoria Barnsley, former CEO and Publisher of
HarperCollins UK and International

THE AUTHOR

Jeanne-Marie Gescher has advised business and government on China for over a quarter of a century. She has lived in Beijing since 1989.

Jeanne-Marie has been honorary legal advisor to successive British ambassadors to the PRC since 1989; she is a twice-elected past chair of the British Chamber of Commerce in China. Throughout her time in China, Jeanne-Marie has also advised policy institutions on the social, human and environmental changes that have taken place and their implications, for China and the wider world.

Jeanne-Marie was born in Canada. She is a graduate of the universities of Durham and Aix-en-Provence, and a member of the Honourable Society of the Inner Temple. Prior to China, she worked as a legal advisor with the International Fund for Agricultural Development (IFAD), as a trade and competition lawyer in Brussels, and as a lecturer in law at the School of Oriental and African Studies (London University). In 2002, she was awarded an OBE for her China work.

ALL UNDER HEAVEN

CHINA'S DREAMS OF ORDER

Sarah & Nick

November 2015

ALL UNDER HEAVEN

CHINA'S DREAMS OF ORDER

JEANNE-MARIE GESCHER

First published in 2015 by
KADUBA HOUSE

www.kadubahouse.com

978-0-9930910-8-7 Hardback
978-0-9930910-9-4 Paperback
978-0-9932206-0-9 eBook
978-0-9932206-1-6 Audio

Design by Five-TwentyFive
Maps by Jamie Whyte

This book is dedicated to my father, John, my mother, Daphne, my sister, Lydia, and to everyone who has ever looked at the sky, and asked a question.

ACKNOWLEDGEMENTS

I am fortunate to have many friends, Chinese and not Chinese, who taught me with their questions, their answers and their stories. Far too numerous to mention, you know who you are, and this book exists because of you. I am also fortunate to have a Chinese 'family' without whom this book could not have been written.

I owe thanks to a number of people who helped me bring the book from the first rough pages to what you will read: Michelle Brown, who was with me through so much of the story, and then held up the sky and enabled me to write; Adam Williams, who read the very first draft and imagined what it could be; James Kynge, whose warning that writing the book would only be the beginning of the work kept me sane; Philip Chapnick, who became my trusted librarian; Helen Wing, whose humour kept everything in perspective and whose poetic wisdom was a rock; Lindsay Levin, whose sharp eye and deep humanity were much appreciated companions; Richard Spencer, who read every chapter and offered a journalist's eye and a philosopher's mind; David Kelly, Rod Wye and Jane Macartney, who read every chapter and applied lifetimes of China experience to their questions; Tristan Kenderdine and Jamie Whyte whose perspective helped me tell the story through the maps; Vicky Barnsley, whose early encouragement was followed with invaluable practical advice; Michael Carlisle, who trusted in the unknown and shared his experience without reservation; Hazel Orme, whose thoughtful edits tamed unruly text; John Bond and Tim Inman at whitefox, who brought the book to print.

I would also like to thank my sons, Theo and Caspar, who lost their mother to a laptop, my parents who lost their daughter to the same (and my father who read every draft with wonderful encouragement), my first husband, Valentin Gescher, who taught me never to give up, and my second husband, Sasi Kumar, who gave me the courage to let the book go.

Tianxi, all under heaven is the ancient Chinese idea that everything under heaven is in the charge of a single Son of Heaven. Out of that idea came another idea: that if the single son could master the understanding of what heaven wanted, then everything under heaven would be at peace. And out of that idea came a dream: the dream of a heavenly order on earth. But what was heaven – and *where* was it? Was heaven a single top-down mind that ordered everything across the four quarters of the earth? Or was it a reflection of the minds and experiences of all of the people who lived under the skies – including very different minds in very different places.

All Under Heaven: *China's Dreams of Order* is the story of the *tianxia* dream of a heavenly order on earth, and of how that dream became the state of China today. It is also the story of what happened when the dream of the state and the dreams of its people went their different ways. Of course, it is the story of China and the Chinese. But it is also the story of some of the biggest questions known to man: what is a state, who are its people, and how do they live together? It may not be our story, but it is a story for us all.

If you try to possess it, you will destroy it:
If you try to hold on to it – you will lose it.
(wei zhe bai zhi, zhi zhe shi zhi)

from the surviving scrolls of the *Dao de Jing* (500 BCE)
composed by Laozi from texts written across the
previous one thousand years

* * *

Only if one man rules all under heaven can all
under heaven uphold that one man.
(wei yi yiren zhi tianxia, qi wei tianxia feng yiren)

Emperor Yongzheng (1722 – 1735)
from a text hung in the Hall of Mental
Cultivation in the Forbidden City

CONTENTS

BOOK I
(From myth to 1911)

Part 1

A Heavenly Empire

(Myth to 206 BCE)

Part 2

Heaven's Heart

(202 BCE – 1644)

Part 3

Whose Heaven?

(1644 – 1911)

BOOK II
(From 1911 to 1989)

Part 4

Up in the City

(1911 – 1989)

Part 5

Down in the Countryside

(1911 – 1989)

BOOK III
(From 1989 to 2014)

Part 6

Great Man

(1989 – 2010)

Part 7

How Many Suns?

(2010 – 2014)

PREFACE

On 1 September 2012, the man most likely to become the next leader of China disappeared. Of course, Xi Jinping might have disappeared a day or two before, but given that his life was lived behind the screen of the Chinese Communist Party, it was only when he failed to arrive at a meeting with Hillary Clinton that he appeared to be missing to the outside world. An empty chair at a later meeting of China's Central Military Commission (the highest military command of the country, of which Xi was vice-chairman) seemed to confirm that he was not only missing to the outside world, but missing in China too.

With only two months before the most important Congress of the Chinese Communist Party to be convened since the time of Deng Xiaoping – one at which a new leader of all would be appointed – foreign journalists went on a 'Xi hunt'. Clouds of speculation followed, while the world's internet found itself awash with questions not only about Xi Jinping's whereabouts (rumours included Xi lying in a hospital, battling Party tigers, or throwing a temper tantrum), but whether he might never return to public view at all (stranger things have happened in China). Meanwhile across the world, deeper spirits began to ask what his disappearance meant both for the succession of power in China and for the economic and political order of everyone whose fortunes were now sailing on the Chinese ship of state. At home, the Party and its presses remained silent.

On 15 September, Xi Jinping reappeared – quietly visiting a science exhibition at the China Agricultural University in Beijing. As soon-to-be leader of a Chinese Communist Party that never explained itself, no explanation was given. Far from heaving a sigh of relief, however, yet more clouds of internet speculation gathered. Was Xi Jinping fighting a bitter battle to remain the front-line candidate to lead China and the Party? Despite China having catapulted to the top of the world in terms of fortune, many even wondered whether its ancient history of dynastic rises and falls was about to repeat itself. Perhaps, just as under the last years of Mao's leadership, the country was really in a secret state of collapse.

China: a country in which the selection of a new leader could not only provoke a dangerous battle of personal power, but also raise the prospect of a root and branch revolution in the very order by which the country was ruled. Could it be that the battle was not just about a man and his job, but about whether the entire axis of China and its 1.4 billion people might shift from a single top-down mind to the voices of the people at large?

Within China, the speculation was wide – and in highly political Beijing, deep. But, as usual, it was all grounded in a story that everyone knew had begun thousands of years ago, shaped by a cast of characters and questions that were echoes of battles fought many times before. The past had certainly thrown up stories far stranger than any fiction. A world of shamans who founded a civilisation on the footprinting patterns of birds. An emperor who became so worried about the rising floods of the Yellow River that he cut off all communications between his people and heaven. Another emperor who was so concerned about the collapsing state of imperial affairs that he created a celestial Jade counterpart with a heavenly court, which every earthly minister was directed to serve as well. A foreign prince who was given the empire simply by turning up and asking for it. And a farmer's son who founded a book club and went on to become master of all. They were tales that seemed to confirm what the Jade Emperor himself had once so wisely observed of the Chinese lands: 'Made up of the essence of both heaven and earth, nothing that goes on among these creatures in the world below should surprise us.'

Perplexed, Chinese speculators scoured the past for ideas as to what might have happened. Heirs to an ancient tradition of burying secret facts in the Chinese language, they pored over every official and unofficial Party sentence for the coded messages that might give them a clue. (With thousands of Chinese characters and only a few hundred syllable-sounds to match them, there is always a wide range of written characters, which, sounding the same as a word too dangerous to write, can carry a hidden meaning.) Guesses were everywhere, but no real clues were found. The 'character code' was, however, very useful to the many who, now convinced that China was on the brink of revolutionary change, used it to bury barbs of meaning in the internet blogs with which they shared their more daring speculations. (They also used the code to make some acerbic observations about life in a land where the whereabouts of a leader is a matter for heaven alone.)

Outside China, the quality of the speculation was rather different. Whereas Chinese minds had always understood the need to think deeply, Western minds had been more concerned to find the shorter, sharper, simpler answer. The observation of a fourth-century BCE shaman-scholar that 'he who perceives the oneness of everything does not know about the duality of it' had not been given much attention beyond China's Great Wall. Chinese with deep insights grounded in long study and experience were told to simplify their ideas for Western readers who could really only be expected to read a paragraph or two. Western minds themselves (many wise, but usually without the benefit of a China education or experience) made sweeping declarations on the basis of the fragments of facts, anecdotes and assumptions that had been gathered in the rush of China's rapid economic rise. Not surprisingly, everyone stayed confused.

The eighteenth of the five-yearly congresses of the Chinese Communist Party (the one at which the future leadership would be confirmed) was eventually convened on 8 November 2012 – a little later than originally expected, and on a date that was not announced until the very end of September. At the end of it all, Xi Jinping advanced to the centre of the stage, flanked by the highest echelon of his newly appointed Politburo. In his first speech to the public, Xi acknowledged the aspirations of the people for better material conditions in good and beautiful lives; he reminded everyone that every bit of happiness in this world has to be created through hard work and labour; and he noted the harmony of the *minzu* ethnic groups (the Tibetans, the Uighurs, the Hui Muslims, the Inner Mongolian Mongols, the Zhuang tribes, and all of the other fifty-two ethnic groups – including, of course, the greatest of all, the Han). Referring to the Party, Xi Jinping observed that metal would have to be turned into iron. Referring to the people, he pointed out that while the capability of any individual is limited, if everyone were united as a single heart and mind, there would be no difficulty that the Chinese people could not overcome. Looking at the challenges facing the country, he declared that the responsibility was weightier than Mount Tai, the way ahead was long and arduous, and the goal was to deliver a satisfactory answer sheet to history.

Every word had been carefully composed. Every Chinese could trace each of his statements about Party, people and country not only to a point in history but to a particular interpretation of China's ancient dreams of order. But few, if any, were clear about what he really meant. A few days later, Xi gave another speech, declaring that it was time for China to pursue its dream: the dream of the 'great rejuvenation of the Chinese nation'. No one was much clearer about the meaning of that either – although, latching on to the tantalising idea of a 'Chinese Dream', the internet, once again, ignited.

China's competing dreams of order are the subject of this book. At the heart of these dreams is the 'story' of China and of the Chinese people. Is there only one story of China as a single beating heart, ruled by the iron will of a single top-down mind? Or is there another story of a China which dreams of a heaven that reflects the minds and hearts of all of the very different people who live beneath its skies? If there are two stories, can they ever be reconciled? And, within the stories, how did the people who live in the lands we now know as China come to have those dreams? Who were these people? How did they think their dreams might come true? What happened to the dreamers? And how did all of those individual stories come together to compose the China that we see – and struggle so hard to understand – today? I believe the answers to these questions will not only help us understand China far better than we do now, but will also help us to think a little more deeply about our own dreams of order – and what they might mean for the world at large.

*　　　*　　　*

All Under Heaven begins in the earliest mists of Chinese time – when shamans travelled freely up to the skies for conversations with heaven. It is divided into three books, and told across twenty-three chapters. There are journeys of exploration and battles of ideas; there are wars, rebellions, conquests and intrigue; there are questions about man and the cosmos, about man's relationship to other men, and about whether man is good or bad. There are also stories about the family, and about fortunes, about blood brothers and goddesses of compassion and about a Monkey King hero whose escapades add a twist of logic-leaping magic to otherwise impossible situations. Across it all, is the sinew-stretching struggle of so many Chinese people, all pursuing a dream of a human utopia which battles against a belief that harmony can only be achieved by a single top-down mind – a belief which becomes strengthened by the idea that the world has become a competition of nation states, each engaged in a desperate struggle for the 'survival of the fittest'. *All*

Under Heaven is the story of the big life of the state and the small lives of human beings, all woven together as one.

The first book takes us from the earliest Chinese times to the beginning of the twentieth century, a sweep of five thousand years. The experiences across this vast span of time contain the roots of all of China's present questions about order, including debates whose battling ideas are repeated today. From a world of shamans who divide into enquiring minds on the one hand and kingmakers on the other, comes the earliest question of whether heaven is a single top-down order delivered by the iron will of a single heavenly son, or whether it is a reflection of the people themselves? And if heaven is a reflection of the people themselves, what qualities would the people need to have for order to be achieved – and could all of the people acquire them? When a war of all against all (in the last centuries before the first millennium BCE) seems to settle the question in favour of a single top-down order, other questions follow. One is whether, to the extent that heaven's order is delivered by the iron will of a single heavenly son, a unity of man required – and if a unity of man is required, across how much of the world's territory can such a unity realistically be achieved? Another is whether, to the extent that heaven's order is delivered by the iron will of a single heavenly son across all of the lands 'under heaven', there is another world in which the hearts of men can freely roam? The questions are difficult enough on their own, but from the fourth century BCE, they are punctuated by conquering barbarians, all with other ideas.

After a thousand years of rebellion and conquest, not surprisingly, the people ask themselves what it means to be Chinese, and whether heaven really cares? By the end of the nineteenth century, and after two hundred and fifty years of rule by the alien Manju Qing, a young generation returns to the idea that heaven should be a reflection of an educated people, and that no state can ultimately survive unless its people are allowed to have independent minds.

The second book takes us across much of the twentieth century – from an 'accidental' revolution in 1911 to Tiananmen Square in 1989, explored through the very different stories of the city and the countryside. This is a time when dreams of heaven as a reflection of all of the people rise, fall, and rise again, only to be snatched away by a Communist Party whose promises of a new people are revealed to be nothing but the iron fist of a single top-down mind. The legacy of the betrayal haunts China today – and the experiences of these seventy years (in the cities and in the countryside) are the battleground of China's arguments about order today. Whose heaven is it? The Party's or the people's?

The third book takes us from 1989 to 2014 – a time in which we see the Party seek to tame man, nature and China's many different races through economic development and the forceful application of unity under the single flag of a People's Republic. It is this taming and this unity that has exacerbated many of the challenges with which China struggles today. With the past now in perspective, we look at the question of China's order from the points of view of the three groups – the Communist Party, the people at large, and the 'intellectuals' who try, like the early shamans, to bring the many ideas into a harmonious order of all. Once again, there are two competing dreams – one of heaven as a single top-down mind, and the other of heaven as a reflection of the people. Which dream will prevail? In the final chapter, we look at a dream of our own.

For the people born to the Chinese world, at the heart of their dreams of order is a five thousand year old question: what does it mean to be Chinese? Which is really the question, common to us all, of what it means to be human, living in the society of other men. As we look at the very human story of China's dreams of a heavenly order – at the big life of the state and at the small lives of human beings, perhaps it is time for us to look again at our *own* ideas of order. What are the qualities that make us human, and in being human, what duties do we have to the wider world of nature and our fellow man? Is it primarily a duty of the people to follow a single 'Son of Heaven' (be that the Communist Party or any twenty-first century god which prefers to brook neither competition nor human questions)? Or is it a duty of the people not just to ask questions – but to so cultivate themselves that the questions they ask contribute to an order which flows as naturally as water, rather than to a disorder that brings heaven down on everyone's heads?

* * *

You might say that this book is a history. It is that, but it is also a story of the present – with some very big questions about China's future and indeed all of our futures. The length of the story of how China came to think the way it does, and the tales of what happened as the Chinese lived it, are powerful influences on how China thinks today, including both the Party's plans for the future, and other people's dreams of something else. Recollections of what worked and what did not work from a thousand or two thousand years before are still regularly considered not only anecdotally within Chinese conversations but by policy makers investigating solutions for a state – as well as by Chinese businesses exploring the world. Not to mention the fact that so much of China's past seems to be an uncanny reflection of the present.

One reason why Chinese thought is generally considered (particularly by the Chinese) to be beyond the understanding of the West is that the story of what happened in China is so long and so complicated that many Chinese themselves struggle to follow it. Most, if not all, Chinese believe that foreigners (not schooled in China, and with a notorious reputation for being more interested in simplicity than complexity) will never really understand it.

All Under Heaven is also a geography. Indeed, for the Chinese, if not for everyone, history and geography march hand in hand. It is the story of how the original heartlands of the Yellow Emperor expanded, contracted and expanded again (many times over). In its expansion and contraction, the question about what it meant to be Chinese became inescapable and, at the moments when the lands of China seemed about to be lost, it became desperate. Was China a place of birth or an idea of order? Could one be Chinese if one did not live in the historic heartlands of China, where so much of what it meant to be Chinese was woven into the very landscape? And if being Chinese was an idea of order, whose idea of order was it? Was it about expressing the ancient idea of *tianxia* all under heaven through a single, all-commanding, top-down mind? Or was it about the embrace of an arguably equally ancient idea of a more 'natural' heaven which 'heard as the people heard and saw as the people saw'?

As a history and a geography, this is not just the story of China but the story of how one-fifth of the world's people have come to think about how order and being human can be reconciled. It is a question the West often overlooks – buried as it is under so many seemingly more immediate or urgent questions, from the state of the economy and the latest swings of the stock market to a changing climate and rising sea levels. We overlook it at our peril. Our ideas of order are what determine how every question – including and particularly the most immediate and urgent – is addressed. China's story holds up a powerful mirror not only to the order of the Chinese Communist Party but to that of the wider world, raising the question of what kind of order we, as a world of human beings, really want. A world that includes not only followers but also leaders – of the governments, the organisations, and the businesses which define so much of the order within which we all live.

Personally, I prefer not to describe this book as either a history or a geography, or indeed any other silo of knowledge or ideas. To truly understand China's story and what it means (and to truly understand the question of human order, and why it is so important), I believe that one needs to read it as the Chinese know it – as the story of a people. This book is not a snapshot of the ten ages of China, and it is certainly not a manual of ten rules for taming China: it is the many tales of what happened when a people tried to find a way to live together. And while it is told in chronological order, the stories within each chapter have been chosen not only for chronological completeness, but for the light they shine on present day Chinese ideas and dreams. I think of it as a puzzle: as you read each chapter, a piece of the bigger picture will fall into place. By the time you reach the final chapters, you will not only understand how the Chinese came to think as they do, but you will also understand their dreams.

*   *   *

I am a barrister by training. It was a profession I chose because I was interested not only in how the big pictures of the world work but in how the many small pictures of individual human lives come together to shape them. I moved to China in 1989 and I have lived there for much of the twenty-six following years. In 1991, I founded an advisory business that has helped a large number of global businesses navigate the seas of a country undergoing extraordinary change. I was always inclined to believe that while professionalism has a value, it is upon the very human qualities of empathy, curiosity and intelligence which our understanding of any country and its people depends, including an understanding of the world of business and economics. My experiences of living and doing business in China have confirmed me in that belief.

As the decades passed, and as China came to be seen more as part of an ever-growing global economy and less as a world of its own, I found that much of the human empathy that had been so important to our clients' early successes was becoming harder for businesses to find. In 2009, reflecting on how to explain to my clients why human qualities were so important even in business, I began to think that an understanding of how China had come to think the way it does about order might be part of the solution.

China not only as the country in which I had spent most of my adult life, but China as the land to which the Western world increasingly looked for its own economic future, notwithstanding the fact that in terms of order, a single top-down mind seemed to have triumphed over the many different voices of human beings for so much of its history. And notwithstanding the fact that the costs of that single top-down mind seemed to be becoming, once again, painfully clear.

I had no idea that the journey to answer the question of how China had come to think the way it does about order would take me back to the beginning of China's time – and I had not at all understood that it was a story which would take me to the heart of some fundamental questions, not least the question of what it means to be a people, what it means to have a state, and what happens to human beings on the long journey to 'civilisation'.

(As for the question of where Xi Jinping had gone and why, nobody can say for sure, but to those who are familiar not just with the 'how' but the 'why' of China's story, the 'missing two weeks' seem to have a lot to do with the remarkable degree to which he has been able to gather up the various reins of power – Party, military and state – with which he presently rules. Far more importantly, however, as you will see in the last part, the fact that he disappeared and reappeared without explanation goes to the very heart of the relationship between the heavenly Party and the people – and to the question of China's human order.)

All Under Heaven is my attempt to reclaim the human qualities of empathy, curiosity and intelligence, and to put them at the heart of one of the most important questions of our time, told through the story of one of the most important countries in our world. Although it is the result of many years of research, it is first and foremost the story of how the people with the single longest unbroken chain of human society came to think about how we order our world. If I have done my job well, I hope that it will not only be a story that will open up a deeper understanding of China and its people – but one that will give us all a deeper understanding of the dreams of order upon which, one way or another, all of our futures depend.

Jeanne-Marie Gescher, 2015

AUTHOR'S NOTE

I make no claim to be a historian. While I hope that *All Under Heaven* presents some thought-provoking perspectives, it is a work that relies on the synthesis of a very wide spectrum of scholarship (from archaeology, anthropology and sociology, to history, philosophy and politics, and much more in between).

Many parts of China's history are highly contested – often because successive dynasties have reinterpreted past events. Some of the most contested parts are to be found in the early to mid-twentieth century; many relate to the founding of the Communist Party and to the stories of key individuals, particularly Mao Zedong.

Much of the contest is between official Party history and relatively recent and more independent 'revisionist' accounts by individuals and historians – most benefiting from access to sources previously closed to scholars, and some, of necessity, published outside China. Many of the revisionist accounts – particularly those of the twentieth century story that draw on first-hand interviews with survivors – are compelling. Whether the revisions are to the recent or ancient past, given that this book is the story of how the Chinese think about order, and given that it is written to put the reader in the shoes of the Chinese people as their story unfolds, I have tried to balance 'truth' with the fact that for many Chinese, the official history (particularly the ancient history) is 'the story' and that for many foreigners, while the official history is rarely unquestioningly accepted, the accepted history has typically been less radically divergent.

The matter is significant – particularly with regard to the story of the Party, which is one not only of idealism but also of inner battles, intrigues and tyranny that have bequeathed a deep legacy of mistrust that can still be seen today. Many of the accepted 'facts' about the Party's opponents (whether people, political organisations or geographies) are questionable. Important examples of tyranny can be seen during Mao's rule of the early Chinese 'Soviet' areas before the revolution, while the true story of the Long March points to terror and intrigue as tools for personal power far more than a self-sacrificing pursuit of utopia for all. To a significant degree, the verdict of history on the events of the civil war and the simultaneous war with Japan owe much to an early exercise of deep propaganda-driven control, which meant that few who were inclined to tell another tale lived to tell it, and of those who did, few dared to tell their truth until relatively recently – long after the event and as many are approaching their natural death.

Where the stories are highly divergent, for example on the degree of terror with which Mao ruled the early Chinese Soviets, I took the decision to write the story as it appeared to the public at large at the time and as it has appeared in the most widely read history books, Western and Chinese, since, and to indicate and describe the divergence in references to the 'revisionist' works in the Short Bibliographic Note.

I hope that I have written the book in such a way that examples of the terror and the intrigues – from the iron rule of the third century BCE Qin Emperor, who Mao saw as a model, to the twentieth century Yan'An Forum on Literature and Art, the Great Leap Forward and the events of the last five years – can leave no reader in doubt as to the fact that much of the Party's order is grounded on a fabric of untruths, which (ostensibly in the interests of wider harmony) the Party's secrecy has protected. I felt this to be the most appropriate approach for a book that has, at its goal, the telling of the story as far as possible from the perspective of the time, the place, and the people whose story it is. At the same time, given the complexity of China's history, and given the fact that the revised version is well told by others whose works I have clearly referenced, it also seemed to be the best practical approach for the reader. The serious China scholar will be familiar with all of the works (traditional and revisionist). The general reader will, I hope, be able to see that there is a difference and to take a view as to whether he or she would like to dig a little deeper into the claimed facts of the Party's history.

For the period from 1989 to the end of the book, I was able to write from both contemporary and scholarly accounts – and I have taken my own experience, which was made in the company of others, both Chinese and foreign, as my truth. This does not necessarily make me right and on certain highly sensitive points (not least the story of June Fourth) it sets me, like many other authors, at odds not only with the official history but also the views of many younger Chinese.

The intrigues of the last few years – particularly after 2012 – have sharpened the contrast between official and independent accounts, and led us from a time when independent truths and official facts could, if one dug deeply enough, be seen side by side, to a time when independent truths have (as so often across history) become 'rumours' whose repetition is not only discouraged but can in fact be dangerous.

As one of China's most famous novelists wrote in one of China's best-loved books (the eighteenth-century *Dream of the Red Chamber*): '*Shenme shi zhende, shenme shi jiade?*' – what is real and what is not real? This question haunts every history of China. And while the story of China may test it to its limits, if we are honest, it is a question that haunts much of the human experience.

A NOTE ON THE CHINESE
LANGUAGE AND VOICES

Chinese words used in this book are generally printed in italics – followed by the English language translation.

With minor exceptions, this book uses the *pinyin* system for translation of Chinese characters into pronounceable English. It works reasonably well, but the following phonetic notes might help:

bo (as in Bo Xilai) is pronounced 'boar'

c (as in cang) is pronounced as 'ts', as in tsar

de (as in Deng Xiaoping) is pronounced 'der'

jiang (as in Jiang Zemin) is pronounced 'gee-ang', with a soft g

nu (as in Nüwa) is pronounced 'new'

q (as in Qin and Qing) is pronounced 'ch', as in chin

xi (as in Fuxi or Xi Jinping) is pronounced 'see'

xu (as in Xu Zhiyong) is pronounced 'sue'

zhou (as in the Zhou dynasty) is pronounced 'joe'

zhu (as in Zhu Yuanzhang) is pronounced 'jew', as in jewellery.

The exceptions include the use of Peking (for Beijing) in the case of Peking University, as it was known in the early twentieth century at the time its story is told; also the use of Chiang Kai-shek as he is still largely known in the West (rather than Jiang Jieshi as he is known in China).

Older texts referred to in the bibliography typically use a different Romanisation system, known as 'Wade-Giles'. Typical examples are the use of 'tao' for 'dao', 'ch'ing for 'Qing', 'ch' for 'zh', 'tzu' for 'zi'.

Having far more written characters than spoken sounds, the Chinese language is rich in homophones. When translated into an alphabetical language, individually different characters can appear to be the same. This is true, for example, of *'ren'*, a spoken word that, depending on the written character, can mean either 'human being' or 'empathy', a quality that is seen as the essence of being truly civilised.

*   *   *

I have written *All Under Heaven* to reflect, to the greatest of my ability, the perspective of the people I am writing about. On this basis, I refer to the people who came to found the Qing dynasty (known in the West as the Manchu and referred to in *pinyin* as the Manzu) as the Manju, as they refer to themselves.

I have also written it to capture, as far as possible, the humanity of the people whose stories are told, and of the times in which they lived. In so doing, I regularly paraphrase rather than quote. This is for two reasons: first, to tame the formality of words that have come down to us in scholarly texts; second, to tame length. All paraphrased voices are marked with inverted commas.

LEADERS AND DYNASTIES

Shamans and Great Men
(? – 1600 BCE)

Shang	Zhou	Qin
(1600 – 1046 BCE)	(1046 – 256 BCE)	(221 – 206 BCE)

Han
(206 – 220)

3 Kingdoms   **16 Kingdoms**
(220 – 280)   (304 – 439)

Southern and Northern Dynasties
(420 – 589)

Sui
(581 – 618)

Tang
(618 – 907)

5 Dynasties and 10 Kingdoms
(907 – 960)

Song	Jin	Southern Song	Yuan
(960 – 1127)	(1115 – 1234)	(1127 – 1279)	(1271 – 1368)

Ming
(1368 – 1644)

Qing
(1644 – 1911)

Republican
(1911 – 1949)

Communist Party
(1949 – ?)

MAPS

*   *   *

Altai Mountains

Taklamakan

Desert

Kunlun Mountains

Bayan Har Mountains

Dangla
Mountains

QINGHAI-TIBET PLATEAU

HIMALAYA MOUNTAINS

Hengduan Mountains

INDIA

Bay of

Bengal

THE HEAVENLY LANDSCAPE
3RD CENTURY BCE

XIONGNU

GOBI

DESERT

Ordos
Desert

Yellow River

ZHAO

YAN

*Taihang
Mountains*

WEI

QI

• Mount Tai

QIN

Lu

Feng / Xianyang
(Xi'an)

• Luoyang

HAN

Shu   Ba
(fell   (fell
316 BCE) 316 BCE) *Yangzi River*

CHU

Yue

EAST

SEA

JAPANESE ARCHIPELAGO

• Nanhai

THE LANDSCAPE
OF THE QING

Altai Mountains

Ili River

Urumqi

Taklamakan
Desert

Kucha

Kashgar

Kunlun Mountains

Bayan Har Mountains

Dangla
Mountains

TIBET

KHAM

QINGHAI-TIBET PLATEAU

HIMALAYA

Chengdu

Lhasa

MOUNTAINS

Dali

Kunming

Hengduan
Mountains

INDIA

BURMA

ANNAM
(VIETNAM)

Bay of
Bengal

Lake Baikal

GOBI

DESERT

Ordos
Desert

Nerchinsk

Amur River

Liao River

Chang Cheng (Long Wall)

Yellow River

Beijing

Tianjin

Yellow River 1853 - present

Mount Tai

Yellow River 1324 -1853

Xi'an
(Chang'an)

Kaifeng

Mukden
(Shenyang)

Shanhai Guan
(Mountain and Sea Pass)

Vladivostok

Yalu River

KOREA

JAPAN

Weiheiwei

Liugong
Island

Qingdao

EAST

SEA

Nanjing

Hankou
(Wuhan)

Wuxi

Shanghai

Yangzi River

Hangzhou

Dongting
Lake

Changsha

Xiang River

Xiamen
(Amoy)

TAIWAN

Guangzhou
(Canton)

Pearl River

Hong Kong

HAINAN

PACIFIC OCEAN

INNER CITY

IMPERIAL
CITY

Peking
University

Jingshan Park
(Coal Hill)

FORBIDDEN
CITY

Tiananmen (Gate of Heavenly Peace)

Thousand Step Way

Daqingmen

Zhengyangmen (Gate of the Zenith South)

Railway Station

OUTER CITY

Temple
of
Agriculture

Temple
of
Heaven

THE FORBIDDEN CITY

Gate of Divine Might
(Gate of the Black Tortoise
during the Ming Dynasty)

Palace of
Heavenly Purity

Hall of Mental
Cultivation

Gate of Heavenly Purity

Moat

Moat

Hall of Supreme
Harmony

Gate of Supreme
Harmony

Meridian Gate

THE PEOPLE'S REPUBLIC
OF CHINA

R U S S

KAZAKHSTAN

M O N G O

Altai Mountains

Ili River

Gulja
(Yining)

Urumqi

KYRGYZSTAN

Taklamakan

Desert

Lop Nur

XINJIANG

Kunlun Mountains

QINGHAI

Xining

GANSU

Aksai
Chin

Ngawa
County

TIBET

K H A M

Chengdu

H I M A L A Y A

Lhasa

SICHUAN

M O U N T A I N S

N E P A L

ARUNACHAL PRADESH

BHUTAN

Y U N N A N

BANGLADESH

Kunming

INDIA

MYANMAR

LAOS

Bay of

Bengal

THAILAND

BOOK I

Things have their roots and branches. Affairs have their beginnings and ends.
To know what comes first and after is to be near the Dao.

The Great Learning, Confucius (551 – 479 BCE)

PART 1

A HEAVENLY EMPIRE

That which was the beginning of all things under heaven.

Yi Jing (1000 BCE; also known as *I Ching*
or *The Book of Changes*)

CHAPTER 1

THE MISTS OF TIME

When Heaven and Earth were yet unformed,
All was ascending and flying, diving and delving.

The Huainanzi (139 BCE; early Han dynasty)

The earth was cold. The forests were wide. The sky was black. Far above the reach of man, a moon of white light stood firm, flanked by stars whose constellations surely held the secrets of everything. Far above the reach of an ordinary man, but not above the reach of all. As the spirits of the dead found their way across the galaxies, watching from *mingtang*, halls of light, huts open to the skies, the most adventurous and curious of the earth-bound scoured the world to find the ways in which they could follow in the spirits' paths. Cloud-piercing mountains were found to offer natural bridges to the heavens for those prepared to climb; dragons, tigers and phoenixes provided willing carriages for those who dared to jump upon their backs; magic stems offered leaves whose juices could sweep a wise spirit to the skies.

Soaring above terrestrial boundaries, the shaman adventurers searched the spirit world for news of heaven's thoughts. Ancestors were consulted on the rains or questioned about the seasons. Those ancestors without the latest news were sent to search for other spirits who, having been longer in the skies, would be closer to the cosmic force that governed all. Answers secured, the exhausted shaman travellers would trace their path back to earth and whisper their reports to those on the ground. These were the shaman *wu*, diviners of the mind of heaven, spirit guides for the questions of men.

Time passed in its thousands of years. The land warmed and, question by question, the shaman *wu* continued to scour the skies for answers. Flights to the heavens were accompanied by peering investigations into the constellations of the stars, supported by observations of the earth so intense that they were almost meditations. And so, within a world that had once seemed consumed by chaos and confusion, patterns of a more orderly change began to appear. From a dark *yin* emerged a light *yang*, from which, in time, a dark *yin* would once again appear. The promise of the 'wood' of spring gave life to an early summer 'fire'. The energy of the early summer fire brought the 'earth' to a high summer's fecundity, whose harvests were gathered by the 'metal' of autumn which yielded in turn to the winter stillness of 'water' in whose icy depths everything would rest before the wood stirred again. Within these patterns of change, the land began to reveal its secrets. Trees and plants opened their edible and medicinal strains, the ground revealed its treasures, and the ever-changing seasons submitted their schedules – and those of all the animal creatures whose activities they governed – to enquiring human minds.

As the secrets of the earth were revealed, and man began to settle on the land, forests that had stood like mountains were felled by axes made of iron. Along a muddy 'yellow' river, which the ancestors had once followed from westerly mountains in a broad meander to a far eastern sea, soft banks of yellow earth now offered themselves to receive the selected seeds of foxtail millet and wild rice, which could feed a man through winter. Cattle and sheep were tamed for human purpose. Chattering monkeys were shooed away, preening peacocks lodged on fragrant grasses, and elephants retreated before the greater order of man. And as more men settled and the world continued with its changes, the shaman *wu* changed with it. Some would become shaman kings: their knowledge of the skies bestowing an unquestionable authority upon a new world of rulers on earth below. Others would become the shamans *of* kings: advisers to men who, with a natural authority over others, were determined to harness the celestial secrets for the taming of nature and the ordering of all.

Yet others considered the idea of kings exercising authority over nature and other men as a folly, which could only bring heaven crashing down on everyone's head. Keeping a quieter, meditating counsel these others would leave the worldly battles to those who were determined to subject heaven and earth to a human order. Taking their spirits to the edges of the settled world, they would continue to insist on talking directly to heaven, whenever earth or its people had a question to ask.

CHAPTER 2

A HEAVENLY PEOPLE

*Bright, bright the heavens above, sparkling the
serried stars; the radiance of the sun and the moon
magnifies the chief of men.*

The Book of Songs (1000–700 BCE)

Across the northern plains, on the banks of the Yellow River, winter had begun its annual retreat. Ice had softened into water; bears and badgers had emerged from their long sleep. In fields cleared within the forests, black-haired men stretched every muscle to pull their ploughs; women, sowing the seed, followed behind. Spring gave way to early summer, just as it should. Rains fell; the skies were streaked with lightning and thunder rolled. Peach trees blossomed, goldfinches sang. Peewits, looking for worms spinning silken cocoons, found their way to the mulberry trees.

Early summer rose to the heat of high summer, just as the flowering sow-thistles said it would. Millet ripened in the fields and grasshoppers threw themselves into their ritual chant of life. The backs of the black-haired people bent to gather weeds in aching arms. Then the high summer's blaze faded and autumn began to whisper in the wind.

8

Up in the skies, the swallows and geese gathered for journeys that would take them far away – and bring them back again when spring returned. Deep in the forests, tigers chased deer while crocodiles snapped in rivers and elephants kept their distance. In the fields, the heavy grain was ready for the sickles. Across days that began before dawn and ended long after the setting sun, the black-haired people, bones aching, gathered the heavy millet by the *gu* before winter's icy fingers crept back across the land.

*   *   *

In the city of Great Shang – the capital of the Shang dynasty, who had long ruled the four known quarters of the world – conversations with heaven had clearly gone well. Across the fields of the second millennium BCE, the seasons had followed their promised schedule. As the rains watered the land, the Yellow River had remained within its banks, and even the locusts had kept their distance. Threshed, the millet had been carried to the storehouses of the city – with plenty for those whose whips commanded the fields. This year there would even be food enough to carry a peasant family through the winter and punishment for none. Not starving, the peasants' lives in the villages at the edges of the fields could continue. Soon enough the winter frosts would bite into the earth. Dark nights would lengthen, the north wind would blow, water would retreat beneath the land, and the earth would send man and beast off to a dark rest. Huddling into caves, or sheltered by walls of mud and roofs of thatch, women's fingers would soon be weaving hempen plants and reeds into rough clothes, baskets and shoes. Meanwhile, the men would be completing the autumn tasks for their masters: walls built, ditches mended, goods called for from all directions. Unless, of course, heaven and the city had decided there were new lands to be discovered or a conquering battle to be fought. Then, cold or not, the muscles of the earth would be raised and none could tell whether or when they might return.

The earth had not always been so. In the long winter nights, wise hearts talked of a time before the fields had spread and the cities had appeared. A golden age of *taiping*, great peace, when men had wandered wherever they wanted and eaten whatever they had hunted or found. Mountains had been crossed in freedom; rivers had been forded at will. Food had been plentiful and peace as natural as the air that everyone breathed. Some thought this was just a foolish dream. But others remembered the whispers of men who still lived beyond the four quarters of the settled lands, black hair flowing freely in the wind and food found a day at a time. Here was a deeper tale, going back to before the beginning of time. And when the sun spun to its nightly rest, willing ears would turn to hear that story of the past, told by tongues who whispered it just as it had been whispered to them.

It was a story that no one ever tired of hearing. The story of a time and a space when heaven and earth had not yet been formed and separated, when everything was still twisting and turning, flying and diving: a *hun mang*, chaos, everywhere. From the chaos had emerged a *dao*, a way that anyone could feel, as long as they were willing to open not just their ears but every human instinct. A *dao* way that could be *felt,* but not described by the limited words of man. Indeed, the *dao* was a name that could not be named: a way that was known and knowable only to itself. It was a trace that was driven by the forces of a *qi*, energy, and by the constant changes between the dark *yin* and the light *yang* on which all the fortunes of life rise and fall and rise again. It was the power that governs everyone's destiny, at the heart of everything that is known. A way that, if carefully consulted, could reveal a natural order for heaven, earth and man.

From out of the *hun mang* chaos, so the wise hearts told, the *dao*, activated by the energetic force of *qi*, had revealed a natural order. Heaven and earth had separated; the one had become two, then three, then ten thousand things, all of them different. Heat and cold had settled into seasons. And where once there had been swirling mists there were now beasts, birds, trees, fish and men. It was a golden age of *taiping* great peace – a time when harmony ruled like a symphony. Man and beast were friends. No one, neither man nor beast, had to be told what to do. And even though heaven and earth were now no longer one, those on earth could talk openly to heaven whenever they wanted, and say whatever they wanted to say.

Of course, sniffed the wise hearts, it couldn't last. In the changing *yin-yang* world of the *dao*, everything had an opposite, which was neither more nor less than part of itself. Order and chaos are one and the same; difficult is nothing more than the completion of easy; nothing is high without a low; without a winter there can never be a summer. And indeed, blue skies eventually gave way to those opposites hidden within them: lightning flashed; rain poured in torrents, and a flood rose, so great that it swept almost everyone away.

Almost everyone, but not quite.

From the swirling waters emerged a man and a woman: Fuxi and Nüwa (some said a brother and sister). Acting swiftly against the torrential forces,

Nüwa shored up heaven with a range of mountains to keep the watery skies from falling again. And when she had secured the architecture of heaven and earth, she went on to mould a people out of clay, into whose cold shapes heaven itself breathed life. Nüwa having balanced heaven and earth, Fuxi studied the relationship between the two. Journeying to the skies and peering at the earth below, true to his shaman spirit, he tried to put himself in the shoes of the cosmos so that he could truly see and understand. Wondering at the majestic *ziran*, 'just as it is', nature, he stared at the stars above so hard that he almost became a part of them. And as he stared and thought, he began to perceive points at which the constellations correlated with the landscape of the earth: clearly these were special places from which man would be able to offer up the sacrifices from earth to heaven, and so deliver order for all.

Fuxi went on to observe the land along the Yellow River: the constantly changing *ziran* nature, and the patterns of the creatures that lived within it. Here, were footprints of birds in the damp ground and, there, on the back of a tortoise, was a magic square of nine smaller squares, a mathematical harmony that seemed to talk of the cosmos and its spheres. From the changes of nature, Fuxi concluded that the earth was engaged in a continuous conversation with heaven. And from the footprinting patterns of the birds and the magic square of numbers, he divined a series of symbols that man could use to communicate with heaven. With such an understanding of heaven and earth, Fuxi realised that the cosmos was governed by a secret code that man – unique among all the creatures on earth – could read, and thereby conduct the greater order of all.

Time turned, the wise storytellers told, and Fuxi was followed by others, who dug ever deeper into the mysterious codes of the natural world. Studying the seasons, testing the rocks, tasting the leaves of plants, flying to heaven for consultations with the spirits and ancestors, Fuxi's successors began to see a greater whole. At one point, the observations of a great man called Shennong revealed the secrets of the soil, from which food and minerals could be coaxed, and of the minds of animals, who could be tamed to become man's servants. Discovering the treasures of the earth, Shennong forged the tools that made planting, harvesting, even fishing, possible on a scale never known before. And seeing himself as just one man among others, he shared his knowledge with a black-haired people who were still sheltering in the trees with the birds. Before long, he was farming with them along the banks of the Yellow River. Everyone worked hard, but the 'great man' Shennong proved himself the hardest-working of them all.

11

More time turned, Shennong passed to another world, and those who had left the trees to the birds gathered themselves into a tribe and chose a leader. The first tribe grew and became many, and as each new tribe emerged, its members identified themselves with a common totem chosen from the vast array of the natural world.

After an epic sweep of time, another Great Man emerged from the people settling in the lands along the Yellow River – one with an idea so powerful that future generations would know him only as the 'Yellow Emperor'. Confident that man's duty was to deliver the order on which the cosmos depended, the Yellow Emperor brought together what had become myriad tribes scattered across the northern plains and settled them as a single people under an order which would be modelled on the patterns of heaven's stars and on the changes of the earth.

Drawing on Fuxi's observations, the Yellow Emperor created a harvesting wealth grounded in the wisdom of an annual calendar, which – based upon a constant and meticulous consultation of nature and the skies – set the seasons to a yearly order. Henceforth every ruler would be able to ensure that heaven and earth remained in an orderly harmony. Inspired by Fuxi's observations of the footprinting patterns of the birds, the Yellow Emperor captured the meaning of heavenly power in the characters of a written language and engraved them onto the metal taken from the earth. Enthralled by Fuxi's observations of the chorusing songs of birds, he tamed the notes of nature to order the human heart with music.

The Yellow Emperor: 'yellow' for the waters of the muddy river along which he had settled the people; 'yellow' for the colour of the watery dragons that carried him up to heaven whenever a conversation was required; 'yellow' for the rains he tamed. And 'yellow' as the colour that would forever be associated with the imperial centre of everything – the beating heartland of a people who would one day be known as the Chinese.

With such a clear cosmic authority, progress had been swift. Medicinal plants were ordered by purpose; fire was tamed to serve man; animals were set to their purposes, nets were woven to catch fish; iron tools were cast to turn wild beasts into meat and work the land; seeds were separated and sown. Altars, raised in locations that mirrored the heavenly coordinates, offered improved communications with heaven and the ancestors. As more forests were felled, villages were settled, and fields were laid in squares as far as the eye could see. Walls were raised from tamped earth – to keep at bay the jealous outsiders, 'barbarians' who had failed to understand the wise order of the settled world. And while some of the oldest shamans (those who considered the only true order to be that of the cosmos and the *ziran* nature) stubbornly continued to ask their questions directly of heaven, a people who had once been scattered now found themselves in an orderly Yellow River world: a *tianxia* order of 'all under heaven'.

For those in charge of the *tianxia* idea, everything went well for a while. But, noted the wise storytelling hearts, by the time the Yellow Emperor's grandson, Zhuanxu, came to rule, the cosmos was a little out of control. A force from the watery underworld – a monster known as Gong Gong – rose up from below to capture the earth above. After a fierce battle, Zhuanxu emerged triumphant. Angry at his defeat, Gong Gong raged against Nüwa's mountain range – threatening to bring heaven tumbling down on everyone's heads. Nüwa (who, like all those who had once lived on earth, was now an ancestral spirit in the skies) did her best to limit the damage, but not before the pillar of the Buzhou mountain had been broken. Henceforth the sky would tilt upwards to the north and the west – while the earth would tilt downwards, the water sliding and settling to the south and the east.

Zhuanxu and his people adapted, but somehow problems in the form of rains, floods and droughts kept coming. Zhuanxu consulted his ancestor, the Yellow Emperor, and made a worrying discovery. From the time of Fuxi, heaven had received sacrifices with pleasure, and trust had been established between heaven, earth and man. Since then, however, the black-haired people had grown in number and younger generations had forgotten the correct order of things: sacrifices were being made by anyone and everyone whenever they wanted, with no regard at all for the rhythms of the celestial world; spirits and ancestors were being called upon without a moment's notice and with little respect; gods (including those ancestors whose earthly glory had taken them closest to the power of heaven) were being constantly disturbed with thoughtless requests. Heavenly annoyance had turned to anger, and anger to rebuff. Sacrifices made were now being ignored; blessings were being withheld. And as the blessings stopped coming down from heaven, so the treasures of the earth were beginning to dry up. Zhuanxu and his people would soon be left with nothing to offer up, even through the most skilled shamans.

Disaster looming, Zhuanxu asked the Yellow Emperor what he should do. The answer was clear: bring communications between heaven and earth under control, and quickly.

Zhuanxu summoned his two most trusted governors. One was commanded to take control of communications with heaven, the other to assume responsibility for ordering the proper conduct of the people. Both would answer to Zhuanxu. From that time on, communications between heaven and earth became a matter for the One, and only the One: the Son of Heaven and ruler of earth. Thus, order was returned to the relationship between man and heaven, and harmony was restored to the world. The responsibilities of ruler, and of the ruled, were clear.

Heaven seemingly satisfied, the wise hearts noted, all went well for a generation or two. Other 'Great Men' rose to lead the people, and the quality of their relationship with heaven continued to improve. Wealth spread across the earth, and an archer named Yi set about igniting the mountains and the valleys so that yet more land could be cleared for more order – more fields and fewer of the ravaging beasts who, once friends, were now stubbornly resisting the advance of man.

The watery underworld, however, remained a challenge. While the Yellow Emperor had tamed its dragons, and while Nüwa had prevented another collapse of heaven, from time to time Gong Gong's fury would still erupt from underground, hurling the waters of the Yellow River far beyond its banks. To those responsible for guiding the harmony of all, the consequences were worrying. Under orderly conditions, the Yellow River looped in a leisurely manner across the land, brushing dry soils with moisture and nurturing fish that would spring into waiting nets. When Gong Gong raged, however, men, women and children were washed away from the banks and surrounding fields, carried off in the river's furious embrace. Dams were repaired and dykes were dug. But heaven inexplicably stood aside.

And then, another Great Man emerged, this one named Yao. Strengthening the dams and dykes, Yao also laboured on communications with the spirit world. Shamans reported on their conversations with heaven and wherever there was a problem, sacrifices were offered to encourage the ancestors to intercede. Eventually, Yao discovered, like Zhuanxu before him, that the problem lay with the people, who were simply not behaving well enough. Arguments were breaking out in every direction. Children did as they pleased without consulting their elders. The calendar was disregarded, and planting took place at all times of the year, regardless of the celestial schedule.

Laws were introduced so that everyone knew how to distinguish good behaviour from bad, and punishments were polished to address the bad. It was not enough. By now, the waters of the river were surging over hills and rising high enough to even threaten heaven. Yao decided that the earth needed a man of such virtue that the people could be tamed by moral example. A long search eventually led to a man called Shun. Burdened with an obstinate father, a dishonest mother, and an arrogant brother, Shun was a man who had nonetheless honoured them all, creating a model of household harmony. Here was someone who clearly understood the importance of order. Yao abdicated in Shun's favour and Shun took up the reins. Like Yao, Shun laboured night and day to deliver the ordering balance of the cosmos on earth. Humility became a compulsory virtue for all, as did the meticulous ordering of everything and everyone. Shaking their heads in disbelief, many of the descendants of the earliest shamans – those who had seen man-delivered order as a folly that would bring heaven tumbling down on earth – retreated to the natural order of the mountains and the forests.

For those fixed on the idea of a man-delivered order, matters seemed to improve. But the monstrous Gong Gong was still far from tamed. Realising that he had reached the limits of his abilities, Shun passed the watery challenge to a man of even greater promise: the son of the minister responsible for public works, whose name was Yu. Having watched his father struggle to control the waters of the Yellow River with dams and dykes, Yu was convinced that the answer lay in a greater understanding of the river and its banks. As clear as Yao and Shun about the all-important duty of keeping a cosmic balance, Yu ensured that communications with heaven were strictly maintained while dedicating an equal attention to studying the challenging changes on earth. Through thirteen years of freezing winters, muddy springs, blistering summers and windy autumns, Yu summoned the spirits to help. Tracking the river, surveying every point on the land through which it passed, Yu even classified the surrounding soils.

At the end of his journey, his hands covered with callouses, and his children strangers to him, Yu announced a plan. From henceforth, the land would be ordered into a grid of nine provinces, each identified by its specific geographic features, and each placed under the command of a local lord. Within each province, Yu gave instructions for the taming of all. The living would have their houses, their villages and their cities; the dead would have their temples; the animals would have their forests and grasslands (those not needed by man himself). Each to its own purpose and place: man and nature, heaven and earth, all at peace.

Province by province, the black-haired people were diverted from the fields and tasked with restoring order to the waters. Rivers were dredged, marshes were drained, banks were raised, mountains were moved. Channels were laid so that the water could be delivered smoothly from what Yu had discovered to be the Yellow River's glacial mountain origins in the west to the welcoming arms of a sea to the east. Wherever possible, the waters were guided over level ground; and where the waters were too wild to be guided, they were divided into two, three, or even more channels. Up and down the land, over hills, across plains and in valleys, forests were felled to open yet more new lands for cultivation. The people were directed not to store the treasures of their land, but to exchange them with others so that each province could specialise in what it did best such that the whole would be in harmony. Once again, matching attention to celestial spirits with a diligent approach to understanding the earth, heaven's order was restored.

As Yu battled against the river, more men of greatness emerged to help him. Among them was a man called Xie, who, like many others who had been helpful to Yu, had been rewarded with a territory of his own. Xie named his land Shang. By now, the old worlds of Fuxi and Shennong were but distant memories. Where Fuxi had wandered among birds and animals, and where Shennong had farmed shoulder to shoulder with others, the one world of their descendants had separated into twos: a great and a small, a high and a low, a chosen few who were closest to the ruler in the great city, and a not-chosen many who were spread across the fields. The chosen and the great settled in high dwellings raised above the earth in places which, fixed by correlation with the stars, were surely grounded in the very thoughts of heaven. The not-chosen were settled below in dugouts carved into the soil, sheltered only by roofs of straw. While the chosen called themselves and their ancestors by family names, the not-chosen were called by their nature: 'the black-haired people'.

Across the next four hundred years, the wise storytelling hearts continued, the rule of Yu (now known as 'Yu the Great') was passed down the line of his descendants – all possessed of an ever-increasing power. As each great ruler passed in turn from the living to the dead, across the Shang cities more altars were built from which yet more descendants could engage in the private 'family' conversations with the ancestors that offered privileged channels to heaven's thoughts. Harvests were offered up as taxes, and as the wealth of the fields flowed into expanding treasuries, so more of Yu the Great's descendants built more new cities, each greater than the last. Meanwhile, the nameless black-haired people, whose purpose was to clear forests and plough fields, reap harvests and battle the envious beasts and barbarian outsiders, stayed close to their fields, exposed (but for their dugout dwellings) to the elements at large. Their labours heavier with each new ruler, the whips applied to keep their earthly bodies in heavenly order eventually became more than some could bear.

In 1600 BCE, a man named Tang – a descendant of Xie and ruler of the lands that Xie had named Shang – announced that heaven had had enough. Gathering together the forces of his Shang army with those of other like-minded local lords, Tang confronted the latest descendant of Yu the Great in a battle which shook the earth. Outnumbered but determined to displace the brutal higher power, Tang, his warriors and their allies fought without fear. Miserable under an unbearable yoke, the peasant armies of Yu the Great's ruling clan looked up and saw a sympathetic sky – at the stars from which the Yellow Emperor, Shennong, Nüwa, Fuxi, Yao, Shun, and even Yu himself, seemed to gaze down in shock at how once-great ideas had turned to tyranny. Seeing hope in the opposing forces of Tang, they dissolved. Heaven had spoken and the world had changed.

And so, the wise storytelling hearts observed, the lords of the land of Shang came to occupy the cities, their leader now the Son of Heaven. Once again, cities became sparkling gems, glittering in a landscape of open fields, linked by the blood of the ruling family. Many in number, none of the cities was greater than Great Shang, the capital ordained by heaven and fixed by the constellations of the stars. Pivot of the four quarters of the earth, it was the central axis of the cosmos whose heavenly energy – the *qi* – flowed through the city and out across the world beyond. A heaven on earth, some said, and so it almost was.

Rising up from the lands around, Great Shang was square, the shape that everyone knew the earth to be. Set within towering walls of earth, it had been fixed by the heavenly compass of the Shang's master of works, the son of the son of the son of a shaman. With turrets soaring above its gates, no ordinary mortal could approach it without trembling at the sight. Temples and palaces had been built on the highest ground; pavilions had been painted; and pillars of pine held up gently curving roofs whose eaves tipped to the skies above. Proud horses and carriages coursed the streets, their passengers bedecked in silk and jade; banners of heavenly power fluttered on the winds. Alongside them, ox and man pushed and pulled the luxuries of life from stores of plenty to the homes of the noble spirits whom heaven had blessed. Amid the clanging and carving, the chiselling and the forging, music seemed to float on the air. And at the great gates, soldiers and sentinels stood on guard. Heaven's order was everywhere.

The city of Great Shang became the heaven of earth, emulated by many smaller Shang cities, which spread like stars in the galaxy of the Shang lands. Surrounded by the nine known mountains, the lands reached to the four known seas in a world that worked in majestic alignment with the celestial seasons, delivering treasures of harvests for the Son of Heaven. Ox bones and turtle shells were treated as oracles, heated and cracked to divine the thoughts of heaven. Sacrifices were made to ensure the continued goodwill of the ancestors. The calendar was observed with humility.

At first, the labours of the people were measured with fairness. At peace with the representative Son of Heaven on earth, the black-haired people had grown in number and the wealth of the Shang seemed to know no end. But as time passed, the labour became harder, the rules tightened and the punishments increased. Confident in the heavenly mandate secured by their ancestors, new Shang rulers sent nobles to clear the way for more new cities to establish an even wider order – all forged by the labours of the black-haired people, and all supported by new fields of plenty, whose wealth of grains would shower like rain upon the Shang.

More forests were burned and, like the phoenix, more harvests rose from their ashes. More mountains were mined for the minerals and stones on which the Shang's earthly powers depended: iron for axes, hoes and weapons; copper and tin for the awe-inspiring bronze vessels which, used to smooth conversations with heaven, seemed to have captured living animals in their polished surfaces; jade for its power to conjure up the virtues of heaven on earth – the endurance of strength combined with the softness of beauty. With a spreading prosperity – and an iron power – many of the barbarian tribes were persuaded to follow the people of the Yellow Emperor with their calendars and cultivated fields. Soon, like all the other treasures of the natural world, they, too, were submitting their tributes to a Son of Heaven who was clearly master of the harmonies of heaven and earth.

*   *   *

The story told, some thought that it made perfect sense: a heavenly order of the Shang settled through their cities on earth. Hard though life was, what fearful chaos might otherwise reign without it? But from time to time, a wilful heart would remember the whispers of the past and wonder.

As day had so inexorably turned to night, summer to winter, and winter to spring, it seemed to the wilful hearts that the early peace of the people had begun to change: more cities with ever-greater harvests to produce; more wars; and now seemingly endless battles against nature to be fought. There were fewer of the animals whose lives had once been so intricately entwined with theirs. No more tigers lying down beside the people; no more monkeys chattering to their hearts' delight; no more of the elephants that had once wandered at will. All had retreated into the ever more distant forests and mountains that lay beyond the settled lands. With them had also gone so many of the shamans who had once read the footprints of the birds and who, in their reading, had been able to see the majestic order of the *ziran*, 'just as it is', nature.

Backs bent, arms aching, the wilful hearts reflected on days begun before dawn and ending long after sunset. In a good year, there would be food enough left to carry a family through the winter, and punishment for none. Not starving, life could carry on. While the cities bathed in the warmth of ancestral blessings, the labouring bodies in the fields would huddle together for survival. And as winter turned the metal of autumn into ice, the calloused hands would labour on in the endless battle against nature and the envious barbarians. More, and more, violent punishments were applied whenever things went wrong. And more men were taken into the warring service of feudal lords – many never to return.

Thinking on these things, those wilful hearts remembered the golden age of *taiping* great peace, when men had wandered at will and eaten whatever they had hunted or found. When mountains had been crossed in freedom and rivers forded at will. When shelter had never been further away than a nearby tree and no one, neither man nor beast, had ever needed to be told what to do or say. A time before communications between heaven and earth had been interrupted, when anyone could talk to heaven whenever they wanted, and say whatever they wanted to say.

Some thought it was just a foolish dream. A world without a single top-down order – how could that be real? Others wondered, remembering not only the stories of the past, but the whispers of men returning from the edges of the world to tell of people whose black hair still blew freely in the wind. And from time to time, captivated by the stories of old, one of the wilful hearts would make their escape in the dead of night, looking for the old world, the world of heaven before the time of the single mind and its punishments, a world of heaven without the order of the Shang.

CHAPTER 3

HEAVEN ON EARTH?

What can be said to be of heaven, what can be said to be of human beings?

Zhuangzi (369–286 BCE)

Eyes fixed forward, ears struck by sharp plucks of strings, the audience held its breath in eager anticipation of the story to come. A *pipa*, lute, thrummed, dragons snorting in the wind. Drums beat to a soft rhythm and firm feet appeared, soldiers advancing to the front. Suddenly a zither hummed and the marchers turned as if to towards the north. As the steps retreated, bamboo flutes whispered: *jiang jiang*, a passing breeze. But not for long. *Cang cang!* Cymbals clashed and strong bodies turned to face the audience, pushing themselves forward as if fording the currents of the Yellow River. And then a single stroke of bronze – *dong* – stopped the air. Two forests of flags fluttered into view as if upon a field of battle: one white, as the fierce metal of the Shang; the other red, as the cleansing fires of the Zhou. Slowly, from the sound of silence came a drumroll; to which was added the sound of small chimes, tinkling like anxious spirits; and then came the wooden clappers, beating the air faster than the watching eyes could follow.

Axes struck, shields were raised and spears flew back and forth. White on red, red on white, the flags battled for their lives, some thrashing forwards, others falling back. Sharp strings plucked for effect threw every heart into the air, only to be followed by deeper notes that pulled them down. Then, just as it seemed that the scene would explode, the fallen red flags gathered themselves up and, leaving the white flags where they lay, stood to a proud attention. Drums beating softly again, their triumphant feet advanced. Some stepped off to the left (east), others to the right (west), and then the two sides turned to join together. Finally, all facing towards the audience and the propitious south, they knelt and touched their heads to the ground. Stone chimes struck. 'Wuhu!' the red flags shouted: 'The iniquity of the Shang is destroyed!' And from the chorus at the sides came the oh-so-familiar refrain: 'It is heaven's mandate! A Zhou king across the four directions – may he be treated as a Son!'

Heaven had spoken and the orderly end had been revealed: the old dynasty of the Shang had lost to the new dynasty of the Zhou. Heaven and earth were, once again, at one.

*   *   *

It had been a long journey. Set on the western edge of the Shang lands, the early Zhou had watched the rise of the Shang, then come to pay its rulers the tribute every barbarian tribe owed to the central axis of heaven and earth. Ever-watchful, it had not been long before the Zhou began to emulate the values of their eastern neighbours. There was wealth to be found in the order of a settled life – not to mention the greater blessings that seemed to flow when conversations with heaven were limited to the single voice of a king. Altars aligned with the constellations of the stars, ancestors regularly consulted, and the power of animals magically captured in the burnished sides of sacrificing bronzes: all seemed to be the hallmarks of a greater mind. Watching, the Zhou had transformed their own rough lands into fields, guided by seasons that seemed as willing to submit their schedules to the calendars of the Zhou as to those of the Shang. Fields settled, the Zhou had then mastered the heavenly art of raising cities to the skies.

Time passed: in the west, the fortunes of the Zhou rose; in the east, the Shang lost their way. In Shang, it seemed, the riches that had flooded from every quarter had been channelled only to the few, and even those few had found that treasures produced only the desire for more. Wealth-yielding fields were never enough, city walls always needed strengthening, once-bright palaces always faded: the need for labour was never-ending – all of it required in double-quick time. And for every barbarian brought to tribute-paying order, others seemed only too willing to test the edges of the settled Shang world, with battles demanding ever-greater sacrifices of the nameless black-haired peasants-in-arms. In the city of Great Shang, wine might flow at the snap of a finger. But across the Shang lands, hearts were silently chilling. Revelling in their glory, the mighty Shang missed the whispers that the smaller Zhou ruler had been so quick to catch: the Shang were losing heaven's trust.

Understanding that heaven would be looking for a new Son, Zhou generals wondered how their fifty thousand spears could ever match the five hundred thousand of the Shang. But the Zhou ruler knew that other spears were prepared to rise up with them, perhaps another hundred and fifty thousand; he also knew that weapons would be only half the battle. Where the spears of the Zhou and its allies would be borne by hearts that beat with courage, those who carried the spears of the Shang had long ago lost their hearts.

Eventually, in 1046 BCE, on the fields of Muye, heaven made itself clear. Bells chiming, drums beating, the spears had flown, blood had poured, and by the end of the day the Zhou had captured the mandate of heaven.

Over the years that followed their conquest of all-under-heaven, the Zhou discharged their ruling responsibilities with humility and awe. Dying shortly after the battle, the Zhou king left a young son to the regency-care of his younger brother, the Duke of Zhou. Clear as to the heavy duty which he held on his nephew's behalf, the duke moved to ensure that the voice of heaven would never be ignored again. The power of the once-great Shang now defeated, the Zhou altars (complete with oracle bones and magical bronzes) were carefully polished so that the conversations with the ancestors could henceforth be conducted from the westerly Zhou capital of Feng. Shamed by their own descendants, the Shang ancestors were invited to adopt the living Zhou as their own. And in the Feng capital, the duke raised a new idea of the ancient shamans' *mingtang* Hall of Light.

Calculated to carry the conversation between heaven and earth, the Zhou Hall of Light was raised on a square floor (the shape of earth) set under a domed roof (the shape of heaven) and divided into nine chambers, mirroring the magic numbers of Fuxi's turtle square. From within its portals, assisted by descendants of the early shamans, the Zhou sent their sacrifices up; and from the observing terraces of the domed roof – open to the moon and stars – the blessings of heaven were welcomed down. A *mingtang* Hall of Light: the place where heaven and earth would come together through man, and from which man, with his sacrifices and oracle bones, would be able to divine the will of heaven and observe the changes of the earth; the pivot of heaven above, earth below, and the four quarters all around; the place where every Zhou decision would be taken, from which every command would be despatched from the centre to the edges, and to which every barbarian ruler would come to pay his tribute.

The foundations of heavenly communications settled, and with trusted members of the ruling Zhou family settled across the land, the Duke of Zhou turned his attention to ensuring the harmony of heaven and earth across what had become a much bigger earth, now including not only the vast lands of Shang and Zhou, but the lands of others who, like the Zhou, had begun to emulate the Shang. Stretching from the Kunlun mountains, in the far west, to the coast of a great sea to the furthest east, it seemed to be a world of its own, wider and greater than anything the ancestors could have imagined. Reaching from the flat, fertile plains of the north to the undulating hills of the south, there was even a tip that touched the waters of another river almost as great as the Yellow River, a river which raged through gorges of jagged mountains seemingly at the southern edge of everything. And scattered across the vast tracts of the land, sparkling like gems, stood the walled cities – cities of the Shang, the Zhou and all of those other 'barbarians' who were emulating the settled and city-ordered world.

With so much earth to order, more cities would be required, and with the surviving Shang not to be trusted and the black-haired people able to muster only the rawest skills of the earth, the Duke of Zhou turned to the wider Zhou family for help. Uncles, nephews and cousins, each carrying a bond of blood across the new and greater Zhou world, and all beating to the single drum of a heavenly wisdom now spreading from the Zhou capital of Feng.

With trusted family settled across the four quarters of the world, the Duke of Zhou then turned to the heavenly duty of man to ensure the wider harmony of heaven and earth within a cosmos of constant change. Clear that the secrets of the natural order lay at the heart of success, he knew that understanding the changes of the seasons would enable him to do his duty best. The path of the moon revealed the first month of the year and unveiled the schedule of the seasons by which the annual calendar could be set. The trajectory of the stars foretold the rains. The warm winds whispered of new

23

life. The high summer brought harvest rewards, the cold winter a silent death. These were the most elemental features of a heavenly order so great that only a fool would see them as either good or bad – and so deep and intricate that only the most observant could hope to understand their course.

With the weight of heaven's expectations upon his shoulders, the Duke of Zhou turned to the shamans' heirs, men to whom the ancient wisdom had been passed from father to son across the ages. Appointed them to serve in his court, he charged them to search their memories for the lessons bequeathed by their forefathers, and to scour the ancient threaded bamboo texts which fathers had left to them. With the knowledge of the past accumulated, they were then to compile a book of wisdom upon which the heavenly empire could be made truly secure. Working night and day, thread by thread, the descendants of the shamans, henceforth to be known as 'scholars', traced meaning across cryptic characters until, eventually, they had gathered the learning into a text that held the wisdom of the changes on which heaven's order rested. The text was entitled *The Book of Changes* (*Yi Jing*), a work that every Zhou ruler (and, indeed, the heads of all of the Zhou families) would be able to consult. With it, every Zhou ruler would be able to discharge his duty to heaven above and earth below. And in discharging their duty, each ruler would merit the mandate that heaven had bestowed.

At the heart of *The Book of Changes* was a simple proposition: the unified symphony of a constantly changing heaven and earth, 'conducted' by the wisdom of man. Solid though the principle of unity might be, it was essential to understand that the forces underpinning it were quite the opposite – a perpetual revolution between the propelling force of *yin* and *yang* opposites. Yin, dark and receptive, yang, light and creative; yin, female and passive, yang, male and active. And – like the undertow within a wave, the seed which becomes a fruit, or even the turning wheel of a carriage – within every yin, was a yang; and within every yang, a yin. The mandate of heaven was not a gift of triumph over earth and all of its elements: it was a duty to observe the myriad features of cosmic change upon which the successful balance of the whole depended. And, with the knowledge that resulted from such an intense meditating observation, the mandate of heaven was a duty to divine the delicate path of the *dao* with which the harmonies of heaven and earth could be perceived and order achieved for all.

The Book of Changes was no manual for a selfish individual. It was, rather, a call to the man who would so humbly devote himself to the task of observing the changes that he might be described as a master of change, or a 'sage'. The effort required would always be extreme. But to the dedicated Son of Heaven – the ruler committed to conducting the harmony of heaven and earth – the prize was the knowledge that, having discharged a duty of cosmic proportions, heaven's trust in him would be secure.

The Book of Changes compiled, the Duke of Zhou then raised a heavenly bureaucracy, charged with constant divination of the *dao* way. No more periodic 'ascending and descending' for consultations with the skies, but a virtuous government of ministers. Each minister was given a specific responsibility, and all were supported by corps of scholars dedicated to the meticulous observation of the changes, with regular reports on heavenly matters, and a constant adjustment of the affairs of earth. With every minister and scholar in his position and his place, each would be aware that the correct performance of his duty was essential for the success of the whole. Equipped with such a virtuous government, not only would the correct policies be divined but they would be adjusted to the changes of the cosmos as and when required. Guided by the *dao*, order would appear as effortless as nature itself.

Following the model of nature, spring would be the time for repairs, when the east winds melted the ice and sleeping creatures began to stir (it would also be a time when no punishments would be permitted that might discourage the birth of new life). In summer, when the sow thistle flowered and the great heat loomed, peasant hands would be dedicated to encouraging the fruits of the land to grow. In autumn, when crickets chirped and the geese prepared for flight, walls would be strengthened, harvests gathered and granaries filled (it would also be the time when punishments were executed, and when wars would be fought). In winter, everyone would rest, like the animals, and everything would be stored away. With the actions of man so carefully correlated to the seasons of the cosmos, there would be no risk of the chaos that might ensue from an autumn arriving in the spring or snow falling in summer.

With spreading lands, orderly seasons, peaceful people and harmony across the spheres, the Hall of Light blazed with heavenly communications and the lands of the Zhou bathed in blessings from the sky. So great was the symphony that even the uncles, nephews and cousins who ruled the cities seemed to conduct themselves like obedient stars in the constellation of the Son of Heaven's universe. Barbarian tribes found their way to the Feng capital to offer tribute, and, as the Zhou had followed the Shang, other barbarians followed the Zhou's example of a settled path to heaven on earth.

25

Indeed, so great were the blessings (and so great the tribute paid) that when the young prince came of age, many were astonished to see that the Duke of Zhou honoured his promise and passed the mandate of heaven to his brother's son. But others nodded knowingly: heaven's changes were essential to the order of the spheres, and nothing mattered more than a star that knew its place in the constellation of the whole.

*   *   *

Two hundred years passed and it seemed to most that heaven's blessings would truly be without end. Riches cascaded into Feng; across the lands, the cities of the Zhou relatives grew into citadels of power; everyone was fed with the abundant grains of the vast surrounding fields. But over time, with blessings in all directions and heaven seemingly satisfied, the dedicated example set by the Duke of Zhou began to wane. As the wealth and power of the Zhou relatives had grown, so their descendants had come to see the territories over which they had been given charge, as fiefdoms of their own. What difference, many of them began to wonder, stood between themselves and the Zhou king? The bonds that had once tied the Zhou world together became little more than an ever-expanding roll of titles and names. The sacrifices, now conducted from every city, multiplied with ever-diminishing meaning. And the music that had once commanded hearts and souls became a ritual without a heart.

Wonderings turned to murmurings, and murmurings to mutterings. Where once respect had flowed across the cities of the Zhou world, by 800 BCE even heaven seemed to be raising questions: the weather began to step out of its seasons, while earthquakes and comets added their own celestial concerns. Anxious to restore their power, successive Zhou kings had hoisted martial banners and ordered their forces to stretch heaven's earth and create a greater wealth with which the muttering relations might be pacified. To the north, the west and the south, barbarian lands had been seized and, briefly, the murmurings were quelled. But the city stars at home were not convinced for long. Blood had long since turned to water. While no one wanted to question heaven directly, every relative with a city was raising his own Hall of Light: the cities began to turn away from the Feng capital and look towards fortunes of their own.

Heaven had waited – no doubt hoping that the Zhou would succeed in ordering the family house. But in 771 BCE, it finally shook. When the

Zhou king led a vast army against one of the most stubborn of the westerly barbarian tribes, the barbarians replied with a force of troops unleashed not only on the field but in a march directly on the capital of Feng. The Zhou world held its breath.

Heaven, however, was not quite ready to withdraw its mandate. Help arrived in the form of a rescuing barbarian tribe that had modelled itself on the order of the Zhou world. Feng was lost (a heavenly lesson), but the barbarian rescuers escorted the Zhou king to a new capital in surviving Zhou lands to the east. The Zhou line had been saved. The heavenly reputation of the Zhou dynasty, though, had not. And while heaven might have saved the Zhou, it seemed undecided as to their future. With no obvious alternative, a weak Zhou king sat on the throne, and the conclusion reached across the Zhou cities was that bets should henceforth be hedged. As the Zhou king raised a new Hall of Light in a new eastern capital, the relative-rulers of the Zhou cities decided to keep their own Halls of Light as well.

Over the next two hundred years, with Halls of Light in every city-state, the Duke of Zhou's *Book of Changes* was consulted everywhere – although few now had the patience to look for its deeper meanings. The rituals were observed, but with minds increasingly narrowed to the possibilities of power, eyes lost their hearts, and everyone's local circumstance was now governed by mere pomp. The Duke of Zhou's idea of everything in its place and with a purpose retreated to the mists of a 'golden' past, and the majestic order of the spheres began to fray, not only within the central Zhou court but within the now-myriad courts of the Zhou world. The rulers of the Zhou's cities began to look for ever-greater scholarly bureaucracies of their own, which, with their prized knowledge and power of writing, could help them keep an independent order. With scholars now less in demand at the declining central court of the Zhou, many were happy to wander.

Side by side with the scholarly bureaucracies, the rulers of the city-states also looked to their armies and generals: as the old order had begun to fray, power had become a competition. Highly prized were those generals who could snatch at a neighbour that might be ready to fall. In an increasingly uncertain world, covenants of peace (written in blood and copied to heaven) became the currency of rule. But with the stakes so high, ambition almost always proved more powerful: the drums of war rolled, the blood of covenants was regularly spilled and, more often than not, heaven was simply notified of a change.

Still under the heavenly umbrella of the Zhou, but with the Zhou now in a celestial slumber, successful stately cities became individual city-states. But without the higher 'golden' order of the Duke of Zhou, within the city states, everyone began to question. Younger brothers questioned the right of older brothers to rule. Men whose place had been to provision the household of a noble began to look to their own fortunes – trading their master's wealth for causes of their own. Rulers of the city-states looked for greater wealth. And in so doing, they offered peasants who had been bonded to the land the chance to replace their labouring duty to feudal lords with taxes payable to the city-state, tied, of course, to the success of a harvest.

Everywhere, once simple lives were exchanged for a game played with the dice of uncertain change. Some won, others lost. The greatest of the losers lost their city-states, their positions or their homes. The poorest of them, peasant labourers who succumbed to a failed harvest, not only risked the forfeit of their land to a tax-insisting city-state but, without land to farm also lost, the ability to exercise the only skill with which they could survive. Merchants became willing buyers of lands buried in the debts of unpaid taxes, and of desperate peasants and their children. And when children became the stuff of trade, few were surprised that theft became a valued talent and violence a price that everyone had to pay.

By 600 BCE, the old story of the Duke of Zhou had faded into a fairytale; unity was a dream of the past. Heaven and earth were parting company at a terrifying pace, and on earth each city looked after itself. Heartfelt reflections on the duty of a ruler to find and follow the *dao* way had long ago yielded to narrow calculations of territory and power. Battles and punishments were the order of the day. The past, and all of its principles, was gone; the future was clearly waiting for a map.

With the old order weakening, new minds expressed opinions. The loudest were to be found among the scholars – those who had the additional advantage of special insights into heavenly thought. But they were not alone. As the fortunes of the city-states rose and fell, the roads of the old Zhou world were travelled by craftsmen and traders whose talents had built the pavilions of power. And as the peasants continued to deliver harvests far more reliably than any ruler kept his promises, even the fields developed ideas of their own. While the Duke of Zhou's *Book of Changes* might have been forgotten by many of those at the heavenly top, down on the ground, copied on to bamboo strips, it was memorised by those who consulted it for themselves – not selfishly but with increasing concern about the state of the collapsing Zhou world. From temple courtyards to marketplaces, along roads and at the edges of fields, conversation flowed in all directions.

By 500 BCE, with the city-states now fat with ambition and increasingly concentrated on the wider opportunities of power, with battles casting shadows across everyone's horizons, and with untrained minds chattering at every junction, demand for the talents of the scholars rose. From the portents of the stars to the choreography of ritual, from the archiving of what had gone before, to the stratagems of power, the scholars' skills were talents an anxious ruler could always use. Those who brought knowledge from afar were particularly prized.

*   *   *

One of the many scholarly officials who decided to travel along the roads of the fading Zhou empire was a man named Confucius. Born in the city-state of Lu, distant descendant of a shaman, tutored in *The Book of Changes*, and each great text that had followed, Confucius had mastered every skill that a scholar-official could acquire. But, like so many others, the state of Lu had fallen prey to men who grasped rank with money rather than acquiring it through virtue. Ruled more by intrigues and machinations than by its Hall of Light, supported more by punishments than shame, the changes of the cosmos had become the least of anyone's concerns. Temples hosted rituals without meaning; pavilions were flooded with music that chimed regardless of the seasons.

Dreaming of the golden age of the Duke of Zhou, but without the independence of an inherited income, Confucius made no public comment, simply doing his best to model his own contributions on the discipline and diligence of the selfless, golden, past. But as he worked his way up the bureaucratic ladder, he wondered how the purity of that past might be recaptured and how, in an age of greed and division, the ruler of a state could become the force of harmony and unity through which a peaceful order of heaven could again appear.

Casting his mind across his own decades of thought and experience, Confucius contemplated the wisdom of ancient shamans. In so doing, he found himself continually returning to *The Book of Changes*, to the tenets that had guided the duke and the rituals that had underpinned his court. Eventually, Confucius discerned a set of ordering principles on which, he believed, the golden age of the past could be restored. Of course, he observed, no ruler should be worrying about life after death: if one had not yet understood life, what could be the point of speculating on matters after

29

death? But, charged with co-ordinating the affairs of heaven on earth, there were, he felt, certain qualities and relationships which would ensure that a ruler could find the *dao* way, and that the people would conduct themselves in a manner conducive to the greater harmony of all.

The first and most fundamental of qualities was *ren*, the empathy, or benevolence, with which all men were born, and which, as the greatest of the ancient shamans had demonstrated, enabled man to identify with the cosmos and his fellow man. Key to all knowledge and understanding – and to the harmony that such knowledge and understanding delivered – *ren* was the attribute that made possible the civilisation of society. It was the essence of humanity. It was what distinguished man from a beast.

From *ren* sprang the qualities of *yi*, integrity, *li*, ritual and *de*, virtue. *Yi* 'integrity' was a matter of clarity and truth. *Li* 'ritual' was not a spectacle of vain glorification but a prompt which, grounded in stories and carried out in the rhythms of music, dance and sacrifices, would choreograph everybody's lives. Constantly practised, it would ensure that everyone remembered his name and purpose, and where he stood in the celestial hierarchy. *De* 'virtue' not only ensured that the Son of Heaven would find the *dao* way of the state, but that the men within the all-under-heaven lands would cultivate themselves to such a degree that they would become *junzi*, gentlemen, and the *dao* would be found and followed by all.

To these, Confucius added the quality of *zhi*: the pursuit of knowledge that would ensure every decision taken was wise. To be complete and reliable, such knowledge would be grounded in a *ge wu*, investigation of things: a constant enquiry into everything. Things present, that could be observed with one's own eyes and heart; and things past, that could be understood by a mastery of the wisdom contained in the ancient texts, such that none of the accumulated discoveries on which the Duke of Zhou's golden age had been founded (and the Yellow Emperor's lands originally raised) would ever be lost.

Each of the qualities identified by Confucius was part of an inner life that every citizen of all-under-heaven, from the Son of Heaven through the heads of families and down to the youngest sons of the land, should cultivate. And the cultivation of these qualities was not to be sought through an abstract reflection on the civilising features which distinguished man from beasts, but as a practical pursuit of the greater order on which civilisation itself is based.

Intertwined with the qualities was an ordering set of family relationships. Each of these would rest on the fundamental principle of *xiao*, the filial piety upon which every household and the greater 'family' of the state depended: fathers at the helm, older brothers above younger brothers, men above women. With each individual family as harmonious as the music of the spheres, the state, which was surely just a gathering of small families into one, would be a symphony, with the ruler above as the conductor of heaven and earth, the chorus of the people below, and the ministers, officials and scholars in between.

Applied by all, Confucius insisted, these qualities and relationships would deliver a new golden age of peace and unity – a resurrection of the golden age of the Duke of Zhou, when the Son of Heaven governed with integrity and respect rather than rules and punishments. And with everyone's eyes returned to the order of heaven, hearts would turn against the selfish pursuit of individual gain that could only ever result in everybody's ruin.

Looking for any opportunity to apply his principles to the government of Lu, Confucius worked as hard as any of the Great Men of the ancient past. Eventually, he became a junior minister to the Duke of Lu. But the city-state of Lu was far too caught up in battling intrigues and machinations for its duke to take any interest in the dreams of a man who seemed to have lost touch with the real world. Eventually, at the age of fifty-four, Confucius concluded that Lu had irretrievably lost its way. Heaving a sigh of regret, he packed his modest belongings and set off to find a ruler who would welcome the chance to build a more solid future by understanding the wisdom of the past.

The roads were long, and the city-states many. At every opportunity, Confucius presented his model of good government: pursue the *dao* way by being a master of change; embrace the *ren* empathy of putting yourself in other people's shoes; hold on to the *yi* integrity which ensures that things are called by their correct names, and that names and purposes are always carefully correlated; observe the *li* ritual which ensures that no one forgets their place in the whole. Keep to the true *zhi* knowledge; hold to the ge wu investigation of things; strive for the *de* virtue of diligence and discipline. And never stray from the concept of the *jia* family as the pattern for all.

The wisdom was clear: be good and the people will follow; cultivate yourself and the order of heaven will naturally appear on earth. Indeed, as Confucius observed, if you cannot cultivate yourself, how could you try to cultivate anyone else? Many fellow travellers who met Confucius on his journeys were quick to see the wisdom of his words – more than words, some suggested, surely his ideas were a manifesto of civilisation itself. But within the gates of every city, Confucius found that the machinations of the city-states were not limited to Lu. Rulers wanted scholarly minds that could supply a quick solution to a problem: increasingly, they wanted military strategists who could prepare a battle plan at will. In a world where everyone wanted to command as much as they could, quick results were everything. True, not everywhere was quite as lost as the state of Lu, but no ruler seemed able to grasp the value of the treasures that Confucius was placing before them.

After fourteen years of travel, Confucius turned for home and applied himself to teaching smaller men the precepts he had prepared. In the disturbing chaos of the time, many came to his door to learn, but none had the power to apply his ideas to the grander scale of government. When Confucius died in 479 BCE at the age of seventy-one, he had little hope that much would change. But at least, he thought, he had lived according to his principles, and taught others to follow in his modest steps. A small star, no doubt, but heaven had its reasons and he had done his best.

Those whom Confucius had taught taught others in their turn. But as they travelled, they found men with much older ideas of a different 'cosmic' wisdom wandering across the troubled lands of the Zhou. Taught by masters of *The Book of Changes*, they had no dreams of holding up the city-states or of conducting heaven and earth for the greater harmony of all. Seeing the idea of cities and states as an epic mistake, they insisted that the only force on earth was that of the natural order of the cosmos – an order within which man had neither responsibility nor power, but to which man could adapt, and in adapting become something greater than himself. Encountering such ideas on the road, Confucius' students found themselves confronted with questions that left them almost speechless. 'What on earth had any human being to do with the idea of order?' was one. 'How could anyone believe that the Duke of Zhou (let alone the Yellow Emperor or Yu the Great) had anything useful to say?' was another. '*Ren* empathy and *yi* integrity? Good principles if you can find them, but if you're looking for them in a city-states then you're wasting your time.'

'*De* virtue?' others queried. 'Nothing but the arrogance of city men who fail to understand that nothing they do can have a cosmic consequence any greater than the sneezing of a gnat.' And as for *li* ritual, their disdain was almost palpable: 'Self-distracting mumbo-jumbo. However much kings and emperors might have wished it otherwise, the *dao* way of the shamans could not be reduced to a handbook for anyone – least of all for a family or a state.'

Expounding on their beliefs, the cosmic thinkers explained to Confucius' followers that the ancient texts from which *The Book of Changes* had been written were not designed to put man under the order of a ruler but were the accumulated wisdom of those who, having humbled themselves before the greater order of nature, had understood that heaven and earth were far more powerful and complex than a human being could ever imagine. Forces that could scarcely be contemplated, no paltry human words could ever describe them – and man tinkered with them at everyone's peril. And as for Confucius' *zhi* idea of knowledge, their contempt was clear: the narrow human identification of what is useful and what is not (beloved of every ruler since the Yellow Emperor) had been nothing but a recipe for the disasters with which everyone was now living. Surely any fool could see that, in the constantly changing *yin-yang* world, it was only those who knew the value of the useless who could understand the value of the useful.

While Confucius' students struggled to answer, the cosmic ideas were being embraced by more and more hearts who were increasingly strained by the troubles of the times. A few, struck by the force of the cosmic proposition, left the city-states to follow its exponents into the mountains and the forest, where man was not at war with nature. Others stayed in the cities but kept the cosmic ideas warm in their hearts, consulting them in the quiet of night, thinking of them when the ups and downs of human life became too much for any man to bear. And many memorised the text of a work known to some by the name its readers had given to its self-effacing author – Laozi, 'old master' – and known to others by its title: *Dao De Jing, The Classic of the Way.*

Composed before Confucius had lived, and in lines whose poetry echoed the mysteries of the cosmos itself, Laozi's work observed that, in a world of changes, the wisdom of the ancient shamans had not been the revelation of a once-and-for-all set of principles designed to give man the power to rule the world. Rather it had been the discernment of a way of thinking and living that, if followed, would bring man into harmony with the natural order. Grasp this simple wisdom, Laozi had written, and the 'myriad things' would fall at your feet. Lose it, he added, and sooner or later everything would evaporate from your grasp. Watching as the ancient knowledge fell on ears deafened with ambition, Laozi had reached the conclusion that the jostling lands of the Yellow Emperor would be unlikely ever to understand its meaning. As the city-states grew ever bigger, he walked to the farthest wall that divided the Yellow Emperor's lands from those of the barbarians to the west, and passed through the Jade Gate into a natural world where man was free to find his peace within the truer cosmic order that governed all.

33

Time passed, and the Zhou's dream of heavenly rule continued to crumble. As many embraced the ideas expressed by Laozi in their hearts, Confucius' principles also gained greater currency, particularly among scholars who saw a renaissance of the golden age of the Duke of Zhou as the only hope for the settled world.

Nearly two hundred years after Confucius' death, with so many scholars wandering between the city-states that they would come to be known as the 'hundred schools of thought', another cosmic mind appeared. This one not only tried to put some of the oldest ideas of the *dao* into words but to set them against Confucius' misguided premise that a simple set of principles could deliver order for the settled world. The name of the man was Zhuang, and he and his work came to be known as (the) Zhuangzi. Taking up the age-old argument against cities and states, Zhuangzi declared that 'good government' was a contradiction in terms: the only order was that of the cosmos, within which man was no more than a speck of dust. In Zhuangzi's opinion, the idea of heavenly appointed rulers was a gross deception, which had simply legitimised the arrogance of man. All that the Great Men of the past had achieved was a tyranny of obstacles that put brambles under everyone's feet and prevented the ordinary human from finding peace. And if anyone on earth truly wanted to look for order, they should stop moving mountains, give up the pursuit of straight paths and accept that the way of the cosmos is as crooked as a brook.

By 400 BCE, with the Zhou Son of Heaven languishing under heaven's seeming slumber, the city-states had flung themselves into a warring race to replace him. Smaller states had fallen to larger neighbours; many had turned their troops against each other. Engineering talents honed in the taming of rivers were now applied to defence and attack: moats to defend one's own walls, and siege machines designed to collapse the walls of others. Peace became a disappearing dream. Covenants and ritual had long ago given way to generals and strategy. Fathers and elder brothers went off to a front and were never seen again; younger brothers followed in their footsteps. For the peasants in the fields, the ravages of war were only a conscription away.

Loaded back and forth, the arguments between the city-states were never short of words. From time to time even heaven was brought into the equation. But it was the chariots, the battle-axes and the armies that won the day. And as the generals fought, the minds of their rulers turned inevitably to the knowledge that would bring victory in the battlefield. 'Know your enemy and know yourself,' urged one general, in his thoughts on war. To which, he added, 'If any soldier, hearing and understanding, fails to obey, he should be despatched to the skies without a moment's hesitation.' The general's name was Sunzi, and one day his wisdom would come to be known as the *Bingfa* – the Rules (or 'Art') of War.

By 300 BCE, with every ruler's attention fixed on winning what had now become a war of all against all, criticisms of the present could only be safely expressed within a carefully constructed code – with all truths masked in observations carefully softened for sensitive ruling ears. But scholarly minds continued to carry their critical questions up and down the roads of the collapsing Zhou world, each seeking new ideas of order that could restore peace to all. In private homes (or in the open chaos of the marketplace), the failings of the present and its rulers were constantly exposed to a searing criticism, with new ideas regularly rising to challenge the old.

One of the newer ideas of order came from a man known as Mozi. A carpenter and master of the 'cloud ladders' used to conquer the walls of enemy cities, Mozi saw the greatest challenge in establishing order as that of preserving the humanity of man. With a deep belief in the importance of man's love for his fellow man, Mozi was sympathetic to Laozi's idea that the cities were the enemy of human hearts. 'Bind the fingers of those who would keep building the city-states,' he argued, 'smash their arcs and plumb lines, throw away their compasses and squares.' The battling rulers, the busybody bureaucrats, the punishing officials and the warring generals were obstructing everyone's way. In a world where misfortune showered down like rain, and where good fortune was as light and evasive as a feather, everyone should stop and think about what it meant to be human. 'More has been forgotten by man', Mozi argued, 'than man has ever learnt; and more has been destroyed by man than man has ever created.'

Mozi then turned to Confucius (as Zhuangzi had before him) and observed that here was a man who, however good his intentions might have been, had rushed off down the wrong path. Looking at footprints rather than shoes, Confucius had misunderstood the ancient ideas brought together in *The Book of Changes*. Obsessed with his hero the Duke of Zhou, he had conspired with the Great Men of the past to create an illusion of human order based on a bureaucratic dabbling that could only make things worse. In reality, Mozi noted, these so-called 'Great Men' were no more than a succession of overactive busybodies who had worn themselves out in a bid to impose a human idea of order on heaven's earth. Forget cities and their states, Mozi argued, discard glory, step out of the yoke of the sacrificial ox and follow the old shamans to find your own simple way in your own simple life, consulting the changes of the cosmos with the same natural instinct with which you take each breath.

Mozi was not the only man with another idea of order. Others looked back to one of the earliest Great Men: Shennong, the original farmer, whose star had faded beside the glittering triumphs of the Yellow Emperor and Yu the Great but who was surely a far better model for an orderly future. The shaman who had discovered the secrets of the soil and of the animals, it was Shennong who had turned the earth into a treasure-trove for humans. And, unlike those who had come after him, Shennong had not tamed rivers or built cities, but had put his back to the plough and worked among the people in a community where every man was an equal brother. Forget the grander visions of delivering a heavenly triumph on earth, these others argued. Forget the cities with their raised pavilions and armies of peasants, who laboured until their backs broke. Go back to the fields and to the very earliest idea of *de*, virtue. Put every hand to the plough, live within the treasures that nature offers and make every heart count.

The many sceptics of Mozi's ideas and the Shennong ideal countered that Shennong's dream had been given up as impractical a long time ago, not least by the Yellow Emperor, who had realised from the age of ten that a people needed a state and that a state needed a ruler with a plan.

Some, however, saw much to be recommended in the dreams of Mozi and Shennong. Guaranteeing human security through universal love, living through sharing, ruling by example rather than force: surely these ideas offered a better route to order than anything that the dreams of the Yellow Emperor (or Confucius) offered. Skip the rituals, cancel the music, and bridge the gap between the rich and the poor: what could be more orderly than that? Many – particularly the peasants and the artisans at the tightly ordered bottom of the city-state world – agreed that Mozi's ideas had much to recommend them.

Those at the increasingly precarious top, however, were unconvinced. The Shennong ideal seemed a little dour. It also seemed to miss the point. The Zhou king was clearly no longer ruling, and mysteriously, heaven appeared to have gone to sleep. But at some point soon, heaven would wake up to the fact that a new ruler was required. The only real question was who it would be. And the only way to find the answer was to keep going to war.

The arguments continued. Those who believed in the essential importance of a Great Man in conducting the harmonies of heaven and earth were convinced that unity within each city-state was essential – how to achieve such unity, however, was as clear as mud. Punishments were meted out in all directions but everyone continued to hold their own opinion, even as the practicalities of order hurtled out of anyone's control.

Eventually, though, the great debates of the past began to narrow. Laozi, Zhuangzi, Mozi and Shennong were increasingly set aside: not only was it clear that men were not equal, but it was obvious that the men of the city-states were not going to take themselves back to small communities in the fields. And then there was the practical observation that Confucius had once made: 'Given that man is neither a bird nor a beast, what is the point in hankering after an ancient time in the wild?' The question of order increasingly turned to Confucius' preoccupation with the self-cultivating order of man.

And in focusing on the idea of self-cultivation as the essence of human order, attention soon returned to the matter of man's nature: was man inherently 'good', in which case he could be trusted to cultivate himself; or was he inherently 'bad', in which case any idea of self-cultivation would be a fool's errand and the only solution would be to bend his nature to a greater will.

Those who argued that man was essentially 'good' pointed to the innate ability of human beings to recognise and accommodate the needs of others, and to a natural sense of shame that responded far better to kind acts of correction than to brutal punishment. Those who argued that man was essentially 'bad' pointed to a deep self-interest, which meant that only the application of painful punishments could lead him to change his ways. The champions of 'man as good' retorted that even brutal punishments seemed to make no difference. The champions of 'man as bad' replied that the punishments were obviously not brutal enough. With death and destruction in every direction, they added, it was time to make it clear that the order of a city-state was essential for everyone's survival; that order required leadership; and that leadership required responsibility.

And heaven? Nobody was really very sure any more what heaven thought – or even if there was one. Some went so far as to argue that every 'fact' of the past was nothing but a mistake, if not a delusion, including the very idea of heaven itself. Others, hearing such words, caught their breath in shock.

With wars in every direction, little hope of peace, and with the minds of the scholars (and everyone else) hopelessly divided, a small number of men left the city-states of the collapsing Zhou world to seek their fortunes in a new state that was rising rapidly from the barbarian west. A rough, dry place where there was no room for contemplation or argument, it certainly had no time to wait for heaven to make up its mind. With the war of all wars to be won and the prize of the old Zhou world at stake, its successive rulers had begun to welcome men of talent from every direction, to join them in facing up to the responsibilities of the time in which they were living, rather than speculating about what a Yellow Emperor or a Great Yu (or anyone else who had lived three thousand years ago) might do.

Leaving one of the Zhou city-states to start a new life in the barbarian west, one scholar observed that while mothers might love their children twice as much as fathers, the orders of a father were ten times more effective; and while a state might not love its people, its orders were ten thousand times more effective than those of any father. The world had changed. As the rising power in the barbarian west had understood, it was time to be hard in the interests of doing good. Laws should be stated clearly and applied uniformly, with neither humanity nor generosity. The good should be rewarded and the bad truly punished as a lesson to themselves and an example to all. And if anyone tried to muddy the waters by appealing to the past to condemn the present, they and all of their family should accept responsibility for the error of their ways – with the forfeit of their lives.

The name of the state was Qin.

CHAPTER 4

A SINGLE HEART

All under heaven are of a single heart's resolve,
gripping a single will.

Qin Shi Huangdi (inscription at Mount Tai, 219 BCE)

The force moved like a dark cloud. The ground trembled. Behind the fortress walls of the Shangdang garrison of the small state of Han, no one in that year of 265 BCE was in any doubt about the cause. Peering into the dust-filled distance, long-feared shapes began to take their terrifying form. A thousand banners beat the air. Ten thousand snorting horses hurled themselves forward in a storm of thundering hoofs. Sharply drilled to order, five hundred thousand pairs of following feet pounded at a heavy pace. Swords swinging at their sides, axes glinting on their backs, first ten thousand soldiers came into view, and then ten thousand more. And still they came, like waves, ten thousand at a roll. Suddenly, a bronze gong struck, the depths of its echo calling a halt. Hoofs and feet obeyed. For a moment, silence hung like a thread in the air. And then the drums began to beat; the thread was cut, and thousands of men rushed forward. At a single piercing command, crossbows were loaded and ten thousand arrows turned the sky to black.

Within the Shangdang garrison it was clear to all that the small state of Han could not withstand the forces of the mighty Qin. The heavenly Zhou king was still sleeping in the east, languishing in a celestial dream. Only Zhao to the north – once a brother within the great Zhou family, now one of the many warring states – could push Qin back behind the western mountains. But would Zhao come? Battles were two-a-penny, the loss of a state was nothing new, and with the idea of brotherhood now a relic of the past, what had Zhao to gain? Messages were despatched with haste, and sealed with a promise: 'Shangdang is Zhao's,' they offered, 'simply for the taking. Anything but a fall to Qin.' Meanwhile, the arrows rained down upon Shangdang's garrison walls, and Qin roamed as the terror of the world.

*   *   *

More than five hundred years had passed since 771 BCE when the heavenly Zhou had fled from west to east. Challenged by a wild tribe known as the Rong, its barbarian rescuer had been a small state at the north-west edge of the Zhou world: Qin. A dry patch of rainless earth locked behind the western Taihang mountains, Qin had only narrow mountain passes to bring it into contact with the settled eastern world. More often described as a 'pack of wolves and tigers' (it had been founded by a horse-breeder with ambitions to join the settled world), Qin was rarely accorded recognition as a 'state'. But having granted himself the title of duke, as he rescued the Zhou from their attackers, the horse-breeder's descendants had not only secured respect but had also stretched his domain: forced to flee, the escaping Zhou had offered their abandoned western lands to Qin – if Qin could wrestle them from the Rong. Where the softening Zhou had failed, the tougher Qin succeeded.

The new Zhou capital had faded into a heavenly cloud, and the once-mighty noble families of the now 'Eastern Zhou' had begun the spiral of battles that would eventually lead to the war of all against all. Standing on the sidelines to the west, Qin had watched the unfolding events with interest: thousands of battling city-states reduced to hundreds, and almost all simultaneously shattering under competing branches of the noble families who had built them. Ambitious sons conspiring to take kingdoms for themselves, jealous uncles seizing opportunities for gain, once-friendly advisers changing colour: the permutations of intrigue knew no end. By 400 BCE, the city-states were battling each other in mutual destruction – and the greatest of them all, Jin, had found itself torn into three: Zhao, Wei and Han.

While the Zhou family and its many city-state had been crumbling from within, the Qin 'pack of wolves and tigers' had raised an army and, learning their lessons scrap by scrap, pushed its way through the rough western mountain passes out to the east and the fertile banks of the Yellow River. When the hundreds of surviving Zhou city-states had been reduced to seven major powers, to everyone's astonishment, those powers included the upstart state of Qin. Struggling to understand how a paltry place could have swelled to such a force, Zhou family minds paused to reflect.

Clearly, it must have been luck. While Qin had the usual barbarian pretensions to the heavenly virtues of civilisation, its rabid population of wolves and tigers could certainly have no place in heaven's order. Their banging pots and swaying bodies could not charm the spheres; their clumsy sacrifices would never achieve the magic of the *li* rituals; their brash brawls held no *yi* integrity; and the brutal animal code by which they lived certainly showed no *ren* humanity.

Somehow, though, Qin turned its barbarian fate to fortune. Even the Taihang mountains, which separated it from heaven's world, had been transformed from an obstructive wall to a defending shield; and the rough lands, which were lucky to see rain, no longer seemed to be a curse but a blessing: forcing the thirsty Qin to push outside and wrest more fertile lands from those who were either too distracted or too weak to answer back. Reaching out to the north-east, Qin had snatched at the fertile banks of the Zhou's Yellow River. Turning to the south, nothing had been easier than to grasp great plains from tribal kingdoms that seemed to have no appetite for war.

Indeed, Qin feats on the battlefield were a marvel to behold – few of anyone else's generals hoped with any confidence to strike them down.

But triumphs of war alone could not account for Qin's run of luck. Powerful alliances had regularly been forged among the other six warring states in bids to defeat the barbarian upstart. In every case, though, almost before the covenanting blood had dried, a whisper or a word crumbled their fragile trust to dust. A king would be persuaded that a brother's rediscovered love was a ruse; allying armies would find themselves led by generals who had no intention to unite; agreed battle plans would be changed at a moment's notice. Defeat seemed to stalk every attempt at unity, and, as often as not, it would be followed by war between those who had come closest to peace. With the oddest spirit behind it, Qin was gaining a foothold in heaven-on-earth. With every battle won, its might expanded. And when its troops had pounded into Shangdang, it had been clear that, unless Qin was checked, nothing short of heaven itself would satisfy its thirst.

When the appeal for help in saving the Han state's Shangdang garrison had reached the state of Zhao in 265 BCE, the calculation had seemed clear: save the Han garrison from Qin and take the opportunity to push the pack of wolves and tigers back behind their mountain passes. Qin's army was mighty but Zhao's was mightier still. The Zhao king had taken time to be convinced but eventually troops were rallied, drums rolled, and a Zhao army marched south under the greatest general of its time – an army so big that surely even Qin would quake at its approach. Arriving in Shangdang in 262 BCE, the Zhao general surveyed the field. Qin had calculated well: every natural vantage point had been exploited, with troop formations meticulously shaped to pitch Qin strength against Han weakness. But, as every general knew, few battles could be won with arrows alone. Far from home, Qin's supply lines would surely be quickly stretched, and even wolves and tigers get hungry. Drawing on nerves of steel and a lifetime of battling experience, the Zhao general busied himself with fortifications and settled his army down to wait.

One month became two, two became three; a year passed and then another. The Zhou world held its breath. At the court of the Zhao state, whispers rustled across the corridors of power, casting barbs of doubt about the general at the front. 'Wasting all this time,' some murmured, 'the stresses of war must have softened his courage.' 'Qin must have been delighted', muttered others, 'that we put such a coward at our helm.' One particular whisper went further: 'Qin is secretly relieved that Zhao has not deployed its greatest living force: a well-born scholar whose mastery of the written texts of past battles has never been sullied by the doubts of any experience of the front; if sent to the field such a highly cultivated brush would surely have the Qin quivering in their boots.'

The whispers reached the ears of the king and led him to wonder if he had somehow missed a trick. It was not long before his doubts led to the recall of the great general from the field, and the advance of the well-born bookworm to the front. Within days, the new Zhao general had marched the army from its cowardly defences and opened up his forces for all to see.

The immediate result was indeed spectacular: the mighty Qin seemed to race away in fear; with the great Zhao army sweeping after them, victory had seemed all but assured. But as the Zhao rushed to what appeared to be the clear front lines of the Qin, a message flew from the back to the front:

four hundred and fifty thousand soldiers deep, the rear of the Zhao army was coming under a storm of arrows from behind. Buried in his books, the new Zhao general had forgotten to look to his rear.

Within less than a day, three years of waiting patience had been lured into a trap. While Qin's supply lines were badly stretched, Zhao's had now been severed; the tide had turned. Qin waited. Cut off, Zhao's troops were forced to eat their dead. With the nerves of their scholarly general made of little more than paper, the bravest of the Zhao soldiers were commanded to follow him in a desperate bid to break out. Courage never wanting, they obeyed. Within an instant, the general was shot down and the four hundred thousand surviving Zhao soldiers were left without a leader. Within days, they surrendered.

As the news spread across the greater old Zhou world, heads nodded sadly: yet another battle lost in the wars that had scarred the past two hundred years; more defeated soldiers straggling home, shamed. When would it ever end? Surrendering its soldiers to Qin, however, the Zhao state had confidently expected the usual *de* virtues of heavenly war to apply. Shangdang would now be Qin, but surely the Qin ruler would return the vanquished troops with the same *ren* humanity that every heavenly ruler ritually observed.

Behind the mountain passes, though, Qin had taken a different view. The charge of heaven demanded leadership, which required responsibility, and responsibility required unswerving attention to the facts. The garrison of Shangdang was indeed a prize, but with such a force of fighting men returned to the ranks, Zhao could always fight again. Better to wipe the board clean and bury the beating hearts of the living in a settled field of death. Four hundred thousand Zhao souls were swiftly despatched to meet their ancestors. Across the old Zhou world, everyone's blood ran cold.

*   *   *

To the few who had taken the trouble to become familiar with the state of Qin, the brutal outcome had been a foregone conclusion. While the scholars of the old Zhou world had been debating the finer points of heavenly order, Qin had been strengthening its might. And just as new ideas had travelled across the warring states, they had also wandered into Qin. Not the finest ideas, of course. A hardy people, Qin had little to commend itself to a Confucius or a Laozi; this was a land that saw nature more as a beast than a gentle path.

But for some of the Zhou world the rough ideas of Qin had a strong appeal. Qin might be barbarian, but within its tough exterior was a glittering metal with a value. Unconcerned with *ren* empathy, for Qin, survival itself was a virtue. Undisturbed by *yi* integrity, Qin minds were quick to grasp any advantage that could twist itself into triumph. And untrammelled by *li* ritual, Qin had no scruples about disguising its men to roam the courts of its enemies.

One man who had seen Qin's breathtaking triumphs from afar was a scholarly son of the distant sibling-state of Wei. A man who had watched the fine ideas of the old Zhou world crumble into the dust of war, and with it the lives of men he had called his friends: his name was Shang Yang. Struck by what he had heard of the fresh energies of the west, in 359 BCE Shang Yang had packed his bags, and, presenting himself to the court of Qin, had been enchanted by what he heard and saw. Here was a land where the past was not even a memory, and where any golden age that might once have existed had long ago been buried along with any soft hearts that dreamt of such a thing. A heavenly family? Nothing but a luxury. Virtue above survival? Pure vanity. Musical harmonies to temper human chaos? A wilful blindness that deserved to fail. If man had ever been good (and it was unclear that he ever had), those days were clearly over. Government by a family fixed in heaven had obviously failed. There might well be a *dao* way; but if there was, it was reserved for the ruler who had the courage to order a state. That Zhou general (Sunzi with his art of war), who had tried to tell the city-states that order was all, had hit the nail right on the head: discipline was everything.

Delighted with the ideas he encountered, Shang Yang sought an audience with the king of Qin. Listening to Shang Yang's praise of the order of his state, the king had been equally delighted: finally a mind from the refined world of the east that understood the wisdom of the wilder west.

Sheltered behind the mountain passes, free from the chattering of idle scholarly minds, and with the full trust of his new ruler, Shang Yang dismissed the state's scholars and transformed Qin ideas into a 'reforming' manual for rule. Clear goals were set: agriculture for food, war for survival, and the people as guarantors of both. The principles were clearly stated: *ding fa yi min* (fix the rules, order the people). Convert all useful knowledge into rules; set down the rules in black and white; and achieve the correct standards of behaviour with painful punishments as reminders that every failure has its price. With Shang Yang's more detailed order, the Qin people were turned

44

into a power that could snatch victory in any war, and could even be trained to order themselves.

For Shang Yang, turning a people into the force of a state was a three-step matter of discipline conducted to a level of detail from which none could escape. The first step was to control the land with registers and maps: registers to keep a record of every human head in the country; maps to divide the land into county units of administration and then to mark every village in the land upon them. The second step was to use the registers and maps to order the population into households, which – each charged with paying its taxes from the produce of its fields and the soldiering of its men – would be constantly available for the service of the state. The third step was to transform the people into instruments of their own command. Learning from the successes of the battlefield (and with family affections seen as a foolish distraction that no successful state could afford), Qin households were ordered together in groups of five, with each household bound to guarantee the orderly obedience of all. Any failure, of any member of any household, to comply with any rule was to be reported to the head of the group, who would report it to the officials above. Those who made their reports would be rewarded with an exemption from military duty; those who failed to do so would be put to instant death: a swift stroke to the waist with a sword.

Seasons were set in stone, calendars were fixed as farming regulations; even seeds were subject to laws for sowing. Depending on their gravity, derelictions of duty attracted anything from a stiff rebuke and a fine, to a mutilation that would mark a man for life. Performance was measured meticulously; production was tallied by the day; and the results (good or bad) were despatched across the country and reported to the ruler himself. Good harvests and productive weaving could earn a holiday from tax. Poor harvests or failure to meet a quota of cotton cloth attracted the white heat of a brand to the face. One rat-hole discovered in a granary would bring the responsible family a sharp rebuke, two would carry a fine, three the slicing off of a foot or a nose. As obvious enemies of efficiency, quarrels and complaints were banished; anyone unable to restrain their tongue would feel the sting of the lash, just as their own lack of discipline had stung the order of Qin itself. There were no exceptions. Out in the fields, heads ducked and bodies laboured. Everywhere, branded foreheads and lost limbs became a common sight. Trust vanished from the land.

But while Qin's fortunes often seemed to defy the natural principles that applied to everyone else, even wolves and tigers have their *yin* and *yang* changes. In 338 BCE, a new Qin ruler decided that Shang Yang's 'reforms' had gone too far. Tutored as a child in some of the romantic ideas of the Zhou, as a man, the new ruler saw the merits of *yi* integrity, and *ren* humanity. He also saw the brutality of ideas that had pushed Qin beyond the pale of proper rule, turning it into a state whose silenced scholars were too ashamed to lift their heads. Shang Yang was executed. But while a sigh of relief momentarily passed across the land, with Qin and the other six 'warring states' still battling to the death, little else actually changed. And with Qin constantly on the brink of war, the harvesting of food and the securing of survival could brook no luxuries of finer taste: the registers and the maps remained, the responsibilities of the households stayed fixed, and the people continued to guarantee the order of their own behaviour to the state.

With matters 'clarified' at home, the new ruler felt free to settle the surrounding world. To the north (present-day Mongolia), long walls were raised where nomadic tribes from the steppes constantly worried at the Qin frontier. To the south, where wild forests and mountains beckoned, softer tribes were vanquished and brought under Qin command: from the lands of the people known as the Shu, the Ba and the Yue emerged provinces that would become known as Sichuan, Jiangsu, Zhejiang and Anhui – on down to the Nanhai tip at the bottom, which would one day come to be the province of Guangdong. Vast pantries of southern plenty: fields of rice, rivers of turtles and fish, mines of bronze, iron and salt, and lacquer-bearing trees; vast scented forests of pine, cypress and bamboo; and herds of elephants and rhinoceroses, which had long since disappeared from the north.

As the new lands were conquered, triumphs of human engineering (the now-shared legacy of millennia of river taming honed over centuries of the art of war) began to turn rough pastures into expanding fields. Water being everything to men of the dry west, Qin turned its armies to the redirection of the rivers which splashed so unevenly across its rocky lands. Wherever a mountain was an obstacle, its rock was heated and cooled until it cracked enough to open new channels to the other side. Wherever rivers were prone to flood, levees – built from thousands of bundles of rock wrapped in bamboo – were raised like walls. Lands that had once been hostage to the vagaries of an unforgiving nature became watered valleys traversed by rivers as tame as the people themselves.

The rivers tamed, Qin's fields spread and, with its population growing, they filled with labour ready for any task. With war never more than a step away, every seam of Qin possibility was mined. Across the fields, the growing army of peasant farmers, trained to fight to the last inch of their collectively responsible lives became a battle-machine-in-waiting. Within the Qin court, minds constantly turned to the destabilising possibilities of whispering campaigns. And while many battles were fought and won, the Qin were proudest of the victory that had put a bookworm at the head of the Zhao army and so had finally won the battle for the Han garrison at Shangdang.

As Qin counted its victories, by 250 BCE, the greatest minds of the old Zhou world were stumped. How could Qin's relentless conquests be brooked? And where on earth was heaven? Enquiring souls began to question everything, not least the thorny question of whether man was essentially good or bad. Looking at Qin's brutality, some held stubbornly to the view that man was essentially good and that the only way forward was to align oneself with the changes of the *dao* and embrace the Confucian virtues that would (eventually) put everyone on a path to a better future. After hundreds of years of war, though, others were less sure. The Confucian principles of *ren* humanity, *yi* integrity, *li* ritual and *de* virtue were all predicated on the premise that man was essentially good. But what if man was essentially bad? Then Shang Yang's *ding fa yi min* principle, fixing the rules and ordering the people into a single unity through punishment, would be a much better idea.

As the warring states continued to battle, more searching souls set off from the crumbling Zhou east to the barbarian west, crossing the mountainous passes into Qin to take a look. Of those who went, many of the younger ones were persuaded by what they saw: fields neatly tended, granaries full, people in orderly awe of their officials, wars won, wealth rising, and not a bandit or robber to be seen. Older spirits, although impressed by the results, held to their stubborn questions about the means by which it had all been achieved. Certainly, they accepted, it was about time that one stopped leaving everything to heaven and began to recognise that heaven's mandate required a strong sense of responsibility for the order of all. But violence could never be more than destruction, they argued, and coercion was a blind hammering of metal that could never win the love of the people. Qin's methods might seem to offer the promise of success, but if an order could never be questioned, surely any state would ultimately be tilting for a fall. Wars might be won, mountains might be moved, but a state unable to hold the hearts of its people could never hope to hold its peace.

One of the many men who travelled to Qin was a district clerk from the southern state of Chu. A scholar who had studied at the feet of one of the greatest Confucian minds, his name was Li Si. Having studied all of the heavenly virtues, like many others, he could not help thinking that while there was a certain scholarly logic to Confucius' ideas, they had clearly failed. Surely, he thought, it was time to accept that the future was Qin. As the surviving states of the Zhou world prevaricated, an opportunity to be part of that future beckoned to him – a chance of finding the kind of influencing success which would come only once in every ten thousand years.

As Li Si packed his bags to leave, his teacher gave him a parting lesson: 'True, the old Zhou world is failing. But its failures lie with its unwillingness to take the time to think. And, true, man is essentially weak and needs a responsible ruler to lead the way. But a responsible ruler is not immune from the order of the cosmos itself. Marvel all you like at the temporary triumphs. But do not forget to fear.' To which, the teacher added: 'When seasons are regulated without a sensitivity to nature, when calculations of loss and gain are limited to numbers, when fortunes are measured in deaths, and when men lose the trust that binds them not to life but to each other – those are the times when man should be on his guard. Grasp your chance at fortune if you will; ignore the abstract portents of heaven; but do not forget to keep a ready eye for the *human portents* that can overwhelm even the greatest of worldly triumphs.'

Arriving in the state of Qin 246 BCE, Li Si seemed to have fallen on the best of times. The previous king had died before his time, and (highly unusually) a wildly successful merchant who had risen to the heights of advisory power had been appointed as regent to the king's young prince. A native of the state of Wei, the merchant-regent had aspired to add a touch of old Zhou heaven to the new Qin success, recruiting a corps of three thousand Zhou-world scholars to bring more of the older heavenly principles into the Qin court. Li Si was included in the corps, and before a year was out, his talents clear, the merchant-regent made him mentor and guide to the prince.

The years of youth passed; Li Si and the young prince grew ever closer. But by the time the prince came of age, the Qin world was beginning to experience a momentous change. Shocked and insulted by years of the outsider merchant's regent-rule, the nobles of the great Qin ruling family had looked for revenge and found it in a rumour. The young king, it was murmured, was a cuckoo, the bastard son of the old king's wife, his father none other than the merchant-regent himself. In 235 BCE, the merchant-regent was sent to his death, and the young king, his position precarious, turned to Li Si. The moment which came 'only once in ten thousand years' had arrived.

Observing the daggers of gossip floating around the court, Li Si's advice to the stunned young king was swift: put the family at arm's length and distract everyone's attention by taking up the unfinished business of the warring states. Whatever rumours might be on the tongues of the restless nobles across the rest of the crumbling Zhou world, Qin was still a force that everyone held in awe. And, unlike the other states, Qin was well prepared: fields of willing soldiers stood ready to march. Victory over the six surviving states was only a command away; heaven's mandate would be as easy to win as sweeping dust from the top of a stove. And in the final winning of the war to end all wars, the young king would not only defy his doubters, but would unify the world.

Li Si's exhortations struck their target. Peasants set to martial training, the fields were turned to armies and the armies began to march. This time they would not return until heaven was Qin's. In 230 BCE they turned to the east and the state of Han. With its Shangdang garrison already under Qin control, the rest of Han fell with little effort.

In 225 BCE, Qin looked to the nearer state of Wei and consulted the terrain. Washed by the waters of the Yellow River, its lands were vulnerable to a flood. The Qin army was instructed to deploy the engineering skills used to master its own rivers, and divert the Yellow River from its natural course. Without the shooting of a single arrow, the Wei lands disappeared under muddy waters. Qin had won again.

In 223 BCE, turning to the south and east, Qin went on to conquer the mighty Chu – a state where warning voices had long ago been silenced by the whispering campaigns of Qin.

In 222 BCE, its path now clear, Qin advanced east and north to meet the state of Zhao. Thirty-two years after the slaughter of Shangdang, the Zhao troops had yet to recover their confidence; a Qin victory was assured. But, never leaving a hostage to fortune, Qin deployed its usual stroke of whispering campaigns. Smoothed with gold and silent daggers, they ensured that the fatal errors of Zhao command were repeated once againthen . Zhao was defeated. Qin moved on to the more distant north-eastern state of Yan: a state whose ruler had once despatched his greatest swordsman to kill the king of Qin. The assassination had failed, and when the Qin troops arrived, the wrath of Qin swept like a tide of natural retaliation.

By the end of 222 BCE, all that remained of the six Zhou powers was the very distant state of Qi, settled on the shores of the eastern sea. Flanked until recently by stronger rivals, Qi had never seen Qin as much of a threat. But as Han, Zhao and Wei had fallen, every road into Qi seemed to invite destruction. Scrambling its army, the Qi ruler directed the defending sights of his generals to the most likely origin of a Qin attack – the west. But in 221 BCE, Qin's forces found their way through the newly conquered lands of Chu to the south and east. Taken by surprise, Qi, the last of the old Zhou states, fell to yet another triumph of Qin calculation.

Li Si's advice had won the day. In fact, it had won the world, as far as Qin knew it. From the deserts of the west to the sea of the east, from the frontiers of the settled north to the tip of the occupied south, all of the lands and all of their people were now Qin. It was a world wider than any the Shang or the Zhou had ever known, with a wealth far greater than anyone's ancestors could have imagined. And with it came a unity that had been forged not from the old ideas of heaven and Confucius, but from the brutal back of a western beyond.

*   *   *

Reflecting on his conquests, the still-young king of Qin, now master of all, wondered how his victory should be styled. No known expression seemed sufficient to capture the scale of his triumph. The word 'king' hardly hinted at the power he had acquired. In fact, no single title seemed to convey the enormity of what had been achieved.

Ministerial heads were scratched; every annal of the past was consulted. *Huang* was one suggestion: 'yellow', the colour chosen by the emperor who had first united the people along the river of the same name and a word which, across the intervening millennia had come to mean the great and central pivot of everything. Certainly, it was a step in the right direction. On its own, however, it was not quite evocative enough. *Di* was suggested as an addition – the suffix of a title given to the greatest of the ancestors whose wisdom and labours had raised the original heavenly lands from the mists of the past. Almost, but not quite, thought the king. Perhaps one could add *shi*: first. *Qin Shi Huangdi*, the first and greatest emperor. The highest title that any mortal mind could imagine, and one that suggested that 'the first' would unquestionably be followed by a second, a third and a fourth – and so on, across the ten thousand years over which the Qin dynasty would inevitably rule.

Title settled, the young king's attention, so carefully tutored in the old ideas of the Zhou, turned to the critical matter of finding the imperial alignment with the cosmos that, alone, could ensure eternal success. Every secret of the ancient texts was consulted to find the colour, the element and the season that would best express the power of his rule. Shang had been the white metal of autumn, Zhou had been the red fire of summer: conquering Qin would take the gripping black power of winter, with its terrifying ice. Black banners, black pennants, black clothes – black everywhere. And as for the essential magical number that would define the power of the Qin state, with the black ice of winter fixed, this was now easy to see: six, *liu*, a number whose written character when pronounced sounds the same as that for 'running water'. The hats of office were ordered to be six measures high, the carriages of state were to be six measures wide – and every carriage that bore the badge of empire was to be led by six horses. The message was clear: winter had arrived; power was complete; order would be everywhere.

The First Qin Emperor then looked at the vast lands that were now a true empire and considered the challenge of command. The old registers and maps, which had covered the original Qin domain, were stretched to cover the newly conquered lands; and every corner was placed under the power of a military governor. To improve the speed of control, highways were added, built the length and breadth of the new world and bringing everything and everyone within the imperial reach. Goods could now be traded in all directions; taxes could flow from the peripheral edges of order to the centre of power without interruption. Pockets of inconveniently placed people could be moved. Prisoners could be despatched in an instant to provide labour wherever it was needed.

As the land settled to a greater productive order, a new capital city was raised to match the triumphal nature of the state: close to present-day Xi'an, its name was Xianyang. The central point of a single top-down order, it sat at the apex of all. With the geography of power now set, commands would pass from the centre to the edges as smoothly as grain, and labour would flow swiftly from the edges to the centre. A single world with single standards for everyone to obey. No special circumstances to be bent by any wind; no exceptions to prove a rule. And to ensure that any competing idea could be swiftly extinguished, every noble family from every old corner of the new empire was wrapped in an icy embrace and escorted to a palace home – in Xianyang.

Empire and capital now ordered, the remaining differences of the old

Zhou world were hammered to a single iron die. Weights and measures – long since fixed in Qin – were set as standards to be observed across the new imperial lands. Coins were carved to a single Qin image. Taxes were paid with a common currency. The ruts of roads followed the single width (six measures) of the Qin carriage. Language was unified: a single spoken tongue with a single script of commands, which no one, however far away, could argue they had not been able to read and understand.

Words put in their place, the occupations of the people followed suit. With the greatest human purposes being the tilling of fields and the fighting of battles, farmers and soldiers were ranked at the top. The ordering of trade being a matter for the state (and merchants being an untrustworthy distraction from imperial business), the purveyors of goods not useful to the First Emperor were despatched to the chilling edges of the empire. As was every other useless person who failed to deliver a value to the state – including any independent minds that had not already been excised from public life. The privileged few permitted to remain and trade within the Qin cities found themselves under constant watch. In the markets, prices were fixed, and towers were raised so that every transaction could be observed by official eyes; brands were kept ready for anyone who failed to obey.

As the grids of Qin were flung like a net across the rest of what must surely be a grateful world, the First Emperor decided that it was now time to observe the ancient rituals and present his credentials to heaven and the ancestors. In 219 BCE, following in the footsteps of the ancient Zhou (and indeed the Shang who had gone before them), he proceeded north and east to the greatest mountain of all: Mount Tai. The peak which had been declared by the earliest shamans to be the highest intermediary between heaven and earth, this was the point at which every great emperor marked the triumph of his rule.

Raising his sacrifices, the First Emperor duly announced the glory of Qin to the skies. And, lest heaven be tempted to forget the spectacular accomplishments of its newest emperor, he paused to inscribe his achievements upon a rock: order fixed with rules and measures, chaos quelled, peace and stability for the black-haired people – in short, heaven established on earth. The messages clearly despatched, the First Emperor and new Son of Heaven journeyed on across his world, seeking out the other mountains his shamans had told him would connect a ruler directly with heaven above.

*   *   *

Returning back to earth (eventually), there was always something to do –
even with an army for a population. There were roads, palaces and dams
to be built, ditches to be dug, mountains to be moved and canals to be
carved, like veins, into the land. Riding a tiger and flogging the sun, the
First Emperor found that there were never enough days in a year to get
everything done: from time to time, he even had to shout at the moon. And
then, up at the northern edge of the world, a troublesome tribe of nomads
appeared – seemingly unaware that the world was now under the order of an
imperial winter. The emperor's most trusted general was despatched to bring
the nomads up to date, with hundreds of thousands of men commanded to
follow him and raise a single, long wall of four thousand kilometres from
beaten earth and stones. Exposed to some of the world's greatest extremes of
heat and cold, the bones of many fell by its side, never to leave. Meanwhile,
in the south, it seemed that other tribes had also not yet understood that
heaven had arrived. More generals were despatched to announce the news,
each accompanied by an army, all charged with building occupying garrisons
to make sure that everyone was clear.

Back in the capital of Xianyang, more palaces of splendour were being
raised to the sky, many with terraces touching the clouds, and all designed
to replicate heaven on earth. A little to the west, a vast park of palaces
appeared: protected by two mountains serving as gates, and connected by a
suspension bridge in the image of the Milky Way, to carry the emperor from
one sparkling palace to the next.

But as the First Emperor had been proclaiming the orderly end to any
history other than that of the Qin, ill winds were gathering close to home.
Earlier, clumsy, attempts at assassination had failed to kill, but they had,
nonetheless, hit a mark: as far as the First Emperor could see, the world was
full of conspiring minds and, quite possibly, some very malevolent spirits.
Summoned to advise, tamed shamans could only agree – suggesting that it
would be best if the emperor were not seen. Walkways were elevated, imperial
pavilions and roads were walled: no expense was spared nor punishment for
any breach. Anyone even suspected of revealing the movements of the emperor
would be sliced in two without question. And as the walls went up around the
First Emperor, any walls that stood elsewhere in the city were ordered to be
pulled down. Security depended upon the people's buildings being open for all
to see, with secrecy reserved for the emperor alone.

The costs were enormous and the labour so great that even the
punishments struggled to keep pace. Branded faces appeared everywhere;

lost feet and missing noses took no one by surprise. Honest men found that they could not help but break laws that were impossible to keep: many became outlaws by default.

Conveyed along covered roads, carried across elevated walkways, the First Emperor seemed oblivious to the terror around him. Did he not know or did he not care? Few had the courage to ask. But in the privileged debates of his courtly scholars, a risky comment was occasionally advanced. And so it was that in 213 BCE, a scholarly Confucian from Qi, who had survived the conquest of his fallen state, stood up and suggested that if the emperor wanted to be secure in his empire both he and Li Si (now chief minister), might like to gaze back to the lessons of the past. Order was clearly desirable; hierarchies were obviously important. But while a world of single-minded commands blindly issued without regard to the qualities of *ren* humanity, *yi* integrity, *li* ritual, *de* virtue or even *zhi* knowledge might work for a time, it was evident to anyone with eyes to see that a protracted tyranny would end in tears. There was also the matter of the greater imperial family to consider: a family which, in the opinion of the scholar, the emperor had foolishly set aside.

A master, like all Confucians, of the history books, the scholar had gone on to suggest that the First Emperor had only to consult the story of the ancient defeat of the Shang by the Zhou to realise that eventually the power of human hearts would out. Men might be bad, but Confucius had a point: virtues were a value. To which he added that families were a treasure too. With the empire at peace, perhaps the First Emperor might like to invite his own relations to return to serve the imperial state.

Responding on the First Emperor's behalf, Li Si was quick to snap: 'Study the past to guide the present? What kind of claptrap are you peddling?' To which he added that no ancestor had ever scaled the heights of human triumph by looking back to the past, and if the scholars had not understood that simple point, what on earth must be going on in the country at large? Announcing that it was time for a new communications policy, Li Si declared that anyone using the past to criticise the present should be put to death, along with their immediate relatives (the common blood obviously carrying a dangerous strain). In addition, with the scholars daring to question the roots of risk, every home should be commanded to burn its books, with the exception of useful works on agriculture, medicine and divination, of which one copy of each could be kept. Confucian minds were buried, the bamboo burned and Qin fell silent.

A year later, in 212 BCE, the emperor, now aged forty-seven, turned to a matter that had long troubled his heart: immortality and the importance of perpetuating his imperial life. On the advice of his shamans, fortunes had been spent on journeys to find a paradise known as Penglai. Set in misty eastern islands, roughly in the region of present-day Japan, it was thought to be the home of eight immortals who held the secret of eternal life. Exploring boats were stuffed with virgins – far more likely than soldiers to be able to tempt the secret of eternity from the immortals. But not a drop of the secret elixir ever made its way back to Xianyang. Meanwhile, every year, the First Emperor's tomb was getting bigger, even as the emperor himself advanced in age: if the shamans' journeys did not find the elixir soon, the emperor might have to occupy the magnificent underworld he had created. One shaman-captain, returning from a particularly promising (and expensive) mission without the promised secret, blamed his failure on a giant sea monster that had suddenly reared out of the sea. Given another ship and a company of crossbowmen, he was told to make sure that this time they reached their destination. Reading their own omens, however, and fearing for the worst, the fastest of the remaining shamans fled from Xianyang. Slower others (including hundreds of equally unreliable scholars who had failed to burn their books) found themselves buried alive. Only the First Emperor's son and heir dared to raise a question: 'It seems a little extreme', the young prince suggested: 'Surely even heaven should have a heart.' Despatching his oldest son and heir to the wintry northern frontier with an order to apply his energies to the building of the long wall, the First Emperor's rebuke was sharp and swift: 'The desert sands and the freezing steppes would be delighted to listen to your opinions.'

The punishment clear, the First Emperor returned to the matter of his own life and death. With the promised elixir of immortality still eluding his grasp, the sea monster that had thwarted the most promising of his missions was now occupying his dreams. Deciding to send his cold-blooded nemesis to a watery grave, in the summer of 210 BCE, crossbows assembled, the First Emperor led an imperial progress to the coast. No longer trusting his ministers, and with his eldest son and greatest general building the long northern wall, he was accompanied only by his palace guards, favourite eunuchs, a younger son and Li Si. When a giant fish was duly observed, it was quickly executed. But in the days that followed, it seemed that the spirit of the fish had fixed upon revenge. A minor illness became a fever, and immortality began to slip beyond reach. An imperial letter was dictated to order the return of his heir. Within a week, in the fire of a Zhou summer, the First Emperor fell victim to the winter of death, leaving the letter confirming that his eldest son should inherit the empire in the folds of his favourite eunuch's robe.

Secrecy being everything, Li Si, together with the First Emperor's favourite eunuch and the younger son, decided that it might be easier if no one knew that the First Emperor was dead. And much easier if the country's greatest general and the outspoken heir were kept out of the complicated picture. Letters were written in the name of the now-dead First Emperor commanding the general and the heir to take their own lives.

Trusting the soothing words of the eunuch and Li Si (and confident that the punishments of law would guard the throne against any inconvenient questions), the younger son, now 'Second Emperor', directed his thoughts to heaven-on-earth and redoubled the building of everything – with no expense spared. The next two years saw rising costs, accompanying taxes, a scarcity of food, an increase in punishments, and so many executions (as arbitrary as they were final) that they became a daily fact of life. Backs almost broken, those who could fled to the mountains and the forests. Those who could not struggled on until the laws became impossible to obey. Faced with a choice between death by execution for a duty failed, or flight to raise a rebellion that might succeed, some began to think that the latter was a better choice. It was not long before the Qin's army of labouring peasants began to contemplate marching to colours of their own.

Sheltered in the covered walkways of his father's cities, and with everyone who ventured a contrary opinion swiftly executed, the Second Emperor might not have known the risks he was taking. Young and new to power, he was easily persuaded by Li Si and the eunuch to preserve his dignity by avoiding any ministers who might be inclined to tell the truth. Meanwhile, out in the open streets, rebels began to rise and blood to run. Li Si's thoughts belatedly turned to the parting advice of his teacher so many decades ago: 'Beware the human portents.' But it was already too late: a whispered word from the eunuch led the credulous Second Emperor to send Li Si first to prison and then to a public dismemberment of himself and all his family.

By 207 BCE, the rebels were so much at large that the state of Qin was struggling to defend the capital of Xianyang, let alone the empire. With the young Second Emperor now increasingly asking questions, the eunuch despatched him to his death. Masking it as suicide, he replaced him with a younger sibling – the 'Third Emperor'. Younger he might have been, but with the human portents now obviously at large, he was not entirely blind. In 206 BCE, with the wider empire lost, a battalion of rebels threatened the gates of Xianyang, and the last Qin ruler – no emperor now – acknowledged the limits of his father's wintry order.

Placing a simple rope around his neck, seating himself in a plain white carriage, the young man rode out of the palace and delivered the imperial seal into the hands of the rebels' leader.

The single heart of the state had been broken – and with it, the single will had fallen, too. Where would heaven go next?

PART 2

HEAVEN'S MIND

Heaven does not have two suns;
the people do not have two kings.

Mencius (372 – 289 BCE)

CHAPTER 1

ONE HEAVEN, ONE EARTH?

*If one grasps the One and does not lose it, one can be lord
of the ten thousand things.*

The Guanzi (compilation of older texts, named after Guan
Zong, 720 – 645 BCE)

A hint of Turkish pastry touched the early afternoon air. Up and down the wide streets, shops offered passers-by an array of purchases while teahouses invited conversations. Camels wandered with a lazy air. Falcons, perched on brocaded arms, flashed talons fit for a hunt. Heavenly horses (fresh from the Ferghana valley of the far north-west) were paraded for a price. Last week's tiger had been sold, but rumour had it that another was on its way. Wrapped jackets of white cotton, well-worn by the people at large, rubbed past the robes of officials where red or green was outranked by blue, with neat caps completing the higher attire. And in everyone's midst flashed coats of many colours, swirling skirts and leopard-skin hats, all marking out their wearers as men of a different breed.

Narrow lanes beckoned with signs proclaiming special wares for sale. A turn to the left and a lane of Byzantine threads would dull the sounds of the market with damasks that tore at the heart, all thronged with Sogdians who knew the stuff of their trades. A turn to the right, and on stall after stall, the wonders of the northern steppes appeared: purple forest furs, red deerskin boots, wild horsehides and heavy saddles of scarlet felt. A few steps to the east, and stands of boxes from Arabia opened up a haze of perfumes and powders: plumes of myrrh and puffs of frankincense. A few steps to the west, and purple-robed monks offered a Buddhist fairyland: scrolls of paradise illuminated with divine Himalayan creatures sitting on spreading pink lotuses; bodhisattva saints carved from amber; and the coral trees of utopian gardens bedecked with brilliant gems. Tucked in a corner were leopard tails, charged with the power to ward off even the most stubborn spirits.

On and on, the market maze continued. Down a lane, the musical instruments of Kucha, conjuring up wild dances, were offered for sale by men with high noses and green eyes. Left, and lapis lazuli appeared from Khotan. Right, and gold sparkled from the princely kingdom of Tibet. Round a corner, books and maps appeared, stirring everyone's imagination with Sanskrit stories inked in Chinese characters, and routes to the west marked along a string of oasis states. On a little further, and heavenly jades from beyond the singing sands of the Taklamakan desert would come into view, followed by mountains of pearls from the shores of Persia, and phosphorescent gems from who knew where. Between it all, cardamom from Kashmir, peaches from Samarkand, and strings of cash counted by Turkish-speaking Uighur lenders, whose blue eyes flashed like gems, and whose talents with money smoothed everyone's trade.

Streets stepped, lanes explored, treasures acquired from the corners of the earth: time passed like a flash of silver. Eventually, the sun began to dip and the drums of dusk began their tattoo. The market gates closing, merchants and customers wended their way into the evening and the city at large. Chang'an in the early Tang dynasty, seven hundred years after some of the foreigners had begun to count the years following their Christ. The city of eternal peace: the heart of China, and the unifying centre of the world.

*   *   *

The concept of 'unifying everywhere' had all begun with horse-borne nomads worrying at the northern walls (although some would later wonder whether it was the building of the walls in the first place that had really caused the problem). A distraction for as long as anyone could remember, the nomadic barbarians tried endlessly to thrust their wild ideas of a roaming trade into the settled Yellow River lands, with roving pillage their resort whenever the inhabitants refused to play their game. What to do with a people who threatened to unsettle everything, and rejected the tradition of tribute paid from the edges of order to the civilised centre? Walls had been the obvious answer.

Unifying the world under his black wintry watch, the First (Qin) Emperor had looked at the northern walls he had inherited with his conquests and decided that they must match the singular strength of his own iron will. Sending his army to push the barbarians back to the grassland steppes where they clearly belonged, he had then redirected their labours to raising the greatest wall ever imagined. Strung with towers, punctuated with garrisons, constantly built and rebuilt, great though it might have been, the wall was named the *chang cheng*, the long wall, and remained a formidable barrier for as long as the First Emperor ruled the world. But with his wall-building general and his eldest son treacherously dismissed to their deaths, the First Emperor's army (like so much of the rest of Qin) had crumbled, and the walls had followed suit.

Watching the collapse of Qin from the steppes above, it was not long before strikes of galloping nomads flashed into the northern lands, pillaging as they went. And it was not much longer before the wealth captured from the settled lands opened an opportunity for an ambitious nomad warrior to sweep across the vast steppes and unite the myriad tribes into a mounted federation of horse-borne power. Three million strong, and riding under the command of a man they called the 'Heavenly Wolf', the nomadic warriors were known to the terrified Yellow River people as the Xiongnu. Looking down at the settled lands below them, the Xiongnu themselves saw one of many sparkling gems in a world which, seen from the spreading roof of everywhere, reached farther than anyone in the settled lands could ever have imagined: to the north and east as far as the ice-flocked seas, and to western places which other worlds would come to know as India, Persia, Greece and Rome.

The Yellow River people, however, had little time for imagining. After the end of Qin, rebels had battled back and forth, not only sacking the once-iron state, but charging against each other too. Year after year, the rubble had risen until, in 202 BCE a rebel named Liu Bang emerged triumphant. A minor official in the twilight of the Qin, he had been in charge of delivering a group of convicts when some escaped. Balancing the certainty that he would be executed for his carelessness against the possibility that, as a rebel, he might survive, Liu Bang chose survival. Founding his own band of men, he eventually defeated every other rebel contender and inherited the wreckage of Qin. Crops crushed underfoot, and pavilions destroyed, one of the most pressing of his victory tasks was to return the peasants to the fields upon which everyone's fortunes had always depended.

Liu Bang set his star for a restoration of unity and gave his family the dynastic name 'Han', after the southern district of Hanzhong where he had built his strength. Styling himself 'Gaozu' (High Ancestor) to ground his rule in the golden past, he welcomed back the surviving Confucian scholars. Brutally silenced by Qin, they were happy to accept a renaissance of the romantic Zhou idea that the mandate to rule was issued from heaven above. Having vanquished the black waters of Qin, Liu Bang then took the fire of summer as his element, with red the colour of all. Raising a new capital – not far from Qin's secretive city of Xianyang – he named it Chang'an, Eternal Peace.

Proclaiming a golden age and rebuilding a city were, however, the least of Liu Bang's challenges. Far harder were the questions of what kind of state he was going to rule, and what, given the fraying edges of the old Qin empire, he was going to do about the age-old problem of the northern barbarians.

Looking, as tradition ordered, to the lessons of the past, Liu Bang realised that they seemed to point, unhelpfully, in two different directions. The first, the model of the Zhou, offered a vision of a heavenly kingdom across the lands inherited from the Yellow Emperor, all governed by a Son of Heaven. Under this model, the Son of Heaven conducted the delicate balancing of a constantly changing cosmos, supported by a body of ministers, officials and scholars whose own spirits (and households) were guided by the Confucian qualities from which order naturally flowed. The second, the model of Qin, presented the same lands as the kingdom of a ruler who, although mindful of the heavenly power, discharged an earthly responsibility to deliver order through a set of rules applied with an iron hand. The soft world of the Zhou had dreamt of harmony and lasted eight hundred years; but only the first two hundred had been truly 'golden', with the last six hundred spiralling through a chaos of human ambition into the catastrophic death and destruction of the warring states and their war of all against all. The iron world of Qin had seen a spectacular rise from dust to triumph, culminating in twenty years of unity grounded in terror, only to collapse from within. Each clearly had its advantages, but both had fallen. While the old Zhou idea of a heavenly order based on cosmic changes and human virtue had much to recommend it, it had failed to avert the rise of Qin. And while Qin had understood that to govern an empire man, like nature, must be tamed, it had failed to grasp the risk that when an iron will cast its people as prisoners, the people would eventually rebel.

Confronted with two seemingly irreconcilable alternatives, Liu Bang decided to combine them. While the Duke of Zhou might have had the luxury of believing men to be good, everyone's experiences over the past six hundred years had shown that goodness was more a matter of potential that could be realised only if the ruling conditions were right. It was obvious, though, that the people preferred the softer Zhou ideas. Accordingly, Liu Bang decided that the state of Han would be formally fashioned after the golden age of the Zhou, but with an imperial interpretation of what Confucius had *really* meant. At the centre of the model would be the pursuit of the *dao* as the particular and exclusive task of the emperor, to which would be added an unquestioning acknowledgement that an effective Confucian rule should be touched with a flash of steel. *Ren* humanity would be dedicated to the single ideal of heaven as an order of all, rather than any individual ideas of good or bad. *Yi*, integrity, would be a formal correlation of names and purposes (let the ruler be the ruler, the subject the subject, the father the father, and the son the son), rather than any matter of personal judgement. *Li*, ritual, would ensure that actions taken would be appropriate within the wider context of the order of the state rather than by reference to any local ambition. And the *jia* bonds of family (fixed with the *xiao* duties of filial piety) would ensure that everyone was bound to the imperial centre.

With the Confucian rule of the Han underpinned by the more practical principles of Qin, the Son of Heaven would be the greatest power on earth. And while Liu Bang's management of heaven and earth would be supported by a bureaucracy of scholars, the scholars would come not only from the ranks of the Confucians but from the ranks of the realists who had been schooled in the Qin's art of crafting effective laws. Confucian or Qin, every scholarly bureaucrat would keep to his particular name and place, with the full force of the law and severe punishments applied to anyone who stepped out of their appointed line. Of course, the laws and punishments were not quite what Confucius had had in mind, but since the First Emperor had burned the books that told everyone what Confucius had actually said, what did it really matter? More importantly, who was there to make a fuss?

Liu Bang then turned to the northern edges of the once-Qin empire, badly battered by the end-of-Qin rebellions and now threatened, once again, by the nomadic barbarians. With the fields returned to their harvests and the mulberry trees again supporting the silk-producing worms, the Heavenly Wolf's nomadic horsemen had been raiding ever deeper into the resettling lands. Of course, the grain and the bolts of silk could have been offered for sale on open markets. But, keenly aware of the heavenly mandate on his shoulders, Liu Bang preferred to keep to the settled order: fixed farming for all, with any disorderly trade limited to the exchange of necessities across the heavenly lands, all carefully controlled by the Son of Heaven, in the faithful discharge of his duty to balance the harmonies of heaven and earth.

Liu Bang's refusal to contemplate a wider trade left the fields easy prey to the forces of the Heavenly Wolf. Harvests were seized, villages set alight, farmers and their families were carried off to the steppes as a warning to the rest. Battling against men whose horses, faster than the wind, seemed to have come from heaven itself, the Han armies struggled to hold their lines.

Reluctantly reviewing the position, Liu Bang eventually warmed to the idea of an 'ordered' trade. A treaty was prepared and signed: silk, grain and wine were to flow north to the Xiongnu; horses, camels and sheep were to come south to the Han. Aware of his heavenly responsibilities, and thinking in the longer term, Liu Bang also suggested that gifts might be sent to the north in the form of Han princesses as brides for steppe warriors and future mothers of steppe children, who, in later years, could be expected to prefer the settled world.

Time passed and Xiongnu horses trickled south, accompanied by men accomplished in the extraordinary skill of shooting arrows from the saddle. As the Han delighted in their new treasures, successive Xiongnu leaders began to consolidate their steppe-wide power by emulating the settled glory of their southern neighbour. Modelled on Chinese cities, great camps of martial tents were raised – although the Xiongnu warned their people against the seductive comforts of a settled life: comforts which no expanse of steppe would ever be able to support and which would gradually eat away at the skills of a force whose fighting spirit depended upon the constant hunt of the wolf.

More time passed, memories faded, and with horses and archery skills now under their belts, the Han began to wonder if the bargain had been a mistake. Too much silk for too few horses; princesses going north but steppe-born children still behaving like wolves; and a treaty by which the northern barbarians seemed to consider the heavenly Han as Xiongnu vassals, even as the treaty itself seemed to be written in dust. When signing the treaty, the Xiongnu had presented themselves as a confederation: as solid as the settled Han. But whenever any question arose about a detail of the terms, the 'solid' confederation scattered into disparate hordes of unruly tribes. Some of the emperor's advisers suggested that it was time to think again. Others, particularly the few Han diplomats and generals who had personal experience of the steppes, argued for caution. Across the entire roof of the world, they warned, no one dared brave the force of the Xiongnu's wrath.

For a time, caution prevailed. But as the decades and succeeding emperors passed, the influence of the generals and the diplomats began to float away, like clouds on a wind. Trade from the Han lands began to slow: fewer bolts of silk, lighter loads of grain, and soon even the princesses stayed at home. And as the stream of treasure waned, Xiongnu tempers frayed. Raiders returned and, pushing ever deeper into the Yellow River lands, harvests again began to vanish, while villages quaked with fear. By 140 BCE, the barbarian terrors to the north had forced the Han diplomats to return ten times to renegotiate the treaty. Each time, the 'renegotiation' had simply increased the pile of tribute (silk, grain and wine) moving from Han south to Xiongnu north, with new generations of Han princesses following in its wake. From the palaces of Chang'an it seemed that the emperor was struggling to balance heaven and earth. And with every failed negotiation, the empire's scholarly officials directed the Han generals to consult their arts of war and find the martial strategy that would finally restore heaven's order on earth.

The most preferred of the strategies advanced was to divide the barbarians so that they attacked each other. This could most easily be achieved by chipping away at the Xiongnu's 'federation'. Individual treaties offered smaller tribes the promise of trade, in return for a promise to ride against their brother barbarians whenever the Xiongnu swept down on the fields of the Han. Some thought this an excellent idea. Others – including generals who had served at the front – were less sure. With Han soldiers being constantly exposed to death, and the outcome of any battle never more than yet another 'renegotiation' of the relationship between the settled and the barbarian worlds, the generals had long ago concluded that the real question was of the very nature of heaven and earth. Given the force of the barbarians, it was a question that needed far more careful consideration.

Certainly, the experiences of the last two thousand years had shown that the heavenly idea of settled fields and a ruling son who was constantly attentive to heaven's cosmic changes was better than anything else known on earth. It was equally clear, though, that each time the Han opened trade with the barbarians, the pillaging stopped and peace returned. Must a heavenly order turn its face against a wider trade from which everyone seemed to benefit? Confucius' cascading hierarchy of relationships seemed to say that there could be only one son at the top. But if one looked further back, cosmic minds had long argued that heaven's order lay not in a single top-down human will, but in a more accommodating meditation on the complicated order of nature. From the earliest shamans who had stepped away from glittering opportunities to advise kings, to the spirit of Laozi with his *Dao De Jing* and the arguments of Zhuangzi about crooked paths, the lands around the Yellow River had been full of men who insisted that order was much greater and more complex than forcing a ruling will upon everything in sight. Surely, added the generals, the unity of heaven and earth lay in the power of an idea, not in the force of a fight.

The bureaucracy rigid with shock, Confucian scholars painted black memorials to the emperor, pointing to the cowardice of the generals as the true cause of all the trouble.

In 141 BCE, imperial patience snapped. A new emperor had come to the throne (one who would come to be known as 'Wudi', the 'Martial Emperor') and decided that the costs of the trade (including the raids and the battles) were now beyond all bearing. The Xiongnu barbarians were not only destroying the farming fields but sat in tight control of rising routes of a westerly trade, which was apparently flowing across the roof of the world to distant lands the Han could only dream of. Determined to end the barbarians' constant challenges to heaven's ordering authority, the Martial Emperor moved to restore the military architecture of Qin. Roads to the North were repaired; walls with their watchtowers were reinforced; and, thanks to the trade in Xiongnu horses, the empire's army was strengthened with a grand new cavalry. Declaring that the world would be turned to the order of the heavenly lands, in 134 BCE, the first of a series of martial campaigns was launched.

The terrain was tough, but the enemy was tougher. Thousands died, coffers were constantly drained, and the Martial Emperor soon realised that pushing the Xiongnu back to their own wild world would be a long battle. Standing firm on his military position, he decided to push forward with the strategy of dividing the barbarians by exploring the possibility of another front to the north and west, in a land that, it had long been whispered, was home to a warrior tribe just as anxious as the Han to push the Xiongnu federation off their pedestal of the steppes. The land's name was Kangju, and the Martial Emperor decided to send a trusted military man to discover whether there might indeed be such a distant ally to be found. The man he chose was called Zhang Qian: a military officer whose battling career had taken him up to the steppes and brought him closer than any other to the Xiongnu foe.

Setting off in a camel caravan, Zhang Qian journeyed beyond the heavenly limits of the Kunlun mountains to the west, and drove deep into Xiongnu territory. A world of deserts as well as grassland steppes, it was not long before the caravan lost its way – and not much longer before Zhang Qian was captured by the Xiongnu. Ten years a captive, Zhang Qian eventually escaped to continue his search for the mysterious Kangju ally, who might turn the barbarian tide. Skirting the deadly Taklamakan desert, whose *kara buran*, black storms, buried men alive, and edging around formidable mountains, Zhang Qian finally reached Kucha, first in the line of oasis states known to thread across the roof of the world. From Kucha, he found his way to Ferghana, home of horses so sleek and strong that they could only be described as 'heavenly'. From Ferghana, he went on to Daxia, the Bactrian kingdom founded by the Greeks and awash with stories of a Sindhu land around an Indus river (present day Pakistan, once part of India) below. From Daxia, on to Sogdiana, with its trading states of Bokhara and Samarkand, and then to the nomadic kingdom of Kangju. There, Kangju's ruler confirmed that the nomadic tribes who roamed his lands did indeed include the sought-after tribe. But, he added, the spark of the rebellion they had tried for years to ignite had long ago blown out. Zhang Qian was ten years too late.

Retracing his steps past the formidable deserts and the blockading mountains, Zhang returned to his emperor in 125 BCE and admitted defeat. Though disappointed that the hoped-for allies had lost heart, the Martial Emperor realised that, in his failure, Zhang Qian might have found the solution to the vexing question of how to manage the wider world. True, he had failed in his goal; but he had opened up lands beyond the Kunlun mountains and found the routes of trade. The Xiongnu were still a powerful threat, but heaven's reach had been significantly expanded. There was indeed a bigger earth, and it was high time that heaven's appointed son stretched his order across it.

Initially, it seemed like a good idea. But it soon became clear that stretching the heavenly lands opened the cavernous 'Confucian-Qin' compromise on which Liu Bang had founded the Han idea of the state. For

Confucian scholars, the matter of order was a simple question of heavenly-imperial command and control. Technically, this was the prerogative of the emperor but, given the complexity of 'the changes' and the many 'things' that had to be 'investigated' in these times of complicated empires, it would obviously have to be delegated to excellent Confucian minds. For the Qin scholars, charged with crafting clear laws and strict punishments, the matter was anything but simple: how was 'unity' to be achieved over deserts and mountains that stretched further than the eye could see?

With the emperor clear that he wanted to unify the world, any question of whether or not the Han armies should advance to the west had already been answered. But how? Once again the past was consulted, and once again, it was the combined wisdom of Zhou and Qin that seemed to offer a solution. An empire that included the vast west would be too big for the Son of Heaven to manage singlehandedly, but the Son of Heaven had many relatives and trusted military advisers to whom, following in the footsteps of the Duke of Zhou, he could give fiefdoms. And where the empire was girded with clear rules (the lesson learnt from Qin), surely the heavenly territory could be successfully stretched.

The matter of unifying the world now settled, one question remained: who would make the rules for the advance to the west and, indeed, everything else in the heavenly lands? Those closest to the Confucian tradition argued that in what was supposed to be a revival of the golden age of the Duke of Zhou, the rules should be written by Confucian scholars, who were clearly closest to the ever-changing mind of heaven. Those of the Qin tradition, schooled in crafting clear laws and strict punishments with nothing left to anyone's discretion or imagination, argued that the rules should be set out by those scholars (realists whose mastery of rule-making, made them 'legalists') with the greatest talent for fixing things in writing.

Certainly the Qin tradition had the advantage of clear commands: highly appealing to any busy emperor. But, as it transpired, the Confucians offered something much more powerful: the fear of heaven above. Every time the rains failed, an earthquake struck, the Yellow River changed its course, or a comet flashed across the sky, the Confucian scholars rushed to their brushes and inked a memorial to the emperor, advising him in no uncertain terms that heaven was unhappy. And if that was so, it must be because heaven's son had failed to apply the right policies. The balancing of the cosmos was the personal duty of a Son of Heaven: a constant and unwavering obligation to ensure that the actions of man and the changes of nature were properly aligned. A momentous task for one man, it was a duty that even the greatest emperor could only discharge with a bureaucracy of loyal Confucian scholars. Looking fearfully up at the unpredictable skies, the Martial Emperor could only agree.

Charged with the emperor's confidence, the Confucian scholars recommended that a new Hall of Light be constructed to ensure the highest and brightest reflection of the cosmos possible on earth. Centred on the Pole Star, it would be the point at which heaven and earth came together in the person of the emperor as the Son of Heaven – and the point from which the Son of Heaven would issue the commands that would bring all together in a unity of everything, everywhere. Every detail of its construction was to be carefully considered. Modelled on the relationship between the sun and the earth, the mystical numbers of Fuxi's magic square were to be embedded in every rafter. And from terraces open to the stars, the emperor's advisers (now fully qualified Confucian scholars rather than soaring shamans) would scour the skies with their eyes and make their recommendations for the order of all.

The Martial Emperor raised the new and greater Hall of Light without delay. No sooner had it had been constructed, though, than it became clear that a new kind of army would also be required. Not more of the cowardly generals who lobbied for trade, but an army of scholars who, in helping their emperor balance the weighty matters of heaven and earth, would 'investigate everything' through a careful consultation of the written word. For this, the scholars argued, a heavenly library would also be required, with a large and constantly expanding number of heavenly books – composed, of course, by the Confucian scholars. Once again, the Martial Emperor could only agree.

Without a moment to lose, the new Confucian army picked up its brushes, and ink was splashed on bamboo. Soon, confident interpretations of everything Confucius had ever said (or might have said) appeared on the library's shelves. To these were added a surprising stream of 'original' texts, which seemed to have re-appeared. Some were described as having miraculously survived the flames of Qin, hidden within the walls of scholarly households. Others were presented as faithful transcripts of conversations with Confucius, passed down from fathers to sons over a mere three hundred years. The texts of the 'recovered' works varied, but the ones most valued by the emperor were those that attached the greatest weight to the laws and punishments of the Qin past – albeit appearing under a comfortably Confucian title.

Under the spreading eaves of the new Hall of Light and its accompanying library, the Confucian ink spread and Confucian knowledge swelled. Then came the question of how a reliable supply of recruits might be found to guarantee the scholarly reserves necessary to maintain the strength of the new Confucian army. The answer was not long in coming. In 124 BCE, a scholar suggested that a Grand Academy might serve a valuable purpose, and a class of fifty was admitted for a course of Confucian study that would equip them to hold office in the heavenly bureaucracy. With every year that passed, the Confucian army expanded, within the Grand Academy and increasingly outside, as alumni took over the most powerful imperial positions across the heavenly lands. And as the Confucian army expanded, so did the number of interpretative Confucian texts – and with them, the Han's Confucian idea that the only topic worth pursuing was the unity of everything. And with the question of unity clearly being something which only Confucian-trained bureaucrats could master, the idea that the Son of Heaven could discharge his duties by waiting for wild tribes of horsemen to see the error of their ways was confirmed as being nothing but the product of a military cowardice. Far from the bureaucrats getting too big for their boots, as the generals had so foolishly argued, the bureaucratic boots were obviously not big enough.

With everyone's duties now Confucianly settled, the Martial Emperor turned to the ordering of heaven's earth. Fortunately, it looked as if heaven itself had understood that the northern barbarians were a problem, and the power of the Xiongnu seemed to be on the wane. The Han armies pushed forward, and the Long Wall, with its watchtowers, was stretched ever further towards the west. Corps of Han diplomats were then despatched to follow in Zhang Qian's footsteps, offering treaties of tribute and trade to the oasis states across the roof of the world. The north at last seeming to bend to the will of the Son of Heaven, the Martial Emperor turned his thoughts to the south.

Softer than the north, and already opened once by Qin, the southern lands spread below that other great river (the Yangzi, flowing parallel to the Yellow River through the lands of present-day Sichuan) to coasts swept by far-off tropical seas. Home to a myriad of southern tribes, this was a world of hot and humid forests, punctuated with peaks, dotted with marshes and touched with strange fevers – not a place where the treasured heavenly horses and their archers could be of any help. Consulting the changes, the Martial Emperor turned to the ruling element of the Han for a vanquishing solution: fire. When flames were thrown at forests, the tattooed men with flowing black hair who lived amid the trees were easily scattered: some to far-off mountains, others further south. Now reduced to a more manageable stubble, the southern forests were populated by Han armies of migrant peasants – and a number of stubborn minds who, asking inconvenient questions in the Han capital, were despatched to serve out punishments at the fever-drenched frontier.

Forests fired and fields sown, the Martial Emperor then commanded the peasant army to raise new cities. As the cities rose, yet more people were sent from a now-overpopulated north, to find new homes in the south. As hundreds of thousands of the Han's northern people flowed south, those southern barbarian tribes who had not managed to reach a rescuing mountain, were invited to tie up their hair, put on some shoes, and learn the arts of the heavenly settled order. Willing to learn or not, it didn't really matter, because the old three-step discipline of the Qin was ready to ensure that everyone was ordered by their name and place: registers and maps to capture everyone in a grid of administrative power; families settled as households, all charged with taxing duties for the state; and groups of households (bound together in fives) guaranteeing the orderly obedience of all.

Heaven was stretching. By the time that the Martial Emperor joined his ancestors in 87 BCE, the territories of the Han spread far beyond even the wildest reaches of the preceding Qin. The cost of the conquests, though, had been great; and the cost of securing the lands thus conquered, was even greater. Even with taxes, the expanded empire found that wealth flowed out of the imperial treasuries faster than it flowed in. The Martial Emperor's successor instructed the imperial officials, now spread across vast lands, to fill it.

With no resources of their own, the officials turned to the smallest of the local households: those who, while they might have least to spare, would also be least able to make a fuss. As time passed, poorer households burdened by taxes lost their lands to richer landowning men with deeper pockets. For those struggling to keep up with the latest treasury gap, moneylenders offered loans against rights to the land. While the rich flourished on solid ground, yet more of the poor lost their fields. With nothing to their name other than the muscle of their arms (and nowhere to sell their muscle other than in markets already stuffed with desperate labour), many struggled in seas of despair. As the Martial Emperor's successor continued to pursue unity across the four quarters of the earth, at home everything was separating.

At the turn of the millennium, heaven issued stern warnings. With forests felled, stripped soils had turned to dust, rains were failing, and even the seasons seemed to falter. Droughts were followed by floods, locusts chimed in, the Yellow River repeatedly changed its course, comets flew, and earthquakes added to the toll. The first century turned painfully to the second, and things got worse. Out in the fields, desperate men began to question whether heaven was indeed to be found in Han. Whisperings turned to mutterings, mutterings turned to bands of self-help – and in 184, a peasant army rose. Wearing turbans in the cosmic colour of the Yellow Emperor, they claimed to be warriors for a new golden age – one of a *taiping* great peace, which went back to the most ancient of times when Shennong had farmed the fields, side by side with ordinary men. Named the Yellow Turbans, the rebels infected so many labouring men with the idea of revolutionary change that they were able to declare themselves the battling vanguard of an independent Kingdom of Taiping. In 189 they presented themselves for heavenly approval in the palaces of the last of the ancient Zhou capitals, one that had become a capital for the later Han: a city now known as Luoyang.

Then, just as it seemed nothing could get worse, the Xiongnu terrors of the steppes, who seemed to have been so effectively vanquished, were replaced by a new and even more ferocious confederated force: the Xianbei.

As the battling price of unity rose, more rebellions broke out and successively weakening and desperate emperors found themselves and their borders increasingly dependent on their generals. With the heavenly empire collapsing, the generals, keenly aware of their power, became warlords in their own right. By 195, the strongest of the generals controlled most of the northern plains of the Yellow River heartlands. Named Cao Cao, in 196, he swept the Son of Heaven off to his own military base. Leaving the emperor with his life and his title, Cao Cao proceeded to try to 'unify' the world himself, albeit through commands issued from behind the heavenly façade. Four years later, his son flung off the pretence and declared a new heavenly dynasty, the Cao Wei, across the north. Before long, he was challenged by two other warlords, each claiming a heavenly dynasty of their own: one, to the south-west (including present-day Sichuan), leader of a new state of Shu-Han; the other, to the south-east (including provinces surrounding present-day Shanghai), the leader of a new state of Wu.

* * *

For the next forty-five years, the unity of the Han world was divided into three kingdoms, each with its own warlord waiting to become the single Son of Heaven. Three warring 'brothers', all inheritors of shared dreams from a past which included the golden age of the Zhou, the iron grid of the Qin, and the compromise of the Han. Each dug deep to find the defining idea of order that would enable them to unify the broken world.

Meanwhile, as the 'three kingdoms' battled each other, in the north the new Xianbei confederation seemed to mirror the disintegration of the land below the Long Wall. The nomadic tribes threw themselves into wars against each other and, as each fought for steppe supremacy, many concluded that the best way to win the roof of the world was by capturing the treasures of the settled Yellow River lands. Posses of steppe warriors swept down, one after another, and it was not long before the Cao Wei in the north fell to a tribe with the dynastic name of Jin. Before long, Shu-Han and Wu fell to the Jin as well.

It looked as if heaven had made a shocking choice: a unifying Son of Heaven from the wilderness of the steppes? But no sooner had the Jin claimed the mandate of heaven, than hordes of other challengers – steppe warriors and Han warlords alike – set out to bring them down. The three warring kingdoms, now fractured into a competing chaos of claims. As greatest battles raged back and forth in the north, more and more displaced people flooded down to the fertile lands of Sichuan and the wider south. Eventually, sixteen kingdoms emerged above the Yangzi River, many led by steppe generals, each claiming a Son of Heaven dynasty of its own, and all looking for advantage over the others. And as the north began to settle to a fragmented order of sorts, southern lands below the Yangzi erupted in a host of competing kingdoms all of their own.

As generals battled, and with the north and the south divided by the Yangzi River, scholars (Confucian and Qin: by now taking the name of their unifying dynasty, they were really they were really one and the same, 'Han') continued to counsel the succession of conquering rulers on the weighty matters of heaven. In the northern kingdoms ruled by men from the steppes, their advice was always secondary to the overriding power of the totem of the wolf, even as the tougher notes of the steppes increasingly crept into northern Han hearts. Meanwhile, in the south, ruled by men who followed the Confucian tradition of a scholarly bureaucracy, and with lands that now included northern migrants raised the Confucian dream as well as softer tribal natures, most of the people's hearts had been won by less rigid ideas, closer to the shaman spirits of the mountains and forests than to any wolf. Indeed, with rain in abundance, and the fruits of nature everywhere, many in the south found it hard to understand why heaven had to order everything.

Changes within the heavenly lands notwithstanding, to the world outside, the people and their language, unified by the Qin's First Emperor under a single spreading heavenly bureaucracy, had come to be known as Qin: Chinese.

*   *   *

Time passed and heaven (north and south) seemed to float, tantalisingly suspended somewhere above the earth. An order of sorts had been established by many dynasties, but the 'unity of everywhere', upon which a truly heavenly order must surely depend, was as elusive as it had been in any warring past.

Then, in 581, a new confederation flew across the steppes. Calling themselves the Sui, they were a force of Turkic people, *Tujue*, who had emerged from the Altai Mountains to the far north-east (present-day Siberia). Journeying across the roof of the world, roaming through the oasis states, they had encountered many travellers from the Sindhu lands and been touched by the meditating order of the Buddha's ideas. Chanting sutras as they wielded the vanquishing power of the horse, they became an unstoppable force. By 589, the sixteen northern kingdoms had been forged into one. A Sui son was sent south to find a bride, thereby marrying north and south together. Within a decade the Sui had restored a unity of order, upon whose firm foundations they then applied the old engineering feats of Qin to build a Grand Canal, stretching from the southern city of Hangzhou to the northern city of Zhoujun (which would, one day, become Beijing). With north and south now firmly reunited, the Sui armies marched east and west. To the east, they snatched at the lands of present-day Korea. To the west, they swept deep into the oasis states that Zhang Qian's journey had opened to trade – lands the Han had held and lost. Across the north they strengthened the *chang cheng* long wall (not yet 'great'), as it had never been strengthened before.

For a while, all went well. The Grand Canal more than served its purpose – trade took to the water, and boats carried rice from southern terraces of plenty to northern plains that were now drying in a climate of change. But the wars of reunification, the building of the canal and the strengthening of the Long Wall had not only emptied the empire's pockets but bitten deep into the people and the land. Legions of young men had been torn away from their families, with many lost to an early death. Fields failing, once again, misery was everywhere. Just as in the ancient times of the Shang, the Zhou, the Qin and the Han, the weight of a single great empire was taking its familiar toll.

Once again, whisperers spread the idea that heaven was changing its mind. Rebels began to rise, and rumours rustled that a new Kingdom of Taiping Great Peace, was on its way.

*   *   *

In 617, as the Sui's rule crumbled from within, the ambitious son of a general in charge of a garrison in the near-west persuaded his father to seize the reins of power and sweep the Sui into the dust. Named Li, both son and father had higher noses than most, with slightly darker skins. Claiming to be descendants of Liu Bang's Han family, like so many people now on the northern plains, the ancestral blood that flowed in their veins clearly included a touch of the steppes – Xianbei and even Turkic people Tujue. In 618, from the old Han capital of Chang'an, Li the father declared a new dynasty, and named it Tang. By 626, Li the son had grasped the throne, under a title that anticipated a glorious reign: Emperor Taizong (the Supreme Ancestor).

Dedicating himself to restoring the vast wealth of the Sui, Taizong, like so many of his predecessors, looked for a stronger unity that would, this time, keep everything together. Consulting the steppes, Taizong found that the world of the Tujue was dividing into an east and a west. As schooled in the idea of 'divide and rule' as any of his Yellow River ancestors, Taizong put all of his weight behind the western side, and within three years, the east was forced into a surrender. Taizong then looked at the power of the western Tujue who now controlled a string of states from the oasis edges of the Tang's west to the far-off lands of Persia. Twisting western Tujue words into jealousies, Taizong sparked a storm within the western Tujue ranks. By 642, he had pulled the rug of power out from under the feet of their rulers. Already the Son of Heaven Emperor of the Tang, Taizong now became a Heavenly Khan of Khans – a Turkic *qaghan* – and ruler of the steppes. Surely this was unity indeed.

But not everyone accepted that this was the kind of unity heaven had in mind. Remnants of the Tujue began to win back friends, and when, in 639, Taizong was forced to quash a rebellion in the oasis state of Gaochang, Confucian officials – who had now learnt the costs of war – began to repeat the old questions of the generals and ask whether Taizong's idea of heaven-everywhere was really wise. Quoting a line of Confucius (one that their Han predecessors had presumably forgotten), the officials pointed to the disasters that had eventually befallen the acquisitive Qin, Han and Sui, and suggested that it would be better to be master of what was close before rushing to seize control over things far away. That wisdom conveyed, they went one step further, concurring with the view of the (now long-dead) Han generals that conquests waged beyond the edges of one's own lands were more likely than not to bring heaven tumbling down upon one's head.

Preferring the older Han-Confucian idea of 'unity everywhere', Taizong was unimpressed. If one is truly dedicated to pursuing the heavenly way of the *dao*, he observed, one has no choice but to chase it to all of the corners of the earth. The Confucian doubters were dismissed. But Taizong had underestimated the Tujue. Hearts burning at his betrayal of both east and west, they determined to displace the interloping 'Heavenly Qaghan'. Unleashing their fury across the roof of the world, they also rained down their rage upon the earth of the Tang.

In 649 Taizong passed the reins to a weaker Tang successor – unfortunately just as a new power was rising to the south-west, known as the *Tubuo*, Tibetans. Taizong had dismissed them as upstarts, even refusing the now-common request for a Tang princess. Expanding swiftly, however, the Tibetans had pushed north and west, biting into the oasis states, and threatening to push the Tang off their already-weakened perch. Looking at the rather difficult lie of the land, Taizong's successor had a change of heart: treaties were concluded and a Tang princess made her way to Tibet. But the battle for the earth had already stretched into realms beyond the charms of a princess. Far to the west, beyond even Persia, the future fortunes of the Tang were being mixed with those of yet another nomadic power. Having seized control of Baghdad, in present-day Iraq, it had risen as an empire of Islam, stretching east across the oasis states of the central Asian roof of the world. As the Islamic power marched east, the wider world seemed not only to be getting closer but carrying a host of unknowable risks.

As one Tang emperor passed his heavenly power to another, imperial envoys struggled to keep abreast of the news. The western lands were clearly complicated – so complicated that it was getting difficult to keep up. Battles in every direction were demanding bigger and bigger armies with the skills to fight across distant desert and mountain terrains. With peasants endlessly despatched for uncertain distant victories, by 740, the Tang decided that their only hope was to invigorate their own fading battalions with tougher commanders drawn from the terrifying steppes. It was a brave decision, but it came a moment too late. In 750, the Caliphate of Baghdad marched into the central Asian lands of present day Kazakhstan and seized a victory over the Tang that turned the roof of the world into a new Islamic west. Soon afterwards, a new Muslim force rose from the Tujue. Calling themselves the Uighurs, it was their leader who would capture the now coveted roof-of-the-world title Khan of Khans: *Qaghan*.

With battles blazing, affairs in the Tang's capital, Chang'an, had become a little fiery too. Already in 685, under an earlier emperor, the Tang armies had been strengthened by wild steppe warriors chosen as officers to lead them into battle. It had not been long before one among their number, a particularly spirited and seasoned commander, caught the attention of the new emperor. Part Sogdian, part Tujue, known by the Chinese name of An Lushan, he had been given charge of one of the Tang's most important garrisons. Contemplating a devastating loss of ordering influence, the Confucian scholar-officials convinced themselves that his swift upwards trajectory could only have been the result of a seduction of the emperor's wife. Determined to recover their positions, they launched themselves into a whispering campaign, rubbing away at the emperor's trust to such a degree that An Lushan concluded (much like Liu Bang, the Qin rebel who became the first Han emperor) that, with little chance of a fair hearing, he would be better off at the head of his own rebel army.

An able man with an easy command of confidence, An Lushan was quickly joined by other generals from across the northern plains, many, like him, with the blood of the steppes in their veins. Before long, the Tang generals had divided, and the country was launched into a brutal civil war.

In 756, An Lushan captured the now-secondary capital of Luoyang and proceeded to march upon the riches of Chang'an. As the imperial court fled, the emperor reached out to the only nearby powers who could overcome his treacherous rebel general: the Tibetans and the Uighurs, who, as heavenly fortune would have it, were already allied. Prices were named in princesses, silk and almost everything else that a desperate Tang emperor could offer; and the secondary capital of Luoyang was recaptured. The civil war, however, raged on. But then the fragile friendship between the Uighurs and the Tibetans fractured and, while the Uighurs held firm, the Tibetans tore away. While the Tang dynasty would eventually restore its power, the price it would pay was more than even a Son of Heaven could have imagined: acutely aware of their own value, the generals who had stayed loyal to the

Tang demanded fortunes of gold, while the Uighurs raised the price of the heavenly horses, whose western trade they now controlled, to that of a king's ransom. Meanwhile, the Tibetans hurled their forces against the empire. In 763, Chang'an itself was attacked. Over the next twenty years, it would be attacked again and again.

In 783, desperate for heavenly order to return, the Tang emperor eventually offered the Tibetans a treaty of equals in return for peace. It lasted just a year. The Tang then turned back to the Uighurs for yet more assistance. But the Tibetans defeated them both, and the Tang emperor found himself (like so many of his unity-pursuing predecessors) at the mercy of generals whose loyalty had been bought. Navigating a chaos of his own making, the emperor felt he had no choice but to pass on the costs of battle to the people at large. Taxes rose – particularly, as always, for the smallest households.

And then, predictably, heaven chimed in. Harvests failed, locusts flocked and, once again, the people – in tatters after so much war – became 'human portents'. Bandits roamed like dogs, and from the embers of a dying dynasty, a host of new rebels arose. Once again, chaos was everywhere.

In 907, the Tang reached the end of their empire and their dynasty. For the moment, the idea of heavenly unity seemed to lose its appeal.

*   *   *

Over the next fifty years, the heartlands of the northern plains were again overtaken by wolves from the steppes, who founded dynasties of their own. Meanwhile, the southern lands (now the richest of all) fractured again into competing dynasties fuelled by disputes of their own. And then, from the north, a Song dynasty rose, founded by a general from the heavenly lands. Briefly uniting north and south, the Song went on to seal treaties with the barbarian wolves, buying a fragile security from the most amenable of the steppe tribes. Under a short-lived peace (and with a smaller idea of unity), the Song managed to conjure up splendours of heavenly treasure, restoring spirits that had been badly damaged by the fall of the Tang to such a degree that dizzying heights of artistic and technical excellence were achieved.

As wealth rose, though, it was not long before emperors returned to their usual denial of the peasants' desperate state. Many imperial scholars held their tongues. But a number of artists painted spectacular images of heavenly order, one or two brushes risked life and liberty to paint the truth plainly enough for an emperor to see. Others, more cautious, applied their artistic skills to bury carefully coded messages of warning in deceptively peaceful images of the natural world.

Meanwhile, on the steppes, the glittering wealth of the Song had caught the eye of another new tribe, the Jurchen, which not only had declared a dynasty – another Jin – with heavenly ambitions of its own, but had raised a terrifying army with which to chase its dreams.

In 1127, the Jurchen-Jin snatched the Song's northern capital, the splendid Kaifeng, and the Song court fled across the Yangzi River to the southern city of Hangzhou. Friends and relations with northern estates too big to abandon stayed behind, where they struggled under a steppe dynasty whose rule felt like an icy winter which would never end. Smaller people followed the Song court south.

The now 'Southern Song' settled in their new capital, with lands reaching to the south-eastern coast, from which they built a navy to protect themselves from the advancing hordes of the north. North and south, everyone whose heart had been attached to the once unified Song dreamt of a day when the steppe usurpers would return to the barbarian wilderness and leave the treasures of heaven-on-earth alone.

While the north lamented, those scholars who had migrated to the softer south looked again at the idea of order. Surrounded by the wealth of plentiful rains and terraced fields, riches rose, and new treasures flourished – from gunpowder, with its fireworks, to the printing of texts, and a delicate drinking of tea.

With a prosperity and leisure denied to their northern cousins, southern dreams returned to the golden age of the Duke of Zhou. Contemplating the memory of a ruler who had so carefully consulted the cosmos, their thoughts then naturally turned to the exhortations of Confucius to establish their order through heavenly qualities and relationships – and to the haunting words of the ancient shamans and their cosmic ideas. The words of Laozi's *Dao De Jing* echoed in their ears: 'If you try to possess it, you will destroy it: if you try to hold on to it, you will lose it.' Also echoing in their ears was the story of Zhuangzi's meditation on a dream about a butterfly, which had left him wondering whether it might have been a dream a butterfly was having about him. Indeed, the tale of the butterfly dream seemed to be a poignant reminder of the ephemerality of everything. In the north, the ancient homelands had once again been caught in the rough embrace of a steppe power. In the south, forests had been felled in every direction. And everywhere across lands where *qilin*, unicorns, had once wandered and

80

where *feng*, phoenixes, had flown, new cities were rising, even as more and more migrating people were floating desperately on earth.

What was real in this world? Scholarly hearts full of questions, the heavenly court saw nothing but a challenge to its order sence of Punishments following, the questioning scholars picked up their brushes and painted images of the natural world in which they buried yet more of their opinions for only the most trusted to see.

As questioning brushes painted coded communications, however, other scholars scoured the texts of the ancient past, searching for the still elusive key to order. Known as 'new' (or 'newer') Confucians, they began to see a grand arc of wisdom that, this time, might really be able to unite the ideas of almost everything in a harmony of heaven and earth. One of the scholars, Zhu Xi, described the arc as more than just having a *ren* humanity, embracing *yi* integrity, and observing *li* ritual. What was really important, Zhu Xi suggested, was the *zhi* knowledge that, founded in the meticulous ge wu 'investigation of things', was essential to the harmonious order of all. To this he added that in 'investigating things' one had to be careful not to be misled by any individual judgement or emotion and to remain constantly guided by the texts that set out what Confucius had thought. Not everyone agreed, but even among those who did, the question naturally arose as to what it was that Confucius had originally thought – and whether any of the texts truly reflected it. After the Qin's burning of so many books and the mysterious resurrection of so many texts, how could anyone know what Confucius had really thought?

For Zhu Xi, the answer was simple. There were, in his opinion, four books, rescued from the flames of Qin in the early years of the Han, which were the authoritative Confucian texts: *The Great Learning*, with lessons on the harmonious pursuit of the *dao* way; *The Doctrine of the Mean*, with ideas of moderation as essential to the balancing of all; *The Analects of Confucius*, with a description of the heavenly qualities and relationships (including the filial piety on which the strength of the family-state rested); and the work of the greatest interpreter of Confucius: *The Mencius*. Insisting that these texts were the key to any successful investigation of things, Zhu Xi declared that if people who traced their origins back to the Yellow Emperor and the shamans before him were finally going to find their order, they would need not *less* Confucius but *more*.

*　　　*　　　*

As the captured north tried to keep its spirits warm, the sheltered south, separated by the great Yangzi River and now with a navy to keep it safe, wrapped itself in its dreams. But the steppe world of the wolves had not finished with them yet. In 1206, a new leader had risen up from the swirling northern tribes to gather together yet another federation. Raised at the harshest edges of the steppe, he agreed with the settled lands that the key to rule was unity, but not the kind that put a single Son of Heaven in charge of everyone (look where that had got the settled people). Rather, it was a unity that took the form of many *different* hearts all beating to the common call of a Mongol wolf. Born in 1162, by 1206, his federation reached across the wild grasslands of the north. Known to his people as the Blue Wolf, he had come to be known across the steppes as Chinggis (Genghis) Khan.

Charging to the west, to the east, then down to the once-Song lands snatched by the Jurchen-Jin, Chinggis Khan treated every battle like a hunt. Seemingly blessed with the magical talents of his totem, he scarcely blinked at the forces arrayed against him. Like every wolf in charge of a hunt, he gathered intelligence like gold, and harnessed the wild temperaments of his warriors into clear sets of rules that seemed to mirror the ideas of the once-barbarian Qin. Men were organised into groups of ten, with a single deserter from a unit triggering the deaths of the remaining nine. For any unit that deserted *en masse*, a hundred would pay the price. Clear as to direction, bound together like a single heart, Chinggis' united warriors tore across the steppes and down into the settled lands below. Besieging Song cities that the Jurchen-Jin had captured before them, they deployed the lessons of siege warfare learnt from Chinese captives whose ancestors had invented them during the centuries of the warring states.

By the time Chinggis Khan died in 1227, the Mongol empire was bigger than anything that the Xiongnu, the Xianbei or the Sui had ever created. Bequeathing it to sons and grandsons, he had commanded them to spread the Mongol idea of unity across the world. In the far west of Persia (present-day Iran), a grandson founded an Il-khanate state. In the lands of the Rus (present-day Ukraine and western Russia), another founded a khanate that would be known as the Golden Horde. Across the steppe lands of the Mongols, another ruled the khanate at home. And in the lands to the south (those of the northern Song, captured by the Jurchen-Jin), yet another grandson, Kublai, proclaimed himself emperor of a new Great Yuan (long-lasting, far-reaching) dynasty. Moving his commanding camp to a once-Jurchen-Jin-conquered area around present-day Beijing Kublai raised his own cosmic city: 'Khanbaliq', 'the great residence of the Khan' (known to the Chinese as Dadu). With Dadu in place, he returned to the further south and the softer Song.

Gathering the captive soldiers of the old Song north under the flag of the Mongol Yuan (and adding inventions discovered in his cousin's Persian world), Kublai led his forces swiftly south. Vast catapults set their sights on solid walls; exploding bombs thundered through the sky. Terror spread, and city after city fell.

In 1276, Hangzhou was laid to siege, the Song navy fell to the Mongols, and their young emperor (surrendered by a grandmother desperate to save his life) was marched away to the north. Taking whatever vessels they had snatched from the jaws of defeat, the Southern Song (and the lost emperor's younger brothers) set sail for present-day Guangdong. But having conquered Hangzhou and captured the Southern Song's navy, the Mongols simply set their own sails and followed them south.

In 1279, the southern coast just off present-day Hong Kong erupted into the greatest sea-battle that the Yellow Emperor's people had ever fought. More exploding bombs crashed in every direction. Flames soared to the sky. One young emperor already lost to the Mongols, his succeeding brother then fell to a fever. As the sea-battle raged, the Southern Song clutched the only surviving imperial son (now an eight-year-old emperor) close to their hearts. Dreams sinking to the depths, they watched in disbelief as Song vessels fell to ships manned by northern cousins – all commanded by men of the horse who seemed to have taken to the water like ducks.

The battle won, Kublai Khan returned to his new capital in the north and proclaimed a bigger heaven with a new son. Meanwhile, the last Song general carried the young emperor to the top of a range of eight 'dragon' mountains on the southernmost peninsula, and jumped with him into the sea. Holding him tight, as man and child flew through the air, the general whispered to the boy that he should not be frightened: when they reached the water below them, the eight dragons would become nine and he would join his father in the heavenly sky. In the language of the Song, the nine dragons were known as *jiu long*. One day they would find themselves tied to a rock called Hong Kong, and known by the name of 'Kowloon'.

Shocked and exhausted, the people who traced their origins across the Song, the Tang, the Han, the Qin, the Zhou, the Shang, and all the way back, through the Yellow Emperor, to Fuxi and his sister Nüwa, looked up at the sky and asked themselves who and what they were. Children of the shamans and the *dao*, inheritors of the soft wisdom of Confucius, the dreams of Zhuangzi and the iron will of Qin, they seemed to have ended up in a watery mess. A people whom heaven itself had breathed into life and who, in their turn, had painstakingly studied the cosmos and measured their every step by reference to heaven's will. But along the way, they had lost their path.

Once upon a time, it had all seemed so crystal clear: a *heavenly* people singled out by their *ren* humanity and their *yi* integrity, by their *li* ritual, their *de* virtue and their *zhi* knowledge; and united by their *jia* families. Under the Han, it had seemed to be even clearer: inheritors of a Yellow River heartland whose very earth held the traces of their story, they had gone on to unite the world under a heavenly order. But then everything had got mixed up – not just the places, but the people too. And eventually, the virtues of a hundred million Chinese had fallen prey to a wolf, who now claimed to be some kind of heaven's son.

What did it mean to be Chinese? And did heaven really care?

CHAPTER 2

A BRIGHT IDEA

Displaying its splendour, the cosmos is filled;
hiding away, nothing is revealed.

Zhu Yuanzhang, the Hongwu Emperor (first emperor
of the Ming dynasty, fourteenth century)

To a casual dragon sweeping overhead, everything seemed to be moving towards its perfect position and place. From the dark of a cold night sky above, the stars of the *ziwei*, purple enclosure – with the Pole Star at their heart – were scattering their energies down like blessings. And under the flickering lamps of a forbidden square of a city set within a city, all hidden behind purple walls, earth in the form of a host of scholarly officials was preparing to receive them. Rising before dawn, red lanterns held aloft, they had gathered like a soft wind at the Meridian Gate, which guarded the innermost walls of the 'Purple City': the southern gate that marked the point at which the emperor's 'forbidden' enclosure met the imperial city, the point at which heaven came to meet earth through its son. Passing from south to north through its lofty portals, they then made their way swiftly on through the Gate of Supreme Harmony, and into the stone expanse of a courtyard that spread beyond.

Accompanied by the soft chimes of heavenly bells, every scurrying scholar searched for the small bronze marker that, set in stone below their feet, ensured that the official rank of each was not only matched with badges embroidered on their silken fronts and backs, but also with the precise position at which they should stand. Those whose badges showed two stately cranes soaring above heavenly clouds knew they would be at the top and front; those whose badges displayed a pair of earthbound quails pecking at the grass knew they would be at the bottom and behind; and those whose badges were composed of pheasants, peacocks, geese, egrets and ducks knew they would be somewhere in between. Shuffling almost done, a whip cracked, official bodies stiffened, and the imperial censors proceeded to step along the ranks – the power of their own particular office proclaimed by the badge of the legendary *qilin* unicorn who could smell good from bad at a thousand paces. A peacock feather out of place here, a sleeve askew there, a whisper off to the left: each misdemeanour was sharply noted and quickly corrected.

As disciplined hearts contemplated heavy prices that would later have to be paid, an altogether different procession began a more sedate advance from north to south. Yellow silk fluttering in every direction, the Son of Heaven was carried as softly as a cloud from his forbidden enclosure towards the Meridian Gate, the point at which heaven met earth. Floating on, across small and silent courtyards, the imperial sedan advanced through the Gate of Heavenly Purity and up the marble steps to the heights of Mount Sumeru, the spreading terrace on which the Dragon Throne awaited. Set under the eaves of the Hall of Supreme Harmony, placed directly under the central Pole Star point of the *ziwei* enclosure, the emperor was now at the centre of the cosmos. Facing south, he was ready to address his officials at an hour so early that the sun had not yet risen to declare the new day. Gathered in the courtyard before him, and facing north, his officials were ready to receive the commands of the day.

'*Xia gui!*' came the command to kneel, and the stiff joints of older age disregarded, hundreds of bodies rippled to the ground. '*Ke tou!*' followed the command to place all foreheads upon the ground, with kneeling bodies dipping their heads to such a position that not even the greatest of them could fail to feel respect. '*Ping shen!*' came the command to rise. All heads now facing into the full force of the wind, eyes fixed expectantly forward, heaven's representative on earth then issued the edicts of the day. As his orders echoed across the ocean of stone, the leopard tails of guarding soldiers stood stiffly to attention, while gilded dragons, tamed from the deep, curled obediently around the pillars of red which flanked his sides.

Suddenly, even the wind seemed to stand still. The imperial edicts announced, the heavenly cloud then swept back to the forbidden enclosures of the emperor's purple city within a city – and the hundreds of cranes, quails and lesser ranks of office stepped off to carry out their duties. On this morning of no particular significance in the year 1500, under the dynasty of the Great Ming, heaven and earth had met. The orders had been given. The day could begin.

*   *   *

The power of Kublai Khan's dynasty had not even lasted a hundred years. Fewer than a million Mongols governing a hundred million Chinese, the Great Yuan had been quick to appreciate the sparkling treasures of the settled world and the ordering value of a disciplined Confucian bureaucracy. But they had been slow to understand the will of heaven, and even slower to understand that the disciplined appearance of an order accepted could always mask a hidden, and very different, point of view.

Early errors seemed to have been easily ironed out. Arriving on the northern plains, one Mongol suggestion had been that the flat fields might be better used for grazing horses, rather than wasted on crops. Fortunately, wiser Confucian minds had prevailed, gently pointing out that taxes from the fields far outweighed the value of even the most heavenly horse. Of course, such a big and populated expanse of land would take a lot of ordering. But so great had been the prescience of earlier dynasties that the necessary layers of bureaucracy were already to hand. True, after a hundred years of battle, trust and loyalty could not be assumed – particularly given the fact that, although valiant on horseback, few if any Mongols had acquired the skill of writing, let alone the art of administration. But the Yuan were part of a much bigger empire, which stretched across the vast roof of the world into European and Middle Eastern lands, with many (particularly Muslim) men of blue and green 'coloured eyes' who were just as good as the Chinese at mastering the power of the pen and would be perfectly capable of overseeing the Chinese bureaucracy. It was not long before the scholarly minds of the old Song officials seemed to settle down to a new prosperity under the riches of a greater 'Pax Mongolica' trade which had surely soothed any temporarily broken hearts.

Once again, cities sparkled, the Grand Canal was extended to the Dadu northern capital, and the routes of the vast Mongol empire were opened up to anyone who wanted to travel to the west. For those in the cities, opportunity seemed to beckon; for those in the fields, it might have seemed that little had really changed. True, there were many scholars whose spirits refused to embrace the new Mongol order, but their dissent, mostly missed by the Mongols, seemed to be limited to the delicate strokes of ink with which their brushes painted visions of rocks, bamboo and plum blossom. Secret declarations of endurance, perseverance and a resolute insistence on the ultimate triumph of scholarly civilisation over any brutal conquest of force: all seemed unlikely to overturn the totem of the wolf.

But heaven, as usual, had a different idea. Cooling over the last few centuries, the winters of the northern lands had begun to turn into a longer, deeper age of ice – and the fragile waters on which the plains depended had evaporated into drought. By 1320, the finely predictable details of the seasons had begun to unravel. First locusts, then famines, and then, sweeping like a scythe, a black death, which cast a pall across everyone's skies. Farms abandoned, any harvests were left to rot in the fields. Canals without keepers, boats lay empty. Rivers without regulators, floods were two-a-penny. Once-piling taxes crumbled like dust. And out of the dust rose armies of desperate men with nothing left to lose, and clouds of orphaned children, for whom chaos had become the stuff of life.

Finding themselves adrift in settled lands, which seemed to have closed around them like a trap, the Mongols struggled to master the costs and complexities of ordering a once-flourishing world, which had now stopped in its tracks. By the middle of the fourteenth century many of the Mongols were muttering that it might be time to go: leave the chaos to heaven, and the coloured-eyed Muslims, to sort out. In 1368, when a rebel Chinese leader stormed out of a childhood lived at the edges of hell, they jumped on their horses and raced back to the steppes.

*   *   *

Zhu Yuanzhang was born to a family of peasants in the southern province of Anhui, and raised an orphan on the charity of a Buddhist monastery. The man who would snap the old lands of the Song back to a heavenly order, he was nothing if not clear about the responsibility of a ruler to rule. Once a member of a brotherhood of bandits, the White Lotus Society, named after

88

the Buddhist goddess of infinite compassion, he swept away the Mongols in 1368. Settling his capital in the southern city of Nanjing, he titled his dynasty Da Ming (Great Brightness).

Styling himself Hongwu (the *Vastly* Martial Emperor), Zhu Yuanzhang set about repairing a country that had been shocked to its core. As emperor, his ideas about order were as simple and clear as those of any rebel peasant: scholars might have an important imperial function but their soft hands would never coax a harvest from the land. And after nearly a hundred years of Mongol misery (not to mention the periodic crises that had punctuated the millennium before) it seemed rather unrealistic to expect that scholarly minds would be able to offer much in the way of practical suggestions to anyone. The road to order did not lie in a book or a brush but out in the villages and the fields. In this simple world, if everybody kept to their proper position and place, and took no more than their moderate needs, the order of a once-golden past would quickly return.

Acting on his convictions, Zhu proceeded to give land to any hand willing to farm it, and to set everyone under the old bureaucratic grid of Qin. The registers and maps would be updated; households would be ordered in groups of mutual guarantee; villages would be set under the supervision of village heads who, in their turn, would be commanded by imperial officials above; taxes would be fixed and quotas for harvesting production would be set for each village, county and prefecture to meet. The occupations of the people would also be recorded, and fixed, in a hierarchy of purpose according to their value to the heavenly lands. In the first and second places there were the scholarly *shi* officials (the brushes of imperial order), and the productive *nong* farmers; in the third and fourth places there were the *gong* artisans and the *shang* merchants (both men who lived on nothing but the hard work of others, with profits always gained at someone else's expense). And given that in any orderly society, the scholars and farmers were the bedrock of everything, Zhu Yuanzhang also declared that every son should follow the same occupation as his father so that the number of less useful artisans and merchants should not increase.

To these rules, Zhu Yuanzhang further added that, from the Nanjing capital down, imperial commands would be relayed to local magistrates set in county towns, whose yamen, official compounds, would become the frontline of the emperor in the fields. Empowered to deal with anything and everything on the ground, their work would include the collection of imperial taxes and the settling of neighbourly disputes. And in order to ensure that everyone across the land was clear about the heavenly nature of the empire, every month, and within every village, the Confucian texts would be read aloud for everyone to hear, with the heads of every village responsible for ensuring that everyone understood. Places fixed and purpose clear, as in the state of Qin, only those whose job was to carry goods from one place to another would need to travel. Canals were cleared and roads were mended, but if anyone wanted to go beyond the distance required to reach a locally approved market, official permits would be required. With simple self-sufficiency the order of the day, the coasts were also closed, and outsiders dreaming of trade with the lands of the Great Ming were told that their offerings were no longer required.

Foundations set, the yields were remarkably swift. Farmers returned to their fields, the fields returned to plenty, roads and rivers carried whatever officially needed to be circulated, and Zhu Yuanzhang was able to address the higher forces of order. There was an empire to regain and an army of soldiers ready for the task.

But the lands were vast and, in Zhu Yuanzhang's opinion, the soldiers were also in need of some stiff lessons in discipline. As were the ministries of scholars whose lofty minds had long ago been proven to lack the practical skills required for reliable rule. Leading from the front, Zhu Yuanzhang rose before the cock crowed, and did not sleep until long after everyone else had found their beds. Military men in the field found themselves led in person by their emperor; those who failed to obey an order were executed on the spot. And from the chief minister, who was closest to the emperor, across the six boards of ministries, which managed every aspect of the realm, ministers and their officials were subjected to the same kind of discipline that the emperor imposed upon himself. Called before the sun rose, they were charged with presenting painstakingly detailed reports, all stuffed with information gathered from every point of the imperial grid and carried to the centre by an army of horse-borne couriers for whom any delay was a punishment and a half. Every official body, high or low, was expected to work for a modest Confucian return. No decision of any weight whatsoever could be taken without the emperor's personal seal. Meanwhile, useful lessons learnt from the Mongols were brutally applied: a secret service, responsible for intelligence at home and abroad, was created; a special corps of censors was established and empowered to investigate anyone at any time (except, of course, the emperor); and all derelictions of duty were met with a Mongol-style public beating which, depending on the severity of the infraction, might easily result in death.

The first decade of the Vastly Martial Emperor's reign passed and, with such meticulous attention to detail, the paperwork of the bureaucracy grew so large that new archives had to be built to hold it. For Zhu Yuanzhang, however, the size of the bureaucracy was hardly a reason to trust it. Indeed, the very cleverness of the scholars made it difficult for the emperor to trust them not to take decisions on his behalf. In 1380, alerted to the fact that his chief minister had abandoned imperial discipline and met with a foreign envoy without his approval, Zhu Yuanzhang turned the full force of his martial attention to the misdemeanour. Arrested on the spot, within a week the chief minister and all of his family were executed. In the weeks that followed fifteen thousand others – anyone who had ever had anything to do with the chief minister – were similarly condemned to death. The emperor's fragile trust broken, the very position of chief minister was itself dismissed. Never again, for as long as the Ming ruled, would such an office be able to stand between the emperor and his imperial affairs. Neither, the emperor decided, would there be any central secretariat trying to weave its own web of power across the six ministerial boards. Henceforth it would be the emperor, and the emperor alone, who would govern the ministries. The only people permitted to help him would be a small number of lowly clerks: too lowly ever to dare to presume, but just educated enough to serve as document-drafting scribes. As the emperor worked across the heavenly day and night, the fields prospered, the empire strengthened, and every suspicion of official obstruction or failure was unfailingly followed with beatings and blood.

In 1394, at the age of seventy, Zhu Yuanzhang died, bequeathing the empire of his making not to the eldest of his surviving sons – a military man – but to the teenage son of his first-born but predeceased favourite son. Raised in the courtyards of the imperial palace in Nanjing, the grandson had been trained by the brush, schooled in the classics, and taught the language of Confucian texts which was so scholarly that only the similarly schooled could understand it. Not exposed to fields of battles or back-breaking ploughs, the boy had never quite comprehended why his grandfather beat and executed so many of the finely educated minds that his own tutors had held in such high regard. While many were surprised that Zhu Yuanzhang had chosen a scholar over a soldier, no one was very surprised when, on his own accession to the dragon throne, the grandson styled himself the Jianwen (Establishing Civility) Emperor, and placed himself firmly on the side of the Confucian brush.

For Zhu Yuanzhang's eldest surviving son, Zhu Di, the appointment of his nephew as emperor was a shock. Sent to guard the northern Dadu city (no longer the capital) against any return of the Mongols, Zhu Di had not only served his father faithfully but, trained on the battlefield and exposed to the harsh reality of peasant life, he had fully embraced and shared his father's suspicion of scholarly skirts. Watching as a faint-hearted nephew raised Confucian scholars to the highest pedestals of the Nanjing court, Zhu Di gathered his army around him and stormed the seven hundred miles from northern Dadu to the southern capital of Nanjing, setting light to the empire as he went. City after city fell to his fury and in 1402, he and his troops appeared before the gates of Nanjing, commanding that they be opened so that he could rescue the nephew-emperor from the pot of scholarly brushes that had obviously put him under a spell. The gates were opened, Zhu Di entered, and the imperial palace, with the nephew-emperor inside, suddenly shot up in flames. With the 'so-called emperor' (surely his father had made a mistake) apparently nowhere to be found, Zhu Di ascended to the dragon throne: not a usurping third emperor, he insisted, but a rightful second, who would style himself Yongle – the Emperor of Perpetual Happiness.

Having raised himself to his rightful saddle, the Yongle Emperor set about establishing the legitimacy of his rule and repairing the empire from the ravages of his own destruction. The establishment of his own legitimacy would, of course, require another battle. Having raged against his father's will and 'lost' the appointed heir, the scholarly brushes struggled to accept him as their emperor – while Zhu Di blamed them and their influence for causing the upset in the first place. Imperial edicts were confronted with official intransigence. The son of his father, Yongle responded with purges of blood – and a redirection of his trust towards his personal household of eunuchs: men without sons to make them ancestors seemed far more trustworthy servants of the present moment than Confucian scholars whose obsession with family and ancestral ritual meant they were constantly contemplating the riches of their own posterity.

With the eunuch-household now in charge and his father's great wealth at his feet, Yongle began to dream of a vast unified empire that would far exceed the reaches of the Mongol Yuan, led by a great new imperial capital to be commissioned for the north. On land, troops were marched in almost all directions: north to push the Mongols further back on the steppes; north-west to wrench them out of the oasis gems; and south-west to reclaim the lands of Annam (present-day Vietnam), once part of the Han and the Tang but which had then been lost to the more local power of the tribal state of the Yue. Adventures on land, however, were just the beginning. Turning his sights to the coast, which his father had so firmly closed for business, Yongle decided that he would outshine Chinggis Khan and his vast land empire with a tribute-receiving embrace of the oceans as well.

With scholarly minds still out of favour, Yongle chose his most trusted eunuch to carry the heavenly glory of the Great Ming out to sea. A tiger of a man-who-was-not-a-man, Zheng He had been born a Muslim. Captured in Yunnan when Zhu Yuanzhang seized the south-west from an outpost of Mongol forces, he had been castrated and sent to serve in Zhu Di's household. Over two metres tall, he became a soldier who fought alongside his master with a courage and skill that few others matched. When Zhu Di as the Yongle Emperor set his sights on the sea, Zheng He was charged with raising the ships to realise his master's dream. From 1403, the shipyards at Nanjing were stretched beyond anything ever known before. Three hundred new 'star-guided' vessels (including sixty-two 'treasure ships') were built within two years. Once completed, they were loaded with the glories of the heavenly empire, and launched on the first of what would become seven great voyages across the western seas. Calling first on the southern coasts of *Yindu*, India, the new Ming navy went on to *Hu-Lu-Mo-Ssu*, Hormuz (southern coast of present-day Iran), *A-tan*, Aden (present-day Yemen), and *Mu-ku-tu-shu*, Mogadishu (present-day Somalia). Treading the waves as they might advance along a highway at home, Zheng He and his crew distributed gifts and titles at each port of call. In return, they received the tribute of the world: lions and leopards, ostriches and unicorn giraffes. There seemed no end to the treasures that the four quarters of the world (once they were clear about the heavenly order of things) were ready to bestow. As Zheng He's ships sailed like clouds across the waves, even dragons appeared to pay a thundering tribute of their own. And when, on a few occasions, a suitable recognition of heavenly authority was not accorded, local kings were taken as captives and carried back to the lands of the Ming for a clarifying audience with the Yongle Emperor, before being returned to the patch of earth that heaven and its Son permitted them to rule.

On 2 February 1421, with the Mongol empire if not quite matched at least imaginatively emulated, the Yongle Emperor unveiled the centrepiece of his dream – a new imperial city on the site of the old Dadu (now 'Beijing', the northern capital). Paid for with a fortune of peasant taxes delivered in the form of grain from across the land, it was a spectacle whose construction knew no bounds. Timbers of forests had been floated along tamed rivers and up the newly restored Grand Canal. Craftsmen and artisans had travelled from across the empire (including the now-secondary city of Nanjing) to deliver the exquisite products of ancient talents and skills. Even the Confucian scholars, who by now had adjusted to the imperial will, joined in the endeavour of conjuring up a city greater than anything man had ever known before (albeit required to work alongside the still far more trusted eunuchs).

Declaring the heavenly mandate for all the world to see, Yongle invited envoys from the four quarters of the world to an audience with the Son of Heaven that no one on earth would want to miss. Carried like a cloud towards the Hall of Supreme Harmony, where he would receive the tribute of earth, Yongle had cause for a confident celebration. Watched by statues of wise tortoises, his heavenly sedan passed through pavilions whose very foundations contained the mysteries of Fuxi's magic square, ascending and descending stairways of loyal dragons that had consented to fix themselves in stone. And everyone's paths perfumed with mists of incense, the watching envoys found themselves floating in a dream of their own, all noting that the mandate of heaven was surely one that would last for ever.

The celebrations over, Yongle returned his attention to the matter of the bureaucracy. Experience had shown him that however much he might doubt the loyalty of his officials, an empire as vast and glorious as the Ming would require something more than a single hand on the tiller of the state. While his father might have been a powerhouse of self-disciplined labour, no ordinary son could be expected to follow that feat. Unable to appoint a chief minister, Yongle decided to work with what he had inherited. The lowly body of clerks created by his father was transformed into a Grand Secretariat, which, headed by three grand secretaries, was charged with guiding and coordinating the six ministerial boards on which the ship of state depended. In keeping with the Confucian tradition of humility (and his own father's emphasis on modesty), pay remained low. But as Yongle delegated greater levels of power to the scholarly officials, experience soon showed that an official life could offer considerable (if less visible) rewards. As humble in their formal appearance as they appeared to be in their imperial remuneration, over time the piles of the officials' personal riches rose so high that they soon began to look like treasure ships of their own.

Unsurprisingly, across the land, interest in an official career grew – and with it an interest in the scholarly books on which such a career was founded. As long as everyone was clear that official positions did not include the right to abrogate any of the imperial powers he might choose to delegate, Yongle was happy to encourage them. Indeed, kept to their proper places, he could see that schools of scholars might be rather helpful. Certainly that had been the opinion of the Song dynasty mind, Zhu Xi, who had insisted that the order of everything depended upon an emperor who could bring heaven and earth into harmony with a dedicated 'investigation of things' through the mastery of the four Confucian books. One just had to be clear that the minds who were doing the investigating had been properly trained.

Seeing the perfect logic of the emperor being at the pinnacle of everything, Yongle put Zhu Xi's wisdom into the heart of the Great Ming, declaring that his ideas should be taught to a new age of imperial officials whose qualifications for investigating things would be tested by the passing of imperial exams. The four Confucian books, which Zhu Xi had so clearly explained were the only authoritative statements of what Confucius had actually meant, were set as texts. To these were added five interpretative classics, which could be relied upon as guides. With these texts, and no others, the imperial curriculum was fixed and a system of examinations was set. Each student would master every Confucian word and every would-be official mind would be bent to the Confucian way of thinking: no essay could be tainted by any other influencing thought or personal opinion. Supervised by the Board of Rites, the rigour of the exams was such that years (often decades) of dedicated study were required before a candidate could hope to craft the kind of literary scripts that would ensure a successful result. And a successful result was essential if a candidate was to unlock the lucrative offices of power: whether in a position at the central imperial heights of the Grand Secretariat and the ministerial boards in Beijing, or at the lesser levels of administering provinces and prefectures, right down to the magistrates in charge of affairs at the lowest (county) level of imperial authority.

With the Grand Secretariat and the imperial examinations in place, Yongle set out an architecture of administration grounded on Zhu Xi's insistence on the critical importance of 'investigating things' under what had become the iron will of the classical Confucian texts. A hierarchy of bureaucratic minds was established, which put the most successful of the scholars closest to the emperor, with everyone else spread across the country at large. Within the imperial city, the 'investigation of things' became an intellectual battle of minds for the greatest mastery of the classical texts upon which any and every argument would have to be won. Across the lands, the 'investigation of things' became a responsibility for local officials to manage local affairs so tightly on the Confucian precepts that there would never be a ripple of a problem to disturb the harmonies of the heavenly emperor's rule – or, at least, not one that the emperor or a superior official could ever hear about.

As Yongle advanced heaven on earth, lesser minds were once again left to count the cost. Lands reclaimed, waterways restored, battles fought, voyages raised, and with a new imperial capital to crown it all, the treasury was struggling to make ends meet. Taxes of grain had been collected – but judging by the number of wandering beggars, peasant backs had borne the brunt of their payment. And while the empire seemed to have far more people than in his father's time, the amount of taxes collected did not appear to have risen. The boards of imperial government in Beijing were asked to explain the gap. But simple facts on the ground were hard to find. Ten-year censuses ordered by Zhu Yuanzhang seemed to have run out of local steam: the tax registers appeared to insist that there had been hardly any increase in the population, even as many of the households clearly fixed in the registers seemed to have disappeared. Suspicious minds had their doubts: local officials looking to supplement their own incomes were very likely burying the bigger population numbers so that tax quotas remained unchanged, and (in exchange for the gratitude of the local rich) spreading the collections of harvested grains more thinly across a wider base – with the greatest taxes, as ever, collected from those who had the least ability to complain (and the least ability to pay).

But the problems in the treasury were not limited to the taxes; and the causes lay as much with Yongle's new Beijing, as with any self-interested local officials. Under the original edicts of Zhu Yuanzhang, the vast majority of the population was expected to be tilling the fields – with trade limited to the essential ordering needs of the empire. When Yongle raised the city of Beijing, though, the demand for materials and crafts had been so great that the studios of the artisans had expanded to become factories of kilns and looms, while the waterways of trade had been opened up like floodgates. With the city completed, rather than returning to their fields, the artisans and the traders had found that hosts of scholarly, and now wealthy, families wanted to emulate the elegance of the capital's splendours with purchases of their own. The kilns and the looms had expanded their production, and the imperial waterways had found themselves carrying ever-greater volumes of splendid objects up and down the land. With everyone piling into the boats of trade, there were fewer hands to till the fields and deliver the taxes of harvests that the empire required. Peasants unable to pay their taxes turned to the moneylending arms of ever-richer landlords, often losing both their lands and their livelihoods. As Yongle's treasury struggled with its income, across the land peasants had been taking to the roads – peddling whatever they could in a pale imitation of the grander trades, and wandering ever-greater distances in an increasingly desperate forage for food. The rich had got richer, and their relentless pursuit of wealth was sinking the straw boats of the poor. Far from the order that Zhu Yuanzhang had dreamt of – where everyone stayed at home in self-sufficient villages – the Great Ming's people were moving all over the place. Some, of course, were merrily moving goods and profits. Others were moving body and soul to wherever a mouthful of food might be found. No wonder the registers did not tally and the taxes did not add up.

Clear as the problem and its causes were to those on the ground (and in the whispered recesses of the court), it was equally clear that any 'investigation of things' should not be allowed to disturb the harmony of the emperor's heavenly rule. Fortunately, heaven was high, and the emperor was usually too far away to see the inconvenient facts. Certainly, while the scholarly officials responsible for the treasury were fretting, the eunuchs who ran the imperial household did not seem at all concerned about the costs. From time to time, of course, the problems became a little too obvious for even the emperor not to notice that the official order of things was dangerously slipping. But the upper echelons of the bureaucracy could always be relied upon to issue reassuring edicts to the officials below: commanding the bottom to do its job and fix whatever was wrong.

And so it was that while the empire was set to the pivot of the Pole Star, the bright idea of the Ming's first emperor was unravelling at the seams. Rather than being bound together in comforting Confucian villages, the people were separating. And even as Confucian lessons about the fabric of the family continued to be regularly read aloud to the people at large, everyone was off in a cloud of their own. Some were busily stashing private balances in their sleeves and calculating profits in rising piles of money. Others were descending to the edges of despair.

*　　　*　　　*

When Yongle died in 1424, sharper imperial eyes – those of his son and, rather swiftly thereafter, his grandson – inherited the throne. Zheng He's voyages were quickly cancelled, and the great treasure ships were relegated to yards where they would gradually turn to dust. Other grand construction projects were slowed to a more appropriate pace, many to a stop. And steps were taken to liberate the farming peasants from a little of their taxing burdens. When Yongle's grandson Xuande (Spreading Virtue) followed his father Hongxi (Great Brilliance) to an early death in 1435, the throne passed to Yongle's seven-year-old great-grandson. A regency of three grand secretaries was created, and the boy was given the reassuring imperial name of Zhengtong (Upright Continuation). While the highly educated grand secretaries held the tiller of the state, in the inner residential recesses of the Forbidden City, the child-emperor was ruled by a world of eunuchs. Men with no complicating dreams of becoming ancestors, they had even acquired a school of their own through which they could master the practical skills of household administration. Banking on a lifetime of future influence, they indulged the young emperor's every whim.

When Zhengtong came of age, he chose to recognise the sacrifices of his eunuchs with a promotion. Once a household, they would henceforth be a bureaucracy, combining the intimacy of daily personal care with powers of administration applied to wider matters of ordering heaven on earth. For the scholarly officials, the unfair competition of a bureaucracy of eunuchs was shock enough, but there was worse to come. Encouraged throughout his childhood to explore every tantalising possibility of his power, the Zhengtong Emperor decided to emulate the conquering glories of his great-grandfather Yongle and set his sights on creating an even bigger empire of his own. A new wall at the northern frontier was surely required; and military campaigns against the now-resurgent Mongols were long overdue. Naturally, the only way to pay for it all would be to raise the taxes.

The grand secretaries looked at the skies, consulted their texts, and wondered what on earth to do. Whenever they were offered an opportunity (which was not often), they tried patiently but firmly to point out that things in the treasury were not quite as glittering as they might appear from the residential recesses of the heavenly city. While the empire might seem to be floating on pavilions and silk, below the imperial capital, there was a world of invisible souls struggling to survive. Seeing that the young emperor was uninterested in such earthly matters, the scholars added that there was another problem to be considered: the weather was taking a turn for the worse and it seemed that heaven might be unimpressed.

Bored with their fussing and preferring to dream of a bigger empire, the Zhengtong Emperor left the important planning to his eunuchs and the messier details to the scholars. And so it was that when the Yellow River again burst its banks, it was the (surviving) poor whose backs were put to fixing it. Here and there, mutterings of discontent turned to local rebellions. But charged as they were with maintaining heavenly harmony, local officials applied every lesson from the Confucian book to make sure that news of the rebellions stayed buried in the fields.

In 1449, boosted by the encouragement of the eunuchs, galvanised by a recent Mongol insult, and tired of listening to scholarly warnings of woe, the Zhengtong Emperor set off on a northern campaign of his own. Poorly provisioned, the emperor and his troops wandered around the edges of the steppes looking for a fight. It was only a matter of weeks before they were sighted by Mongol scouts. And once sighted, it was only a matter of moments before the emperor was captured: a prize for the Mongols to wage against a future bargain. Official minds aghast, it was obvious that Zhu Xi's recommended Confucian texts were not going to be of much help in resolving the situation. It was equally obvious that the 'household academy' of the eunuchs would struggle to offer advice. The emperor was captured, not dead. Yet without a heavenly son on the throne, there could be no heavenly bureaucracy – and therefore no heavenly empire. Zhengtong's younger brother was swiftly pushed into place and proclaimed as the Jingtai (Exalted View) Emperor. Having doted on the older son and disregarded the younger one, the eunuchs struggled to absorb the shock. Heaven, however, has its mysteries. In 1450 the Mongols suddenly returned the Zhengtong Emperor to Beijing. Having already replaced him with his brother, the grand secretaries did their best to keep their preferred younger emperor on the throne and Zhengtong off the stage. But a strange illness kept the Jingtai Emperor confined to his courtyard, and after a host of tempestuous weather conditions rattled everyone's nerves, the imperial guards were summoned for a change. Zhengtong (now restyled 'Tianshun' – Obedient to Heaven) was carried to the Hall of Supreme Harmony, and under the cosmic light of the Pole Star, pronounced the Son of Heaven – for a second time.

Obedient to Heaven ruled for another seven (rather angry) years. Determined to settle accounts with those who had kept him off his throne, punishments were thrown like missiles in every direction, and only those who learnt to polish their tongues could find any fortune in the change. Most were relieved when the Zhengtong-Tianshun Emperor died in 1464, and was followed by his oldest son, the Chenghua (Accomplished Change) Emperor. By that time, though, the world outside the Forbidden City had clearly parted company with the original Ming dream. As the scholars buried themselves in the classical Confucian texts (essential to the winning of any argument at court), yet more peasants were floating across the countryside. Conversely, those lower down the occupational hierarchy – the artisans and the merchants – were struggling to keep up with demand for their goods. Fuelled by the rising wealth of the scholarly officials, demand for practical and precious objects was going through the roof. Indeed, the trading of everything had become such a popular occupation that it was difficult to remember that the place of the artisans and the merchants was at the bottom of the social pile. Imperial disapproval notwithstanding, barges of goods sailed up and down the waterways in such force that some wondered whether there would be any space left for the water, let alone the imperial vessels whose transports of taxes-in-grain delivered the revenues on which the empire depended. And along the Grand Canal, within the walls of every city and town, and at the points at which two roads met (or where local rivers met with the canal), markets sprang up like harvests – or weeds, depending on one's point of view.

As the goods moved, so did the money. Not the clumsy copper coins of empire, but new private paper, flying back and forth across the imperial highways. Not at all the dream of an emperor, these were personal promises to pay created by families and even whole villages who could not, even if they wanted, dream the farming dream. Born into parts of the country where grain simply refused to grow (the hilly lands and mountains of the south-east, for example, around present-day Wenzhou), the families and villages who created the new paper were led by men who had come to see trade as a necessary alternative to farming, and the profits of trade as just another kind of harvest. Sons had been sent across the vast Ming lands to sow the seeds of supply and demand, matching them in complex webs of exchange, with harvests in the profits of the paper money that their families printed.

While many considered that the first Ming emperor's dream of a simple society was being rightly updated, to the scholarly officials responsible for the treasury (and to the magistrates responsible for collecting taxes in the empire's currency of copper coins and grain), it was beginning to look like a nightmare.

*　　　*　　　*

In 1487, a new emperor came to the throne, at the age of seventeen. Titled Hongzhi (Great Good Order), he worked hard to live up to his name. The officials were set to strict Confucian standards, and Hongzhi himself did his best to follow the shining example of his greatest ancestor, the first Ming emperor, Zhu Yuanzhang – not least in applying himself daily and directly to the matter of governing the lands. At the same time, after nearly a hundred years of grand and reckless imperial expenditure – and with the idea of a land of farmers having failed to capture the imaginations of so many of his ancestors – Hongzhi did his best to steady the ship of state. One scholarly suggestion was for the empire to take over production and trade. In this way, prices could be reliably fixed for the benefit of the people, and private exchanges could be prohibited, thus ensuring a tidy profit for the treasury. Various attempts at such an order were made, with particular attention paid to the most essential of commodities. But no sooner was an edict passed than quick local wits opened up new seams of profiting possibility. Officials applying the new imperial rules regularly found themselves blinded by sleights of hand on the ground, and those who managed to retain their sight were soon persuaded, for the usual gratuity, to believe that whatever it was they thought they saw, their eyes must have been deceiving them.

Looking at the tangled web of intrigue, one brave (or reckless) scholar who had reached the heights of the imperial court in Beijing suggested that the best way to protect the people might be to look less to the state as trader and more to the state as a guarantor of rules that were fair to all. The Hongzhi Emperor noted the suggestion with approval. But the Grand Secretariat and the Board of Revenue, both of which had profiting interests of their own, were unimpressed. Imperial astronomers anxiously reported an azure comet plummeting to the south, and noted that the moon was wandering off its usual course, even as a heavenly earthquake was shaking the north-west: with which, imperial attention was successfully redirected to more pressing matters of ritual and morality. Aware, however, that something needed to be done to head off any human portents of rebellion, punishments were eased and, in extreme crises, grain was redistributed. Far too difficult to solve without disturbing their own incomes, the troublesome matter of trade was pushed to one side.

Hongzhi's 'Great Good Order' came to an early end with his death in 1505. Following his father, a thirteen-year-old son ascended to the dragon throne, styled the Zhengde (Upright and Virtuous) Emperor. By now, the rich had become very much richer, and the poor had almost fallen out of everyone else's sight. At the narrow top, every thread of profit was carefully calculated. At the broad bottom, the peasants found themselves under the despotic rule of a god of copper, whose greed could never be sated. For those with money, the acquisition of things became a consuming passion, even as the delivery of an honest day's work came to be seen as a fool's paradise. Lanterns lit up every market. Objects of beauty spread in every direction: paintings and porcelain, silks and scents, jade and jewellery, and everywhere, the exquisite furniture of a grand new life. Indeed for the rich, the question of how to spend their accumulating fortunes had become a far more pressing question than whether or not they should have accumulated it in the first place. Old-fashioned ideas of virtue and humanity had long ago been swapped for handy books to teach the new man with money how to spot true value, and how to avoid a fake. Meanwhile, more and more peasants were getting lost in an underworld from which there seemed little chance of escape. Muttered observations that heaven had receded into the distance seemed to have more than an ounce of truth.

Surrounded by a heavenly bureaucracy revolving around a throne meticulously placed under the Pole Star, the young Zhengde Emperor himself quickly concluded that it mattered little what he did. The bureaucrats and their books were in a galaxy of their own, which clearly had nothing to do with him. Mesmerised by the art of war and Yongle's adventures – but, after Zhengtong's unfortunate kidnapping by the Mongols, not even allowed to think about going into battle – he decided to create his own palace army and conduct field exercises within the imperial city. Soldiers on active service at the northern front were swiftly recalled for a more heavenly duty, and soon, the imperial days – and the imperial city – were occupied with military manoeuvres. Intoxicated by stories of the front told by returning soldiers, Zhengde decided to liberate himself from the stuffy closed quarters of the Forbidden City. A Leopard House was raised in the wider imperial city, where he would be far freer to mix with his men and where it would be very difficult for the scholarly sleeves to pester him with the daily questions of order that any fool could tell had nothing to do with real life. Having deftly removed himself from the cloying presence of the officials, he then suggested that any important questions which might require imperial attentions could be given to the eunuchs: they not only understood his need for independence but could also be relied upon, if any further opinion were ever needed, to consult the more experienced soldiers under his own personal command. Shocked Confucian officials could do little more than resort to volleys of stately memorials and petitions – so many of them that the emperor eventually decided to limit his replies to brutal and public beatings.

With such an emperor, few of the scholars were surprised when the weather took a sudden turn for the worse. Dragons (now seen as messengers of heavenly displeasure) rolled into clouds of thunder, pulling every inch of water from the earth, and then showering it back as red rain. Even fewer of the people were surprised when the human portents began to rise. When the Zhengde Emperor eventually died in 1521 – from complications after falling out of a fishing boat on yet another adventure – the heavenly bureaucracy heaved a sigh of relief. Unfortunately, he departed without leaving an heir.

With Zhengde's sudden, unregretted, departure, the officials moved quickly to rescue the Confucian integrity of the heavenly empire from the eunuchs. Consulting the classics and the family, they tried to find, and justify the appointment of, an imperial candidate who would see things from the scholarly point of view. A fourteen-year-old cousin was found whose rectitude seemed to offer the greatest promise. With Confucius rather rigid about the importance of family lines, the genealogies were meticulously consulted. Unfortunately, once consulted, they seemed to support a number of les attractive candidates instead. The greatest of the scholars stretched every possible interpretation of the texts until they found a solution: the now-dead Zhengde Emperor could posthumously adopt the young cousin and thus transform him into a son and heir. The boy was placed upon the throne, and confident in their selection, the officials styled him the Jiajing (Admirable Tranquillity) Emperor.

Within a month it was clear that any idea of tranquillity was nothing but an illusion. Confucianly educated and thus filially pious, when informed of the plan, the new emperor refused to be adopted, explaining that if he cut himself off from his own dead father, he would be unable to make the necessary ancestral sacrifices. And if he was unable to make the ancestral sacrifices, then he could not possibly satisfy the greatest ritual responsibility that Confucius had given to man. Scholarly heads were scratched. The young man (already emperor) suggested that if one were going to get into the business of a posthumous reordering of family relations, it would be far better, and more acceptable to him, if it were his father, rather than himself, whom Zhengde adopted. In Confucian terms, the new emperor's logic was unassailable. But as the officials scoured the classical texts and the genealogies, they realised that if the father were adopted rather than the son, the dragon throne might be opened to a flood of competing family claims. The scholarly officials politely suggested that the new Son of Heaven might like to think again. He would not.

Once again, a battle of the brushes ensued – but Jiajing stood firm. After three years of heavenly distraction, one day in 1524 the several hundred officials who kow-towed before the emperor at every morning audience assembled as they always did. But this time they refused to disperse. Remaining prostrate before the Hall of Supreme Harmony, they pressed their position in a masterful display of *li* ritual as an imperial instrument of shame. 184 were arrested; brutal beatings followed. Still the officials stood their courtyard ground. In the stand-off, however, one senior minister by the name of Wang Yangming looked beyond the black ink of the classical texts and saw a much more fundamental problem: one that was certainly at the heart of the present crisis, but if the truth be told, had haunted the Ming for over a century. It was a problem that had nothing to do with Jiajing and everything to do with the question of what Confucius had really meant when he talked about 'investigating things'.

In the Song dynasty, the scholar Zhu Xi had made it clear that any 'investigation of things' should be exclusively conducted through the officially approved classical texts. With Zhu Xi's opinion having been adopted by the Yongle Emperor, the fabric of the Ming dynasty's reign – from the imperial examinations to the arguing of every point of policy – had been predicated on the supremacy of the written word. But had Zhu Xi really been right to limit the investigation of things to a fixed set of classical books? Senior minister that he was, Wang Yangming dared to suggest that he had not. Surely, he argued, in asking everyone to 'investigate things', Confucius could not possibly have been referring to four books and five interpretations that had not been written until after his own death. If Confucius had been concerned with investigating things, he must have been referring to things in the real world during the time of his life. In which case, insisted Wang Yangming, he must have been telling everyone to exercise their own innate human judgement as to whether an idea was good or bad. Concluding that no intelligent mind worth its salt should need an ancient textbook (however much of a classic it might be) to tell it what was right and what was wrong, Wang Yangming suggested that the officials should stop pestering the new emperor and let him investigate the matter of his ancestry himself.

For a court of bureaucrats schooled in the four books and the five classics, the senior minister's ideas were nothing short of treason. But listening to a few, having managed to retain the power of independent thought, agreed that he had a point: the texts were indeed a tyranny that had been burying schools of fine minds not only for the last hundred years but across the

104

millennium and a half which had passed since the time of the Han. As one of Wang Yangming's bravest followers observed: 'Confucius never instructed anyone to learn Confucius.' It was, the follower argued, the tyranny of an imperially constructed Confucian*ism* (rather than what Confucius had actually thought) that had buried schools of talented minds – a tyranny that had also deprived every imperial scholar of the simple human power to look at any plain set of facts and draw his own conclusions. No wonder the empire was in such a mess.

Jiajing eventually triumphed in his battle of conscience-over-Confucianism, and was permitted, at least in the matter of the ancestors, to do what he himself thought right. Tranquillity, however, was not to be won. As the oldest son of his father's princely household, Jiajing had been raised to be the summit and centre of everyone else's world. It was this quality that had enabled him to stand up to the scholars with as much intransigence as required. Unfortunately it was also a quality that made him cruel: so cruel to those around him that at one point his concubines attempted to strangle him. The concubines failed and were brutally executed. But by then Jiajing had become convinced that the Forbidden City was a nest of hostile vipers. Following the example of Zhengde and his Leopard House, he took himself outside the purple walls of the Forbidden City and set himself up in a palace in the wider imperial city beyond. From there, like Zhengtong, he directed the affairs of the empire through a small group of trusted advisers (mostly eunuchs) from without. In any event, like Zhengde, imperial power was of limited interest to him beyond the possibilities of pursuing his own pleasure – and the important matter of extending the span of his own life. Jiajing went on to dedicate most of his energies to exploring the power of mercury in acquiring the immortality that had eluded everyone's ancestors. Devoting himself to the mysteries of alchemy, he left the reins of state in the hands of the eunuchs. Corruption soon stalked the land: even the passing of the examinations or the acquisition of an imperial office could be purchased. And with a cruel heart now representing heaven, violence began to spread out from the imperial city like a plague.

Over the next forty years, the Ming lands spiralled even further out of heavenly order, even as wealth continued to soar to the skies. Those in the cities and towns pursued precious objects and spectacular clothing; those languishing in country estates did everything possible to follow their example. Honest officials disappeared, replaced by men who, as like as not, had purchased their positions in the new market for official situations. Even those who had not purchased their positions were usually willing to sell their decisions to someone who offered a high enough price. With the local magistrates as much a part of the corrupted fabric as anyone else, disputes between rich and poor could have only one outcome, even as resolving disputes between the rich became a matter of finding the highest price. Trust between the people became as elusive as the elixir of eternal life. With all eyes fixed on using any means to get to the top, and everything and everyone seemingly up for sale, ambition seemed to become a virtue – and whenever ambition was thwarted, rage was quick to follow. Oddly enough, although it was the poor who had everything to rage against, it was those with the greatest wealth who were most likely to fly into an incandescent anger – venting even the tiniest of thwarted whims with tempers that left the objects of their rage in terror for their lands and lives. For those who could afford it, order was everywhere.

When Jiajing finally died in 1567, the throne passed momentarily to his thirty-year-old son who took the title of Longqing (Great Celebration). Dead before the end of his thirty-fifth year, in the short time that he ruled, Longqing nonetheless managed to appoint a grand secretary who was ready and able to confront the chaos of the country. His name was Zhang Juzheng. One of the leading scholars of his time, Zhang was a man who believed that if one knew what was right, one had a moral obligation to do it. Corruption was placed at the top of his host of issues: a plague that had been allowed to spread as if carried by a pack of rats that were greedily gobbling up every inch of heaven. Costs were cut and taxes were reduced for the poor. Zhang even tried to tackle the age-old riddle of there being more people everywhere except in the registers upon which the imperial taxes were raised, and a country-wide survey of land and people was launched. The fortunes of the imperial treasury were revived. But few of the gains survived Zhang Juzheng's death in 1582. A posthumous assassination of his character not only left his family in ruins but prompted a purge of official positions, which removed almost everyone who had ever agreed with any of his reckless ideas.

Longqing was succeeded in 1572 by a nine-year-old son who would rule under the title of Wanli (Ten Thousand Ages) for nearly fifty years. Few of those years were easy. As a boy, the son had been advised by the sternly moral Zhang Juzheng, and by the time Zhang died, the still-young emperor had decided that things in the Forbidden City were being taken a little too seriously. Once again, the scholarly officials were left to settle their battles on their own. And, looking fondly at the eunuchs who had raised him from childhood, Wanli followed those of his predecessors who had concluded that they would probably make a better job of everything, with a lot less fuss. The scholars kept their official positions but with their influence reduced to dust, most of their highly educated hearts divided into factions. Before long they were at each other's throats. The few scholars who tried to step aside, foolishly thinking that the whole point of office was sacrifice of the self for the greater purpose of a Confucian order, were viciously attacked by peers who wanted to keep things simple and get rich quick. The same few were also exposed to the searing judgements of their families: fathers and relatives who had made heavy investments in securing a son's examination success, and who had no intention of sacrificing their own returns.

The best and most fortunate men took the opportunity to retire from official life to pursue a more meditative existence, far from the reaches of Beijing. As they retired, the eunuchs were offered their positions. Some of the eunuchs were appointed as tax collectors, others as heads of imperial enterprises responsible for the essential commodities of the empire. With more opportunity than time or dedication, they quickly delegated as many of their responsibilities as possible to local thugs and mercenary officers, who were more than willing to step into the breach.

In 1586, yet another ritual dispute arose. This time, the problem was the Wanli Emperor's desire to leave the empire to his preferred third son, rather than to his eldest, as Confucian tradition required. The most senior officials decided to make a stand and stick to it, withholding their co-operation until the emperor changed his mind. Exasperated at the lock in which the bureaucracy held his powers, from 1601 Wanli refused to make any kind of heavenly appearance at all. Every day for the next twenty years, the heavenly officials gathered before dawn and, scuttling to the Hall of Supreme Harmony, prostrated themselves before the terraced summit of Mount Sumeru and an empty dragon throne.

As the older officials battled on their knees, a number of younger scholars, sharply schooled in the classical texts and newer to the heavenly game, decided that it was time for a change. In 1604, the bravest of them founded a faction of their own. Naming themselves the Donglin (East Forest) Academy, after a Buddhist temple at which a respected Song dynasty scholar had once taught, they gathered in the same Wuxi city as the temple, in a southern world that seemed safer than Beijing. Applying a moral compass to the state of heaven on earth, the young members of the academy argued that things could never have come to such a pass if the senior officials had been men of integrity. Nor, they added, could it have happened if the eunuchs had been kept in their place and the Grand Secretariat had not risen across the generations to acquire a power close to that of the emperor himself.

Confucianly trained, and seeing filial piety, rather than personal advancement, as a virtue, the Donglin scholars declined to form an institution that might be seen as questioning Heaven's Son. Their activities were limited to intellectual discussions across literary clubs. But for all of their learning and studious care, they underestimated the depths to which both the senior officials and the eunuchs would go to retain the order of the day. They also underestimated the power of two devilish institutions which had been established in the past. The first was the imperial censorate, created by the first Ming emperor within the scholarly bureaucracy. Able to inspect anyone at any time without rhyme or reason, the imperial censorate pursued the individual members of the Donglin without a measure of heavenly integrity or humanity. The Donglin scholars suffered, but when the Wanli Emperor died in 1620, they were still alive. At that point, however, the eunuchs, led by one of the most calculating and tyrannical imperial servants of all time (a man by the name of Wei Zhongxian), decided to take matters into the hands of their own secret service: the *Dong Chang*, Eastern Depot. Originally created for the personal protection of the first Ming emperor, its greatest power was torture. The Donglin Academy was brutally destroyed – and all of those who lives had touched its members found themselves in the grip of the most terrifying of the Ming dynasty's secret powers.

For the next seven years, a pack of wolves in the shape of a household of eunuchs controlled every inch of the corridors of power. And once again, the weather howled at the injustice of it all. Heaven pretended to rule: first through a young emperor (Taicheng, Great Goodness), who came to power in 1620 but was mysteriously ill for most of his year-long reign; and then through a teenage emperor who took the name of Tianqi (Heavenly Opening). In 1627 both Tianqi and Wei Zhongxian, the tyrannical eunuch, died. The imperial city heaved a momentary sigh of relief at Wei Zhongxian's departure. A new emperor (Chongzhen, Honourable and Auspicious) ascended to the dragon throne; and the empire dared to hope.

The new emperor tried his level best to live up to his name. But as a boy of sixteen who had never been expected to rule, he struggled to do more than hold his place. Unresolved, the problems of the past prowled at large. The tyrannical eunuch was gone, but so was much of the flower of the Ming's intellectual youth. The lands at large were now governed by the lord of silver, with demons riding at his side. Nine out of every ten people were drowning in the mud of poverty, and one in every hundred was floating without a home. As the people were being washed away, official papers rose within the imperial city like mountains while the treasury lay bare. Proclaiming a restoration of the ideas of integrity, humanity and the conscience of the individual, Chongzhen cut every possible cost in sight. Desperate to please – and desperately aware of the chaos into which the heavenly lands had fallen – he even issued an edict commanding every head in the land to purge their evil thoughts, so that heaven might forgive them all.

Proclaim as he might, good and bad, Chongzhen's officials were exhausted. Cut as he might, the imperial revenues had dried up. Up and down the highways, the times resembled those dangerous days at the end of the Mongol Yuan. Orphans and refugees floundered amid throngs of men whose misfortunes had turned them into bandits. Unpaid soldiers stood ready to serve anyone offering a coin. Cities, towns and villages found themselves hostages to bands of blood brothers who, exhausted by the tyranny of local powers, raised their flags and, lighting torches of flame in every direction, looted at will. The hungry, having exhausted the bark of the trees, turned first to clods of earth, and then to the rotting corpses of their fellow men. Perhaps in protest, a freezing shock of weather locked the Yellow River into the metallic grip of ice. Floods and droughts, famines and locusts, earthquakes and epidemics: heaven unleashed them all.

Many no longer had the energy to hope. But, as in the past, there were some who, spurred by rage and driven by a desire to free the people from a rule that had so clearly lost its way, found a spirit of rebellion.

Meanwhile, as the heavenly lands began to rock, beyond the Long Wall and up on the steppes, the old Mongols were being challenged by yet another rising tribal power, this one calling itself 'Manju'. Settling at the north-eastern edges of the Ming lands, on a peninsula that curved around the eastern sea, the Manju had begun as one of the tribes that had been offered preferential trade as part of the age-old strategy of dividing the barbarians. Situated at such close proximity to the Ming, they had had ample opportunity to observe the treasures of heaven-on-earth, and had been quick to note the fading of the Ming dream. When, predictably, the trade turned to border battles, the Manju had invited any Ming official who wanted a better life to join them as they raised a new kingdom: one patterned on the greater ideas of heavenly order, which the Ming themselves had obviously forgotten. As the Manju rose and the Ming crumbled, the border became a constant battleground, even as heaven's treasury struggled to cover the cost. Decorated generals wept at the sight of troops sent to battle with neither weapons, food nor dress. Victims of the final economies of desperation, those soldiers who stayed with their battalions offered their lives, again and again. Seeing brothers sacrificed to a Ming dream that had lost its mandate to rule, many deserted, abandoning the tattered forces of the empire to join the new armies of rebels now pushing towards Beijing.

Among the deserters was a man called Li Zicheng. Born a shepherd, he had long ago lost his sheep, floating from one itinerant job to another until he became first a soldier, and then a rebel in command of his own small band of men. His band became a conquering army and in 1644, having captured Chang'an (present-day Xi'an), he looked east and saw Beijing standing almost defenceless on the plains.

On 24 April 1644, Li Zicheng advanced into the city, quickly laying any objecting Ming forces to rest. Within the innermost recesses of the Forbidden City, the Chongzhen Emperor was in no doubt that heaven wanted a change. Walking out of the now-unguarded Gate of the Black Tortoise at the north of the Forbidden City, he marched up a hill that had once been raised to provide a *feng shui* shield for the back of the imperial household. Unable to face his ancestors for shame, the Chongzhen Emperor humbly tore a strip of yellow silk from his imperial gown, tied it in a noose and hanged himself from a tree.

The 'bright' idea of the first Ming emperor had come to a very bad end indeed.

CHAPTER 3

THIS WORLD AND BEYOND

When I watch this benighted world's devices I despair;
but where else can I go?

The Book of Songs 700 BCE

Shuffling through leaves touched with early-morning dew, the old master pushed softly on. Appearing and disappearing, the hint of an upward trail stretched through a mountain landscape of shadow and light: the omnipresent *yin* and *yang*. Soft bends in the path presented bamboo groves where leaves brushed the master's passing shoulders with respect. Stalks yielded with grace to the gentle steps of a thoughtful mind. Every now and then, a sudden turn took his feet to the brink of a precipice along which he calmly placed one precarious step above another, even as his hands felt their way forward, inch by inch. Eventually a clearing was reached: soft earth below, and above, a midday sun casting its beams, like blessings, on rocks that towered above. Flat and firm enough to provide a simple perch for a human life, the clearing was also sufficiently and far away from the dusty flatlands of the settled plains that few from the settled world below would care to follow in his wake.

Nearby was a wood: space for a simple hut, with trees providing

111

the necessary timber for a home, and branches ready to supply a roof. Underfoot, roots tethered in the ground would provide a simple sustenance, and in the near distance, the sound of a gurgling stream promised water for drinking and all necessary reflections. Surrounded by plants and trees, as the seasons turned, flowering chrysanthemums would offer beauty and tea, while bushes of varying shapes and sizes would offer up the wilder infusions of leaves that could carry a questioning mind on its journeys to the mysteries of the world beyond. In the heat of summer, a cool coppice of low spreading pines would offer an ancient shelter. In the cold of winter, twigs and branches would fuel a warming fire. By day, the sun would offer a natural warmth. By night, the moon would spread the land with light enough to read. Night and day, clouds would come and go, offering the eternal wisdom that their mists described so well: 'Try to possess your desire and you will lose it. Let it go and it will be yours for ever.' Up before dawn, dancing late into the night with the moon, quietly watching, gently meditating, the master had found a place where the secrets of the ever-changing cosmos could be explored in all their splendour.

Down in the cities below, rushing here and there, frantic minds would, of course, still be raising and demolishing their earthly empires, oblivious to all but the most pressing of ambitions. Their air full of words, their eyes flitting from one glinting prospect to another, their hearts would be lost even to themselves. But that was a world away. From this simple perch above, looking out across the beckoning ridges of a thousand misty mountains, one could see clear to the Kunlun west where heaven truly meets the earth. Breathing in the silence, one could never forget that any deeper meaning was always well beyond words. Nothing false, nothing real: only a treasure beyond compare.

Of course, every now and then a curious heart would try to pay a visit, imagining that heaven was a place and clumsily clambering up stone steps that some had carved into the sides of rocks to take them to it. The most observant might even detect the hints of a human life – the smoke of a fire not long extinguished, a trail of dust swept with recently fallen leaves, a patch of glowing chrysanthemums by a hint of a hut. But the master would never be there to be seen. Off to heaven or just wandering amid the forest's pines – who could ever know? Seeing the shadows fade like the early-morning mist, even the most persistent would eventually heave a sigh of regret and turn their steps reluctantly back towards the plains.

But as they made their way down to the boundaries of this world, their hearts would yet be tugged by the dream of what might lie beyond.

* * *

It had all begun so long ago, in that *hun mang* chaos from which the idea of a *dao* way had beckoned like a siren, eventually revealing a natural order sustained by a force of energy known as the *qi*. As heaven and earth had separated, and the seasons had formed, out of those swirling mists of everything and nothing had come beasts, birds, trees, fish and eventually (with Nüwa's help) man. In that most ancient *taiping* great peace, the original 'golden age' where man and beast had lived in sympathy with one another under a heaven that seemed to spread as far as the mind could wander, children had lain down with tigers, everyone had chattered to the birds, and carefully contemplating eyes had pierced the secrets of the stars. Fuxi had observed the symphony of numbers from the magic square on a tortoise's back, while other revelations had leapt out of the mysterious natural world. And while more and more men had foolishly concentrated on gathering ever-greater piles of grain, deeper minds had never stopped peering at the treasures of ideas hidden within the physical terrain. Some had plumbed the depths of the inner cosmos, meditating until their spirits stepped into another world. Drinking the offerings of plants, they had climbed onto the backs of willing beasts and soared to the sky for a conversation with heaven above. Feet back on the ground, they had stared at the footprints of the birds and found yet more heavenly messages. And with every day, they had danced in the changing rhythms of the seasons and found themselves in the presence of an order that caused them to catch their breath with awe.

Time, of course, had turned, and the soft creative *yang* had become a harder *yin*. Lesser hearts had captured the magic and cast it into bronze vessels of power, which ensnared gullible human minds. Meanwhile, the myriad sounds of the skies had been ordered into melodies of music, with every note becoming a prisoner of somebody's composing power. So much attention-catching music that it was hardly surprising that everyone lost their senses. Bundling the people into obedient tribes and settling them along the banks of a yellow river, the most narrow-minded of men had taken the mysteries of the earth and turned them into nothing but the cluttered facts of clouded minds. Yet it was these narrow-minded men who had come to be seen by a foolish world as 'great'. The one had become two: those who wanted to understand the mysteries of the cosmos, and those who simply wanted to order the earth. Even the people of the earth had been divided into a high and a low. While the humble Shennong had tilled the fields shoulder to shoulder with his fellow man, it had not been long before cities had risen and the fields had fallen to the command of the high. Advised by once-shaman spirits who had abandoned the skies for a more profitable pursuit of the order of man, the high had then taken the crests of birds and turned them into hats, whiskers had been transformed into fringes, and furs had been replaced with the silken produce of worms in mulberry trees for clothes.

Then Yu the Great had divided the land into nine ordering provinces. Forests had been tamed with flames, mountains had been opened with gunpowder, rivers had been twisted and turned until none of them, least of all the Yellow River, knew what they should call their beds. Ordered by the high, the low had found themselves as farming hands, set to fields of labour that seemed never to end. The shapes of provinces and fields had been engraved into maps, and the acquired names of the people had been scored into registers, gripping all like chains. The order of the spheres had become the order of man. And the infinite promise of the cosmos had shrunk to the power of a glittering city at the helm of a state.

The Duke of Zhou had tried to recover that most ancient of the golden ages. Gathering together whatever lost wisdom he could find in the bamboo strips and the memories of the surviving shamans who had remained true to the order of the cosmos, he had put it all into his *Book of Changes*. But setting a book as a guide, it was hardly surprising that later generations had lost the point. While *The Book of Changes* was a masterpiece, once its mysteries had been written down in words, narrower minds had lost the light and seized upon the illusion that the cosmos was a chaos that could and should be ordered into something more convenient for man. Trying to recover the Duke of Zhou's dream five hundred years later, Confucius had doubtless been well intentioned, but what a fool. Caught up in the ropes of the settled city world, he had not been able to see the powers that truly were. Mixing up the order of the cosmos with a set of rules for man, he had done more damage than many of a lesser mind. It was said that he had once encountered Laozi and quickly understood that he had missed something. But if that was the case, the meeting had come far too late: fixed on saving the city-states, Confucius had already lost the plot.

114

Laozi had tried to help, leaving the legacy of the *Dao De Jing*. Opening with a warning to the reader not to be mesmerised by the written words of any text, if any spirit could have conveyed the mysteries of cosmic order, it was surely this. But as the city-states rose in arrogance and power, spread across the land, it was hardly surprising that he himself had chosen to escape the settled world. This world or something else? It was a choice that every spirit of heart and mind was forced to make. Stay, and lose any possibility of discovering the *dao*; or leave, and look for a mountain or a forest where you would be free to find your way.

Some had tried to have their mooncake and eat it. Confusing the simple life of humanly ordered villages with the mysteries of the cosmos which only an inner meditation could reveal, they tried to recreate the old world of Shennong – the one in which a ruler picked up his own hoe and ploughed his furrows in a community of equal men. Later, when Liu Bang as first Han emperor had rewritten the past, it was not only Confucius' works that had been recast. Some even tried to stitch together Laozi's ideas about the *dao* with the Great Man triumphs of the Yellow Emperor, stuffing them both into Shennong's egalitarian seams. But that 'big idea' had only turned the *dao* into an 'ism', offered up for the benefit of those who simply wanted to order the earth. And then, all sorts of mumbo-jumbo had appeared, including an idea that the Yellow Emperor and Laozi were at the head of a pantheon of heavenly gods, with the *yin* and the *yang*, the five elements of wood, earth, fire, metal and water (not to mention the elemental energy of the *qi*), all wrapped up in a hocus-pocus that would eventually deliver not just equality on earth but immortality for everyone: a whole new idea of a *taiping* great peace.

Of course, by that point, the waters of the earth had been well and truly muddied by the 'unity' the Han held so dear. Sent off to embrace the rest of the world in the heavenly dream, the Han generals, however, had come upon something rather unexpected. Encountering caravans of trade, they had found golden statues of a meditating man folded in the robes of merchants and accompanying western monks. It soon became clear that the precious treasures of the near-west included a jewel of an idea, which, rather like the *dao*, had been narrowed into an article of faith. Unaware of the existence of Gautama Siddhartha (the Himalayan prince who became the Buddha), many assumed that the meditating statues were of Laozi, who, having made it to *Yindu*, India, was now bringing his ideas back to the heavenly lands. On closer inspection, however, and with a little conversation and reflection,

115

most realised that the man represented by the statue was someone rather different: a prince with a dream of justice and human compassion, offering a promise that there was a place for everyone in a land called Nirvana. This was obviously something very different from Laozi's ideas, although, translated through the many trading languages of the steppe world, it was hard to be clear about what exactly it was. Rather confusingly, everyone who mentioned the place called Nirvana also talked about a 'Buddha nature', which released man from human suffering by melting him into the ocean of a single cosmic consciousness. And somewhere in the baffling descriptions there were strange ideas which talked about *maya*, illusions, that had to be lost, and *sunyata*, an emptiness in which there was no individual self. Mesmerisingly beautiful, it was all a little bit strange.

The simple words of trade failing to convey the truth, travelling imaginations had been stretched and everyone had got confused. And so it was that with a dearth of good translators, the basic elements of the foreign and the familiar wove themselves together. *Dharma*, cosmic duty, became the *dao*, way; *sila*, self-restraint, became *xiao*, filial piety. Nirvana became *tian*, heaven (a world floating somewhere above the earth where the ancestors conferred with the gods). 'Buddha nature' became the Confucian virtues, and the Confucian virtues – *ren* humanity, *li* ritual and *yi* integrity – were paired off with the Buddhist precepts of non-violence, truth and celibacy. None of these ideas were really diametrically opposed, just sufficiently out of focus for nothing to be clear. One idea, though, stood out on its own, even as it seemed almost impossible to believe. Apparently, there was a real Buddhist kingdom on earth. Far away in the mountainous west, it was a place where every horizon was lit with glittering temples, the lands were swept with monasteries, and a king sat down among his people and, offering them food of his own, bowed his head to a monk. A heavenly kingdom that put compassion before considerations of order: now that was truly a novel idea.

As the Han had set off in pursuit of unity, the Yellow Emperor's people received lesson after lesson about the costs of the settled world. Every triumph, and even the losses, had to be paid for in taxes on grains that came from harvests reaped by working hands. And as the triumphs and the losses had piled higher and higher, the peasants had been pushed first into seas of despair and then into storms of bandits. To which, the weather had then added its own flooding judgements, with epidemics of famine and disease following in their wake.

Pushing the barbarian tribes back beyond the Long Wall in the north, and pulling the distant oasis states under the single heaven on earth, the glittering carriages of wealth had retreated behind their own city walls. Struggling to survive in the fields outside, the peasants began to appear like shrunken monsters: faces black, skin as rough as mulberry bark, feet twisted in strange directions. For the people at large, survival had become a matter of chance, with any hope of charity being far more likely to come from the poor than the rich. In such a world, was it any wonder that the minds in the fields wandered to the stories of the most ancient of the golden ages – not the golden age of the Duke of Zhou, but the earlier time of *taiping* great peace, when men had wandered wherever they wanted, and eaten whatever they had hunted or found, when the weather had cast its blessings on all of heaven's people, and when anyone could talk to heaven whenever they wanted, and say whatever they wanted to say. And while some chided them for their foolish dreams, foolish or not, the dreamers were many.

While the fields dreamt of that ancient time of *taiping* great peace, many of those who had come across the Buddhist idea of a heavenly nirvana began to think again. The pursuit of the elusive *dao* seemed to require a meditating order of human hearts. Even Confucius had observed that the golden age of the past could be rediscovered only if men would set their hearts straight. Perhaps those Buddha followers had hit upon something important: if an understanding and practice of the Buddha ideas merited the organised faith of a 'Buddh*ism*', with its temples and monks, then surely the ideas of the *dao* should be given the respect of a 'Dao*ism*' as well.

It was not long before a new text emerged, known as *The Taiping Jing: the Classic of Great Peace*. Dedicated to the resurrection of an earthly order of Taiping Great Peace, it included all of the roots and branches of the shamanic past: the *yin* and the *yang*, the five elements of spring wood, summer fire, higher summer earth, autumn metal and winter water, and, of course, the wider wisdom collected in *The Book of Changes*. To these were added the shamanic wisdom of meditation and the teaching of a style of breathing that would guide the heavenly *qi* towards earthly harmony and could even prolong the life of man. Under the heavenly guidance of the Yellow Emperor and Laozi, and led by an earthly representative in the form of a Celestial Master, the people could indeed be guided back to the purity of the past. Thoughts would be cleansed of disharmony, individual paths would be corrected, and as the proper practices of breathing and eating were taught, the people would be protected from any diseases in this world and be able to find their way to an immortality which would mean they never had to worry about the hidden terrors of any world beyond. Individual hearts and minds corrected, heaven would be happy, and peace would be secured: the peace of the people, and of the seasons and the weather upon which everyone's lives depended.

In 142, a scholar had stood up and declared a dream. Born in the northeast but serving as a magistrate in the Jiangzhou commandery (present-day Chongqing, once part of the central province of Sichuan), his name was Zhang Daoling. Describing his dream to the Jiangzhou people, Zhang said that he had been visited by Laozi, who had commanded him to purify the Han of its destroying decadence by seeding a vanguard of penitent people. A kingdom was to be declared in which the purity of each individual's life would be so great that peace would be guaranteed and immortality would be as natural as the air. Listening, the people of Jiangzhou thought about their own dreams, and the stories of their many different pasts. Some were descendants of families that had been sent south by the First Qin Emperor in the wake of the early southern conquests. Others were later-arriving migrants, who had floated in on the recolonising waves of the Han. But many were the descendants of the Ba people whose Ba state had first been conquered by the Qin and again by the Han. Looking at his motley flock, Zhang Daoling had invited everyone, Han Chinese and Ba alike, to join him in a movement to raise a new order of Taiping Great Peace, led by himself as Celestial Master, and supported by a celestial bureaucracy. Everyone would confess the sins of their past and find their illnesses cured. Cleansed of their sins, cured of their illnesses, inhaling and exhaling in harmony with the cosmos, they would be a community of brothers and sisters, united as the single breath of the people's peace. Lost by the decadent dynasties of the past, the blessings of heaven would return. All that was required to join was a contribution of five pecks of rice to a common pot from which everyone would eat.

For a people labouring under the taxes of the unifying Han, the vision was intoxicating. Backs breaking, many of the Han migrants were quick to join the new community. Dreaming of regaining their lost independence, the Ba also saw in Zhang Daoling's dream the possibility of a greater freedom from the iron fist of imperial rule.

Time passed, the Han dynasty weakened from within, and in 156 Zhang Daoling passed away. But his son and grandson followed as Celestial Masters in his footsteps. The taiping dream spread across Sichuan and beyond: envoys of the Celestial Masters not only went up to the Zhang family's north-east heartland, but even reached into the souls of imperial officials, who, like the people, were now struggling with the turmoil of a crumbling power. By the beginning of 184, the movement which saw itself as the 'breath of the people's peace' had acquired the colour of a rebellion and a name after a cloth: 'Yellow Turban', after the yellow as the colour which had come to mean the centre of everything, and after the scarves the peasant rebels wrapped around their heads. Led by spirit troops and generals, the peasant rebels swept across the land like a purifying wind. And as the rebels fanned to the east, west, north and south, in a mountain-wrapped valley in deepest Sichuan, an independent 'Daoist' kingdom was proclaimed: the Taiping Kingdom of Great Peace.

Across the year of 184, the Yellow Turbans inflicted shocking defeats upon the imperial Han army. Startled by the speed with which these 'human portents' had spread, the Han Emperor promised everything to the warlord-generals of his garrisons if only they could remove the blight of peasant rebels from the land. The sweeping body of the Yellow Turbans was defeated within a year. But the Taiping Kingdom of Great Peace survived in its Sichuan valley for another thirty years of celestial self-rule. And when it finally collapsed, its many limbs scattered rather than disappeared, continuing to break into rebellions for decades, if not centuries, to come.

The defeat of the Yellow Turbans had come at a high price. It was not long before Cao Cao, the great general, took advantage of the weakness that the rebels had created, and kidnapped the emperor. The emperor lost to a warlord, it was not much longer before the whole of the once-unified Han lands splintered into three (more temporal) kingdoms. Three warlord-led kingdoms, all in pursuit of a single heavenly mandate, which would bring everywhere back under the order of a single heavenly son. Each warlord ruler armed with the same ideas of the *dao* and the same Confucian texts, and all guided by the *Art of War* which Sunzi, the master of military strategy, had written during the time of the Warring States.

With such a common past, each of the competing rulers looked for the great idea that would give them a defining advantage in the present. One (ruler of the Kingdom of Shu-Han, whose lands included part of present-day Sichuan) was directed to a hermit, whose thoughts were said to be as sharp as crystal and whose talents apparently included an ability to call down cascades of rain. Indeed, so great and so mysterious were the man's powers that, although his name was Zhuge Liang, he was widely known as the 'Crouching Dragon'. When the Shu-Han ruler suggested that the Crouching Dragon call upon him

119

for an audience, he was informed that this was a man who did not call upon anybody, and rarely allowed anyone to call upon him. The ruler swallowed his pride and made the journey – several times – to persuade the Crouching Dragon to give up his lair for the Shu-Han cause. Refusing all distractions from a meditating life, and without the least interest in who might be running the settled world, Zhuge Liang remained intransigent – until the ruler hit upon the argument that a meditating mastery of the cosmos would be worth nothing if the physical world collapsed.

Entering Shu-Han service, Zhuge Liang brought with him treasures of uncluttered concentration: a deep knowledge of astronomy, a cosmic mastery of the changing principles of *yin* and *yang*, and flights of shamanic imagination which left other minds far behind. It was not long before the Shu-Han scored a string of victories, almost all from situations that had appeared to be certain jaws of defeat. Stories of the Crouching Dragon's powers flew across all of the Three Kingdoms, becoming a force of their own. A favourite was the story of how, trapped by a general of the opposing Kingdom of Wu, Zhuge Liang played a leisurely game of chess on the walls of a city, in full view of the encircling Wu troops. So brazen was the game, and so great was Zhuge Liang's reputation, that the Wu general assumed it must be an ambush and withdrew his men.

The best of the Zhuge Liang stories, though, the one that shot itself into everyone's heart, was the battle of the 'borrowed' arrows. Set on the banks of the misty Yangzi River, it unfolded when the Shu-Han were about to face the other of their two opponent kingdoms: the Cao Wei. Arriving at the appointed place of battle after a long and exhausting march, the Shu-Han found that their troops had run out of arrows. Spirits already tired and fear now beginning to rustle through the ranks, Zhuge Liang stood calmly on the banks on the river and looked for the *dao*. Consulting the elements around him, he listened to the wind, watched the clouds, observed the bend of the river and its currents – and reflected on what he knew of the enemy warlord, and on the likely state of mind of the Cao Wei troops assembled on the opposite side of the river. Everything considered, Zhuge Liang told the Shu-Han ruler that they would 'borrow' some arrows from their Cao Wei enemy. Eyebrows were raised, but a squadron of Shu-Han ships was summoned up for a sail, and a crew was created not from standing soldiers but out of bales of straw, bound and clothed to look like men. The evening mists fell, and silent feet were commanded to lead the ships up the river towards the Cao Wei camp, pulling on from the Shu-Han bank. As expected, sharp Cao Wei scouts were quick to spot the shadowy movements in the mist and instantly informed their general of an impending stealth attack. Congratulating them on their powers of observation, the Cao Wei general roused his archers from their rest and ordered them to shoot a hail of arrows towards the waiting Shu-Han ships. As the arrows settled obligingly into the straw, the Shu-Han troops erupted with applause. That night, the Cao Wei troops tossed and turned, wondering what kind of trick had been played at their expense, while the Shu-Han slept soundly in the knowledge that the Crouching Dragon had fooled their enemy before the battle had even begun. The story of the borrowed arrows spread like wildfire – and for every ear that heard it, then and thereafter, the deep wisdom of the *dao* became the promise of a secret inner power that could snatch a saving miracle from the trembling terror of any threat.

In 300, long after the death of Zhuge Liang, the Three Kingdoms eventually shattered into sixteen in the north, and a succession of short-lived dynasties in the south. Many of the new northern states had been founded by steppe rulers, who had already embraced the travelling ideas of the Buddha; now they carried them into the settled world. As Daoist Celestial Masters were gathering souls both north and south, in the northern plains of nomadic conquests Buddhist temples began to rise on the horizon. Offered a choice, many stayed true to the dream of Laozi's Taiping Great Peace. But others began to float towards the Buddha, whose soft face seemed to promise a much simpler compassion and an even more tantalising dream: a world free of an all-controlling heaven, one where even a king might sit down among his people, and bow his head to a monk. A dream where the people would be free talk to heaven whenever they wanted, and say whatever they wanted to say. As the heavenly lands had separated, so, once again, had their human hearts.

As the temporal kingdoms battled, within the Daoist world, two new celestial kingdoms were founded. One, naming itself the Kingdom of Great Perfection, was raised (in 306) in the old Ba lands of central Sichuan. Claiming a direct descent from Zhang Daoling's old Taiping Kingdom of Great Peace, its Celestial Master took the name of Li. Although it lasted for less than fifty years, just like the old Kingdom of Great Peace, its followers scattered to all corners of the country, bringing with them a belief in a coming apocalypse, which only those who sought the grace of the *dao* could escape – and the idea that their salvation would be delivered by man called Li.

The second of the celestial kingdoms was more successful. Rising (in

424) in northern lands conquered by one of the Buddhism-embracing steppe tribes (known as the Northern Wei), it was founded by a Daoist priest who also claimed a link to the old Taiping Kingdom of Great Peace. Declaring, like Zhang Daoling, that he had been visited by Laozi, the priest told the ruler of the tribe that while he might be labouring under a delusion of Buddhism, he was in fact a reincarnation of the Perfect Lord of the Daoist Taiping Great Peace. The revelation resulted in the conversion of the ruler to Daoism; and a large part of northern China became a Daoist state. The Daoist priest was rewarded with an imperial title; and as the Taiping Kingdom of the Northern Wei stretched, Buddhism was purged like a plague. Buddhist images and texts were set to flames; Buddhist monks were despatched to whatever world awaited them beyond. And as each Buddhist pagoda was smashed to the ground, it was replaced with a temple dedicated to the new Daoist idea.

Like the earlier Taiping Kingdoms of Great Peace, however, the Daoist hold on the north did not last long – no longer than the death of the steppe ruler who had been converted by the dream. Bloodied, but by no means defeated – and never really wrenched from the hopeful hearts of its followers on the ground – Buddhism returned to the northern plains. While the old Daoist temples were left to stand, new temples raised the Buddhist idea to even greater golden heights, with vast images of the Buddha carved into the towering cliffs of the north-eastern landscape.

But the Taiping Great Peace did not suffer its fall from northern grace in silence. While the dreams of a Daoist kingdom might have been suspended, whispers of a coming apocalyptic reckoning were spreading and becoming louder by the year: Laozi would return in the shape of an avenging saviour called Li, and under the purifying sword of that saviour, the Daoist good would once and for all be freed from everything Buddhist and bad. As the northern Daoists waited for their avenging Li, the earthly representatives of both persuasions found themselves competing for the people's souls. Buddhist and Daoist alike, monks began to call upon every charm they could muster, borrowing the best of them from each other. Miracles were declared from all directions. And the stage was set for a tussling dance of celestial ideas that would last for centuries to come.

As the north battled for souls, down in the south, a softer style of Buddhism had been arriving on boats, carried by the trading winds of the southern sea. In the early years of the fifth century, an entirely new Buddhist idea arrived in the southern garrison of Guangdong – in the form of a south Indian monk who was wandering under the name of Bodhidharma (*bodhi* being the name of the tree under which Gautama Siddhartha had become the Buddha; *dharma* the Sanskrit word for actions that correspond with the cosmic order). The monk had come out of present-day Kerala, walking through south-western lands that had once been Han (and before that the lands of individual tribes) and were now home to a host of different southern kingdoms. Teaching as he travelled, and broadly following in the steps of other Indians who had gone before him, Bodhidharma eventually found his way to a monastery that had been established by an earlier Indian monk. Set on Mount Shaoshi, in the thick of *lin*, woods, its name was Shaolin.

Offering to teach for his keep, the monk shared the secrets of a martial art he had learnt in the Indian south: a skill of hand-to-hand combat known as *kalaripayattu*. Shaolin's monks were trained to fly like lightning, strike like thunder, and appear silently behind an opponent whenever he least expected. Lessons taught, Bodhidharma then turned his body to face a wall and spent the next nine years sitting in a waking silence. When he left the Shaolin monastery, he bequeathed an art that, combined with Daoist ideas about the cosmic energies of the *qi* and the constant movement of *yin* and *yang* change, would come to be known as *tai qi*. He also left the inspiration for a new method of meditation so powerful that, developed under later Chinese monks, it would come to be described as 'the sound of one hand clapping'. Named *chan* (a transliteration of the Sanskrit word *channa* for meditation), it would eventually travel from China across the sea to Japan – where the character for *chan* would be pronounced as 'zen'.

Back up in the north, in 589, when the Tujue finally united the many battling northern and southern states under the single dynasty of the Sui, Buddhism came with them. While the Sui ruler (Yang Jian, both Tujue and Han Chinese) formally sealed his victory with a marriage, he also appealed to the common compassion of a Buddhism, which had now, albeit by very different routes, found its way into both the north and the south. Under the Sui, the heavenly lands were touched with glittering Buddhist temples, all stroked with graceful groves of bamboo and sheltered by lofty pines, and all intoning the charms of golden sutras. To these, Yang Jian added a string of pagoda-like stupas, each holding a relic of the Buddha as a talisman of his ideas. Yang Jian did not ignore the fact that the north had been swept with Daoism – or that Daoism had become a faith with many following hearts. Acknowledging the equality of the Daoist idea, he permitted the Daoist temples to continue their dreams. But taking note of the Daoists' rather stormy history of rebellion – and clear that any other worlds, whether Daoist or Buddhist, would naturally compete with the temporal order of an empire – he also created an imperial bureaucracy devoted to the management of both the Buddhist *and* the Daoist realms. Temples and monks of both persuasions were ordered to register with the state; and anyone wishing to leave the productive purpose of the lay life for the meditations of a monastery was required to secure an official certificate of ordination.

Firm foundations laid, Yang Jian then followed his own Buddhist heart. Climbing to the tops of mountain peaks from which earlier emperors of the heavenly lands had proclaimed the successful fulfilment of their duty to heaven above, he described Buddhist bodhisattvas floating on clouds. Noting the ancient proclamations engraved on mountain rock – not least, those of the First Qin Emperor – he acknowledged them as little more than the footnotes of a foggy past. Instead, on sacred places that had once been seen as fit only for the single conversation conducted by a Son of Heaven, Yang Jian raised a host of Buddhist temples and monasteries designed to lift everyone's hearts and conversations closer to the skies. Gifted Chinese hands, inspired by the wider vision of the Buddhist world, and trembling at the thought of the endless wheel of an unenlightened life, then picked up their brushes and painted images of elaborate layers of reincarnating Buddhist heavens and hells. Touched with golden sutras and protected by the precious relics of the Buddha, gems of temples conjured up dreaming visions of other lives. And the lands of the north became increasingly devoted to the pursuit of nirvana by a people whose past had left them in desperate search for the justice, compassion and truth of another world.

As the Sui offered a Buddhist route to paradise, Daoist hearts began to grumble. Daoist dragons muttered in dark caves; Daoist tigers growled in their lairs; Daoist tortoises drew in their heads in disbelief at the parlous state of affairs; and Laozi, the greatest Daoist of them all, was said to be sighing to himself like the wind. As the Sui praised the Buddha for his blessings, Daoist priests reminded everyone of cosmic warnings of apocalypses that had not been heeded. By the early 600s, while Buddhist souls meditated on mesmerising sutras, a new generation of Heavenly Masters and followers were not only raising their eyes to their own Daoist heaven but were anxiously watching for the second coming of Laozi – in the form of a man called Li.

Confidently expected since 512, Li's arrival had obviously been delayed. Heavenly calculations had been made again, and although no one was prepared to set another date, hopes had risen that it would not be long before the saviour arrived and led his people back to the promised Taiping Kingdom of Great Peace. Buddhism might be rising to the rafters, but every time there was a flood, nodding Daoist heads muttered about the punishments of heaven, and pointed to visions of Laozi appearing across the skies. Added to which, dragons were now regularly seen blowing flames in the clouds above, with mysterious verses appearing on the air chanting magic numbers and pointing out meaningful colours for everyone's attention. With every flood, every vision and every floating dragon, more and more rumours spread of an imminent reckoning that was about to sweep the Sui away.

Deaf and blind to the Daoist dreams, however, the Sui continued to build their world, adding the flourishing triumph of the new Grand Canal, the digging of which tore hundreds of thousands of men from their fields. The higher the Sui glory rose, the more deeply the labouring people suffered. And the more deeply the people suffered, the faster rebellions began to rise up all over the place. By the early 600s, the latest descendants of the Celestial Masters had decided that the time must surely now be nigh. In 617, the warlord in charge of a Sui garrison in the near-west was persuaded by his son to seize the reins of power and sweep the Sui into the dust. No one was surprised when his name turned out to be Li. As visions of a jubilant Laozi were widely reported to have been seen in the skies, bigger than ever before, Li father and son presented their celestial credentials for all to hear and see, and announced the founding of a new dynasty of the Tang. True, they had obviously useful military credentials, but their fitness to rule was grounded on the fact that they were surely none other than the descendants of Laozi himself.

*　　*　　*

Once the dust of rebellion had settled, the new Tang dynasty declared a return of the age of *taiping* great peace. As filially pious descendants, the Lis raised Laozi and the Daoist idea from what had been the margins of the Sui's Buddhist world to the highest peaks of imperial faith. Daoist scholars were invited to join a new bureaucracy, which would serve a now Daoist imperial court – albeit one that would continue to be grounded, like all preceding dynasties, on the practical principles of Confucianism. When Li, the son, proclaimed himself the Taizong (Supreme Ancestor) Emperor, Laozi was given the even loftier title of Taishang Xuanyuan Huangdi (Supreme, Mysterious and Primordial Emperor). As Daoist temples, and the calendars of Daoist festivals spread, imperial ears were also opened with a greater sympathy to the warnings of court officials who, both Daoist and Confucian, reported their collectively deep concerns about the dangers of the Buddhist faith. Millions of misguided souls had stepped out of the settled life, they argued, abandoning their filial duties and now wandering about in the meditating emptiness of monasteries dedicated to a devilishly foreign idea. Burying themselves in clouds of sutras, they had left their loyal brothers to carry the burdens of farming and to provide the labour for imperial construction and war. While others toiled, these turncoats were worshipping gilded figures of mud in rituals that were nothing if not barbaric. Having taken vows of celibacy, they were also a threat to the most fundamental of all of the Confucian heavenly beliefs: the duty of sons to revere their fathers. And if celibate Buddhists no longer had sons who could revere any fathers, then it would not be long before everyone started to question the value of the family, and with it the essential and unquestioning submission of every human heart to heaven's imperial Son.

Increasingly urged to 'do something' about the people who had been seduced into the Buddhist world, the Taizong Emperor searched for a solution. As the reincarnation of Laozi, he was sympathetic to their concerns. As the Son of Heaven with an empire to run, he fully appreciated the importance of having obedient heavenly offspring. But having reached the pinnacle of temporal power, he was also anxious not to offend the millions who had stubbornly attached themselves to the Buddhist call. Neither was he quite ready to sack the Buddha who, judging by the miracles which the Buddhist monks proclaimed was still a power to be reckoned with. Assuring the Celestial Masters that they were closest to his heart, he declared that he would protect the Daoist faith, and vest full imperial trust and confidence in the Daoist priests. With Laozi now the greatest of the imperial ancestors, it was the Daoist priests alone who were qualified to supervise the appropriate ritual offerings. But as aware as the Sui of the dangerous power of the 'other world', the Taizong Emperor was careful to set limits on the numbers of temples and monks, and to apply them to Daoists and Buddhists alike.

Out of imperial favour but still known for its deep compassion, Buddhism continued to attract a mass of faith. It also inspired a lot of searching questions about the Indian lands from which it had originally come. And, with translators still in short supply, these included a number of questions about what the Buddhist texts really meant. From time to time, frustrated with the twisted tongues, brave Buddha-following hearts had set off from the heavenly lands to try to find the truth for themselves. Following in the footsteps of Zhang Qian, one intrepid monk set off to India in 399, risking his life across the Taklamakan desert and the *kara buran*, black sandstorms, that were the terror of man and beast. Returning safely, much to the surprise of everyone (not least himself), he brought back astonishing tales of another world where tribute really *was* offered by kings to monks. He also brought back stories of a remarkably happy people, who, unlike those in the heavenly lands, were free to roam wherever they wanted and even free to farm any open piece of land at will. In 629, another monk decided to go and dig a little deeper: his name was Xuanzang.

The times were challenging. Rebellions in the Tang world had unsettled imperial spirits, even as a new confederation of Turkic tribes was gathering up a storm at the northern frontier. Imperial permissions for travel abroad, never easy to secure, had been suspended, and Xuanzang's application for a pass was denied. But Xuanzang was not only curious, he was also driven by a dream in which he had seen the sacred Buddhist mountain Sumeru, standing at the centre of the cosmos. Surrounded by sea and seemingly impossible to reach, in his dream a sudden wind had carried him to the top and shown him a view that surpassed all others. After such a revelation, the mere matter of an imperial prohibition was not enough to stop him. Xuanzang set off for the Jade Gate at the west of the settled world, the same Jade Gate through which Laozi had once departed. Arriving, he waited for the cover of night, and slipped silently out of the heavenly kingdom.

Travelling west, the young monk passed across deserts whose perils were almost too numerous and terrifying to recall: the black sandstorms that buried men alive, and singing sands that turned to flames. Eventually, he found his way to the bustling Turfan oasis, then on to glittering Samarkand and from there to Bactria, present-day Afghanistan, once battled over by Alexander the Great. Eager to learn, Xuanzang listened to everything that the inhabitants of the oasis states could tell him, then pushed on across the mountains of the Hindu Kush, struggling over trails deep in snow, and even deeper in bandits. Finally, he hit upon a path that carried him down into the valleys of the northern Sindhu lands. Over the next sixteen years, Xuanzang travelled across a wider India and observed a living – although if truth be told, a now slightly fading – Buddhist world. Starting at Gandhara, where Bactrian Kushan kings had carved huge images of the Buddha into their own towering cliffs, he went on to Nalanda, which thousands of Buddhist teachers and even greater numbers of students had transformed into the greatest centre of knowledge the world had ever known. From Nalanda,

Xuanzang wandered on, further west and far to the south, touching every Buddhist temple and mind that he could find. On his way back to the east, travelling through northern India, he was even invited to attend a grand Buddhist Council – attended by no less than two Buddhist kings.

By the time that Xuanzang returned to Chang'an sixteen years later, in 645, he had acquired hundreds of Buddhist texts and a new understanding of the Buddhist idea, which would sharpen everyone's translations. Although he had crept out in the dead of a 629 night, he was welcomed back as an exploring hero: the man who had gone further than any descendant of the Yellow Emperor before him, pushing knowledge of the Indian world to the west to unimagined heights. Opening his imperial arms wide, the Taizong Emperor invited him to exchange his monastic vows for any one of a host of imperial positions. Humbly declining, and wary of the risks, Xuanzang suggested instead that he write an account of his journey to satisfy the imperial curiosity. Retiring into the safety of his own Buddhist heart, he then set about translating the treasures he had so painstakingly carried home.

In 649, the Taizong Emperor passed on to another world. Daoist or Buddhist? So deep had been his conversations with the returning Xuanzang that no one could be entirely sure. On earth, however, the still-Daoist throne passed to his son, the Gaozong (High Ancestor) Emperor, who seemed to have no interest in Buddhism at all. More temples were raised to Laozi; more heavenly titles were added to Laozi's name. Once again, the old sacrifices were made to heaven, raised from mountains that, once blemished with Buddhist colours and names, had now been firmly reclaimed for the Daoist glory of heaven and its son.

The Gaozong Emperor ruled for thirty-four years. When he eventually joined the ancestors, he passed the throne to a young son under the regency care of the boy's mother, his second wife, Wu Mei. An earthly force to be reckoned with, after seven years as regent, in 690, Wu Mei raised herself to become First Empress in her own right (she would later be known by the imperial name of Wu Zetian, Flourishing Heaven). Across the imperial bureaucracy, Confucian brushes unleashed storms of outraged opinion. Wu Zetian stood firm. Dismissed from Confucian favour, she decided that, while the Confucian bureaucracy had its uses, it was time to turn everyone's hearts back to the Buddhist faith. Within the blink of a year the shocked spirits of the imperial court – Daoist and Confucian alike – saw their positions of influence disappear. To emphasise her point, the court was then transported from what had become the Daoist trenches of Chang'an to a Buddhist reinterpretation of the old Zhou capital of Luoyang. Once installed in Luoyang (and declaring the foundation of a new dynasty of Zhou), Wu Zetian raised her own Hall of Light, constructed according to all of the heavenly principles inherited from the ancient shamans and gathered together by the Duke of Zhou – and with a grand statue of herself, as a Buddhist Bodhisattva, set in the middle of Fuxi's old magic square.

Contemplating her heavenly position, Wu Zetian then turned her attention to the imperial titles that adorned her name. Keeping all those she had inherited from the Daoist-Confucian heaven, she added a Buddhist flourish: 'Maitreya the Peerless' – a reference to herself as the reincarnation of a famous 'future Buddha' who, having found enlightenment, declined to take up his rightful place in nirvana and instead returned to earth, determined to save the world. Now the Maitreya Buddha in an imperial heaven, Wu Zetian opened the lands of her empire to Buddhism, like a pool of shimmering lotuses. Mountains recently returned to the Daoists recovered their Buddhist names. Buddhist temples were bestowed with imperial fortunes. And the treasures of the Tang's unified riches, with their spreading conquered lands and sparkling trades, were turned towards those monasteries that put the Buddha at their heart.

Wu Zetian eventually floated away from the earth in 705, no doubt finding a place in what had become a Buddhist pantheon of the skies. On her death, the flower of Buddhism was swept aside, and imperial attention was firmly redirected to the dao. Daoist hearts leapt in relief, and the Celestial Masters were quickly returned to their heavenly positions at the old court of Chang'an, restored to its position as the capital. Within ten years of her death, her grandson (Xuanzong, 'Mysterious Ancestor') was setting the Buddhist monasteries alight and redirecting charitable donations of gold and jewels to other causes. Monks were firmly reminded of their filial duty to place parents and the emperor above any distracting Buddhist dreams. And anyone unable to provide an official certificate of ordination was returned to the farming fields. Meanwhile, Laozi's *Dao De Jing* was declared the most important of all heavenly works (required reading for all), and Laozi himself acquired yet another heavenly title: Tianbao (Heavenly Treasure). But Tianbao notwithstanding, the Buddhist spirit did not disappear. While the bigger temples struggled to survive the redirection of imperial donations, smaller temples remained. And the Buddhist sutras, learnt by heart, were secretly sheltered by loyal souls hoping for a future change.

Over much of the next century and a half, the lotus floated out of imperial favour. A symbol of enlightenment for its power to grow in splendour out of the muddiest of water, the flower of Buddhism was nothing, however, if not resilient. From time to time, depending on the nature of the emperor, purging flames were unleashed just to make sure that everybody knew which celestial kingdom was in power. But after each and every outburst, the stubborn lotus would open its petals once again, blossoming ever more brightly than before. Each time, Daoist and Confucian officials would mutter darkly that foreign ancestors were not to be welcomed in heaven's lands. But as the years passed, up and down the wider streets of Chang'an and out across the empire, it was increasingly the Buddha's temple bells that chimed most clearly, the images of Buddhist bodhisattvas that gazed down with the greatest compassion, and the soft Buddhist sutras, murmured on chanting Buddhist processions, that coloured the best days of earthly life. And while charity was provided by Daoists and Buddhists alike, Daoist alms were distributed on strict family lines, whereas those of the Buddhist monasteries provided for all of the poor, even those without a family.

Eventually, in 860, after 150 years of celestial ups and downs, the imperial tide turned again. A new emperor, the son of a father who had secretly found much to recommend in the Buddhist idea, returned the Buddha to the highest peaks of imperial favour. Once again, Tang riches poured into Buddhist temples and Tang hearts followed the lotus: stupas and pagodas sparkled with gold; the Buddha's birthday became a festival for all; and, lighting the streets of every new spring year, a lantern festival shone the brightest of Tang lights on departed Buddhist souls. So great was the emperor's devotion, that even the relics of the Buddha's bones were worshipped.

*   *   *

When, a hundred years later, in 960, after a brief tussle with yet more northern tribes, the Tang gave way to the Song, the Confucians finally decided that it was time to take a look at their own articles of faith. Always sharply focused on the temporal order of things under the Tang they had experienced something of a battering from the competitive spirits of the Daoist and the Buddhist worlds. Slowly, however, they had learnt the lesson that, great though the heavenly classics might be, the people of the earth needed something more than books. Pondering the possibilities, new Confucian thinkers stretched the Han interpretation of the Confucian idea

130

to embrace the cosmological elements of the Daoist Great Peace. Just to be on the safe side, they added a golden stroke of Buddhist compassion. While everything remained firmly within the old trinity of heaven, earth, and the emperor as a Son of Heaven who united both in cosmic harmony, the newest version of Confucianism had a stronger emphasis on the idea of charity as a quality of human life.

The Confucians were not the only ones to revisit their beliefs. In the eleventh century, a Song dynasty emperor found himself facing the typical heavenly challenges of northern warriors: bad weather, failing harvests, and a peasant people who were losing their way. One night, he had a dream in which a Jade Emperor appeared from the mists and promised him a triumph over all. Waking up to an earth that delivered nothing but trouble, he was reassured when a favour-seeking scholar-artist presented him with a painting of harmony in the form of a majestic mountain where men and women wandered in a land of plenty; it was entitled *Early Spring*. Aghast at the lie, a braver scholarly artist decided to tell the truth with a set of darker brushes. Painting a picture of desperate men, women and children, blown by buffeting winds, stung by storms of sand, and wandering through a chilling landscape, dotted with stumps where trees had once stood and dashed with ponds so dry that anyone could pick up a rotting fish, he called it: *Floating People of the Earth*, and delivered it to the emperor. Staring at the shocking images of the 'floating people', the emperor had a quiver of human conscience. But not for long: official spirits ensuring that the reckless brush was despatched to the feverish south and, looking to the skies for blessings, the Jade Emperor was raised to some of the highest imperial honours that a desperate Son of Heaven could confer: 'Highest Author of Heaven, of the Whole Universe, of Human Destinies, of Property, of Rites and the Way; Most August One; and Grand Sovereign of Heaven'.

One hundred years later, another Song dynasty emperor would confer yet more honours on the Jade Emperor, adding an entire celestial bureaucracy to be served by the imperial court. Replicating every imperial position on earth, every official was commanded, henceforth, to serve their celestial counterparts as a natural extension of their earthly duties. To ensure that the punishing possibilities of such an extension were fully exploited, the terrifying powers of the Buddhist deities who presided over the lower levels of hell were also incorporated into the heavenly pantheon.

But the Jade Emperor and his new bureaucracy seemed to be as vulnerable as any of their mortal counterparts to the events of this world.

In 1276, when the Song finally fell to the Mongol Yuan, it was a shaman spirit, Tengr, who took pride of place, touched by strokes of Buddhism from the western steppes.

Settling themselves into the saddle of a greater power, and with a weather eye to efficiency, the Mongols were happy to let the Confucian officials keep their new-found faith in a Jade Emperor, and the celestial bureaucracy was retained for everyone's good order. Confucian hearts were not, however, fooled. And although not every official felt able to make the dissenting journey up to remote mountains of retreat, many retired into their studies and conjured up other worlds with brushes of poetry and painting. Carefully coded to avoid Mongol detection, these were just as clear a protest as anything that might have been said out loud. The Mongols found themselves serenaded with soft images of the natural world – delicate scenes of rocks, bamboo and plum blossom, all of which seemed, to their untrained eyes, to be evidence of nothing but a foolish Chinese love of natural beauty. To the trained Chinese, though, the painted images were piercing daggers of defiance. Bamboos swaying in the wind might look to the invading Mongols like pictures of a rural idyll, but to Song dynasty hearts they were declarations of a Chinese endurance that would outlive any steppe usurpers. Plum blossom flowering in winter was nothing less than a silent statement that the heavenly idea would ultimately triumph over the brutality of even the greatest northern force.

As heaven would have it, the force that ultimately swept the northerners back to the steppes did not come from scholarly brushes but from the peasants who, as usual, had borne the greatest of the burdens. More than half of them had died in the catastrophes of icy drought, famine, locusts, and a Black Death that haunted the last decades of the Great Mongol Yuan. Many of those who survived owed their lives to the undiscriminating charity of Buddhist monasteries. Open to all, beyond offering a rescuing bowl of soup, these spreading refuges offered lessons in writing characters so that even a peasant could learn to chant the sutras. And the chanting sutras held the promise of a future world in which men could free themselves from the material chains.

When Zhu Yuanzhang, the rebel who became the first Ming emperor, swept into the Mongols' northern Dadu capital, he and his followers rode under the military colours of a secret society that called itself the White Lotus. Buddhist in inspiration, it was dedicated to watching for the reincarnation of the Maitreya Future Buddha – the very same Maitreya Future Buddha adopted by Wu Zetian, representing the idea of a spirit who would save hearts struggling in the present world. The White Lotus Society was also dedicated to the restoration of a world in which men would live simple lives with no personal possessions, free from the torments of desire. While the first Ming emperor would later lose his trust in everything (from Buddhists to chief ministers), the dream of another world on the present earth, a simple land populated by people with simple wants, would become the foundation of his empire. Buddhist in inspiration, it was not so different from the older dream of resurrecting a Taiping Great Peace. Ultimately, the dream would be betrayed by a wealth his own great order had paradoxically created – swept away by the reign of a son whose pursuit of pomp and glory would unleash a tide of trading greed in which the worst of hearts would flourish and take root. But it was a dream that would long outlive the Ming.

Meanwhile as the Ming rose from glory to glory, attention increasingly turned to 'another world'. For the Ming emperors, and for those officials who could afford to emulate them, the greatest interest was in avoiding death with a personal immortality. Buddhist or Daoist, it did not really matter which persuasion a priest followed, as long as he could guarantee an eternity of life. In the event, it was Daoism's inner alchemy, with exotic concoctions of gold and mercury inherited from the desperate dreams of the First Qin Emperor, that proved the most seductive: not only to emperors but to officials as well. Outside the Forbidden City, though, the vast majority of the population was more immediately concerned with understanding whether and how 'another world' might help them navigate the challenges of this one.

Both Buddhism and Daoism offered the promise of salvation. Indeed, after a thousand years of competing for Chinese souls, their boundaries had become rather blurred. Popular Buddhist bodhisattvas had been 'borrowed' regularly by the Daoists' ever-expanding pantheon of gods; and the Song dynasty's Celestial Bureaucracy had come to include so many Buddhist layers of heavens and hells that even Laozi would probably have got lost.

By the middle of the Ming dynasty, the two faiths were no longer life- and death-defining choices, but alternative guides with which to navigate the tempests of the present world – while doing one's best to optimise one's chances in whatever might come next. Daoists continued to offer ancient wisdom: breathing techniques for instant help in the face of malicious influences; dragon slips of paper on which requests for celestial assistance could be written, then swiftly swept up to heaven in a puff of ethereal smoke. Buddhists, now also amenable to the idea of earthly rewards, offered their own particular forms of magic. These included drawing on the mystic arts of India's ancient Tantra and the promise that, since every human being represented a union of all universal energy, everyone always had everything that they could ever need. As many a Buddhist monk advised, just repeat a bodhisattva's name over and over in a deep state of meditation, and enlightenment, with its freedom from the painful wheel of life, would suddenly dawn.

To all of this, of course, everyone added the ancestors. These were not to be confused with the terrifying hungry ghosts – those men, women and children who had departed from this world in violence or misery and who should be carefully kept at bay. The true ancestors were the spirits of the departed who had floated peacefully up to heaven to join the others who had graced the earth – and whose descendants maintained the requisite filial sacrifices. Naturally there was a hierarchy, with the greatest of the departed (the Yellow Emperor, for example, or Laozi) obviously becoming gods. But while other ancestors might not have made it to the status of a god, a deceased relative who had reached the dizzy heights of ministerial office could clearly catch the attention of the highest heavenly powers more easily than someone who had simply swept the floors. Trusted as guides to the favours of the spirit world, sacrifices to such ancestors were readily and regularly made, with Confucian exhortations about the importance of ritual duly observed.

Consulting all of the available pantheons, those pursuing practical professions then added men whose fabulous talents must surely have catapulted them to the status of gods. Carpenters put their faith in Lu Ban, a god of a man who had constructed magnificent city buildings in Confucius' state of Lu, and even set a wooden falcon to flight. Goldsmiths favoured the laughing face of the Maitreya Buddha, whose popular depiction with a big belly (not quite the same image as Wu Zetian had chosen) was a reassuring promise of material success. And candidates for the imperial exams dedicated their sacrifices to the god of literature, Wendi, and his two assistants: one giving out the grades, and the other offering special protection for those who had not properly prepared.

Meanwhile, the Confucian scholars realised that, without the power of magic, Confucianism had become little more than a hat. It was high time, they decided, that Confucius became a god. (Covering their bets like everyone else, they also decided that he should become a Buddha as well.) Refreshed with a direct stake in the court of the Jade Emperor, the Confucians created a pantheon of their own – with a host of scholars to keep the Great Man company. Meanwhile, growing as fast as it could, and borrowing from everywhere, the court of the Jade Emperor became as big and as complicated as the imperial bureaucracy on earth, and just as demanding. Every minister was charged with submitting an annual report to the Jade Emperor, with all earthly promotions and demotions contingent upon the success with which it was received. Noting the efficacy of such reports in improving order, the idea was expanded to include everybody's households, with a 'Kitchen God' despatched to take up residence in each one. Charged with constant surveillance, the Kitchen God would be summoned to deliver his report to heaven at the spring festival of every New Year.

One way or another, and not surprisingly, by the end of the Ming dynasty, paperwork was everywhere – with mountains of imperial paper on earth easily matched by the smoke of written petitions addressed to the relevant celestial authorities and burnt to ensure that they reached their heavenly destination.

While the rich and scholarly conjured up ever more elaborate visions of other-worldly support, the peasants, however, took their usual, far more practical, view, worshipping the gods of local rivers and woods. But with the arrival of the celestial bureaucracy, their troubles spread beyond the greed of earthly landlords and the full force of periodic floods and storms of heavenly temper. With an empire of imperial gods and heavenly assistants now reaching directly into the most private corners of a human life, even heaven itself seemed to have become a foe. Who could withstand the pressure of a local official who had teamed up with a god? And with Daoist temples typically beholden to the highest family on the local land, even the power of the rich now reached to the skies. Fortunately, though, those gods who had been co-opted into imperial service were often open to a deal – and not all of the gods had joined forces with the rich. The Kitchen God offered the most obvious opportunities for persuasion. A resident spy in everyone's hearth, when he flew up to heaven to deliver his annual reports, there was not a family on earth who did not try to smooth his lips with honey before he left. And there was always Cai Shen, the god of wealth, who rode on the back of a tiger: stealing from the rich to give to the poor, he satisfyingly shot everyone's enemies with pearls that exploded like bombs.

At the top of almost everyone's heart, peasant and gentry alike, was the Bodhisattva of Compassion: Guan Yin. The Mother of Mercy who had become part of every pantheon, she was clutched with particular fervour to the poorest of hearts. Close beside her was Guan Yu, a bear-like general who had fought alongside the Crouching Dragon Zhuge Liang in the service of the Shu-Han ruler. Never leaving his master's side unguarded, Guan Yu had also made it his business to ensure that the weak on any side of a battle were always protected. After his death, Guan Yu had become a god of war with a very special characteristic: for those who could not look after themselves, even the mention of his name could be counted on to scatter any demon, even one in official clothing. And while Guan Yin and Guan Yu towered above all the others, they were only the vanguard of a world of divine rescuers who could be called upon by the poor, the downtrodden and the betrayed. Even Zhuge Liang himself became a god – a man whose mastery of the *dao* gave everyone the confidence to challenge their fate.

Other much-loved gods included an outlaw called Song Jiang. An honest man pushed into banditry by lost battles with local tyrants, his Robin Hood escapades terrorised the early decades of the Song dynasty. They would later become immortalised in a popular novel known to those who read it (and to the many more who heard it read aloud) as the *Outlaws of the Marsh*. Hidden in mountain lairs, so the story told, Song Jiang and a band of outlaws who had suffered similar fates used their blood to turn themselves into brothers, then mastered the art of turning cliffs, rocks and trees into natural weapons and defences. Over time, the outlaws succeeded in creating a kingdom of their own under the nose of the emperor. No one was surprised that, in death, Song Jiang became a god.

Then, of course, there was Sun Wukong: the 'Monkey King'. Bouncing into heaven on a bag of tricks, his was the spirit which showed everyone that even the lowest of the low could twist the celestial bureaucracy into knots that not even the greatest official spirit could unpick. The figment of a writer's imagination, his tale told in a novel entitled *Journey to the West*, the monkey became as real as any other god who had started as a mortal hero. Despatched to accompany the Tang dynasty monk Xuanzang on his journey to the Indian west, the monkey acquires a magic stick of such power that, with a simple *bian!* (change!), dragons could be tamed, oceans moved, and even the Jade Emperor taught a lesson or two. Flashing like lightning, whirling in circles, swooshing over thousands of miles in single cloud-somersaulting leaps, the monkey wreaks havoc in heaven and protects his monk with all the skill of a Shaolin warrior. Refusing to be dazzled by the heights of others' learning – and insisting that any conversations be conducted in the common Chinese of the ordinary people, rather than the rarefied language of the Confucian scholar-officials and the gentry – he defeats even the cleverest scholarly minds. By the time the monkey brings Xuanzang safely back to Chang'an, he has managed to show heaven, earth and even hell that courage and a good dose of plain speaking can triumph over any demon and all officials. Printed by the presses that powered earth's greatest literary bureaucracy, immortalised by the travelling troupes of actors and puppets who trod the highways and waterways of the empire, the story of the Monkey King would become far more famous than many an emperor – and much better loved.

As the Ming dynasty cycled towards collapse, many dreamt of leaving the dusty and often terrifying flatlands to find a retreat at the top of a mountain. But few were able to make the journey. For those who stayed behind, however, it was always possible to find another world – a place full of gods with hidden sympathies, populated by bands of heroic hearts who would join with you to fight for justice whatever the imperial odds. Concealed in deep cracks so secret that terrestrial celestials could not reach them, these heroes were a world of brothers who shared their plans only with those who were willing to mix their blood in a common cause. Schooled in all of the arts of celestial wars (Buddhist, Daoist and Confucian alike) they relied on nature to provide their weapons, and fought with bare fists so skilled that they could outwit any sword. Driven by causes so heartbreaking that heaven itself would weep, if only it could hear them, their battles were fought with the unshakeable conviction that Guan Yu, the god of war who so loved the people, would never fail to stand guard at their side.

This world might be fraught with danger and distrust, but there was always something else.

PART 3

WHOSE HEAVEN?

The Lord of Heaven is Heaven itself.

The Yongzheng Emperor (1722 – 35)

CHAPTER 1

SOMEONE ELSE'S SKY

He who wears the great circle of heaven as his hat
will take the great square of earth as his shoes.

The King of Huainan (139 BCE; early Han dynasty)

Snow was still on the top of the mountains when the message arrived. Lapping softly against the walls of the Shanhai Guan, Mountain and Sea Pass, the waters of the Eastern Sea still had their winter chill. The Manju north had been rather quiet in recent months, but home reports from Beijing had brought nothing but tears and alarm. Decades of droughts and famines, locusts and bandits had finally given way (as everyone knew they would) to a rage of rebellions, which had swept across the land. Unpaid and hungry, the generals of the Ming army had been forced to choose between the heavenly honour of their emperor and the earthly growls of their soldiers' stomachs.

Even so, little had prepared General Wu Sangui, the commander in charge of the Shanhai Guan garrison, for the devastating strokes of black ink that were delivered into his hands on 24 April 1644. Li Zicheng's rebel force had arrived in Beijing and was sacking everything in sight; overwhelmed with shame, the Chongzhen emperor had taken himself to another world; distraught at a chaos they were powerless to control, the city's greatest

140

officials were quickly following the emperor's suicidal suit; it could not be long before the rebels would advance on Shanhai Guan, now the last bastion of the north. One of the greatest and last surviving of the martial talents of the Ming, General Wu Sangui drew in his breath and looked up to the skies. Despatched to defend the eastern end of the Long Wall and protect the Ming from the latest horde of barbarians in the north, he found himself in charge of perhaps the only pocket of peaceful heaven left on earth. It would be only a matter of time before Li Zicheng and the rebels would storm the 150 separating miles to find him. Suddenly the barbarians seemed more like friends than foes.

Saddling his horses, Wu Sangui turned them north to Mukden, the capital of the Manju, with an offer that surely no barbarian could ever refuse: join us in defending the Ming against the rebels, and the trading gifts of heaven will know no bounds. Seeing an unexpected opportunity, the Manju's regent leader, Dorgon, had quickly agreed. Within a month Li Zicheng's rebel troops appeared at the Mountain and Sea Pass. Dorgon and Wu Sangui were ready. Dorgon's barbarian men were easy to spot: heads shaven at the front, long hair plaited at the back; masters of the horse, demons of the bow and arrow. But it was Wu Sangui's troops who were to lead the charge. After months of no pay and wearing uniforms that had seen far better days, they would have been difficult to distinguish from their rebel brothers had they not sewn patches of white cloth onto their backs. By noon, both sides of the Ming (soldiers and rebels) were close to exhaustion. And then, suddenly, heaven seemed to intervene: a whistling wind appeared as if from nowhere and, gathering up the sand of the shore, cloaked the battlefield in a yellow haze. Men and horses scattered blindly. The time for the barbarians' horse-borne talents had come. The Manju cavalry in their element in storms of dust, Dorgon unleashed them into the fray. Arrows firing with immaculate precision from the back of every horse, the Ming rebels turned and fled.

In the days that followed, Wu Sangui's exhausted Ming army struggled to recover its breath. Dorgon's exhilarated barbarian forces rode on, pushing the Ming rebels back towards Beijing. On 5 June 1644, holding the line in Beijing, Li Zicheng saw the storm advancing and raced a retreat to the far south. In the echoing silence of the following day, rumours whispered that a real crown prince was about to arrive from the north. Perplexed, but determined to be prepared for every possible heavenly eventuality, a few surviving scholars found an imperial carriage and ventured out to meet him, whoever he might be. Scanning the horizon in vain for an appropriately imperial procession, a dusty horseman suddenly appeared. A dagger at his waist, and the front of his head sharply shaven, this was clearly no Ming prince. Dismounting from his horse in a single swift jump, the figure introduced himself politely to the small gathering in a passable Chinese: 'I am the Prince Regent Dorgon,' he said. 'The young crown prince will arrive in a while. Will you allow me to be your ruler?'

With the imperial city in ruins behind them, and no other crown prince in sight, the only sensible answer seemed to be 'Yes.'

*   *   *

Over the following days and months, those whose horizons had been limited to the skirmishing courtyards of Ming Beijing had to catch up with decades of news and events from the north – and quite a bit of older history and geography as well. Still shocked at the dramatic turn of events, they found that the story was a little long, but at the end of it things were quite a lot clearer.

It appeared that for most of the last 150 years, while emperors, scholars and eunuchs had been battling with each other in the imperial city, yet another group of barbarian tribes had been rising in the lands to the north-east of the wall. Horse-borne hunters, they had emerged from a world of heavy forests stuffed with hides, feathers and furs, and washed with sparkling streams, full of leaping fish and treasures of pearls. Each tribe had a different name and story to tell. Some traced themselves back to Chinggis Khan and the Mongol Yuan, others to waves of steppe barbarians who had been storming in and out of northern China for a thousand years and more. As time had turned, twists of weather and clashes of ambition had regularly scattered them to the four directions – only to push each of them out against unexpected others. Those pushed to the south had traded with or raided the Chinese lands. Those pushed to the north had found themselves in a wide steppe world that rolled into the northern tundra of Siberia, before opening on to the shores of an Arctic Sea. Those pushed to the west had found themselves pressing against the Mongols, the Uighurs and the Tibetans. And those pushed to the coastal east had found themselves in the company of Ming migrants who, looking for new lands and a better life, had settled around an inner (Yellow) sea above the Long Wall, in an area known as Liaodong: just above the secretive peninsula of Goryeo, Korea, which dropped down into the even bigger East China Sea. From time to time, marriages and pacts had pulled the various tribes together, supported by the common threads of Chinggis Khan and Buddhism: Chingghis Khan, whose confederated empire had conquered almost all the world; and a Buddhism that had long ago transformed the Mongols into a land of lamas, whose spirits exercised a powerful force over all steppe hearts, whether Mongol or not.

Charged with guarding the wall, Ming generals had been meticulous observers of the rise and fall of alliances across the steppes. Responsible for keeping the northern tribes at bay, they had regularly deployed the old Han strategy of offering the rewards of trade to one tribe on condition that it would help them to defeat the others. At one point a group of the once-mighty Jurchen, known as the Jianzhou, was selected for advantage. With the borders guarded by the Ming army, the trade had been tightly controlled, but richly rewarding. The Ming were in constant need of powerful horses, ginseng, pearls and furs, while the Jianzhou had an insatiable demand for the tea, silk and weapons of iron which could be traded across the wider steppes. Trading fortunes rose, and as time passed, the Jianzhou, like so many barbarians before them, came to appreciate the finer values of a settled life.

At one point, and with an eye to an improving education, the chief of the Jianzhou's Aisin Gioro clan sent his son into the service of a Ming general, who had settled his household not far from the Jianzhou Jurchen lands. As expected, the young boy added the Chinese language to his tongue and, watching and learning, he observed the Chinese ways with interest. He also buried himself in the tales of their heroes. The story of Zhuge Liang and the 'borrowed' arrows gripped him with excitement; the adventures of Song Jiang and his band of brothers on their outlaw marshes kept him awake deep into the night. And although, like all steppe boys, the triumphs of Chinggis Khan held the greatest power over his imagination, he could not help but be captivated by the stories of the men of the settled lands. By the time his father died – during one of the Ming-incited battles of the tribes – the boy, named Nurhaci, had become a young man of twenty-three. Left with little but a few family suits of armour, he decided that the time had come to create a new force on the steppes.

Over the next thirty years, Nurhaci rose to the top of his Aisin Gioro clan, and the Aisin Gioro clan rose to the top of the Jianzhou Jurchen tree. Led by Nurhaci, and united behind a dream of recreating Chinggis Khan's triumphs, the Jianzhou Jurchen campaigned across the lands, east and west, north of the Chinese wall. Befriending, trading, marrying, capturing, threatening (and, where threats failed, attacking), Nurhaci forged the path in every possible way. With each step gained, the strands of many different nomadic people were gradually woven together, not into a single way of thinking but into a unity of many ideas. One of the Mongol tribes directly descended from Chinggis Khan became such an ally that even brothers could not have been closer. Tibetan warriors brought hearts of steel; Tibetan lamas added the deeper spirits of the Buddhist world. Chinese and Koreans – many captured as the spoils of war – brought the reading and writing power of the brush as well as Confucian thoughts on the hierarchical order of the heavenly family, which seemed to make a lot of sense. And everyone brought their languages: Mongolian, Tibetan, Turkic, Korean and Chinese to name only a few.

Riding, hunting, archery, falconry and fishing remained the essential skills for Nurhaci's people. But as their wealth spread, more and more of the Liaodong lands were put under the plough – to be farmed by peasant soldiers captured from the Ming. Villages multiplied. Some became so big that they were almost like cities, and it seemed only right to put walls around them. In 1587, Nurhaci raised a capital, Fe Ala, on top of a hill. Meanwhile, Jurchen men were organised under fighting 'banners' and ordered under a military command; their hearts, however, were free to wander wherever they wanted: Buddhist bodhisattvas, gods of mountains and rivers, the old Mongol Tengr god of the sky (who, as the Mongol brothers had explained, was really just another way of thinking about heaven): all were worshipped at will.

As Nurhaci's power rose, he became khan of the steppes, and as khan of the steppes, he applied the Chinese lessons learnt in his youth to his own people, ensuring that they were consistently reinforced with the firm Manju discipline of the hunt. Villagers were ordered into military units and charged with hunting for animals or men, as well as tilling the fields. The spoken sounds of Jurchen were translated into a written script, which used the Mongol alphabet (itself taken from the Persian script), for its form. With a written language in place, Nurhaci then commissioned a written story of his people. Tracing their ancestry across the tribes of the vast and varied lands, it was a chronicle that counted among its heroes not only the Jin dynasty of earlier Jurchens (those who had once conquered the Northern Song), but also Chinggis Khan, and Kublai Khan's triumphant conquest of the Southern Song, from which he had raised the Mongol dynasty of the Yuan. Tales of glorious deeds were gathered from all over the steppes, and dreams of heroic hunters, with vanquishing bows and arrows, promised to grip every reader's heart. As the history neared completion, Nurhaci decided to give his new and great collection of people a name: Manju – the brave.

Across the steppes, the Manju had become a force that every other tribe had learnt to respect. To those in the settled lands below the Long Wall, they were just another confederation of barbarians. But in 1616, Nurhaci caused something of a stir. Issuing a list of grievances against the Ming, he accused their generals of inciting the tribes to fight against each other, and their officials of abusing his trading people. To his list, Nurhaci added the claim that his own father's death had been the result of the Ming's meddling interference in tribal affairs. Reparations were demanded which, if not forthcoming, would be met with Manju measures. Occupied with its own concerns, and supremely confident in its heavenly position, the Ming ignored Nurhaci's demands. The threats became attacks. Over the next seven years, piece by piece, starting with Liaodong on which the Chinese had settled above the Long Wall, land was successively captured, culminating in the prize of Liaodong's provincial capital, Shenyang. Nurhaci renamed it Mukden, Rising Power.

When Nurhaci died in 1626, his son, Hong Taiji, took on the Manju cause. Turning the conquered lands into a granary for his own people, he invited the Chinese scholar-officials of Shenyang-now-Mukden to remain in their places and create a mirror of the Ming bureaucracy, for the Manju. 'A healthy animal', he explained, 'finds a tree and climbs it; the wise minister finds a ruler who serves him; the southern dynasty has come to the end of its natural life; its time and course have been exhausted.' Watching the collapsing catastrophes of the late Ming, a number of Ming officials in Shenyang could only agree. Convinced that heaven was about to inflict yet another violent change in its mandate, they accepted the Manju invitation.

Hong Taiji turned his sights to the Mongol west. Dreaming of Chinggis Khan and of the Mongol conquest of the Song, he reached out to the nearest tribes of Mongols, who had been slow to join the Manju idea, and wrapped them into his swelling ranks. At one point, rewarded with the gift of the long-held and much-treasured imperial seal of the Mongol Yuan, he decided that it was time to proclaim a new, Manju, dynasty. Observing the now crumbling corruption of the once-bright Ming below the wall, it was not difficult to strike upon the name that would put them on notice of his unifying intent: after the disaster of the 'bright', Ming, Chinese idea, he would call it Qing: the dynasty of the pure.

By 1644, when Wu Sangui appeared with his offer of a trading reward for help in defeating the Ming rebels, Hong Taiji had died, leaving Dorgon, his half-brother, as regent for his very young son. With the Ming dismissing the idea of a purifying Qing dynasty as the foolish dream of an upstart barbarian, Wu Sangui's offer gave Dorgon quite a surprise. But while Wu Sangui might not have appreciated the force of the Manju ambition, for the Manju the idea that they might one day acquire the mantle of the once-heavenly Ming was far from a fantasy.

*　　　*　　　*

The crown prince was only six years old when Dorgon led him to the Hall of Supreme Harmony and placed him on the throne – styled as the Shunzhi (Humble Rule) Emperor. The throne itself had been an unexpected gift, but it would take all the years of Shunzhi's short reign (he died at the age of only twenty-three) and twenty years of the rule of his valiant son thereafter, to bring all of China under the purity of Manju Qing rule.

The battles on land were initially led by Wu Sangui. With Dorgon installed as regent before he had fought his own way back to Beijing, Wu Sangui had found the tables turned: it was Dorgon who offered Wu Sangui 'a reward' if he would help the Qing to push their conquest to a successful conclusion in the south. Wu Sangui had little choice but to accept – although, having read, like Nurhaci, the same stories of the Crouching Dragon, Zhuge Liang, and the outlaw, Song Jiang, he almost certainly decided that his co-operation would last only until he was able to turn the tables once again. Flanked by horse-borne Manju bannermen, and supported by Portuguese gifts of cannons (the Portuguese as keen as the northern barbarians to get permission to trade), Wu Sangui advanced to the south and south-west, sweeping away waves of rebel armies, all led by someone claiming descent from the ruling Ming family. With Chinese fighting Chinese, it must have seemed as if heaven had truly washed its hands of its people. By 1670, however, the battling south was finally subdued. Wu Sangui's promised reward was delivered: a princely title and governorship of the remote south-western provinces of Yunnan and Guizhou, which he had done so much to pacify.

No sooner had his efforts been imperially recognised than Wu Sangui declared his own colours. Proclaiming Yunnan as the heart of a new and ambitious state (optimistically called the 'Great Zhou'), Wu Sangui marched east and north. Announcing alliances with other loyalist Ming generals, he served 'Manju' Beijing with notice of his intentions to reclaim the entirety of the lost Ming lands. Indeed, Wu suggested, having completed their temporary heaven-sent task, perhaps the Manju might like to retire to their old Liaodong – naturally with the grateful thanks of the Chinese people.

With Wu Sangui and his rebel generals armed against them, it took the Manju Qing another ten years of battles before the lands of the south and south-west were truly pacified. Eventually, though, and largely because the Chinese people saw Wu Sangui as a traitor at-heart, his rebels were trampled in the dust.

But as the mist of war on land lifted, off the coast of Fujian, another force of resistance appeared to have risen, this time out of the sea. Anchored on the coast, it was led by the son of a sea-faring family called Zheng.

The Zheng were merchants who, as a result of Ming prohibitions on coastal trade, had become 'smugglers'. Combining a natural trading talent with a prodigious mastery of maritime maps, they had woven a watery empire of their own, sailing up and down the island-fringed coast of the country and trading with ships visiting from further afield. When the Spanish conquest of Mexico had washed everyone's coasts with silver, the Zheng family found itself drawn into an explosion of Iberian trades around the Asian seas. But in 1644, the arrival of the Manju Qing had split the family. Father and uncles had pragmatically transferred allegiance to the new Qing, but a son, Zheng Chenggong, insisted on declaring eternal loyalty to the Ming. Sharp of mind and keen of heart, he set about creating a loyal Ming navy, with a fortress in Xiamen (Amoy), the sea as his battlefield, and his family's network of smugglers as his crew. By 1651, he controlled a force of more than two thousand ships, becoming the most powerful ruler of the southern waves. By 1655, he had matched his navy with a land army, which then attacked cities across the now-Manju Qing lands of Zhejiang and Jiangsu, including the first Ming capital, Nanjing.

No longer smugglers but loyalists with a heavenly cause on land and at sea, Zheng's troops were trained to win the hearts of the people – just as the fictional heroes of the *Outlaws of the Marsh* had done hundreds of years before. By the time that the Qing, hitherto preoccupied with Wu Sangui, were able to fling their forces at them, it looked as if it was all too late: local hearts and minds had been won across vast swathes of land, and the terrain seemed almost impossible to capture. The Qing decided that the best thing would be to clear the coast, banishing the local population from within twenty miles of the sea. Not even a plank of wood was permitted to set out on the waves. The coast secured, the Qing forces then battered Zheng's fortress in Xiamen. Rich in the wealth of its vast trades, Xiamen was able to hold out. But by 1661, Zheng decided to find a fortress a little further away. Looking out across a stormy southern sea, his eyes fell on a beautiful island: named 'Formosa' by trading Portuguese, it would come to be known as Taiwan.

With an indigenous people of its own, the beautiful island had already become home to a steady trail of Chinese, who had been sailing out of the tumultuous and regularly trade-banishing mainland for centuries. From the 1620s, it had begun to attract the ambitions of the Spanish and the Portuguese, both keen to find a foothold in a world of rising Asian trade; they were soon followed by the Dutch. Zheng Chenggong's trading army dislodged them all, and the Manju Qing suddenly found themselves facing a Ming power on an island that few of them had ever heard of before. Zheng Chenggong died of malaria shortly after his arrival, but his son, Zheng Jing, took up the family empire. Transforming Taiwan into the hub of what would become a great Ming-pretending maritime empire, the Zheng family's trades confidently reached across South East Asia, all grounded on an 'imperial' order that included both Confucian academies and Ming-style taxes. For twenty years, Taiwan flourished as an independent power, while claiming the right of Ming loyalists to rule over the lands of the Qing. But eventually, in 1683, Shunzhi's 'valiant son' was able to turn the full force of the Qing's attention to the Taiwan straits. In the ensuing war, the Zheng were defeated and offered an honourable return to the mainland. Taiwan, including its own indigenous population as well as the harbouring Ming loyalists, was wrapped into the bureaucratic embrace of Fujian province, and the fishermen, who had been banned from the coasts, were allowed to return home.

Challenging though they were, however, the Wu Sangui rebels and the sea-trading Zheng had been only the most obvious of a number of rebellions seeking a restoration of the Ming. Most had been dealt with on battlefields, but some could only be addressed with a brush. Following the moral example of the Chongzhen Emperor, in the months after the fall of the Ming (and in successive waves afterwards), many Confucian officials committed themselves to suicide, paralysing not only the capital but almost everywhere else as well. Others chose to register their protest by wandering into Daoist retreats: climbing to the tops of mountains for a hermit's life or retiring into silent studies in the country estates of family homes. Battle as hard as they might on land and at sea, with less than two million people to China's (albeit exhausted) hundred million, the Manju knew that a successful conquest of the heavenly lands would depend on their ability to return the fields to farming. For that, they would need the bureaucratic talents of the Confucian scholars.

Commanders of the archives, masters of the refined art of managing the bureaucracy of order, diviners of heavenly virtue, and interpreters of earthly changes, the scholars were an imperial force that no emperor could live without. The tax-delivering foundations of any heavenly rule, they were essential not only in the capital of Beijing and the cities of the empire but also across the spreading fields. This was the world of the Confucian fabric: one that went beyond magistrates appointed by the empire to include a wider 'gentry' of scholarly officials who, while retired, continued to busy themselves with the local order of things, together with their sons who, embarked on the decades of learning required to achieve success in the imperial exams, hoped to inherit everything. Dedicated from birth to the idea of filial piety, the gentry's support of local magistrates was typically rewarded with blind eyes turned to taxes: even heaven could not have afforded the true cost of their unpaid services.

The early capture of Liaodong and its Shenyang-now-Mukden capital had given the Manju important insights into how the Chinese imperial order worked. It had even given them a starter-corps of officials, who were quickly catapulted to bureaucratic prominence in the newly Qing capital of Beijing. But with waves of suicides and hermit-like retreats, it was not enough: more scholarly bureaucrats were urgently required. With Dorgon ruling as regent, the young Shunzhi Emperor had been set to a Confucian education, which, it was hoped, would win some scholarly approval and stem the suicides. To further reassure the scholarly class, the imperial examinations were resurrected. Candidates, however, were few, with many of the country's greatest scholars refusing to attend. Matters had not been helped by the fact that one of the earliest edicts, issued by Dorgon as regent, had insisted that the scholars, like everyone else, display their commitment to the new and greater Manju 'family' by following the practice of wearing their hair in the style of the Manju 'queue'. Foreheads were to be sharply shaven, with hair plaited neatly in a single long tail at the back; punishing measures were applied to anyone who failed to obey, including those who argued that the queue should not apply to the Chinese, who were obviously of a very different 'family'.

More suicides followed, and more scholarly minds took themselves up to the mountains or into their studies. The edict of the queue was not rescinded. The Chinese part of the greater Manju sky was going to have to fall into the pure Qing line. But the vacuum of scholars was a worry. The regents and their all too few Chinese advisers scratched their heads. Special attention had already been given to mastering the Confucian knowledge in a bid to recommend the dynasty to scholarly minds: trained to be a model Son of Heaven, the Shunzhi Emperor was steeped in the classical Confucian texts. Sacrifices were raised at every possible opportunity; every imaginable ritual was meticulously observed. So desperate were the Manju Qing to please, that the Bureau of Astronomy (under the all-important Ministry of Rites) retained the services of a German Jesuit to help them predict not only the detailed changes of the seasons on which the agricultural calendar depended, but the eclipses through which heaven so often chose to speak. The Jesuit (one of many in the Qing lands of the time) seemed happy to offer his talents for the privilege of touching heaven's skirts; indeed Jesuit hopes were high that his meteorological calculations would bring the Confucian world round to a Holy Roman way of thinking. But while the accuracy of the Jesuit's predictions was noted, scholarly hearts remained unmoved.

Shunzhi's 'valiant son' had been eight when his father died in 1661. Named Aisin Gioro hala i Hiowan Yei in Manju, the boy also took the imperial name of the Kangxi Emperor (from the Confucian ideal of *kang*: peaceful prosperity). Already well on his way to the classical Confucian education that would surely, this time, win the war of minds, with the country under the rule of a council of regents, the young Kangxi had been settled in a quiet corner of the Forbidden City, with the Hall of Mental Cultivation as his own personal Manju camp. As he grew older, it became clear that the boy would match prodigious scholarly talents with the kind of fighting spirit that might one day turn the Qing into a truly great power. At the age of thirteen, in 1667, Kangxi threw off his regents. At fifteen, he issued his own 'sacred edict' setting out sixteen Confucian maxims for the guidance of all of his Chinese subjects. At twenty-three, he took the hitherto unheard-of step of permitting a group of young scholars to set up a society of their own, and to do so in a corner of the Forbidden City. At twenty-five, with the assistance of the young scholars, he set a special Grand Examination, for which candidates could only be nominated (and thus, which only the stubbornest of vain minds could resist). A few years later, he added another temptation: an imperial literary project that would tell the history of the Ming (with many scholars already penning histories of their own, the idea that their words would acquire the official seal of an imperial history had a powerful appeal). Confucian minds beginning to bend, no one had been surprised when, in 1683, Kangxi finally brought the island of Taiwan into the lands of the Manju Qing.

By 1685, Kangxi had become a thirty-year-old emperor who was both clear about his own will, and thoughtful about the practical dreams of his Chinese people. Rebels tamed on land and at sea, scholars charmed, the Ming lands, devastated by decades of war, had been restored under the greater order of the Qing. Farms abandoned by landlords had been returned to harvests; peasants had been offered lands of their own with which to start anew. Rivers and canals had been reclaimed from the clogging silt of neglect. With the continued assistance of the Jesuits, calendars were being successfully set; and with the seasons returned to order, the cash of crops and the following trade rose higher with every year that passed. Taiwan secure, fishermen and traders had been allowed to go back to sea and the pirate watchtowers of the dark Zheng family past had been redirected to the collection of imperial taxes on trade. Judging by the gentler weather, even heaven seemed happy. Trained for perfection, however, Kangxi looked out across the once-Ming lands and realised that they were only part of the much bigger Manju dream. With the heavenly lands in order, he looked to the north and the wider world above the long Chinese wall.

*   *   *

Some, like the Manju, thought it was about time the empire expanded. Others, with more painful memories of conquests lost – and everyone with a sense of history – wondered where on earth it would all end. Certainly, in the forty years that had passed since the Manju had taken the dragon throne, much had happened in the steppe world. All of it was complicated, and while it included other powers as well, it almost always involved the Mongols.

Returning to the steppes after losing their Yuan dynasty, the Mongol heirs of the unifying Chinggis Khan had first descended into a tumult of battling clans and fluctuating federations, and then they had split into a northerly west and a southerly east. It was the Mongols of the southerly east that Nurhaci's son had swept into the rising Manju world – a people who had taken the Manju name and whose lands, falling under Manju control, had come to be called 'Inner Mongol'. The Mongols of the northerly west had been a different matter. Not directly controlled by the Manju, their wilder lands were known as 'Outer Mongol'. Rising and falling in successions of battling federations, the Outer Mongol lands seemed to switch between war and peace as quickly as the seasons, and their history was so full of twists and turns that it could reduce even the greatest scholar to tears. Unfortunately,

151

it was a history with a direct bearing on Kangxi's dreams for the expanded future fortunes of the Qing.

When Chingghis Khan divided his empire, he had left the lands at the far western end of the steppes – then known as Rus, now present-day Russia – in the hands of a grandson who controlled what would come to be known as the Khanate of the Golden Horde. Trade had been encouraged and city-states had emerged, each with princes of their own. Time had passed, and eventually a line of princes had risen from present-day Moscow, who, having learnt the art of war from the Mongols, eventually chased the Golden Horde out of their lands. Pushing them back east across the steppes, and noting the treasures of timber, gold, feathers and furs which came from the east, the Moscow princes (by now titling themselves 'tsars') also battled every oasis khan they met along the way. By the time that Nurhaci had been born in 1559, with the help of Cossack 'pirates' (who traced their own roots back to the nomadic hordes that had roamed the early forests of Europe, with traces of steppe blood acquired over time) they had swept from west to east. Finally conquering the tundra lands of present-day Siberia, the descendants of the Rus had become 'Russian' neighbours of the steppe tribes, including the Manju.

With a new power suddenly at their side, the northerly western Mongol tribes – seen by the Manju as the Outer Mongols – struggled to maintain their own unity. Battling against each other, they had turned to the still formidable powers of Tibet for spiritual support. Inhabitants of a vast land of mountains and grasslands to the south and west, once valued allies of the Tang and then terrifying foes, the Tibetans had once been a formidable military force. By the middle of the Ming dynasty, while their temporal powers had diminished, they had embraced Buddhism with such intensity that their lama teachers had become the spiritual leaders of the steppe world. With many different Buddhist schools within Tibet, the Mongols (like most of the other Buddhist steppe powers, including the Manju) had come to be spiritually led by the teacher who, as the recurring reincarnation of the Bodhisattva of Compassion, was known as the 'Ocean of Learning': the Dalai Lama. With both Mongol and Manju sons regularly trained under the Dalai Lama's supervision, in 1651 the Shunzhi Emperor (Kangxi's father) had even submitted the Manju Qing dynasty to his eternal spiritual authority. Whatever other heaven or sky they might look up to, every ancient power across the steppe world understood that the influence of the Dalai Lama was far greater than that of any temporal king.

It was in 1677 that Kangxi first sensed that the affairs of the north-west would eventually need Manju military attention. At that point, Wu Sangui's rebels and the Zheng maritime empire had still been at large, but Kangxi found time to receive the usual tributes of the northern and westerly world. One of those who delivered the tribute on behalf of the ruler of a small Outer Mongolian tribe was the young lama-trained son of its ruler: the tribe was the Zungar, and the son was called Galdan. Galdan had gone on to build a federation of Outer Mongolian tribes. And as Galdan's territory and ambition had risen, Kangxi had received messages from the old oasis states asking for Manju Qing assistance in repulsing his attacks. Kangxi admired Galdan's ambition but the idea that a young upstart might be trying to resurrect Chinggis Khan's great steppe confederation was a nagging cause of concern. True, Galdan's campaigns were small and far away, but the rapid advance of what had become a vast Russian empire had shown that even a small problem could quickly become a bigger one. There was also, as always, the great uncertainty of what the all-important opinion of the Dalai Lama of the time might be.

As soon as Kangxi had rid the Manju empire of the Ming restorationists, he picked up his imperial brush and wrote to all of the Mongol khans, informing them that the time had come to talk. Setting a date, he added that the spiritually all-powerful Dalai Lama would, of course, be invited. The talks were convened in 1686, with the question of Galdan's oasis state conquests at the top of everyone's list of concerns. With opinions raised against him, and unhappy at the way the winds were blowing, Galdan mounted his horse and left. Before the year was out, the eastern (Inner) Mongols, who had stood with the Manju, found themselves under a Galdan attack.

Guided by maps helpfully drawn by the Jesuits, when Kangxi heard about the attack on the Inner Mongols, he was convinced that, while Galdan was a worry, the real problem – and probably the destabilising cause of everyone's problems – was the advance of the Russians into the steppe lands. The vast distance between Moscow and Beijing made imperial communications difficult at the best of times, to which was added the further complication that neither side could speak the language of the other. But Russian ambition had made them neighbours, even though no one, neither Manju, nor Russian, nor even Jesuit, was clear about where exactly the borders were. Matching Jesuit maps with what the Manju Qing knew of their own tribute-payers, Kangxi laid claim to the territory south and east of an expanse of water that the Ming had once called 'the Northern Sea' but which was known on the steppes as 'Lake Baikal'.

Kangxi's position was communicated to the Russians, in Latin and through the Jesuits. The Russians responded by pointing to a host of trading posts established well to the east of Lake Baikal and deep into the earliest Manju heartlands. Kangxi's answer was simple and clear: a string of battles was fought. On each of the occasions on which he emerged victorious, however, Kangxi was perplexed to find that as soon as his troops left in any serious number the Russians returned and behaved as if nothing had changed. Strong of will, under normal conditions Kangxi would never have given an inch. But in the back of his mind he saw the worrying prospect of another battle, one in which Galdan and the Russians were united and, blessed by the Dalai Lama, swept the Manju Qing entirely off the map.

In 1689, a treaty was struck at Nerchinsk, which gave neither side exactly what they wanted but offered enough for them to come to terms. In exchange for permitting the Russians to trade with the heavenly lands – and subject to a corresponding Russian duty to pay tribute – Kangxi secured a clear border at the western end of the steppes. This left Galdan's Mongols, and indeed everyone else on the steppes (other than the Russians and the Manju Qing), without a land to call their own. Galdan, who had deeply impressed Kangxi with his bravery, was offered an amnesty. But his heart was set on independence; the Zungars and the Manju Qing went to war. By 1696, Galdan's Zungar forces had been defeated and within a year Galdan was dead – but not before he had reached out to sympathetic spirits in Tibet, and not before his Zungar tribe had gained a foothold on the Tibetan plateau.

Over the following years, the Zungars regrouped under the leadership of Galdan's nephew, with Lhasa as their base. Fortified, they then launched themselves across the old Outer Mongolian lands, which the Manju Qing had ceded to the Russians. The old northern 'Mongol' problem had suddenly become a 'Tibetan' problem as well. By 1720, older now and tiring of the endless to-ing and fro-ing, Kangxi determined to settle the matter once and for all. Strapping cannons to the backs of camels, and throwing every soldiering force he had at the coldest and highest terrain his troops had ever had to master, he eventually forced the Zungars out. Order was restored to Lhasa under the watchful gaze of a resident Qing, amban adviser, and Kangxi proclaimed himself saviour of the Buddhist faith. Ruler of heaven, earth and everybody's sky, he was now also brother-at-heart of an endlessly reincarnating Dalai Lama, who was henceforth to acknowledge the universal power of the Manju.

*   *   *

When Kangxi died in 1722, he left a Manju world wider and richer than
Nurhaci's wildest dreams. Forced to grapple with both the rebel forces of an
unsettled Chinese world and the endlessly swirling dust of nomadic warriors,
nothing had been easy. Seated as confidently on the back of a horse as in
the Hall of Mental Cultivation, however, Kangxi had achieved great prizes.
A vast territory had been won, now spanning the once Ming and Mongol
worlds; tribute flowed from all respectful directions (including the upstart
Russian tsars); all of it was blessed by the Dalai Lama; and the Chinese lands
that had been so very hard to win were not only now lying tame at Kangxi's
Manju feet but eclipsing even the greatest productive heights of the Ming.

Kangxi's prizes clear, the imperial scholars had also come to see that
heaven had no favourites (Ming or Qing) as long as an emperor could rule.
Where once the Ming had struggled against the idea of making money, the
Manju Qing (with their own early fortunes grounded in the trading of ginseng
and fur) were demonstrating the value of the typical steppe opinion that
the people could work out their money affairs far better than any emperor.
Coasts that had once been cleared were now full of people; fishing villages
were on their way to becoming bigger ports of call. Peasants had flocked
back to the land, multiplying in such great numbers that they were now
spreading everywhere: flattening surviving forests, draining marshes, raising
dykes, digging ditches, and creating villages at every possible point. Grain
and rice were sweeping across the fields, silk was tumbling from mulberry
trees, cotton was spreading, tea was rising up like a terraced treasure. And
whenever the peasants had a moment to spare, they took their cotton and
wove it into anything that could be sold to make an extra copper coin. And
on the spreading back of the rising prosperity, merchants returned to the
roads and the waterways, rebuilding fortunes and threading together new
and ever-deeper routes of exchange. Markets appeared at almost every
crossing, whether of roads or rivers, many growing into towns: struck up
by trade and unconstricted by imperial city walls, they were open to all-
comers and free to expand. With such a peaceful prosperity in place, Kangxi
was able to fill the imperial treasuries with taxes on trade, even as he kept a
promise to his father that taxes would never again strangle the peasants in
their fields.

The lands of the Manju Qing basked in a new glow, but not everyone
was impressed. In a far-off place that nobody other than the Jesuits seemed

to have been to (its name sounded like 'Rum') there was a somebody who called himself the Pope. Claiming to be a heavenly power on earth, it seemed that he had no understanding at all of the achievements of the Qing. Described by the Jesuits as their 'father' and 'the greatest ruler on earth', he had distinctly fuzzy ideas about heaven, and no Confucian manners at all. Apparently, he talked to someone called God, a man in the sky with a long beard who sounded a bit like the Jade Emperor and whom the Jesuits saw as the greatest of the heavenly powers, even though he didn't seem to know anything about the Son of Heaven at the centre of everything. Certainly, whatever the Pope was, he had become far too big for his boots. And given that the Jesuits seemed to be so devoted to Kangxi and his conquests, it was all a bit confusing: scanning the stars, offering mathematical equations, translating barbarian languages, fixing the clocks of heavenly time, scurrying around the roof of the world with their maps and dictionaries; some of them had even learnt to read the classics of Confucius and openly acknowledged that they had a lot to learn.

Not everyone in China had appreciated the Jesuits' worth. Even Kangxi himself had some serious reservations when he was told they were intent on resurrecting the old great peace idea of heavenly taiping kingdoms, albeit marching to the call of a man named Jesus, rather than Laozi. In 1692, however, the Jesuits' scientific ideas cured Kangxi of malaria and, balancing up the good and the bad, he decided to let them stay – although, it would seem prudent to redirect their obviously prodigious talents to some less sensitive areas of the Manju world: the design of an exotic garden of perfect brightness, the *Yuanming Yuan*, as the setting for an imperial summer palace, for example.

It had all been rather a shock, therefore, when, rather than expressing any gratitude, and pointedly not congratulating Kangxi on any of his territorial triumphs, the Pope from 'Rum' insisted on an extraordinary principle with which no one in their right minds could possibly have agreed. According to 'Rum', heaven was that man in the sky with the long beard, who, they insisted, had created the world in six days and then (obviously exhausted) had needed to take a rest. From such a flimsy intellectual foundation, the Pope had then had the temerity to proclaim that any Chinese who accepted these ludicrous ideas was directly under the imperial power of Roman Christendom, rather than that of the Qing. More specifically, the Pope had then insisted that, as his subjects, they should immediately stop making sacrifices to the ancestors. In Kangxi's opinion, anyone who could believe that the world had been made once and for all in six days must be completely mad. And if the Pope could not learn better manners – or appreciate the power of a constantly changing heaven, which obviously went far beyond a man in the sky – then, however long a beard he might have, the empire would be better off if no one was allowed to make any mention of the so-called 'Christian' idea.

*   *   *

When Kangxi died in 1722, after a reign of sixty-one long and rather extraordinary years, he was followed by a forty-four-year-old son, who had had quite a lot of time to think about the empire he was going to inherit. Taking the imperial title of Yongzheng (Righteous Justice) the new emperor sent a clear message that he would be consolidating what his father had achieved. Steeped, like his father and grandfather, in the Chinese classics, and most at home in the Hall of Mental Cultivation, Yongzheng was a highly accomplished scholar. He was also, like his father, extremely proud of what he considered to be his far more important Manju roots. While the classical texts might have given him a deep understanding of the fine details of Confucianism, in Yongzheng's unwavering opinion it was his Manju family's qualities as highly disciplined horsemen, hunters and archers that gave them their heavenly right to rule. '*Manjusai fe doro*,' he was often heard to remark, in approving tones: 'the old Manju ways'. With which, edicts were regularly sent to his bannermen, exhorting them to remember their inheritance: 'Stick to the saddle and be brave!' Not words, of course, that the settled Chinese, sheep as they seemed, would ever be able to understand.

From the earliest days of the Manju, the ruling Aisin Gioro clan had been aware of the risks that a settled life posed. Riding, hunting and archery had remained firm features of the Manju world even when they had settled as the Qing. Every Manju, man, woman and child, continued to be organised into banners of military units. And whenever they were not engaged in active battle, every fighting bannerman's energies were directed to the highly ordered hunt of game. Indeed, from the moment of their conquest of Beijing, everything in the Chinese lands and in their own Manju homelands had been organised to reflect the importance of the hunt. Just as the bannermens' tents surrounded the central tent of their emperor on any military or hunting expedition, the old palaces of the imperial city had been rearranged so that the camps of the military banners surrounded the 'inner city' of the court. (As part of the rearrangement, the scholarly Chinese officials had been removed entirely: placed outside and to the south, with day passes for any bureaucratic business that required their presence within.) As soon as Kangxi's conquests had tamed the battles at the borders, he had immediately created a vast spread of carefully cultivated 'imperial hunting grounds', devoted to the constant training of every bannerman in the highly skilled art of the hunt.

Thickly forested, full of lakes and streams, the imperial hunting grounds were painstakingly managed to ensure that the large beasts, on which the success of the hunt depended, were given everything they needed to thrive. Stocked with valleys and glens, the hunting grounds were also carefully punctuated with clearings into which the abundant game could be skilfully driven. Divided into military units trained to think and act like disciplined packs of wolves, the Manju bannermen were then sent in their thousands to practise their hunting skills for months at a time. Rules were strict; discipline was sharp. Each unit was put in charge of a large forested area of its own and, fanning out to encircle their designated territory, each man was given a precise position of his own to hold. Once in their places, all were required to work together: each advancing in concert with the rest of their unit, everyone concentrated on drawing the circle gradually tighter. Successfully executed, large, increasingly frightened and highly dangerous beasts would be corralled into a centre within which they could be expertly held for the kill. Only the greatest intelligence, the most acute alertness and the most vigilant observation of their prey – with the highest co-ordination of physical movement and mental skill between each man and his horse and across the pack as a whole – could deliver success. The bannermen were expected to be nothing less than masterly wolves on horseback: failure was met with punishment, brave success with rewards.

Observing their rulers' dedication to the hunt, a number of Chinese whispered that the Qing were nothing other than barbarians. One, rather recklessly, published his opinion, citing the texts of ancient Zhou dynasty officials as authorities on the barbarian nature of the northern tribes. The whispers did not last long: many were arrested and some not seen again. And the man who had published his point of view was swept up by the new emperor, Yongzheng, who sat him down and gave him a lengthy lecture on how barbarians were nothing other than civilised men waiting in the wings.

Immaculately trained, and with a sharp military attention to the detail of everything, Yongzheng was always keen to set an example. He was also aware of the paralysing (not to mention mischievous) potential of an imperial bureaucracy. Leaving the scholars to carry on with their daily business, he set up his own Office of Military Intelligence, conveniently located to the immediate south of the Hall of Mental Cultivation in which he spent so much of his own, studious, time. Trusted correspondents were invited to deliver secret memorials in individual caskets to which only the emperor and the individual memorialist had a key; replies were sent by the same secret means. It was not long before the Office of Military Intelligence became the heart of the empire. The formal mechanics of Confucian order continued but the real power of the dragon throne narrowed to a secret box, a shadow, and the fierce eye of an emperor who was determined to personally tackle every sign of disobedience he could find.

Seeing the welfare of the people at large in much the same terms as that of the beasts of a hunting ground (both needed to be nurtured), Yongzheng was careful to pay attention to their material needs. Martial eyes were directed to tackling the famines of wayward weather, as well as the floods of any rivers that might decide to slip their leash. Imperial budgets (inflated not only by his father's wars, but also by an expanding population) were personally examined down to the smallest copper – and slashed. Quick to see the costs of corruption and the value of eradicating it, Yongzheng announced a moratorium on punishments for those who told the truth; and, with the help of the secret memorials, chased those suspected of taking a bribe down every possible corridor. On closer inspection, however, it was often discovered that some of the reported corruption was a matter of officials taking the initiative to raise levies for essential such projects overlooked by the imperial budget. Yongzheng accordingly suggested that all local levies be put on a more formal footing, with magistrates co-ordinating local gentry fund-raising on behalf of heavenly Beijing, and with any and all local funds first delivered to the provincial treasuries, from which more senior, and more visible, imperial officials could then spend them back. In that way, reasoned Yongzheng, the local people would be clear that, whatever the details, the real source of support was the emperor's concern for the welfare of all.

Even the most honest of expenses were put on notice: garrisons at the outposts of the empire were directed to take up local farming in order to earn their own keep. And as spending was scrutinised, so new revenues were explored. Long recovered from the devastating Ming rebellions, by 1720, breaking all previous bounds, the Qing's Chinese population was now approaching 250 million. However much money might be saved, more would need to be raised: more wealth-creating income would need to be generated for the people; more taxes would need to be raised for the state; and somehow more of something would be needed to help replenish a soil that had become so overworked that it was beginning to give up its ghost. One obvious way to help everyone get richer, and to relieve the pressure on the earth, would be to tease new fields from hitherto unused, and therefore 'wasted', land. Another would be to help the peasants grow more food, and faster. Loans were provided for sickles, hoes and cows; and everyone was introduced to the new seeds of potato and maize, discovered in the recently opened American world.

Yet another way to help everyone get richer was to improve the returns from the remote south and south-western lands. Many of these areas, including the provinces of Yunnan and Guizhou, were occupied by the descendants of tribes. Some had been there as long as anyone could remember; others were the descendants of northern tribes who had been pushed south by successive conquering expansions. Looking at their lower levels of productivity, Yongzheng declared that the tribal people should get a better education from the settled world. Confucius seemed to offer the best place to start, followed by a more 'heavenly' approach to local affairs than any of their own chiefs had been able to achieve. Once the essentials of bureaucratic order were set in place, forests were felled, surviving marshes dredged, rivers diverted, dams raised and dykes dug. And when a stretched production on the mainland was still not enough to feed the burgeoning people, imperial eyes turned to the possibilities of Taiwan. Now safely embraced within the province of Fujian, and with its original inhabitants clearly too barbarian to be able to make best use of its natural advantages, the island was opened up to as many mainland settlers as might choose to go.

Yongzheng's rule was far shorter than his father's: thirteen years in all. But his hard work left its mark. The Chinese lands had been firmly placed on the footing of the Manju hunt, silent whispers had been encouraged to flush out disobedience, all game had been nurtured for a greater wealth, and the net of the empire had been tightened so that few could escape. No one was very surprised when, in 1735, Yongzheng died, at the age of fifty-seven.

*   *   *

In the year of his father's death, the imperially titled Qianlong (Enduring Glory), Yongzheng's fourth son, inherited a vast Manju empire. Adorned by a host of tribute-paying neighbours, it also included a China that was richer in people, land and trade than ever before: all achieved through the discipline of the hunt and the intelligence of the wolf.

Fiercely proud of the towering achievements of his father and grandfather, Qianlong determined to be even clearer about the ruling qualities of the Manju. Books with even a hint of Confucian disapproval were burnt in their thousands; any voices that had openly used the word 'barbarian' were summoned back to court and put straight on any misunderstandings. It was not, the misguided opinions were told, because the Manju had learnt to become Chinese that they were no longer barbarians – anyone could do that. It was because the 'barbarian' Manju were a superior race: true wolves on horseback who had not only learnt to corral the useful ordering talents of the settled Chinese man, but had even managed to tame the dangerous excesses of the scholarly brushes. Unsolicited opinions, endless preoccupations with what Confucius thought or didn't think, not to mention an inexplicable pride in the fact that their complicated language had so many layers of meaning that no one could actually tell the truth – how on earth could anyone have thought that the Chinese could govern themselves? As far as Qianlong could see, it was the so-called 'barbarians' – the Manju, and the Mongols before them – who had created the truly great empires, while the Chinese had achieved little more than two thousand years of bickering, with any attempts at a 'greater unity' usually ending in tears. While Confucianism certainly had its values for ordering the settled world, opined Qianlong, for the true potential of the heavenly lands to be realised, a wolf on horseback was required.

With Qianlong keen to prove his point, his father's spartan cost-cutting was set to one side and the splendours of the Manju mind were displayed for all to see. The imperial hunting grounds were stretched beyond anyone's imagination, literary projects were raised to the skies, and the Forbidden City was converted into a veritable museum – with sumptuous palaces, sparkling porcelains and spectacular paintings as far as the eye could see. With the most obvious way to demonstrate the greater quality of the Manju Qing being through the size of the empire itself, it was not long before Qing troops were back in the saddle.

At first, Qianlong sent his bannermen and their accompanying Chinese troops to the south-west, around present-day Yunnan: commanded to pacify a Miao tribe whose people had not quite understood that being conquered meant doing what you were told. Judging by the huge numbers of Miao willing to sacrifice their lives for a long-lost idea of freedom, it seemed a difficult lesson to learn. Not long after that, Qianlong found that the lesson needed to be repeated in the wider west as well, largely as an unfortunate result of what Yongzheng, his father, had done in Tibet.

Troubled by the same Mongol problems in Lhasa that had worried his own father (Kangxi), Yongzheng had wrapped the eastern parts of Tibet – an area known as Kham – into the settled Chinese province of Sichuan. True, the result had been a bigger Sichuan, but with a Sichuan west that was now full of a Kham Tibetan people, who were anything but settled. By 1747 the Kham were foolishly flinging themselves against a tightening circle of Qing control. In a tug of wills that looked as if it would never end, Qianlong was forced to send his troops to fight a war on mountainous precipices at the western edges of Sichuan. It would take thirty years to win. In 1750, however, he was also obliged to race his troops up to the western north. The old Zungar Mongols, who had so terrorised his grandfather Kangxi's reign, had once again risen up and unsettled the fragile Tibetan peace. Qianlong's troops managed to restore a certain order. But by then it was patently clear that any permanent solution to the Mongol problem was going to require control of a much bigger piece of the western sky. Instead of returning his troops to Beijing, Qianlong pushed further north and west, into lands across which the Zungars regularly roamed. Advancing through the old deserts, and into the oasis city-states, Qianlong instructed his generals to conquer everything in their way.

As the old oasis states were conquered by the Qing, in a bid for peace, Qianlong offered to soften their losses by conferring Qing titles on their leaders – all followers of Islam. Meanwhile, Tibetan lamas were pacified with warm invitations to spread their spiritual blessings in an imperial Beijing, which, after a hundred years of Manju rule, was beginning to glitter with Buddhist temples. Steeped in the painful lessons of the ancient past, Confucian officials not only frowned at the temples but looked aghast at the vast and unfamiliar deserts that were now being brought back into the empire. There would be consequences, they warned.

Some pointed back to the Han dynasty and the expeditions that had followed Zhang Qian's journey to the west – campaigns which had opened up such a tinderbox of northern trouble that one might easily argue they were the sparks which eventually led to the disastrous thirteenth-century sea battle when everything had been lost to the ships of a Mongol navy. Others pointed to the later travails of the Ming against the Mongol north – lands where the Long Wall had proven to be nothing but an expensive frontier, with costs so high that in the end everything had crumbled, including the wall itself.

Qianlong was unconvinced. Tracing his own Manju inheritance to the power of the steppes, he saw the failures of earlier Chinese expeditions to the west in simple terms: they had just not understood the ordering discipline of the hunt. And as far as the Long Wall was concerned, any horseman worth his saddle could have told them that the idea of raising a pile of bricks to keep out horsemen was nothing but a foolish fantasy. Ignoring the squawks of his scholarly officials, in 1768 Qianlong rolled his new western conquests into a Qing province. He called it the 'new frontier': Xinjiang.

For the next thirty years, Qianlong would march his Manju bannermen and his now much larger force of Chinese troops, up and down, left and right, conquering the world as he went. In so doing he would, like his father and his grandfather before him, bring to bear the full authority of the hunt, including a careful attention to the welfare of the settled people whose fate, like that of every captive creature, he held in the palm of his hand. By the end of his life, he was able to congratulate himself on leaving the legacy of a moderately well-off people to his son and heir: an exemplification of the *xiao kang* ideal of modest prosperity that Confucius had once declared to be the hallmark of a good ruler – and which had been the inspiration for the *kang* character of his grandfather's name. Qianlong also, however, quietly noted that the future might be a little different. Counting off the costs of his triumphal conquests, the pacification of tribal rebellions, and the feeding of a large and growing population which regularly broke out in plagues of brotherly bandits (not to mention the costs of the hunting grounds, the literary projects and the palaces), he suggested that unless everyone tightened their belts, disaster might be looming.

While the discipline of the hunt had guided his every campaign, abroad and at home, Qianlong had always set his sights on something much, much greater. Wearing the circle of China's heaven as his hat, and carrying the totem of the wolf, which Chinggis Khan had known as the power of the Tengr sky, Qianlong had not measured his own achievement by the Chinese ideal of a Son of Heaven. Dreaming of himself as Manjusri, the Buddhist bodhisattva of wisdom, he had pursued the very different dream of being a *chakravartin*, a conquering wheel. First imagined in the plains of India, where it had been immortalised by the towering achievements of the ancient Indian emperor Ashoka, then whispered for nearly two thousand years across the steppes, before finding its way into the Buddhist realm, his was the ideal of a wise and universal ruler whose carriage wheels were so great that they could roll in whichever direction he wished, without any obstruction at all.

When Qianlong died in 1799, it was in the confident belief that he and the Manju Qing were not rulers of this piece of sky or that: they were emperors of emperors, universal rulers not only under heaven but across all the earth, before whom everyone should tremble and obey.

CHAPTER 2

RIVERS OF FORTUNE

A hundred thousand households of one determination –
how else can one run a business?

Hankou, seventeenth-century poem by Jia Shenxing

As a brisk breeze blew among the masts, choppy waters bumped thousands of brightly coloured hulls against each other, all packed as tightly as the scales of a fish. Even then, more fan-tailed sails hauled in for anchor, rising with sudden swells of fortune, only to drop into a following slough; all jostling for an inch of advantage. Not that many in the bustling early 1800s were paying them much attention. Stretched out along the shores as far as the eye could see, the junks were a permanently floating warehouse with the riches of everywhere daily pouring from their decks, all unloaded by an army of porters whose swift movements seemed to beat to an eternal drum.

The biggest of the junks had fought their way up or down the oceanic Yangzi. Fighting the current up from the sea-mouth of Shanghai, their hardened crews rowed and pulled treasures of silk and lacquerware gathered from across the south, up the mighty river; and when the rowing became impossible, men accustomed to the breaking of their backs descended from their boats and hauled the crafting cargo up the river from the land. Floating down from the mountainous tropics of Yunnan, braving rapids and hairpin bends, their flat-bottomed hulls carried precious minerals and timbers, stopping to collect harvests of rice and wheat along their Sichuan way. Smaller junks, built for narrower waters, sailed down the river Han, carrying northern cloth and salt, all hoping for a higher southern price. And then there were the sampans. Poled in from thin streams of rivers which threaded all around, they were the simple carriers of everything a village might want to sell in the market of markets, the city where the great Yangzi crossed the mighty river Han and everyone met for a trade: Hankou.

All sterns (large and small) set to the shore, bare feet and narrow shoulders picked up the slack without dropping a beat. Headmen commanding from the quay, sacks and cases were hauled ashore by the hundredweight and despatched, either to waiting shoremen or to another junk or sampan, which would carry them along lesser rivers to their contracted destination. Hempen sacks slung on to bent backs, heavy cases suspended from both ends of bamboo poles slung across shoulders, the porters ran to orders so heavy that only the bitterest, *kuli*, strength could serve. As they ran, the porters, 'coolies', chanted mantras of bitterness-eating endurance on tongues that spoke in the languages of far-off fields. Turbaned heads bent to the ground, the red rafters and glittering gold of Hankou's splendour passed them by. Mighty pavilions, they had been raised by new men on whose calculating minds the biggest trades depended – men who had, themselves, come from many different places to find the spot where river met river and fortunes could be made.

Standing on their piers of plenty, as the coolies pulled below, these new 'Great Men' peered out across the floating warehouses: scanning the horizon of waiting masts, counting the junks that were angling for a bay beyond, and considering the tally of profit and loss which the trading day would bring. For the coolies, all that really mattered was the crowded path around their feet: the clattering hoofs of donkeys, whose tails swished in their faces, the running feet of sedan chairs bearing someone to a temple or a teahouse; the wheelbarrows zigzagging to a market; the hawkers casting around for a customer; and the myriad hurried Hankou souls – all pushing hard, this way and that, to reach whatever particular dream their personal heart was pursuing. Counting off the bitter paces to the end of a hard day, the coolies' thoughts were fixed on the slivers of metal with which they would be rewarded, and the bowl of noodles they would buy.

Meanwhile up above, on the piers of plenty, the higher souls of the Great

Men lit celebrating shots of fire-powder, all crackling like guns. For those able to lift their eyes above the ground, flurries of red paper dust could be seen exploding like a bountiful cloud. Fortunes for the truly fortunate, from the market of markets, which was everyone's home.

*   *   *

Set in the centre of China, at the confluence of two of its mightiest rivers, over the past thousand years Hankou had gradually become the beating heart of the Manju Qing. A market that had become a city, it was a cauldron of trade into which, one way or another, all of China's waterways eventually poured their wealth: the Yangzi, the Han and all of their tributaries; the tributaries of the tributaries; and here and there, connecting canals, dug by ancestral engineers for circulating purpose, with the greatest of all being the Grand Canal constructed so long ago by the unifying Sui. From the time of the Tang, mountains of rice, grain and salt had been travelling up, down and across the many rivers of the land. By the time of the Song – with the land divided north and south along the Yangzi's line – the great river had become the lifeline of a smaller but richer southern empire: one in which the god of wealth had an increasing pride of place. Even under the 'bright idea' of the first Ming emperor, simple goods had continued to flow, including heavy taxes gathered in grain and passing through Hankou. And by the end of the Ming's first century, the idea of a land where everyone would stay at home had vanished like a puff of smoke, replaced with an empire of trade.

Of course, the trade had really exploded with Yongle's fifteenth-century building of the city of Beijing. As the new northern capital had risen to the skies, rafts of pavilion-raising timbers had been floated up to its hungry gates, with copper and iron following suit. Precious porcelains, heavenly silks and lustrous lacquers had been added to their train: all necessary adornments, gathered from the finer southern cities for the Son of Heaven. As the scholars and the gentry sought to emulate the imperial splendour, flotillas of junks and sampans had found themselves carrying returning trades of cloth, salt and grain from north to south, and increasingly being asked to strike out in other directions: wherever anyone was eager to acquire the splendours of a consuming life. Stuffed in sacks and packed in cases, goods of every description sailed north, south, east and west – so many sacks and cases that as the Ming advanced in years, the imperial barges had often had to push for a place on their own overcrowded waterways.

The first Ming emperor's dream of a simple life had faded: but who was there to question the change? If ever someone in Beijing raised a querying eyebrow, palms could always be crossed with silver, and if that didn't work, the goods could always be concealed below the decks of seemingly honest junks or, even better, hidden under the planks of the very smallest sampans, which could pass under anyone's nose. At the height of the Ming, while the dreaming imperial city had little idea about the detailed ways and means, the empire was floating on a rising triumph of trade, much of which was passing through Hankou.

When Hankou first flourished as a market, few could have imagined the heights it would reach. Trading ever more ably on the differences across the empire, the once simple market had soon become a town. Food and all of the daily necessities of life arrived by water, and money flowed out with the tide. As individual fortunes began to rise, firmer foundations had been settled, and it had not been long before the usual pavilions of splendour had started rising to the skies. As the market-town spread, its fortunes were built on the principle of being open to everyone. No official magistrate had a hand in its design, its builders had never subscribed to the heavenly idea that a city must have walls, and those who raised its riches had never been the kind of scholarly gentry who saw themselves as having a responsibility for any surrounding fields. Well before the end of the Ming, Hankou had grown to challenge the size of a city, without receiving a single stroke of approving official ink. By the time of Qianlong's death, it had become, outside the imperial capital, the richest city of the Manju Qing's world. And while the ancestral spirit of the first Ming emperor must have watched from heaven in horror, for the Manju Qing its prosperity was simply an illustration of the most fundamental principle of the hunt, applied to the population at large: 'Store wealth among the people.'

The greatest beneficiaries of the Manju's hunting principles were, as under the imperial dynasties before, those families whose fathers had been well enough placed to understand and navigate the currents of change. Confucianly trained, imperially examined, and with large heavenly families to please, the fathers were scholarly officials who had seen nothing wrong in applying the powers of heavenly office to recoup the great investments made in their own prodigious education. Imperial compensation rarely sufficient to keep food on an official table, let alone a banquet, silver had been found by mining the seams of imperial opportunity. For those charged with raising taxes, it was a simple matter of adding a supplementary fee – call it the cost of carriage. For those charged with running the emperor's factories of silk or porcelain, it had been the addition of a personal interest into the trading equation. And for those responsible for applying the regulating edicts of the state, all that was required was the turning of a blind eye – while delicately indicating that a gift was required.

Whichever direction the profiting opportunity came from, the silver had piled up. And the higher it got, the quicker attention had turned to the possibilities of how to spend it. Most expensive, but most rewarding, was the purchase of one of the state's many trading monopolies with which the empire vainly tried to control its prices. Salt, that staple of everyone's life, was one of the most highly prized, iron was another: anyone able to acquire a position in either of those trades instantly acquired a licence to print money. More affordable, and very popular, was a patient and ongoing acquisition of land. With the peasants carrying the burden of almost everyone else's taxes – and borrowing from money-lending landowners to keep themselves afloat – the small patches of land that the first ruling emperor had intended every man to own had, over time, been transformed into a currency of desperation. Unable to pay their taxes and repay their loans, once the bullock, the plough, next year's harvest and any surviving daughters had been sold, the only remaining way to settle the mounting debts was to sell the land itself. Patch by patch, small men reduced to penury had sold their fields to silver-rich officials and their related gentry. Land sold, shoulders that had once pulled their own ploughs, pulled the ploughs of landed masters instead. The emperor had his treasury; and across the imperial world, the wealth of the scholarly officials rose on the ink of their heavenly credentials to inherit the land.

That, at least, was the dream. But with big families and the offices of empire limited to the lifespan of a successful examination candidate, the vast estates were difficult to hold beyond a few generations. Not every son could master the exacting literary skills required to follow in a father's official footsteps – and without a well-placed scholar in the family, land would almost certainly be lost. Fortunes were spent on tutors, books and decades of learning. But few fathers managed to repeat their own success through their sons; and even fewer managed to repeat it through a grandson. Constantly aware of the risk of losing everything, by the time the Qianlong emperor jumped into his father's saddle in 1735, China's landed gentry was beginning to hedge its bets. Confucian study for everyone, and nothing but Confucian study for the eldest upon whose shoulders all family hopes depended. But with the tragic lessons of human failure scattered across the fields for all to see, as time passed, younger sons were also trained in the more mathematical equations of trading profit and loss.

The mastery of arithmetic was essential – protecting the family silver required a scrupulous accounting for every copper penny spent; and an understanding that any future expansion of wealth required a close relationship with officials charged with the empire's local affairs. And just to make sure that no son ever forgot his place, founding fathers wanting to preserve their families' fortunes applied their literary talents to creating genealogies which not only reminded everybody of the descending order of who was related to whom, but also included detailed sets of rules about what could be spent and when. Written and read like edicts, the genealogies were compendia of rules intended to govern the conduct of every following son. They were, however, only good as far as they went: they could try to slow down the rate at which a fortune was spent, but in a world of rising prices, there was a limit to what even the most successful could do – and they could certainly not raise a new fortune from the ground. With this in mind, wherever a son or grandson failed to pass the imperial exams, fathers and grandfathers did their utmost to ensure that they made themselves indispensable to more successful candidates, who would be in a position to share their wealth. Imperial officials, charged with raising money for an emperor's dreams, were to be given every possible assistance. And given that local magistrates were never attached to their own home districts – too great a risk of corruption – they were always in need of helpful guidance on perplexing local decisions. Grounded in the local lands, familiar with the up and down fortunes of the local people, who else could be better placed to advise on general matters of judgement, or offer an opinion on which groups of households might most easily yield the taxes the emperor required. And if anyone in the higher orders of the imperial office wanted a wife – first, second or third – dutiful daughters were always in ready supply.

For quite a while, some of the gentry even dreamt that the poorer farming households could become traders, albeit in small ways: weaving everything they needed, their households already produced an array of clothes, hats, shoes and baskets from the meagre land they farmed. Indeed, almost every field of grain had been edged with patches of cotton plants so that when the ploughing, sowing and reaping had been done, hands idled by winter could turn to making the cloth that, rolled into a bundle, could be taken to the nearest market to sell. With little hope of affording a textbook, let alone passing an imperial exam, peasant hands, particularly those in the harder north, had needed little encouragement to apply every spare moment to a spinning trade. As times had toughened, weaving goods for sale had become as much of a necessity as the harvest itself. It had not been long before men from the trading towns, alerted to the possibility of a profit, had come in search of industrious households, offering 'putting out' commissions for the peasants to weave at home. And it had not been much longer before the fruit of those peasant looms was washing into Hankou. The peasants certainly became sellers, but the profitable position of trading in the middle passed to those who ran the markets. Lands lost, peasants in penury, by the time Qianlong left his *chakravartin* wheel, bequeathing the legacy of a much bigger population and a much hungrier treasury, the cloth that went to Hankou was increasingly being followed by its makers: newly landless migrants desperate to find a foothold in which to survive.

*   *   *

When Qianlong's son, the Jiaqing (Great Celebration) Emperor, rose to take his father's seat, the imperial costs of the last hundred years were well on their way to becoming a nightmare. Empire-stretching conquests had exacted a painful price, as had misfit tribes battling against the conquerors, and hungry peasants rampaging as brotherhoods of blood. When the imperial books were opened after Qianlong's death, the worst of everyone's fears was confirmed. Having fallen victim to a friendship with a Manju bannerman, who bore an uncanny resemblance to a departed and much-loved concubine, Qianlong had opened up the imperial treasury to satisfy his beloved's every desire. The bannerman had seen no reason to contain his greed: family, friends, wider relatives, all had been woven into every imaginable budget – as had the 'special expenses' that the bannerman himself had claimed. One way or another, under Qianlong's reign half of the imperial revenues had found their way into other people's pockets. By the end of his life, the imperial treasuries, so full of cash at the beginning, had been emptied and the dream of imperial frugality, so dear to his father Yongzheng, inspired nothing more than a sneer.

The problems that Qianlong's son Jiaqing inherited were not limited to silver. While 'storing wealth among the people' had repaired the fortunes of many, by 1799 the population had reached three hundred million, and even after Kangxi's reclamations, the land upon which everyone's fortunes depended was struggling from the relentless demand for ever-greater harvests.

With so many forests felled, any surviving stand of trees had been axed for the increasingly profitable returns it could yield; and with so little land for so many people, every foot of earth was supporting a family of many mouths. It was hardly surprising that the weaving of cotton cloth had gone back to being a necessity for survival. But still the population kept growing.

As if that was not enough, Qianlong's ideas for reclaiming land from surviving forests and marshes seemed to have created some devastating, if unintended, consequences. Where northern farmlands, long cool and dry, had been protected by a canopy of green, they now found themselves threatened by dusty deserts. Similarly, rain-swept southern slopes, once held together by the roots of trees, turned into muddy landslides, sweeping away crops and burying the peasants in their wake. And wherever a marsh had been reclaimed for a paddy field, it seemed that a flood was sure to follow – on the paddy field itself, and up and down the rivers all around. It was one thing to flatten the forests and fill in the marshes in the expectation that new land taxes would more than cover the costs, but now that many of the lands were beginning to fail, who would cover the costs of fixing nature?

The problem was a knotty one. While it was the Son of Heaven (whose father had spent the family savings) who had the responsibility for managing the wellbeing of the imperial lands, it was Hankou that was reaping the fortunes of trade. Carrying everybody's food and taxes up and down the country, and receiving ever-greater tides of bitterness-eating labour, as sea-borne trade expanded, Hankou was also carrying a rising quantity of Chinese treasures destined for foreign shores: cotton, silk, tea, porcelain, lacquer and lanterns, all gathered from across the Chinese lands, and almost all of them passing through Hankou's watery markets before journeying across the seas.

The old Ming solution of raising taxes was a tempting one. Since wealth had been 'stored among the people', it was surely time for the people – at least, the richer ones – to share it back with the empire. But Jiaqing's great-grandfather Kangxi had promised that imperial taxes on land would never rise (and, indeed, had it not been for Jiaqing's father's devotion to a bannerman, the books might well have balanced). It would be a brave great-grandson who was prepared to face a towering ancestor with such an act of filial disobedience. With barely enough money to keep the imperial household going, let alone the burgeoning empire, other solutions would have to found. The imperial cloth would have to be cut to the size of its purse. And more of the costs of empire would need to be transferred to the private accounts of the gentry, whose fortunes had been built on the scholar-official titles of fathers and sons.

In terms of cutting the imperial cloth, the obvious place to start was with the officials. Compensation should, of course, remain Confucian and frugal – certainly the officials seemed to have managed well enough across the centuries. From the courtyards of imperial Beijing, where self-important scholars always seemed to have too much time for their own learned opinions, it also seemed sensible to put a stop to the creation of any new bureaucratic positions. It would, of course, be hard on the tens of thousands who were studying themselves blind in the confident expectation that, once passed, the imperial examinations would naturally deliver a promising situation; but they were young, and needs must. It would be particularly hard on the magistrates. Charged with tax-collecting, peace-keeping, dispute-resolving, water-taming and morality, they were generally responsible for keeping the harmonies of heaven in place in every local county – in an era when some county populations were now edging past a million. But, having passed the imperial examinations, their wits should be more than quick enough to cope with the changes.

In terms of meeting the wider costs of the empire, it was time to look a little more closely at the gentry. A lot of officials had retired to country estates, and all had sons and grandsons who, with fewer prospects in the imperial bureaucracy, were now lounging longer in the wings. The heart of the gentry, they had always been more than willing to share the imperial burden: surely, they could be relied upon to help a little more. Sitting on personal fortunes accumulated over the years, they could also afford to fund any necessary heavenly projects a local county might require. True, no one ever liked to spend their own money, but confused though the ancient empire might have been in many ways, it had always been crystal clear about the filial piety on which everyone's heaven – from the emperor down to landlording fathers and their tenanted estates – depended. As Confucius had observed so astutely: 'Family is everything.'

Hankou certainly had more than its fair share of wealth. As the tides of trade had washed up in its waters, so its shores had become a popular home for anyone with a bargaining turn of mind – whichever part of the empire they might have been born in. Truth be told, the greatest of them usually seemed to have come from a handful of provinces in which they had first monopolised fortunes from salt, tea, timber and other natural treasures, and then bet the profits on financing trade up and down the empire. The mountainous Shanxi with its natural wealth at the northern end of the Han River, was one; the fertile land of Anhui to the east was another. From wherever they came, in Hankou the greatest of them had gathered together under the pavilions of their individual provinces and ordered their trades and themselves with the tried and tested principles of the Confucian family and its values. *Dao, ren, yi, li, zhi* and *de* – the emphasis and the meanings had changed a little over the past two thousand years but the principles were the same: *dao*, the mastery of change; *ren*, putting yourself in other's shoes (these days, particularly a brother's); *yi*, the integrity which ensured that names and purposes were constantly correlated; *li*, the observance of ritual obedience, which ensured that no one forgot their place; *zhi*, the knowledge that ensured that every profitable opportunity was exploited; and *de*, applying yourself to whatever the task at hand with such discipline that the energies of heaven would constantly keep you afloat.

With mountains of silver at their disposal, the migrant merchants had spared no expense in raising the guilds which would order the interests of provinces or trades, complete with portals of piers and palaces of halls from which the changes that affected everyone's fortunes could be mastered. From the piers, each guild managed the boats of its members. From the palaces, temples were dedicated to the spirit of the god of wealth, while inner halls set out the rules and regulations that every member would observe. By the time the Jiaqing Emperor was looking for families to share the burdens of empire, it was not only to fathers and sons that he looked, but to the guilds as well. And remembering the early trade in pelts and pearls on which the fortunes of his own Aisin Gioro clan had been grounded, Jiaqing noted with pleasure how happy it was that such a good Manju idea of using trade to store wealth among the people should fit so easily with the Confucian idea of the family, and how strange it was that the Confucian Ming had failed to see its virtue.

*　　　*　　　*

With piers of fortune rising for Hankou's merchants, for a while even the lowest tides seemed to be touched with silver. But by the time Jiaqing passed the heavenly lands to his son the Daoguang (Bright Way) Emperor in 1820, for those at the bottom of the pile, the idea of wealth being stored among the people had become nothing but a dream. With the land too exhausted to support the peasants, and cotton cloth no longer a source of relief but an essential labour, the poorest families were clutching any available wooden plank and floating to Hankou. Under Qianlong, the city had already become a babel of migrant dialects and accents that few could understand. The well-placed corners in which someone with a few pennies could hang a trading hat of their own had long ago become firmly occupied. And as more people came, even the bare-handed positions, from barbers and bakers to tailors and fortune-tellers, even the more skilled boatmakers, were also filled. For those floating in at the later time of his grandson, Daoguang, it looked as if every inch of opportunity had already been covered. But although all of the obvious trades were more than adequately represented, it always seemed that if one squeezed hard enough there would somehow be room for yet another sturdy pair of shoulders, or yet another basket of something more to sell. More barbers, more tailors, more singers of stories, more tellers of fortunes, more hawkers, more beggars than anyone could ever imagine. And swarming along all of the shores, more would-be boatmen and coolie porters ready to sweat even harder than the men before them. Indeed, Hankou seemed to have discovered a new trade in the labour of desperate men with nothing to sell but their ability to endure: *chi ku*, as the peasants called it – eating bitterness. If you could take enough of that desperate fruit, you might just survive.

With everyone, from top to bottom, all constantly contemplating either triumph or destitution, there was, naturally, a heavy interest in respite. From the calculating top (where every trade was a risk) to the bitterness-chewing bottom (where every morning of life-extinguishing endurance might be one's last), at some point or another in the working day everyone wanted to find a soft cloud they could call their own. And, like so many other things in Hankou, the cloud that everyone dreamt of arrived up the Yangzi, on a boat.

The magical powers of opium had long been understood by Daoist alchemists: shaman successors who had been exploring other worlds since the beginning of time, not to mention helping anxious emperors in their search for the elixir of eternal life. For many centuries, opium had even been grown to imperial order in the easy tropical climate of the south: full of masculinely creative *yang* properties, Ming emperors had spent fortunes procuring its powers. Soon the scholarly officials were following suit, with exquisite pipes finely crafted for more popular appeal. And then the wider families of the scholarly officials began to pick up the habit: wealthy wives shut behind protecting walls and languishing in boredom; stressed sons who thought they might explode if they had to read another studying book. Eventually everyone with a headache or a twinge was turning to the poppy for relief, as were the labouring backs and shoulders that needed bitter strength. With simpler sticks of wood for pipes and the magic sold in tinier pinches – and cut with cheaper properties – it became a universal fixer, far better than a meal. Observing the relief acquired, even Hankou's merchants had been quick to see how opium could also be a treasure, certainly valuable for its profits, but also offering a dose of personal comfort when negotiating the often-stormy seas of trade.

By the beginning of the 1700s, opium had already become a dangerously captivating power. One of Qianlong's brothers had been an addict, and their horrified father, Yongzheng, had banned its use by anyone for anything other than medicinal purposes. But time had passed, the stresses of wealth had risen and the power of the poppy had grown. Before long, southern fields were struggling to satisfy the volume of demand, and with many growers favouring a faster production, quality began to be a challenge too. By the time the Daoguang Emperor came to the throne, in 1820, cases of opium were not only arriving in Hankou from the southern fields but from the southern seas as well. Handled initially by Portuguese mariners keen to insinuate themselves into the currents of South East Asian trade, they were later delivered by British traders who had fields of Indian poppies to sell, and a lot of silver to make.

Confucian values notwithstanding – or perhaps because it was just so hard to live up to them – taels of family silver were smoked away. Entire estates then followed in their wake, all puffed into clouds by otherwise dutiful fathers and sons. Even the attentions of the imperial troops were captured by the pipe. Shocked by the news that the empire had failed to vanquish a tribal rebellion because its soldiers had been floating on a cloud of opium, Jiaqing tried, in vain, to banish it completely. But the cost was not limited to the gentry's estates and the security of the realm. With Indian opium increasingly flooding in on British ships, taels of silver were rolling out; and as the taels of silver rolled out, the price of silver at home soared to the skies. What had begun as a problem of an imperial addiction was ending up as a crisis in the balancing of the books. And imperial displeasure notwithstanding, across the failing estates and in dark city dens, the charms of opium seemed to conquer all. Hankou traded on.

In the early 1830s, a string of poppy tales began to float in on Hankou's rivers: apparently the imperial officials had once again been commanded to flatten the opium fields, and once again the coasts were being cleared. Hankou paid them little heed: it was not the first time, it would certainly not be the last, and it usually didn't last for long. Following whispers confirmed that there was little to fear: with Guangdong's port of Guangzhou ('Canton' to twisting Western tongues who first heard of it in the local Guangdong language) exclusively appointed by the emperor to handle all trade across the southern seas, the local merchants had been quick to realise that the sea-faring barbarians had mountains of opium to sell. And although there was an imperial ban on the selling or buying of opium in China, the southern coast was fringed with thousands of tiny islands: all one had to do was send a smaller junk or a sampan to meet the foreign ships off the mainland's shore. Silver handed over, the forbidden treasure then swapped ships and the smaller vessels – craftier at navigating the narrowest rivers of the empire and always in need of a cargo – carried it off across the watery highways and byways until they reached Hankou. Heaven being high and, usually, far away, it seemed as if the problem was solved.

By 1835, with Hankou now supplier of clouds of pain-relieving pleasure to a grateful empire, its fortunes were riding higher than ever before. There was a bit of a squall in 1839, when heaven rather unexpectedly decided to investigate Guangzhou's 'port affairs' in the person of a highly Confucian official named Lin Zexu. Known as a stickler for smugglers, it was obvious to all that he would need careful handling. As expected, the Guangzhou merchant brothers were given a serious telling-off, with promises of future perfectly heavenly behaviour insisted upon, accompanied by hellish pictures of punishment for anyone in need of persuasion. As the exclusively appointed imperial traders of everything, the Guangdong merchants were also ordered to ensure, on pain of death, that the barbarian traders dumped every ounce of opium in their holds. Apparently, it wasn't easy to get the barbarians to understand the need for this, but eventually, after a year of fussing, three million pounds of poppy dust were finally handed over and Lin Zexu poured them into the sea. 'The risks of trade,' Guangdong's merchant brothers sighed, 'but once the waves have washed this particular harvest of opium away, it shouldn't be long before the stickler for smugglers is called back to more important imperial duties, and everyone can get on with the business of trade.'

Up in the centre of the country, Hankou had not been consulted by the Guangdong brothers, but it couldn't have agreed more. Floating in a world of its own, the empire's emporium had found a silver lining to the cloud of poured-away losses: when the southern opium was thrown into the water, Hankou merchants made fortunes from the opium in their stores. True, there were quite a few sons and fathers who, smoking away their estates, were now losing their fortunes even more quickly than before. But fools were everywhere in the world, and one man's loss was another's gain. Firmly anchored at the heart of the merchant world, Hankou's trades were bobbing up and down very nicely, thank you; and if one kept one's Confucian wits about one, the rafters of fortune could still reach to the skies.

Of course, there were always killjoys. Some said silver was a problem – but as far as Hankou's teahouse conversations could tell, it was nothing that the clever merchant-bankers from Shanxi had not been able to fix. Paper notes might not be popular with an emperor who preferred to receive his taxes in silver, but for the merchants they were an obvious means of smoothing trade, with the added advantage of creating a whole new industry of exchanging money. Then, of course, there were the usual old Confucians, muttering in their studies about the shame of Hankou's splendour. Mutter they might: every day brought another junk of eager peasant hands clinging to Hankou's shores for dear life. But while the burred accents of the migrants might be impossible to understand, they were willing to eat any amount of bitterness to get their toes into the city's waters. Pick-pockets, however, were certainly a problem: with so much of the countryside washing up, penniless, in Hankou, they were becoming a natural pest. They, and perhaps even the bitterness-eating coolies themselves. With the price of opium so high that many of the coolies were having to eat their bitterness raw, some in the trading terraces suggested that things might start to get a little bit bumpy on the streets.

In 1841, the self-satisfied merchants of Hankou began to hear some stranger stories. Having lost their opium (and clearly untrained in the Confucian ways), the barbarian foreigners had apparently thrown down their anchors in a temper and insisted on compensation. When they (obviously) had not got it, they had gone one step further and demanded the right to sell whatever they wanted, to whomever they wanted, up and down China's shores. Although Lin Zexu – still in charge of 'port affairs' – had been very clear about the heavenly principles, the barbarians had loaded their arguments with gunpowder, and were now training their sights up and down the coast. No one was quite sure what to make of it all. But as the southern merchant brothers got themselves snarled up in the spat, Hankou's trades continued even more buoyantly than before.

At one point, one of the foreign ships had the temerity to sail up the Yangzi, and Hankou jaws dropped in disbelief. But once its strange curiosity had apparently been satisfied, the ship seemed to understand that no barbarian could ever hope to match the trading powers of the Hankou merchants, and turned back down the Yangzi to the mud-flats of Shanghai. That being the case, it was quite a shock to hear, less than a year later, that the emperor had suddenly given the Western barbarians an imperial licence to trade not only in Guangdong's port of Guangzhou but in a clutch of other ports up the coast, as far as and including Shanghai. 'Treaty ports', they called them. To which were to be added millions of taels of silver, which the foreigners had demanded as 'reparations', for heaven's sake.

But what could one expect from the Manju Qing? As everyone up and down the country knew, barbarians themselves, they clearly could not be depended on to understand the heavenly lands, let alone be relied upon to keep them safe. Having squandered their early fortune on conquests and the corrupting charms of that greedy bannerman, was it any wonder they didn't have the necessary forces for a fight? How on earth the emperor was going to find the money for the reparations was anybody's guess. But as far as Hankou was concerned, heaven really was high and, whatever his troubles, the emperor was far away. Guangzhou and those coastal 'treaty ports' might be experiencing a few problems, and a lot of cheap foreign cotton was probably going to be working its way up the Yangzi, but Guangzhou's loss was probably Hankou's fortune, and cotton, after all, was just another trade.

For the next few years, Hankou's teahouses settled back to their usual roaring business. Even the opium dens were going great guns. Whether as paper, silver or even the odd old-style copper coin, the cash was flowing. Most of the merchants were so busy calculating the constant rise of their accounts that the wider world of human beings seemed not to exist. From time to time, some visiting curmudgeonly Confucian would start lecturing on the idea that the rich were vying with each other for splendour while the poor were being squeezed to death. There were even madmen (when had there ever not been?) who had started muttering about ominous vapours rising and a darkness beginning to spread across the earth. No one paid them much notice.

But then, even stranger tales began to arrive from Guangdong. Particularly the one about a failed imperial scholar who was talking about a new Taiping Great Peace. As if all of the Taiping Great Peaces of the past had not taught everyone more than enough about how dangerous they could be. Special breathing, confessions of sins, brothers and sisters dreaming of a pure land where everyone could be equal *and* immortal: one way or another, every one of them had been swept away – as often as not betrayed by the very idiots who had dreamt them up in the first place. Usually, some northern barbarian had then ridden down to take advantage of the chaos.

Those close to the south explained that this particular scholar had failed his exams so many times that he had not only lost his head to visions, but had started to mix them up with one of those foreign ideas: the one about the man with a long beard in the clouds. Of course, the idea of a man in the clouds was nothing new, but this one wasn't Laozi: it was a foreigner with a bigger nose and a beard, that character the Jesuits chattered about until Kangxi had thrown them out – the one whose English name sounded something like 'god'. And as if that was not enough, the scholar was now declaring that he himself was none other than the brother of the old man's more famous 'Jesus' son. Well, what could you expect if you opened up your ports? The madman's name was 'Hong something' and apparently he was not just railing against the Manju Qing (well, who wouldn't rail against that barbarian shower?) but against Confucius as well. Of course, it would not be the first time that someone had had a bone to pick with Confucius, but it was very rare that anyone dared to stand up and speak their mind. For the settled Hankou merchants, it was all a bit confusing. But while the stories about the deranged scholar kept floating in from the south, Hankou, nestled in the beating heart of China, and with all the seasons turning as usual, continued to trade.

In 1847 and 1848, however, it began to look as if there might indeed be a few problems. A drought in neighbouring Henan, then a famine in southern Guangxi were both a bit too close for comfort. Calculating hearts duly noted that the cost of grain would go up, and proceeded to buy as much as they could. Even those most absorbed in their abacuses began to wonder if heaven was about to turn. Boatmen shipping in to Hankou had been muttering about hard times in the north for a few years now – along with tales of yet more of the kinds of rebellion that always blew up when heaven was unhappy. Apparently, the peasants were anxious about cheap foreign cotton flooding across the country: for the northern lands, which had so few other crafts to offer, this was obviously going to cost them dear. That and the fact that, with not much money in the imperial treasury, the Grand Canal was not being dredged and had become too silted for many to use. Even inland traders were shifting their cargoes to the coast; it looked as if the boatmen were also about to lose their jobs.

Was any of this really any different from the past? More people, less land

and less land that could be farmed; empty coffers in the imperial treasury and a gentry who would rather buy a city palace than dig their hands into their pockets for a peasant in need. There had always been poor peasants, and they had regularly raised local rebellions – so much so that the idea of *human portents* seemed to have become a bit of a mantra. Someone had written an essay about the origins of the present problem during the time of the Jiaqing Emperor (and been banished for his pains): twenty times more people than there had been a hundred years before; not enough land or food to go around; and a lot of the rich eating so much and buying so many things that they were swallowing the food of future generations. What to do? As even the smallest schoolboy was taught, the times were constantly changing and the cultivated man simply had to find a way to adjust. And as every trader knew, fixed as it was at the heart of the empire, the source of Hankou's fortunes might change but the direction of trade was almost always up.

In 1850, the problems of the empire suddenly rolled a lot closer when the Yangzi River burst its banks not far from Hankou. Oceans of fields were swallowed under water and floods of washed-away families suddenly floated into Hankou. Then, in 1851, the news went from bad to worse. In the company of twenty thousand men, the deranged scholar 'Hong something' (Hong Xiuquan was his name) had proclaimed a Heavenly Taiping Kingdom of Great Peace and raised a 'Heavenly Army', which was now marching north up the Xiang River valley with the riches of Hankou clearly in its sights. Word was that its numbers were swelling with every village they passed. Of course, everyone had known Hong Xiuquan was on the move. But rebels were always moving somewhere, and no one had thought it would come to this. True, rumours had been washing up since the previous year that ten thousand men had gathered under the Taiping banner on a mountain in Guangxi, with hundreds more joining every day. But Guangxi was such a long way away.

It had been a little more worrying to hear that, in addition to converts to Hong Xiuquan's mad visions, the Heavenly Army's numbers included members of other, much older, brotherhoods of men. The old White Lotus Society was one – the brotherhood with which the first Ming emperor had swept himself to power and which had been erupting periodically into northern rebellions ever since. The Heaven and Earth Society was another: a well-known brotherhood, dedicated to ousting the Manju Qing, its ranks had long ago been swollen by a host of Shaolin monks, after their loyalist monastery had been destroyed by that other rebel, Li Zicheng, who had marched against the Ming. There was even a society called the Three Harmonies – although heaven knew what could be harmonious about a rebellious brotherhood. Who could have known that these brotherhoods talked to each other, and that their members could have reached such a mass? Now it seemed that, although many were primarily dedicated to the overthrow of the Manju Qing, the brotherhoods were also committed to the rise of every peasant, with the idea of joining everyone together in one great harmonious family of brothers, which any peasant willing to share his blood was welcome to join. Nor was it just the peasants. As the Grand Canal had clogged up, with jobs lost to the corresponding rise of coastal trades, it seemed that the crews of canal-plying boats had pledged their blood to a heavenly order of their own – and now they had decided to throw in their lot with the Heavenly Taiping Kingdom of Great Peace.

Breath held, Hankou watched and waited, quizzing every boat and sampan that arrived. Then, in the early December of 1852, news arrived that the Heavenly Army (one million and rising) had arrived at Dongting Lake, just south of Hankou. Awash with thousands of empty boats, the banks of the lake also happened to be piled with guns and ammunition abandoned from the rebellions of Wu Sangui, two hundred years before. Trading minds quickly made their calculations: it would be only a matter of days before the peasant hordes sailed into the Yangzi and climbed aboard the floating emporium of the empire. Everyone who could rushed to the piers in a bid to escape; only the very richest made it. By the end of the year, Hong Xiuquan's Great Peace lovers had indeed sailed into Hankou's fortunes. Silver and food had been redistributed for all. And the beating heart of trade had stopped.

Slow to understand the threat and almost as slow as the Hankou traders to catch up, the imperial troops were nearly as far away as the emperor when the city fell. With Hankou under its control, and hundreds of new recruits joining every day, Hong Xiuquan's army moved on. Three months later, the once-capital of Nanjing was captured and declared the capital of a new Taiping 'Southern Empire'. As the Qing imperial troops mustered to confront the Heavenly Army in the south-east, pent-up anger began to explode in almost every other quarter of the country as well. Tribal people who wanted their own worlds back, brotherhoods of men who wanted justice: north, south, east and west, there was not a corner that could keep its peace. At one point, it even seemed as if the Heavenly Army would capture the new treaty port of Shanghai – but then suddenly a Small Sword Society popped out of nowhere and occupied it before they could get there. Some said the Small Swords were cousins of the Heaven and Earth Society, others insisted that they were just another branch of the Taiping Great Peace lovers. Most, however, realised that when a man has nothing left to lose, it doesn't really matter what he joins, as long as it promises help.

In 1854 Hankou would be saved, only to fall again. In 1855, it would be saved once more. Meanwhile, the rest of the Yangzi world descended into a battling hell, which would last until 1864.

In the end, their saviour, and the saviour of the Manju Qing, was a Confucian scholar who had never fought in a battle, let alone led a battalion of troops. His name was Zeng Guofan. Ordered by a desperate emperor to raise an army from his home province of Hunan (just south of the Yangzi and home to Dongting Lake), he succeeded by appealing to everyone's sense of Confucian values. Painstakingly searching for the *dao* way, he consistently expressed the *ren* humanity, which put himself and his men in the shoes of the people. Insisting on an *yi* integrity, which matched people up with their places, he did nothing without a dedication to the pursuit of *zhi* knowledge, which went well beyond the learning of books. Applying a *li* ritual to the order of the ranks, he never departed from the *de* principle of a disciplined virtue. Indeed, Zeng Guofan seemed to be the incarnation of everything that Confucius had ever taught. As the Qing's imperial army foundered (bereft of funding and now famous for scattering at the sound of a gun), Zeng Guofan raised an army from a ragtag bunch of Yangzi peasants, and created a host of local 'fund-raising' bureaus to persuade the gentry-merchants of central China to pay for it all.

Raised from the home villages of its soldiers – and with each recruit properly paid, reliably fed and organised under the strict Confucian bonds of father to son and older brother to younger brother – by 1855 Zeng Guofan's army was a force to be reckoned with. Known as the 'Xiang Army' (after a river in the Hunan province), across the next ten years it would battle the Great Peace lovers up and down the Yangzi while tackling every other upstart rebellion that was cashing in on the chaos.

By 1864, when the ancient and more recently Taiping capital of Nanjing had been restored to the Qing, it would be seen as an army of Confucian heroes standing stark against a Yangzi landscape that was now in shreds. The battles had been followed by famines and plague, once-fertile fields had turned to tangles of weed and dust, with the bones of thirty million dead scattered across the landscape. Stunned survivors could only look on in shock. Heaven had certainly winnowed out its people. Many more would be lost in the years it would take for the shattered earth to find its feet.

* * *

Well before the end of the rebellion – a rebellion of such a size that many would whisperingly describe it as a civil war – Hankou's surviving merchants returned to the remains of their once-gilded city. Threading their way through the rubble of their rafters, they began to resurrect the floating emporium from its watery grave. As they worked, they applied every Confucian virtue in their books. Heaven may have taken its toll but the Qing's remaining people would need their rivers of fortune if they were to rebuild the past. Fathers gathered themselves and their sons together; guilds reached out to their members. Surviving souls without a patch of land to stand on sailed in on every possible sampan and offered their shoulders for the task. The order of trade painstakingly restored, everyone then set about rebuilding the glittering palaces and piers. Back in business long before the final triumph of Zeng Guofan's Xiang Army, more stories floated in of how the Western barbarians were redirecting their own fire against the rebels, lest heaven completely collapse.

Then in 1861, news arrived that the emperor had given the British barbarians yet another imperial licence to trade – this one for Hankou itself. Good luck to them, the merchants thought. After everything Hankou had endured, there was little that a volley of foreigners could teach it. And in case the foreigners hadn't noticed, the rise of Zeng Guofan's Xiang Army had proved, beyond the shadow of a doubt, that their Confucian spirits were more than equal to any barbarian trade which might be thrown at them.

Looking out at the waters, however, and listening to the tales of the washed-up people who had floated in, some of Hankou's number did begin to wonder about the peasants in the lands around: rags and bones, clutching at the straws of an exhausted earth. Rumour had it that tides of them were not only flooding back into Hankou, but into the bonds of the brotherhoods as well. A world of secret societies where a family of blood brothers was all. If the past had been a problem, what on earth would the future bring?

IMAGINE A PEOPLE

Heaven sees as the people see;
heaven hears as the people hear.

The Great Declaration (from now lost pages of the *Book of Documents*, second millennium BCE, referred to by Mencius)

The black ice of winter had bitten deep into the northern peninsula that curled around the inner gulf of the Yellow Sea. Outmanoeuvred in a chilling sea-battle in late 1894, the ironclad dreadnoughts of the Beiyang northern navy had slipped back behind a sheltering island base, which sat just off the coast in the bay of Weihaiwei. By all rights, they should not have lost the Battle of Yalu. With bigger ships, and more of them – all fitted with the latest Krupp German guns – they should have won not just the battle but the war as well. But, as was so often the case, sighed Admiral Ding, imperial meddling, wanton corruption and cowardice all seemed to have got in the way. Gunners had been deployed before they had received any training. Shells once fired turned out to have been stuffed with porcelain and cement. Then the captain of the fleet's much-prized armoured turret ship had preferred to duck out of the line of fire rather than take a hit that would have saved the day. A damaging exercise with painful lessons for all to learn.

Now sheltered by the generous length and convenient hills of their base on nearby Liugong Island – and protected by newly armoured fortresses along the shoreside bay of Weihaiwei – the fleet would at least have time to get its positions clear before venturing back for a more successful kill. Somewhere out there on the Yellow Sea was the navy of the Greater Japanese Empire: a smaller fleet but with fleeter ships; a chain of command that seemed to run like a clock; and a cunning grasp of strategy that always seemed to find the weakest flank. For now, however, the Beiyang fleet was at home, tucked under the protection of artillery designed by the best of naval minds. On either side of the island, booms had been spread to keep out any Japanese opportunists who might try to get past – each spiked with mines, and all guarded by submarine torpedoes lying in watchful wait. And just to make sure that nothing had been left to chance, the Krupp cannons on the shoreside were fully armed, with the sight of each one facing firmly out to sea. They wouldn't, of course, be needed: the Beiyang navy had no immediate plans to move. But this time no one was leaving any fortune to Fate – not where the clearly crafty Japanese were concerned.

As the old (lunar) year entered its last January month, temperatures plunged to 26 degrees below freezing and snow stormed across the skies. Admiral Ding turned his attention to his sailors and set about reminding them how to fight. At one point, there was a bit of a distraction: the Japanese attempted a clumsy landing, foolishly trying to take a heavily armoured fort to the west. Finally, something the Qing forces could easily rebuff. A week later, as the old Year of the Horse prepared to depart, the Liugong Island base relaxed its guard a little, cracking an armoury of fireworks to scare away the hungry spirits and welcome in a new Year of the Sheep.

Then, just when all seemed so quiet both at land and at sea, the Beiyang fleet exploded. Pummelled with shot and with black clouds of destruction in every direction, Admiral Ding peered towards the shore and saw the Krupp guns of the landside fortresses firing towards his harbouring ships with a faultless military precision. Jumping to clear orders, gunners were loading and firing the cannons like clocks. Newly hoisted on their turrets was the flag of the Rising Sun.

*   *   *

The Manju Qing had needed to learn a lot in the decades after Zeng Guofan raised his Xiang Army to stand against the Great Peace-loving Taiping rebels.

Much of it was simply catching up on what had been happening in the rest of the world across the previous hundred years. But a lot of the learning had had to be grasped at the height of the Taiping rebellion – with the added obstacle of a new emperor Xianfeng (Great Prosperity) who rarely managed to face up to challenges of the present, let alone the future.

It seemed that two hundred years ago, something called the 'sovereignty of nations' had been dreamt up at the barbarian edge of the world. Not surprisingly, given the barbarians' limited education, the idea of a *dao* way was completely unfamiliar to them – as were the Confucian principles of *ren* humanity, *yi* integrity, *li* ritual, *zhi* knowledge, and *de* virtue. Apparently, when it was first conjured up as an idea, the sovereignty of nations did three things. First, it divided the world into individual countries, each defined by physical borders and populated by people who were 'citizens' of the state. Second, it seemed to agree that the merchants of every state could trade with each other, and even put their silver to work in each other's countries. Third, it declared that anyone within those sovereign states could practise whatever version of that barbarian Christian faith they liked (there seemed to be a lot of them). And then on top of it all (hardly surprisingly, given the poor foundations of these barbarian thinkers) someone called *A-da-mu Si-mi-te* (Adam Smith) from that very barbarian island of 'Great Britain' had magicked up a truly shocking idea of an 'invisible hand': a notion of self-interested greed, which he managed to convince everyone was far more natural than any *ren* benevolence. Arguing that this 'invisible hand' was such a positive force of nature that everyone should kowtow before it, *Si-mi-te* had gone on to insist that the idea did not just apply to individual 'citizens' but to the 'sovereign states' as well. Even the youngest of the Qing scholars could see that it was wrong – and any scholar worth his salt could easily point to its patent errors of morality. But the barbarians had raised a rather fat god, by the name of John Bull, who seemed to have told them not to bother with a discussion, just to repeat themselves, again and again – always louder, and, wherever possible, over the barrel of a gun.

Unfortunately for Confucius and the Manju Qing, John Bull's guns first arrived at just the point when the costs of the Qianlong emperor's conquests were taking their toll. Lin Zexu (the diligent official despatched to sort out the opium 'port affairs' in Guangdong) had made the obvious Confucian arguments against the *Si-mi-te* idea. But the barbarians had simply fired their guns, and in 1842, it had seemed best to give them what they wanted (five southern coastal ports for trade and a rocky island with a *xiang gang*, fragrant port, that the foreigners called Hong Kong) and hope it would be enough. Of course it was not. Within a year, the British barbarians had come back, with an addendum insisting that no Briton visiting China should ever be subject to the vagaries of heavenly justice again. A year later, they had been followed by others from the West: French and American frigates demanding (and receiving) much of the same. Even that had not been enough. Sixteen years later, in 1856, pointing to the small print of the treaty text, the British had returned in the company not only of the French and the Americans, but the Russians as well. Their demands constantly rising, across the next two years, they had sailed their guns up and down the coast, forcing the Qing to split their forces even as they struggled to defeat the inner threat of the Taiping rebellion as well.

In 1858, and again in 1860, the Qing acceded to the ludicrous demands: in all, another eleven treaty ports, leases on other lands, and the left bank of the north-eastern Amur River (heartland of the Manju Qing, including Lake Baikal) to be ceded to Russia – which would now be free to sweep right across to the Pacific Ocean. To this was added shipping freedom up and down the Yangzi River, travel anywhere in China for any of their barbarian people, and more 'reparations' (for the now-additional battles they claimed they had had to fight just to get the Qing to give in). On top of all this, the barbarians insisted on a right to post official representatives to the imperial capital of Beijing. (There had also been a punishing assault on the splendid *Yuanming Yuan*, the 'Summer Palace', which the Jesuits had so thoughtfully designed.)

With everyone's ancestors turning in their graves, the Xianfeng Emperor had died an early death. Under the heavenly title of Tongzhi (Restoring Order), his five-year-old son had been raised to the throne. This was naturally under a regency – one that began as a council of many and ended up as a partnership of two: the boy's mother, Yehenara Cixi (Xianfeng's unusually forthright concubine who henceforth styled herself the Dowager Empress), and a talented half-brother of the Xianfeng Emperor, Prince Gong.

While imperial minds had found it hard to concentrate on the barbarians during the years of the Taiping rebellion, in the twenty years that followed, the Manju Qing (Prince Gong in particular) worked hard to understand the new Western barbarian world. Not that anyone wanted to accept it, but since it seemed to have so many guns, there must be something to learn – and clearly it was not going to disappear. Somehow Confucian talents were going to have to find a way around the madness, but it was hard to know where to begin.

Even the question of names was a problem. This was hardly surprising given the fact that any foreigners had no idea of the intimate relationship required between the name of a thing and its purpose. Under the Manju, the heavenly lands were now called Da Qing Guo (the Great Qing Empire), although the people themselves were still referred to as the *laobaixing* – 'the old 100 names'. But the uneducated foreigners kept talking about something called 'China', and referring to 'citizens', who seemed to be some kind of people who had a voice and an individual importance of their own: nothing that made much sense to anyone in the heavenly lands.

Behind the vexing problem of names was (as Confucius would have understood) the far more difficult question of how any of these new ideas could possibly work within the heavenly hierarchy of everything. Every emperor knew how to order a world in which barbarian rulers diligently studied the Confucian ways in the hope that they might become, if not part of the lands of the Son of Heaven (a privilege reserved for only the most diligent of the barbarians), at least acknowledged as tribute-paying states entitled to exchanges of treasures and, when required, protection. But what worked under a heaven where those not born to the Confucian wisdom were simply waiting to join it, seemed to have no place at all in a world of independent 'sovereign states'. Instead there were strange ideas with even stranger names: 'comity of nations', 'extraterritoriality', 'most favoured nation'. They all tripped off the tongues of the foreigners with the smoothness of silk. But whenever a foreigner was pressed to explain them, it seemed to come down to a wolf-like competition for raw wealth and power. True, the foreigners seemed to have a little bit of an idea about the *ren* humanity and the putting of oneself in others' shoes – one of their favourite principles, on paper at least, was about the mutual and equal sovereignty of states. But they seemed to have no idea about the *dao* way with its changes – let alone *yi* integrity, *li* ritual, *zhi* knowledge, or *de* virtue. And they certainly didn't seem to understand the importance of unity under a single heavenly mind. Indeed, they seemed to have no understanding at all of the deep morality that underpinned everybody's cosmos – or any interest in it.

Shocked at the new ideas they were being asked to learn, the imperial officials muttered against the madness of the barbarian ideas. But Prince Gong (who had a wonderful grasp of the Confucian classics) suggested that one could hate the evil that a barbarian in his ignorance might do, but one should not hate the barbarian himself. Reminding everyone of Confucius' exhortation to 'be kind to men from afar', he suggested that, with a little patience, even these Western barbarians could surely be tranquillised over time. To which he added, that with enough self-cultivation and discipline, the *de* virtue of heaven would find its feet again. 'One must remember, however,' he counselled, 'not to call them barbarians – off in their own dark cloud at the edge of the world, and never educated in the Confucian classics, they cannot see themselves for what they are, and they do not like to be reminded that they are not at the centre of everything.'

In 1861, a new office was created to try to deal with the problem of the foreigners as the unnatural phenomenon they clearly were. Charged with exercising a single central responsibility for what would obviously be the highly specialist task of dealing with the foreign 'sovereign states', it was simply named the *zongli yamen* (the general management office). A whole new corps of scholarly officials was recruited; all were instructed to apply their Confucian spirits to 'investigating the things' of the foreign world, and understanding as much about the barbarians as they possibly could. Obviously the four classical texts would not be enough: a translation bureau was created so that the *zongli yamen* scholars could read the same books as the foreigners. Every possible tome on international law was read, and then subjected to the same dissecting scrutiny the scholars applied to their own Confucian texts. Foreign newspapers were also discovered – and found to be particularly helpful. It seemed that in their inability to comprehend the towering importance of unity under a single heaven, the foreigners were perfectly happy to publish all sides of every argument. This was extremely useful in providing the scholars of the new *zongli yamen* not only with invaluable tuition, but with rather effective ammunition as well. Indeed, after a while, the new foreign texts did not seem to be so difficult at all – it turned out that the literary mastery of the Confucian canon could be a powerful skill: once one had learnt the basic barbarian principles, how could three thousand years of bureaucratic experience not be useful? There was a little bit of a problem with the fact that the foreigners did not always keep their word – but once one understood that this was the case, adjustments could easily be made on one's own side as well.

Years passed, and as the *zongli yamen* grew in confidence, special academies were created to teach the geography and customs of the foreign world. In 1871, a group of young scholars was sent abroad to study the mathematics and the engineering that seemed to have made the foreigners so strong. In this, they had been advised by a man called Yong Wing who, in his youth, had found his way from Guangdong to America and Yale University, from which had graduated in 1854. But nothing to do with barbarians was ever easy. Now settled in the treaty ports and protected by their 'treaty rights', the Westerners had created cities within cities (more like fiefdoms), particularly in the bigger ports of Tianjin and Shanghai. Barbarian boats were now trading up and down the Yangzi, stopping off wherever they wanted. And from the boats had descended legions of their own fanatical followers of the skies, who were wreaking havoc wherever they went. Men, and even women, called 'missionaries', now insisted on pushing themselves into the most extraordinary corners, all in the name of that man with the white beard who they said was everyone's 'king'. It was hardly surprising that a position in the *zongli yamen* was one of the most stressful posts any scholar could get. But there was an art to managing these foreign devils and, over time, a number of scholar-officials liked to think that it was one they were becoming increasingly good at mastering.

* * *

As Beijing's bureaucrats tried to work out how to adapt the mechanics of the imperial bureaucracy to the demands of 'state sovereignty' and, wherever possible, to adapt 'state sovereignty' to the more familiar mechanics of the imperial bureaucracy, the wider gentry and merchants began to explore new ventures of their own. Nowhere was this done with greater energy and imagination than in the province of Hunan.

Home of the Confucian general and genius Zeng Guofan, sitting to the south of Hankou and the neighbouring province of Hubei, and host to a number of towns and cities of its own, Hunan's capital city was Changsha. The lands of Hunan had also once been home to one of the greatest of the Warring States – a splendid state by the name of Chu. Eventually falling to the unity of the Qin, the people of Chu had, however, never lost their stubborn sense of having an independent heart. Not surprisingly, over the next two thousand years, few of Hunan's scholars had ever succeeded in entering the senior ranks of the imperial bureaucracy, which had made the rise of Zeng Guofan to the heights of imperial office all the more extra ordinary; a veritable vindication of what it meant to be Hunanese. Successful in entering the scholarly courtyards of the empire, Zeng's subsequent triumph in raising the wildly successful Xiang Army had so touched his fellow Hunanese that they saw in his example the inspiration for a broader 'self-strengthening' of the Hunan world.

191

Triumphant, Zeng had certainly been. In 1852 when the Qing empire had needed an inland freshwater navy to launch against the Taiping Heavenly Army, Zeng Guofan had not hesitated to search out the necessary ship-building talent required. As far as he could tell, what was really needed was gunboats, but neither he nor anyone else in land-locked Hunan had ever seen one. Undeterred, he called upon the Confucian feelings of the merchant brothers in the south, who suggested three shipyards; each was invited to send the best of their hands to help build the basic boats. Somehow working out how those foreigners had managed to attach brass guns to the sides of a boat without sinking everyone on board, Zeng had the new 'model navy' ready within two years.

In need of a bigger army, Zeng Guofan had then sent his most trusted aide back to his home province, neighbouring Anhui, and told him to repeat the recruiting successes of Hunan.

When, in 1862, the empire had needed an even bigger navy, Zeng hit upon the idea of asking the scholar Yong Wing, then just recently returned from Yale, to take himself back to America to buy whatever was needed to build an arsenal at the Shanghai mouth of the Yangzi River, in the region of Jiangnan. Unperturbed by the inconvenient fact of an American civil war, Yong Wing had gone back to America and, within a year, returned with everything required. And as far as technical skills for maintenance were concerned, Zeng noted that there were now, rather conveniently, a lot of foreigners sailing up and down the Yangzi. No doubt some of them would be available for hire to explain whatever his army and its friends could not work out for themselves.

By the time the Taiping rebellion ended in 1864 – with a battle in the heavenly capital of Nanjing that had destroyed thirty thousand lives – it was clear to everyone in Hunan, and, indeed, across the wider world of the Yangzi, that the answer to the problems of the day would not be found in the imperial city of Beijing. Hijacked by the Qing more than two hundred years before, the capital was in the grip of the barbarian Manju spirits; now burdened by foreign reparations, their empire was broke. The true answer lay in the self-strengthening powers of scholarly men like Zeng Guofan. Not just scholars in office, but a wider body of gentry, merchants and even retired generals whose *fu* wealth, and *qiang* power, had saved the day: 'self-strengtheners' all. With fields decimated by rebellion needing to be restored for everyone's food, it was now clear that everyone's future would also increasingly depend upon the city and its ability to gather together the new *fu qiang*, wealth and power, of the gentry, merchants and retired generals on which Zeng Guofan had so successfully drawn. Hankou had been rebuilt by its ordering families of guilds; Hunan's Changsha (also attacked by the Taiping rebels) had likewise been rebuilt with the capital of self-strengtheners. Other cities had followed suit. All of them had been guided – and bound together – by the Confucian virtues. Where the empire and its emperors struggled, it was Confucius – at least the most up-to-date idea of what Confucius had meant – and the self-strengtheners who had really won the day.

In the decades that followed, self-strengtheners – from Hunan, from senior official posts in Beijing, and from across other provinces – set about building the basic blocks of a new Confucian world. Following Zeng Guofan's example of the Jiangnan arsenal in Shanghai, arms and defence came first. Then came the taming of nature and the resurrection of harvests, with the building of factories to produce the necessary articles of life for the *laobaixing* people at large. Cotton and bamboo were particularly favoured commodities – with the industrial production process starting with the old 'putting out' system, which the merchants had introduced into the village households of the desperate fields. To these foundations were then added schools, academies and societies, through which the new (mostly technical) knowledge could be spread.

Wherever required, the local fund-raising bureaus that Zeng had established for his army were replicated – now dedicated to the task of raising funds for whatever local construction might be needed. And whether from city pavilions or rural estates, the gentry organised battalions of local labour to take on a more formal responsibility for the rivers, dams, ditches and everything else that the harvests required.

As the fund-raising bureaus were replicated and the rural militias were raised, the gentry wrapped themselves up in the fabric of the greatest common experience and network they had: the imperial examinations. As brutally difficult as ever, few candidates passed them without several attempts; indeed many took and retook them without ever passing. Travelling to Beijing for the highest of the tests, over the final days of anxious preparation, friends were made from across the country, with many forging bonds that would endure through the thick and thin of their lives. With such a fabric of relationships in place, it was not only funds and rural battalions that could be raised by the gentry but any family sort of a society, for any kind of a task: patrolling streets against brigands, flattening roads, raising lamps to light streets, not to mention a host of other new scientific possibilities that had been introduced by the foreigners. Even the foreigners' novel idea of a newspaper was adopted. Initially launched out of the foreign settlement within Shanghai, these remarkable printed pages charged themselves with picking up any and all good ideas, then distributing them across the country for everyone to read.

Up and down the land, the new 'Confucian army' set itself to transforming the chaos left by the Taiping rebels into a new order. The strongest roots of the new order were in the capital cities of the provinces, where indeed the strongest roots of the Chinese world had been since the time of the ancient Zhou. The branches of the new order were scattered across the country: wherever there were gentry, merchants and retired generals to be found. Its communications ran across the world of examination candidates, whether successful or failed, now strengthened by a growing printed press. The founders and leaders of it all were men whose scholarly talents had made them powerful officials, and whose merchant money had made them not just traders of scale but owners of vast wealth. For the first time in two and a half thousand years of being at the bottom of the ancient hierarchy of human productivity, the merchants had found a pride of place in a new Confucian world. Heartened by a rising *fu qiang* wealth and power, the new Confucian army was a model for an old empire, which simply grew and grew.

* * *

While the new Confucians were going from self-strengthening strength to strength, however, the seas of the Manju Qing's new world were anything but calm. In fact, from 1870 onwards, the waters had become distinctly choppy. The *zongli yamen* might have been congratulating itself on a number of lessons well learnt, and the self-strengthening 'new Confucians' might have been rebuilding Da Qing China from citadels in cities and the countryside alike, but, far and near, barbarians seemed to be intent on raising a havoc of hell with extremely inconvenient and selfish ideas all of their own.

The biggest trouble-makers were always going to be the Western foreigners who had arrived by sea – particularly those who had decided to push their 'God' into every possible Confucian life. By 1870, they had set up missions in all sorts of directions, with some of them deciding to 'rescue' Chinese children into orphanages. Anyone could have told them that the local populations would struggle to understand where the children were going. And so it was that, before long, someone started rumours that the missionaries were in fact merchants – trading in Chinese children. Naturally, riots erupted.

In the June of 1870, a particularly messy misunderstanding resulted in the death of a Chinese official in Tianjin from the barrel of the French consul's gun. This was swiftly followed by the murder of the French consul, and then by a riot that nearly burnt the whole of Tianjin to the ground. As always in such situations, the foreigners loaded their gunboats, and the now ageing Zeng Guofan was pulled out of retirement. But this time, even Zeng could not really help. Buoyed by their successes up and down the coasts, the foreigners insisted on something ludicrous to 'repair their losses': the foreign missionaries who had caused all of the trouble in the first place were not only to be allowed to go wherever they wanted and do whatever they wanted, but wherever they were, and whatever they were doing, the Great 'Da Qing' Empire was to be held responsible for the safety of their lives. Everybody – at least everybody Chinese – knew that such a state of affairs would only bring down more trouble on everybody's heads. But, as was usually the case, the foreigners simply shouted ever louder until they got their way.

As if all of that was not enough, the various conquests made by Kangxi and Qianlong began to collapse. In 1871, a barbarian tribe on the once-renegade island of Taiwan killed two Japanese fishermen. Claiming that the Qing clearly had no idea what was going on in that or any of the other southern islands that sat between the two lands, the Japanese proceeded to occupy the nearby thread of the Ryuku islands. With everything else that was going on with the sea-barbarians from the West, no one in the imperial bureaucracy had the heart for a fight. Then in the same year, up in the north-west, a stubborn Muslim, who had pronounced himself the King of Kashgaria – even exploring treaties with the Russians and the British – decided to launch an anti-Qing rebellion in the bare lands of the Ili Valley (part of present-day Xinjiang). Embarked on building an empire of their own, the Russians used the rebellion as an excuse to occupy the lands themselves. Only the spending of an imperial fortune managed to save the wider north-west, and even then the Qing ended up losing the Ili Valley to the Russian tsars.

The only bright light on the horizon was down in the Yunnan south-west, where, after decades of disaster, things had seen a rare but marked improvement. There had been the final end to a twenty-year rebellion of Muslims, who somehow felt they had not been treated as well as everyone else in the heavenly lands. It had taken a while, but eventually their 'southern sultanate' was finally brought back under heaven's powers, and its so-called ruler, Sulayman ibn Abd ar-Rahman (better known by the easier-to-pronounce Chinese name of Du Wenxiu), had fallen. And then there had been the (hopefully final) pacification of a stubborn misfit tribe in Yunnan's neighbouring province of Guizhou, who seemed to think that the land they lived on was their own. Some patches of blue in an otherwise distinctly cloudy sky.

But these small gains notwithstanding, as far as the Manju Qing were concerned, the decade just got worse and worse. In 1876, a British official surveying the border with neighbouring British-Indian Burma managed to get himself killed by one or other of the Yunnan tribes (there were so many that no one quite knew which). That had ended up with a letter of apology to Queen Victoria (something the *zongli yamen* was becoming rather good at), and another four treaty ports. Then, in 1882, a group of Chinese bandits, who had settled on the border with the tribute-state of Vietnam, got themselves into a fight with French explorers looking for trade. France lashed out at Vietnam and Vietnam naturally called upon its protectors, the Manju Qing, for help. Sensing that things could easily get dangerously out of control, the *zongli yamen* did its best to negotiate for a quick peace. But in the end the Qing found themselves in a one-day war with France. In fact, it didn't even last a day: in just a single hour on 23 August 1884, the French navy destroyed the Nanyang (southern) fleet. The peace that finally followed put Vietnam under French dominion – and reduced to an illusion the idea that the Qing empire could protect its tribute states.

It was only a matter of time before the other wolves circled. Russia pushed ever closer to the Manju's north-eastern homelands, looking for any excuse to start a war. Japan, watching from its archipelago of easterly islands, began to sense that the Qing's failings might lose not only the Da Qing empire to the Western barbarians but the rest of Asia, including Japan, as well. Having been forced to strengthen themselves as the result of an American ultimatum – and with the worrying example of the Qing's travails so close to its shores – the old Tokugawa shogunate had opened to the outside world and built its own new 'sovereign state', forged with samurai steel. An enlightened 'Meiji' rule had followed, complete with the first constitution and parliament outside the West, and a rise in industry, which took everyone by surprise. Within the space of twenty years, the scattering of islands once seen by the First Qin Emperor as nothing more than the misty Penglai home of the immortals had become a rising power.

With a Japanese empire rising, it had not been long before the Korean peninsula found its way into everyone's sights. Another state that had long paid tribute to the heavenly lands, when a rebellion erupted there in 1884, both the Manju Qing and Meiji Japan raced to the Korean court. In that encounter the Beiyang army came out on the winning side. But within ten years, the Qing found themselves at war with Japan over the terms of a broken treaty. It was at this point that the redoubtable Admiral Ding had found himself on the Yellow Sea battling the navy of the Greater Japanese Empire – and eventually losing the fleet. On 25 January 1895, two weeks before the final attack, Admiral Ito Sukeyuki, commander of the Japanese forces, had written a letter to Admiral Ding – once a friend with whom he had discussed the common question of how to adapt to the new Western barbarian world. Urging him to surrender, and offering him a temporary refuge in Japan until the Qing empire eventually (and inevitably) fell, Admiral Sukeyuki wrote: 'It is not the fault of one man that has brought the Qing dynasty to this position. The blame rests with the errors of the Government that has long administered her affairs.' Admiral Ding chose a loyal opium death. But by 1895 Admiral Ito was not the only mind in the East who thought there was something badly wrong with the Qing.

*　　　*　　　*

By the 1890s, back in Zeng Guofan's province of Hunan (the ancient state of Chu, from where, more recently, the new Confucian army, with its ideas of self-strengthening, had emerged), younger minds had been watching everything. Like most others in the heavenly lands, they concluded that the Qing had had their time. But looking at the situation from the perspective of Hunan, the young Hunanese had a more distinctive point of view. After thirty years of self-strengthening, *fuqiang* wealth and power had certainly defeated the Taiping rebels and rebuilt much of the country. But had anything really changed? In Beijing, another infant emperor had come to the throne in 1875, adopted by the Dowager Empress and titled Guangxu (Glorious Succession). Imperial rule, for all of the good it was doing anyone, seemed to have been reduced to a strange Manju family affair. Of course, one couldn't expect much from conquerors who had run out of steam. But were the Chinese self-strengtheners any different? *Fu qiang* was all very well for a while, but the heavenly lands had seen it all before. Sooner or later, wealth and power would always fix itself at the top and nothing but ignorance, poverty and blind dependence would settle again across the always much bigger bottom. While the latest Confucian fabric of order might bring a sparkle of pride to the eyes of the wealthy, underneath, the vast spreading foundations were composed of nothing more than the creaking shoulders of men who, across the imperial ages, had been taught to serve and never question.

In the Changsha capital of Hunan, highly educated young minds began to stretch their thoughts back to the ancient independence of the state of Chu. Thinking on the past, they saw in their mind's eye a happier world governed by men who had been allowed to talk to heaven whenever they wanted, and free to pursue their own destiny whatever it might be. They also remembered how the Chu state had initially been eaten away by conspiracies of Qin whispers, and then destroyed by the First Qin Emperor, vanishing as if it had been a dream. But had it really disappeared?

As Hunanese hearts dreamt of a long-lost past, someone pointed to a secret classic that been written during the tumultuous times of the Ming. Presenting a rather different perspective from that of the single heavenly mind, it was not a text that had ever made it into the imperial curriculum (in fact, it had been hidden in fear). But its words had been rediscovered and quietly published in 1829 under the tempting title of *The Treasures of Chu*. And what a treasure it was: a compendium of secret writings from the oldest Chu minds, prepared by a brave Hunanese scholar in the Ming dynasty, who had patched surviving fragments together and pulled them into a single secret text. Hidden for so long, it was these newly rediscovered words that had led Zeng Guofan's Hunanese friends to encourage him to take up the idea of raising his Confucian army in Hunan.

The Treasures of Chu might have inspired their fathers to raise an army to save the empire. But as far as younger minds in 1890s Hunan were concerned, those fathers had completely missed the point. The magic of Chu had nothing to do with restoring a colonising empire – and everything to do with the heart and courage of an independent state led by independent minds.

If one wanted to understand the wonder of the state of Chu, the young Hunanese argued, one had simply to look at the story of the heroic poet-prince, Qu Yuan. Born in 340 BCE, he became a selfless and patriotic minister who, quick to perceive the rising threat of the iron state of Qin, urged his king to confront the rising power a hundred years before the final devastating battle. But the king's heart had been turned by those in Chu whose palms were already being crossed with soft Qin gold. Qu Yuan had been sent into a heart-breaking exile. And from beyond the borders of his much-loved home, he had watched the early battles of Qin against Chu with the anguish of a man whose warning cries had been cut to silence. Despairing at the treachery and corruption, when the Chu capital fell to Qin Qu Yuan cast himself into the Miluo River, hoping to find his way to another world where ordinary men could still talk to heaven. Before he left this world, however, he crafted an epic description of his own battles with the greed and betrayal of this world and of his subsequent journey to heaven in search of something better. Memorised by scholars across the ages, it was a poem that had given two millennia of despairing heavenly hearts the courage to keep looking for another kind of world.

To the younger scholarly minds of Hunan, the greatest treasure of Chu was Qu Yuan himself. A poet prince who had given his home and all he loved to protect the greatness of Chu, he stood for the idea that every scholar had a duty to his inner heart and the greater good of being human. Betrayed by lesser men, he had left his Hunanese descendants with a lesson: heaven was nothing to do with an empire that flattened everything in its advance, and nothing at all to do with a 'unity' that did nothing but destroy. Quite the contrary: heaven was the power of an individual mind to talk directly to a ruler whenever one wanted, and to separate truth from lies. At the height of its power, the state of Chu had been a land where good ideas had been shared by men who could think for themselves – even the ideas of Laozi and Confucius had been read across Chu – and where bad ideas had been seen for what they were. Looking at the state of the present, the young minds decided that nearly two thousand years after Qin's treachery, it was time for Qu Yuan's Hunanese descendants to stand up for the truth.

What did the young Hunanese think was the truth? Taking Confucius' belief in the importance of *ren* as empathy, a young intellectual by the name of Tan Sitong set out the answer in a book called *Ren, On Humanity*. Resisting all pressure to prepare for the stifling imperial exams, Tan Sitong read widely, thought deeply and wrote his mind with little care for the consequences. On the Manju Qing's troubles with the foreign world, he observed that the only really bad thing the foreigners had brought was opium – and the Qing should have been strong enough to deal with that themselves. And as far as the last thirty years of the *zongli yamen* were concerned, the 'general management office' seemed to have achieved a triumph of literary twists (now presented as the high art of 'diplomatic discourse') without solving anything at all.

On the self-strengtheners, Tan Sitong's thoughts were even sharper: the only power worth having was the power of the people – and they had lost that long ago when the Yellow Emperor had become the Son of Heaven, when Zhuanxu had cut communications between heaven and earth for everyone except the emperor, and when the First Qin Emperor had forced the idea of a single top-down mind on everyone, including the people of Chu. Since then, it had been nothing but a line of power-hungry emperors whose greatest achievement had been the deadening of everyone's minds.

In Tan Sitong's opinion, while the Taiping rebel leader Hong Xiuquan had been madly muttering about Jesus Christ being his brother, his millions of followers had been desperate people simply looking for a change. And although Zeng Guofan had indeed been a remarkable man, he had stuck his Confucian colours to the wrong mast: shoring up the Qing when what was really needed was for the Manju to go home – and for the very idea of an empire to end. Misguidedly attaching themselves to Hong Xiuquan, the Taiping supporters had not, in their hearts, been wrong. The problem was that, after millennia of not thinking for themselves, the people had lost the ability to work out how to create and run a new world of their own. Having, long before, lost the ability to speak for themselves, the only thing left to them had been the wild rebellions in which the peasants had been regularly erupting over the previous two thousand years. For anyone with any surviving intellectual power whatsoever, the rebellions were an irrefutable confirmation that the very idea of *tianxia* all under heaven was a problem: without the power to talk to anyone above them, death and destruction had been the people's only possible voice. Self-strengthening was nothing but a dangerous delusion – with the only real 'strengthening' being that of the snare in which the people had been held for so long. The *fuqiang* wealth and power at the top was simply masking a *mangliu*, blindly floating misery, across the vast bottom: all in the pursuit of a great state that would eventually destroy not only man, but nature too.

For Tan Sitong, the time had come for China's youth to dig deep into the past and come up with something new: to go back to the most ancient of the golden ages, when human beings had minds of their own, and think. Awoken by the thinking experience, they could then forge a new future in which the Chinese people would rediscover the power of independent thought, and share that power with a state they felt they could call their own. The essence of it all was Confucius' idea of *ren* humanity, or empathy: put yourself in other people's shoes and in so doing understand that the future is a fabric composed of *everybody*'s dreams – not just a commanding plan imposed from the top. In fact, *ren* was neither more nor less than the art of 'being human'. And if (as seemed quite likely) all of this was too difficult to be achieved across the vast spread of the Da Qing empire, Tan suggested that the province of Hunan should just return to being an independent state of its own, from which position of independence it would then be able to inspire a wider revival of the old Chu way. And while it might take a revolution to secure Hunan's independence, once secured, other provinces would be able to follow. Newspapers might be able to light torches to touch thousands of minds, but the time for idle words alone was over. The world had changed and those who knew the truth about the past now had a duty to act. If there was to be a state, it should be able to think for itself. For a state to be able to think for itself, it needed a people who could think for themselves too. And in thinking for themselves, the people would need to ask themselves the question of what it meant to be human.

The self-strengtheners could not have been more shocked. After everything that the last fifty years had thrown at the Qing lands, finally *fuqiang* wealth and power were firmly in their grasp. Yes, of course, if one went back to the time of the Duke of Zhou and the Confucian classics, some of the greatest scholars had recognised that the people should be esteemed by their ruler – but no one, in any of those texts, had ever suggested that the people should 'esteem themselves'. Counting off all the challenges that the Da Qing empire faced (a formidable list), one of the leading self-strengtheners dismissed Tan's ideas as the 'delight of foolish people', based, he argued, on a fundamental misunderstanding of the heavenly fact that (like any phenomenon of nature) the only purpose of the people was to explain their feelings so that the ruler could set the right path. Any idea that there should be more than one ruler (or more than one opinion) was nothing less than treachery; and anyone who thought in such a way was clearly not Chinese.

*   *   *

Tan Sitong's was not the only mind thinking about a state populated by a people with independent minds. Nor was Hunan alone in thinking that it had once all been very different, and could yet be different again. Down in Guangdong there were other scholars, who, while seeing the need for change, had not yet given up on the imperial exams, and had also not yet given up on the possibility of a more peaceful evolution.

One was a thirty-seven-year-old man renowned for his mastery of the classics, even though his independent ideas had delivered a string of failures in the imperial exams; his name was Kang Youwei. Turning his vast classical expertise to a searing reconsideration of the Confucian texts, Kang had produced scholarly proof that the great literary edifice on which the heavenly empire had been built, was based on nothing but deceptions and lies. It had, indeed, all gone wrong when Zhuanxu cut communications between heaven and the people of the earth. But it was under the great deception of the Han dynasty that the rot had really set in. Bent on advancing the martial Wu Emperor's desire for a single heaven across the four directions, Han scholars had used the flames of the First Qin Emperor's earlier book burning as an excuse to rewrite the past. With this, the imperial scholars had excised an older idea of heaven as a reflection of the people – a heaven that hears and sees as the people hear and see – and replaced it with the idea, based on books of their own which claimed to be an authoritative Confucian canon, that heaven was whatever the Son of Heaven said it was. The imperial interpretation of 'what Confucius meant' had become a tyranny over everybody's minds. Pale imitations of past wisdom had been passed off as 'rediscovered' lost works, even as they had buried older debates about what it meant to be a state, what it meant to be a people, and what it meant to be human. Their own scholarly heads filled with the blind, and blinding, arrogance of the self-appointed wise, they had piled the people onto a raft of nonsense that had been compounded by the vanities of every successive dynasty over the past two thousand years. The early questions about a state and its people had not been solved – they had simply been buried under two millennia of imperial (and imperious) rule. And as for the even earlier question of what it meant to be a human being, that had simply been swept under the carpet of the state.

With the courage and conviction of a mind that questioned everything, Kang Youwei then advanced the greatest heresy to have been heard for two millennia or more: there was no duty to a mythical Son of Heaven, only the duty of a ruler to the people who were heaven's ears and eyes. And, had it not been for the Han dynasty, the people, being essentially sensible, would have been perfectly capable of working out an order of their own all by themselves. All they had needed was the freedom to take responsibility for themselves and for each other. With such a freedom, there would have been no need for a Qing empire at all, let alone a Ming, a Song, a Tang or a Han – just a world in which local communities governed themselves in one

Da Tong, Great Unity. Not the self-interested unity pursued by ambitious emperors keen to grab as much earth and sky as they could, but a truly great unity of all the people to rule themselves – and one that would eventually include everyone across the wider earth as well.

As Kang Youwei inked letters of his ideas for others to read, he acknowledged that the achievement of a *Da Tong* Great Unity might take a while and that it would only be achievable by progressing through stages. But in the end, he argued, a truly 'harmonious society' would appear. On the journey to this future utopia, the first and most important step was to get the people themselves to stop behaving like sheep. Somehow, tired hearts had to be transformed from the old fatalism (one that, after millennia of being silenced, had come to expect nothing more than whatever it was given) into a shining belief that destiny was something the people could build for themselves. Such a future, built by such a people, could not help but be glorious.

As to how to get from here to there, Kang Youwei was convinced that it should be achieved as peacefully as possible. Given where they were, Kang reasoned, the safest course would be to persuade the young Guangxu emperor that the time had come for the people to be released from the Confucian bonds of 'the family' (family as imperial state as well as family as household), and for self-cultivated individuals – whichever positions they occupied in either of the state or household hierarchies – to be able, respectfully, to speak their minds. But heaven was high and the emperor was far away: how could a simple imperial examination candidate catch the emperor's ear? Kang decided to start with a book of his own. He called it *Da Tong Shu, The Book of Great Unity*.

One of the oldest and most scholarly of the imperial examination candidates, Kang Youwei had acquired the respect of many of his peers and juniors. One of his juniors was a younger neighbour and fellow scholar by the name of Liang Qichao. Studying for the imperial exams (but struggling) Kang Youwei had become a tutor, and then a very close friend. While Kang worked on his *Book of Great Unity*, however, Liang thought less about the grand scheme of things and more about how to take the next practical steps. It seemed to him that the most immediate problem was that, after thousands of years of believing in a Son of Heaven, no one in Qing China had any idea about what a state of people – a 'nation' as the foreigners seemed to call it – really was. Certainly, since the Western barbarians' arrival had so forcefully demonstrated that the Qing lands were not the centrifugal middle of a flat world but, rather, a single point on a round globe, a lot of ink had been spilt in trying to understand what it meant to be a sovereign state. It had not taken the *zongli yamen* long to understand that it was something more than the ruling dynasty of the time, and that it also required a clear idea of territory. Yet it seemed to be a lot harder for them to get their heads around the idea that for a territory to be a nation it also had to have a people.

The Manju idea of *Da Qing Guo* (the state of the Great Qing Empire) was little more than an insulting description of the fact that the Manju had conquered China. Certainly, it could not be seen in any meaningful way as a description of the people who lived there. The foreign idea of 'China' was not much better – just the result of an ancient tangled twisting of the name of the upstart Qin state that had not only unified the Warring States but had 'unified' their people into nothing more than a million arms of a central imperial power. But the *tianxia* all under heaven idea had now been proven by Kang Youwei to be a dangerous myth that had swept away thousands of years of human minds. And the idea that the rest of the world should eventually be embraced within a perpetual expansion of an all-under-heaven dream that had been shown to be a lie, could surely now be seen to be ludicrous. If the foreigners had done nothing else good for China, at least they had surely made that madness a little more unlikely.

Even the new word for 'country' – *guojia*, 'state family' – which the *zongli yamen* had cobbled together like so many translations of foreign things, was a complete misunderstanding of what was required to be a nation. A *guo* (state) was nothing more or less than the old city-states from the time of the Zhou; and a *jia* (family) was simply the old idea of everyone being in their ordered place, with the emperor at the top, fathers next, sons (in order of birth) below, and women at everybody's beck and call. Where was there any mention of the people at large – the peasants – who, although highly esteemed by the Confucian hierarchy of occupations, never seemed to count?

For Liang Qichao, the solution was obvious, but it was clearly going to take a lot of hard work. The people were going to have to change the way that they saw themselves. Where to start? Tempting though it might be to think that the scholarly gentry might lead the way, judging by the last few thousand years, being literate – even magnificently literate – did not necessarily give one a sense of being human. In fact, it often seemed to do quite the opposite: a point that was obvious to anyone whose mind hadn't been twisted by an imperially Confucian education. Meanwhile, Liang noted, after thousands of years of being scattered like sheep, the now 450 million peasant people had become a sea of ignorance and superstition. And after an eternity of imperial divide and rule, the only thread between the scholars and the people was the Confucian idea that everyone's order depended on the peasants at the bottom doing whatever they were told. If the men and women now held captive under the Manju Qing were going to become a nation, and if the nation was going to have a people, everyone (scholars and peasants alike) was going to have to think again. The scholars would need to understand that they were but one part of a greater unity. And the peasants would need to understand that they were not just a hapless collection of arms and legs but had minds and a reason of their own. Obviously this was not going to be easy for anyone, and after so many millennia of imperial deception, there would be very few independent minds available to help. But if the so-called heavenly lands were going to move beyond the pattern of repeated rebellion, there was no other way. Looking at the state of the empire's affairs, there didn't seem to be a moment to lose.

Considering the past and the present, Liang Qichao concluded that the obvious first step would be to create small communities of people, with each community learning to apply their minds to local questions. Being local, and using all the faculties of being human, it was reasonable to suppose that they would care enough about the results that everyone, not just the gentry, would voluntarily roll up their sleeves and put their hearts and souls into the tasks at hand. Not at all to be confused with Zeng's self-strengtheners (who were simply little emperors in disguise), this would be a true 'people', who would include both the top and the bottom, working together side by side. Eventually, argued Liang Qichao, it was obvious that the empire would have to become a republic, and that a constitution would be required to ensure that no ruler could ever cut off communications with heaven again. In the meantime, Liang Qichao decided, it was time to take up the idea of a society of people who were committed to changing minds.

Where better to start than by splashing it across the printed press?

*   *   *

In 1897, Liang Qichao was invited to put his thoughts to the test. A group of young Hunanese had persuaded the reforming governor of Hunan to open a new kind of school in the provincial capital of Changsha. The group included Tan Sitong, the author of *On Humanity* – who had by now gone on to found Hunan's first newspaper. Within the classrooms of the new school, Chinese and Western studies were to be mixed, and a curriculum was to be taught that had nothing to do with the classical Confucian texts of the imperial exams and everything to do with the practical tasks of building a nation. Offered the position of lecturer-in-chief, Liang Qichao leapt at the chance and soon found himself swimming in the company of fellow minds. Conversations between Liang and Tan Sitong went on long into the night. Indeed, with so much to talk about, the pair rarely remembered to eat; and if one of them ever travelled, the letters they sent each other were enough to fill more than whatever suitcases they had taken along for the trip.

There was, indeed, a lot to talk about. As 1897 turned to 1898, things in Qing China could hardly have been worse. After the Beiyang fleet had been lost in the disastrous sea battle of early 1895, the Japanese victors had extracted a treaty of Shimonosekei, which (apart from the usual punishing reparations) put neighbouring Korea under the 'protective' wing of Japan, and rolled the island of Taiwan into the Japanese state. The Japanese were also allowed to establish industrial factories wherever they wanted on the mainland of the Qing. Given that all of the foreign powers had acquired a 'most favoured nation' right to enjoy any additional privileges that any of them might somehow acquire, this meant that all of the foreigners could do the same. Looking at the new map of Qing China (seemingly now a blank page as far as the rest of the world was concerned), the other foreigners had then decided that they needed a little more territory if things were going to remain in any kind of a balance. Russia demanded ports on the Yellow Sea coast of Liaodong. Britain decided that, in that case, it would need Weihaiwei, in the province of Shandong, on the opposite side of the Yellow Sea. Then, of course, Germany needed something on the Shandong coast as well (it chose Jiaozhou Bay, present-day Qingdao). And then, to the shock of almost everyone in China, and to the extreme consternation of Japan, Russian engineers, protected by a Russian army, began to lay a Trans-Siberian Railway right up to the Pacific Ocean and its inner 'Sea of Japan', ending at Russia's Siberian city of Vladivostok ('Ruler of the East'), directly facing Japan's northern island of Hokkaido.

Around the rest of the world, newspapers carried cartoons of a gigantic China feast where the 'Great Powers' gorged at their respective corners, and the remaining Chinese land became smaller by the day. At home, newspapers began to carry stories about an idea that had come out of Britain and had apparently swept across the rest of the Western world. The theory of a man named Charles Darwin, it described an evolutionary earth within which the fittest species were 'naturally selected' to survive. To this, a man called

Herbert Spencer had added the observation that it was not just species of plants and animals who were engaged in the process of 'natural selection' but the species of man as well. Indeed, according to Spencer, the world of man was engaged in a great battle for the 'survival of the fittest'. Putting the two ideas together, the foreign powers seemed to have concluded that only those who possessed the necessary military and human strength to win would survive. Many thought that it all sounded remarkably like the battle of the Warring States that had followed the collapse of the ancient Zhou dynasty. And it certainly explained why the foreigners were competing so hard with each other to eat China up. Some wondered whether the foreigners knew that what had followed the Warring States was the iron state of Qin.

Reading the articles, however, and pondering over the new ideas, many began to think that, while questions about nations and citizens were obviously important, a far more urgent question was now looming: if the foreigners kept battling over Chinese soil, how much longer could Qing China survive? And if there were not a Qing or a China, what would happen to the people who lived on these lands?

Gripped by the sense that time was running out not just for what the rest of the world called 'China', but for 'the Chinese' as well, Liang Qichao, Tan Sitong, Kang Youwei and other like-minded friends travelled to Beijing in January 1898. Another round of imperial examinations was due to be held – and with many Chinese contemplating the possibility of extinction, even the more imperially minded scholarly officials were beginning to appreciate the urgency of the situation. One, a high-ranking official and friend of Kang Youwei, promised to ensure that even though the empire only received memorials penned by senior officials, any suggestions that Kang and his colleagues might make would find their way to the personal attention of the Guangxu Emperor.

The friends prepared a series of memorials, modelled on the highly successful reforms of Meiji Japan, and each with a recommending strike of thunder designed to bring Qing China back from the brink. The first of the recommendations was that the Guangxu Emperor should throw off the dead hand of the Manju court (including that of his imperially adoptive mother, the Dowager Empress) and make it clear that he was committed to reform. The second was that a new 'office of ideas' should be set up at the gate to the imperial city, with the purpose of discovering new talent and ideas – and making sure those ideas got past the bulwarks of bureaucracy to the emperor. The third was that a new 'bureau of government reorganisation' should be established to create a blueprint for a host of institutional changes, which, complete with a 'government of all the talents', would be committed to the eventual achievement of a National Assembly, with rule through the law of a constitution rather than by the unbridled power of a single imperial mind.

Reading the memorials, the Guangxu Emperor decided to take advantage of a temporary absence of the Dowager Empress (on holiday at a new Summer Palace built in the outskirts of Beijing), and act. In June 1898, an imperial edict announced that Qing China would henceforth pursue a policy of root and branch reform. In the following days, Kang Youwei was summoned to the Forbidden City to meet and talk with the emperor; and in the weeks that followed an astonishing cascade of reforming edicts was announced. A number of them were accompanied by appointments that leap-frogged Kang, Liang Qichao and other scholarly youths into senior positions of power. Rafts of imperial rot were addressed. The imperial examinations were to be rescued from the cloying classics by a new attention to 'substantial studies': subjects such as current affairs, that might help in the governing of a country. New schools, and new curricula for all schools, were to be created, all teaching the mathematics and science on which the foreign barbarians had built their sovereign states. Wasteful and obstructive ministries were to be abolished, with self-interested self-strengtheners to be removed from their helms. All ministries were to submit any proposals to the rigour of a national budget. Last, but by no means least, the Beiyang navy was to be replaced with a new fleet, this time supplied with proper ordnance and equipped with men who were trained in how to use it. The bigger ideas of a National Assembly and a constitution were not immediately accepted but, looking at all of the other edicts, few doubted that they would eventually find their time.

For those who liked to peer into the shadows, it was obvious that the emperor had entered uncharted and dangerous waters. But over the summer of 1898, hope rose like spring. Quite apart from the youthful ideas that began to populate the dusty Qing bureaucracy, from across the land paper messages flooded into the new 'office of ideas'. Some of the messages were exquisitely brushed by the most educated of hands. Others, inked in big, clumsy characters, had obviously been painted by the working fists of farmers and fishermen. Hands or fists, all had been written from the heart.

For a hundred magical days, Beijing and the towns and fields of the great Qing empire sparkled like the stars. And then, on 19 September 1898, the

Dowager Empress appeared in the Forbidden City cloaked in a cloud of rage. Alerted by a senior group of self-strengtheners, who saw their new Confucian world about to be reformed away, she had broken off her holiday and raced the imperial carriages back to the Pole Star of the empire.

The imperial city held its breath, waiting for the storm to break. Within two days, another edict appeared in the name of the Guangxu Emperor: no sparkling dream but a kowtow confession that, although nominally the Son of Heaven, he was clearly not fit to rule. The edict concluded with the announcement that, after repeated supplications, the Dowager Empress had graciously agreed to resume the regency of his youth. The edict issued, the Guangxu Emperor was then confined to the Forbidden City, from which he would never again be permitted to have a conversation with an outside mind. The heady edicts of the hundred-day summer were cancelled; and imperial orders were issued for the arrest and execution of the memorialists, as well as any other scholars who, having been in Beijing for the imperial examinations, might have been party to the plot.

Most of the memorialists and scholars, including Kang Youwei and Liang Qichao, managed to escape, fleeing to Japan where the Meiji reforms had created a number of schools and colleges ready and willing to share their new ideas with brave new Chinese minds.

Most, but not all. Tan Sitong had stayed behind, determined to stand his independent ground. On 24 September, he was arrested. Three days later, his mind was swept from its body with the swift stroke of an imperial sword.

*　　*　　*

In exile, the memorialists travelled along similar but different paths. Kang Youwei scoured the seas, looking for men who might be able to help him rescue the emperor from his palace prison and, in so doing, throw China and its people a lifeline. In 1900, he attempted to raise rebellions in the city of Hankou and the province of Anhui. But lines of communication got tangled up with distance, and yet another group of martyrs fell to the imperial sword. The losses were painful but Kang did not give up.

Meanwhile, Liang Qichao, now in the more open schools of Japan, set about exploring what the rest of the world had to say about how to be a citizen. Many of the other memorialists followed him, increasingly joined by a rising tide of youth looking for any and all ideas that might save the independence of their country and their own minds. As part of the journey of learning, in 1902 he launched a new journal with the title: *Xin Min, New Citizen*. Full of articles on every imaginable independent idea, it was regularly posted back to China for those at home to read. Safe in exile, Liang wrote prodigiously and questioned even more: what was it that made a nation, and how did a people fit in?

In 1903, keen to understand the land of freedom in which President Lincoln had made the now-famous 1863 Gettysburg Address, Liang Qichao travelled to America. 'Government of the people, by the people, for the people': a fistful of words that had not only changed America but had also deeply touched Chinese hearts who, across the separating Pacific Ocean, had heard it as a whisper. But once in America, and observing powerful men engaged in what seemed to be their own form of self-strengthening, Liang Qichao had been unconvinced. America's freedom from an imperial ruler seemed to have resulted in rule by its own self-strengthened rich. And looking at the streets of New York, it seemed to him that freedom had come at such a cost to equality that it did not appear to be at all the kind of freedom that the Chinese people needed.

While Liang Qichao retained his respect for the American ideal, he noted carefully that if even America, with all of its great regard for the people, could not manage to create both freedom *and* equality, then China had better beware.

* * *

Back in Qing China, as the shock of the palace coup of 1898 gave way to an anxious 1899, it was as clear as ever that it was not only a library of scholars who would have to understand the need for change if the Chinese lands and the Chinese people were to survive. Black and white newspapers, launched from the extraterritorial safety of Shanghai but read up and down the country, were now spreading the fears of thousands, for everyone to read.

The newspapers were also carrying reports of a new army of patriotic rebels, who had decided that enough was enough. Rising in a rage from the north-east (now home to British Weihaiwei and German Qingdao, not to mention a host of missionaries off on frolics of their own), the rebels declared that it was time the foreigners left – and if the Manju Qing could not get rid of them, they would do it themselves with their 'boxing' fists. To those who looked carefully, the usual sparks of human portents had been present for a while: a flood, a drought, a famine – all on lands where local cotton had lost its market to foreign imports of cheaper factory cloth, and where families who had once had a spinning wheel to cling to now had nothing but dust. To the 'Boxers', however, the greatest culprits were the foreign missionary devils. Free to go wherever they wanted, protected by the talisman of an 'extraterritoriality' that meant they were immune to the local justice of a magistrate, they had dug themselves into villages across the north, insisting that the kitchen gods be ousted, that the temple festivals be closed, and that anyone who converted to Christianity should be subject only to the order of their God.

With the missionaries waving their treaty-given rights in everyone's faces, feuds had followed. In missionary-occupied villages, the rules of the land had been replaced by the 'laws of God', applied by men who could not speak Chinese and who had no idea about the relationship between a name and a purpose, let alone the Chinese principles of the family.

Hardly surprisingly, heaven had become extremely upset and, of course, the rains had failed. Hunger had begun to prowl, swiftly followed by the rise of new brotherhoods of men. Spirits were called upon, and a school of ('plum flower') boxing had been founded to give even the poorest man a transforming confidence in his ability to fight. Rooted in millennia of mixed-up Daoist and Buddhist beliefs, the brotherhoods of men also discovered magical talismans and 'invulnerability charms' guaranteed to protect their simple boxing fists against foreign guns.

Armed with the combined powers of Laozi, Buddha and Guan Yu (the god of war, who never failed to protect the weakest), the leaders of 'the Boxers' urged them to fling the foreigners out of the land: rip up the railway lines that Russia was laying across the north-east; smash the telegraph poles with which the foreigners seemed to be communicating with each other at the speed of light; and wherever, and however they could, apply their fists to throw the foreign devils out. A forgotten people on forgotten fields of misery, most – peasants and small landlords alike – saw the Boxers as heroes from the stuff of the old stories. Propelled by the energies of so many nightmares, the various brotherhoods swept across the north-east, like a surging ocean.

In June 1900, the tide of the Boxers began to lap at the edges of Beijing. From the seclusion of a new Summer Palace, and with not much else left for the weakened empire to rely upon, the Dowager Empress decided that it must be a gift from heaven. Declaring that they should be allowed to try their magic in defence of the Qing, she offered the services of the surviving imperial army to help. Aghast that the Qing were prepared to unleash a killing tide of boxing rebels on any and all foreign souls, the foreign powers turned their embassies into fortresses and prepared for a vanquishing war.

Over the next two months, forty-five thousand foreign troops were poured into the treaty-port of Tianjin, commanded to fight their rescuing way to Beijing and, as they advanced, to defeat Boxer rebels and imperial troops alike. Eventually, Beijing was reached and the embassies were liberated. But by the time the foreign troops had command of the city, hundreds of foreigners and thousands of Chinese Christians (not to mention tens of thousands of Boxers and others caught up in the fray) had been killed. In a chilling confirmation, if ever one were needed, that the foreigners were truly nothing more than barbarians, the foreign troops then sacked Beijing. As the city burnt with flames of rage, the foreign powers composedly sat down to compile their more formal demands: nine hundred million taels of silver, including interest, to be paid over thirty-nine years, with customs duties and taxes as guarantees; executions of Boxer rebels and of senior officials who had supported them; a moratorium on imports of arms; and twelve more cities to be opened up for foreign occupation.

From his exile, Kang Youwei noted that, amid the great foreign insistence that desperate peasants be executed, not one of the foreign powers had taken the opportunity to request the release of the imprisoned Guangxu Emperor. For Liang Qichao, it was just another example of what happened when a territory was seen as nothing other than a conquest, and when a people had no voice.

In the months and years that followed, China's youth flooded out of the country. Having given up on the empire and its examinations, many of the voyagers were now 'independent scholars': students looking for anything to help them save their country. Most found their way to Japan: geographically close, grounded in similar Confucian ideas, and with a written language that had been heavily influenced by the characters of Chinese. So many students went to Tokyo that the headmaster of the city's Higher Normal School opened a special academy for them, with a curriculum designed to 'strengthen China'. Deeply thoughtful about what the Chinese might need, the curriculum included not only instruction in the Japanese language necessary to enable them to read the vast libraries of Western texts, which Meiji Japan had translated (much easier than learning to read them in English), but a host of Western subjects designed to strengthen the students' forces for the tasks ahead: science for the mind, morality for the heart, and physical education for the body.

Not all of the voyagers went to Japan. Britain and France were popular destinations, as was the American power whose forceful example had so deeply influenced Japan. And not all of the voyagers, wherever they went, were travelling under their own steam. After the dust of the Boxer rebellion had settled, America converted some of the 'Boxer reparations' it received into scholarships for Chinese 'Boxer scholars' to study the new and transforming sciences of America. And the Qing empire sent a number of students to learn the special skills of Western self-strengthening: the kind of skills that had won Japan the Battle of Weihaiwei (and destroyed the Beiyang navy), while putting Western boats and railways on Chinese rivers and land. Whatever the origins of the students, by 1906, eight thousand of them – independent scholars, Boxer scholars, imperial students – had not only floated to Japan but on to bigger beacons of the wider world.

Encountering the outside world, the students read and learnt beyond the imagination of their fathers. More importantly, whether independent or imperially sponsored, they found a common conversation among themselves as well. With Qing China seemingly about to sink, they stretched their minds as far as they possibly could in the desperate hope of saving their Qing-conquered land. And as they were learning, they set about creating societies that would share the new knowledge, and hopefully also begin the process of change upon which the survival of their homeland would depend.

Works read in foreign languages were translated into Chinese and posted home, for friends and relations to read, and for newspapers to print. There was a wealth of ideas to be found among the great mind-changing foreign texts. One had been penned by a man called Ma-ke-si (Marx) whose utopian idea for a new world seemed to have a lot in common not only with Kang Youwei's *Da Tong* Great Unity, but also with the ancient dreams of a golden age of *taiping* great peace, where all men would be equals. In 1905, a wave of Marx-inspired strikes and rebellions washed across Russia and a political party following Marx's thinking almost achieved a revolution. In 1906, a Marxist 'Communist' Party was founded in Tokyo – and Marx's *Communist Manifesto* was translated into Chinese. In the same year, in Paris, a group of Chinese students established an anarchist society, which they called 'New World'.

To the students, it seemed that it was not only China that was changing, but everywhere. And while Qing China seemed to be at particular risk of drowning, the idea of a people rising up to save their country and themselves

213

seemed to have spread well beyond the Chinese lands to include all four of the directions of the world.

* * *

By the early 1900s, while Chinese students were learning about revolution abroad, young minds at home were thinking about raising a revolution of their own. Their numbers were being strengthened by returning students from Japan and the West. But many were beneficiaries of a modernisation of schools and academies that the Dowager Empress and the imperial self-strengtheners had decided to create in a desperate attempt to shore up the flagging fortunes of the Qing (a belated recognition that while change was challenging, a continuation of the past was perilous).

Many of the most questioning minds were to be found in Hunan's capital, Changsha, where the idea of education for independence rather than exams had already taken root. Inspired by both the ancient poet-prince Qu Yuan and the more recent Tan Sitong and his work *On Humanity*, the goal of Hunan's youth was first to prise Hunan's lands out of the grasping and incompetent hands of the Qing and then, province by province, to rescue the rest of China as well. Comparing themselves and their situation to the battle between Sparta and Athens, they dreamt of an independent 'nation', which would start at the bottom instead of the top. Qu Yuan was to be vindicated and Tan Sitong's dream was to come true: two thousand years of imperial top-down bureaucracy was to give way to a republic that, founded by and for its people, would be able to stand as strong as the greatest mountain. From village to county to province, each ascending level of human community would have its own self-governing order. And at the root of it all would be a people who would be given the first and greatest quality of a 'citizen': the ability to govern themselves. In 1903, drawing on an American work, *On Civil Liberty and Self-Government*, read in the usual translated Japanese and prefaced by none less than the president of Yale University, they set out a plan for the self-government of Hunan – and decided to found a revolutionary society to bring their dream to life.

Recognising that any 'revival' of Hunan (let alone the whole of China) would require a fight, and taking a leaf out of the now-numerous revolutionary Russian texts, the young Hunanese also founded a Citizens' Military Education Society. Dedicated to teaching the art of assassination, it set the Dowager Empress Cixi firmly in its sights.

Over the first years of the new century, the young Hunanese reached out to anyone and everyone who might be able to help: patriotic Hunanese merchant-gentry with funds to spare, and ancient brotherhoods of men committed to getting rid of the Qing. Successful assassinations turned out to be more difficult than they had imagined. But while they did not succeed in blasting the Qing out of China, or even assassinating Cixi, they did bump into a man who thought he might be able to help. A Chinese, born in Guangdong, his name was Sun Yatsen.

Educated in Hong Kong and in the then still independent island of Hawaii, Sun Yatsen had had an eclectic childhood, one that had given him an enviable eloquence in the English language, and roots in communities of overseas Chinese in the Pacific West. Seeming to be a magical bridge to the wider world, through his Pacific links, he had become closely acquainted with a 'lost' world of Chinese: men and women who had been sailing away from the lands of China ever since the times of the Tang, the Song and the Ming. Long the stuff of fantasy, it turned out that while many of them had gone on to make fortunes across Asia, a number had also found their way to wealth across the Pacific. Of course, the vast majority, those who had left in the last fifty years, had travelled as labourers, indentured to the mines and plantations of foreign empires. Some, however, applying both the same *chi ku* ability to eat bitterness that had sustained Hankou's labourers, and the Confucian principles that Zeng Guofan had used to raise his Xiang Army, had become wealthy traders, and even industrialists. And while many of those crossing the Pacific had found their fortunes in America, a number, including many of the most successful, had stopped in Hawaii, keeping their links with all.

Shocked by the rising chaos of the Qing, Sun Yatsen, like many other Chinese overseas, had watched events in Qing China with as much concern as the students. In 1891, supported by the funds of wealthy Hawaiian Chinese, he had founded a Revive China Society. Then, in 1896, calling on the Chinese embassy during a visit to London, he had been whisked off the street by secret forces loyal to the Qing. Eventually, Sun had been released and, writing a book about his kidnapping, he had become a Chinese hero, instantly recognisable around the world. Having held his breath in hope across the hundred days of the Guangxu Emperor's short-lived reforms, like Kang Youwei, Sun had tried to instigate a revolution. Without schools of willing students to hand, he had then reached out to one of the strongest of China's secretive brotherhoods: the Heaven and Earth Society. While

Sun's uprisings were no more successful than Kang Youwei's, his powers of overseas funding – incalculably heightened by the fame of his kidnapping – were far greater than those of any students at home.

Plotting his revolution, Sun Yatsen was as aware as Liang Qichao that if China was to change, it would need to find its people. But while Liang Qichao tried to understand the mechanics of *building* a people, Sun, more familiar with the West, turned to America and the ideas of Abraham Lincoln: ideas which were much more concerned with the question of the government of a people who already existed, rather than the awakening of a people in the first place. Touching only lightly on the vast difference between the nameless bitterness-eating bodies spread across the fields, and those migrant hands that had already managed to get themselves to America, Sun repeated Lincoln's mantra: 'Governance of the people, by the people, and for the people'. Rephrasing it as three breath-catching principles for a new China, he declared that it was time for the country to raise up a *minzu* people, who would be conscious of being a nation, a *minquan* republican government which would be guided by a constitution, and a *minsheng* people's state to provide for the livelihoods of everyone. Rich in foreign connections, but poor in links to the youthful energies of mainland China, when Sun Yatsen heard of the Hunan students and their dreams of revolution, he saw an obvious opportunity to build a more united force.

The Hunanese students were less enthusiastic. With little access to money, they were certainly struggling to get their dreams off the ground. But when Sun suggested that they join together, many thought it a distinctly bad idea. While Sun was looking for a new China, the students were looking for a Hunanese independence, out of which might *later* come the independence of the greater Chinese people, not only from the Manju Qing, but also from the ancient imperial deceptions that had so dulled everyone's minds. Divided, other students argued that while Sun might not have a clear enough understanding of the situation on the ground, he obviously had the power of a patter and a world of wealthy connections, both of which could help Hunan succeed. The rest of China might not yet be ready, but if Sun could help Hunan recover its independence, what did it matter if the wider Chinese dream had to be postponed?

To many of the students, however, Sun's vision was not only vague, but dangerous. A state of all the Chinese people when no one seemed to know who the 'Chinese people' were and a number did not seem to care? Notwithstanding a lot of complaining, and with allowances made for a few exceptions, the scholarly class did not seem to be all that anxious to throw off the tyranny that had bound them to emperor and empire for the last two thousand years. True, the Hunanese did not have much beyond their hearts, but in those hearts, they held a strong sense of who they were and what they wanted. Where the myriad of Chinese people were often described as a scattered tray of sand, Hunan was a firm foundation. And where many Chinese, scholars and peasants alike, often seemed to be a flock of sheep-in-bondage, always looking for a Great Man ruler who could come to their rescue, the young Hunanese were nothing if not clear about their dream of Hunan as an independent state, grounded on the idea of individuals whose independent minds were both a value in themselves and a value for the state as well.

In the end, the collapse of yet another Hunan rebellion in 1905 tipped the scales in Sun's favour and the two forces combined to create a *Tongmenghui*, United Alliance Society, to defeat the Qing. But the divisions remained and few (at least in Hunan) were in any doubt that Sun's dream was dangerously underdeveloped. Nor were they in any doubt that the United Alliance Society they had agreed to was united for one thing and one thing only: the violence necessary to bring a final end to the rule of the Manju Qing.

*　　*　　*

While the revolutionaries had been searching for success, the self-strengtheners had eventually come to realise that the Manju Qing were running out of ideas. In the aftermath of the Boxer rebellion and the foreign invasion that had followed in its wake, there had been no army left to speak of. And with foreigners having forcibly secured the right to pour their own capital and equipment into China to create fortunes of their own, some of the self-strengtheners began to see that while Kang Youwei's ideas of a popular *Da Tong* Great Unity, were clearly extreme, he had been right in his insistence that reform was urgently required. A few had even gone so far as to suggest that some of his more practical ideas might have a grain of sense. Obviously the one about local self-governance was out of the question: no one was going to contemplate the chaos of 450 million Chinese specks of sand deciding what to do for themselves. But some of his more practical suggestions might make for a stronger empire – one better able to stand firm against the foreigners, as well as against any Chinese who had got the wrong end of the stick.

From 1901, under the influence of the self-strengtheners, a new series of edicts had begun to appear, reintroducing many of the changes Kang Youwei had originally suggested (and for which the Guangxu Emperor remained under palace arrest). Obviously, the most important place to start had been with the money. With China's fortunes now mortgaged to the foreign powers seemingly until kingdom come, it had been clearer than ever that only the gentry merchants would be able to finance any of the necessary changes – and that, as usual, all of the work would need to be done by the bitterness-eating peasants. This time, however, the self-strengtheners were to apply their talents less to the promotion of their own individual interests and more to strengthening the empire.

The old guilds (of Hankou and everywhere else) were to be organised into 'chambers of commerce'; and, given the importance of trade and new industries in the strengthening of China, the chambers of commerce would be closely bound to the state. A new and better army was also to be raised; and considering the travails of recent years, police forces were to be introduced as well. These had been obvious improvements. But Kang Youwei and the memorialists had also been right about the importance of ideas, and the need for a new bureaucracy with a more open mind. A new Bureau of Government Affairs was to be established to receive ideas from anyone and everyone, and to think (in a truer Confucian spirit) about which ones might work. Alongside it, a host of new ministries were to be created: with good practical ideas once identified, the grand bureaucracy could demonstrate its own new ability to think beyond the classics and start getting on top of everything. The imperial examinations, already modified, would be abolished altogether, replaced with modern schools designed to teach the best of what was Chinese and foreign, with the same kind of firm focus on science and engineering skills that had clearly carried the foreign powers to such conquering heights. And, given that the central imperial state was the most important ship of all, the provinces were told to dig deeply into their pockets, and start to pay off the imperial debt. Where more money was needed, taxes would have to rise – and if the taxes were not enough, then more money would simply have to be printed.

To the astonishment of all, even the memorialists' idea of representative public assemblies was floated: places where locally elected people could gather together and express their views. Of course, Kang Youwei had not got that quite right. Naturally, all of those 'elected' would have to come from a pool of people who had been carefully selected before anyone could choose to vote for them. And any decisions that the voters might make would have to be sent up to Beijing for the careful consideration of the imperial bureaucracy before any confirmation could be made. Heaven, obviously, would always know best.

From within the courtyards of the Forbidden City, it had all seemed like an excellent idea. And it had certainly seemed to be an improvement to many of the old self-strengtheners outside. But, seemingly oblivious to the revolutionary plots around them, as the years of the first decade passed, some of its wider enthusiasts began to have second thoughts. Taxes seemed to be rising by the month and, with new presses printing money, the value of the Qing's currency seemed to be falling through the floor. Pockets shrinking, a new selfishness began to rise. In the countryside, gentry-merchant owners of estates, anxious to shore up their family fortunes, set their fields to producing whatever cash crops the outside world wanted to buy, leaving peasant mouths to find their own food.

Meanwhile, in the expanding towns and cities, a new generation of the rich was taking root: country gentry who had left the land to find new fortunes, merchants whose wealth continued to soar on an empire of trade, and industrialists – who were mainly traders who had decided to invest their profits in factory futures. Even literary talents, once restricted to the imperial exams, were now turning their attention to the making of money.

Factories began to rise, more private hands began to bank, new steaming ventures of the boat variety shipped goods across the land and abroad. Peasants who had failed in the fields flooded into the towns and cities in a desperate pursuit of work. Many, cheap and long trained in eating bitterness, there seemed to be no end to the hours they were willing to work. And then there were the foreigners – now trading and raising factories of their own. Although, as the Hankou minds had so presciently predicted, most of them had turned out to be just another opportunity. Hardly seeming to know up from down when they ventured out of their coastal enclaves, they usually left the running of their businesses to the locals, and it was naturally the locals who decided how much of the profits to share.

Some thought that the only real problem was the self-strengtheners who, notwithstanding the new imperial edicts, were once again weaving empires of selfish wealth within the reforms. Self-strengthening for the state was once again turning into self-strengthening for the officials of the state. Had it ever been otherwise? With millennia of experience behind them, and little understanding of the present, the gentry and the officials were picking up the tried and tested measures that had yielded imperial scales of riches across the millennia of the past.

Others saw a new and more worrying version of an older problem. As new industrial wealth had risen to city rafters, a growing tide of peasant hands had become city labourers; squeezed together within the city walls, they were now grumbling for higher conditions. Calls for days off and better wages had become a mantra, and every now and then a rabble-rousing strike would break out, auguring much bigger and darker clouds. While the ship of the imperial state was congratulating itself on its self-strengthening wisdom, and while the gentry-merchants were working on managing the ambitions of the self-strengthening officials, a small but rising number of voices was beginning to wonder if the ship could possibly withstand a storm. The answer, whispered at first, then inked a little louder in the newspapers, was that any ship was only as worthy as its captain and its crew.

With the Dowager Empress Cixi as captain, and with the crew a host of self-strengtheners who were completely cut off from the scattered specks of the people, unless someone found a way to turn the people into citizens, and soon, it would be only a matter of time before everything ended up in a wreck.

* * *

In 1908 the Dowager Empress died, departing from this world only a day after the death of the still-captive Guangxu Emperor. Many quietly noted the coincidence of timing, which only she would have been able to explain. A two-year-old Manju prince (Pu Yi) was gently placed upon the dragon throne as the Xuantong (Declaring Unity) Emperor. Yet another regency began, this one under the cautious reins of the young boy's father, Prince Chun. Eyebrows were raised and hearts sighed.

Later that year, however, just as imperially reforming edicts had promised, the first steps were taken towards establishing a National Assembly in Beijing, with a written constitution promised by 1917. And before the end of the year, twenty-two provinces held elections to see which voices would be chosen to represent them. Anyone was able to stand – as long as they had been pre-selected by the imperial bureaucracy. And anyone over twenty-five was able to vote – as long as they had a serious education or a pile of silver. Once elected to provincial assemblies, in the following year, the assemblies would meet to elect from among their own number those who would then go on to be representatives in the promised National Assembly. No one, however, was quite clear how any of this was expected to work – the constitution would not appear for another nine years.

A few inconvenient student voices argued that, given the delays, everyone should take control of everything and organise it themselves. This was not at all what the imperial state wanted to hear; neither indeed did many conservative others think it sounded like a good idea. By this time, however, more serious critics had decided that, interesting though the imperial reforms might be, they were too little, too late, and obviously the work of an empire that had not yet understood the root cause of its problems. With Sun Yatsen establishing secret branches of the United Alliance Society abroad, chests of silver were flooding in to fund the revolutionary attempts of brothers at home. As more secret branches of the society had been established within China, uprisings were being shaken into action, guns had been stashed in corners, assassins had been trained, and bombs had been prepared. The ranks of the members were flooded not only with revolutionary students, but with older others who had lost their imperial illusions – including a number of military men. They were also flooded with brotherhoods of blood, which had long been preparing for war against the Qing: the Heaven and Earth Society and the White Lotus among many others, all promoting one version or another of the three ancient harmonies of heaven, earth and man. So many were these brotherhoods that the missionaries who came across them had given them all the old Greek name for 'three': the Triads. Whatever name they marched under, the swelling number of revolutionaries was increasingly being wrapped up into the secret heavenly families, led by men who were turning everyone's desperation into a power of their own.

*　　*　　*

In the event, the revolution was an accident. On 9 October 1911, just across the river from Hankou, in the Wuchang capital of Hubei (right next door to the province of Hunan), a revolutionary bomb-in-the-making exploded in an unlucky pair of hands. As injured underground revolutionaries were rushed to hospital, imperial troops swarmed to what had until then been a secret headquarters. Arriving at the premises, they executed three of the surviving revolutionaries summarily on the spot. Registers containing the names of other members (closed books that included the names of many imperial soldiers and their officers) were then swept off for inspection. Those who managed to escape – and particularly those revolutionaries in the ranks of the army – realised that even though the bomb had jumped the revolutionary gun, if they did not rise to the occasion now, everyone whose name was in the registers would be damned.

Before the light of 11 October found its dawn, the 8th Battalion of Wuchang Engineers mutinied, with transport and artillery units rushing to join them. By the end of the day, the chambers of commerce had pledged their support (and much of their silver), and Wuchang became China's first revolutionary city. The entire province of Hubei then declared itself an independent republic, led by a rather reluctant general who, under the circumstances, felt he had little choice. Within two weeks, Hunan's own revolutionaries rose up and declared an independent state of their own. Across the following months, revolution by revolution, many of the other provinces followed suit. In America, raising money for the revolutionary cause, Sun Yatsen read about the explosions in the *Denver News*.

For a revolution, it was all remarkably peaceful – more so than many of the failed attempts that had gone before. Little blood was shed, and the overwhelming support of the army meant that order was largely maintained. Largely but not completely: after nearly three hundred years of conquest and the near-loss of the country, the massacres of Manju, which broke out by popular accord, could not be helped.

The only real problem was that since the revolution had taken even the revolutionaries by surprise it did not have a leader. And since the revolution did not have a leader, there was no one to talk to the new child-emperor; although it was reasonably clear to all that, even if consulted, neither the child-emperor nor his regent-father would have any idea of what to do. There was, however, an accomplished self-strengthener waiting darkly in the wings. The old commander of the Beiyang army, and a meddler whose past machinations had included the betrayal of the Guangxu Emperor's dangerous dreams to the Dowager Empress Cixi, he was a man whose ambition for power had few if any limits: his name was Yuan Shikai.

Pretending to be an honest broker, Yuan convened a meeting of the imperial government and the revolutionaries, at the end of which the young emperor issued the last of his imperial decrees. The lands of Qing China, including the lands of those provinces that had jumped the gun and declared an earlier independence, would become a republic, and Yuan Shikai would lead them until elections could be held at the end of the coming year.

On 12 February 1912, the emperor formally abdicated. Over the course of the remaining year, the National Assembly was returned to try to be of whatever service it could. Given that it had been intentionally created without the power to do anything, this was a feat that few, even in the assembly itself, had any confidence it would be able to achieve. And with a written constitution, with its promise of a rule of law, still five years away, it was obvious that it was not going to be of any immediate help. With the members of the assembly unclear, the population at large was even more in the dark. 'What is a republic?' was one popular question. Others included: 'Where has the emperor gone?' and 'When is he coming back?'

Sun Yatsen had recently returned from America, and many assumed that Yuan Shikai would yield in the face of his greater popular appeal. But the Beiyang army was now firmly in Yuan's hands, the 'independent provinces' were being ushered back into the fold, and no one who had read their history really imagined that Yuan would stand down without a fight.

Facing a constitutional crisis without a constitution, in the National Assembly, Sun called on the elected representatives to organise themselves into groups of ideas ('political parties') and raise the assembly arguments on which national political decisions could be forged. To start the ball rolling, he changed the name of the United Revolutionary Alliance to a *Guomindang* National People's Party, opening up its membership to anyone in the National Assembly who wanted to join.

Before long, everyone was launching parties – with banners of them fluttering in all directions. Many of the representatives did their best. But with so little experience, and representing so many different grains of sand, within the year almost everyone in the Assembly was hurling arrows at everyone else, regardless of which party they might technically have joined. Outside the National Assembly, puzzled observers looked on in dismay. And outside the heartlands of the Chinese people, those on the edges of what had been the mainstay of a Manju empire, and was now the Republic of China, decided to take their chance at an independence of their own. While a republican flag had been raised in the unifying colours of all of the five peoples whose lands had been embraced by the Manju (the Han descendants of the Yellow Emperor, the Mongols, the Tibetans, the Uighurs and even the Manju) the Mongols and the Tibetans stood up to say that they would rather find their futures on their own. (The Uighurs would have done the same if a warlord had not put them in their place.)

In the last months of the Chinese lunar year (across December 1912 and January 1913), elections were finally held. For all of the battling (or, perhaps, because of it), the *Guomindang* National People's Party won a clear majority. Sun Yatsen stood to be a popular president – and a rising revolutionary star within the young ranks of the *Guomindang* was confidently expected to become prime minister: his name was Song Jiaoren. But on 20 March 1913, while waiting for a train to take him from Shanghai to Beijing, Song fell to the bullet of an assassin's gun. Yuan Shikai's hand had not been on the trigger but whispers attached his name to the death.

By the end of the year, elections notwithstanding, Sun Yatsen was in exile in Japan, Yuan Shikai was still president – and, as president, he ordered the expulsion of the *Guomingdang* from the National Assembly. It did not really matter, because the following year, Yuan Shikai dissolved the Assembly altogether, declaring that the whole idea had been a terrible mistake: 'Too many arguments,' he observed, 'not enough results.' According to Yuan, the Chinese people were confused – even heaven was confused. It was time to go back to the old single top-down order of the past.

Critics of every colour were silenced, opinions were discouraged, newspapers were prohibited from publishing anything that might be detrimental to the 'republic's peace'. Across the country, military governors were appointed to each and every province, all reporting directly to the president. In 1914, as a war of the world broke out in Europe, Japan, allying itself with the British and the French, occupied German-held lands in the Chinese north. Less than a year later, it would follow up its occupation with a list of 'twenty-one demands' for wider power in the Chinese lands; demands which Yuan Shikai struggled to contain. In November 1915, a 'special' representative assembly was convened exclusively for the purpose of unanimously appointing Yuan Shikai as emperor of a new 'Chinese Empire'. 'A collection of persons makes a family,' the new emperor observed, 'and a collection of families makes a state.' But, in Yuan's imperial opinion, a republic would achieve nothing other than the destruction of all.

In early 1916, wrapped in the protection of an armoured car, and with imperial robes on order, Yuan Shikai travelled to the Temple of Heaven – the blue-roofed altar with which his Ming predecessors had reinterpreted the ancient Hall of Light. Following in the footsteps of every ancestor who had gone before him, Yuan obediently presented the sacrifices of earth to a waiting heaven above. With as little sense of irony as the emperors of the past, he then announced his imperial title: Hong Xian, Constitutional Abundance.

BOOK II

Speak in the language of the time in which you live.

Hu Shi (1891 – 1962)

PART 4

UP IN THE CITY

Our million hearts beating as one.

March of the Volunteers (written by the playwright Tian Han
in 1937; now the anthem of the People's Republic of China)

CHAPTER 1

MIDNIGHT

One by one, the white clouds set off to leave,
Vanishing into the distant oasis.

The Weak Flame of a Star, Xu Zhimo (1922)

Soft autumn winds blowing from the west, the train sped across the flat northern plains. Above, a bright blue rainless sky; all around, the vast expanse of a dry earth fending off the advances of a hungry desert. As steam billowed into temporary clouds, a whistle pierced the silence of the land. Passing camels loaded with coal lifted their heads and, from the windows of the train, excited eyes peered towards the horizon. There, at the edge of everything and nothing, was a vision like no other: the walls of a city appearing like a mirage. Destination in sight, the engine picked up its pace and soon guarding towers appeared, lapped with an ocean of yellow and green tiles, all sparkling in the sun of a rising day. Within an instant, or so it seemed, the thick walls of the *Zhengyang*, Gate of the Zenith South, stood before them: portals of power open for the day, terraces above floating towards the heavens.

Carriage doors eagerly opened, boxes and baskets clutched to anxious chests, feet of many descriptions touched the ground, some leathered in shoes, others embraced in soft cotton slippers, the smallest ones tipped with playful tigers – all were swept into the arriving tide and carried towards a waiting chaos outside. Silken robes rubbed shoulders with tailored trousers; bowler hats jostled with bare heads; military uniforms surged to the front. Once into the sparkling light of a 1918 day, chaos pushed and shoved. With passengers pouring on to the street, mules, carts and rickshaws edged ever closer in search of a fare. Then a gathering of engines scattered everyone to the side. Shining in their metallic glory, a pair of Dodges and what seemed to be a Citroën purred into waiting place: ready to float a sturdy warlord, a rising official or a 'money devil banker' smoothly off to a conversation or a club.

*　　*　　*

The Zhengyang Gate of the Zenith South had once been the foremost guardian of the imperial dragon, the boundary between the *nei cheng* Inner City heaven, and the *wai cheng* Outer City of the people's earth. The towering point at which every passing Chinese spirit had paused to observe the force of heaven, only the fewest of the few had ever entered through its portals, but whispers of the wonders of the Inner City had long flooded the crowded lanes of the Outer City of Beijing. A world of walls behind which sat the glittering pavilions of the greater family of the emperor: each arranged as courtyards of low buildings with tiled roofs of yellow or green; all sitting like squares on a chequerboard; the whole partitioned by narrow streets so straight that the eye could see from one end to the other.

Those few who had passed through the Zhengyang Gate into the Inner City had swiftly found themselves at the Gate of the Great Qing from which a 'thousand step way' – a dragonly avenue, which guarded by Manju bannermen and long enough to humble even the proudest heart led to the Tiananmen Gate of Heavenly Peace. Flanked by lions fixed in heavenly stone, across the top of the pillars of the gate hung a set of characters that every Chinese scholar knew by heart: *jieshou yutian, anbu zhiguo*, receive the mandate of heaven and peace will reign. Through the gate, trembling visitors entered the Imperial City within: a world of spreading gardens and contemplative courtyards. And then, ahead, the Meridian Gate: entrance to the 'purple', or 'vermilion', city beyond: a city forbidden to all. Set below the Pole Star and its surrounding *ziwei*, purple enclosure, constellation, it was a city wrapped within an Imperial City that was itself wrapped within the wider Inner City around; hidden behind walls within walls: the secret heart of the heavenly empire.

But that was before, when Beijing had a dragon emperor and heaven was a power before which everyone trembled, and most obeyed. By 1912, however, the six-year-old Manju who had once pretended to be the Son of Heaven had lost his imperial voice, silenced with the childish pleasures of a now echoing 'Forbidden City', which stood like a shadow of its former self. The scholarly officials had gone to serve the new Republic. Even the guarding Manju bannermen, now surplus to the reduced requirements, had found themselves cast into the Outer City, joined by Manju princes and princesses for whom the imperial world had become nothing but a dream. Reduced to the status of a barbarian prince who had lost even his own original Manju lands, floating on the fortunes of an uncertain world, the young emperor was protected only by an army of eunuchs, all bent on strengthening themselves with the treasures of five hundred years of imperial silk, jade and gold. With the walls of the Inner City already breached by a railway and roads, the wider Imperial City had soon been opened up to a public view: once-hidden courtyards and gardens were swept out of their dreams, and the Tiananmen Gate of Heavenly Peace was exposed to the city at large.

The winds had changed. Indeed, they had changed so much and so often that many wondered whether the idea of a heavenly order would ever return. And if it did return, whether the hope of a *ren* humanity (the Confucian principle that the Hunanese Tan Sitong had turned into a revolutionary dream) would still be alive. While the Japanese had held their ground in what had once been Germany's northern lands, Yuan Shikai's imperial reign had lasted less than a year. Within days of its announcement in late 1915, newspapers reported that the military governor of south-westerly Yunnan had declared the province's independence. Over the coming months, other southern provinces below the Yangzi followed suit, and continued to do so even after Yuan Shikai offered to cancel the imperial idea. With the south separating, and the idea of a single new empire on its way to an illusion, by June 1916, Yuan himself was dead. Beijing, now a Republican pearl, momentarily dropped into the hands of the same reluctant general who had been pressed to take the helm of the independent Hubei Republic after the 'accidental revolution' in 1911.

In 1917, the reluctant general was ousted by another, who declared the restoration of the Qing (and of the young emperor). Then a group of generals stormed Beijing, declaring the restoration of the Republic, and commanding the young emperor to abdicate once again. A 'new' National Assembly was convened which, since no one had had any time to call any elections, was simply populated by the same men who had been elected for the first one. Led by a general named Duan Qirui, most of them represented no other interests than their own.

Just as in the distant past of the Three Kingdoms, the generals had split, returning the provinces and cities to individual fiefdoms, each ruled by a warlord who dreamt of unifying everything, with himself on top. And then Sun Yatsen, returned from exile, resurrected the Guomindang in the south. In the messy mosaic of competing cannons, north and south divided.

In Beijing, the National Assembly continued to proclaim a republic, but the people were not convinced. With China once again a world of fiefdoms and warlords, what on earth could it possibly be a 'republic' of? Certainly nothing that seemed to have anything to do with the people. The lands of the north had become a particular question mark. Japan and Russia were still staring warily at each other over the barrel of China's vulnerable expanse. Russia was insisting on a Far East of its own, across lands that stretched to the lapping edges of the Pacific Ocean. Japan, which had sided with the British in the First World War (obviously so named by barbarians who had never heard of the ancient time of the Warring States) was insisting that the security of its island archipelago depended upon putting a stop to the relentless spread of the Western powers across the lands of the Chinese north. Meanwhile, representatives of the wider European powers were still quartered in the capital, not to mention being firmly anchored in the country's treaty ports. Chinese self-strengtheners had raised new industries in central and southern cities, but it was still Western banks that owned the foreign tracks of trains and telegraph lines that spread across the fields, and Western science that seemed to own so much of the wider Chinese world.

So desperate were the times that even the land itself seemed to be for sale, and certainly its people. In 1916, with the republican treasury in a parlous state – and doubtless a Republican pocket needing some cash – someone at the precarious top had had the bright idea of trading China's bitterness-eating labour for a victory deal: trenches were to be dug in France in exchange for a return of the northern Chinese lands that the Germans had taken in Jiaozhou Bay (present-day Qingdao), in the event that the Allies won the war. The deal struck, nearly a hundred thousand peasants had set sail from nearby British-controlled Weihaiwei. At the end of the war, with the British and French victorious over the Germans, popular Chinese hopes anticipated a rare reversal of Western territorial fortunes.

On the evening of 2 May 1919, Beijing waited with bated breath for the decision of a European conference that was to decide the fate of the northern lands. Hearing the news on the ground, Chinese journalists in Paris tapped out a telegram that would be everyone's despair: Europe's Versailles had decided that the German lands in China would be given to Japan. The people of Beijing first gasped in disbelief – then realised that, with each and every general out for himself, Duan Qirui, the general who controlled the northern military (and with it the National Assembly in Beijing), had secretly struck a different trade. In return for a Japanese advance of the softest of loans, not to mention a few personal arrangements, the once-German lands had been promised to Japan by the Republic itself.

Two days later, on 4 May, Beijing exploded in protests, led by a student youth that had come of age only to find its future had been traded across the sea. Less than a decade had passed since a revolution had been won (admittedly accidentally). But the gap between heaven and the people was as wide as ever, with the new heaven populated by a rapid succession of self-strengthening 'emperors' who were as keen as any of their ancestors to grab as much earth and sky as they could, even as they sold the heavenly lands from under the people's feet. Had China learnt nothing from its past?

Equipping themselves with banners, the students boldly proclaimed what they believed to be the greatest words of liberating wisdom discovered in studies abroad: 'Mr *Sai* Science', and 'Mr *De* Democracy'. Mr Science to ensure that the ideas of both the state and its people would be grounded in objectivity, rather than distorted by personal self-interest and ignorance. Mr Democracy to ensure that an independently minded people would be able to guarantee an independent state. Armed with outrage, they carried themselves on a throbbing tide to the edifice that seemed to make their point, the place where heaven met its earth: the Tiananmen Gate of Heavenly Peace. Once there, they were joined by multitudes: pressing hearts who had been pushing and pulling at everything just to make ends meet, teachers who shared the students' rage, and exploding souls whose enterprises had brought them riches, but whose country could not hold an honest peace.

By the end of 4 May, the home of the government minister most conspicuously responsible for the loss of the lands had been burnt to a cinder; and many of the students had been marched to jail. Before long, neighbouring northern warlords arrived to stamp a stronger authority across Beijing's rebellious streets.

In the months and years of chaos that followed, any surviving belief in a Republic vanished into a swirling world of warlording battles for a once-imperial capital that had become nothing more than a northern prize. At the end of 1924, the latest ruling northern warlord expelled the Manju prince, the last emperor, from the Forbidden City, where he had remained, clasped like a cast-off pearl, for so long; he also cancelled the National Assembly.

With warlords prowling, the flood of Beijing's once-heavenly wealth trickled to a stream, even as a tide of desperate refugees flocked to a city that was losing its walls. The palaces with all their imperial families and courtiers were turning to dust. The streams of heavenly retainers that had once kept everyone in silk had been cut asunder with the end of the empire. Across the wider city, everyone's diminishing savings had become the city's principal float. Scholars had been replaced by a new corps of 'Republican' officials. And as once-orderly streets were transformed into a chaos of competing claims, soldiers and beggars had captured the roads. Tan Sitong's old dream of a *ren* humanity, let alone the newer lodestars of science and democracy, seemed a long way away.

*   *   *

Dedicated to the service of the Son of Heaven, Beijing had always been a city unlike any other. Far away from the industrious citadels of Hankou and Changsha, never a bustling treaty port like Tianjin, Shanghai and Guangzhou, the production of the practical had never thrived in this capital set on a dry northern plain. While emperors had risen and fallen within the Imperial City, across the Outer City at large, it had been the crafting and consumption of luxury that had kept everyone afloat. Set behind grey walls, brushed by willow trees and passed by unwitting camels, the magnificent residences of once-scholarly officials had been a world of pavilions and courtyards, each with a name, a meaning and a delicate purpose, and all needing just the right furniture of a civilised life. With an ideal of 'five generations under a single roof', heads of households had commanded, and servants had procured: officials' hats and tailored gowns for the master of the house; silk slippers, feathered fans, embroidered skirts and jackets for wives; carved lacquer boxes and cloisonné vases for beauty; lanterns for light; paper and ink for painting; books for young and scholarly minds. Chattering in the streets as they went, maids had fluttered from their gates to procure the necessities of the scholarly courtyards: silk thread, reed mats, pig bristles, soap and candles for daily life; and mountains of duck, rice, pork and wines to keep the banquets flowing. And as the great households reached out for their requirements, in the *hutong* alleyways all around, the purveyors and makers of everything that the courtyards needed had crafted simple lives of their own.

By 1925, however, with the last emperor gone and his scholarly officials long stood down, many of the purveyors of imperial dreams had melted into the tides of pedlars, vegetable vendors and prostitutes, all looking for a living. Who could now be in need of an official's hat? And with their husbands' minds surplus to requirements, which scholarly wives could still afford silk slippers and embroidered skirts? Many, declaring Beijing an unlucky place, had floated south, particularly to the foreign emporium of Shanghai – where the promise of wealth rose on waves of industry and trade, protected by treaties and gunships which had become far more reliable anchors than those of the shifting Chinese state. Meanwhile, the old skills, passed from fathers to sons from the beginning of Beijing time, and rarely written down, were fading like memories.

As the past became a dream, though, the new was arriving everywhere – relentlessly. With the once-separate Inner and Outer cities now open to all, in the modern spirit of the times every ordering mind, whether Republican official or newly successful warlord, had a wild idea for transforming Beijing into a Paris, London or Berlin. As the Imperial and Inner cities were exposed to everyone's gaze, once-secluded avenues opened up for everybody's progress. The temples, from which a long succession of Sons of Heaven had dedicated the seasonal rituals and sacrifices, became, for a small entrance fee, public parks. Walls were breached or dismantled entirely. Gates that had guarded for hundreds of years were stood down to make way for the new. Free from the constraints of the walls and gates, the tracks of trains were matched with widened, asphalted roads; the trains themselves were soon followed by trams. Courtyards that had stood for generations found themselves swept away for the passage of a general's car. A telephone company brought distant voices into privileged homes (as often as not, with the conversation carrying sons and daughters off into dreams of new lives either in Shanghai or abroad). And as troops of warlords increasingly marched across the streets, the Forbidden City, relieved of its heavenly duties, became a museum.

Once governed by their own scholarly gentry, the people of Beijing found themselves not only under the corrupted orders of a Republican government, but under the barrels of warlords' guns. They also found themselves under the scrutiny of a novel phenomenon – a local 'Beijing government' which, working both with and around the warlords, seemed to think that its purpose was to tell everybody what to do. As the new government tried to re-imagine the city with an architecture fit for the new, even as spaces and vistas opened up, distances were shrunk by the new means of transport and communications. From within what had once been small pockets of Confucianly ordered people, everyone now emerged, blinking, into the new order of a single, and very earthly, city. In the new 'public interest', which only the government's officials or its police could define, the old Outer City and its people were pushed this way and that.

Shops that had served neighbouring imperial and official customers for two hundred years or more found themselves ousted by trams. Some sank with the fortunes of their once affluent clients; others moved to new avenues of consumption especially built in new streets with new names separated from old and now lost worlds. Wangfujing (named after the place where a 'Prince's Well' had once been) was one; Xidan (so-called after an elaborate 'West Gate' that had once stood in its place) was another. Suddenly, the brazen advertising of one's wares which flouted every Confucian principle, seemed essential for survival. Billboards appeared, full of the Western ABC alphabet that foreigners seemed to prefer. Electric lights were switched on to dazzle passing eyes. And anniversaries of establishment were regularly celebrated with a firecracking bang. Old stock was replaced with new – and the new was usually either foreign or produced in a part of China so far away that it might just as well have come from abroad. With everyone selling everything at any time of the day, night or year, even the order of the seasons was forgotten.

But as the shops called for greater custom, the market upon which they depended was following its people, and fading by the day. The old meaning, once threaded into the heart of Beijing, and into the very essence of what it meant to be a *Beijing ren*, Beijinger, had been cast to the wind. With so many sons and daughters departing for Shanghai, fewer and fewer families could claim 'five generations under a single roof'. And the names of the pavilions and the courtyards of the magnificent residences of once scholarly officials no longer corresponded to any kind of order.

Purposes lost, meanings, identities and even names struggled to survive. Temples found themselves converted into factories, or left to the birds: who was interested in talking to ancestors when the past had been revealed to be a lie? Lanes that had once carried so much chatter lost the crafts after which they had been named, and then fell silent. A number of the *hutong* alleys found that what had once been unique about them was scarcely even distinctive anymore: fourteen *jing'er*, wells; seven *tangzi*, ancestral temples; and sixteen *biandan*, carrying-pole, alleys. Many were obliged to change their names. Others found that the names of the past were no longer considered respectable enough for the new order of the 'public' world: *gou yiba*, Dog Tail Alley, was changed to *gao yibo*, Old Man with High Morality; *ji zhua*, Chicken Feet Lane, became *cui hu wan*, Emerald Flower Creed; even the *lu shi*, Donkey Market, was changed to *li shi*, Respect the Scholars bazaar. As the changes were painted onto the streets, though, Beijing's people kept the old names firmly in their hearts and on their lips – in the stubborn belief that clinging on to the human fabric of their past was the only way they could save the future.

The new Republican world even ate into the filial hearth of the family home. *Li* rituals with which sons had dedicated themselves to fathers, and a *zhi* knowledge devoted to studying the Confucian classics, had obviously lost their purpose. With the Son of Heaven a receding memory, which son was going to sacrifice himself for the greater family? And with imperial examinations long gone, what was the point in learning any classics? Indeed, with the classics revealed as nothing but a grand deception, who would want to read the words that had kept everyone in chains for two thousand years? The employment of classical tutors trickled to a stream, and the great *Xiao Jing*, *Classic of Filial Piety*, which had once governed everyone's position in the family like a rod of iron, gathered dust unopened, its lessons for children on what it meant to be Chinese cast aside, along with the past. For those who could afford the expense, the teachings of the *Xiao Jing* were replaced with new and different classes. Lessons on the English language that seemed to be everybody's future, were particularly popular, usually followed up with a place at one of the many new colleges that had been opened in Beijing. For those who could not afford the expense, libraries and lectures were offered by the government on a host of subjects, to which were added the chattering meetings of new societies and dedicated to the creation of a new Beijing, for a people who were clearly becoming new.

Sons and even daughters now looked outside the family to the possibilities of a more individual and modern success. Sons looked to new industrial or professional opportunities; daughters stepped out of their Confucian bonds to see themselves with opinions and futures of their own. Without an imperial treasury on which to depend, everyone in Beijing, other than a general, was looking for an income. It was not easy. The Republican government had few positions to offer in the city, and although some adventurous spirits had bravely opened factories, capital for industry was in short supply. Added to which, every line of production was exposed to the ravages of a much wider national market where competition was everything. No longer required within the courtyard households, small *xiao min*, small people, looked for possibilities as shop assistants or clerks in the offices that were beginning to appear under any available roof. Out on the street, in the world of the smallest people (the rickshaw drivers and the travelling sellers of anything that could possibly be sold), survival had become a strategy that was crafted one day at a time. With cash much thinner at the top, and with troops of warlords now in occupation, little of value trickled into the lives of these lower orders; and whatever did was often commandeered by regularly rampaging soldiers who were rarely paid.

As Beijing struggled with the shock of the new, further south, Shanghai rose and rose. Carried high on the wealth of its foreign treaty status, and cycling cash in the freewheeling uncertainty of the times, the smoke of its ever-expanding factories billowed into the air, even as the waters of its mighty river groaned under the weight of the biggest trading ships on earth. Flush with foreigners congratulating themselves on having found the freedom of an international fiefdom (known as 'Shanghailand'), the treaty-given 'foreign concessions' had become a magnet for everyone. New factories with foreign capital and tools, fresh presses printing newspapers and magazines for thousands, money to pay for the new city skills of doctors and lawyers, and modern enough minds to want it all. Unlike Beijing, this was a city that seemed to turn to the, very different, order of trade. And while the presence of the foreigners was a historical affront, their ruling powers seemed to have taken to the task of local government with an inspiring efficiency – even though they made a shocking distinction between the 'purity' of the city's Western residents and the yellow skins of any 'visiting' Chinese.

But behind the face of Shanghai, as every Chinese knew, sat the same local forces that ruled the rest of the land: warlords, who saw the city as part of their own fiefdoms from which they dreamt of eventually 'uniting' the broken Chinese world; and the leaders of the secret brotherhood societies, whose 'families' owned almost every labouring man. Meanwhile, stuffed into factories, labouring hands were struggling more than ever. From time to time, erupting into protesting strikes, they were met with the barrels of guns.

With the whole country gripped by warlords of one stripe or another, a slavish poverty was gnawing at hundreds of millions of feet. Even as a glittering train was carrying those at the top to some of the greatest riches on earth, ever-greater tides of human misery were descending upon cities seen by every peasant as beacons of desperate hope. New Shanghai, old Beijing, those who could make a living were feasting on the crumbling heaven, even as those who could not were descending into the furnaces of hell. The past had gone. The new that seemed foreign in every respect. Survival was becoming harder by the day, and the *ren* idea of being human was becoming ever more difficult to sustain. What China would become was anybody's guess – and everybody's question.

*   *   *

As the old struggled with the new, the young were grasping the future with an energy denied to their ancestors. Those who had studied abroad in the last tumultuous decades of the Qing (whether as exiles or voluntary voyagers) had finished their foreign courses and many had returned. Slightly older and wiser, they had not, though, lost the conviction of the earlier rebels that a new order was required. Kang Youwei's *Da Tong* dream of a great unity to free the people from the deadening chains of a deceiving empire had changed forever the way in which they saw their future. While the dreams of Tan Sitong, Kang Youwei and Liang Qichao – of a people as human beings who could think and act for themselves – had become a beacon for almost everyone. Back in the changed, and still changing, fortunes of the new Republic, however, the returned students encountered the rubble of a revolution that had clearly been hijacked and was now struggling to survive. Some turned around and sailed back to the foreign world; others anchored themselves in Shanghai. Both were places where the future seemed a little more secure. But many, looking at the warlording chaos all around, decided it was time for an educated Chinese mind to set itself the task of finally addressing the errors of the past in the hope that, this time, the future might be different. And, as the early revolutionaries had so clearly explained, if that was to happen, the people were going to have to find a voice.

Of the thousands who had come back and stayed, some of the most questioning minds found themselves swept into the vast imagination of a once-revolutionary by the name of Cai Yuanpei. After studying in Germany and France, Cai had returned to Beijing and in 1917 had taken up the presidency of Peking University. Known (after its red brick walls and its four storeys) as the *hong lou*, red building, it sat on a busy thoroughfare just a short walk from the towering Tiananmen Gate of Heavenly Peace. Sunlit trees sparkling on a small front lawn, from within its gates the outside chaos of Beijing was clear for all to see. Trams clattered past, rickshaws vied with mules and bicycles, beancurd sellers plied their trade, swaggering soldiers shouted raucous jokes; and the thin hands of wretched beggars reached out for any possible passing coin.

Within the *hong lou*'s sturdy brick walls, however, was quite another world. Corridors home to the energies of youth, eager voices chattered on their way to class. Lecture rooms regularly erupting in debating shouts, silence would suddenly fall to the mesmerising observations of some of Republican China's greatest masters of words and new ideas. One of the most loved of its teachers was a mind who had returned from America in 1917. A philosopher, by the name of Hu Shi, he had early on stroked a thoughtful brush across an intellectual page, crafting a call to think. As warlords were loading their cannons back and forth, and as the battles of the past seemed to be rewriting themselves by the day, his compelling characters had painted a thundering storm. 'Write with substance', he had argued, in one of the most authoritative of the new journals, 'don't imitate the ancients, eliminate old clichés, speak only when you have something to say and, above all, speak only what is in your heart – and only in the language of the time in which you live.' In short: tell the truth, as you see it.

Under Cai Yuanpei, Peking University became the energetic eye of the storm of new ideas that had been sweeping across China since the early 1900s. Carried back on the wings of students returning from abroad, written in letters sent to parents and friends, copied into pamphlets and newspapers for wider distribution, idea upon idea – now increasingly translated directly into Chinese – tumbled into the university's classrooms. After Liang Qichao had founded his *Xin Min* (*New Citizen*) journal from Tokyo in 1902, a host of magazines and journals introducing new and foreign ideas had spread like wildfire. In 1914, from a small group of Chinese students at Cornell University, a *Ke Xue* (*Science*) journal appeared. Mailed, like *Xin Min*, direct to China, *Ke Xue* translated a whole new world of science for a country whose ideas had, until so recently, been firmly fixed on heaven. The following year, from within the foreign fortress of Shanghai, something even newer had been launched: a journal entitled *Xin Qingnian, New Youth*.

Founded by a philosophical revolutionary whose intoxicating thoughts had, the previous decade, led thousands of hopeful hearts to imagine the toppling of the Qing, from its very first edition in 1915 *Xin Qingnian* was a call to the energies of a student youth. Opening with an article written by its founder, its pages declared the power of the young to renew the old, and their responsibility for shaking off the bonds of other people's ideas. In so doing, and for the first time ever in the all-under-heaven lands, it conjured up the idea of a student spirit: students at university, students at school, students from every walk of China's new life, high and low, including many of its new rich; students as people who wanted to learn, and all looking for ideas about what a new order might be, and where in that order they might find themselves. The philosophical revolutionary was a man called Chen Duxiu. In 1917, Cai Yuanpei invited him to join Peking University as dean.

Ideas about the order of man were everywhere: what it was, what it wasn't, whether it could ever truly be found, how it might be built, and what the individual could do. Order and society, society and science, science and people, people and order: ideas from everywhere, and seemingly all at once. From the translations of earlier students who had gone abroad at the end of the nineteenth century (many returning as revolutionaries and then teachers), the thoughts of distant foreign minds were once again conjured up for examination: John Stuart Mill on liberty (the quintessential importance of the individual and the tyranny of the majority); Charles Darwin and natural selection (the 'tooth and claw' of survival in the natural world); Herbert Spencer on the 'survival of the fittest' (natural selection applied to the society of man, including both people and states); Thomas Huxley on evolution and ethics (why good is better than bad); Nietzsche on the nihilistic idea that the only truth was that of the scientific force of human will. Not to mention the man who had come up with the idea that had triggered the changes on which so many of the new ideas had been predicated: Adam Smith and his *Wealth of Nations* (why self-interest can be a positive good). To these were added Tolstoy's searing portraits of people whose lives had been changed by their times, and Ibsen's heroes and heroines who challenged destiny, and sometimes won.

Ideas were not only conjured up from minds of the students' own time but also from other places: Bertrand Russell's logical revolt against abstract ideals, and his passionate conviction in the forging power of experience for human transformation; Einstein's insistence that science was a human endeavour – with human beings like the atoms on which everything depends, and human morality an essential part of any equation; James

Joyce's *Ulysses*, which turned a country into a character of epic proportions; Shaw's transformation of theatre into moral debate; and John Dewey's ideas of education and his psychology of man (why the mind and voice of each individual human being is important, and why real change is never a sudden fact but always the slow result of an evolutionary sequence).

To all of these were added the great works of Chinese who had sacrificed so much for the dream of being human: Tan Sitong (the human conscience of individuals as the essential foundation of any truly independent state); Kang Youwei (a unity of people, rather than the deceiving and dividing powers of a single top-down mind); and Liang Qichao (a new people, informed by a responsible press; both taught and unified by societies that the very human people would create themselves).

Across all of the ideas – the foreign and the Chinese alike – three common strands seemed to stand out as key to everyone's future: the empathetic conscience of man as a ren, human being; the 'science' of actual facts; and the essential importance of some form of 'democracy' as a means of ensuring that the voices of the people were able to keep a truly independent state on track. Tumbled together, the treasury of works – scientific, philosophical, political, literary, foreign and Chinese – came to be known as a 'new culture'. Not 'culture' as a frivolous excursion to the opera, but culture as the crucible of ideas that made one both human, and Chinese. And 'new culture' as an essential component of what would be required to finally 'imagine a people.'

For Cai Yuanpei, as president of Peking University, the ideas translated into practical questions: what to teach, how to teach, and where? It seemed that one only had to open a magazine to find new knowledge splashed across a page – accompanied by the energetic debates of a quickly growing forest of Chinese minds. Highly educated, hungry for answers, impatient for change, all of the voices insisted that whatever new order arose, and however much it might be inspired by the myriad of ideas around the world, it would be nothing if it was not Chinese. The chaos of ideas was a garden of delights. But even knowledge needed an order of sorts – particularly one that had its sights set upon securing the independence of hundreds of millions of minds. Cai began with a university senate, grounding the pillars of thought in the principles, and responsibilities, of organisation that his liberated students would need to learn as their own societies grew.

Turning his attention to what would be taught, Cai opened up the doors of the *hong lou* and invited a pantheon of Chinese spirits to raise a powerhouse of ideas. Hu Shi had been beckoned to teach philosophy, with a department populated by thinkers drawn from worlds away. And, back from Vassar, Chen Hengzhe was invited to teach the history of the West – the first woman to be given a lecturing voice. To these were added visiting Chinese authors who brought some of China's most powerful stories to life. By far the most inspiring was a towering mind by the name of Lu Xun. A writer of novels and poetry, he was also the man whose invention of the 'critical essay' had inspired a generation to write with searing questions rather than quotes, and whose *Diary of a Madman* – a short story with a haunting image of China's imperial past as a cannibalistic deception that had eaten the country's youth – had left no one in doubt about the urgent need for change.

Establishing his faculty, Cai Yuanpei also searched for a mind that could bring order to the clutter of journals, magazines, newspapers, books and scripts that were now piling up in every direction. For this, a chief librarian was uncovered in a political economist with a deep interest in what it meant to be Chinese. Freshly returned from Japan, he was an enthusiast of the Russian Revolution – indeed, he was famous for sending a congratulatory message to Moscow on the success of the recent Bolshevik triumph. Not to mention a talent for bringing the chaos of paper under filing rule. His name was Li Dazhao.

Cai Yuanpei's ideas of learning went well beyond the narrow classroom and the library. In the gaps between lectures and the twilight evenings that followed, he seeded a sea of societies. Launched for everyone and anyone (student of Peking University or not), they gathered in a borrowed study here, on an open spread of grass there, or in a teahouse: wherever a conversation could be had. A Confucian society was created to pick at the fragments of the old ideas and see if the ancient principles held any surviving value for the new. A society for the cultivation of morality was launched to explore what might be possible in a world where every heavenly principle, and many human ones, seemed to have collapsed. A university press committee was founded; a society for painting and art appeared; a patriotic comrades' society for women took root; and a *hu zhu* mutual aid society opened new doors. A central point in a galaxy of new ideas, everyone flocked to the pillars of Peking University – hub of the new magazines, journals and books that were turning thousands into students – even if it was only to touch the edges of its dreams.

Given the deep relationship between the university and the wave of ideas for a new Chinese future, the students and teachers of Peking University had watched with enormous interest when Liang Qichao had travelled thousands of miles to Paris to observe the Peace Conference the foreign powers had convened in Versailles in 1919. Committed to the creation of a 'new people', he represented both himself, and a body of minds who were determined that foreigners should understand that, even if the Republic's government was too timid and corrupt to speak, China was home to a population of human beings, and that those human beings had a voice. Letters written for home soon showed the depths of the challenge. Not only were the foreign powers squabbling among themselves but it was clear to Liang that Europe and America had no understanding at all of what had been happening on the Chinese lands. Liang had spoken as loudly and as clearly as he could. But when the 'great Western powers' had decided that Germany's Chinese 'possessions' were to be transferred not to China but to a preferred Japan, it was clear that neither he nor the Chinese people had been able to speak loudly enough in a world that was obviously governed by the 'surviving fittest'. Back in Beijing, when the voices of rage rose in the burning protests of 4 May, many of Cai Yuanpei's most promising students had been among those swept off to jail; within months, Chen Duxiu would be arrested for his role in the protests, and forced to stand down as dean.

By the end of that day, though, and for the first time in thousands of years, scholarly Chinese minds had found a public voice. Over the coming days and weeks, the voice would fly, first as letters to friends telling the tale of a spirit found, and then as a throbbing tide crashing against the biggest cities and the smallest towns, both north and south. The spirit was the old Hunanese idea of independence: an independent state, guaranteed by the independent minds of its people. And it was now firmly tied to the idea of a strong and unified nation, as free of meddling foreign powers as of its own corrupt officials. The throbbing tide was the old 'scattered tray of sand', which now included the voices of labourers and the minds of scholars who had become students, both raising the banners of 'Mr Science' and 'Mr Democracy' aloft with every wave. 'Science', as the empiricism that would ensure that no imperial scholars could bury truth in sleeves of silk. 'Democracy', as the voice of the people that would ensure that the human truth would always be told.

The great wave of May Fourth did not bring down the government of the Republic on that late spring day. But in carrying intellectuals and labourers onto the streets of a common cause, it set off a tide that would eventually sweep away the order of the Chinese world.

* * *

In the heady aftermath of the 4 May protests that had become a May Fourth dream, more students and would-be students had flocked to Beijing. With its Peking University and its questioning students, it was a once-imperial city that had become a citadel of ideas and a beacon of hope. Visitors also arrived from afar: intellectuals from all over the world, as eager to learn as to teach. Many were scholars, some were authors; a few were revolutionaries. And so it was that on a summer's day in 1920, a man from Moscow had called upon the university's chief librarian, Li Dazhao. Representing Russia's newly established Communist International organisation (a 'Comintern', founded to forge a brotherhood of independent non-imperial states), the visitor had read Li Dazhao's congratulatory letter on the success of the Bolshevik revolution and wondered whether China might like a Communist Party of its own. Minds meeting, Li leapt at the suggestion, and Chen Duxiu (now no longer dean of Peking University, living in the relative freedom of Shanghai) was invited to lead the new Party organisation – and to spread the conversation to other Chinese cities selected for the launch of small Communist groups. Within months, the Party was established, with Li Dazhao and Chen Duxiu formally recorded as the Party's founders, and Chen Duxiu, the man with the most obviously revolutionary credentials, elected general secretary.

The first of what would become the Party's many 'Congresses' was planned for July 1921. The sentinels of nervous and trigger-happy northern warlords across Beijing made the European-controlled Shanghai a safer city for the meeting; although even in Shanghai, secrecy seemed to be the best order of the day. In all, fifteen men came together on 23 July. Thirteen of the men were Chinese, representing the fifty-three individuals who had so far signed up to join the Chinese Communist Party; two were representatives of the Russian mothership, Comintern. Also attending (although rather on the sidelines) was Li's toweringly tall assistant librarian. Invited more for his enthusiasm than any Communist credentials, he was an odd fish. From Hunan, and from a richer peasant rather than a scholarly family, he seemed to have taken his education into his own hands, leaving the foothills of local schools for further studies in the provincial capital of Changsha. There, he had attached himself to a highly regarded scholar, the brother of one of the founders of the Citizen's Military Education Society (created in 1903 to train revolutionaries to kill), and a friend of Chen Duxiu. One thing had led to another and the scholar had gone to Beijing. Following him, the young man had found his way to the library shelves of Peking University. His name was Mao Zedong.

Permitted to sit at the margins of the university's Marxist Study Group, Mao found his comments were invariably disregarded. Having been a student in Changsha in the spring of 1911, it was true that he had observed the violence of the first – accidental – revolution, but he had few if any Communist credentials. And although he seemed to have read a lot of the relevant literature, from Kang Youwei and Liang Qichao to the foreign ideas of Rousseau and Marx, and the all-important social Darwinian theories on the survival of the fittest in the battle of the human races, he seemed to have given little thought to much beyond his own education. Rather confusingly, he was also devotee of the First Qin Emperor and of the destructive force with which the Qin people had been transformed into a brutal state – a devotion that was rather oddly combined with a passion for the stories of the Crouching Dragon, Zhuge Liang, the Monkey King, and the bandit *Outlaws of the Marsh*. Not surprisingly, his contributions always seemed to be a little offbeat. But as a native of Hunan, and with a useful pair of hands, in 1920, he had been given the chance to open a bookshop in Changsha to sell the Party's literature. By the time of the Party's first Congress in 1921, the bookshop had found its feet. A Hunanese twang, a clumsy education and an admiration of the wilder ways notwithstanding, perhaps this was a man who could get a few things done.

*　　　*　　　*

Back in Peking University, at the time of Comintern's initiation of the Communist Party, the order of everything had still been a matter for debate. In the avalanche of ideas that had arrived from across the world, many of the big things seemed certain and were fairly easily agreed upon by almost everyone: nationalists, Communists, reformers, intellectuals, and even the few remaining Confucians. A stable government that did not suppress, arrest or kill its youth was obviously required. A written constitution that protected the people from the risk of any imperialist ruler putting themselves above the law, was key. Also essential was an objective and empirical science with which a modern nation would be able to raise the industries that could employ the people and secure the state – and with which, after nearly two thousand years, 'things' could finally be truthfully 'investigated'. At the heart of the investigation would be, as it had been before the accidental revolution, the question of how to create a people who accepted a responsibility both for their own personal actions and for the security of the state, including the livelihoods of all the other people who lived in it.

Other things, however, were neither quite so clear nor so easily agreed. How, in the grip of warlords and in the face of an ambitiously rising Japan, could China navigate its way back to statehood – let alone create a constitution that could both proclaim rights *and* protect them? How, with its broken and starving people, could the country's human hearts be lifted above their misery, and their minds be freed to build a new and better world? And, most importantly of all, how, after millennia of a seemingly inevitable cycle of all-under-heaven rises and falls, could the dream of heaven be finally fixed to the Pole Star of the people's will? United on many of the fundamentals, to these more difficult questions, nationalism and Communism offered very different answers, not to mention the wider competing claims of a now-humbled Confucianism, as well as an early anarchism that continued to attract.

As the competing claims were bandied back and forth, Peking University's department of philosophy proposed two interesting but quite different ideas. The first idea was offered by Hu Shi, who brushed another article with a self-explanatory name: *Study More Problems, Talk Less of 'Isms'*. Noting that progress is not achieved in an evening, Hu urged his friends and peers to see civilisation as a patient study in solving problems: 'Bit by bit, drop by drop, one by one'. China and her people would need to find their own way and, like the crossing of any great river, there was not a map or an 'ism' to guide them: everyone would need to feel their best way forward, using whatever stones they could find.

The second idea was offered by one of the rare surviving Confucianists, a man called Liang Shuming. Having spoken to many visiting foreigners, and having read the reports of Liang Qichao (no relation) on his journeys across the wastelands of post-war Europe, Liang Shuming said that he had been struck by a rising European questioning of the value of science when applied without human morality. Indeed, noted Liang Shuming, the European questioning had been so great that, in his letters home, Liang Qichao had urged everyone in China to think again before following the West on a course that might carry everyone over a cliff. Reflecting on Liang Qichao's warnings, Liang Shuming cast his thoughts back across the history of great civilisations, and to the 'human will' that had shaped them.

There were, Liang Shuming said, three great wills in the history of mankind – expressed by three great, but very different people. The first was the will of the West: a world where man saw himself as having a duty to tackle nature. The second was the will of Oriental China: a world where man felt an obligation to bend to nature. The third was Asian India: a world where man set aside his will, and recognised that his only true nature was the inner, and also greater, cosmic self. For Liang Shuming, these were not so much competing perspectives, but rather an evolutionary sequence that would unfold, rather like a novel, across the future span of human time. The Western beginning was man's engagement in a righteous battle of reason. The Chinese middle was where man bent his own desires to a greater order grounded in the harmony of all. And the Indian end was the understanding that the physical world (both man and nature) was an illusion.

Seen as an apologist for the Confucianism that had been used to justify thousands of years of a single top-down imperial rule, Liang's ideas were swiftly dismissed by the students. As were India's illusions, presented by the mesmerising figure of Rabindranath Tagore but considered to offer nothing but a distraction from the important task of revolutionising the order of man. And while Liang Qichao and Liang Shuming had both urged caution in pursuing Western science without considering the importance of a human morality, it was the impartial objectivity of science that seemed to many to offer the best possible chance of cleansing the heavenly lands from the arbitrariness of imperial power.

The debates about order and civilisation continued, and in 1923, a powerful mind at Beijing's other great university (Tsinghua) stepped forward with an observation of his own on the question of science and morality. His name was Zhang Junmai. Agreeing with Liang Qichao and Liang Shuming on the matter of science and man, Zhang noted that, while the objective powers of empirical science had a value, science without the subjective moral compass of human feelings would be a dangerous thing. Within days, a geologist-biologist by the name of Ding Wenjiang swept off a searing reply. Science, Ding retorted, was nothing if not absolute, and to think otherwise was to open the door to a return of the imperialism of the past. Liang Shuming was mistaken: there was only one world to be considered, and that was the material one which could be objectively measured. And as far as risks to the ordering civilisation of man were concerned, the greatest risk was a failure to understand that ideas of a spiritual world could never be reconciled with the facts of a material life, for the simple reason that the spiritual world deceived all who floated on its clouds.

With both positions published in the *New Youth* journal, the arguments of Zhang Junmai and Ding Wenjiang were marshalled for everyone to consider. Few were in any doubt as to the importance of the question: was order dependent on the quality of morality and the human heart, or was it simply an empirical challenge to be met by the scientific talents of the mind? At stake was everyone's future: which of these two competing ideas would be most likely to ensure that the single top-down mind of the imperial past would never be able to return?

Backwards and forwards the characters raged, with *New Youth* and its pages the battleground, and not an end in sight. Eventually, Liang Qichao stepped in. Trying to bring peace to the bitterly divided factions, he insisted that he had never said that science had no value, only that human feelings and science needed to be looked at together. Ding Wenjiang's fury was not assuaged. Flourishing an inky full stop, he proclaimed that human feelings had no place in science. At which point, Hu Shi added some ink of his own. Worried that a world which accepted subjectivity could toss China back to the heavenly superstitions of its imperial, Confucian and even Daoist past, he reluctantly decided to agree with Ding Wenjiang.

*   *   *

As the battle of man and science raged in the corridors of the universities, out on the streets, the cannons of the military powers were getting louder by the year; with the energies of the censors following suit. After the May Fourth arrests, a tightened security led to the constant fear that any mind that seemed to question the fragile authority of the guns could be snatched off the street at will. Those at the greatest risk were students with an interest in the new Communist Party: clearly contemplating a second revolution, and obviously training young bodies for the cause, the Party was seen as the shadow behind an increasing number of uprisings and strikes. But even with the risk of an arrest (and the likelihood that an arrest would result in a brutal punishment), the ranks of its student members were growing. Chilled by the changes in the political air, in 1922 Cai Yuanpei had returned to the foreign world to think about what might come next. Beijing's clouds continued to darken; and judging by the news reaching the capital, events in the far south were also getting a lot more complicated too.

In 1925, Sun Yatsen, still everybody's original revolutionary hero, passed on to another world. In the years before his death, he had lost and then recovered his position at the controlling top of the Guomindang, regaining his influence through an acceptance that the Guomindang would henceforth be organised on a strong military footing. With warlords in control of many parts of the country, Sun had also built a friendship with the new Communist Russia and its international 'Comintern' organisation: Russia's Communist Party having demonstrated an ability both to launch a revolution and to keep a revolutionary party in power, Sun had been as keen to learn its skills as Chen Duxiu had been happy to accept its invitation to found a Chinese Communist Party. Concerned that such a large and important neighbour should not fall victim to the guns or the charms of the still-imperial West, Moscow was prepared to hedge its bets and pay heavily for success. Looking at the military force of the Guomindang and the youth of the Chinese Communist Party, it suggested that the chances of a successful second revolution would be stronger if the two were to join together in the necessary battles against the would-be imperialist warlords who had hijacked the first revolution – not to mention the worrying Japanese.

Members of both parties, Guomindang and Communist, had had their doubts, to say the least. Those within the Guomindang responsible for raising funds from Chinese industrialists were shocked at the idea of an alliance with a reckless group of Communists who wanted to bring down the very factory foundations of *fuqiang* wealth and power on which any strong Chinese state would depend. Almost everyone within the Communist Party was equally shocked at the idea of an alliance with a militaristic group of capitalists, who were nothing but bourgeois self-strengtheners. Some within the Communist Party even ventured to suggest that Russia's experience of a Moscow-led rebellion was, in any event, hardly relevant: after the failure of the accidental 1911 revolution launched from the city of Wuchang, surely the ultimate Chinese uprising was far more likely to come from the countryside.

Within the Guomindang, Sun Yatsen had deftly dismissed his doubters with a reminder that Russian help would be essential in evicting the foreign imperial powers from China's lands. He had also noted that, wherever the Russian revolution might have come from, it was the force of Lenin's organising skills that had transformed the explosions of an uprising into the iron power of a solid state.

Within the Communist Party, Chen Duxiu addressed his own doubters with a lecture on Marx, a personal observation, and a fact. Marx, Chen noted, had not only been clear that revolutions always came out of cities, but in describing the stages necessary for every society to pass through on its way to a Communist utopia, he had expressly stated that it was essential

250

that the old feudalism be replaced with an industrial capitalism that would trigger the labouring classes to rebel. To this, Chen added his view (shared by many in a young Communist Party whose membership included a number of highly educated minds) that, whatever Marx might have said, any future China would need to include not only the labouring classes but also the intellectuals who had always been the conscience of China, as indeed they were the driving force of the new Party. Given that intellectuals needed education and the luxury of time to work out what to do, they would naturally have to come from the very 'bourgeois' classes that were members of the Guomindang. To all of this, Chen added a final practical argument: although the selfish capitalists of the Guomindang would eventually be ground into the dust of any real revolution, their skills and experience in the art of war, not to mention their guns, would be essential if the Communists were ever to defeat the warlords.

In 1923, the Guomindang and the Communist Party had pooled their very different dreams to forge a 'United Front'. Moscow opened up a Leninist education to both, and the Guomindang invited the younger Communist brothers to join their Whampoa Military Academy in Guangdong. Sun Yatsen despatched the most trusted of his own younger men to Moscow to learn not only the art of winning wars but that of securing an enduring political power as well. So close was the co-operation with the Chinese Communist Party, and so promising were some of the young Communists, that the Guomindang even welcomed some of their most talented members into its own official ranks.

It was not long, however, before the differences in the dreams had begun to tell. When one of Sun Yatsen's favoured students returned from Moscow to lead the Whampoa Academy, he declared that the combination of proletarian Marxism and iron-will Leninism with which the Russian Communist Party ruled its state, was not for China. While Confucianism might have failed in many ways, the ideals of personal virtue and family harmony were far too deeply rooted for such a brutal discipline to prevail. In his personal opinion, the only way that China would be able to tame her warlords and defeat the foreign imperial powers would be to learn from the lessons of the nineteenth-century self-strengtheners, and build the *fuqiang* wealth and power that would eventually conquer all. Born Jiang Jieshi in the province of Zhejiang, to the West which learnt his name through the Cantonese tongue of the far south, he would come to be known as Chiang Kai-shek.

Chiang's pronouncement split the Guomindang. Some continued to support Sun's pragmatic alliance with Moscow and its Chinese Communist Party. Others, particularly the industrialists on whose support the Guomindang so heavily depended, sided with Chiang, insisting that the Russian Communists were barbarians, and that the Chinese Communists were nothing but wolves in their midst. Before the dust could settle, though, Sun Yatsen died from his own longer battle with cancer. And while a lefter leaning rival succeeded him as chairman of the National Government, it was Chiang, as commander-in-chief of the Guomindang's National Revolutionary Army, who had the power to change the lie of the land.

In 1926, with warlords still at large, and the Guomindang and the Communist Party bound together in their United Front, Chiang Kai-shek announced a 'Northern Expedition' to storm the north from the south. Nearing warlord-controlled Shanghai in March 1927, the Communist brothers were asked to raise workers' militias in diversionary strikes. As the strikes were unleashed, the righter wing of the Guomindang argued that there was little point in success if it brought down the very industrial pillars that were supporting them. With his sights firmly set on a self-strengthened China that would be able to tame the warlords, get the foreigners out of China's lands, and ensure that she was 'fit to survive', Chiang decided that the time had come to cleanse the country of the Communist dream.

So it was that on 12 April 1927, as the forces of the United Front arrived at the outskirts of the Chinese quarters of Shanghai, Chiang Kai-shek commanded the Communist flanks under his command to lead the advance, in concert with the organised militia of the city's workers. With secret orders already delivered to the Triad brotherhoods, and with the silent support of the foreign powers, he then ordered his own Guomindang battalions to swoop down upon the Communists and the workers' militias alike. Across the following days, the Triads and the Guomindang purged the city of Communists, union members, brothers-in-arms and anyone else known for their left-leaning sympathies. Three hundred were executed; a thousand died. Over the weeks and months that followed, convinced that Communism would tear up the material foundations of a future industrial Chinese state, Chiang turned his sights to tracking down every other heart that looked as if it might be Communist – and executing it. Within a year and across the country, hundreds of thousands of others had been pursued to their deaths.

Shattered by the betrayal, surviving Communists did their best to find each other and regroup; but by the end of 1927, the Party was in tatters. Li Dazhao was captured by a warlord and executed; Chen Duxiu was forced to resign for the fatal error of recommending the Party's collaboration with the Guomindang. Meanwhile, a still minor Mao Zedong, increasingly captivated by the scientific possibilities of revolutionary destruction – and always keen on country guerrilla ways – suggested that he be given an army of peasants to raise an autumn harvest uprising in Hunan. The uprising struggled to take off and then fell, but Mao was able to secure the all-important charge of a troop of men. Advancing further south and up to the protecting mountains that sat between the provinces of Jiangxi and Fujian, Mao led them to a safer haven in a desolate place known as Jinggangshan, the Jinggang Mountains.

With the heavenly order once again divided, Chiang Kai-shek marched on.

*   *   *

When the Guomindang arrived in Beijing in 1928, they did not bring quite the kind of order the city had hoped for. The incumbent northern warlord was despatched, but it was clear to Chiang Kai-shek that other warlords were simply waiting in the wings. With the Guomindang's forces now severely stretched, it was hard to see how they could be kept at bay. A series of reluctant alliances with the most amenable of the warlords seemed the best bet of all bad options, and with these settled, Chiang, now elevated to top of the Guomindang, moved what little remained of the Republican government south, to the old Ming capital of Nanjing. As the government's offices moved, so did its remaining officials. With Beijing's fortunes already fragile, many wondered how the city would survive.

Then, in 1931, the Japanese declared a new land in the Chinese north. Already occupying the old Manju capital of Mukden (Shenyang), with the wider once-Manju lands of Liaodong and the eastern part of Inner Mongolia, Tokyo declared a new Manjuguo state (Manchuria), with the discarded Manju Prince and last Qing emperor, Puyi, as its monarch. By 1933, the lands around Beijing were not only home to fluctuating corps of Guomindang-allied warlords, but were also under the sights of nearby Japanese guns.

Northern fields trampled to dust and any dreams of a heavenly peace buried in fear, yet more refugees began to flood into the once-imperial capital for a future that could surely be no worse than their past. Many of the incomers turned to pulling the rickshaws that had once roved the streets and lanes: so many, that a trade which had once provided a living wage now struggled to offer even survival. Others found their way to factories that flickered in the half-life of sixteen-hour days, seven-day weeks, at wages that could scarcely clothe and feed. With every hand hungry, even children queued for work. Rag-picking became a jealously guarded profession; many survived on the bones of someone else's meal. Soup kitchens became a fixture. And from time to time, misery would break out in bands of brotherly feeling, complete with uprisings and strikes.

Meanwhile, across the country Chiang Kai-shek was turning the social Darwinian idea of the survival of the fittest into a new mantra for a Guomindang Nationalist state – complete with a 'New Life' idea for a return to the ancient morality that had always been grounded in 'self-cultivation'. Telegraphing extracts from Confucius' *Analects* to government officials, city industrialists and the supporting gentry across the countryside, he exhorted them all to remember the ancient virtues of *li* ritual and *yi* integrity, to fortify the bonds of filial piety, to rediscover Zeng Guofan's self-strengthening spirit, and to remember that, in the words of Confucius, 'When the wind moves, the grass bends'. Responsibility and discipline were all. As in the latter decades of the Manju Qing, redoubling their efforts to strengthen the state, the officials and the gentry harnessed every family relationship they could think of to build towers of self-serving wealth and power. As the self-strengtheners' wealth and power rose, so spread the desperation that forced others to sell their children on the street.

What to do? Over the next four years, the question echoed around the now fading teahouses, batted back and forth across tables that had seen better times. A Chinese world without a Son of Heaven had been shock enough. A Chinese world without a heavenly family had seemed a recipe for chaos. But a nation of individuals all selfishly fending for themselves? And a city where everyone might be technically a citizen, but where the very fabric of life that made them human had disappeared? Beijing's orderly past was gone. Memories had already been lost, along with the imperial gates and the walls that had carried them. Crafting skills were disappearing without a trace of ink to hold their light. And while Sun Yatsen's last-century dream of a nation of people, guided by a constitution which provided for the wellbeing of all, had once captured the popular imagination, with a million people in Beijing, and four hundred million in the wider Chinese world beyond, it was difficult to see how it could possibly come true.

There were, however, some cheerier spirits. Looking at the relics of Beijing's imperial beauty, these wondered if the city's treasures might be able to create a future not just for the city but for its human beings as well. If

Beijing could not find the industries that seemed to keep other cities afloat, why not trade in the past and all of its memories? Itinerant carts with *dagu* drums were already soliciting the unwanted past, turning it into second-hand items and antiques to pay for the present. Surely, abandoned palaces and temples could be reopened for visiting souls? Thinking about the value of the old, the mayor of Beijing had an idea: why not offer the city and its imperial dreams as a story to sell? Turn the old crafts to the tune of new customers: outsiders, whether foreigners or even other Chinese, who might not have that special Beijing ability to see the meaning in every detail but who would surely love the tales that had been woven into the hearts of every *Beijing ren*.

The tapestry was certainly rich. The kitchen god, who made an annual new year report to the celestial Jade Emperor (and the honey which everyone applied to his lips to make sure that the family fortunes would be safe for the year to come). A god of wealth, who stole from the rich and gave to the poor, riding in on a black tiger and shooting his enemies with pearls that burst like bombs on impact. There were even stories in the dust that annually stormed the city, straight from the sands of the stretching deserts beyond. Then there was everything else that Beijing had to sell: gliding swallows with whistles tied to their backs, turning blue skies into song; pomegranate trees with goldfish bowls guaranteeing families of sons; red everywhere for luck. Twelve ways to cook a fish; sixteen ways to eat a chicken; sweet and sour plum sauce; noodles with a special heavenly flavour; candied fruits skewered on a stick, not to mention the special spring pancakes rolled in sesame oil. All treasures that only Beijing knew how to make. Operas with swishing sleeves, rolling eyes and clanging gongs; the market at Tianqiao with its puppets and stilts in eye-commanding colours; astrologers who could see the fortunes of the future; story-tellers with clappers to catch the ear; songs that told the tales of centuries; mechanical mice which jumped at the tickle of a hair; bird-shaped lanterns which could flap their wings – Beijing had it all. Surely somebody would want to buy? But try as hard as the dreamers might, it soon became clear that midnight could not be postponed.

In July 1937, a Japanese wind swept past the Long Wall and made its way down to Beijing. Circling the city, just like the yellow sands that dusted Beijing's streets with their storms, the wind choked off food and supplies. It was only a matter of time before the city would fall to the Japanese idea of order.

Some chose to stay, accepting the future with a Daoist resignation.

Others wanted to leave, but where to go? To the new Guomindang capital of Nanjing? To a Shanghai that seemed to have become an imperialist New York? For the hardiest youth, the choices even included a new Communist city, which had been founded in the caves of a far-off place called Yan'an.

Back at the Zhengyang Gate of the Zenith South, the railway station heaved with uncertainty and confusion. Willow and pigskin suitcases battled with baskets, bedding and pots. Fathers and sons, wives and daughters, surviving maids and servants: all tumbled on to the trains. The heavenly order was long gone. The city and its people were moving – but no one was quite sure where.

CHAPTER 2

A BRAVE NEW WORLD

The Golden Monkey wrathfully swung his massive cudgel,
And the jade-like firmament was cleared of dust.

Mao Zedong (1961)

As the red curtain parted, five thousand pairs of wondering eyes looked up from the near-dark of the war god's temple. With little room to breathe, let alone move, bodies were locked in concentration and hearts were spellbound at the sights. Singing the *Rice-planting* Song, and stepping the *Defeat Japan* Dance, the energies unleashed on the stage before them seemed to know no bounds. Somewhere on the makeshift boards there was supposed to be a famous face, someone called Ding Ling – a writer *and* a woman. But it was hard to tell in the blaze of so many brightly performing faces. As the bombs pounded outside, the sights and sounds of the stage were enough to help everyone set aside their troubles for an evening's delight: brothers and sisters gone to heaven could be momentarily forgotten, and tomorrow's food was a problem for another day.

For the performing troupe of the Front Service Corps of the 8th Route Army it was a night like many others, only bigger and the culmination of a journey that had begun months before. Donkeys loaded to the limit, they had left the caves of Yan'an in August, following the waters of the Yan to its Yellow River master. Passing through the seasons, red banners had first flapped in soft breezes, then whipped into autumn winds. Crossing rivers by stones, advancing to the front line of the province of Shanxi, they had worked their way across a fragment of China's vast north-eastern lands: *Heijiapu* black family store, *Yancheng* salt city, *Zhangjiatan* family rapids, *Heishanguan* black mountain pass. Wherever they had gone, men, women and children, dressed in the tattered straw and the handwoven cotton of the land, had flocked to their path, eyes filled with hunger but hearts brimming with hope.

The Front Service Corps had not been the first to pass along the way. Red volunteers had come before them: unbinding women's feet, tracing characters on sandy ground, teaching skills that would stretch the land to feed its people, and standing up to landlords who had once ruled all under their own particular spot of heaven but were now being sent to the bottom of the peasant pile. By the October night when the performing troops arrived at the war god temple in the city of Linfen (a major stopping point on the prized railway that was attracting so much of Japan's exploding military might), they had seen the Communist countryside and it was good. As their voices strained to reach the furthest listening rafters of the full-to-bursting temple, and as their feet jumped to the beat of a revolutionary song, victory seemed only a leap away.

*　　　*　　　*

Arriving in the Jinggang Mountains in late 1927, Mao Zedong had set his company of followers to the task of creating a Communist stronghold of their own. Battered by competing instructions from surviving upper echelons of the Party's Central Committee, he applied a set of his own ideas: grounded on the historical example of the First Qin Emperor, touched with his observations of the rough violence of the 1911 revolution and its following years, and shaped by his own thoughts on Marx and Moscow. Keen to make his mark, the results included local rallies to celebrate the arrival of his forces with public executions of landlords.

The Party was a little uncertain about the maverick that had sprung from their midst, but with Communists constantly at risk of arrest and execution in the wider Chinese world, news of Mao's stronghold spread and new recruits began to arrive. When one of the largest units of the newly formed

'Red Army' came looking for refuge, his wild outpost acquired a certain standing, and even Moscow, now banker to the Party, took note. Soon the Jinggang Mountain base was struggling to hold the rising tide of refugees and Mao's revolutionary ambition. In 1929, Mao moved the base to join up with another of the Red Army's units, further south and deeper into the mountainous province of Jiangxi.

Encountering other ideas of the Communist dream, battles arose about whose Party it was. Sheltered by the mountain mists, Mao confronted them with his own revolutionary principles, touched with a hint of Qin: whispers were spread, red blood ran, and eventually unity was achieved. Intrigued, but still uncertain, and with Moscow's treasury watching, greater Party powers began to find their way to Mao's red enclosure. In November 1931, Mao proclaimed Jiangxi as a 'Chinese Soviet Republic', with the county town of Ruijin as its capital. Within a month, the highly educated and much admired political commissar of the Party, Zhou Enlai, arrived to assume command. Soon, the earth below was ringing to rumours of a Communist state hidden in the mountains. And as the Soviet Republic of Jiangxi swelled, Chiang Kai-shek turned the sights of his forces to encircling a world that seemed to have appeared out of nowhere.

By 1933, now with nearly a hundred thousand men, women and children in the Jiangxi Soviet, yet more of the Party's leaders began to arrive. Looking at the skies of Guomindang planes, they realised it would be only a matter of time before Chiang Kai-shek destroyed them. Snatching at Mao's maps, they decided to move: not only eighty-six thousand of the people who were deemed fit to march but the pots and pans, the files and field phones that made up the daily necessities of life and the furniture of the Party's order. Thanked for his efforts, but with his voice now diminished by a Party suspicion of his Hunanese twang and his country-guerrilla ways, Mao and his then, third, wife were attached to the tail of a march that some suspected might be very long indeed. Departing in October 1934, over the next 370 days, navigating some of China's harshest nature, encountering tribes that no one had ever heard of, pushed to the edge of their own existence and humanity, they walked six thousand circling miles from south to west and north. A year later, in October 1935, the surviving fittest arrived on the northern plains of China, in a once-proud and ancient city that had shrunk to a remote and isolated market town. Surrounded by soft loess mountains where almost everyone lived in caves, its name was Yan'an.

Between leaving and arriving on what would come to be known as the 'Long March', seventy-eight thousand fell by one wayside or another. Traipsing in and out of some of China's remotest provinces, the marchers passed through the hunger of lands where food was nothing but a dream, under burning sun, through piercing hail, freezing snow, and under almost constant clouds of squabbles about direction, tactics and survival. As they marched, Mao Zedong worked his way up from the tail to the front, seemingly propelled by a superior grasp of strategy in the unpredictable terrain of the wild, although those closest to him were less convinced. With lectures offered to everyone who followed him, he seemed to have a deep appreciation of the harsh lessons that needed to be learnt from the past – and a high regard for the calculating ruses that had led to the triumphs of the ancient Qin. The costs to the Long Marchers were high, but the Moscow treasury, which was funding all, seemed pleased with progress. Victory seemingly snatched from the jaws of defeat, and a number of messy internal battles resolved, the Communist Party acquired a new Soviet Republic in the north-east, and a new chairman: Mao Zedong. The greatest prize, however, was a story to end all stories: the triumph of red hearts over almost every adversity that man and nature could contrive. As the survivors, now joined by rivers of new recruits, began to carve themselves into the caves of the new Soviet-city, Mao was wondering who might be able to tell it.

*　　*　　*

When, in 1927, Chiang Kai-shek had launched the Communist pogrom across the country's cities, not everyone had fled. One of those who had stayed in Beijing was an impecunious young poet by the name of Hu Yepin. An ardent Communist, he was also the lover of a young writer, Ding Ling, who, having captured the newly independent female spirit in the pages of one of China's most popular novels, found herself clasped to the heart of Chinese youth. Travelling to a Shanghai which was now twitching with guns of its own, despite keeping to his own shadows, Hu Yepin fell to the greater forces of the dark. Arrested on the orders of the Guomindang, on the night of 7 February 1931, he was executed with a shot.

Within a year, Ding Ling had penned his story. And having pitched the first of many young stars into the constellation of the Communist Party's heroes, she found herself seen as a threat by the warlords and the Guomindang, and as an inspiration by thousands of young Communist hearts. Two years later, she was placed under a house arrest that would last for three years until, in

1936, a band of Communist brothers arrived to help her escape. Disguised as a Guomindang soldier, accompanied by some of her rescuers, Ding Ling, the heroine of so many dreams, carried her pen to the sanctuary of the new Communist city in Yan'an. Pushing her way on mule and by foot across the gruelling miles to her destination, wondering not only whether she would ever get there but whether, even if she did, the Communist dream could possibly survive, she constantly remembered the final characters with which she had brushed her tribute to Hu Yepin: 'When will it be light?'

When Ding Ling eventually arrived in Yan'an, the now-chairman Mao was quick to understand the nature of the treasure that had appeared from the dark. Famous for her works and her dazzling circle of literary friends, Ding Ling had the power to tell a story and make it real. By 1938, two years after Moscow had once again pushed the troops of the Guomindang and the Communist Party to unite in order to defeat what it considered to be the greater Japanese foe, hers was a talent that had become one of the greatest prizes in a Communist armoury now fixed on a propaganda battle against the Guomindang idea. Looking out across the vast expanses of the old Chinese world which had yet to be touched by the Communist dream, Mao decided to despatch Ding Ling to the performing boards of the front line in the company of the Front Service Corps of the 8th Route Army. Arriving back in Yan'an in late 1938, her mission accomplished, Ding Ling's literary senses had been sharpened by a first-hand understanding of the lie of China's land. Like every other new arrival, she was then sent to the Party's Revolutionary Central School to train her mind.

Taught by brothers returned from Moscow, Ding Ling found that she was listening to the lectures of new Yan'an friends who were also rising Party stars. One was the powerful Party secretary for all of northern China, Liu Shaoqi, who delivered a directive text entitled *How to be a Good Communist*. The lesson was apparently simple: at all times and on all matters, take account of the Party's interests as a whole, and put them above any possible personal considerations. Beyond the formal lessons and across the many quiet evenings, Mao Zedong added personal thoughts of his own, largely delivered over the dinner table in the cave that he shared with his new, fourth, wife, Jiang Qing, a young actress recently arrived from Shanghai.

Away from the front, Ding Ling found that time in Yan'an passed slowly, particularly for the thousands of highly educated young intellectuals who had arrived. Students of all ages, artists, authors, historians, poets, scientists, doctors, lawyers, economists, linguists and every other mind that could be imagined: many had fled the 1937 advances, particularly its bombardment of Shanghai; all had come to build a new and stronger China. Ding Ling noticed that not all of those who arrived were permitted to stay; minds apparently too rooted in bad old ways of thought were discarded or returned. Those who stayed were given a Communist education, and set to their appointed tasks. Some were despatched to carry out peasant education and land reform. Many of the men marched to wherever the northern front had most recently moved. Left behind, their wives – women who were only following battle-commanding husbands – found themselves, like so many others sitting behind the lines, with little to do.

From the multitudes who successfully passed through the revolutionary education, Ding Ling found herself among the chosen few who were offered a cave, a clackety typewriter, and a chance to describe the new world. Looking at those around her, she watched as the organisations of the new Party city grew from within the caves. There was a central committee to craft the decisions of the day, and a Party school that would make sure that intellectual minds understood the rules of Mao's order, while forging more detailed socialist principles for the future. There was also a *Liberation Daily*, a newspaper to tell Yan'an what was going on at home and abroad, a journal to tell the tales of a Communist life, and a Propaganda Department, whose job was to tell the story of the Party and its Yan'an caves, to teach the new young Communists the Party line, and to tap out the Communist promise of a brave new world across the wires of the land. The dream was for a revolutionary order delivered not by a single man or even by a top-down government, but by a unity of the mass of the people at large. A challenge indeed.

With so many beings, all in such a remote location, and with those behind the lines not always having enough to do, Ding Ling found that authors and editors were everywhere in demand: a policy here, a story there, a poster to catch an eye, not to mention essays to teach the new Communist lessons. And everywhere, writers were required to make sure that '*i*'s were dotted, '*t*'s crossed, and that intellectual logic kept up with the Communist page. But with the Party's institutions telling everybody not only what to do but what to think, Ding Ling also noticed that questions were beginning to play like fountains, particularly for the authors and artists who, like herself, had been trained to look for the truth on which the all-important order of the human heart was surely grounded.

As far as Ding Ling could see, contradictions were everywhere. While almost everyone had risked life and limb to get to Yan'an, the Party spirit whose word she was supposed to be spreading seemed to be floundering on many fronts. As an overzealous top seemed to be trying to reorder everyone's ideas, loose-ended minds were making an industry out of idle chatter, with those offended being quick to rally troops in their support. Meanwhile, leaders of the front (and the rear) appeared to find a ready supply of new wives, pushing first choices far from inconvenient sight. Food and pay gravitated to the top. Democracy appeared to have twisted into a funny turn where only some votes seemed to count. And equality seemed to have been upended, with some people very clearly at the top, and a lot of others focused only on how to climb up after them. Blind bureaucracy was everywhere; and some people (particularly Mao) just talked and talked. While it wasn't always obvious what they meant, there seemed to be a rule that everyone had to listen to them. Where in this new city of caves, she wondered, was the dream of being human?

Finding their feet in a confusing new world, the authors and artists began to ask their questions out loud. What exactly was the Party's position on science and democracy? And why was it that the Party was constantly telling everybody not just what to do but what to think? Mao, the one-time assistant librarian, now chairman of the Communist Party and in charge of achieving a revolution, listened. And as he so often did with everything, he gave a series of lecturing lessons in reply. Starting with science and democracy, he explained that the two were really one and the same thing. To which he added that in the new scientific world, the real goal was not the messy 'old democracy' of the National Assembly on which the Republic had clearly floundered but a 'new democracy' on which a successful revolution could be built. 'New democracy' was apparently as simple as a scientific equation: in the new Communist world, there was only one truth, which was the truth of facts. The facts of such a new world could either be made by evolution or by revolution. Communism was committed to the path of revolution. And the primary fact on which the new Communist world would be built was the will of the mass of the people (the working and peasant classes) to rule – as a result of which, the state would eventually wither away. The Communist Party being the vanguard of the people, the will of the people was of course the mind of the Party. Any other mind was an enemy.

As far as telling everybody what to think was concerned, the answer to that, Mao noted, must surely be self-evident. It was, once again, a matter of science – with objectivity being everything, and subjectivity being the greatest danger of all. Obviously the only true revolutionary thought was the objectively scientific one that reflected the real will of the mass of the people. Liberalism, with all of its bourgeois ideas about the importance of the individual, was nothing but a subjectivity that had to be combated as the enemy of the people's will. The greatest risk of subjectivity was with those scholarly minds who always used twisting ideas to trick the masses into settling for a past in which they were endlessly trodden underfoot. But the revolution had declared war on the past with its highly educated minds winning wars of words with claptrap. Naturally, therefore, the Party would need to teach those intellectuals who wanted to serve the revolution what to think.

Drawing his lectures to a close, Mao suggested that those who wasted their time on questioning and complaining should take a look at the wars: the war of the classes, the war with the Guomindang, and the war with the Japanese; with Chinese men, women and children dying real Chinese deaths. Freedom was nothing more than the understanding of historical necessity, and the use of that understanding to change the world. Darwin and Spencer had understood it, with their ideas of the survival of the fittest; and the First Qin Emperor had understood it long before them, bringing an end to the Warring States and unifying the lands that had become the Republic of China. Of course, Mao concluded, the Party and Yan'an could always improve. But the real battle was bigger than most understood: it was not just a battle between the classes of the workers and the peasants on the one hand, and bourgeois landlords and intellectuals on the other, it was a battle between the old individual self and a new revolutionary being who understood that the triumph of the masses was the prize.

Ding Ling took her notes. But like many of the authors and the cleverer minds, she found them a little hard to understand. The revolution was being conducted to deliver the will of the people, but the only voice of the people was that of the Party. As sole producer of the opinions that could be classified as scientifically objective, it sounded as if the Party could not be questioned – in which case, surely everyone in Yan'an was becoming little more than a 'scientific' cog in a greater machine. Where was the art of being human? And if the idea was that there weren't supposed to be any human beings, who on earth would tell the truth? Mao seemed to be saying that truth was a matter of science, reserved for the objectivity of the Party. But hadn't it been precisely that way of thinking which had delivered the tyranny of thousands of years of emperors, a tyranny that had only just been thrown off? Surely, thought Ding Ling, and many others, they must have missed something in one of the lectures. While it might make sense on complicated matters of Communist theory, Mao's ideas on scientific objectivism couldn't possibly be meant to apply to the daily ups and downs of human life. Somewhere, there was obviously a mistake.

In 1941, one of the authors asked Mao if the Party had a policy on literature and art. Observing that, with a war to fight and millet to bring in from the fields, there hadn't been much time, Mao suggested that the authors might like to work on it themselves: 'Base it on my thoughts on new democracy,' he added.

Gathering together, Ding Ling and the authors thought and thought; but the more time they spent thinking, the more the editors began to press for copy – anything to fill the hungry pages of the *Liberation Daily* with something other than what had become the boring back and forth of a slow war. Eventually, mindful of a duty to deliver something, and still convinced she must have failed to understand the detail of Mao's lectures, Ding Ling obliged with a paper recalling the 'critical essay' that Lu Xun, the great revolutionary author whose works were so much admired that they had become classical Party texts, had created: a revolutionary form of an essay that was not designed to meet the artificial standards of the old imperial examinations but to shoot piercing arrows of criticism into the institutions and ideas that stood in the way of revolutionary change.

Within weeks, it was clear that Ding Ling's 'bourgeois' mind had wandered off the Communist path. Standing to open a new Party school in Yan'an, Mao squarely addressed the problems of the Party; and his observations had nothing to do with any 'critical essay'. Repeating his view that the subjectivism of individual opinions was a muddled currency, he addressed his words to intellectuals who gave themselves airs, and sharpened his sights on individuals who wanted to put themselves in the limelight. A sickness had emerged, he warned, hindering everybody's revolutionary progress: it would have to be cured. In the weeks that followed, once again, the cleverest minds seemed to be very slow in getting the point.

Ding Ling (among the slowest) proceeded to pen another paper, this time suggesting that it would be better if there were less empty theorising, more talk about real problems and, in light of the growing number of leaders discarding old wives in favour of younger models, a little more attention to the moral conduct of males. Ding Ling was not the only one to write or speak. Another who picked up his pen was a young journalist and writer with a fierce dedication to the integrity of truth – a truth that, in his subjective opinion, was the only possible foundation for any human order. His name was Wang

Shiwei. In early 1942, Wang spoke his mind through the same critical essay that Lu Xun had used to tear apart the feudal past. 'Wild lilies,' he wrote, using nature as a masking metaphor for inconvenient human voices, 'are the most beautiful of the flowers in the hills around Yan'an and, slightly bitter to the taste, they have the greatest medicinal value.' With the free and open skies of nature behind him, Wang Shiwei then launched his thoughts on the troubles in the Yan'an world. Crawling obsequiousness, inhuman arrogance, a sense of criticism as a crime, special wifely interests who hid their own petty privileges behind a shield of anti-bourgeois principle. A place of light but also a place of dark, where great minds seemed to occupy themselves with petty passions. And, like a shadow at the edge of sight, a place from which emanated the constant threat that the expression of any different idea would bring down not only heaven but the Party on your head.

As Mao himself had once observed – and Wang Shiwei had seemingly not heard – a single spark can start a prairie fire. And so it was that on 2 May, as soft breezes heralded a north China summer, a Yan'an Forum on 'Literature and Art' was convened with a group of seventy or eighty participants from among the intellectuals in the caves. As had become the Party custom, Mao Zedong was invited to provide the opening and closing address. '*Tongzhimen!*', Comrades!, he shouted in his usual emphatic tone. 'Literature and art for who?' he demanded. 'And literature and art for what?' 'Authors,' he advanced, 'might think that it was literature and art for intellectuals, but they would be wrong: literature and art were for the workers, the peasants and the soldiers. And authors,' Mao continued, 'might tell us that literature and art were all for the love of man and nature, but they would clearly be wrong. The only story worthy of being written and painted is the story of man's power to change the world through a revolutionary force of will with which each heart struggles to conquer its treacherous individualism and all combine together to triumph over the chaotic forces of nature, including the chaotic forces of men who have failed to understand the need for change.' 'Literature and art may have some practical value in advancing man towards his socialist destination,' Mao went on, for the benefit of intellectuals who were clearly struggling to keep up, 'but not without a literary and artistic criticism which remembers that nobody's ideas or thoughts should put themselves above the Party.' To which he added that a new order would require not only a military army of its own but a *cultural* army too. Closing with the ominous observation that a Rectification Movement had already been established to 'rectify the rectifiers', Mao expressed his confidence that the literary and artistic comrades would understand the need to 'move in the direction indicated'. More darkly, he noted that those 'still lacking in knowledge and understanding' would find themselves in difficulty: subjective minds that had so far failed to grasp the revolutionary force of literature and art would have to change.

No one had long to wait. Ding Ling was one of the first encouraged to criticise herself, instructed to do so in the new objective language of the time. And then on 27 May, Mao Zedong chaired a special committee to consider the case of Wang Shiwei. In a process that was as personal as it was official, Mao's deputy was his trusted and feared head of security, Kang Sheng, while the interrogators included a representative of the maligned chattering classes: Kang Sheng's wife. Questions were fired, silence was not permitted; and to every one of Wang's muffled answers, a volley of 'Nonsense!' was shot off in reply. Behind the scenes, deprived of sleep and food, Wang Shiwei was taken across a seemingly endless day-and-night process of thought reform, whose violent criticisms were designed to twist the muscle of his humanity, and break every thread of his mind.

On 8 June 1942, a thousand 'cultural troops', drawn from schools and organisations across the Party city, were gathered for an all-out attack. Reminded of their revolutionary duty to turn against even the most loved of one's family and friends if they held on to the wrong ideas, literary peers were invited to add their criticism to the guns.

Nearly a year later, in April 1943, after months of crippling detention, Wang Shiwei was formally arrested, and the rectification spread like wildfire, paralysing the caves with its purge. Advising Yan'an's 'specialists in literature' to pay attention to the wall posters that the Propaganda Department had now plastered across the Party city, thousands were questioned and criticised until they dropped with exhaustion. Once-sparkling minds struggled to tell the difference between black and white. Anyone who could, left. For many, it was clear that they were no longer free to leave. Not least, Wang Shiwei himself. Derided as a 'Trotskyite' (after the Russian revolutionist whose 'errors of thought' had been seen by Stalin as a threat to the survival of Communist Russia), and denounced as a bourgeois mind, Wang was condemned as an enemy of the people. Incarcerated in the bowels of Yan'an, from time to time, he was invited up to the sunshine: presented to visiting foreign journalists, as an example of open Party minds.

Meanwhile, as the 'cultural' battle for everyone's thoughts was being fought within the caved fortress of Yan'an, Mao spread his troops across the wider northern countryside, apparently fighting for national unity, although those closest to him noticed that Moscow and its wider machinations seemed to be commanding a lot of his attention – as had been the case for some time.

Years before, in 1936, with Japan's forces growing and China's defences undermined by a civil war, a desperate warlord had kidnapped Chiang Kai-shek. Ever fearful of Japan's imperialist advance, Moscow had stood behind the warlord and, long armed with Chiang's son as a 'friendly hostage', forced Chiang to accept a second United Front with Mao Zedong. Once united, and as the Japanese proceeded to advance on China's cities, both had been instructed to concentrate their attention on defeating the Japanese. It was not easy: in 1937, large parts of northern China, including Beijing, fell to Japanese control; Shanghai was bombarded and occupied; the Guomindang's capital of Nanjing was besieged. Retreating up the Yangzi to Wuhan (a trinity of Hankou and its sister cities of Wuchang and Hanyang created by the Republic), within a year, that too was lost. By the time that Wang Shiwei lost the freedom of his thoughts, the Guomindang had retreated further up the Yangzi, to the inland Sichuan city of Chongqing, the world had gone to war, and both Nationalist China and Communist Russia had joined the Western allies against an axis which included Japan. As the battles with Japan had escalated, fought over Guomindang strongholds in China's cities, Mao had found himself struggling with a battle of his own: holding on to Moscow's attention (and its funding) as Chiang-Kai Shek and Stalin sat on the same side of the Second World War.

Mao's struggles with Moscow would continue as Russia eventually turned its own far eastern forces to wrestling the northern Chinese lands from the grip of the Japanese. In 1945 Chiang and Stalin found themselves on the same winning side, with Stalin holding large parts of northern China surrendered by Japan. In 1947, however, drawing closer to America, Chiang declared a constitution and a new National Assembly for the Republic of China, Mao decided that the time for his own final push for power had come. With Japan now defeated, Chiang Kai-shek moving ever-closer to America, and Mao in tight control of the Chinese Communist Party, Moscow eventually agreed.

There would be two more years of battles on the ground before Mao could finally announce a revolutionary victory over the majority of the lands of China. But on 1 October 1949, flanked by his central committee, he ascended to a viewing terrace constructed at the top of the Tiananmen Gate of Heavenly Peace. As an autumn wind blew, he announced the 'liberation of the masses' and the Communist Party's fulfillment of the dream of a People's

Democratic Dictatorship. Waving to what would be described as a sea of radiant faces, the revolutionary notes of the *March of the Volunteers* were played: 'One million hearts beating as one: march on!'

Just over a month later, down in the last Sichuan stronghold of the Guomindang, Chiang Kai-shek led his defeated troops on to the boats and planes that would carry them to the once-renegade (and for most of the last fifty years, Japanese) island of Taiwan. Remembering Sun Yatsen, their broken hearts sang the anthem of an older dream: *Sanmin zhuyi*, the Three Principles of the People. Singing of a government of the people, by the people, for the people, they chorused: 'one heart, one soul; one mind, one goal'.

Once again, the single dream had divided and the old question returned – what did it mean to be Chinese? For Wang Shiwei, it was a question that had long since floated away: when the Party city of Yan'an had set off towards its liberation of the Chinese lands, he had been taken to the silence of a remote valley and, with the swing of an axe, his head had been severed from his heart.

*   *   *

As early as January 1949, when the People's Liberation Army captured the once-imperial capital, Mao and the senior ranks of the Party explored new offices in the Zhongnanhai, Central and Southern Sea, gardens, in a corner of the Forbidden City. It had quickly become clear to the Party and its generals that decades of uncertainty had created a mountain of chaos. Mountains of rubbish lay all around, food was in dangerously short supply, money had no value, and even the trains had lost their tracks. The People's Liberation Army was ordered to step in and clean up the rubbish, a duty which, to the considerable surprise of Beijing, it discharged with revolutionary efficiency.

Looking at the wider problems, the Party also realised that the city had been deeply damaged by refugees. The most visible damage had been inflicted by those flooding in: tens of thousands of incomers, who had washed up, like a river, from the countryside, in search of shelter from the guns, carrying hunger and disease in their wake. On closer reflection, though, it was clear that the loss of those who had followed the Guomindang, would also have a cost: the many who had left included a number of the city's greatest talents.

The choice to stay or leave had not been easy. In the chaos of two decades of warlords and war and the uncertainty of any outcome, many of the students who had raised the roof of Peking University had not known which way to turn. Everyone had heard whispering stories of Yan'an and its strange ideas, not to mention its hidden prisons (some had even heard whispers of a tyranny which had started in the earliest of Mao's mountain years). Given, however, that the caved city was already home to many friends from the past, some decided that the whispers must have been the propaganda weapons of a Guomindang desperate to win the war. Certainly, everyone had seen the lengths to which the Guomindang were prepared to go for victory. Guns in everyone's faces, arrests at every turn and the Yellow River unleashed as a weapon against the advancing Japanese (a desperate attempt to save Wuhan, with the unfortunate consequence that hundreds of thousands of Chinese peasants had been swept off to watery graves). Not to mention the fact that the corruption of the Guomindang's selfish self-strengtheners was so vast and deeply rooted that it seemed to have been directly inherited from the dying embers of the Qing. Those who left had decided that the known world of the Guomindang would be safer than the mysterious caves of the Communists. Those who had stayed had decided that 'red or white', Beijing was a city like no other.

Looking at the efficiency of Mao's cleaning up, many of those who had stayed behind began to think they had probably made the right choice. Clear about the importance of discipline, the Red Army's generals had trained their troops in three revolutionary 'modesty and prudence without arrogance', 'plain living' and 'hard struggle'. Armed with these mantras, from the earliest days of their entry into the capital, the troops of the People's Liberation Army had introduced themselves politely to the people and set themselves up as examples. Unlike the cold guns and the barked commands of the Guomindang and their warlords, the rules for the cleaning-up operation had even been thoughtfully announced to the public in the press: 'three main rules of discipline', 'eight points for attention'. Rather than the nightmare everyone expected, the entire process seemed to be a masterclass in revolutionary order. Roads were cleared to the tune of cheerful songs, damaged property was restored to rightful owners; and the human misery that flooded the streets was either gathered up and encouraged to go home, returned to healthier feet or sent respectfully on to a better life beyond.

By the 1950s, the wider order of the city was being systematically restored. Trains and trams were returned to their tracks, radios broadcast programmes, newspapers reported events, markets set out their wares for sale, shops reopened their doors to trade, and the poorest were presented with work and food. After so many years of destruction, even more of the early doubters dared to dream that the 'liberation' would be exactly what it promised: a change of past misfortune into hope.

Curious about the changes around them, many of Beijing's people turned to their much-loved bookshops, consulting the works of Marx and Mao Zedong to get a clearer idea about what they could expect from the new order of the Chinese world. Opening crisp new volumes, they learnt that man is determined by his society, and that if man studied society scientifically, he would be able to change his fate and usher in a golden age of socialism where everyone would have what they needed. That seemed to make sense. Reading further they noted that when the scientific force of human will (objective thinking) is applied to serve the people, a new abundance can be achieved, rubbing out the differences between manual and mental labour, erasing the gaps between the cities and the countryside, and evening out the inequalities between rich and poor. Reading the conclusion of one of Mao's own works, they saw that a 'new democracy' had been established, one that was dedicated to guaranteeing the Democratic Dictatorship of the People, with the Communist Party as the revolutionary guarantor, and with the eventual 'withering away' of the state as the goal.

Thinking on the chaos and destruction of the past two decades, it all seemed perfectly reasonable. Indeed, to those who were familiar with the past, it sounded rather like Kang Youwei's late nineteenth-century idea of a *Da Tong* Great Unity. Looking at the trains, the telegraphs and the telephones, even the cars and the very polite tanks, many began to whisper in admiration that there seemed to be no end to what this new science could achieve. Apparently, all it required was a more objective perspective on how to make things work for the better order of all. Well, that and a sharper attention to the idea of class.

According to Mao (and Marx before him) class was everything. Digging deeper into the books, Beijing's people read that idle landlords and imperialist compradors had no place in the new world. Well, that had been obvious for a long time and most of them had already left, following Chiang Kai-shek to Taiwan or some other part of the capitalist world. Those who had been friends and neighbours would be missed, but if things went well, perhaps they would come to realise that they had underestimated Mao's dedication to the people and, chastened, would return with new and redder hearts. As for those landlords and compradors who had failed to flee in time, they would, just like everyone else, have to learn to adapt. Then there were the 'rightist' bourgeoisie. According to Mao, these were people who claimed to be all for a change, but didn't want any kind of a revolution that threatened to put their own personal limbs to labour. Fair enough: it was obvious that everyone was going to have to learn some lessons, but hopefully a better, more selfless, people would come out of it all. Within the broad ranks of the bourgeoisie, though, apparently there was a higher and a lower. The higher bourgeoisie were people who just wanted to live off capital rather than turning their minds to any kind of labour: they were apparently scarcely any better than the landlords and the compradors. But almost anyone with that kind of capital had picked up their belongings and gone, and if they had stayed behind they would just have to take their lessons. As for the lower, petty, bourgeoisie, these were students, teachers, clerks, and shop-keepers: the people who had kept the capitalist ship afloat. That seemed to cover quite a few of those left in Beijing. There was apparently an argument in the Party that they were, in fact, a higher-bourgeoisie-in-waiting, but before writing them off as a socialist risk, Mao was apparently willing to let them prove themselves with an offer of service to the people at large.

And then there were the people at large, the proletariat who had been propelled to the top, which had obviously been the whole point of the revolution. The most advanced of these were the factory and railway workers who had laboured hardest for the strikes of the past. Also included were the craftsmen, shop-workers, rickshawmen, street cleaners and pedlars: men and women who had been a little slower to understand the call of change but who, while they might not have read their Marx or their Mao, were really at the heart of everything. That seemed to account for most of the rest of Beijing. The greatest number of people across the country at large, and now the dictatorship of all, it was this proletariat which was to dedicate itself to the elimination of the oppressive classes, including the treachery of tricky minds. Where once the peasants and workers had pinned their hopes on secret brotherhoods of men, they now appreciated that stronger measures were called for: an elimination, once and for all, of the classes who had stood against them, with a root and branch re-education of bourgeois minds so that they could never again use their clever tongues to climb back on top. To do this, of course, having been so oppressed by the upper classes for so long, the people would need ongoing revolutionary help. And after twenty-eight years of battling, it was precisely that help which the Communist Party, vanguard of a revolution that would take some time to achieve, would provide.

Reading the Communist texts, it all seemed very ambitious. As Mao himself had pointed out, it might take twenty years before the golden age of socialism finally arrived. But if everyone played their part, it seemed as if victory would deliver a bright new future where the state and all of its powers would gradually be eliminated, and everyone's needs would be met: the people would be equal and free.

* * *

As the people familiarised themselves with the principles of the new revolutionary world, the Communist Party's bureaucrats got down to the business of recreating the administering machinery of Yan'an in the much grander city of Beijing. Party leaders having replaced their caves with spreading courtyard homes in Zhongnanhai, attention turned to the maze of new ministries that would now be required. Meanwhile, with the Party stretching its wings in the freedom of the capital, and with mountains of work to be done, new recruits to the Party were welcomed on a daily basis.

For those who had experienced the greatest bitterness of the past, the changes were intoxicating. More questioning minds held their judgement. Some thought on the millennia of Taiping Great Peace dreams, which had risen and failed so often before. Others, understanding that this new society was clearly going to promote the cause of the common man at others' expense, wondered whether there would be a place for everybody – and what would happen if you didn't want to join in. Eventually, however, encouraged by what they began to see and read, a number of the sceptics decided to get on board. Passers-by seemed to find a new spring to their step, people smiled in greeting, and the harrowing memories of the recent past became distant ghosts. Revolutionary songs were taken to heart; children sang in the streets. Inspired by the Communist victory, students were moved to join the new youthful organisations for singing and drama; and everyone was encouraged to join the collective physical exercise on which health and strength depended. Beggars who had been taught new working ways reappeared as street performers of revolutionary dances, celebrating their own reform. Handcarts selling snacks at the roadside were emblazoned with exhortations to join the spirit of the times: *Gong he!*, Work together!, *Gong he!* And after a while, those who had insisted on holding on to their questions began to seem a little bit selfish, with increasing numbers of newly converted minds observing that perhaps they had something to learn.

Of course, nothing was going to be easy. After decades of war and destruction, how could it be? The essentials of life were in short supply, and the means of producing any kind of wealth had been blasted out of existence. Newspapers printed under the Communist star explained to Beijingers that living in a city was a privilege to be earned. Editorials urged them not only to reform their thoughts but to embrace frugality and equality with their hearts. Consume less electricity and water; offer to take a reduction in your pay. And if you were one of those lucky enough to have a courtyard or a business, think about what might be possible if you opened your profits to the workers, and your rooms to people in need.

Schools were asked to cut their courses to a more efficient cloth: fewer hours, fewer subjects, fewer years; less attention to academic tricks; more attention to the discipline that trains a young body to endure, and strengthens the revolutionary resolve to build a better world for the common good of man. Families were told to think twice about how they fed themselves and raised their children: in the pursuit of a glorious future, a big consuming city was an extravagance no one could afford. Along the streets and alleys, once-idle housewives were encouraged to step out of working in the home to find a purpose in a life outside: set up a committee and become a revolutionary, sweep the neighbourhood, look after the sick, sort out arguments. Barbers, pedlars, noodle-sellers and owners of small corner shops were all pushed into groups that would be collectively owned by all of their members (although how, on earth, that was going to work, nobody knew). And the newspapers, in addition to carrying everyone's daily reminders, were asked to match their stories to the new revolutionary goals: irresponsible rumours were to be swept to the past; revolutionary heroism was to be printed on the front page.

As Beijing's residents were set to a new order, some were surprised when they were required to register at local police stations, and then told to help the police in keeping track of everyone. But apparently, the Guomindang had their spies everywhere, just waiting to tip the city back to the chaos of the past. Residents were to live in their registered homes; visitors were to present themselves to local police stations for checks; strangers were to be reported whenever and wherever they might appear. And everyone received a *hukou* passbook that confirmed a right to live in the city – as long as you didn't do anything so terrible that it might be withdrawn.

Attention then turned to work. Not just the earning of an individual living, but the dedication of everyone to the Communist goal of achieving the productive abundance that would deliver equality for all: work was to become everybody's purpose. In 1953, a Five Year Plan was drawn up to set out what the country needed and how it would be achieved. State-funded industrial production was to put China onto a solid socialist track, creating a footing firm enough to enable the country to catch up with the obvious benchmark of the imperial and capitalist West. With inputs and outputs fixed by the Plan, the state went on to raise or acquire factories to get production on the road. Workers were told that they would need to live closer to their place of work and that, once at work, they would need to dedicate their hearts to revolutionary heights of production. How to achieve this? Part of the answer was the creation of *danwei*, work units, to unite the people with their workplaces, all under the leadership of a new corps of 'Party cadres'. And where would the Party cadres come from? Taking volunteers with the correct class credentials, the Party school was training them as fast as it could.

Before long, loudspeakers were calling everyone to the early morning exercises that would prepare them for a day of work. Committees were created to carry out whatever non-productive work – from cleaning to security – needed to be done. Meetings to hear government announcements were helpfully convened on site. Welfare groups were established to make sure that everyone had the bare essentials. And with everyone still needing to learn the art of objective thinking, study groups were raised to teach Marxist purpose and human responsibility, together with the fervour that every successful revolution required. To all of this was added a system of *dang'an* personal files to make sure that everyone stayed on track. And for those who lost their way, groups of peers were gathered to voice the criticisms that could clarify right from wrong – guided, of course, by the Party cadre in charge.

Businesses acquired by the state took the new working ideas to heart and reorganised themselves accordingly. The collective groups of sundry spirits – the barbers, peddlars, noodle-sellers, corner-shop owners and any other local community service providers who had cared to join – did their best to follow suit. Everyone was clear that productivity was key: the industrial kind of productivity which would deliver China into self-sufficiency, and for which cities with their large collections of people were so ideally made.

The order of work settled, it was also clear that a high degree of organisational efficiency would be required if the city was to afford to run itself. District municipal administrations had little value to offer and came at a high cost: they were more consumers than producers. Conversely, the people themselves were a revolutionary force, an ocean of labour that could be applied not just to industrial production but to the business of running the city itself. Costs could be further reduced through the institution of the new 'mass organisation': whole troupes of people organised under 'All China' banners. Dedicated to everything from women to work, and from youth to the disabled, they would be an essential part of a Democratic Dictatorship of the People in which everyone would have a voice, as long as the voice was at one with the Party's revolutionary stand. No more need for unions in the factories, or for anyone to argue individually for whatever they thought they wanted: the mass organisations would take care of it all.

The people, the newspapers and productivity all set firmly on the tracks of the brave new world, everyone dug deep to display the revolutionary courage that would make the dream come true.

*　　*　　*

Contemplating the new model of scientific man he was creating, Mao turned his sights on the architecture of the city in which it was all taking place. Standing on the terrace of the Tiananmen Gate of Heavenly Peace, he was asked by the mayor of Beijing what kind of view he would like to see. Looking down the ancient 'thousand step way', and observing the still-remaining flanks of tiled roofs, glittering yellow and green below, Mao paused for a moment, and then replied: 'A forest of chimneys'. Quickly concurring, the mayor, Peng Zhen, declared it 'an excellent idea'. New city officials were commanded to commission a plan from Beijing's most famous architect: a Princeton-educated scholar who had developed an encyclopaedic knowledge of the imperial buildings of Beijing, and who, braving the revolutionary changes, had offered his experience and skills to the service of the People's Republic. The son of Liang Qichao, the early revolutionary who had gone on to launch a school of journalism at Peking University, his name was Liang Sicheng.

So familiar was Liang Sicheng with the structure of the city to which he had dedicated his life that he had no need to stand and look at anything. Without being asked, he knew that the Inner and Imperial cities – with the Forbidden City at their heart, and with their heavenly chequerboard of princely courtyards and dividing lanes – were not fit for the kinds of practical purposes that Mao had in mind. The courtyards were treasure troves of an ancient beauty and painstaking skill that were testaments to the great art of Lu Ban (the god of carpentry to an ancient city built of wood) and, indeed, to the very idea of what it meant to be Chinese. The dividing lanes were so narrow that they could scarcely carry a car, let alone a truck. Unaware of the transforming scale of Mao's dream, Liang thought he saw an obvious solution: keep the heart of China's government in the centre of the city, but locate the critical functions of bureaucracy, industry and knowledge outside the remaining walls. 'Imagine the People's Republic as a paradise for all,' he suggested. Outlining his idea to Beijing's Party bureaucrats, he went on to explain that the walls and their surrounding moats could be turned into a people's park, with tunnels underneath to carry any vehicles that needed to pass. Originally constructed to be wide enough to carry ten horses abreast, the walls could easily accommodate gracious walkways for the workers. Curving all around the old Imperial City, the moats could offer boating and fishing to ease the spirits of the masses at the end of a hard-working week. But Liang's ideas could not have been further from Mao's material mind. The imperial city of the past was nothing but an enemy of the revolutionary future. The walls came down.

The architect's subjective thinking noted, Liang Sicheng was then invited to self-criticise the opinions that had led him to disagree with the will of the people at large. But Liang was not the only one to shed a tear at the idea of the old walls falling. And while the walls were monumental, they were not the only problem to have struck those minds that wanted to hold on to their own powers of thought. Mao's views on the scientific force of human will were clear, but the single-minded ordering from the top was becoming rather hard to distinguish from the imperial edicts of the past.

After two revolutions in fifty years, both of them fought so that the people could have independent minds and voices with which to express them, many had begun to mutter that the promises of the past were not being kept. Looking at the *danwei* work units, with their study groups and their insistence on Party cadre leadership, university professors argued they were an assault on the academic spirit. Finding themselves wrapped into a mass All China Federation of Trade Unions, workers pointed to an even deeper contradiction: just because 'the people' were in charge of the Republic, didn't mean that the Republic's factories were always in the right. The All China Federation of Trade Unions would need to decide whether it was on the side of the factories or the workers – and if it wasn't on the side of the workers then new trade unions should be created to make sure that everyone was represented. And then the lawyers chimed in, arguing that even in socialism one needed to be clear about duties and rights – including the duties of the new People's Republic, and the rights of the people at large.

'Quite right,' replied Mao in 1956. 'We should all be clear about our responsibilities.' 'Why not let me hear your individual suggestions and we can let a hundred flowers bloom and a hundred schools of thought contend?'

Eager minds inked their subjective thoughts onto enthusiastic pages and pasted them up on walls for everyone to see: 'too much top-down decision making', 'too many bureaucratic rules' and 'a stifling of individual energies and ideas' seemed to be the gist of it all. But everyone had their own particular point to make. Across the city, on almost every *danwei* work-unit door and wall, posters appeared, detailing complaints about things that were not working, with well-intended ideas for solutions, including the suggestion that it was all perhaps a bit too much for the state to do on its own. Perhaps, suggested the posters, the people (the real ones on the ground, rather than the abstract ones who were theoretically in charge of everything) ought to lend the state a hand. Even the old landlords and compradors (those who had survived and obviously forgotten the lessons of peers who hadn't made it) ventured to add a splash of their own: after eight years of socialism, wasn't it about time they were allowed into the people's fold?

At Peking University, a wall was dedicated to 'democracy', decorated with posters criticising the Party for the failure of its revolutionary promise of a Party for all. As reports of the postering treachery reached Mao, it seemed that the voice of Wang Shiwei (executed, but apparently by no means buried) was everywhere. Even Ding Ling seemed to have forgotten her newly learnt lessons: gathering together with groups of authors, arguing that taboos on subject matters and styles would inhibit human creativity and jeopardise the country's reconstruction, she was once again spreading her dangerously subjective ideas.

The brutal rectifications of Yan'an having cost more than a fair number of Party lives, many of the Party's leading spirits (not least Zhou Enlai, once Mao's superior, now vice-chairman of the Party and Mao's premier) thought that the questioners – the doctors, lawyers, scientists, historians, authors and artists – had a point. If the country was going to be reliably rebuilt, surely every qualified mind needed to be able to tell the truth as they saw it. As the ink splashed across the posters, and as Party minds joined in, it was clear to Mao that these subjective opinions were just the kind of revolutionary risk he had been warning about.

Mao told himself that he should have seen it coming back in 1953, when Stalin had died of his stroke. Krushchev and the other Russian brothers had started pawing over the legacy of Stalin's 'personality politics', even as they had begun to bite each other's backs. Not surprisingly, three years later, unreliable Hungary had erupted with a bunch of intellectuals who wanted a more subjective life, and the Russians had nearly lost it.

Stalin's personality had fallen out of favour in Moscow and Russian winds of change were blowing towards Beijing. While his own (Mao Zedong) thought was now the most popular of all the national Party pieces, those bureaucratic men in skirts in the Party quarters of Zhongnanhai had already taken to wondering whether Mao's personality had become too much of a cult. 'Perhaps it might be time,' they suggested, 'for Mao and the Party to adjust to more dignified positions, with Mao formally a little higher but in reality more towards the rear. *Honorary* chairman perhaps?' Oblivious to the foolishness of their bureaucratic preoccupations, they even took to suggesting that the adoring public should be encouraged to sing the hugely popular '*The East Is Red*' (with its vision of Mao as a great sun without whom there would be no China) a little bit less.

True to his guerrilla spirit, Mao bided his time and conceded gracefully. As he bit his tongue, though, his mind had already begun to turn to the intellectuals who were plainly at the root of a confusion of bureaucratic preoccupations better suited to the time of the Ming. True, the bureaucrats and their specialist skills had their uses. But, chronically unable to rid themselves of their subjective bourgeois thoughts, they had failed to understand the bigger revolutionary picture and were now leading everyone up the wrong path – at what cost? Time and again, he had submitted grand schemes for revolutionary change to Party committees; almost all of them had been buried by men who lacked the courage to live the dream. A bunch of chickens who seemed to be more like women with bound feet, their petty cowardice was threatening to bring the soaring triumph of the revolution down to earth with a thud.

Contemplating both the revolutionary risks of the subjective intellectual minds outside the Party, and the treachery of his own foot-dragging bureaucrats within, Mao chose to reply with a (long) lecture on contradictions – that tricky law of opposites, which meant that it took the objectivity of a truly revolutionary mind to be able to work out what was what. Not sure that his words had conveyed his message clearly, Mao followed it up with another sharp lecture on class. 'There are good class elements,' he explained, 'who understand the importance of being on the left of everything. And there are bad class elements,' he continued, 'who, after all this time, still do not appreciate that the left is where they need to be.' The gist of it was that anyone who criticised the Party was obviously one of the latter – bad class and a bourgeois 'rightist' to boot.

The lecture delivered, but to little obvious effect, Mao decided that it was time for everyone to get the point. That old Beijing bourgeoisie of intellectuals, who could have bent to the revolutionary wind but had clearly failed to learn their lessons, were not to be trusted. Just as bad were the city's workers with their ideas of unions to champion petty personal interests: a would-be bourgeoisie, if ever there was one.

The message as clear as he could make it, across the early months of 1957, Mao flooded the Party School and its cadres with his own preferred opinions. Looking to the population at large to support him, he turned to the *danwei*s and suggested that they raise a cultural army of popular opinion which, manned by everyone's friends, relations and work colleagues, would report those whose hearts were not in the revolution, and, in so doing, demonstrate that they themselves had overcome their own subjectivity and banished any and all emotional loyalties to the back of beyond.

By the end of the year, three hundred thousand intellectuals had been declared 'rightist' enemies of the people. The worst offenders were charged with counter-revolution, and despatched to another world. Others were marched off with their arms in the twisting helicopter position, and expelled from the city: clearly undeserving of its revolutionary riches, and obviously in need of the kind of re-education that only the peasants in the countryside could provide. For those lucky enough to stay in Beijing, the working day would acquire a little more discipline and a sharper attention to the *dang'an* personal files that daily recorded the colour of everyone's hearts.

For those expelled from the city's ideological purity – the ones who had not been sent to jail, or to labour camps, or committed suicide during the harrowing struggle sessions launched against them – the fields were waiting. Among the exiles, was Ding Ling.

*   *   *

As the city was emptied of its questioning minds, a cloud of silence settled. The streets lost a bit of their shine, and many faces looked a little heavier. But socialism seemed to have a boundless energy, and Mao marched bravely on.

Having thought about the challenge of beating the imperial and capitalist West, to say nothing of withering away the state, Mao had concluded that, on its own, the danwei was too small to guarantee the industrial scale of success required. Something bigger and more ambitious was needed: obviously not a city, with all of the consuming distractions and clutter that the Party had struggled so hard to tame, but something dedicated to realising the essential productive purpose of the city. Mulling over the possibilities, Mao contemplated the factory. Not just one factory, but many factories. And not just factories producing goods for sale, but satellite factories and workshops, conveniently delivering whatever materials the leading factories needed – and equally conveniently, relieving the leading factories of the discarded materials and waste which were left behind. Indeed, not just factories, but every other kind of entity that would enable the workers to concentrate their time and attention on the productive tasks in hand: tailors, barbers, schools, post offices and essential shops for basic needs. Simple dormitories and housing, tightly packed to fit everybody in, so that everyone and their families could live close by and concentrate their efforts on their work. Industrial productivity would shoot to the stars, and whenever the Party had anything to announce or teach the masses, everyone could be easily gathered together for the kind of meeting that would improve the efficiency of everyone's thoughts.

Seeming to search for an idea, though, Mao had, in fact, long ago found his answer: what was bigger than a danwei but more tightly organised than a city? A commune. A tremendous step towards the withering away of the state – even as it got rid of all the layers of meddling bureaucrats who might otherwise get in his greater visionary way.

Hearing of Mao's dream, the bureaucrats scratched their heads in consternation. Of course, Russia had its large organisations in the countryside, but no one, beyond the few who had read their French history, had ever heard of a commune in a city before. Neither did anyone have much of an idea of what it should look like. Being bureaucrats, those responsible for running city administrations wondered how the new 'communes' could possibly be fitted into the geographic districts into which the city had always been divided. Given that the state was supposed to disappear, they also wondered how the communes would deliver any kind of order. Meanwhile, bureaucrats in the Party struggled to understand how the communes would fit with the Five Year Plans.

Explaining that the whole point of a commune was to get rid of the wasteful city bureaucracy – not to mention simplifying planning by pushing as much production as possible through communes, rather than lots of smaller danweis – Mao redirected the local city bureaucrats to new jobs, and set the central Party bureaucracy to redesigning the Plan. Minds confused, but revolutionary spirits trying to please, the bureacracy set off to try to work it out.

For the businesses of the state – the army and the essential industries, like iron and steel, which had been acquired or set up from scratch – the proposition seemed relatively easy. For work and workers already anchored in the Plan, the Party cadres simply had to identify empty adjacent spaces, and invite related producers to join them in the new higher efficiency. The collectives, however, were more of a challenge. Building a motley collection of individuals into a danwei had been difficult enough, but how could one conjure up something the size and complexity of a commune out of a bunch of collected livelihoods on the streets? And, not included in the Plan (and thus not supported by any budget), where would the collectives get the cash? Inspired by Mao's challenge to revolutionise society with discipline, energetic Party cadres soon came up with an answer. In the absence of any money from the state, the members of the small collectives would just need to do their own self-strengthening, and provide according to their means. Collective members who still had private businesses would have staff and buildings they could contribute; surviving small landlords would have courtyards that could easily double up as workshops, and even dormitories for the night; workers could contribute their wages; and everyone with a pair of hands could offer their labour or skills.

Some were enthusiastic, others more sceptical. But with the disappearance of so many of the flowering minds who had dared to ask their questions, most were quick to read the writing on the wall. There were, however, a few stragglers who seemed slow to get the point. Some wondered if they could hire others to do their work for them; others asked how much profit each individual would be able to take. Hadn't they bothered to read the books? Quiet chats – as many as required and as late into the night as necessary – soon set them to rights. With little or no money to rub between them, paper-makers remembered their skills, shoe-menders offered their tools, housewives delivered their sewing machines, and the unemployed offered their time. Courtyards were soon commandeered for production, managers with Party cadre credentials emerged, and the larger factories of the state were approached, either in search of an invitation to fill an empty space or for some sort of productive order that could squeeze the collective misfits into the circulation of the Plan.

With the danweis of the state enterprises now marching into communes, and smaller collectives somehow finding a niche within the Plan, newspapers began to report industrial miracles by the day. Party confidence rising, in early 1958, a second Five-Year Plan was introduced to usher in a Great

Leap Forward. Industry would rocket, and the precocious steel production of imperialist-capitalist Britain would be overtaken in fifteen years: that should show the Russian brothers that China was a serious contender in the Communist world. With similar innovations to be introduced in the countryside, the fields would be able to support everyone with bumper harvests that would fuel the cities' industrial success.

Looking at the details of the paper projections, bureaucratic minds that had successfully survived the treacherous straits of the Hundred Flowers campaign, began to feel a little queasy. But the horrors of the following Anti-Rightist campaign ensured that, even in the highest corners of Zhongnanhai, very few flowers bloomed. Daily models of productivity appeared in the pages of the newspapers. It was even said that a city had risen from the middle of nowhere in which industry and agriculture had been combined, and where everyone did everything with almost nothing – and all without a single human cost. Factory workers were divided into teams, with competitive targets set for all. The people were invited to imagine a new China: one where, once the ground of hard work had been laid, everyone's needs would not only be met but they would all have more time to do whatever they wanted. Once achieved, such a country would become the envy of the once-so-vainglorious foreign world.

Inspired by Mao's supreme confidence, on the ground, and undisturbed by the paper details, many hearts began to beat a little faster. Perhaps 'the great sun rising from the East' had a point about those questioning rightists: maybe they really had been slackers who had not been able to understand the greater revolutionary purpose. Inspired by the cause of the common good, workers set aside personal families and their problems, turning their energies to the 'big family' of the commune and the even 'bigger family' of the state. Practical problems of making meals and the daily care of infants were solved with communal dining halls and industrial nurseries. And with the countryside now producing just the kind of bumper harvests Mao had said they would, even the weather seemed to be showing some revolutionary fervour: the sun shone on fields, and food seemed to pour straight on to open tables. Hope began to soar. Housewives who had never worked before got so excited that they forgot to eat, sleep, or even go home. Students, inspired by stories of superhuman men who had defied the odds to achieve the impossible, saw themselves as revolutionary pioneers, readily accepting assignments to work in whatever factory needed them. And with everyone keeping an eye on the ambitious targets for iron and steel, backyard furnaces were built wherever there was a space, with pots, pans and pipes contributed for the good of the nation. In awe of their achievements, Mao penned poems as paeans to the wonders of the mass human will.

But while many hearts rose, some remained heavy, intent on counting the cost of it all. Working hours had stayed the same but under the Democratic Dictatorship of the People, endless meetings had been piled on top. Dormitories were opened up to constant inspections. Thoughts, and the personal files that recorded them, were subject to constant scrutiny. Permissions were required for everything. Without the approval of a Party cadre, nothing could be done. Bonuses for extra hours ('to each according to his work'), marriages and travel, all needed a stamp; and the job of stamping appeared to have acquired a spirit of its own, with a strong preference for the reddest hearts of Party members. And while good class backgrounds seemed to have no trouble in getting whatever approving ink they needed, those whose backgrounds had any sort of a question found that the ink had usually run out. The heavy hearts bit their tongues: Mao's poems were clearly not for them.

*　　　　*　　　　*

Mao's own heart set on revolutionary heights, he had left the details of the communes to the bureaucrats and the Party cadres, addressing his thoughts to a jubilant contemplation of the more constructive possibilities of socialism. By mid-1958, it was clear to him that a new China would require a new capital. The old capital, built for a ritual consumption of China's people and things, should not only give way to new productive purpose, but also to monuments that would recognise the triumphant will of the masses. Across the 1950s, palaces and walls had already given way to the productive future, and factories had risen for the glory of all. Now it was time to create a Communist cityscape for the nation.

Casting his eyes across the remaining imperial indulgences, Mao's sights fell on the Tiananmen Gate of Heavenly Peace. Where the avenue of the 'thousand step way' had once conveyed humble subjects to the gate which marked the point at which heaven met earth, Mao imagined a vast square, big enough to hold 'a million' people: a parade ground for everyone (including the army), and a taming of the past to serve the present. Of course, a lot of the clutter of the surrounding imperial buildings would need to be removed. And if the square was to serve the practical purpose of marching people and military parades, there would need to be some sort of a boulevard, running east to west, and wide enough to accommodate the troops.

Once imagined, it was only a matter of applying revolutionary hands to make the dream come true. With the tenth anniversary of the formal October 1949 declaration of the People's Republic advancing, what better than ten monumental edifices as revolutionary testaments to the triumph of socialism in Chinese hands? In early 1959, newspapers announced a contest for designs, and a thousand architects were invited to liberate their imaginations. Within a few revolutionary weeks, plans for ten vast buildings were completed and approved: a Workers' Stadium to host mass games; the biggest railway station in China, from which revolutionary trains could set off to the remotest of China's corners; a Military Museum to celebrate the triumphs that had won the peace; hotels to welcome foreign guests and visiting 'overseas Chinese'; a Diaoyutai State Guest House to display the socialist power of China to the visiting world; a Cultural Palace for all the different tribal 'nationalities' who were part of the great Chinese people. And at the centre of the city, commanding the two corners of the new Tiananmen Square closest to Zhongnanhai and the wider Forbidden City, a Great Hall of the People, and a Museum of the People's History.

Inspired by socialism, each of the great new buildings was designed to put the purpose of production into the heart of the city. Utility and efficiency were evident; beauty would take a little familiarity to see. With brash positions on vast new avenues, all of the monuments would oblige every passing eye to look in their direction. Concrete columns would push their way to the skies. Cavernous façades would summon up the sense of a much greater 'Man'. Heavy roofs would draw sharp lines between this world and any misguided ideas of the next. Each edifice would be bigger than anything that China had ever seen, and all would be a capital reminder of the power of the revolutionary will.

Plans having been produced at lightning speed, work soon followed. Ground was broken in April – less than six months before the sun would rise on 1 October 1959. Clearly, a triumph of man would be required. Mao was confident. Hearts still thudding after the shock of the Hundred Flowers and its following Anti-Rightist campaign, few of even the greatest Party stars dared to urge the caution that many of them felt would be wise. Of those who did, Zhou Enlai was the only one to remain standing, although not without a lecture. Across the countryside, tons of solid materials were torn from the earth, while tens of thousands of peasants were invited to leave their fields and raise the revolutionary city. Military principles were applied to annihilate all obstacles; revolutionary songs were sung to raise the spirits high; feats of human endurance became matters of daily fact. As Mao had so confidently predicted, in the world where the will of man created history, success was to be theirs.

As the sun rose on the morning of 1 October 1959, the ten monumental edifices were ready for inspection, and Tiananmen Square opened its arms to receive an anniversary parade. Trucks pressed past in carefully geared formation; cannons and howitzers followed. Silver F5 fighter jets streaked across the skies. Green battalions of soldiers marched in the tightest of blocks; the navy followed in shipshape squares. Advancing eyes swept up and to the right, to the towering spirits on the terrace of the Gate of Heavenly Peace who were beaming with pride: eleven thousand military men on a marching display, with not a single step out of place; all followed by seven hundred thousand representatives of the people, advancing a hundred and fifty abreast. Trumpets trumpeting, pipes piping, drums beating, cymbals clashing, the notes of the *March of the Volunteers* conducted them all.

Up in the clouds, red lanterns swaying in a gentle breeze, Mao Zedong, the sun of the East, waved to the masses, with Zhou Enlai and the galaxy of Party stars standing loyally at his side. For those below, the slogans of the times flooded everyone's hearts and minds: 'The East Wind overwhelms the West Wind!' 'Work hard, struggle upstream, build more, better and more efficient socialism, faster!' '*Renmin gonghe guo wansui!*, Long live China!

It was a ten-year triumph; a revolution that had overturned a revolution; a battle that had swept aside every occupying foreign power; and a victory that had delivered a People's Republic into the heart of once-imperial Beijing. And with the temples of socialism now successfully raised to the skies, the peasants were invited to return to their fields: the city was not for everyone.

* * *

As 1959 passed into 1960, the winds began to change. In the dining halls of the communes, food began to lose its flavour and there was a lot less of it than before. No one was quite sure what was happening but rumour had it that the harvests, which had seemed to romp to abundance in 1958 and 1959, were beginning to fail. The Great Leap Forward seemed to have foundered.

From the commanding heights of the capital, 'pests' were blamed – certainly insects, but possibly even pests of the foreign human kind as well. Whatever the cause, food was thin, and the workers were getting thinner. Suddenly the sun seemed to have dimmed a little. Factories that had conjured up storms of orders found that demand was slimming down. The state managed to keep its enterprises going, together with their iron bowls of rice; but many in the collectives began to feel more than a pinch of struggle. With too little food coming in from the countryside to feed everybody, any remaining recent migrants were returned to their village homes. Still the hunger growled. In the quiet gardens of Zhongnanhai, Mao forgot about razing imperial palaces and raising chimneys, and set a model example by digging up the mulberry trees that graced his courtyard, and replacing them with chillis and corn.

Ever-present in the posters splashed across the communes, a radiant Mao continued to spread his blessings. But out across the city, as the pangs of hunger were followed by a loss of steam, the purpose of production lost its power to command and inspire. Hearts stumbled, and hands began to slow. Anxious to raise the people's spirits, the leading lights of the Party looked for inspiring images and words. A rising star conjured up a model soldier by the name of Lei Feng, who, having braved the bitterest of winds to keep the Chinese people safe, had lost his life in the course of his productive duties; images of the hero appeared on posters everywhere, as a beacon for all. And another volume of Mao's selected works appeared on the spartan shelves of bookshops: being 'recommended' reading for all, it flew off them just as quickly. A new campaign was launched through the danweis, this one supposed to be all about 'cleaning up': apparently not only had the fields collapsed, but someone at the top had noticed that some of the Party cadres in the canteens had been feeding themselves and their families first. As with all such campaigns, though, it started out as one thing and ended up as quite another. Before anyone knew it, it was all about class struggle and criticism: of oneself and everyone else. Few doubted the warmth of Mao's personal sun, or the integrity of the people at large, but red hearts were beginning to think that something in the city was not quite right.

By the spring of 1961, while Mao's personal sun continued to glow, the nightmare of the Great Leap Forward's failure was seeping through the upper echelons of the Party. No one in Beijing (or anywhere else) could be sure of the exact numbers of the dead, but many in Zhongnanhai were aware that millions of Chinese had disappeared; others, less close to Party policy, were beginning to guess. Natural disasters and foreign conspiracies were invoked, but most at the top of the Party knew that the dead were victims of a mass campaign whose revolutionary fervour had created an 'objective' fabric of lies so scientifically unassailable that they had stamped out human truth.

Mao, aware of the human costs but refusing to sacrifice the scientific force of the revolution for the sake of a few mistakes, threatened to remove his colossal personal appeal from the Party altogether. And the Party – aware that it was Mao's great personal sun that kept them all afloat – was anxious not to step any further on his toes. Skirting around the chairman's sensitivities, some of the Party's bravest leaders – Zhou Enlai, the premier, Liu Shaoqi, the Yan'an author of *How to be a Good Communist* (who had become president of the People's Republic), and Deng Xiaoping, vice-premier and increasingly Zhou Enlai's right-hand man – tried to bring the calamity under control, suggesting an easing of the scientific principle that had eliminated the corrective powers of subjectively human judgement from the decision-making equations. It was not easy.

From time to time, however, encouraged by anxious minds behind Mao's public posters, one or two small weeds had begun to push their heads above the grass. One was a Party writer and accomplished historian, by the name of Deng Tuo. Having tapped out an 'anonymous' suggestion in 1957 that the 'politics of simpletons' should be discarded, he had been swiftly sacked from his position as editor of the *People's Daily*, the Party paper. But Deng Tuo's brave words had earned him a number of clandestine friends, not least some in the upper echelons of the leadership who saw the idea of constructing a country without a drop of human truth as a disaster in the making. When it had become clear to anyone with eyes to see and a stomach to growl that something had gone very wrong with the Great Leap Forward, Deng Tuo bravely returned to his typewriter.

As far away from the countryside as anyone else in a city, Deng Tuo decided to consult the pages of history to see what lessons might be found. There, he came across a host of stories that seemed to tell a similar miserable tale: someone at the top blindly telling everyone what to do at the bottom, and everyone at the bottom too scared for their skins to have the courage to speak up. Moving on to consult the more recent past, Deng Tuo found a series of Mao's old speeches: those from the very early days, when his thoughts had seemed to urge a mastery of facts and to embody an earthy common sense. Heir to the same literary codes with which earlier imperial scholars had tried to protect their lives, he produced a series of articles that seemed to shower Mao with praise, while leaving careful readers in no doubt about the real, and very critical, nature of his ink.

By the late summer of 1961, Deng Tuo was regularly contributing a column to the *Beijing Evening News*. Entitled '*Evening Chats at Yanshan*', it was a series of coded essays and observations, with the 'evening chats' easily recognisable as the endless lectures Mao had been delivering since Yan'an. 'Yanshan', Swallow Hill, not only sounded like Yan'an, but was also instantly recognisable as another ancient name for Beijing: 'Yanjing', Swallow City, once the capital of Yan, one of the last of the Warring States to be conquered by Mao's greatest hero, the First Qin Emperor. Character by character, Deng Tuo shot arrows of derision deep into his typewritten text. 'Some people have the gift of the gab,' he tapped, 'they can talk endlessly on any occasion, like water flowing from an undammed river. After listening to them, however, when you try to recall what they have said, you can remember nothing.' Secretly, subjective hearts smiled as they read the words. With Mao seemingly not a reader of the *Beijing Evening News*, Deng Tuo continued to type.

Though close to his seventieth year, Mao was not yet a spent force. Withdrawn from a Party whose other leaders seemed determined to thwart the perpetual revolution which would change the destiny of man, Mao quietly set his sights on the still-adoring masses, and waited for an opening. In 1965, it came in the form of a play staged in Beijing.

Entitled *Hai Rui Removed from Office*, the play told the story of an upright Ming dynasty official who had lost his job after attempting to protect peasants from a calamitous imperial decision. Quite possibly guided by Mao's wife, Jiang Qing (the one-time Shanghai actress who had now risen to become China's cultural tsar), a literary critic with Party ambitions read up on his history and, in the wake of the catastrophic Great Leap Forward, informed the head of Shanghai's Propaganda Department that the play was a disguised attack on Mao. Mao was delicately alerted, the author of the play disappeared from view, and a critique of the play's 'subjective errors' was published to set the public straight.

With Mao already clear about the need to replace his closest lieutenants with new men who better understood the importance of 'objective thinking', some of the most powerful Party members had already begun to disappear into the bowels of the Party's investigating offices, invited to the kind of thought reform and struggle sessions from which even the strongest minds would dream of suicide. And as the subjective minds disappeared, a *Little*

Red Book began to appear across the country. Spread by Mao's newest rising star – a senior military man by the name of Lin Biao – it was composed entirely of quotations of Mao's words. For an innocent youth who still saw Mao's red heart as the greatest treasure of the revolution, a copy quickly became the most treasured of possessions.

And then, in the early months of 1966, it became clear that Deng Tuo's columns had been read far more widely than he had appreciated. Opening the newspapers, he found that he had become the leading headline in a mass press campaign, with Jiang Qing accusing him of 'using cultural sophistication as a mask for bourgeois restorationism'. Branded an enemy of the people, before the inevitable struggle sessions could begin, Deng Tuo jumped to his death.

*   *   *

The winds of yet another revolution were now quickly gathering pace. Judging from their own personal experiences, it seemed to the youth that the problem must be the petty minds of lecturers and danwei leaders. Whether in the universities or communes, it was all the same: endless bureaucratic meetings telling them what to think and do; study groups to check their inner thoughts; cleanliness drives; dormitory inspections. Orders here, there and everywhere: none of this could possibly have come from their hero, Mao. The glittering dream of a revolution had faded to a mechanical power and, given Mao's grand vision, it must be the Party's officials who were to blame: a sparkling socialist future hijacked by bureaucracy. As 1966 arrived at the dangerous date of May Fourth – with all of its 1919 memories of a people betrayed – university students and young workers alike clutched their *Little Red Book*s and hurled themselves against those who seemed to be trying to derail Mao's dreams.

In the early summer, finding himself subjected to a rising pile of Party complaints about an unruly youth, Mao let it be known that his heart was with the students and the workers. In July, keen to demonstrate his fighting fitness, he swam for two hours in the Yangzi River. Then, contemplating his own corps of busybody bureaucrats, he observed that anger was actually a form of revolutionary spirit. On the campuses of the universities and in the rooms of middle schools, an ocean of students, struggling under the commands of teachers and facing the prospect of more of the same in commune life beyond, saw that Mao had, as ever, understood the matter completely. When Mao went on to suggest that the students *fa fen du qiang*, draw strength from anger, few needed much encouragement. Taking him at his word, they flung off the shackles of the teachers and the danwei leaders and decided to create a revolution of their own.

On 5 August Mao inked a big character poster claiming that 'leading comrades' had taken a bourgeois stand against the revolutionaries, and exhorting his followers to 'bombard the headquarters'. On 8 August 1966, the newspapers carried a Party piece announcing a new stage in the perpetual revolution, one in which the stubbornly subjective minds of the past would finally be brought under the revolutionary will of the people.

On 18 August, tides of students from across the country swept into the newly created Square of Tiananmen for a promised audience with Mao. Fearing that the bureaucrats were going to try to bury their hero, they had wrapped red bands around their arms, and appointed themselves as a personal protective cordon: the *hong weibing*, Red Guards. Orderly in anticipation of Mao's arrival, and clutching precious copies of the *Little Red Book*, they chanted his quotations like mantras. And then, like the great red sun they knew him to be, Mao appeared on the terrace of the Gate of Heavenly Peace, offering a revolutionary blessing to the will of the people, whatever that might be. 'Throw off the Four Olds,' Mao exhorted: old customs, old culture, old habits and old ideas. 'Make way for the Four News,' he shouted: 'new customs, new culture, new habits and new ideas'. To which he added: 'Without destruction there is no construction.'

Once a vastly popular hero, Mao suddenly became everybody's god. As more mass rallies followed over the coming days and weeks, the students looked up to the commanding heights of his big character poster and its exhortation to 'bombard the headquarters'. Which headquarters? For the young Red Guards, it was the schools and universities, sources of the greatest tyrannies against youth, which seemed to be the most obvious. The students' rage unleashed, lessons were suspended, exams were postponed, and suddenly teachers and professors found themselves in the midst of the rightist ranks, and in the line of the revolution's fire.

Still battling against his own demons within the Party – petty minds that had been unable to see the Great Leap Forward in the historical glory of its revolutionary purpose and were still bent on obstructing his dream – within a few months, Mao generously expanded the ranks of the 'Cultural' Revolution to include anyone and everyone who had a grievance against someone sitting on top: 'Why shouldn't a revolutionary democracy embrace all of the oppressed, including the children of the old bad class elements as well? Ink,' he declared, 'should flow freely for all, and posters should be everyone's prerogative.' To this he added that, while violence was to be avoided, if the energies of youth discovered the means to produce their own rockets and artillery, who was he to stand in their way?

Every authority was instructed to give the students all necessary support for their revolutionary battles, not least providing the names, addresses and *dang'an* personal files with which they could launch the struggles that, one way or another, would rid the Party of its foes. It was not long before the remains of some of China's greatest minds and hearts were being pulled from fish-ponds, or picked up in pieces after precipitous flights down stairs. Everywhere, the old made way for the new and, quickly becoming old itself, the new found itself the target of the next revolutionary idea.

By the end of 1966, Beijing's communes and their factories had joined the universities as permanent pitches of battle. Production for purpose slowed and regularly came to a halt, save for the rockets and artillery that the Red Guards were now producing from workshops they had commandeered. As some suggested that the city's traffic lights might be better off flashing red as the colour for 'go', the palaces, temples and shops that had so far survived Mao's vision of a forest of chimneys, fell to the wrath of youth; many of their owners followed suit. Poems and paintings, family photographs, relics of the ancient past, and any surviving figures of the gods and heroes of the 'other world': all were fed to the flames of an anger that was directed to rid the present of the past. And as the past went up in smoke, many of the capital's greatest hearts gave up their ghosts, including an architect with a foolishly unscientific love of Beijing: Liang Sicheng.

Over the following two years, proclaimed by Mao as the 'soldiers of a new democracy', the revolutionary youth determined to ensure that no busybodies at the top could destroy Mao's dream that the people should have their 'will'. Youthful sights expanded to include everyone and everything that anyone could argue was a counter-revolutionary tyranny.

Among the targets were the surviving students of Cai Yuanpei's Peking University. Now in their middle age, their May Fourth dreams of science, democracy and the art of being human were swept away by the great crime of a subjective thinking that dared to question a leader who was clearly heaven's sun. Teachers and danwei leaders having already been dismissed, parents came next. But as every battle won seemed to result in some busybody or other rising to the top and telling everyone else what to do, after a while there were so many targets that it was hard to keep count. Factions fought factions; counter-factions fought back.

Meanwhile, Mao retired to his personal train, and the surviving Party leaders (those who were still alive and not in the avenging clutches of the Red Guards), trembled behind the gates of Zhongnanhai. Outside, the students' 'objective' army battled, released from any subjective ideas of being human. And as fear stalked the nation and millions jumped or were jumped to their deaths, the subjectivity of emotions became nothing but ammunition in the hands of those who could rise above history and human nature. Darwinian evolution had followed the teachings of Nietzsche and Marx; nature had been submitted to the revolutionary will of the people at large. Order had come from a cave; the material world had triumphed. If it didn't quite make sense, not to worry: fight every subjective thought ferociously and obey the masses, whether you understand it all or not.

After two years of rage, with even the city now at war with itself, Mao conceded that it might be time to invite the army to restore the peace and rid Beijing of a youth that had gone too far: 'Send them up to the mountains and down to the countryside'.

CHAPTER 3

THINKING AGAIN

What is right the previous day,
Could be wrong today.

Great Chant on Observing Weiqi, Shao Yong (poet-
philosopher, eleventh century, on the Chinese game of 'Go')

Simple chairs low to the ground, shoulders hunched forwards, the players
pondered their positions. A rising moon had tempered the fiery heat of
the sun, the whisper of a wind had tugged away the cobwebs of the day;
willows wept as they soughed in the warm evening breeze. With life and
death on the board, chests had been stripped to their vests; teeth were being
sucked in deepest concentration. And every now and then a fan was waved
to attention. Friends leant forward and murmured grave observations. Not
even the simplest of them would make the mistake of thinking that this was
just a game of chance. In the struggle for territory, every move would bring
a change and only the most prepared of players would be able to scan the
terrain and grasp the possibilities. As the black and white stones struggled
to encircle each other in the *weiqi* game of 'Go', one would win, another
would lose. And while the coins and notes of *renminbi*, the people's money,
were nowhere to be seen, the assembled company would be keeping a silent

tally of the ups and downs of the evening in their heads, with a certain reckoning to come.

*   *   *

In the late 1960s, after the rages of the Red Guards had been redirected to the countryside, Beijing's people found themselves in a very grey world indeed. With the collapse of the Great Leap Forward, and the chaos of the Cultural Revolution, Mao's star had definitely dimmed. It had then been further eclipsed by a decline in his health and a marked retreat from public view. Across the danwei work units of the capital, the state-owned factories were now running at close to empty; the collective workshops had almost given up the ghost. Iron rice bowls had thinned; ration books, long a fact of life, were stretched beyond their limits. The population having grown, small rooms struggled to squeeze everyone in. The idea of simple, selfless housing for productivity had lost its revolutionary appeal: with shared kitchens, queues for bathrooms, and paper-thin walls that left no one with any peace, privacy had become a dream, and sleep not much easier to find.

Outside on the streets, there was little relief. Roads were empty, buses were scarce, and any destinations on offer were unlikely to be any different from the place where one was already standing. Most of Beijing's shops had shut their shutters long ago; those that were still open offered little to tempt the eye. Electric lights and waving red banners had faded. Thoughts of anything other than necessity had become little more than a hallucination. Toothpaste and toiletries, light-bulbs and glue were the fabric of Beijing's existence, with cigarettes and peanuts for a treat. Once in a while, a rich red blanket or a small television might make an appearance in an otherwise dull shop, but they would be set so high above the reach of the spartan counters that everyone knew they were destined for an official purse beyond the possibilities of an ordinary man. Anyone brave enough to ask for the impossible was likely to be met with a quick 'mei you', 'not available', snap (or, rather, 'not to the likes of you').

Those who asked were few. The last ten years had taught everyone that serving the people was a principle reserved for speeches. Amid the winds of every campaign, the masses had watched factory heads and cadre officials pay far more attention to advancing their own careers than pursuing any truly socialist construction. It was obvious to all that the Democratic Dictatorship of the People had become not just the dictatorship of the Party, but the dictatorship of every Party official who stood above your head. But after scouring the four directions for the bare essentials of daily life, hardly anyone had the time or the energy to argue. Fridges were a fantasy, and queues were the stuff of conversation: so long that every meal was like a military campaign. Beyond the queuing and the endless danwei meetings, life in Beijing seemed to have little to offer, particularly to its youth. Even work was a matter of bureaucratic allocation. And apartments were in such short supply that marriage was a matter of camping in the corner of an already-crowded parental home, with brothers and sisters just more of the clutter that made it hard to breathe.

Grey walls, grey factories; and after twenty years of industrial energy, even the sky itself was beginning to look pale. Firecracking spring festivals had long ago lost their colour, temples had been lost to dormitories, fortune tellers had been redirected to futures in socialist reality, and the motley pedlars who had once sold jumping toys and sticky sweets in hutong lanes had become the stuff of fairy-tales. Even the huge poster-faces of the revolutionary heroes were fading. And whenever a study group was convened to hear about a new speech or an announcement, the hours were spent in yawning, with eyelids struggling not to close.

Minds tried to wander to a more colourful future, but few managed to conjure up the dream of a life beyond. The socialist spirit had narrowed to swapping for the essentials of everything; and the only hope of a better future seemed to lie in the calculated pursuit of personal advantage, with eyes sharply fixed on climbing up the iron rungs of Party power. Marx was long dead, Mao was fading and, as both of them had been at such pains to point out, any idea of heaven above them was nothing more than an illusion. 'Leng leng, qing qing', a cold and dreary world.

*　　*　　*

Life had also had its challenges behind the closely guarded entrance to Zhongnanhai. Over the course of the previous ten years, as the dream of the Great Leap Forward had collapsed and the avenging Cultural Revolution had first raged and then whimpered, Mao had turned his remaining revolutionary sights on the Party people immediately around him, in a 'cultural' backlash that had carried off a number of those who had once been the Party's brightest lights. Deng Xiaoping had been revealed to be a 'capitalist roader', as had Liu Shaoqi, one-time successor-in-waiting to Mao and the man who had once tutored everyone on *How to be a Good Communist*. Both had been guilty of recklessly suggesting that the Great Leap Forward had been a step too far – to which Deng had added the heresy of agreeing with a suggestion, made by Zhou Enlai, that Four Modernisations (of agriculture, industry, national defence, and science and technology) would get the Party out of its economic doldrums – adding that black cats could be as good as white ones, as long as they caught the mice. Deng was sentenced to time in a southern tractor factory; Liu Shaoqi was beaten to a brutal death. Then the man Mao had brought in as a replacement successor, Lin Biao, had turned out to be a clandestine counter-revolutionary as well (heaven's punishment was a plane crash). Judging by the loudspeakers, the greatest stars of the day now seemed to be Jiang Qing, Mao's wife, and a gaggle of men who clung to the hems of her revolutionary trousers. In fact, so strong had the pull of these new stars become that many in the Party began to wonder if Mao's ageing sun had any energy left.

Of course, the treacherous ups and downs of what went on within Zhongnanhai were, as they had always been, mysteries to everyone outside. But if the gusts of wind coming out of its gates were any indication, by 1973 heaven was struggling. Mao's health failing even further, China limping from one grey day to the next, even Zhou Enlai was now looking haggard. The only man to have survived his own opinions, having escaped the terrors of the last fifteen years, he found himself the unspoken victim of a new campaign that, mysteriously to most, linked him to Confucius. Apparently, the two shared a slavish attention to human values, a preoccupation with questions, and a lack of conviction about the historical triumph of the kind of iron-willed ideas that had made the First Qin Emperor ruler of all. Confucius' principles – considered to be both subjective and imperial – had made him an 'enemy of the people'; Zhou Enlai's sympathies with the people were deemed an 'unfortunate mistake'. Zhou was able to survive with his position relatively intact, but not his health: few were surprised when rumours of a ravaging cancer floated out.

In 1974, though, spring brought a change. At Zhou Enlai's request, Mao reluctantly agreed to return Deng Xiaoping from the countryside, and resurrect him as a vice-premier, albeit on a very tight leash. Once restored to Zhongnanhai, Deng realised why Zhou had risked Mao's wrath to bring him back. What had been clear in the tractor factory was even clearer from the capital of the country: over the years of struggle and across the land, far from rising, proletarian production had almost come to a halt. Indeed, if one factored in the disasters, it was probably in retreat. Abandoned to fluctuating revolutionary committees, planning had become a piece of paper fluttering in the wind. Thrown to the mercy of the fates, food and every other item of daily human and industrial necessity had become a matter of a Marxist wing and a Maoist prayer. There was not a moment to lose.

While the gates of Zhongnanhai remained just as closed as they had always been, out on the streets those who had the time and inclination to listen to the loud-speaking broadcasts that daily assaulted everyone's eardrums began to hear strains that made them wonder if Deng's return might be a hint of a thaw. But Deng, as trained as Mao in the shaman-guerrilla ways of the ancestors, bided his time; life in the city continued in its Communist routine; and the stars who had stayed closest to Mao continued to sing the praises of the communes and every other revolutionary hymn Mao liked to hear. In 1975, however, Deng began to speak his mind. Emphasising that the past was, of course, a revolutionary triumph to be proud of, he observed that it might now be time for some self-strengthening – of the kind which had enabled Zeng Guofan to rescue China from the rubble of the Taiping rebellion. Gathering up his courage, Deng repeated Zhou Enlai's earlier idea of Four Modernisations, suggesting that, in addition to applying the best of their own abilities to catching up with the times, the Party should energise the country with some capital imports from the West.

Weak though Mao was, the idea did not last much longer than the Guangxu Emperor's hundred-day reforms. Rising from their Zhongnanhai courtyards, a loyal gathering of left-leaning East Winds gathered into a gale: 'launch ourselves into the Western capitalist breach once again', they gusted, 'have you learnt nothing from the past?' Battered by anti-bourgeois sentiment, Deng was invited to criticise himself.

*   *   *

In January 1976, with the East Winds still in a rage, Zhou Enlai passed to another world. To many across Beijing, the loss of the Party's most human heart was both a sadness and a shock. Gusting hard, the East Winds scarcely seemed to notice. Three months later, though, on the 4 April eve of the ancient *qing ming*, grave-sweeping, festival – a day when everyone visited the graves of the most beloved of the ancestors – Beijing's people decided that it was time for Zhou Enlai to receive some respect. Advancing, in their hundreds and thousands, to the Tiananmen Gate of Heavenly Peace which had now become Tiananmen square, they made their way to a monument the Party had erected to the memory of its revolutionary martyrs. Bearing poems and banners as well as wreaths and flowers, they poured out their tributes to the ghost of the departed Zhou.

Returning the following morning, however, the crowds found that the square had been swept clean and the open spaces of yesterday had been cordoned off. Spirits already high, a hundred thousand Beijingers rose up and swept the barriers away. Sacrificing the vehicles of the police patrols to the attention of a higher god, they then raised their voices in a mighty protest against Jiang Qing – Mao's wife, and the woman who had unleashed the flights of propaganda with which the Cultural Revolution had been turned into a war of all against all – and the three others who, as members of her 'Gang of Four', were being presented as the demons who had betrayed everything.

In the midst of the protesting chaos, two new banners flew high. The first proclaimed an end to the seemingly eternal rule of the First Qin Emperor. The second demanded the return of the original spirit of Marx that had, once upon a time, promised a new golden age of equality in which the people would be freed from the imperial conditions that enslaved man. The forces of the People's Liberation Army were summoned and by dusk the hundred thousand had disappeared. Some had been arrested, others molested, but in the pointed silence of the next day, it was difficult to say whether or not they had been defeated. Blamed for the chaos, and still not forgiven by the East Winds of the Party for his resurrection of Zhou Enlai's Four Modernisations, Deng was set aside again.

Three months later, in the July heat of summer, nature joined the general rebellion and Beijing rocked. A hundred miles to the east, an earthquake shattered the steel city of Tangshan; factories and dormitories in Beijing shuddered. The People's Liberation Army rushed to demonstrate its constructive credentials. But some of the older people of Beijing suspected that they might all be missing the deeper lesson of nature's rage. And then, on 9 September, as if to make the point, Mao Zedong was carried off into the darkness of an eternal night.

Less than a month later, on 6 October, Jiang Qing and her cronies were arrested. Over the following weeks and months, a stream of official broadcasts began to report the nature of their crimes to the people. Colourful detail was released across the newspapers and on the rare black and white televisions; deeper digests were delivered in the danwei work units. The reports described a treachery so cunning and evil that even the reddest hearts were shocked. The Cultural Revolution, it appeared, had been nothing but a game played by the Gang of Four: a choreography of chaos, in which the Chinese people had been played as puppets on a stage of breath-taking ambition. The pitched battles, the lost youth, the hounded, the wounded, and the dead; all had been for naught. While the Gang of Four's guilt was assured by their arrest, it would be five years before they were brought to a very public trial in Beijing. (When the trial eventually took place, the benches stuffed with a host of journalists waiting to observe her fall, Jiang Qing would declare that she had only done what Mao had instructed her to do, and that she, as a victim, had simply done her best to return an eye for an eye: *chi shenme, huan shenme*, you give as good as you get.)

As the people digested the extraordinary news that the Cultural Revolution had been nothing more than a soap opera, old hearts sighed. Not even a hundred years had passed since the Boxer Rebellion, with two revolutions and sacrifices beyond imagination, yet the petty spirits of emperors and empresses had managed to enslave the people once again. Younger spirits, those who had spent years of their youth adoring Mao's revolutionary sun only to find themselves transported to the desolation of the countryside, felt as if the very earth had been pulled out from underneath their feet. Winter passed to spring, and in the stunned silence of the city, those youths who had managed to smuggle themselves back from the countryside began to reach for their ink, penning secret poems and critical essays so black that even the strongest Party hearts would have fainted.

By the summer of 1977, with factories now going so slow that they were hardly moving, Deng was back. Clear that the communes had been a mistake, and with the factories now even deeper in the red, he repeated his call for the Four Modernisations, with science and technology at the helm. While the Party was still stuffed with a number of East Winds to whom his ideas were heresy, in December of 1978 it was Deng who rose to command the pulpit at the Party's annual ('plenum') meeting. And when Beijing woke up the following morning, the news was everywhere: 'Emancipate your minds, seek truth from facts, come together in unity. And if you have something on your chest, don't be afraid to say it'. To the Party's cadres, Deng added another note: 'Class struggle is over; get ready for change.'

The single-minded Five Year Plans, which had controlled every branch of production and consumption, had sapped the life from everything. The time had come for a triumph of man over his landscape – a *jingji fazhan*, which the West might blandly translate as 'economic development', but which every Chinese would recognise as nothing less than a repeat of the ancient taming triumphs of Great Man over nature. While Mao Zedong Thought would remain the guiding star for everyone, the idea of perpetual revolution was to be quietly set aside. From now on, the Chinese world would march to the more practical tune of the Four Modernisations. And although everyone knew that the Chinese people were made of such mettle that one year of their efforts would equal twenty of anyone else's, Deng suggested that even the mighty Chinese might need to take a rest from time to time. The hard work having been done, perhaps it was time to allow the foreign barbarians to contribute some of their own science and technology to the sparkling socialist future that was still beckoning to all.

The East Winds rose in yet another gale of anti-bourgeois rage, but Deng once again declared that one should not confuse the colour of one's cats with the matter of catching mice. Science, he stated (as opposed to the messier 'literature') was a force of production, just like any other. And scientists could be patriotic members of the proletarian working class, just like their labouring peers. That did not, of course, mean that the heaven of the Democratic Dictatorship of the People would change; and it certainly did not mean that scientists could go about expressing reckless intellectual opinions whenever they felt like it. Indeed, just to make sure that they didn't, Deng declared that he would set the Four Modernisations under the clarity of 'Four Cardinal Principles': keep to the order of the socialist road, uphold the dictatorship of the proletariat, uphold the guidance of Marxism-Leninism and Mao Zedong Thought, and uphold the leadership of the Communist Party. Think of them as four guarantees, he suggested, to ensure that the Four Modernisations don't jump off their tracks.

*   *   *

As Deng was battling with Zhongnanhai's East Winds in the late 1970s, 550 miles to the south, a group of students was hungrily scribbling equations on to the flimsy pages of their books in the dusty Hefei capital of what had become one of China's poorest provinces, Anhui. Enrolled in the University of Science and Technology, newly reopened after the tumult of the Cultural Revolution, they were listening to a lecturer whose classes were unlocking the secrets of the cosmos, and whose ideas, while clearly advancing the Four Modernisations, were on a clear collision course with the Four Cardinal

Principles. The lecturer's name was Fang Lizhi. Wrists taut, minds clutching at every scientific stroke, each of the students was aware that they were sitting in the presence of China's greatest scientific mind. By the end of the class, Einstein's ideas about relativity had been explained. And then the questions had really begun: questions about Newton's older 'truth' that time and space were fixed and absolute, and about Einstein's challenging proposition that the cosmos while finite, was a still-expanding fireball in which time was speed (velocity), and space was constantly expanding.

The science was hard enough, but for the students in that dusty lecture hall the wider 'cultural' questions were even harder. Across the ups and downs of the last thirty years, astrophysics, and science in general, had taken a beating. After 1949, the science societies, journals and research faculties that had proliferated in Republican Beijing had been 'liberated'. Research institutes had been released into a single Chinese Academy of Science; journals and societies had been rolled into the All-China Confederation of Special Societies; and the scientists of the past had been ordered to serve the masses. Every institute had been instructed to free itself from its 'subjectivism', and all had been introduced to a new world of Party science, grounded in the 'single scientific truths' of Marxist and Mao Zedong Thought. But it had not been long before the scientists had been seduced by Mao's invitation to let a hundred questioning flowers of thought bloom. Revealing their true bourgeois colours, in 1957 China's scientists had become some of the most important catches in Mao's following Anti-Rightist campaign.

With the industrial challenges of a Great Leap Forward to deliver, the more useful scientists had been returned to the city and offered a chance to redeem themselves under a Twelve Year Science Plan whose goals included a satellite, two bombs, and propelling China to the top of the world in the mastery of quantum physics (the science of sub-atomic particles, which fascinated Mao, and the 'solid-state' building block on which China's new industrial future was being planned). In the event, the reprieve had been short-lived. Having successfully tested a nuclear bomb in 1964, and confronted with a Party of foot-draggers who seemed so easily seduced by the twists of subjective minds, Mao had reappraised his priorities: scientists might have a productive value, but the cost of any intellectual's subjective opinions was always far too high.

Never had the problem of subjective minds been clearer than in the case of Einstein. A man whose ideas about relativity had ignited young Chinese minds in the 1920s, upon closer Party inspection he had failed the most basic political tests. The posthumous personality cult that had grown up around him was an obvious problem – as were his later literary works. Writing a book under the outrageously subjective title of *The World As I See It*, Einstein had argued that the state was made to be the servant of man, and that man was on no account to become the slave of the state. The really fatal flaw, however, was the fact that Einstein's theory of relativity was wholly incompatible with the unassailable science of the far greater Marx. Einstein's logic posited an expanding but ultimately finite universe. But as everyone who had read their Marx knew, the universe was infinite, expanding by the constant energies of change. It was what Marx and Engels had described as *dialectical materialism*, and what Mao (aware of the yin and yang changes) described as the law of contradictions: a universal unity of opposites which was also the propeller of the constant revolutionary struggle through which the Chinese masses would ultimately overcome the feudal imperialist past and achieve their Communist dream. Einstein had got it wrong.

Abstract though the matter of relativity might seem to many, for Mao the importance of an infinite universe was both practical and critical. In practical terms, it was a matter of the power of man to triumph over circumstance – a perpetual revolution in which a new world of scientific humans would learn to put the interests of the masses above those of the individual. Objective minds over subjective opinions: wasn't that what science was all about? In critical terms, it was nothing less than the ability of the Chinese people to triumph in the battle for the survival of the fittest and reach their goal, not by a random wave of happenstance, but by the determination of scientific man to establish new facts on the ground.

Putting the practical and the critical together, the question of the nature of the universe was not an idle philosophy to be debated over dinner tables, but a fundamental truth on which every action should be predicated, and from which no individual spirit should be permitted to deviate. To see the world otherwise, as Einstein so obviously and erroneously had, was to infer the existence of a divine creator and to accept the idea that every subjective individual should be able to talk to him – a reckless chaos that the Yellow Emperor's grandson Zhuanxu had (rightly) banished from the settled lands. As every Marxist scientist knew, not just in China but in Russia too, the only creator of anything was the objective will of man (more conveniently described as 'the people'). Of course, Mao acknowledged, one should not be surprised to get such subjective sophistry from scientists who, like all intellectuals, were captives of their own personal minds and not to be trusted with any collective, let alone revolutionary, cause. But, he continued, a true revolutionary leader should steel himself to fight against them, tooth and claw. Just as with the other intellectuals, the battlefield would be the printed page – and the mind would be the prize.

By the time the Cultural Revolution was launched in 1966, accusations against Einstein had become common fare in the *People's Daily*. Then in February 1968, a middle-aged school-teacher from Hunan had advanced to deliver the final blow to Einstein's treachery. Clutching a carefully crafted paper, he had climbed aboard a train and traveled to Beijing, at the invitation of the Revolutionary Committee of the Institute of Physics at the Chinese Academy of Sciences. Delivering his thoughts, he had hit the nail on Einstein's error-filled head and unveiled a whole new scientific theory fit for a revolution: Einstein's theories were nothing but a mischievous attempt to assert the supremacy of the bourgeois capitalist classes over the heroic working classes; they were also a failure to understand that there could be only one principle for the cosmos, scientific or otherwise, and that Marx, or more particularly Engels, had already found it, with the idea of dialectical materialism. The preposterous, limelight-catching idea that the universe was guided by a constant speed of light was nothing but a devious trick: an attempt to present Western science as the centre of everything. But the Chinese masses, asserted the school-teacher, were not to be fooled. Grounded on the breath-taking clarity of Mao Zedong Thought, and ignited from the East, a proletarian scientific revolution was on its way. The West, as usual, had got it wrong: Einstein was not a scientific hero: he was the greatest of all of the reactionary bourgeois minds to tread the intellectual boards of the twentieth century.

Thinking again, it had become clear to the powers of the Cultural Revolution that the errors could not be limited to Einstein: it was not only relativity that was wrong, but much of the rest of Western science too. All it took was a clear standpoint to see the truth, and that was easily supplied: a Mao Zedong Thought Study Class for 'Criticising Reactionary Bourgeois Standpoints in Theories of Natural Sciences'. Blessed into existence by Mao, it added a critical mass to the science of the people and put the surviving scientists firmly in their place. Those still unable to appreciate the errors of their ways were struggled to their deaths, or reassigned to the countryside to think new and different thoughts. With each research institute experiencing a revolutionary nightmare of its own, surviving Chinese scientists entered into a seemingly endless struggle against the dark.

Mao having concluded that the cost of the scientists' risky subjectivity was far too high, the attention of the Red Guards had been directed to the University of Science and Technology, laboratory home to some of the most hopeful projects in China's science world. Fearing for its safety, Mao's bureaucrats put it out of sight in the far-off province of Anhui. It was not, however, far enough. No sooner had it arrived in 1969 than the Red Guards were alerted to a group of its rightist scientists who had escaped the revolutionary net. Fang Lizhi was one of them. It mattered little that he was the greatest scientific graduate of his era, or that he was the brightest star in the pantheon of living Chinese scientific minds. It mattered little that he had been tasked with conjuring up the solid-state physics whose equations were to form the building blocks of China's new industrial future. Initially confined to a cowshed, Fang would eventually be banished to the reforming labours of a mine.

Finding himself in the bowels of China's yellowest and dustiest earth, Fang had not been entirely without company. Before he left his library, he had managed to snatch up a forbidden book with his belongings; its title was *The Classical Theory of Fields*. It was not the solid-state physics on which his mind had been told to concentrate but a detailed analysis of the various physical fields of the cosmos and what happens when particles collide. It also included a description of Einstein's theory of relativity. With nothing else to occupy his thoughts, Fang turned its pages over and over in the dead of every night, until he knew the text inside out. By the time the storm of the Cultural Revolution had died down and the scientists (those who had survived) had been recalled from purgatory, Fang Lizhi had fallen in love with Einstein and made a quantum leap into the astrophysics of the cosmos, far ahead of anyone else in the Chinese field.

In 1971, as the Cultural Revolution's gales began to blow themselves out, Fang was returned to Hefei, this time to a brick factory that was under orders to produce a constant supply of building blocks for the soon to be resurrected University of Science and Technology. Carrying the cosmos in his head, Fang's hands made bricks while his counter-revolutionary thoughts secretly leapt across the equations of a higher truth. And then, in 1972, he was released from the brickworks and returned to the classroom with instructions to stick to Mao's facts. But the call of the cosmos was too great. Defying Mao's 'immutable principles' of dialectical materialism and an infinite universe, Fang Lizhi set about exploring the unfinished depths of Einstein's equations.

Within months, supported by new advances in radio-telescopes which probed the cosmos and proved with the power of the eye that the galaxies were moving away from each other, Fang published an article in China's *Physica* that rocked the Party. He called it 'A solution of the cosmological equations in scalar-tensor theory, with mass and blackbody radiation'. He could simply have called it 'Big Bang', for that is what it was. Where steady state theory postulated that matter was static (constantly created and recreated), the cosmological equations of relativity indicated that matter was dynamic (expanding like an exploding fireball), fuelled by forces far beyond the power of even the most scientific of men. More to the political point though, in proposing the idea of an expanding universe, Fang had drawn on the very idea of Einstein that Mao had seen as the great heresy of relativity: the universe was finite. The idea of heaven as an infinite propulsion of a perpetual people's revolution had hit a rock.

With the printing of his paper, Fang broke all Party taboos. Engels was directly contradicted; Mao's cosmic viewpoint was imploded; and the heretical Big Bang theory was laid out in black and white for everyone in China to see. Outraged Party spirits advanced column inches against his science, and a crusade against cosmology was launched. Fang was unmoved.

When Deng had launched the idea of the Four Modernisations in 1975 – with a firm focus on science and technology – the rage unleashed against him had been provoked in part by the fact that science itself had become a cosmic heresy which threatened to unravel the most fundamental tenets of Marx, Engels and Mao Zedong, upon which the logic of the Party depended. As quietly as they could, Party minds who agreed with Deng's direction worked hard to protect the surviving scientists in general and Fang Lizhi, the country's greatest scientist, in particular. Sticks and stones were stayed; and Fang was advised to keep his thoughts to himself. Seemingly deaf, however, to the East Winds which were blowing around Zhongnanhai, in the same year of 1975, Fang Lizhi published yet another paper. This time, he invited a debate on the even bigger question of 'truth'.

From the commanding perspective of outer space, where the earth appeared as a single tiny dot, Fang argued that no theory should be above the theoretical challenge of an individually questioning mind. Neither, he argued, should any idea, 'scientific' or otherwise, be free from the observational test of subjective human eyes. There was no such thing as an 'objectively scientific' question that could be resolved by a quick consultation of Mao's quotations, with any tests limited to a snappy deduction sketched on the back of a Marxist principle. Marx himself had not only emphasised the importance of empiricism but he had argued against placing blind trust in an omnipotent 'supreme'. And one of Mao's most famous declarations was that truth could only be discovered from facts. If Marxism, and Mao's interpretation of it, were to be claimed as a science, then its proponents would have to start conducting themselves like scientists, starting with a more dedicated attention to the truth. Arguing that if one faithfully followed the Communist logic, no one should be afraid of the truth, he even added that it was not beyond the realm of scientific possibility that if everyone were actually allowed to tell the truth in their work together, maybe one day China might even be able to show that there was indeed a dialectical spirit of materialism embedded in the Big Bang.

The matter at stake, advanced Fang, was so important that it went well beyond principle and even physics. It was nothing less than the order of man. The disasters of the Great Leap Forward and the Cultural Revolution had more than proved the point that science without a human mind to ask human questions was a disaster that could push man beyond the edges of survival. Zhang Junmai had been right all those fifty years ago when he had argued that, while the objective powers of science were valuable, without the moral compass of human truth, science was a dangerous thing. Ding Wenjiang, with his idea that a scientific truth was an unquestionable absolute, had been wrong. True they had both been doing their best to protect the country from a return to the feudal-imperial past, but by now the lesson should have been learnt: there was not, and never had been, anything wrong with China other than an ancient fear of the people speaking their minds. But this ancient fear of the people speaking their minds had become China's greatest risk: truth was essential to the survival of human beings. And it was out of the minds of the people's questions that the truth was to be found, not out of a dictatorship that told everyone what to think.

Brought back into the fold of the Party's science institutions, and advanced to the front of China's bid to make up for lost scientific time, Fang was not only catapulted to a higher rank within the University of Science and Technology, but also presented for conversations with leading Western cosmological lights. Fang's ideas turned his lectures into the most popular intellectual journeys in China. Publishing his thoughts both in scholarly articles and in a host of essays and papers crafted for the people at large, he pushed and prodded at the contradictions of science under the single mind of a state. And as Fang pushed and prodded, students in Beijing and other cities began to splash their ink across big character posters, and to plaster them across any and all available walls.

Deng found himself in a dilemma. Scientifically speaking, Fang's logic was hard to argue with. But the question of order was quite another matter. A hundred years of chaos had already passed since the troubling memorial that Kang Youwei and Liang Qichao had presented to the Guangxu Emperor. And while Fang was arguing for truth, an open mind, liberty for individual action, and a heaven within which more than one idea could fly, Deng was counting the bodies of China's rebellious past and calculating the odds of achieving the order that it was the Communist Party's responsibility to deliver. Whatever Marx might have said about empiricism – and whatever Einstein and Fang Lizhi might say about truth, history from the time of the First Qin Emperor onwards had taught that only the firmest grip could maintain a steady state. Lessons from Lenin (who, with his own arguably Mongol background, had presumably inherited much of the same kind of wolf-like thinking as the early Qin) confirmed it. Life under Mao had reminded everyone that being Chinese was about learning to live with contradictions rather than insisting on an absolute truth. And the Republican past before him had clearly shown that the very size of the empire made it impossible to accommodate everybody's voices, however 'scientific' they might be.

But while Deng grappled with the contradictions of science and truth, Fang kept on with his arguments, and other well-educated minds seemed to think it was time for them to stand up and offer their 'truths' as well. All around him, Party minds began to falter. The terrifying possibilities of the unknown seemed to be opening up before everyone's eyes. Why on earth, Deng wondered, could intellectuals never learn the art of keeping quiet?

*   *   *

As Deng and his Four Modernisations had advanced towards the Party's pulpit in the early winter of 1978, younger minds had been scribbling down secret thoughts of their own. Aware since the arrest of Jiang Qing that they had been betrayed by the Cultural Revolution, for the last few years they had kept their poems and essays close to their hearts. But in the autumn months before Deng had risen to speak, they began to splash the ink of their anger in big black character posters across a quiet grey wall close to one of Beijing's busiest streets. With little else to do in the long winter evenings, it was not long before Beijing's bored people (torches always at the ready) found them.

Noting that the stabbing criticisms of the treachery of the Cultural Revolution supported his own arguments about the need for a more productive future, Deng initially stood back. Indeed, the searing stories of betrayals, tortures and deaths that appeared on television night after night – all having been carefully attributed to the Gang of Four still awaiting their trial – only emphasised the urgency of reform. Referring to the constitution of the People's Republic, Deng announced that anyone who wanted could write a big character poster: what could be wrong with allowing people to express their views? Instantly famous, the quiet grey wall quickly acquired a name of its own: the 'Democracy Wall'.

Over the weeks that followed, though, the posters began to challenge Deng's call for everyone to unite together in a great new future. 'What unity?' they raged. It was obviously not only Mao's wife and the Gang of Four who had been spitting on the people: it was every Party cadre who had swept up the wealth of the people's labour and put it into their pockets. Bold splurges of ink told of Party cadres raising red pavilions for themselves, and even pulling down historical landmarks that had stood in their way. To which the posters added black strokes of anger at the spying danwei work units, at people being disappeared for daring to speak their minds, and at the imperialistic style of order, which meant that those at the top were always right. Here, there, and everywhere, the reckless ink of the posters shouted out reminders to everyone that where the *ren* respect for human beings was banished, heaven eventually always fell down on everybody's heads.

On 5 December 1978, only weeks before Deng would reach the Party's pulpit and exhort everyone to 'emancipate their minds', a poster appeared that shocked even Deng. Quoting Einstein, it went on to ask a simple question: 'If China is to have Four Modernisations for productivity and science, shouldn't there really be a Fifth Modernisation: namely, the voice of the people whose hands and minds will be doing the work, and who will be the only ones in a position to know whats really working and what is not?' Mistakes, the poster argued, were inevitable: a fact of life. To fear them was to put oneself under the shackles of the imperial past that had always told everyone to shut up. Recklessly, the poster-writer had even signed his name: Wei Jingsheng.

Deng quickly discovered that Wei Jinsheng was one of those young people whom Mao had sent to the countryside in the Cultural Revolution – a boy who, having lost his education, had reappeared in Beijing as an electrician. Proletarian, or bourgeois intellectual? Confusingly both, it would seem. But, in Deng's opinion, it did not matter. Before long, Wei's argument for a Fifth Modernisation was condemned as 'counter-revolutionary' and Wei himself was detained in Beijing's Qincheng jail. In the spring of 1979 he would be sentenced to fifteen years in its cells.

Meanwhile, back in Hefei, Fang Lizhi, now with a string of scientific successes to his name, was continuing to fire yet more volleys of his own from his lectern, following them up with column inches in a press that was now joining the fray. If China's minds were going to be subjected to the contradiction of a Democratic Dictatorship of the People led by the members of a Party, how could any Four Modernisations, let alone science, ever flourish? Critics were challenged to a debate, and students were instructed to stretch their thoughts. Relentless in his insistence that minds had to be free, Fang was also ruthless in his attacks on the suggestion that the Four Modernisations could succeed without Wei Jingsheng's Fifth. With every one of Deng's calls for a scientific revolution to propel China up the ranks of the world, Fang fired off yet another riposte to the effect that a narrow-minded attention to technical detail would never unleash a scientific spirit, and that setting targets in the absence of truth would only nurture the risk of lies, with catastrophic failure as the prize.

As the guns were loaded back and forth, Deng, now under attack from both the left and the right, revised his liberal position on the posters: anyone using their ink for counter-revolutionary purposes would be arrested. As winter turned to the spring of 1979 (with the annual April *qing ming* sweeping of the graves of the better loved ancestors; followed by the dangerous 4 May and its sensitive memories of Mr Science and Mr Democracy), Beijing's officials were ordered to tear down the posters on the offending Democracy Wall. Such irresponsible splashes of black on white, Deng declared, had no place in the socialist world. If anyone felt they had something important to say, a more orderly wall would be provided: one where everyone putting up a poster could register their name and their danwei, and take full responsibility for whatever characters they chose to paint.

The Democracy Wall returned to its old grey bricks, and older hearts, sighing once more, stayed at home. But younger spirits with courage took up their pens again. Walls now far too closely watched for anyone's safety, this time they printed their words in pamphlets, and gave them out by hand. Each one was different but there seemed to be two common threads. The first was that the last twenty years had been nothing but a catalogue of the same imperial errors that had been repeated dynasty after dynasty over the last two millennia. The second was that man was born to be human. One brave spirit seemed to sum it all up with the observation that it was always the 'inhuman' humans who managed to grab the fruits of everyone's labour and congratulate themselves on their own civilisation; and it was always the 'human' humans who ended up working so hard that they scarcely looked human at all. They were words that carried almost the same price as that paid by Wei Jingsheng: fourteen years in jail.

*   *   *

Spring turning to summer, the pens and the pamphlets went underground, and Deng tried to get on with the business of the Four Modernisations and the pursuit of productivity, including a brave rehabilitation of once-bourgeois scientists, and the invitation to foreigners to contribute their science and technology to China's socialist future. Recognising the enormity of the task, he reminded everyone that even the greatest river could be crossed only by feeling for the stones. There would be advances and there would be setbacks; mistakes were inevitable; some would have to get rich first before others could join them. And while it was important to have a clear goal in sight, it was equally important to understand that a truly successful revolution would take a lot of time.

Meanwhile, the old East Winds continued to blow, occasionally gathering into positively electric storms. Deng's Four Modernisations were described as nothing less than 'peaceful evolution', that conspiracy of words with which a 1950s America had imagined that China could be seduced out of Communism – the one against which Mao had solidly charged every Party mind to guard. Deng's ideas were decried as a treachery that would carry the Party into the clutches of Western capitalism as effectively as any revolution had overturned the imperial past. Aware that he would need to establish some new facts on the ground as quickly as possible, Deng repeated the mantra of the Four Cardinal Principles (keep to the order of the socialist road, uphold the dictatorship of the proletariat, uphold the guidance of Marxism-Leninism and Mao Zedong Thought, and uphold the leadership of the Communist Party), and then scoured the country for more practical ideas.

In 1980 a popular moderniser from Hunan province was appointed general secretary of the Party: his name was Hu Yaobang. In the same year, another moderniser who had recently been Party secretary of Sichuan was invited to become premier of the People's Republic. A man famous within

Party circles for having rescued Sichuan (China's 'breadbasket') from imminent starvation with an embrace of rebellious peasants who wanted to grow crops on their own plots of land, his name was Zhao Ziyang. With two modernisers at his side, the Four Modernisations as his core objective and the Four Cardinal Principles as a protection against criticism from the left and the right, Deng began to spread his own winds of change.

Intellectuals who had been exiled to the countryside were welcomed back to the city; renegade peasants secretly farming personal plots were heralded as advance heroes of a new 'household responsibility system' which would free everyone from the clutches of the communes. Trade with the West was encouraged for cash returns, and the southern coasts were offered for factories into which the foreigners could pour their science and technology. Of course, the foreigners would not be allowed to spread across the whole of China. But if one applied a little bit of the Monkey King's down-to-earth logic, there was no reason why they could not build their factories behind walls that would keep their capitalist pollution from tainting the revolutionary purity of the rest of the country: *jingji tequ* as they were announced to the Chinese, 'special economic zones' for the tongues of the West.

With modernisation now being launched across China, Deng Xiaoping looked at the state of the cities. Observing the promising results of the 'household responsibility system' in dismantling the old unproductive communes of the countryside, Deng decided it could become the model for industrial change. Why not adopt the same logic for the factories and put them on to *chengbao*, contracting-out, arrangements that would let a factory head contract out the machinery and keep the profits, as long as he delivered the bulk of its production to the state? Once again, the East Winds raged: with all productivity fixed by Five Year Plans, how could any private production be undertaken without bankrupting the country? And if factories were run for profits, what would happen to the prices? Deng replied that anything could be managed if one just applied a little Monkey King logic. Why not split the prices into two? One, low, price for quotas of goods to be sold to the state straight from an enterprise's factory gate; and another, higher, price for additional goods that could be bought by people with a little cash to spare, in markets that wanted more.

The Monkey King logic seemingly fit for any purpose, Deng went on to look at the increasingly pressing question of overcrowded housing as well. Reminding the people of Beijing of the privilege and the responsibility of living in the greatest city in China, he noted the revolutionary zeal of the

1950s that had led to a huge leap in the size of the population. It was now time to look at the capacity of the capital to keep up. With the Urban Planning Bureau closed since the bombardments of the Cultural Revolution, and with architectural minds swept away along with almost every other relic of the past, a long-overdue survey of the city and its housing was to be conducted.

Once completed, the survey confirmed what every older Beijinger knew: thousands of chimneys had touched the sky, and the imperial heart of the city had been pierced. The few temples and palaces that had not been converted into workshops and dormitories, or transformed into Party pavilions, were crumbling in the wind. And the sea of yellow and green tiled courtyard houses, once an uninterrupted spread of mesmerising beauty, survived only as lonely puddles in the mud of a now very grey world. To Deng, however, thinking a little more like Mao, the survey told rather a different story. Looking at facts rather than fairy-tales, one could see that the question of overcrowded housing could not only be solved, but in solving it, a rather productive new industry might be created as well.

Factories so indulgently spread across the chequerboard of the old Inner and Imperial Cities were instructed to sell their (now very central) land and premises for a profit, and to use the proceeds to house their workers in cheaper places outside the heart of the city. New homes could then be built so that everyone could get a little more space and the chequerboard could be opened up for those with money to build. Looking at plans for high-rises, relics in the Urban Planning Bureau muttered about the need to protect the low-flying spirits that had swept the city's skies for centuries. But they were easily dismissed: the city needed to accommodate its multiplying population in higher storeys, and no one had seen a spirit for nearly a century. If someone was ready to put money on the street, why would anyone object? The faster the houses went up, the more money would be made. If the cat caught its mice, what difference did its colour make?

The question of housing addressed, Deng then announced that it was high time for Beijing to brush off the dust of its last thirty years, and put a little consuming spring in its step. Shops in the danweis had been all well and good in the past, but given the constant shortages and the changes, why not allow the peasants to bring their produce to an open market, and cut the queues? While they were at it, why not have a beancurd seller on the street as well? Repeating his cat mantra, Deng explained that letting people make a little bit of money on the side was not, after all, such a bad idea. Come to think of it, even though the priests and the fortune-tellers should obviously keep their superstitions out of the city, there was no reason why the temples couldn't open up for a profit-making fair or two. And when festivals came around, why not explode a little shot of profit-making red, and crack a bit of fire? Emancipate your minds!

Beijing's people did not need to be asked twice. Spread out on pavements for popular inspection, eggs and chickens fresh from the countryside flew off the streets. In the shops, even television sets began to come within reach. Temples, whose eaves had long been colonised by pigeons, sprang back to life as markets. Many of them specialised in the sale of what Beijingers had come to call 'the army, the air force and the navy': armies of crickets trained for betting battles, air forces of caged birds offered for heart-conquering songs, and navies of two-tailed fish, flashing the treasures of their golden scales for luck. It was not long before the army, the air force and the navy were competing with the three new 'must-haves': a watch, a bicycle and a sewing machine. After thirty years of ups and downs, perhaps socialism could deliver something, after all.

With housing under orders, and consumption on the rise, by 1985 Deng was suggesting that Beijing should begin to see itself as a model for the rest of the country. The experience of the last forty years or more had shown that, however important agriculture might be, everybody's future was going to be in the cities. With southern coasts raising factories of modernised production, Beijing should not just catch up but step ahead as well. Before long, a scientist recently returned from a study tour of Silicon Valley came up with the idea of turning a university village on the outskirts of the city into a special purpose park for computing. China's academics, the scientist argued, were more than ready to start earning some money, and America had proven that when minds and enterprise came together, sparks could fly. The village's name was Zhongguancun. Tracing its roots back to the Ming dynasty, since the 1950s, it had been designated as the site for the relocation of Beijing's earliest universities. Before long it was rising with new businesses – and inspiring the city to start thinking about copying the southern special economic zones with industrial parks of its own.

With Beijing now setting a capital standard for other Chinese cities to follow, Deng encouraged Beijingers to raise their sights yet higher. Now that minds had been emancipated, they should begin to think about a more daring dive: out of the iron rice bowl, and into the rushing sea of every man for himself. More of the state-owned and collective factories that could not turn a profit should be cutting their losses and handing themselves over to *chengbao* contractors, foreign or Chinese, who could deliver returns. Meanwhile, workers without a job should try and come up with ideas of their own; and the prices of everything should begin to compete.

Some spirits were very enthusiastic; others were less sure. Life in a money-making city seemed as if it might be a lot more complicated than it had been in the grey old past. Taking their cue from Deng's encouraging speeches, however, the most energetic people rushed ahead, chasing money wherever they could, encouraging government officials to take their courage in their hands and approve a fresh idea, even if the ink of an approval was not entirely dry. Those who hesitated watched with growing unease as the grey but familiar world of the iron rice bowl changed. Workers on factory floors woke up to find that a *chengbao* contract had turned a comrade with a useful connection to a Party official into a boss. Settling down to the new management, they then found that their hours had been stretched, and the pressure to perform was rising by the day. Many were to be released from their jobs; and almost every older worker, with or without a job, was to be despatched to more affordable housing beyond the limits of the city. Families who had lived in Beijing for centuries found themselves cast into an outer-city wilderness that even the buses could not reach.

Struggling to come to terms with the change in their fortunes, Beijingers then watched as *hou men* back doors suddenly appeared everywhere. Playing games of *weiqi*, Go, on evening streets, they also watched as new bosses rushed off to wine-washed banquets. Going to work in the morning, they passed comrades on the stairway who were on their way to the airport for officially funded 'study tours' in some foreign country or another. As like as not, in every case, the lucky person in question would be jumping into one of the shiny new black foreign cars that had begun to appear around the city, all with windows delicately darkened. Soon the apartments of neighbouring officials were being stuffed with televisions and sofas, or emptied onto carts carrying the furniture of old lives off to new pavilions where water and electricity flowed freely, with kitchens and bathrooms that would never need to be shared. Reaching deep into their pockets for the rising price of a cigarette, and any other comfort or essential, it was obvious to everyone on the streets that their own hard work was paying for the lot. Condemned to the queue, while the benefits were going to those who had found the back doors.

As the gathering possessions and the rising pavilions went from strength to strength, the price of everything just kept climbing. Revolutionary righteousness was fading into the mists of memory, and the edifice of the Four Modernisations was becoming shot with cracks. What had seemed like a good idea in the beginning was increasingly looking like a problem. Yes, Deng had warned everyone that they would have to take a small step backwards in order to get themselves firmly on the road to the golden age of socialism, but they had not expected the pursuit of productivity to take on the bitter unfairness of the imperial past.

*　*　*

With Beijing now divided on the question of whether the future could be both red *and* richer, Fang Lizhi had not given up in his quest for truth. In 1984, his international prizes propelled him to the vice-presidency of the University of Science and Technology. But by 1986, across Hefei and other cities, more posters were being splashed across more walls, and the writing on the walls was bringing more and more people onto the streets. Spreading like wildfire across many of China's cities, the protests began to wash up like an eternal tide against the Tiananmen Gate of Heavenly Peace. Discouraging the protests for fear of the violence they might provoke, Fang Lizhi nonetheless welcomed the open minds. The truth was the rock on which everyone's future was grounded, he argued. However hard it might be to hear it, and however unknown or unknowable the answers might at present be, it was the duty of the intellectuals to tell it. Within the Party, East and West winds began to battle, and Deng tried to quell the squall.

Meanwhile, on the people's streets, Beijingers were becoming anxious. Prices were rising even faster than before. And the higher they rose, the quicker everyone rushed to a queue, anxious to stock up on the essentials of life before they slipped out of affordable grasp. Everyone scrabbling for the shops, the tiniest of savings flew out of the banks. At the same time, with labouring hours rising, but jobs under pressure and wages frozen, factory workers turned their sights on the All-China Federation of Trade Unions, the Party organisation founded in the 1950s which had promised (wider scepticism notwithstanding) to look after the workers' interests. Ever-ready with its Party broadcasts, always quick to collect its members' dues, its energies had never stood up for any of its members, and in the recent years of 'modernisation' its eyes had become blind to the racing cost of everything, and its ears had turned to cloth. Brothers united by their labour, the workers decided it was time to stand still and strike.

Recognising the 'contradictions', Deng dug deep into the theories of Leninist-Marxist thought and, like the ancient hero Zhuge Liang, looked for the wisdom that would bring two seemingly incompatible principles together in the harmonious unity of one. Eventually, he found the answer in Marx's stages of socialism. In the zeal to reach the socialist utopia, Deng declared, China had failed to read the small print. Marx had not suggested that the people could rush from the feudal imperialism of the past straight into socialism. What he had, in fact, said was that one had to pass through the lower stages of capitalism before the great triumph of socialism could be reached. While Mao and the people were to be congratulated on their revolutionary fervour, if true socialism were to be achieved, there was no alternative but for everyone to retrace their steps and create the capitalist industry over which they had leapfrogged in the past. That said, Deng reminded the people that no other socialist state had ever tried to conjure up a capitalist past, that mistakes would be inevitable, and that it might be an idea to take things a little more slowly, perhaps even take a pause. With a number of minds, not to mention factories and prices, already marching forward, it was not clear how this could be done. Obviously, though, the state would not be withering away for quite a while. Belts were tightened, targets were cut, and the Four Modernisations were told to go so slow that it seemed as if they had stopped.

But the factories and the shops did not appear to be listening. Prices did not go down; wages did not go up; and as 1988 unfolded, even those hearts that had embraced the storms of change in the hope of a more colourful future became uneasy.

Then in the summer of 1988, an image of the Yellow River washed across the screens of everyone who had managed to acquire a television set, announcing the beginning of a series that would take everyone back across thousands of years of history. It's title was *Heshang, Deathsong of the River*. And just like the Yellow River, it carried its viewers from floods to famines, from self-strengthening to foreign imperial powers, and from Confucianism to Communism. It portrayed the pent-up rage of the people that periodically erupted into a nightmare. And it led, relentlessly, to the conclusion that, at the root of almost every Chinese problem, was the single self-deceiving idea that only those at the top could be right.

Staring at their screens, the television viewers almost fell off their chairs. No eyes watched more closely than the young ones in Beijing's universities. While Deng's dreams had promised a better world, invisible bureaucrats were assigning every graduating talent to a government-appointed purpose, with never a choice about what kind of work they might personally like to pursue. Unless, of course, as it had always been, they were members of the red royal families that could always conjure up the best and most desirable of jobs for themselves.

The past, it seemed, was indeed destined to repeat itself.

*   *   *

In early 1989, seventy years after the 1919 protests that had so boldly paired Mr Science with Mr Democracy, and just ten years after the Democracy Wall, Fang Lizhi wrote a letter to Deng Xiaoping, asking for the release of Wei Jingsheng. Signed by many of his peers, Fang published it openly for all to read. Deng limited his reply to the Four Cardinal Principles: the order of the socialist road, the Democratic Dictatorship of the People, the supremacy of Mao Zedong and Marxism-Leninism thought, and the leadership of the Communist Party. He also issued orders that the fast-arriving, and now highly inconvenient, anniversary of May Fourth was not to be celebrated with any reference to 'Mr Science' or 'Mr Democracy' but with a call to *ai guo*, love the country. Fang hit back with the simple observation that 'Truth does not distinguish between localities'. In China as anywhere else, he insisted, one should be able to love the country *and* love the truth as well.

Just over a month later, on 15 April 1989, uncomfortably close on the heels of the annual April *qing ming* festival, another veteran Party soul departed: this one, the modernising Hunanese, once-general secretary of the Party, Hu Yaobang. Already set aside by Deng for a failure to crack down on the unrest of 1986, Hu Yaobang's spirit seemed to stand as a heavenly reminder of all that was going wrong.

On 17 April, five hundred students appeared on Tiananmen Square to pay their respects to the man who had seemed to stand a little closer to the people. Over the following two days, on the square and in the streets around, the five hundred became five hundred thousand. University classes were abandoned: replaced with posters, ink and pens. A vigil was taken up opposite the gates of Zhongnanhai. A few days later a 'committee of students' asked for a voice in the newspapers, as well as an open and clear account of the riches acquired by Party officials.

Met with stony silence, a few days after that, a small gathering of students moved to the steps of the Great Hall of the People, the revolutionary monument to the people's proletariat. Digging deep into Beijing's memories of the past, they knelt in an ancient act of supplication to request an audience with the Party's imperial powers. Zhao Ziyang, the other moderniser who had re-revolutionised the fields of Sichuan, once premier and now general secretary of the Party, was abroad, and it seemed that not a single other Party heart could be found to receive the students in his place. Instead, a reply was delivered in the form of an editorial in the Party's *Peoples' Daily*, denouncing the 'conspiracy and turmoil on Tiananmen Square' as 'nothing less than a class struggle which is doomed to fail'. With teachers, workers, journalists and ordinary Beijingers coming out to meet them, the students gathered their courage and began to march to a common cry: *renmin wansui!*, 'Long Live the People!'. As they passed along the roads of the city, shop doors flew open in encouraging applause, buses were brought to a halt, and lollipops and even *renminbi* notes were thrown towards the marchers like votes of support. As April tumbled towards May, the posters only got louder: 'What is truth?', 'Why can't this poster be published?' and 'Beijing belongs to the people'.

4 May arrived, with its 1919 memories of student calls for science and democracy, and of the fact that so many of those early students had been the earliest founders and supporters of the Communist Party. Zhao Ziyang, now returned from his travels, and talking more openly to some visiting foreigners, let it be known that, in his opinion, the students had a point. Back doors should never have become a fact of life; Party officials and new bosses should not have been moving into new pavilions; the press had better and more important things to write about than the empty rhetoric of the past; and at a time of modernisation, questions should naturally be asked. Zhongnanhai shook with shock, but by the middle of May, with Beijing now afloat on a sea of youthful hope, Zhao Ziyang had become a beacon – and Zhongnanhai was beginning to look like a remote and renegade island.

Worryingly for the Party, the students were far from alone. Defying the mothership of the All-China Federation of Trade Unions, a Beijing Workers Autonomous Union also appeared under blazing banners. With twenty thousand members calling for the fat cats to slim down, it seemed as if all the shop floors in the capital were sending someone to turn up in the square. As labour turned up in rising numbers, armies of bookish researchers arrived to join them. Marching under the banners of enterprises that included both state and private production, their slogans pointed not only to a voice for the people, but more specifically to the matter of a constitution, and to a rule of law that would apply to the Party as well as everyone else. Journalists from radio, print and television abandoned the rules of reporting-to-order and joined the crowds, raising their own flags of truth. On 13 May, hundreds of students sat down for a hunger strike. By 17 May, the square was awash with a million hearts seemingly beating as one. Street vendors offered up their wares for free; pickpockets declared a moratorium on theft. As the square swelled with ever-greater numbers, and while the students waited for the Party to come out of Zhongnanhai and have a conversation, everyone sat down to long debates about what it meant to be Chinese.

On 19 May, after weeks of chilling winds blowing across the courtyards of Zhongnanhai, Zhao Ziyang stepped out of the gates. With an understanding that the Party's minds were more fixed, and harder, than anyone on the streets could know or understand, he made his way to the square and the students. 'I am sorry that I didn't come earlier', he apologised, with tears in his eyes. 'Please be patient. The situation is very complicated. It will take time. We can talk. Please eat.'

Later that day, the students abandoned their hunger strike. But as the sun rose the following morning, stronger powers in Zhongnanhai pronounced a martial law, commanding everyone to go back home. Beijing stayed on its streets. Declaring that 'stability is everything', Deng Xiaoping stood the capital's own military garrison down on grounds of a suspected sympathy. Replacement convoys of soldiers were summoned from the provinces to take control of the city: hearts hardened by orders that told them 'a counter-revolution' had broken out. Alerted by journalists who had broken their boundaries weeks before, Beijing's people flocked to the city's intersections and turned themselves into human barricades. Sleeping on the streets, asking themselves and those around them how the People's Army could turn against its own, stubborn men and women transformed themselves into popular guards. Calculating spirits were transformed into warm red hearts; and those whose souls had prided themselves on just getting by, began to break into smiles. Army convoys were surrounded by doting grandmothers – even as their drivers looked up to find paper blinds shielding the road ahead from their view. Soldiers in their trucks looked down to see nimble Beijing fingers letting the martial air out of their tyres. As days turned to dusk, anyone venturing out of an evening found the soft breeze of early summer carrying the patriotic voices of ten thousand people singing the tune of the *March of the Volunteers*: 'Arise, arise, arise! Our million hearts beating as one'.

As 3 June moved towards the midnight that would carry it into 4 June, tanks from the strongest corners of the country finally pushed their way forwards. Trucks thick with troops followed in their wake. Called up from the depths of Inner Mongolia, the men had been prepared for war, and told only that a corps of terror was striking at the heart of China. Tanks rolling towards Tiananmen Square, squadrons of soldiers chased young spirits who rushed into the surrounding narrow streets where willow-treed shadows seemed to promise shelter. Bullets flew like arrows; once-beating hearts fell like broken birds; blood ran like ink.

Watching the past appear yet again, heaven might have wept. But, if it did, no one on earth was allowed to see its tears.

PART 5

DOWN IN THE COUNTRYSIDE

When the wind blows, the grass bends.

The Analects (attributed to Confucius, 551 – 479 BCE)

CHAPTER 1

SNOW IN SUMMER

Make a new people.

The Book of Documents (second millennium BCE)

Dirt underfoot, a whiff of the earth in everybody's nostrils, man and nature were once again putting on a spectacular display. Drums had drummed, and bells had rung, but by the autumn of 1926 no one in Hebei's Ding Xian had needed to be told when and where the market would appear. Near and far, everyone had descended for the day. Bales of straw spread left and right; ruddy apples and warm pears piled towards the sky; proud cabbages stood to command the attention of passers-by. Here and there, chickens scratched in wicker cages, while pigs and piglets grunted in crates; children struggled to keep charge of scrawny goats with minds of their own. Tables offered up mountains of grain: scales ready and waiting for a buyer to appear, as strident voices called out their fare. Woven mats and baskets were presented on the ground for inspection; seeds were spread out for discerning eyes. Worn brown hands clutched precious coins; and every now and then, long and prosperous coats counted strings of cash. Over by a grove of trees, blacksmiths, carters and barbers had set up shop under sheltering branches: shoes for a horse, wheels for a carriage, and a shave for anyone in need. The crowd heaving, few failed to find a familiar face and exchange the age-old greeting of the fields: *chi fan le ma* (have you eaten)?

Those who lived nearby had left their village before the crack of dawn. Those coming from further away had walked for a day or more. Some had hit the road with a single pig and a hope. Others, with a little better luck, had pushed their produce in a creaking cart. The richest of all had been carried on the wealth of a horse or an ox, hauling wagons whose wheels turned with little human effort across the bumpy land. But, once arrived, even the tiredest of feet and the poorest of pockets found a sight to put a spring in their step: jugglers and storytellers for anyone with eyes to see and ears to hear; medicine men entertaining their way to a hopeful sale; letter-writers dashing black characters across white pages. Over by the temple, as always, there was a show of puppets: evil landlords, dark officials and heroic peasants, all caught up in a dance of dramatic delight. For those with a coin or two to spare, the possibilities were endless: *miantiao*, noodles, spun in front of one's eyes before being poured into a bowl of steam; sweet *bing*, cakes, warm from the griddle. And this year, something quite, quite new. All the way from the city of Beijing, and all for free, a group of students and teachers had come to bring the future to the past: lectures with lanterns, conjuring up a magic that seemed to be called science; stories about seeds that burst with bumper crops; promises of new pigs whose fat bellies would dwarf anything known before; and demonstrations of pumps that could cut hours of labour from an irrigating day.

Then, just as the moon was rising – when some thought that heaven must surely have run out of its wonders – an opera appeared with an even stranger tale: the story of a peasant who had learnt to read.

*   *   *

Ding Xian county had not always harboured such high spirits. Set in the heartlands of Hebei province, two hundred miles south of Beijing, it had first appeared as a military garrison under the Tang dynasty's founding emperor, Taizong. Four hundred years later, it had become a county seat, its soft wealth and simple harvest songs poetically captured by a Song dynasty magistrate who was also a scholarly poet. Behind official walls, a Ding Xian county town had risen, home to a succession of tax-collecting and dispute-resolving magistrates. Outside the walls, the county over which the town presided spread across an undulating expanse of fields, scattered with villages, each dotted with the households that brought them into life.

For almost a thousand years, the fields had turned from season to season; feasts and famines had been ushered in by the alternating changes of rain and drought; heaven had smiled and frowned. But in the past few hundred years, the winds of change had brought more than their fair share of trouble. With paltry sums of imperial remuneration, the magistrates had sought an ever-greater affinity with the self-strengthening families, whose wealth was always ready to buy a blind official eye. Taxes had continued to be spread more heavily across peasant lands; and disputes between landlords and peasants were always resolved in the formers' favour. The headmen of the villages had gathered the taxes like bitter harvests, local thugs had backed rent collections with whips, and the additional cost of anyone's shoe-leather used in collecting the taxes and fees had naturally been charged to the peasants' accounts.

Preoccupied with the state of the treasury, in the last few centuries, official observations of the heavenly changes had dulled, even as the northern peasants spent all of their energies in trying to deal with the vagaries of the local land and weather. Soils protesting under pressure, forests lost to timber, the clouds seemed to float past without distributing a drop of rain. Most accepted the changes as part of nature's wisdom – just like the periodic floods, droughts, frost and hail, not to mention the inevitable failures of crops, and the following deaths. Indeed, after millennia of heavenly sliding, even the fact that disputes were typically resolved with a clink of coins was accepted as part of life on earth, as was the fact that if anyone from the fields ever wanted to object, there would always be a ready pair of arms to twist their necks until they saw sense. Those who fell behind with rents, taxes, or both, were naturally forced to go to a money-lending landlord for a loan, with rates fixed by the level of desperation rather than any market, and interest collected on interest as a matter of course. Whenever the harvests faltered, the price of grain would naturally rise. With the gentry and the merchants placing their bets on the changes, grain acquired by the ton and stuffed into the gunnels of granaries would be held back for as long as possible in order to boost the bumper profits that the inevitable failed harvest would bring. For those who could not afford anything, there was always a patch of land to be sold. And if the land was already gone, then there were the assets of wives and daughters (even sons, if things were really desperate) which could always command a price: an exchange that, as far as the calculating landlords and officials could see, would give the peasant the added benefit of less future expense.

Working without a stop, pouring their sweat into the ploughed furrows of a northern land that had become as hard as metal, beasts of burden had become a luxury which few could afford. Barely earning enough to feed themselves, let alone their families, Ding Xian's peasants had eaten their fair share of bitterness. In a heavenly land of two thousand counties and three hundred thousand villages, each with its own particular troubles with nature, and all with their troubles of landlords and officials, they were not alone. But while nature seemed to have taken a particular turn against the now treeless and exhausted soils of the north, Ding Xian's peasants had often been able to count themselves luckier than some. Remembering the exhortations of Confucius to put oneself in other people's shoes, in parts of Ding Xian county, the gentry had done their best to open up their doors to the peasant poor. On festival days, benevolence had been spread for all to see; and whenever an ancestor merited a celebration, the poorer branches of family trees had been invited to join the lower levels of a feast. From time to time, the White Lotus and other secret societies had even offered hope of serious change – although, in the end, their rebellions had usually come to naught.

But then the foreigners had come, with their cheap cotton and their interfering god, meddling in things they never understood. For a few years, from 1898, it really looked as if the Boxer rebels with their talismans might be able to get rid of them. In the end, however, their boxing fists had failed to match the power of the foreigners' guns, and the price of their failure – levied in time-honoured tradition through ever higher taxes and levies on the peasants – looked as if it would be paid until kingdom come. Remembering a song from the travelling opera that passed through from time to time, peasant minds tilling the fields often dwelt on the thrilling dream of a good official who would free them from the corruption above. But, as the tale itself told, that was a dream that was as likely to come true as snow falling in summer.

Not long after the Boxer rebellion failed, though, a would-be imperial scholar from the most powerful family in the county (one who had failed to pass his exams) had come up with the hitherto unheard of idea of improving not just the lot of his own family, but everyone else's as well. Villages were brushed up for a self-strengthening dream, streets were renamed after the Confucian virtues, trees were planted, and schools began to open their doors to peasant minds. But then, in 1912, the emperor disappeared. Heaven knew where he had gone, but when black clouds of warlords arrived, the scholar with his self-strengthening ideas retreated behind the walls of his courtyards, the villages sank back into their dirt, the schools closed, and an uneasy silence settled over the fields. Plagues of unruly soldiers began to march across the crops. As always, the old hearts sighed: nothing good ever lasted.

*　　*　　*

By 1918, two hundred miles away from Ding Xian, the eager halls of Peking University had begun to turn their minds to the question of the countryside. Most of the students, like their lecturers, were the sons and daughters of gentry scholars and merchants: a youth whose lives had been blessed with the wealth of their families' spreading lands, even as their protected eyes had failed to see the burden of the peasants' bitterness-eating labours below. Returning from Japan, Europe and America with ideas of revolution in their hearts, they had revisited the comfortable country estates of their youth, and received quite a shock. Where childhood memories recalled spreads of grass blowing in soft winds, minds opened up by studies abroad saw a destitution that their younger selves had missed.

Observing the fields of suffering, most had confidently, and even hopefully, expected to hear a sudden thunderclap of rural rebellion. Hearing only silence, they had reflected upon the past and pondered. The late nineteenth-century revolutionaries had told everyone to 'imagine a people'. But it seemed that the peasants were just a soporific mass of straw who only roused themselves when the harvests didn't appear. At which point, they gathered into brotherhoods of men, hopelessly calling upon heaven to give them a Taiping Great Peace; and, when that could not be managed, they would dream of 'a good official'. Minds mesmerized by the seasons, senses dulled by the earth, hearts frozen by the hail of rents and taxes: beyond the harvests and the occasional brotherhoods of men, the only thing the vast majority of the population seemed to care about were the wooden gods who ruled their hearts like little demons shouting from their temple heights. No wonder the foreign gunboats had been able to sail themselves into the coastal cities; no wonder the coastal cities had become treaty ports of foreign empires; and no wonder the northern lands of the new Republic were still being carved up into the humiliating territories of foreign powers.

Seeing the students' confusion, in 1919, Li Dazhao, the chief librarian of

Peking University (who was also the convenor of Peking University's Marxist Research Society, and a political economist with a passionate interest in the question of what, after all these millennia, it meant to be Chinese) inked a challenge to the students. 'Go down to the countryside and wake the people up' was his suggestion. 'See if you can start to repair the wreckage left by your fathers; and while you are at it, cleanse your own hearts with some purifying labour in the fields.' Elaborating on his words, he explained that ideas about Mr Science and Mr Democracy might be flooding into China's cities and lapping at the edges of bigger towns, but the countryside was still in the dark. Instead of the students following in the ancestors' scholarly examples, it was time that these intellectual flowers started to roll up their sleeves and build the kind of bridges to the countryside that would ensure the peasants would not only be found but never lost again. Peking University's students took up the task. Dedicated to going down to the countryside, the movement was flooded with volunteers, all ready and willing to go and find the missing peasant people, and wake them up. Although, since few, if any, of the students had ever actually spoken to a real live peasant in the flesh, no one was quite sure what on earth they would say to them when they did.

Prepared for the unknown, and fortifying themselves with tobacco and tea, quilts and cameras (not to mention the odd flask of foreign medicinal whisky), the students found that they had arrived not a moment too soon. In 1921, the north-eastern areas of China which surrounded Beijing (Ding Xian included) had once again experienced the disapproving flick of a dragon's tail: no rain, then no harvest, and then nothing to eat other than the bark of a tree – and then even that had run out. Stomachs sank to skeletons; the price of a patch of land, or a wife, fell to a few days' food. In the opinion of some in the cities, it didn't last long – just long enough to winnow out the numbers in the villages, and to sort the wheat from the chaff. Confronted, however, with the stunned faces of those who had survived, the students began to see quite another side to the popular story of an indolent peasant past: less a tale of peasants who had gone to sleep, and more the tragedy of a desperate people who had got lost – if, indeed, there had ever been a time when the bitterness-eating peasants had really been attached to the imperial whole.

Hearts touched, the students looked and thought again. Never part of the walled and gentrified world of Confucian ideals, untutored in the complicated classical language of scholarly minds ('Chinese Latin' as some described it), across the millennia, the long-suffering peasants had tilled the fields for everybody's food, even as they had occupied a silently bitter world of their own. Save, that is, for the moments when, desperate, they had erupted like a storming force of nature, only to be branded as bandits. Really, they were the earliest of revolutionaries who had not just failed to find their luck, but had failed to find anyone who could write their story so that others could read it and understand. And so it was that five thousand years after the time of the Yellow Emperor, these black-haired people were still invisibly tucked away into small villages where the sight of a floating sleeve was never the bearer of any news other than a tax, and where a bus or a train to any other kind of place was donkey-cart-hours away. Waking with the sound of the cockerels, not sleeping until long after the sun went down, this was an invisible world of men, women and children who worked from dawn to dusk for barely enough food to survive.

Thinking even deeper, though, the students began to realise that this was also an invisible world of men, women and children who knew nature like the backs of their hands, and who, while their bowls were never full, had nonetheless kept a song on their lips for as long as anyone could remember, not to mention stories in their hearts to tell their children as hungry bodies tried to sleep. While the peasants could obviously do with a better life, it was the students themselves who had the most to learn. But none of the peasants' past had ever been written into a book, and given that the city had never had any use for their knowledge, little of what they knew could even be described in the lofty scholarly language that the city had made its own.

Descending upon the villages in their quest for a nation, Peking University's students received a lesson in what it meant to be a people, and the true meaning of Li Dazhao's words came alive. On closer consideration, the city with its minds was less a citadel of omniscience, and more a corruption of the honest, hardworking man, not to mention a betrayal of the peasant. Conversely, the countryside turned out to be a wealth of buried treasure: man in daily encounters with a wisdom of nature which no city person had any experience of; songs and stories which no city ears had ever heard before. Clutching their notebooks, the students found themselves wooden stools to sit upon, and stroked down every possible fact from the newly discovered world. Meanwhile, astonished at the arrival of a scholarly youth that had never in any peasant's memory shown any interest in the fields, the peasants themselves could only stop and stare. Or at least, the simplest of them stared. Those who had their wits about them took themselves swiftly off to the safety of their homes, confident in their expectation that somewhere at the bottom of all of this was bound to be trouble.

*   *   *

As Peking University's students were discovering new rural horizons in the countryside around Beijing, other young minds were finding Chinese peasants in the unlikeliest of foreign fields. One student came across them unexpectedly in France. The youngest son of a Sichuan line of scholars, he had gone, like so many others, to look for China's future in the New World. Accepted at Yale University, Yan Yangchu (or James Yen, as he would come to be known by his foreign friends) found himself mesmerised by Woodrow Wilson's ideas that rulers should have principles, that governments should judge themselves by their ability to raise a new and better world from the devastating cinders of the First World War, and that any decisions taken for the people at large should be explained in terms which could be understood by the ordinary man on the street. Desperate to be part of putting such ideas into action, in 1918 Yen volunteered to help the Western soldiers and civilians whose lives had been overturned by war. He soon found himself in France, at the tail end of the Western Front, a member of a delegation organised by the American chapter of the YMCA.

Arriving in France, young American volunteers were assigned to work with displaced Europeans; Yen was sent to look after a corps of Chinese peasants. Masking his disappointment, he remembered that these were men whose desperation had, in 1916, led them to the British recruiting stations of Weihaiwei. From there they had travelled across the seas to dig trenches for a war between countries whose languages they could not speak – traded away by a self-strengthening Republican government looking for loans and personal shares, rather than the return of the northern lands held by Germany, for which their labour had originally been pledged. It was on these foreign fields that he encountered a Chinese peasant for the first time in his life, and on these foreign fields that he came to the same conclusion as the students in Beijing: the son of a scholar had far more to learn from the peasants than anything they might learn from him. Hearts willing to eat more labouring bitterness than he had ever imagined possible, these peasants were men whose only ignorance was of books, and whose stamina and determination put every scholar he had ever known to shame. Before long, Yen's disappointment turned to exhilaration.

Not only unable to speak English or French, but also unable to read or write the characters of their own Chinese language, Yen decided to give the front-line peasants the education they had missed – on the fields of France.

Working in their midst, teaching the strokes of the most essential characters, one by one, Yen gradually gained their trust. As he did so, the unknown stories of a people who had suffered for so long and in such silence began to tumble out like water from a broken dam. Stories of such suffering they would break the hardest heart, they were more than enough to inspire Yen to try to think of how he could make their learning easier. While he might not know what to do with a plough, teaching was something that Yen had been born to.

Listening to his peasant corps, and digging into his own ideas, Yen decided to set aside the textbooks written by scholars, for scholars, and to create a new set of lessons. Written in the ordinary language of the Chinese north from which the peasants came, it would limit itself to one thousand carefully-chosen, basic characters which represented the essential reading and writing words of daily life. As Yen began to teach, characters aside, with every lesson, came a torrent of questions: questions about the world whose trenches they had been building, for a start; questions about home; and all of the other questions which, based on nothing more than rumours run amok in the darkness of eyes that could not read, revealed the anxieties of desperate men. With his students studying to the point of forgetting to eat, Yen decided it was also time to start a newspaper. Short and to the point, its four pages of articles opened up everything under heaven, in words that the peasant students could read and understand.

In 1920, with the war over and his peasant students packed on to ships bound for home, Yen returned to China. By 1921 he had persuaded the YMCA to fund a literacy campaign to teach labourers in Chinese cities how to read and write. By 1923, thinking about what might be possible if whole villages of peasants could be taught the magic of the brush, Yen had reached out to like-minded Chinese friends and peers for support in founding what he called a 'Mass Education Movement', the MEM. Lessons would be delivered in the fields and offered at the times of day, and in the seasons, permitted by the farming calendar. Subjects would be chosen which would introduce the peasants to new scientific ideas as well: breeds of pigs which could offer more meat; seeds which would produce bigger yields; and simple pumps which could irrigate dried-out northern fields at prices the countryside could afford. After millennia of being left out of the country's scholarly conversations, China's peasants were finally going to be joined up with the minds of city cousins who were emerging from citadels of learning which most of the peasants had never even heard of.

Not surprisingly, news of James Yen's MEM spread quickly. Volunteers, particularly students, rolled up in promising numbers. Other helpful minds, ones with deeper pockets as well as a few with valuable skills to share, followed in their wake. Then, in 1925, the elderly head of a family in a Hebei county presented his lands for service. Disillusioned by the competing banners of the early Republic's political parties, and exhausted by a decade of battling against warlords, the scholarly Mi Qianshan told Yen that his home county, Ding Xian, had been waiting for decades, if not centuries, or a millennium, for something like the MEM to arrive. Within a year, Mi Qianshan had offered up the entire county of Ding Xian as a laboratory for the MEM's new countryside.

Peasants were invited to classes not only in how to read and write, but also in how to understand the science of the far-off city world. And with an entire county as a laboratory, the MEM was able to dig deeper into the local earth to find out what was needed than any of its founders had imagined might be possible. Reading and writing were an important beginning, but if the countryside was going to be able to talk to the twentieth-century cities, there was not only a world of science that needed to arrive, there was also a world of local, natural knowledge that the MEM's city minds were going to need to learn.

Bubbling with excitement about its possibilities, Ding Xian began to attract the attention of scholarly Chinese minds, including many trained in America. Once on the ground, and gradually getting a better understanding of the countryside – the rhythms of its seasons, the stuff of its soil, the falling of its rains – the scholars began to think about what new ideas might help the peasants find their way to a more heavenly future. Which new breeds of animals? What new crops and seeds? Soon Ding Xian's cabbages were the envy of every market for miles around, and their pigs were winning almost every possible prize. Meanwhile, for Peking University's students – some Communist, but most just believers in their own 'new culture' way of imagining a people – 'back to the village' became a powerful mantra: chanted not only by themselves, but by some of the most talented minds of the time.

*　　*　　*

While the MEM had concentrated its thoughts on the Ding Xian pocket in the north, down in the far south, another young scholar had been looking at quite a different county. Youngest son of one of the richest landowners in Guangdong province's Haifeng county, like so many others of his age, he dreamt of 'imagining a people'. In 1917, he had gone to Japan to study. In 1918, his heart had risen to the skies when he heard the news that the old imperialist Russian empire had been transformed into a revolutionary Bolshevik Republic. In 1919, it fell back down to earth with a bang when the Chinese journalists of the country's *Da Gong Bao* newspaper tapped out the words which told everyone that the imperial powers at Versailles had rewarded the trench-building labour of China's peasants, not with a return of the northern German-held lands to China, but with the transfer of those lands to the rising imperial power of Japan.

Returning to Haifeng in 1921, Peng Pai accepted his family's suggestion that he take up an official position in the county's education bureau. Full of ideas from abroad, he was keen to try out some experiments of his own: new schools, a modern curriculum, and young educators whose tasks would include the teaching of revolutionary thoughts on the importance of building solidarity between teachers and their pupils.

With such an imagination, it was not long before Peng was relieved of his official duties. Brothers, uncles and cousins were shocked at the reckless independence with which he had squandered the opportunity of an official career. But Peng rejoiced in his freedom. Looking at all of the things that needed to change, he decided to carry his dreams of solidarity up the local mountain, stand himself at a busy crossroads, and shout out his ideas to every passing peasant. 'Year in, year out', he called, 'you work in the fields until you drop dead, while your landlord sits at home with a book. Meanwhile, selling those you love to pay back a money-lender, you have forgotten the thousand years of labour that the greedy landlords have stolen from your hands.' Of those who had any time at all to stop and listen to something that had nothing to do with the fields (not many), most thought he was mad. Indeed, a number muttered that he sounded like that Great Peace fanatic Hong Xiuquan, the one who had conjured up the Taiping rebellion seventy-five years ago. 'Look where that had got everyone,' they added.

After a few days of talking to thin air, a sympathetic soul named Zhang finally stopped to listen. Taking pity on Peng, he offered him some advice. 'If you want any of these labouring hands to pay attention to your arguments, let alone believe that you might be speaking from your heart, you had better learn the local language. And while you are at it, you should think about trading in your soft silk gown for something simpler, in the rough blue cotton line.' Quick to learn, and desperate to teach, Peng asked his new acquaintance if he had any other advice to give.

That evening, after his own day's labour was done, Zhang returned with a group of his friends and offered Peng Pai an education in the mind of the peasant, with suggestions on how to get the peasants to lend him their ears. 'In a world where rent collectors are nothing but armed thugs,' they explained, 'one where taxes and fees are dreamt up quicker than a cock can crow, where lands are seized without explanation, where talking to an official is harder than getting into the Forbidden City, and where everyone has been taught, with beatings, that obedience is a survival skill, finding a peasant willing to trust an outsider will be almost as hard as finding the eternally elusive good official.' 'But', added one of Zhang's friends, 'you could create a band of brothers which would certainly catch their attention.' Peng was only too willing to take his advice. By the end of the evening, the new friends (Peng the scholar, Zhang and his associates) had agreed to work together, and the Haifeng County Peasant Union was born.

Over the coming weeks, with Peng Pai under the tutoring wings of his new peasant brothers, they walked across the mountains, calling in to every village, and inviting anyone and everyone to come for a talk. Conversations always limited to the evening ends of working days, lanterns were lit, at Peng's expense, and more brotherly spirits were ignited. Within a few months, five hundred brave peasants found the courage to risk the beatings threatened by officials and landlords, and joined. As a contribution to the new common cause, each advanced a copper coin. Within a year, the Peasant Union had twenty thousand member families. A Peasant Manifesto was inked for all to see. Each member was given a small card testifying to his membership, with a list of the principles by which the Union would abide. Among these, was the capital idea that all of the members would apply their minds and pool their resources for the challenges ahead: land to be tamed, families to be helped, and landlords to be addressed on an equal footing.

Bit by bit at first, and then with something of a rush, the pile of copper coins began to rise. Soon, fields were being turned into open schools, and the Peasant Union was teaching its members the science of accounts. Henceforth, it would no longer be only the landlords who could read the registers of rent. Hills that had been stripped bare over centuries of desperation, were being replanted with trees, and a peasant clinic appeared. Even travelling operas were being organised to set new revolutionary stories to old peasant tunes.

Confidence gathering by the day, the Peasant Union then turned its attention not only to helping the peasants resolve their own disputes – something which the magistrates had rather neglected across the centuries – but to tackling the trickiest challenge of all: standing up to the landlords. Having watched the ways of the magistrates from the courtyard of his family's power – and having grown up with a landlord for a father – Peng Pai was full of advice. 'Think of them as paper tigers,' he said 'big shadows which will jump in fright if anyone ever really stands up to them'. Seeing Peng Pai resolve seemingly impossible problems, the peasants turned to each other and asked themselves who needed a magistrate if one had a Peasant Union – and what, indeed, could the gentry landlords do if the peasants stood together?

With Peng Pai at their side, drop by drop, the peasants lost their fears. Soon their ideas were beginning to flow like southern water. 'All of these labouring hands,' ventured one, 'trundling their individual goods to market, only to find that the landlord-middlemen step in to take the profit. Why don't we make the markets without them, and keep the profits ourselves?' 'So many problems', suggested another 'but so many of us to help. Why not stand together and be the charity that a neighbour might need?' Peng Pai's heart swelled with a warm pride as he saw the very people that he was 'imagining' begin to appear at his side. Introducing a new lesson, he suggested that next time anyone higher up held out a palm to be crossed with silver, the peasants should reply not with a coin but with Sun Yatsen's three simple principles of the people: *minzu, minquan, minsheng* – government of the people, by the people, and for the livelihoods of the people. Warming to the idea, the peasants' own hearts began to swell. 'If the landlords really cut up rough', shouted some, 'why not take a leaf out of the Crouching Dragon Zhuge Liang's book? We could just pull up the stones that mark the boundaries between their fields, and leave them to jump at each other's throats!'

Bold words shot across the peasants' secret meetings. No one was in any doubt, though, that if they were truly going to become 'a people', then the landlords were going to have to learn some bitter lessons of their own. And if the landlords were going to be learning some bitter lessons, then the peasants had better get ready for the inevitable beatings.

But the peasants were as brave as Guan Yu (and all the other ancient outlaws who had since become gods). By 1926, the Peasant Union had spread across Haifeng. Naturally, the landlords branded Peng Pai a 'bandit chief'. But the unionized county of Haifeng was gaining ground, becoming a legend among peasants across the wider province of Guangdong. Everyone was looking with wonder at Peng Pai, and wanting to learn from his revolutionary ideas. Sharing the thoughts of their unknown brothers in Ding Xian, and having heard the same travelling opera song, many turned their eyes to the sky and wondered whether, perhaps this time, snow really could fall in summer.

*   *   *

While Ding Xian was discovering a wondrous spring in what everyone had thought would be a never-ending winter, and with Guangdong imagining the miracle of a mid-summer snow, up in the old Changsha capital of Hunan province, Mao Zedong was getting on with his own business of finding a foothold in the next revolution. Going back and forth between Peking University's library and the Changsha capital, he was applying a prodigious energy to the possibilities of a change in power and building relationships with anyone and everyone who might offer him an opportunity to be part of the advance. Asked to create a Cultural Book Society to promote the Party's literature, he joined up his work with the new efforts of the American YMCA, encountered through the person of the now-returned James Yen.

Hearing about Peng Pai's Haifeng Peasant Union, Mao suggested a few ideas for peasant militia movements in the countryside of Hunan. And when, as part of the Moscow-brokered 'United Front' of the Guomindang and the Communist Party, he became leader of the Guomindang's Peasant Movement Training Institute (the brainchild of Peng Pai, who had joined the Guomindang in 1924) he adopted as many of Peng Pai's ideas as he could. To which, he added the benefit of his own family experience: son of a farmer whose three acres made him a landlord even though he was little more than a rich peasant.

In early 1927, when the Guomindang and the Communist Party were still brothers in revolutionary arms, Mao penned a 'Report on an Investigation of the Peasant Movement in Hunan'. In it, he listed 'fourteen great achievements' of work conducted so far, including: overthrowing local landlords and tyrants, spreading propaganda, igniting brotherhoods of peasants, education, and mutual help and co-operation. As a conclusion, he advanced the idea that the revolution was going to come from the fields. While Chen Duxiu, leader of the Communist Party, followed Marx and Moscow in their belief that revolutions always came from cities, given that nine out of every ten Chinese people were living in a village, it scarcely seemed an unreasonable point of view.

The members of the young Communist Party divided between those who agreed with Marx and the Moscow brothers, and those who thought that, in China, the revolution would come from the fields. One who agreed with Mao was Li Dazhao, once his chief (librarian) at Peking University. But while Li Dazhao and Chen Duxiu stood shoulder to shoulder on questions of intellectual conscience and freedom, Li was unable to move Chen's Moscow-led conviction that it would be the workers labouring under the inhuman conditions of the factories who would bring the revolution to life.

When the Communist dream was smashed in the treacherous Shanghai massacre unleashed by the Guomindang in April 1927, however, the Party began to shift. Sun Yatsen now dead, and any and every heart which looked as if it might be a Communist red being chased down, the Party shattered into a host of individuals struggling to survive. Hounded out of the cities, the remnants of the Communists did their best to find each other and regroup in the countryside. Dreams of a city-led revolution, at least a revolution led from any Chinese city, were shattered. That year, the Party moved its annual congress to Moscow, with delegates travelling across the border disguised with beards and hats.

In the months following their return, the battlefield moved to the countryside, with brave individuals from the fields volunteering to take up the lead. Among them, having transferred his allegiance to the Communist Party and vowing that his Haifeng peasants would hold strong against what would obviously be devastating landlord attacks, was Peng Pai. In the southern cities of Guangzhou and Jiangxi, uprisings rose, but the Guomindang's military forces smashed them down. Further up the country, Mao Zedong made his suggestion of an autumn harvest uprising for the fields of Hunan, with a peasant army to be put under his own command. And when his uprising fell, he took the opportunity to lead the company into the Jinggang Mountains and build his own Communist base.

* * *

Back up in the north-east lands around Hebei's Ding Xian, the shifting fortunes of the Communists, the Guomindang and the warlords had been having an impact of their own. When the Communists scattered in fear for their lives, and with many of Peking University's students if not active Party members at least sympathetic spirits, the fragile peace of the University's *hong lou* red brick building had been rocked. And then Chiang Kai-shek decided that it would be better to leave the north in the hands of allied warlords rather than try to hold it himself, and swept the central government out of Beijing and off to the Nanjing south. James Yen and the MEM did their best to stick to their own guns and hold on to their belief in the possibilities of snow in summer, but the lands of the north were edging further into chaos.

Ding Xian's future was now a little cloudier, but it had already conjured up a lot of magic, and it continued to work. In 1927, the MEM acquired the additional novelty of a new-fangled 'social surveyor'. Fascinated by the relationship between labour and society, the social surveyor was the son of an American soap-maker who had partnered with a candle-maker to create an industrial fortune: the candle-maker's name was Proctor, and the social surveyor was Sidney Gamble. Gamble had first travelled to China with his parents in 1908. In 1918, he had returned to Beijing with the YMCA, of which he was a devoted member, to apply the new science of social surveys in China's challenging world. By 1925, early surveys around Beijing were disrupted by the warlords. Gamble, now a friend of James Yen, suggested a study for Ding Xian: Who were the peasants? How did they live? What did they think? And, apart from tilling the fields, what sort of crafting labours did they do? When the survey was completed, the results pointed to a host of practical steps with which the peasants could be imagined into a people. Within a few years, Ding Xian had acquired four hundred People's Schools with classes grounded not on city textbooks but actual village life; fifteen thousand students and a host of alumni villager-students trained to teach; household associations; a youth group; even an association for the very young. Most important of all, Ding Xian found a conversation with the county's leaders, and even their support.

Suddenly the route to the future seemed a lot brighter. Friends, relations and alumni pooled their labours, and roads and bridges appeared. Village elders who had lost their way were replaced by younger representatives – not just chosen, but elected, by the village at large. A radio station appeared, full of local news. A *Farmers' Weekly* magazine followed: printed on a single big sheet of paper so that it could be conveniently pasted on to a wall for all to read. In 1929, even as a Great Depression settled in the West, sending dark clouds towards China, a ten-year county plan was crafted, with careful attention paid to Ding Xian's strengths and needs. Weaving hands were organised into co-operatives; trading minds were added to ensure that any profits found their way back to the pockets of Ding Xian's people. Not long afterwards, diagrams of how elections worked were being drawn on to pamphlets, and scattered around for everyone to consider the wider possibilities of imagining a people in the countryside.

In 1932, the idea of health as a way of life was added. Lighting up Ding Xian like a lantern, it was the brainchild of a man named Chen Zhiquan. Often described as a 'medical bolshevik', Chen had a number of new ideas about how to keep the people healthy – as opposed to the desperate remedies that tried to treat disease. Lessons in public health were held in the open air; the songs of travelling operas were adapted for support; ideas about cleaning water wells and washing hands were aired for all to hear. And with no possibility of creating an army of qualified doctors for the countryside – there were not even enough for the cities – villagers were trained to become a front-line in the fields.

By 1933, James Yen's MEM had become the government of Ding Xian. Headquartered in the old Temple of Culture, feted by representatives from the provincial government above, even recognised as a protected territory by the warlords around, its ideas on everything from cabbages and pigs to teachers and health workers were now flying across the country with wings which no one had ever dreamt of, albeit in skies blackening with the advancing clouds of war.

With its trail-blazing successes, Ding Xian was not short of company in its adventures. While local Hebei newspapers and magazines had covered its story, by the early 1930s, its trials and triumphs were being carried by newspapers and magazines across the country, reaching across a much wider world of students and intellectuals. Pockets of Ding Xianism were popping up all over the country, south as well as north – and Ding Xian itself had become a model for a new China. The wildly romantic imagining of peasants as a people was beginning to go beyond a dream, inspiring not just more of the students and intellectuals to roll up their sleeves and offer themselves as volunteers, but even some of the gentry, the merchants and the industrialists.

From the pulpit of Peking University's philosophy department, Liang Shuming (the Peking University professor who had argued that China's greatest contribution to the world was the Confucian idea of man as a virtuous spirit who bent his own desires to adapt to nature) set off in search of a county of his own. Convinced that Confucius' original principles held great value for mankind (not to be confused with the Confucianism with which imperial dynasties had raised tyrannies of top-down minds), Liang Shuming restated the virtues which city scholars should carry to the fields. The ren humanity of putting yourself in other peoples shoes; the yi integrity of names and purposes; *li* ritual as the remembered choreography of common lives; *zhi* knowledge as a pursuit of learning that included investigating 'real' things with one's conscience, rather than mechanically applying the texts of the classics; and the *de* virtue of doing everything so diligently that one would never fail. Principles clear, Liang Shuming raised his own practical bridge between the hallowed halls of city-centred knowledge and the villages that had always sat at the edge, and in so doing, forged a link between the present and the past. Liang's dream was to give the peasants the possibility of creating a governing order of their own: a village life within which everyone would put *ren* empathy at the heart of their values, grounded in the rhythm of daily rituals designed for the common good, and all guided by virtue like the north star. Call it 'rural reconstruction', he suggested.

Then arrived another scholar, fresh from the London School of Economics. The son of a poor gentry family, who had braved the seas to study the science of sociology, his name was Fei Xiaotong. In London, he had been inspired to look at the different functions of a community and, having understood how they worked, to see how such an understanding might be applied to change. Returning to China, Fei had gone to the far south-west province of Yunnan, where he had used his learning to write up the stories of China's villages in ways that captivated everyone's imaginations. 'To city eyes, the countryside might seem like a scattered tray of sand', Fei observed. 'But if you look more carefully, you will see that what is actually there is much more of a fabric of threads all woven together.' Battered and torn by centuries of neglect as the villages were, Fei agreed that it was not always easy to discern the fabric, but if only everyone would take the time to look, they would see that there was still a warp, a weft and a pattern to be found. And recognising that there was still a pattern, why on earth would anyone want to add a bloody revolution to the miseries of the earth?

Looking at the factories now sprouting across the cities, and at the industries sweeping up migrant hands, Fei Xiaotong addressed himself to the Guomindang, whose power now spread across so much of the land. 'Stop parroting the West', he argued, 'anyone with eyes to see can tell that it is a world obsessed with cities which behaves as if the countryside was a cosmic mistake and assumes that man, better made for factories, has nothing to do with nature.' Then, listening to the Communists and their Marxist theories, he turned to offer them an honest opinion as well. 'Stop chattering about 'class' as if everyone lives in a textbook, and look at facts on the ground.' And then he addressed himself to by far and away the vast majority of the people: the men and women who were neither on the Guomindang right, nor the Communist left, but were standing in the middle hoping only for a wider security with which they could return to peaceful lives: 'Roll up your sleeves, brush off your dusty Confucius, and start thinking about how to build a truly Chinese world where everyone can live together, without forgetting the blindingly obvious truth that nothing worth having can be achieved in a day or even a night.' Cities could rise, but no one should forget that China and its people were grounded in its fields. And if the fields and the people were to survive, the trading minds harboured in the cities would need to co-operate with the peasants, including helping them to find a way to raise some manufacturing possibilities in the countryside, while ensuring that the peasants could profit from the wares of their own labour.

Printed on the pages of newspapers up and down the country, news of Ding Xian's triumphs, Liang Shuming's Confucian journey, and Fei Xiaotong's sociological remedies spread across the land, all described as 'rural reconstruction'. North and south, the future of the rural world became the centre of almost everyone's attention. And as the population read its newspapers, there arose an increasing understanding that the biggest problem of all was the fact that the cities and the fields had been pulled apart – and in that process, the ability of the countryside and any peasant to earn a livelihood was rapidly disappearing. Crops were being farmed for exports and cash rather than food; cotton cloth and crafts were being surrendered up for copper pennies before being sent on to the cities by traders, who were the only ones who made a profit. With the peasants working every hour that any god could give them, it seemed that only those who could find their way into one or another of the 'rural reconstruction' projects, would be able to change their fate.

For James Yen, Liang Shuming, Fei Xiaotong, and all the other 'intellectuals', including the Peking University minds, rural reconstruction was not just a question of the survival of the peasants – nor even just a matter of imagining a people from a scattered tray of sand – it was a matter of creating the foundations of a country which would include *both* cities and the countryside, and where each could learn from the other. And unlike the millennia of the past, the new intellectuals would not be stroking coded characters of disapproval onto scrolls of paper, but would put their own shoulders behind the ideas. Bit by bit, and drop by drop, the dream began to take shape. Here, there, and in more places than one could have ever imagined, rural skills and city minds began to come together. Rural co-operatives (for manufacturing and trade as well as farming) sprang up like bumper crops, all organised by the people themselves. Village hopes began to rise with hosts of enterprising ideas; even as those in the cities began to imagine a different future. It was a stubborn dream of snow in summer: one that almost came true.

*   *   *

Meanwhile, down south in the Jinggang Mountains, while news of James Yen's educating ideas and Ding Xian's prize-winning pigs no doubt reached Mao's ears, it was the dream of a Communist state which had taken hold – with Peng Pai's idea of Peasant Unions an inspiration, but the lessons of the First Qin Emperor as a guide. Peng Pai's idea, but without Peng Pai. Arrested at a secret meeting in Shanghai in 1929, the desperate attempts of Zhou Enlai to rescue him failed. On a late summer's day, refusing even under torture to give up his dream, the great heart who had led his peasants not just to imagine snow in summer but to make their dreams come true was executed by the Guomindang.

In that same year, Mao Zedong carried the kernel of Peng Pai's ideas from the Jinggang Mountains to Jiangxi, to a bigger base spread across thirty thousand square kilometres of mountainous land that would become a Chinese Soviet Republic. Not yet the vast fields of the north, but home to three million, mostly peasant and widely scattered, people. And then in 1934, while others up and down the country were trying to imagine a people, and with the battle for the 'survival of the fittest' raging between the Guomindang and the Communist Party (not to mention within the Communist Party itself), the Party decided it was time to march on.

CHAPTER 2

LEAPING AHEAD

Discover truth through practice.

Mao Zedong, 1937

The red heart arrived in Liu Lin village on a late winter's day, disguised as a donkey driver. Of course, whispers of a Communist army had floated in before: the one that was supposed to be dividing up heaven and earth into equal pieces for the poor. But in these dry lands of yellow earth, far from anywhere, truth and hope were always hard to tell apart.

As ragged as the poorest of the villagers, the donkey driver found a shelter at the fraying edge of the village caves, where the meanest of the dwellings tumbled into the fields beyond. Over the nights and weeks which followed, smuggled glances led to tests of cautious words until, eventually, everybody at the bottom of the pile knew exactly what colour he was. With the landlords' militias scouring the countryside on full Guomindang alert for any cunning Communists, one couldn't be too careful. Like-minded souls carefully identified, in the dark corner of a field, under a moonless sky, the donkey driver revealed himself as a revolutionary from Xi'an. The whispers were true, he murmured in a tongue that was clearly not from the fields. 'There is a Red Army and it is on its way. Tell no one except the poor. If you want to help, organise yourselves into a peasant union and create a company of rebel soldiers of your own.'

Over the months that followed, whisper by whisper, bravely independent spirits conjured up a Peasant Union from the fields, together with a company of rebel soldiers they could confidently call their own. It was not long before treacherous ears reported events to the landlords sitting behind their fortified county town walls, and no time at all after that before the landlords' militia appeared in the fields with their spears and swords. But, with the donkey driver always behind them, the company of rebels was prepared. As so often across the past, the heroic stories of the *Outlaws of the Marsh*, and the dazzling exploits of the Crouching Dragon, Zhuge Liang, had been scoured for strengthening inspiration. With only wood for weapons, bayonets and rifles had been carved and covered in silver paper to make them glint menacingly in the sun. With only fireworks for gunpowder, firecrackers had been hurled over the walls of the officials' courtyards in the dead of night, attracting a returning fire which, just as in Zhuge Liang's great battle of the arrows, sapped the ammunition and the spirits of the landlords' side.

At one point, the chairman of the Peasant Union was captured and taken to the county town, where he lost his head to a warlord's sword. But the Union stayed strong. By the end of the following September, battles fought and won amidst the corn, Liu Lin's land and that of its neighbours was sitting under a new heaven – one where the poor could till the fields without having to pay taxes, or even rent, where justice was free for all, and where not a single landlord could be found.

By the end of the year, the donkey driver was gone. By night, he had helped them plan not only their defences but their future. By day, he had put his shoulder to the plough with the best of them. When a fragile field had slid off its precarious slope, he had been the first to offer his ideas and his labour to try to restore the loss. If a family had needed a helping hand, he had been there before they had even asked. At every meal, he had eaten the same cabbage as everyone else; and if there was ever any corn, he had never, ever, taken a grain more than the rough hands next to him. When he had left, he had taken only one gift, the simplest of all to give, for those whose home it was: a hand-sketched map of the lay of Liu Lin's land and that of all of the surrounding villages, including every secret path. 'I will be back', he promised, 'and when I return, I will not be alone.'

*   *   *

The 'drop by drop' approach taken up by James Yen, Liang Shuming, Fei Xiaotong and the Peking University minds had worked well for a while. But the tides of the time had been unwilling to wait. In 1937, the Japanese army had swept across the north of China, and into its county towns. With no troops to protect them, as the Japanese poured through the northern gate of Ding Xian's county seat, the MEM workers, and everyone else who wanted to follow them, picked up whatever they could carry and clattered out through the gate at the south. Like brothers and sisters in the cities, each had to make his or her own choice about where to go. Shanghai was a muddy battlefield of what had become a second Sino-Japanese War, and the Guomindang, having lost the even bloodier battle of Nanjing, were moving on to the central cities of Sichuan.

For anyone ready to convert to the Party's faith, Yan'an always offered an open door. Many of the MEM members sympathised with the Communist idea of equality, and few were fans of a Guomindang whose self-strengthening seemed to have engulfed its forces in clouds of corruption. But the rising stories of the Communists' battles against questioning minds – and worrying whispers about Mao's darker ideas of order – were as disquieting for the MEM sympathisers as for others. Unsure, many decided to stay within the guns of the Guomindang's world. Once again, Chinese minds divided: some made their way to the Shaanxi plains around Yan'an, hoping that Ding Xian's lessons could be taught in a new Communist world. Others, including James Yen and many of the MEM's organising volunteers, followed Chiang Kai-shek to Sichuan, eventually landing in the inland port of Chongqing that, by the end of 1938, had become the latest capital of the country.

Yen and his followers might have congregated in the industrious city of Chongqing, but none of them had given up on their dream of a new countryside. Soon, they dug themselves into the nearby Sichuan county of Beipei and tried to build yet another new world. Peasants were taught to read and write, new breeds of pigs were raised, new seeds were sown, better pumps were installed for spreading water, schools were opened for all, health was taught as a way of life, and co-operatives were created for rural industry, with markets added for peasant trades. Beipei became Ding Xian all over again – with the added ideas of Liang Shuming's rural reconstruction and Fei Xiaotong's rural enterprise sown deeply into its soil. Although physically located within the territory of the Guomindang, few of the MEM adherents had any attachment to Chiang Kai-shek's version of the national dream. Tired of disasters, weary of broken promises, shocked at troops who seemed to see the Chinese people as their personal property – and with a government now suspiciously scrutinising every word for subversion – they were also worn out by the daily assaults on what anyone could say. From time to time, some would even wonder whether the future might not be better in Yan'an after all. Indeed, for many of those brave enough to touch the banned pages of the Party's propaganda or tune into its secret radio signals, Mao's thoughts on 'new democracy' began to seem not so bad. 'An enlightened and progressive China', he promised. Well, everyone could do with that. But that was the stuff of evening conversations, those moments when, after a long day's labour, Chinese hearts would ask themselves the age-old question: what did it mean to be Chinese, and where on earth was heaven?

Then, as the Second World War finished, America poured its dollars into the Guomindang's lap, not only to fight the Communists but to support the idea of rural reconstruction which was now seen as the best means of saving China. James Yen and others like him sighed. While dollars were always helpful, it was not money that China's countryside needed: it was a sympathetic bridge between the rural and the city worlds – and time. In any event, with corruption now rife across the Guomindang's Republic of China, the chances of those dollars being used for much other than strengthening the pockets of individual officials seemed slim. With the best will in the capitalist world, once again, it looked as if the peasants and the villages were going to find themselves at the bottom of the pile.

With the civil war now resurrected, the rural reconstructionists raced, like the ancient Nüwa, to shore up as much of a heavenly countryside as they could before the black skies collapsed on to earth. With whatever narrow threads of energy left to them, a few took the time and gathered up the courage to tell Chiang Kai-shek why they stayed in a countryside controlled by his troops. It was certainly not because they believed in the Guomindang's censorship or revelled in its corruption. They stayed because, while they might not be able to say whatever they wanted, at least – and unlike the stories that were whispered out from Yan'an – their hearts still had the freedom to be silent.

*   *   *

In 1947, two years after the latest war of the world had ended, and as competing ideas about order became the central theatre of China's post-war battles, Mao surveyed the landscape from his Yan'an caves. A lot had changed. After Japan lost its war, its northern Chinese lands had been occupied by Russia's Soviet Republic. Eventually, long after any movable industrial parts had been expatriated to Moscow, the older Soviet brothers had turned the territory over to their younger Chinese brothers. The Chinese Communist bases in the north now included some of those MEM members who, disillusioned with the Guomindang, had decided to stay where they were and look for their future with Mao. Meanwhile, the 8th Route Army, whether in companies of troops or as individual donkey drivers in disguise, had spread out, not only fighting against the Guomindang for territory, but also actively reaching out to capture peasants, body and soul.

Every successful battle seemed to open up fields of possibilities. Peasant unions and rebel soldiers had united in the creation of a new heaven and a new earth. Where stories ran riot about Guomindang troops ransacking granaries and trampling across fields, every 8th Route Army soldier was a Guan Yu guardian, straight out of the magical stories of the past. Famous for fighting fiercely on the side of the poor, they conquered land from the landlords, and were said to be redistributing it to the peasants, even helping them plant their corn as well. Where the Guomindang's troops scorched the earth in a desperate attempt to flush out Communist spies, every 8th Route Army commander was a Zhuge Liang Crouching Dragon who scoured the landscape for any and every possible means of winning a battle without harming the people at large. Rumours that muttered otherwise were nothing but Guomindang lies.

Not surprisingly, with new models of old brotherly heroes, stories were told of how many peasants, men, women and children, were willing recruits. Eager to do anything to bring about a new and better heaven, no task was too burdensome. In the dead of night, barefooted bands of brothers (men who knew the lie of the land better than the backs of their hands) climbed up poles and cut the Guomindang's communicating wires. By the light of day, from the vantage points of their fields, peasant eyes observed Guomindang troops moving this way and that, and when they got back to the village after the sun had gone down, they whispered what they had seen to brothers who were now messengers for the donkey drivers. Nothing was too daunting to learn or discover. No one, not even a child, was too young to become a hero.

With Moscow adding capital support, field by field, county by county, the north of China turned red. And when, on 1 October 1949, the Party's radios reported the magical story of Mao Zedong waving to the people and announcing the dream of a 'People's Republic of China', the fields exploded with joy. Strings of firecrackers crackled like guns, children raced around like miniature airplanes, pedlars appeared from nowhere with threads of fruit, and everyone put on their best blue cloth.

In November 1948, with the Communist flag firmly planted on northern soil, Mao's troops had turned south. Zhou Enlai had sent word ahead that James Yen, and every other patriotic mind, would be welcome in the coming People's Republic. Yen, more suspicious than ever of Mao's darker ideas, set sail for America. Once again, the MEM members and followers divided. Many followed the Guomindang to the refuge of Taiwan – not because they wanted to live in the corruption of the Guomindang's orders, but because they feared that the Communist Party might be the worse of two evils. Others decided that, red or white, China was China, and it was hard to be Chinese anywhere else. Yan'an had been full of friends from the past: surely things could not be that bad. When the dust settled, wouldn't everybody realise that they were all pursuing the same dream?

*   *   *

Waking up to the new dawn of the People's Republic, it seemed as if the sun was going to shine over every rural river – so Ding Ling's stories told. If the Party's land-reforming cadres did not arrive today, they would certainly be coming tomorrow. And once they arrived, the 'autumn accounts' with which landlords had once terrified their tenants, would be settled to a different tune, with all of the land divided up and shared out, and everybody treated the same. After thousands of years of tyranny, the days of tilling somebody else's fields looked as if they would be finally over.

Gathering together the land-reforming experiences of the earliest Chinese soviets and Yan'an, Mao marshalled his thoughts on how best to proceed. Like all Great Men, he began by consulting the past. The old idea of a hierarchy of four occupations – *nong* farmers, *shi* scholars, *gong* artisans, and *shang* merchants – had obviously been an imperial mistake. The *shi* scholars had risen to the top of the pile, eventually becoming lords of lands that they did not farm themselves, and then rushing off to the city to live new lives of ease. The *shang* merchants, pushing their own way upwards, and trying to become *shi* scholars in the process, had turned the countryside on its head, and then torn off to the cities for an even more profitable life. Left behind in the countryside, the *nong* tillers of the land had fallen to the bottom of the heap. Meanwhile, and depending on the quality of their

349

skills, the artisan *gong* had gone in all directions – some up, some down, and some staying where they should have been: an industrious rung above the unproductive merchant *shang*.

It was time to wipe the imperial slate clean – and what better cloth to use than the scientific logic of Marx. Applying the simple divides of class, rather than the more difficult idea of imagining a people, the countryside was reconstructed again. First on Mao's list were the idle landlords, those who had lived off everybody else's labour. They now belonged so far down the bottom of the pile that one really shouldn't worry if some of them fell off. Good riddance to them. *Chi shenme, huan shenme,* as the old wisdom went: you get as good as you give. Then there were the 'rich peasants', those with a bit of extra land that they rented out to others while tilling a lot of the fields themselves. They should go down to the lower levels of the pile, just above the idle landlords. After that, there were the 'middle peasants', who worked their own land. Obviously, they should be a cut above the rich peasants. Then came the 'poor peasants', tenant farmers and others who worked for a wage. They should sit just above the middle peasants, quite close to the top, and be given a piece of land of their own. And then there were the 'hired hands', those with nothing to their name but their labour. Reaping the greatest rewards of all, they would now get a piece of land of their own, and rise to the top of the pile.

With class now in control, redistribution was the order of the day, and not just of land and status. Anyone who had possessions beyond a wok or a pot was told to gather them up and be ready to share them out equally in order to restore (even if only in the smallest way) the great injustices of the past. Not, of course, including the animals and the ploughs: they would be put in the fields so that the Party's land reform teams could somehow work out who should be able to use what, and when.

Over the course of the next three years, the Party's land reforming cadres worked their way across China's vast lands, visiting almost every imaginable corner, no matter how remote. It took a while: as Mao Zedong had once said, 'when night falls in the east, the west is still lit up; when darkness covers the south, the north remains bright'. By the time they arrived in some villages, they found that the villagers had already executed a rough justice of their own. And in many places they found themselves obliged to right not just the wrongs of the past, but recent ones as well: strong voices who had put themselves at the top and pushed the weakest out, and local thugs who had decided that anyone who owned any land at all, even if it was small or as unyielding as rock, should be instantly despatched to another world. There was a lot to teach, and a lot to learn. With the landlords toppled from their perches, many of the peasants could scarcely stop from pinching themselves: had snow really fallen in summer? Others, however, were convinced that it could not last: surely, it would only be a matter of time before the sky changed, and the landlords, whether alive or as the hungry ghosts of the dead, would come back, grab their land, and give everyone a beating.

Meanwhile, there was a whole new language to learn, with the lexicon of class rankings replacing the old Confucian relationships, and fixing everybody into new revolutionary places. Naturally, everyone wanted to be a poor peasant or a hired hand: heroes, who were entitled to the best redistributing returns. No one wanted to be a rich peasant: condemned to a cloud of suspicion, it was not much better than being a landlord. Being a middle peasant seemed all right, but it was a bit too close to the dangerous rich peasant status for the liking of most. These challenges aside, it was also clear that not everyone should be celebrating. The surviving landlords and rich peasants were quivering in their boots: lucky to escape with a bashed-up body, many of their peers had died in the rages of anger that had been poured upon their heads. And then, according to the Party, there were the counter-revolutionaries hiding in the straw of village life: men and women whose hard hearts secretly yearned for a return to the past; bad elements who worshipped wooden gods; and those who harboured subjective dreams about the older rural reconstruction. They would clearly need to be rooted out.

Trained to find the enemies of the people, and guided by quotas from the top, the Party's work teams organised the villagers into meetings and instructed them in the Yan'an arts of struggle and self-criticism. It was soon clear to all, though, that truth was not an easy commodity – it usually took a beating to bring it out. But to many, it seemed the truth was just the icing on the cake: an important question of justice, obviously, but once the bad elements had been settled under the Democratic Dictatorship of the People, where they belonged, they would be cleaning pigsties, sweeping the streets and carrying anything and everything that the village leaders ('on behalf of the people') might require. The really important thing – the magical snow-in-summer thing to which every once-downtrodden heart should be directed – was the fact that each peasant would have a piece of land which he could call his own. Backs applied to the hoes and the ploughs, horses available to lend a hand, with everyone expected to help everybody else, and the fields about to be washed with plenty, surely everything would soon settle down.

* * *

Installed in his spreading Zhongnanhai courtyard, by the early 1950s, Mao was receiving regular reports about the affairs of the countryside. The early achievements had been highly encouraging: red flags waving as far as the eye could see, landlords tamed or eliminated, land for everyone who deserved it, and harvests rising. Under the guidance of the Party's workers, peasants had even elected their own village leaders, to replace the tyrants of the past.

But looking at the bigger picture, Mao was a little concerned. While many people should have been satisfied beyond their wildest dreams, as the seasons turned and the meetings continued, there seemed to be a lot of fussing about who got which piece of land, and whose fields were weeded first. There was also a lot of complaining about class-classifications. Not to mention a lot of revelling in thoughts of new clothes. As if that were not enough, there was also a lot of whining about 'too many meetings', even as everybody wanted to have a view of their own. 'New democracy' was where the will of the people was protected by the guidance of the Party. But somehow the peasants had got the wrong end of the stick and were launching themselves into a kind of 'extreme democracy' where everybody chattered about their personal opinions, and no one gave the blindest bit of notice to the revolutionary principles at stake.

It was not long before Mao reached the conclusion that the peasants were incapable of understanding that what had been achieved was not about satisfying the individual wills of hundreds of millions of Chinese people but about creating a greater revolutionary will of the people at large. Fields and donkeys were as nothing compared with the prize of a truly socialist world where everyone would eventually own everything, and even the state itself would wither away. Just as Sun Yatsen, still a hero to the Communist Party, had promised a government of the people, by the people, for the people. Not *individual* people but, represented by the Communist Party, 'the people' as a whole. Seeing selfish subjectivism in every direction, hearing the constant refrain of peasants wanting nothing more than to create their own personal paradises on earth, and in so doing, constantly criticizing everything, Mao came to the conclusion that it was time to move the revolution on. The peasants needed to understand their place in the new China: a China which not only had to attend to its affairs at home, but which, in the battle for the survival of the fittest state, also needed to ensure that it was strong enough to keep any imperial foreigners out as well.

As Mao worried about the quality of peasant minds, his thoughts naturally turned to the fact that the country's power to defend itself among the endlessly competing nations of the world would now have to come from the cities and their industries. If the city industries required for China's 'survival of the fittest' battle were going to be able to grow, it was the countryside that was going to need to fuel and feed them. True, Fei Xiaotong and the old rural reconstructors had been playing around with manufacturing co-operatives in the countryside, but these were nothing more than chicken feed in the bigger scheme of things. Given the fuzzy and rather selfish thinking that was going on in the villages, however, the Party was going to have to have to deliver some further change. Step-by-step was the answer: better not to panic the peasants with too much information in advance. Old habits die hard, and even revolutionary peasants would need time to get used to the rather contradictory idea of an order in which the peasants who had battled for the revolution were now to devote themselves to the industrial success of the cities.

The first revolutionary step would be for the peasants to pool their land into mutually helping and very local 'co-operatives'. With this achieved, and with everyone's confidence won, the second step would be to ask the peasants to express their revolutionary gratitude by selflessly folding the co-operatives (and their own land) into bigger collectives: still local, but now under the county governments of the Democratic Dictatorship of the People rather than the old villages and their heads. Obviously, quite a few people were going to mutter about the loss of land so recently acquired; but those who did would simply be revealing themselves as just the kind of bad elements that needed to be eliminated. With the collectives organised under local county government, the need for a third step would then become obvious: with a little better organisation, the collectives could be pooled together into vast 'communes' for economies of scale. Scale achieved, the communes would be able to manage themselves, and the wasteful job of local county government would disappear. The state would start to wither away, and Marx's utopian dream (or was it Kang Youwei's dream of *Da Tong* Great Unity?) would begin to appear.

Clear about the broad direction required, Mao looked at the maps and started to think about a plan. As far as he could see, the ancient foundations

353

were encouraging. Two thousand years after the First Qin Emperor, the faint traces of his commanding genius could still be seen in the ancient grids of central power which had been flung like a net across the country at large: a patchwork of twenty-five provinces, each with a capital of its own; thousands of county districts and towns; and millions of village settlements spread across endless fields. To any keen Chinese eye, the order was clear: the provincial capitals had been the seats of imperially-appointed governors; the county towns had been the seats of imperially-appointed magistrates, supported by a loyal gentry; and the village settlements had been, and still were, where the majority of China's now six hundred million men, women and children lived – all bound together in groups of households, with each one guaranteeing the obedient peace of all. Truly, thought Mao, the First Qin Emperor had done more for the Chinese people than any other emperor since.

In the intervening millennia, however, the clarity of the Qin genius had become muddied by far lesser men. For a start, the tight central control which the First Qin Emperor had so wisely insisted upon had gradually been eroded until the provincial governors and the gentry were doing whatever they wanted, taking care only to ensure that the fiction of the simple Confucian ideal was maintained. In such a world, it was hardly surprising that everyone else had fallen to thinking only about themselves: families in the fields weaving cloth to sell to others for extra handfuls of coppers; artisans making all sorts of frivolous gadgets; merchants leaping at the chance to sell anything they could get their profiting hands on; and even scholars jumping on the bandwagon. With all of that going on, it was even less surprising that by the end of the Qing, messy market towns had further clouded the simple order – hundreds of them by the time the first revolution had exploded in 1911. But by that point, the wisdom of the First Qin Emperor's genius had been well and truly lost. Then had come forty years of Republican chaos: warlords everywhere, and Guomindang variations on self-strengthening mixing up farming and trade. Factories had been scattered wherever an individual mind chose to put his ideas or his money, and a number of peasants had ended up dabbling in industry, whether at home or in the cities, instead of minding the fields.

It was as clear as crystal that the picture was not only wrong, but dangerous. After one hundred years of humiliation at the hands of the imperial powers, even a half-educated schoolboy could see that the countries of the world were engaged in a bitter battle which only the fittest would survive. Likewise, any half-educated schoolboy could tell you that the deciding factor in this battle would not be how many fields one had, or who had them, but whether or not those fields, together with any ponds and seams of minerals, were marshalled for the collective good. The 'collective good' was, of course, the delivery of the cities of the harvesting surpluses necessary to fuel the industrial productivity on which China's strength – and survival – would depend.

Contemplating the facts on the ground (and drawing on the experience of the bigger Russian Soviet brothers not to mention the ancient Halls of Light), Mao was persuaded that the solution lay in the creation of a new Party-led central government commission which would be charged with building the urban industrial triumph required for survival. The same commission would also decide, in meticulous detail and on a five-yearly basis, exactly what everyone, in the countryside and the cities alike, needed to do to make it happen. Order and production would go hand in hand, all under a Five-Year Plan. The most important and urgent questions were how to increase the harvests as quickly as possible, and how to get them transferred to the cities at as low a price as possible, so that industry could rise. Production quotas for grain, the most essential harvest, seemed to be the obvious answer. Given that the peasants were still at the earliest stage of farming their own land (not to mention stubbornly insisting on getting the best prices), while they might be allowed to keep other produce for their own family needs, all sales of grain would need to be made to the central state itself. That should get the harvests up, and keep the prices down.

In 1954, the first Five-Year Plan was put into action. With the stroke of a central brush, Mao instructed his lower Party officials – and the lower Party officials instructed the village leaders – to inform the peasants that, while they could keep the land they had been given, from now on, they were going to work in co-operatives. Not the old kinds of co-operatives where villagers organised themselves, selling their produce on messy rural markets, but new ones, organised by the Party, with everybody's grain, as the most important crop, sold only to the central state. While they were at it, the officials should tell the peasants what grain quotas every village would have to meet, and the prices they were going to be paid. Lots to do, no time to lose, the revolution was only just getting started: a 'little leap forward' should do the trick.

As might have been expected, reaction in the fields was mixed. The old poor peasants were rather enthusiastic, unable to believe their luck that someone else would take on the job of organising everyone to help each other. Conversely, the old middle and rich peasants were rather upset by the loss of the power to set the terms and prices of their own sales of grain. Once they had got over their initial shock, however, many started trickily seizing on the details. 'How much of our fields do we have to turn to grain?' was a common question. 'If this is a democracy, who says that everyone has to join a co-operative?' was another. Trickiest of all, though, was the question that only the cleverest asked: 'If everyone has to contribute their fields and produce to a quota fixed by Beijing, whose land is it anyway?' Mao began to see that it was not just the bourgeois city intellectuals who had a lot to learn.

By and large, the Party officials and village leaders patiently explained the logic of helping a neighbour – and the necessity of defending China in the wider battle of nation states. They also reminded everyone that they could still keep a small plot for their own family needs. But with the questions continuing, some of the Party officials and village leaders found themselves pushed beyond the limits of their patience. With many peasants unwilling to join the co-operatives, the most stubborn heads were dealt a beating. And in the new registers which the Party had taken to keeping, a little black question mark was placed by every name which raised an inconvenient objection or just refused to join: a clear sign of a clandestine counter-revolutionary. More meetings were held, the arts of struggle and self-criticism were practised over and over again, and for those who really could not learn from their mistakes, punishments were to hand.

Strengthened by the struggle sessions and the punishments, the powers of the Party's local cadres seemed to climb. But quieter questions began to whisper on a few suspicious people's lips. One was the obvious query about why, given that the revolution had been won by the peasants from the fields, it was the cities and their industries that were going to get the benefits of the grain. Another (noting that the peasants – who, after all, were really supposed to be the new rulers – were going to submit themselves to the greater will of the people, and that the Party was going to decide what that greater will was) mischievously asked who the Party was going to answer to. The natural response to the first question was that the peasants still had a lot of lessons to learn. The answer to the second question was a sharp and simple snap that over the last five thousand years, heaven had never submitted to anyone. 'But if that was the case', persisted the thickest minds, 'why had there been a revolution at all?'

* * *

Summer turned to winter, winter turned to spring; seeds were sown, fields were ploughed, and soon a year had passed. By 1955, the first of the three steps – the creation of nearly a million new co-operatives – had been taken, and the principle of mutual assistance for a greater common good had been repeated. But, still clinging on to the idea of individual plots of land for their own household needs, the peasants had once again managed to miss the point. And their petty ignorance was reflected in the less-than revolutionary results. While the co-operatives' grain harvests were promising, they were as nothing compared to the bumper crops of the other produce – from apples and potatoes to chickens, ducks and eggs – which the peasants' individual plots sent off to market.

Getting a little impatient, Mao decided to move things along to the second step (collectives) as quickly as possible. In the same year, 1955, he issued an updating announcement in the name of 'the people': it was time for the peasants to concentrate all of their energies on production, rather than worrying about their own individual marketing. From now on, they should selflessly contribute all of their land to a host of new collectives, with Beijing deciding what they would need for their own consumption – after a careful consultation of what the cities and their hungry industries required. And for the avoidance of any tricky doubts, 'land' would include not only the fields, but also any orchards, chickens and ducks.

This time, there were a lot more questioners in the meetings. But after some sharp 'clarifications', the majority bit their tongues. Following up on the logic of the collectives, in 1956, Mao decided that it was time to close everybody's markets. Appearing as regularly as the seasons, part of the rhythm of everybody's country life for centuries, the peasants could scarcely believe their ears. Mouths opened, ready to complain. But then Mao's city suggestion that a hundred flowers should bloom ended with the brutal purge of the Anti-Rightist campaign – and three hundred thousand questioning intellectuals ('rightists') arrived in the countryside. And those were just the ones who had survived. The fate that awaited anyone who could not keep their revolutionary tongue under control was now clear for all to see. Party officials at all levels made sure that the new position was clearly communicated to the villagers at the bottom: even the most constructive criticism was going to come at a cost so high that nobody would want to pay it. And there would be a particularly punishing cost to any local Party official or village leader who failed to keep a firm lid on local opinion: yes, there had been a revolution but now that up was down, and black was white, the old idea of obedience had to be restored – obedience to the Democratic Dictatorship of the People, of course.

Back in Beijing, Mao, impatient to fuel the industrial revolution with bumper crops from the fields, decided to crack on to the third of the steps. Time to gather the collectives into even bigger 'communes'. Local government would disappear and, just as under the First Qin Emperor, every household would work in production teams, organised under production brigades. Henceforth, regardless of local land conditions, production goals, crop choices and farming methods would be set by the central mind of the Party and its government, rather than by the individual peasants on the ground. Irrigation systems would be stretched as far as the eye could see; wells would be dug to sparkle like subterranean stars; dams would be raised to tame rivers; roads, canals and bridges would be produced to speed the expanded harvests up to the cities.

With the lessons of the Anti-Rightist campaign still fresh, complaints were few, and those who dared to express contrary opinions were quickly struggled straight. In 1958, a second Five-Year Plan was announced, and the revolutionary idea of a *Great Leap Forward* was announced, with the twin goals of catching up with Britain's steel output within fifteen years, and firing the furnaces of industry with a doubling in the peasants' production of grain. And just to make sure that everybody could give their full attention to the targets set, communal kitchens would also be created so that nobody else would have to cook. 'More, faster, better, cheaper' would be the slogan of the day. With these efficiencies in place, the countryside would deliver mass bumper harvests, and any inconvenient outbursts of local nature could easily be contained. China's industrial productivity would rocket: more grain to feed the cities, and with the communal kitchens feeding the people, everyone's woks and pots could be fed into local furnaces, which would increase the national output of steel as well.

Every official was aware that Mao expected revolutionary harvests. They were also aware that, in the Party scheme of things, their zeal would be matched against that of their neighbours, and their personal futures would be held to ransom too. Encouraged by strong crops in recent years, many Party cadres in the countryside saw an opportunity to make their revolutionary careers fly. Clear as to Mao's expectations, when Beijing asked for local estimates, almost all of the officials decided to demonstrate their Communist credentials with a robust embellishment of the harvesting volumes they expected to achieve: what harm could a little confidence do?

As the 'estimates' were delivered, the old heavenly facts – that nature was rarely predictable, and that bumper harvests tend not to come in strings – were conveniently set aside. Also set aside were the more revolutionary facts that a number of peasants were now being despatched to the cities to build new industrial factories, not to mention the raising of the triumphant ten-year anniversary monuments in Beijing. Across the communes, Party cadres took the estimates for fields expected to produce five hundred kilos of grain, and bumped them up a bit. Up in the county towns, Party officials, just as keen to establish their revolutionary credentials, and with the added advantage of city thinking that nature always had room to stretch, added a zero, here and there. Further up in the provincial capitals, higher Party officials, keenest of all to bask in the revolutionary sun, and furthest away from any inconvenient idea of what nature could really do, doubled everything. By the time the estimates arrived in Beijing, the scale of their ambition would have been seen as preposterous by anyone who had ever spent any time on the land (or indeed anyone who had not been petrified into silence). But no one on the land was asked for their opinion. Planning the strategy that would enable China to catch up with imperialist Britain in fifteen years required only the clearest, and most objective, of city minds.

Estimates presented, the quotas were set, central purchases were made at the usual low prices, and the grain was ordered to be loaded onto trucks and boats. From there it would travel to the cities, whence it would either be distributed for urban consumption or loaded again on to ships bound for foreign countries who would pay an industrially-valuable US dollar price. As trucks began to move the vast volumes of grain out of the countryside, villagers and lower level officials who had not been privy to the higher level embellishments raised surprised eyebrows. Some even dared to question whether there would be enough grain left in local granaries to feed the peasants themselves. Needless to say, the questioners were put firmly into their obviously counter-revolutionary places, and the loaded trucks and boats continued to move out. Mao was ecstatic. All it took was a bit of revolutionary fervour and the Chinese talent for working hard: catching up with Britain in fifteen years? With this kind of zeal, they might manage it in two or three.

By the early months of 1959, a cold dawn of truth began to spread from under the moonlit facts – at least to the Party officials in the countryside. In the communal kitchens, food was now running out before the last peasants had got to the front of the queue. And in many parts of the country not only were the villagers getting hungrier by the day, but quite a few bodies seemed to be tumbling by the wayside. Still eager to make their numbers, the officials put the early deaths down to an unfortunate run of natural events, and turned their attention back to pushing the limits of production in the fields. The peasants were exhorted to 'dig deeper, irrigate better, sow ' those seeds whose packages carry the biggest promises of yields – and sow them closely'. To which was added an instruction for the commune leaders: 'Whatever you do, make sure that when the next time comes for the trucks to be loaded, by hook or by crook, and regardless of the tears of any hungry onlookers, the quotas are met.'

Already wobbling on weak legs, day in, day out, the peasants were sent back to the fields to force the earth into revolutionary action. Following planting instructions from the top, almost no one had the stamina to argue that many of the new ideas were taking everybody backwards, rather than leaping anything ahead. At the end of every day, exhausted by labouring targets fixed for men who were eating enough to work – and disheartened by planting seeds so closely that they would never be able to grow – the peasants could only join the communal kitchen queues and hope that whatever was left in the pot would be enough to carry them through to another day.

It was never enough. Up in the Shandong north, the peasants returned to that desperate diet of the worst of the imperial times: tree bark and chaff. In other parts of the country, they foraged for whatever might keep the aching pains in their stomachs at bay: roots, wood, grass, and any and every insect, whether it crawled, or jumped, or flew. Dogs no longer barked, chickens no longer clucked; children stopped running. In the most unfortunate of counties, whole villages became hungry ghosts. Those who had a breath of life left in them began to whisper rhymes as old as the Ming dynasty: tales of times of famine, when beggars were so poor that they had only children left to sell. This time, in their desperation, some would even eat their dead.

*　　　*　　　*

In April 1959, the government of the Democratic Dictatorship of the People quietly sent a report to Mao noting that twenty-five million people across fifteen provinces did not have enough food to survive. Mao observed that this must be a temporary crisis – an understandable problem when transforming such a big country with so many mouths to feed, and one that the local officials were surely more than capable of fixing. 'No need to reduce the amount of grain that the state is procuring for the cities', he commanded, 'the revolutionary spirit of the peasants will sort it all out in the end'. Down in the countryside, each commune became locked in its own official secrecy. With every Party official acutely aware that Mao was counting on them, most decided to bury the mounting evidence of their 'revolutionary fervour'. It was not easy. Dead bodies, mounting by the day, were demanding to be buried in the dark of night. Meanwhile, starving individuals kept trying to make their way to buses and trains, hoping to find food elsewhere, and seemingly oblivious to the fact that if anyone outside knew what was going on, their local officials would lose their jobs – or worse. Worrying round the clock, the officials came up with the idea of 'dissuasion' stations to round up the complainers before they could leave. Prison cells were stretched to hold the most unco-operative complainers until they could see sense – or until the prison's food ran out; in which case, the problem was solved.

A rather bigger problem, however, was the mountain of counter-revolutionary letters, which clearly had to be stopped. Missives to friends and relations, some even recklessly addressed to higher Party officials in Beijing, they included desperate alerts of what the people of the individual communes assumed was just a local disaster, with each of them begging those outside and above to come and help. Reading all the mail was obviously an impossible task, but the postal service could easily be suspended. In some parts of the country, peasants who had not understood their place in revolutionary history rose up in riotous anger, and had to be beaten into silence. (On the positive side, this did mean fewer mouths to feed.) As if all of that was not trouble enough, from time to time an individual official or a commune leader would begin to get cold feet and think that it might be time to own up to the over-estimates. Only heaven knew how such subjectivists had managed to survive this long. With the power to bring the hounds of hell down from Beijing, they were beaten like the drowning dogs they clearly were. Casting aspersions on excellent situations, could they not understand that there was a bigger revolutionary truth at stake – not to mention a number of official careers and lives?

*   *   *

By the end of 1959, with Mao describing the Great Leap Forward as a uniquely Chinese combination of Marxism on the one hand and the First Qin Emperor's wisdom on the other, some of his comrades were feeling uneasy. As hunger touched Beijing, a few of the most senior leaders made disguised visits to their rural family homes. Seeing once-lively villages worryingly quiet, and with relatives willing to talk, they soon understood that hunger was stalking the fields. Delicate questions were asked and anxious local officials conjured up the better-fed people from the dying ranks to put on a reassuring display. But, eventually, even the most imaginative of officials began to run out of steam. By the spring of 1960, it was crystal clear to those in the senior echelons of the Party (as it had been clear to almost everyone in the lower ranks for the last two years) that China's countryside was engulfed in a mass famine. It was also clear that the people's desperate cries for help had been smothered by the very same men and women who only ten years earlier had been revolutionary heroes.

Astonished at the ability of the people to eat so much bitterness in so much silence, some noted that if China had been like any other country in the world, the troops would have had to be sent in long ago. Others replied that if China had been like any other country in the world, Party leaders who had faced hails of bullets on fields of war would never have trembled before Mao like a herd of sheep. Not all of the local officials, however, had stayed silent. While many in the countryside battled to keep the truth separate from facts, there were, as there had always been, heroes; and in Beijing, a handful of brave Party comrades finally forced Mao to acknowledge that something would have to be done. By the summer, the flow of grain from the countryside to the cities began to slow, and the courageous comrades began to enquire into the causes of the nightmare.

In the end, the enquirers concluded that it was all the product of 'five winds', each of them contagious. The first was a 'communist wind', which had stripped the peasants of even their pots and pans. The second was a 'commandism wind', which had seen local officials rise as gods. The third was an 'exaggeration wind', which had transformed so many wild dreams into paper facts that no one had any idea what was really going on. The fourth was a 'chaotic directives wind', which had every bureaucrat tripping over his own orders in an attempt to defeat the logic of nature. And the fifth was the 'cadre privilege wind', which meant that, at the end of any day, the soup ladles were always firmly in the hands of the Party's officials: men and (and women) whose bowls were always filled first, and to the brim, regardless of how many hungry mouths were standing behind them in the queue.

Within a year, the courageous comrades succeeded in putting a question mark over the communes, and Mao was under heavy pressure to think again. But the revolution was not finished with the countryside yet.

WINDS, AND MORE WINDS

*These creatures in the world below were compounded of
the essence of heaven and earth; nothing that goes on there
should surprise us.*

The Jade Emperor to his ministers in the Treasure Hall of
the Holy Mists of the Cloud Palace (*Journey to the West*, Wu
Cheng'en, seventeenth century)

Long Bow village was asleep when the brigade office fell. Momentarily
unifying under a single banner in the spring of 1969, the Red Guards from the
cement plant, the Rebel Regiment from the railway repair shop, and the Mao
Zedong Thought Red Guards from the middle school – all of them supported
by a motley young crew from the nearby power station – broke down its door
with little effort. A quick shine of a torch over the obvious hiding places, and
the seal which held the stamp of the brigade's power had been seen, seized
and carried off to a new home in the pocket of the youngest and least obvious
suspect. Mission accomplished, everyone went home to bed.

Over the following days, news of the 'power seizure' travelled fast, and
the rebels found themselves in rising demand: other brigades were ripe for
a takeover and there was also the bigger prize of the commune itself. Before

long, the villages of the Taihang mountains in the Shanxi north were locked in so many cultural revolutionary battles that nobody knew which way was up. Loyalists defended the old guard; young rebels fought for a new one; both old and new accused the other of betraying the revolution. Few, if any, of the onlookers could tell who was right or wrong.

If the truth be told, the holders of both sides of the lines looked suspiciously like the great-grandchildren of the old feuding families whose battles for local power had been tearing the village apart for centuries. A hundred years before, one of their feuds had divided the village into a north and a south. Even when the north of the country had gone to war (Communists against the Guomindang; everyone against the Japanese) they had continued to prosecute their old enmities, albeit against the backdrop of bigger battles. Then had come the Communist revolution and the struggles against anyone who looked like a landlord. Although both sides had lost a lot of their richer numbers in those battles, poorer relations seemed to have picked up the cudgels, opening up yet another succession of struggles. In the early years after 1949, the fights had been about whose new fields should be irrigated. A decade later, they had graduated to the often life-and-death question of who should hold the soup ladle in the communal kitchens. Things seemed to have died down a little in the Great Leap Forward years, but then there had been that wife-snatching incident a few years back (more of a bride-to-be really, but jealousy ran too deep to be mindful of such fine distinctions): that obviously hadn't helped.

And then heaven had sent down troubles all of its own. Who would have thought that a *Cultural* Revolution would come to the countryside? Surely something like that belonged with all those battling intellectual brushes back in Beijing? But somehow, like most bad things, it had found its way to the fields. Investigating work teams had descended from the county town to inspect the old 'bad elements' and 'class enemies' and, before anyone knew it, new revolutionary whispers were blowing all over the place.

The first whispers had pointed to brigade team leaders who had become too big for their sandals: punching others to make a point, while cooking the village books on the side themselves. Then the counter-whispers had followed: pointing to rebel heroes who had hidden nationalist pasts, or even secret Japanese connections. Was Whiskers Shen really a man who could be trusted? And what about Little Shen, was he the solid revolutionary that he pretended to be? The mass meetings had only made things even more confused: points and counterpoints scattered in all directions, jumbling up not only the present and the past, but the real and the imagined as well. Blasted out on loudspeakers, directives from Beijing had been hurled by the left and the right, each convinced that the magic of acoustics transformed their own particular black into white. Opposing positions had plastered their posters across village walls, one on top of another, with each layer covering up the bad ink of the one before. And then the clubs, spears and knives had appeared, with battles breaking out on the threshing floors of the granaries, and sacks of grain becoming spoils of war.

The shop floor of the nearby railway commandeered, machine tools were now turning out artillery and shells. Anyone who could hid behind their doors. Those who tried to keep up with the times found themselves having to change the scores by the day. One day, the Mao Zedong Thought Red Guards were holding the railway yard in an alliance with the May Fourth Regiment (whoever they were); the next, the Rebel Regiment had seized the middle school, and were advancing on the railway yard. Every now and then, someone's ink would run dry – or the shells would run out – and a strategic retreat would have to be made to the county town. Once in a while, the loudspeakers would succumb to a technical fault, which made it harder to know who was up and who was down. But at least the village could get some sleep: heaven had not completely lost its heart.

*   *   *

It all started with the 'Four Clean Ups' in 1961 – Mao's idea of cleaning out the bureaucrats who, in his opinion, were the biggest problem. But, of course, that was yet another one of those good ideas from the top which always seemed to end up badly in the fields. After the Great Leap Forward had floundered in famine, more individual leaders, some disguised as peasants, had smuggled themselves into the countryside to find out what was really going on. Apart from the discovery of the five winds of communism, commandism, exaggeration, chaotic directives and cadre privilege, the reports that returned to Beijing showed that there were other reasons to worry as well. Not only was local peasant knowledge still being ignored but the commune leaders were putting themselves above the people in ways that were threatening the revolution itself. Those in charge of communes close to cities had taken to farming their own personal plots of land, and selling the produce on nearby black markets. Others, further away from the city's black temptations, had traded chickens for back door payments, confiscated grain from out-of-favour peasants, awarded themselves more work points than their labour merited, and gambled with commune funds. Whether near to the cities or far away, a number had even taken up the old world practice of buying child brides. With friends and family aiding and abetting, and few peasants daring to raise a subjective flag of objection, was it really any wonder that the commune leaders had become new local emperors?

While Mao might have lost his footing on the Great Leap Forward, it seemed that his warnings of the rise of a new bourgeoisie-gentry had been sharply on the mark. True, Zhongnanhai had divided over the communes in the aftermath of the famine: should they be the only means of farm production, or would productivity be higher if the peasants were allowed to keep some land on the side for themselves? But one thing everyone had seemed to agree upon was the importance of cleaning things up.

Since the bourgeois rot obviously included bureaucratic spirits in the cities, tens of thousands of officials were despatched to learn the lessons of manual labour at the hands of the peasants. At the same time, it was agreed that the local officials needed to be taught some lessons about the duties of a revolutionary spirit. Commune accounts should be subjected to the harsh light of an outside scrutiny, work points should be clarified (how many points for how much work), commune assets should be ticked off against inventories, and the granaries should be inspected against actual levels of production.

As ever, opinions had differed (deeply) over how all this was to be done – and by whom. For the senior leaders (still the same old 'foot-draggers' as far as Mao was concerned) this was a delicate matter that should be managed by the Party itself ('internal housekeeping'). But for Mao, the matter was far more important than a famine – it was nothing more nor less than the rise of a new bourgeoisie and as such it went to the heart of the revolution, requiring nothing less than the purging energies of the mass of the people at large. This time, the senior leaders seemed to win, and Mao, rather surprisingly, lost. Party work teams were despatched to investigate communes across the country, and the masses with their inconvenient energies were either herded into the fields, or called to attend endless meetings where their criticisms could be safely batted in other directions: particularly towards the reserves of old landlords and other bad elements who could be recalled to a continuing round of struggle. And if ever the reserves ran low, new class enemies could always be found. Senior Party leaders congratulated themselves on keeping the heat down; Mao muttered that the only way to really solve the problem would be to let the masses off the leash.

Skulking in his Zhongnanhai garden in 1963, Mao consulted the landscape and came across a model northern commune by the name of Dazhai. With a truly revolutionary leadership and workers, it seemed to be a commune that had genuinely transformed its fields into a miracle of production. Terraces had been laid like slanting walls, tunnels had pierced perpendicular cliffs, dams had blocked rivers to drain new lands; even mountains were said to have been moved. Noting the proud sweep of red flags flying above its fields, Mao invited its leader – clearly someone who understood the importance of revolutionary science and its power over nature – to stand by his side. And with the revolutionary man standing by his side, he then invited the heads of every other foot-dragging commune to come and 'learn from Dazhai'.

When not praising Dazhai to the skies, Mao also watched as his new rising star, Lin Biao, set about telling the story of the revolution's success. A man of towering military credentials, and a comforting supporter during the critical assaults from the bureaucrats at the end of the Great Leap Forward, in 1963, in a stroke of propaganda genius, Lin suggested the idea of a soldier in the People's Liberation Army as a revolutionary hero to raise the people's spirits. Named Lei Feng, he was described as a truly red heart who never failed to put others before himself. While those who hear the story wept, revolutionary resolve was indeed strengthened when the people were informed that he had died, at the age of only twenty-two, in the line of duty: struck down by a telephone pole which had been hit by a reversing army truck. Lei Feng's diaries were distributed into the hands of Mao's adoring public, with a personal inscription written by the great red sun himself, to the effect that it was the People's Liberation Army which had the most to teach the people (presumably including the rest of the foot-dragging Party as well). A Party wind (the exaggeration wind, perhaps?) then carried Lei Feng's diary down to the countryside, accompanied by a fervour of revolutionary work teams to help keep the endless meetings awake. A year later, Lin Biao followed up his success with a collection of Mao's quotations – binding them into a *Little Red Book*, initially for distribution to the troops and then offered to the wider masses. But by 1965, exhausted eyelids were drooping once again, and after the work teams had gone back to Beijing, few remembered their lessons. For those who did manage to pay attention, however, it was clear that some important writing was beginning to appear on the wall.

*   *   *

While the peasants were being taught about model revolutionaries, from 1963 the city youth were being told that they should be learning from the peasants. Arguing that books were a simple, and ultimately damaging, form of education, Mao had suggested that the city students should advance their studies through practical labour in the countryside. 'Bad class' students (those studying under the shadow of their parents' mistakes) listened particularly attentively. Relegated to the bottom of every lesson by their teachers, their backgrounds had condemned them as permanently 'bad eggs': runts of a litter whose higher-born, 'red class', peers were wholly justified not only in pushing them into lonely corners, but kicking them as well. Hearing Mao's suggestion of countryside studies, the desperate ears of the bad eggs seized upon what seemed to be a promise of redemption: volunteer for the fields, and finally get to bask in the warm rays of the Great Leader's revolutionary red sun. Hands had been quickly raised, and over the next few years, the villages had been invited to welcome a number of student volunteers – whether they wanted them or not.

It had not been long before the student volunteers realised – like the earliest sudents who had gone down to the countryside forty years before – that they had a lot to learn. In a world of mud and flies, few lessons from the classroom held any value. As far as life in the fields was concerned, the only marks that mattered were work points; and the peasants were far too busy trying to survive themselves to have any time to show city youths what to do. Some of the students managed to get themselves into schools – as teachers of muddy village children. Most, though, were set to the muckiest of tasks: carrying the stinking buckets of ordure that no peasant ever really wanted to touch, and which surely even a pair of soft city hands could manage. From time to lucky time, some were invited to tell an evening story to leaders of villages who had never seen the wider world: tales of tall buildings, which frankly beggared belief, and stories of Mao, the Great Leader, waving from the terraces of the Tiananmen Gate of Heavenly Peace: a god who, the students assured everyone, was really a man. Summer turned to winter, winter turned to spring and, desperate to prove that they were better than the bad blood of their parents, the bad class students pushed themselves to eat the labouring bitterness on which the countryside survived.

In the late summer of 1966, letters arrived from parents in Beijing with news of a Cultural Revolution and of a new, elite, army of young Red Guards that had adopted Mao as their commander, and was 'bombarding the headquarters'. With the Party citadel of Zhongnanhai seemingly unscathed, the students in the countryside were as confused as their city peers as to where and what the headquarters were. But as the months passed and more letters arrived, it seemed that schools and universities had somehow become battlefields; and in the ensuing chaos, the very teachers and professors who had pushed the bad class students to the bottom of their schoolrooms had been revealed to be treacherously bad elements themselves – in disguise. Remembering teachers who had battered their knuckles with rulers and stung their hearts with class enemy taunts, many of those who read their parents' Cultural Revolution news thought that it was not before time. Some even wondered if they would now be able to go home. But as they read to the end of the letters, they found that Mao was calling upon the Red Guards to wage a war of 'perpetual revolution' and launch a campaign against the 'Four Olds' of customs, culture, habits and ideas. Hard as the countryside might be, their parents told them, they were better off where they were.

As the summer of 1966 turned to winter, the letters told of a twist. Somehow the Red Guards had split into two, and started to fight each other – and then a new front had opened up altogether. This one was not led by the usual 'red class' vanguard, but by groups of students, from middle schools as well as universities, who had picked themselves up from the bad class floor, and launched a defiant rebellion against red classmates who had once been their tyrants. Expecting the next lines of the letters to tell them that the bad class upstarts were being rounded up by the army, they were astonished to read that Mao was encouraging them. In the perpetual revolution, Mao was now calling time on the idea that the red class students were the only natural revolutionaries, and urging the rest of the city youth to rise up in the name of the oppressed masses – whoever they were – and against incumbent powers of any and all descriptions. 'Call it the Great Democracy', Mao said. Taking him at his word, the bad class students still in the cities had apparently done just that, calling themselves the *Rebel* Red Guards. With Mao now supporting a revolution of all against all, ink was suddenly free, posters could be plastered everywhere, and every student of every faction could chase down every counter-revolutionary in disguise, whoever and wherever they might be. They could even have the trains. According to Mao, China was a big country, and the trains were there to serve the people; the students should be sharing their revolutionary experiences with whoever they liked, and the carriages could take them wherever they wanted to go.

Before the year of 1966 was out, the bad class volunteers no longer needed letters from home to tell them what was going on: waves of Red Guards and Rebel Red Guards were washing up in the countryside's county towns. Already on the ground, and for once in a position to steal a march on even the reddest of the good class elements, the bad class youth were determined to make their mark. Ink pots at the ready, they splashed paeans to Mao in every direction. And alert to every shifting loyalty in their villages, they also offered their services to turn the old wrongs of the countryside upside down. With trucks and loudspeakers regularly commandeered for official revolutionary purpose, it was not long before 'power seizure' winds were beginning to blow across the fields.

*   *   *

When the cities had exploded in youthful rage, the peasants had done their best to continue their essential hoeing, planting, weeding and harvesting, in the silence of the fields. But with new waves of city students being carried by the trains to provincial cities, and then catching carts and trucks to county towns, the countryside found itself caught up in the heat. Paper and ink available on demand by official decree, wherever the students went, big character posters followed in their wake. When the posters went up, many of those in the countryside who felt badly treated by the recent revolutionary past suddenly saw an opportunity to turn the tables. Old scores could be settled in new directions, and, hardly believing their luck, those who had lost earlier battles, began to hope that past wrongs might now be righted.

As the months moved on, though, the stories from Beijing began to acquire a much darker air. The score-settling in the capital had now apparently turned to war, with university campuses and city communes becoming battlefields. Factories were burning like fires, while struggle sessions, power seizures and torture had become daily facts of life. Any and all education had been thrown out of the schools, and, with everyone busy with the perpetual revolution, productivity had come to a standstill. As the red ink continued to splash down from Beijing, the peasants began to get concerned.

They were not alone. Up in the revolutionary capital, even the inhabitants of Zhongnanhai were wondering how long their portals would be able to stand strong. Eventually, the People's Liberation Army was asked to put out the rebellious storms, and Mao agreed that all of the students who were ticking like bombs in the cities (in middle schools and universities alike, not only in Beijing but across the land) would have to go. 'Go where?' the bureaucrats had asked. The peasants could scarcely believe their shocked ears when news of the answer trickled down to the fields: 'to the countryside'.

*   *   *

What had been an eager countryside adventure for the Red Guards in the early seasons of the Cultural Revolution became more of a punishment when the Party announced that every youth now had to leave the city. It was one thing to sweep down into the fields on a train and a truck, knowing that you could go home at the end of a week – but quite another to find that you were going to follow the bad class students into a rural exile that might never end. But Mao had spoken, and the People's Liberation Army had backed him up – although with the busybody bureaucrats still at large, many wondered whether Mao, the leader of their student hearts, was really free to speak his own mind. Across the cities, work teams were summoned to scour the academic registers, and the name of every student, from middle school through university, was matched with an individual village and told to be ready to go. Well, not quite every name. Single children who could point to dependent parents would be allowed to stay, as would older students who could show that they already had a job. Not to mention, of course, the sons and daughters of parent-cadres who had, in all the chaos, managed to keep their official positions of power. For the rest, however, bags were packed (clothes only; books, banned, were only for the bravest pockets) and trains were boarded.

With stories of countryside hardships having filtered back to the cities in letters, and with no one able to tell the new wave when, or even whether, they would ever be able to come back, many students left with heavy hearts. Others, built of sterner stuff, imagined themselves as new Lei Fengs: models of Mao's revolution, ready to go and serve the peasants with all of the lessons that a city could teach.

No sooner had the students' soft shoes touched the country mud, however, than they realised that the travails of the past were just the beginning. While it seemed to have escaped the notice of the powers in Beijing, once on the ground it was obvious that there were only so many people that a field could hold, let alone support. How on earth could eighteen million students be squeezed into a countryside that was already buckling under the revolutionary strain? The brigade teams were already hard-pressed to match work points with enough of the basic food on which everyone depended. And while teaching seemed the most obvious job for the students, places were in short supply. Generally speaking, a village had only one school and one teacher, and in many cases, that one place had already been taken by the 'bad elements' who had been first to arrive. True, there was always a need for someone who could count and read well enough to keep the village books, but all the villages in China could not find room for the ocean of students who were being sent in their direction.

As the students struggled to absorb the enormity of their new situation, for the most part, the peasants tried to do their best: squeezing harvests to feed the millions of extra mouths; making do, themselves, with less. Helpless in the face of nature, early student dreams of Lei Feng heroics were quickly dashed. Exhausted before the farming day was done, plagued with lice, sleepless with the shock of a life without family or the surviving entertainments of the city, few were able to till the land to any noticeable effect. Even fewer were left with energy for any of the other tasks which needed to be done just to survive. When new buildings were grudgingly put up to accommodate the students, it was the peasants who had to raise the bricks. Not surprisingly, the buildings looked much more like granaries than living quarters – the villagers were looking ahead to more productive future uses, and hoping that the students would not be staying long. They were not the only ones.

For their part, the students, some as young as thirteen, others old enough to have been graduating if their worlds had not been turned upside-down, looked up in dismay at the countryside's endlessly boring skies. Pitched battles prompted by periodic power seizures offered occasional opportunities for action and glory, but as far as the students could see, the results were only ever yet another reshuffling of local interests. Obviously, the outcomes were important to someone at the top – and the diversions were certainly welcome – but in terms of a revolution, nothing ever seemed to change the lot of the peasants below. From time to time, electrical faults and damaged limbs offered some the possibility of applying the elementary principles of city knowledge and experience. Once in a while, peering at the earth beneath their feet, and scouring the memories of past biology lessons, one or two even managed to unravel the mysteries of unco-operative soils. But revolutionary purpose was hard to come by, and time in the fields passed as slowly as eternity. Up before dawn, to bed before dark, not much to eat, no books to read, no films to watch. There was only the squawk of a loudspeaker for any kind of broadcast, with *The East is Red* replayed over and over again. Either that, or yet another exhortation to 'learn from Dazhai'.

In April 1969, parental letters announced the end of the Cultural Revolution. But as far as the students in the countryside could see, their parents had been misinformed: there were even more power seizures going on in the communes than before. A few months later, more letters arrived, this time announcing the fall of Mao's designated successor (Liu Shaoqi, author of *How to be a Good Communist*, now apparently found to have been a treacherous wolf in Party clothing) and the rise of his successor, Lin Biao. Still loyal to Mao, student hearts broke at Liu Shaoqi's betrayal, and hoped that Lin Biao would be a more worthy successor. But none of it made any difference to the monotony of their imprisonment on the land. Out to the fields and back again, day in, day out, with only blaring loudspeakers and the odd pitched battle to punctuate the peace: when would it ever end?

Everyone looked for an edge or an opportunity that could carry them back to the city; few found one. From time to time, a 'lucky' soul (almost always someone from one of the reddest families) managed to swing the ailing parent or the miraculous job that could secure the coveted chops and approvals required to get them back home. No one believed the bit about the parent or the job – one way or another, there was always a *hou men* back door at the bottom of it all. But it didn't really matter. With the city and home a fading memory, and nothing but cocks crowing, seasons changing and endless boring meetings to mark the passing of time, no one believed in anything very much any more.

And then, in 1972, letters arrived that sank the students' spirits even further: Lin Biao, the military man who had replaced Liu Shaoqi as Mao's designated successor, had turned out to be nothing but a 'renegade and a traitor' himself. The news was so big that the peasants heard it on their grapevines even before it hit the village meetings. Two traitorous men discovered to be standing at Mao's right hand in the course of just a few years? Confused, the peasants asked the students what on earth was going on up in that heavenly Beijing.

Cast adrift from a city which had once been home, now as perplexed as anyone else, the students could only shrug their shoulders with the rest of them. Nothing made any sense anymore.

With the fall of Lin Biao, the students' dashed dreams now turned to strategies for escape. Distance and money were not the only obstacles. There was also the *hukou* net of official registration that continued to cloak the country, just as it had in the time of Qin. Now registered as rural residents, like the peasants, if they wanted to shift from the countryside to the city they would have to get a clutch of approvals which only the best connected could secure. With a bit of luck and courage (and a lot of dinners for those willing to help), one could probably smuggle oneself into the city. But without ration cards and a job, staying there would require the co-operation of a lot of family and friends: family to keep them in food, friends to keep their silence. With every passing year, the redder classes of students pulled every possible family connection to make it back to the city. And up and down the country, every other family scrimped and saved to find the money to cover the costs of the favours.

While a number made it back, many were left behind with a rising fear that they would never be able to leave – that, and an anger which ate deep into hearts which now sensed they had been betrayed. Education had become nothing but a memory, and the only hope of a job if they ever made it back to the city would be that of a labourer at best. What if they never made it back? As far as they could tell, they would never see their families or a city again. Left to their own desperate thoughts, some threw themselves into wells. Others cast their minds back to the giddy heights of the early Cultural Revolution and wondered what on earth had happened. Yet others, in the depths of their misery, began to look again, beyond Liu Shaoqi and Lin Biao (the so-called 'wolves in Party clothing') to Mao. The peasants were right: what on earth was going on?

*　　*　　*

When Zhou Enlai had died in 1976, and Tiananmen Square had been flooded with a hundred thousand Beijingers, more letters arrived in the countryside, describing the crowds that had overwhelmed the standing guards, all of them demanding an end to the counter-revolutionary terror of the 'Gang of Four'. The stranded students knew exactly what that was all about: the crowd had clearly included a lot of smuggled 'returnees' from the countryside, the angry flotsam and jetsam of a lost generation. If they could have made it out of the fields, they would have been at the square themselves. Living lives without an education, employed in factories, or not employed at all, those 'lucky' ones had obviously reached the same conclusion as their student brothers who were still in the countryside: they had all been nothing but sacrifices in a greater battle of heavenly tigers. And as sacrifices, like thousands of years of other Chinese, they had never stood a chance. No wonder the anger of the crowds had known no bounds.

This time, though, the winds carried on changing. And changing so quickly that in September 1976 the students in the countryside got the news of Mao's death direct from local Party officials before any letters arrived. In October, reports arrived that the Gang of Four had been arrested and finally 'smashed'. Deng Xiaoping, now restored as vice-premier, had called a formal end to the Cultural Revolution, and then promised 'Four Modernisations'. Given that the Four Modernisations would obviously need some educated minds, the students wondered if, perhaps, they might finally be released. It almost seemed too much to hope for. Indeed, for many, it was. Thinking through Deng's modernising ideas, the stranded students soon realised that time had passed and left them all behind. After a decade or more in the countryside, even if they could get back to the city, what could they possibly have to offer anyone? But now, at least, it was official: they had been betrayed by a Cultural Revolution which had been nothing more than Mao's wife spitting on her enemies. In December 1978, when rumours filtered back of Wei Jingsheng's poster asking for a Fifth Modernisation (a voice for the people) the students could not have agreed more.

* * *

While the Four Modernisations gathered pace in Beijing, gusts of change began to appear in the countryside as well. Whispers started to circulate that individual peasant households might be given plots of land to farm for their own account. If it was true, it wasn't a moment too soon. After a decade of calls to 'learn from Dazhai', not to mention the turbulence of the power seizures, few of those in the countryside felt any better off than they had been before the Great Leap Forward – and most seemed to think that things had gone distinctly backwards. Without a patch of land to call their own, and under the constant gales of commandism, chaotic directives and cadre privilege, many peasants had reached the conclusion that it didn't really matter what they did; and actually, given the exhaustion of the soil, less would probably anyway be more. Feet dragged to the fields as slowly as they could, hoes were cast aside as soon as the afternoon sun gave the slightest indication that it might be winding down. Up and down the country, still under productive pressure from the top, brigade team leaders struggled to marshal their troops to push for yet another bumper harvest – and largely failed.

Here and there, however, seeing the exhaustion of the fields and the desperate fortunes of their families, brotherhoods of men had begun to meet together in the dead of village nights, sealing secret pacts to change their fate. While the Party might have put the fields under the iron will of the communes, these brotherhoods decided that if they didn't start separating out some plots of their own soon, everyone's futures – and all of their ancestors' wisdom – would be lost. Aware of the counter-revolutionary risks they were running, the brotherhoods agreed that, if the worst came to the worst, each surviving member would look after the families of the fallen.

But then Deng Xiaoping had come searching for ideas that might restore the harvests of old, and the secrets of their plots had become harder to keep. By 1979, their treachery had been outed; but retribution failed to fall. Instead, with a leap of Monkey King logic, the Party secretary of Sichuan (Zhao Ziyang) suggested to Deng that the rebellious peasants might have hit upon the very solution he had been looking for: a household responsibility system for the fields.

Deng was quick to grasp the possibilities. Henceforward, the communal grain quotas would be divided between the peasant households. Each household would be given an individual plot of land from which they would have to deliver up their share of the quota, but from which they would also be allowed to keep any surplus, whether as food for themselves, or to take to the side of a road and start a new local market (or better still, load on to a borrowed donkey and cart off to a nearby city or town).

Many rejoiced, but not all. And as always, everyone had their questions. The most common questions were: 'How will the land be divided?' and 'Who will do the dividing?' Others included: 'What will happen to the animals and the tools?'; 'What will happen if your particular plot of land can't deliver its yields?'; and 'What is going to happen to the communes?' And while a number of the stranded students had by now given up and resigned themselves to life in a village, many continued to ask their own now-dull question: 'When can we go home?'

The obvious answer to the dividing of the land was that the people would do it themselves – through the brigade team leaders, of course. Smiles fell a little at the mention of the brigade team leaders being involved, but any kind of new spring was better than the long winter that the communes had been. As far as the question of the communes was concerned, Deng promised that they would be faded out: their bureaucracies would be turned into new 'township' governments which would sit between the government of the county town and the leadership of the village. Some thought it looked as if everything was going back to the past. But if the peasants could once again decide how they were going to farm the fields, why should anyone complain?

As for the students, they had already had their answer in 1978, when Deng had finally acknowledged that they were right to want to come home. Indeed, he had added, it was also time that the peasants were released from the burden of looking after them. But the Four Modernisations had not yet got sufficiently off the ground to create the city jobs and apartments that would be required. Just a little bit more patience, and they would eventually be released.

*　　　*　　　*

The biggest gusts of change were in the south, under the strength of a supporting gale from Beijing. 'Household responsibility' was indeed an important contribution to the Four Modernisations but, in the countryside, more was needed. Once again, Deng scoured the past for inspiration, and consulted every element of the present for ideas. As he scoured and consulted, he found himself looking at the wider lands of China: the renegade province of Taiwan; the Malayan island of Singapore to which numerous boat-borne Chinese had floated off across the centuries before; and the lost rocks of Hong Kong. Looking at all of these 'Chinese outposts', he saw that a host of modernisations had been already achieved with the help of some 'special purpose' ideas. In Taiwan, special parks were bartering low wages for Western technology; in Singapore, overseas Chinese were trading on family ties across vast sweeps of Southern Asia; and in Hong Kong, not only had one of the world's greatest markets been created, but, in a stroke of genius worthy of the Monkey King, it had also been successfully separated from any reckless Western ideas of democracy. Oddly enough, the separation had begun as a British idea.

Looking again at the map of China proper, Deng saw a southern coastal countryside full of modernising opportunities. Studded with old ports that had once been lost to foreign treaties, it was also a land of fishermen who had since seen limited trade, and a hinterland packed with peasants at the back. With the southern coast so close to rising markets, special purpose possibilities seemed to be everywhere. Hard against Hong Kong, the southern east could not only tap into a harbour which traded with the world's imperial capitalists, but it could also find a way into the currents of the overseas Chinese anchored in Singapore. Far away from Beijing, and full of fields, the coastal hinterlands could easily be fenced off as parks without the Communist empire having to change its colours. True, Hong Kong and all the other overseas Chinese ports were full of traitors from the imperial past (not to mention escapees from the more recent revolutionary present), but the wealth of the overseas Chinese successes was a pearl of a prize that any crouching dragon would take.

By the end of 1979, four locations had been carefully chosen to host a set of new 'special economic zones'. One of them came with the rather unprepossessing name of 'deep ditch': Shenzhen. Name aside, however, Shenzhen, like all of the new zones, offered two invitations: one, to the capitalist-imperialist West to send its science and technology, another, to any and all overseas Chinese relatives to send back any spare cash which they might not need, to give their mainland cousins a hand. For many of the peasants tilling the chosen fields, it suddenly seemed as if snow might once again fall in summer. From Shenzhen's deep ditch, a walled city of factories rose; well, more of a clutter of fences around a constantly expanding construction site, but within the fences were construction and factory jobs for lucky recruits. Across the surrounding villages, families found that long-lost relatives with money began to reappear like dreams. Within a few years, Shenzhen had grown so big that it was jumping its walls, with factory owners offering jobs to anyone, and always eager to lease yet more fields on which to spread their greater productivity. When those who wanted to work on a production line, but did not want to lease their fields for factories, began to worry about how they could hold down a job *and* till the fields, the special economic zones were granted a magical dispensation which allowed the peasants to hire peasants from other parts of the country to come and do their work.

Within a few years, as Deng had hoped, the communes around Shenzhen were all but relegated to the past. The villagers found themselves spoilt for productive choice: Buy a tractor to rent out for a fee? Rent out a village fish pond? Open a brick works? The opportunities seemed endless. And as the southern coasts took to modernisation like ducks to water, many across the rest of China's countryside began to wonder how they could catch up with the future too.

*　　*　　*

Scouring the countryside for inspiration, Deng soon found that pockets of prosperity were breaking out all over the place. The greatest number seemed to be in the provinces around Shanghai, with the most successful of all in a long-forgotten place called Wenzhou.

Sitting on a south-eastern fringe of rocky hills, Wenzhou was a land of towns and villages screened from the rest of China by the Yangdang mountains, and threaded into the waters of the East China Sea by a myriad of tiny islands. In ancient times, before the period of the Warring States, it had been home to the independent people of the Yue. With long subtropical summers, its local breezes had always been quick to conjure up typhoons; and with little flat land, it had been the despair of emperors dreaming of settled fields.

By the time of the Song dynasty, the Wenzhounese had been stubbornly insisting on a more practical school of heavenly thought which was as happy to trade as to farm. There was even a tale that one of the emperors had once resorted to exchanging its people with those of a poorer province, in the confident expectation that this would finally rid the Wenzhounese of the pernicious trading idea. But the Wenzhounese had won – the trading ideas were simply transplanted to a whole new part of the country, while the new arrivals in breezy Wenzhou were quickly converted to markets.

By the time of the Ming and its idea that everybody stick to the fields and villages, Wenzhounese sons were already spread across the country, and the local hills and mountains were as unlikely as ever to become fields; the Wenzhounese had had no choice but to defy the imperial wisdom of the day, trading in the shadows of family networks, supported by private paper for money. And at the end of the Ming dynasty, few were surprised when the Wenzhounese had emerged as supporters of those members of the Donglin Academy who argued that the 'investigation of things' required on-the-ground human judgement rather than an iron-clad reading of the classical texts. Even during the times when the Ming (and later, the Qing) had cleared the coasts (the Ming to put an end to the disruptive trade with foreigners; the early Qing to put an end to the Zheng family of Ming pirate-loyalists) the inhabitants of Wenzhou had either climbed over the Yangdang mountains to keep up their domestic trade routes, or taken to their boats with bundles of cash and hulls full of crafts and settled in other worlds, albeit trying to keep close connections with home. Naturally, secrecy became an essential trick of their trade.

By the time of the Qing, Wenzhou's networks had spread across the country and abroad, supported by a long-established system of private paper, issued like money to cover the risks. And when the 1911 revolution had pulled the rug from under the Qing floor, the Wenzhounese found themselves in their element. Cash-rich families extended credit north and south, with overseas brothers ready and willing to support any sons who wanted to try their luck abroad.

But all that was long ago, before the revolution and its communes flattened everything to the uniformity of a Five Year Plan. Or was it?

When the Communist Party had been founded in nearby Shanghai, the Wenzhounese, always quick-witted, formed an independent local branch of their own, which naturally funded itself with levies on local factories. When, nearly twenty years later, Mao's branch of the Communist Party captured the country, the local Wenzhounese Communists simply bent with two winds: receiving central orders from Beijing, but applying them in the breeze of local conditions. As Beijing deepened the countryside's co-operatives into collectives and communes, each new central directive was translated as yet another request for increased yields – with similar central edicts, directed to the factories of Wenzhou's towns, being interpreted as well-meaning, but misguided, thoughts on how to improve local production. Naturally, central work teams had made inspecting appearances, but these had been regarded as temporary obstacles to endure – certainly not reasons for a fundamental change of heart. Of course, every now and then a local leader had to take a fall for the benefit of everyone else. But such ccasional sacrifices – struggle sessions and stints in jail – were seen as investments in keeping Wenzhou's productive ship afloat, with every act of official selflessness rewarded with an ever greater share of the profits.

Over the following two decades, Wenzhou continued to play its age-old game of central cats and local mice. As fields were tended for public display, a significant manufacturing underground was maintained, with factories quietly subcontracting to family homes, traders silently plying their wares across family connections laid centuries before, and deals sealed in the dead of night by men who were born blood brothers. Deng Xiaoping might have been astonished when Wenzhou announced its ten thousand town and village enterprises. But for the people of Wenzhou, and all of those who traded with them, it was nothing more than the sharing of a well-kept secret.

*   *   *

Shenzhen had its special purpose, and Wenzhou had its secrets. After decades of tilling the fields, by the 1980s peasants in other parts of the country were beginning to search for their own modernising qualities. With most of the villages hundreds of miles away from a city, and without the benefit of Wenzhou's centuries of networks and experience, it was not easy. But casting their minds back as far as they could possibly go, it did not take them long to realise that no one in the countryside could think of a time when an official had not been interested in a profit. And come to think of it, no one could remember a time when a relationship with an official had not been worth its weight in gold. With the communes being broken up, and with the leaders of the communes and the brigade teams going off to join the new township governments, a number of bright minds looked at what was being left behind and wondered. The chicken coops, orchards, saw mills, cement plants and repair shops which had all once served the communes were now being sold off for a song. Indeed, most of them had already been earmarked for officials thinking about their own personal 'modernisation'. But with government jobs on offer in the new townships, many surmised that the officials might appreciate a village partner: someone who would be willing to buy up local productive assets at the songs they were being sold for, and share the future returns. In that way, the officials would be able to pursue their own bureaucratic futures, and everybody could get a foot in the game.

Not everyone was keen. Particularly unenthusiastic were those who watched from the sidelines and saw chickens being swept up into other people's hutches, the incomes of the saw-mills disappearing into somebody else's pockets, and orchards tumbling into a neighbour's ready hands. Soon, though, it was clear that everyone who wanted to be anyone was arming themselves for modernisation. The arms? 'Twenty-shot pistols' of cigarette packs, 'hand grenades' in the form of bottles of wine, and 'explosive satchels', full of the biscuits which always smoothed the course of the countryside's trade. Watching the fruits of thirty years of bitter labour vanish into dust – to say nothing of all the struggle sessions and the fallen bodies – hearts as cynical as the stranded students asked themselves some questions. One of the most obvious questions was: 'If we have all been working for the same kind of work points all this time, how come some of us can afford to buy the very means of production themselves?' Equally obvious was: 'Who's paying for the cigarettes?'

With the leaders of the communes and the brigade teams now busy with the new bureaucracy of the townships (not to mention personally productive enterprises on the side), and with the old idea of 'to each according to his work' well on its way to becoming 'to each according to his enterprise' it was difficult to find anyone who had the time or the inclination to answer. Old hearts sighed. Gone were those dreamy days when someone would help out a neighbour without charging a fee. At this rate, 'household responsibility' or not, it wouldn't be long before the peasants were working for someone else again, and city fat cats were appearing to buy whatever could be sold: where on earth had the revolution gone?

The peasants were not the only ones with the questions. Watching the transformation of the countryside, the still-stranded students, now in their twenties and thirties, who had lost their youth to Mao's revolution, could scarcely believe their eyes.

*   *   *

On 1 October 1980, those once-students who had not already managed to smuggle themselves back to the cities were (in principle and subject to the paperwork) finally to be allowed to return. But after all this time, not everybody wanted to go: some had married in the countryside, and could no longer leave; others had come to the wistful conclusion that with no possible qualifications for any kind of city job, the past was better off left as a dream.

Those who did go home, found themselves greeted by shiny new posters carrying visions of a high-rising city world, and the sight of heavy trucks shuttling backwards and forwards along rapidly-building streets. Remembering the old posters that had once carried images of revolutionary workers, and recalling the open streets in which their own dreams had once roamed, many of them wept. Picking up their pens, they began to write the stories and poems of everything they had experienced and seen. Careful to keep their scribblings underground, they were more than willing to share them with each other, and with the handful of outsiders whom they felt they could trust.

In 1986, and again in the spring of 1989, they would find their way to Tiananmen Square, hoping against hope that heaven would finally be ready to listen. For over twenty years, they had leapt forwards, only to find themselves thrown backwards, and all for somebody else's dream. If snow were ever going to truly fall in summer, something would have to change.

BOOK III

Those who rule are supported by those who are ruled.
This is a principle accepted by the world.

Mencius (372 – 289 BCE)

GREAT MAN

*The sage assesses the affairs of the age and
prepares himself in response to them.*

Han Fei (280–233 BCE)

CHAPTER 1

FULL SPEED AHEAD

*He perceives the laws of Heaven and Earth; He discerns
the ways of demons and gods ... his mind clearly orders all
planets and stars.*

Journey to the West, Wu Cheng'en (seventeenth century)

It was night when the special train pulled out of the railway station. Wrapped in the winter of early 1992, the streets around stood silent. Few had noticed the dark cavalcade of cars that seemed to glide through the dusk; and no one had witnessed the large family make its way to the waiting platform. Except, that is, the appointed sentinels of the People's Liberation Army, and the escorting five-star general. 'A holiday in the south,' was all that the Party had been told: much deserved and long overdue for the small spirit upon whose personal energies everyone in China had come to depend. All other engines stood down for the night, the carriages of the special train pulled out of the station and, picking up speed, chugged devotedly down towards the Yangzi, leaving the sparkling stars of Beijing's *ziwei* purple enclosure behind. By morning, the first of the carefully planned destinations had been reached: the accidentally revolutionary city of Wuchang (sister of the old Hankou heart of river fortunes; both now part of the much bigger industrial powerhouse of Wuhan).

Standing on the platform, waiting for the doors to open and the greatest of the surviving revolutionaries to descend, the small group of high provincial officials assumed that their task was to wish him and the sixteen other members of his family a happy holiday. By the time the slight figure had climbed back into his carriage twenty minutes later, they knew that a holiday was the last thing on his mind. Feet barely touching the ground, his parting words had been sharper than a north wind: 'Do more, talk less, cut the boring meetings, drop the endless reports. And next time I see you on television, you had better be talking change.'

As the special train sped off down the line, bound for Guangdong, the momentarily speechless officials gathered up their wits and reached for their phones. Wires charged with electrifying currents, the urgent message to their southern colleagues was short and simple: watch out, this is not a holiday – a revolution is on its way.

* * *

Time had passed slowly since the flaming summer of 1989: productivity had chilled, and even the miracles of Wenzhou had come to seem as ephemeral as a mirage. Stunned into silence, young and old, workers and intellectuals alike, the people had retreated from Tiananmen: the gate which had become a square, the place which had once stood for communications between heaven and earth. Zhao Ziyang (Deng's premier and once-annointed successor, who had become general secretary of the Party) had been retired to his own courtyard: a courtyard with a curtain drawn across it, in case anyone dared to think about a conversation with the man who had clearly been responsible for encouraging the bourgeois student spirits which had nearly brought heaven down on the Party's head. Within the Party, criticisms and self-criticisms had been made, all in true Yan'an style. Trained in Moscow, Zhou Enlai's adopted son, Li Peng, had succeeded Zhao Ziyang as premier, becoming the leading light of the left-leaning East Winds. And a new general secretary (and anointed future president) had been appointed in the form of a safer, if less heroic, pair of hands, belonging to a southern engineer by the name of Jiang Zemin.

The battle had been hard and had spread out beyond China, to the wider Communist world. By the end of 1989, Hungary had given up its socialist senses, East Germany had lost its wall, and Romania's people had despatched their own general secretary, Ceausescu, to another world, with a simple bullet of justice to the head. Then Moscow – the red star that had set the Party on its early course – had been captured by soft hearts whose *glasnost* openness had been causing havoc for years, and whose *perestroika* fiddling had already pulled the rug of power from under the feet of the once almighty Soviet State. Scarcely credible to the Party faithful in Beijing, by 1991, Lenin's Russian dream had simply vanished in a puff of inexplicably faint-hearted smoke.

Behind the gates of Zhongnanhai, the biting East Winds had once again gathered in whispering corners, before raising themselves into full blown gales of leftist virtue. Directed towards Deng, they even included gusts from Deng's own appointed successor, Jiang Zemin. 'The storm', they grumbled, 'has been a long time coming. And if everyone had been on their Leninist guard, the Party would have done something about it before.' Some pointed to that ill-fated day in December 1978, when Deng had taken command of the Party pulpit and announced that everyone should emancipate their minds. Others insisted that the weather had changed long before that: in the aftermath of the Great Leap Forward's famine, when weaker Party spirits had lost the courage of their revolutionary convictions in their rush to get the harvests back. One or two argued that the gathering clouds of havoc had been there from 1949. Others suggested that they had been there long before, from the Yan'an days or even the Jiangxi Soviet: all part of the primeval struggle between the true revolutionaries (those who understood the need to master stubbornly subjective minds) and the bourgeois-liberals-in-disguise (those who were simply playing revolutionary games).

Whenever it started, the East Winds had argued, it could no longer be ignored. While Deng might blame the students' counter-revolution on the 'peaceful evolution' conspiracy of the American capitalist West, everyone knew that the real question was about the Marxist-Leninist-Mao Zedong order of the Communist Party itself. What were the 'Four Modernisations', other than a treacherous capitalist shot of bourgeois liberalism across the bows of the striving socialist state? What was 'productivity', other than an old imperialist trick designed to distract attention from Marx's central question of class struggle? Exactly what kind of Leninist discipline had anyone expected to see when Fang Lizhi and the other intellectuals had been welcomed back into the fold and then sent off on hundreds of scientific journeys to the West, only to return with the treacherous sutras of capitalism?

Had anyone really thought that the bureaucratic delusions of household responsibility for peasants, and *chengbao* factory contracts, would not bring back precisely what Mao had predicted: wine-soaked bosses, rising pavilions, runaway prices and panic in people's hearts – not to mention an entire revolution betrayed?

'For that matter,' the East Winds continued, 'who, or what, was Deng Xiaoping?' 'Revolutionary hero, in the mould of the great self-strengthener, Zeng Guofan? Heaven help us.' 'Rising sun, in the footsteps of Mao Zedong? Well, only in the sense that his black and white cats had almost brought down the same heavenly catastrophes as the Great Leap Forward.' Truth be told, Deng looked a lot more like the Monkey King whose own *Journey to the West* had created all that chaos in heaven. *Bian!* with his magic stick, and a sudden directive had appeared declaring that the only thing which mattered in socialism was getting rich. *Swoosh!* with his cloud somersaults, and state-owned factories had been left to flounder in the mud, while towns and villages threw up untamable enterprises, and southern coasts went back to being temples of foreign factories. *Flash!* with his spells, and suddenly everyone was rushing to multiply productivity four times in ten years. And all the while, Deng had been mesmerising everyone with his endlessly repeated Four Cardinal Principles (keep to the order of the socialist road, uphold the dictatorship of the proletariat, uphold Marxism-Leninism and Mao Zedong Thought, uphold the leadership of the Communist Party), as if a mantra could defend anyone against anything. There was only one way to move forward, and that was to keep to the Leninist discipline, never forget Marx, and never relax the Party's guard against the bourgeois liberals – whoever they may be.

By the November plenum at the end of 1989, fired with the confidence of impending victory, the left-leaning winds had regained control of the pulpit. Declaring that weeds of bourgeois liberalisation had, once again, risen within the ranks of the Party, they announced that it was time to root them out. And then, echoing Deng's own insistence that stability was everything, they set out their principles for revolutionary order: any and all ideas of markets would need to give way to the primacy of the Five Year Plan; the rush for productivity would need to be braked to slow; and the coasts, with their special economic zones, would just have to cool their heels.

Deng was not surprised. In fact, he told himself he should have seen it coming. Zhao Ziyang's foolish heart had blinded him to the responsibilities of socialist power with Chinese characteristics. Talking, as they had done in the early years, about the respective importance of 'democracy' and 'law', Deng assumed that Zhao had understood them in the same way as himself. 'Democracy' as a once-and-for-all revolutionary choice in favour of a Communist Party, which would thereafter be trusted and left alone to take the right decisions at the right time, and whatever the circumstances. 'Law' as an improvement in the clarity of rules for bureaucratic efficiency – and certainly not something to be allowed to obstruct the necessary actions of the revolutionary Party. How could he have known that Zhao was dreaming of the kind of democracy that would let every speck of sand in the tray stand up and say whatever it wanted? Let alone a law that would have the misguided idea of putting itself above the Party's guns? But he should have realised that a man like Zhao would easily be carried away by those imperially-capitalist liberal winds. True revolutionary hearts would never have been so easily fooled. Confusing 'socialist production' with 'bourgeois liberalism' was a fuzzy kind of thinking which would never have won the revolution. Mixing up 'mind emancipation' with an uncontrolled blossoming of subjectively independent thoughts was a surefire recipe for disaster: with that kind of confusion the Party would not even have made it to 1949. But none of Zhao's mistakes changed the fact that ideas that failed to feed the people were never going to deliver the socialist utopia that Marx or any of them had dreamt of, nor the fact that feeding the people was not a betrayal of Marx.

Listening politely to the pulpit pronouncements of the left, Deng acknowledged that mind emancipation was a challenge, and that the most vigilant of the Party's present-day spirits would be required to ensure that the ghosts of the past stayed buried. No one wanted the Four Modernisations to be betrayed as the 1911 revolution had been betrayed by Yuan Shikai and the warlords. But it was for this reason that he had set the Party under the careful guard of the Four Cardinal Principles, and why he had so firmly resisted Wei Jingsheng's counter-revolutionary call for a Fifth Modernisation. And as everyone could see, his prudence had been rewarded with an ultimate triumph over the counter-revolutionary treachery of Tiananmen – something that the Russian brothers, with their *glasnost* and *perestroika* had obviously failed to achieve. Unlike Moscow, here in the Chinese People's Republic, the proletariat was still a dictatorship of the people under the leadership of the Party: how else could they have avoided Ceausescu's terrible fate? The Communist Party was still leading: weren't they still in power? Marxism-Leninism-Mao Zedong Thought was still the lexicon of everyone's ideas: would anyone in the Party dare to put forward a single idea without grounding it carefully in the Communist classics? And for those who were paying attention to facts on the ground, in the lands of the Chinese People's Republic, the socialist road was still advancing – or at least it would be if those East Winds would stop their whining.

His opinions expressed, and his steam gathered, Deng then pushed on to make his points about China's socialist future. Since 1958, far from catching up with Britain, China had fallen down to the level of Ouagadougou (Africa, for those who needed to consult their maps). Markets were not the exclusive prerogative of the capitalist West, even as planning was not the exclusive prerogative of socialism. If anyone was casting an anxious eye over their shoulders towards a crumbling Moscow, the lesson they should learn was that the shift towards the kind of productivity that could compete with the West needed to be faster, not slower – albeit tightly controlled by the leadership of the Party. There was a train in the station, ready to take China and its socialism to a glorious future. If everyone didn't jump on it, quickly, the opportunity would be forever lost.

But Deng's observations fell on ears deafened by their own sense of triumph. Rounding on his recollections of the past (and keeping their remarks to the secret recesses of the inner Party, lest any outside spirits should get confused), the East Winds replied that the only real problems the Party had had in forty years of successful revolution were Mao's Great Leap Forward and the Cultural Revolution. In the Great Leap Forward, Mao's excessive ambition had 'drained the ponds of the collectives, in a pursuit of flying fish'. But before that, everything had been plain sailing: a golden age where the necessary battle against bourgeois liberalism had stood shoulder-to-shoulder with the taming of markets by a planned command. As for the Cultural Revolution, even men like Mao could make a mistake: '70 per cent right and 30 per cent wrong', as Deng himself had once put it, was not a bad verdict in the scheme of history. A couple of mistakes did not change the logic of a revolution. It was time to go back to the socialist basics.

'Socialist basics?' Deng repeated, in an effort to control his temper. As far as he could see, the East Winds didn't have a clue. Zhongnanhai had simply gone back to being that Yan'an cauldron of bored wives with nothing better to do than tell tales and stir up trouble – if, indeed, it had ever really been anything else. With thoughts like these, Zhongnanhai would become the centre of nothing but its own hot air.

Retreating to the quiet of his own company, and reflecting on the urgent need for fast action if the train was going to keep moving ahead, Deng had decided that the solution was not going to be found in the classically Communist corridors of Beijing. Thinking about it, he told himself that he should have seen that earlier as well. When had anything sensible ever come out of a central cave? Across the story of China's time, wisdom had always come from the provinces – the places where men were men, and truth was always based on practical facts. Say what they would about the capitalist fringes of the coast, it was in cities like Shenzhen and Shanghai where the future would be found. Of course, there would always be a need for a centre to make sure that everyone ultimately pulled together. But the trick was for the centre to make sure that the provincial spirits aligned, without disrupting their energies.

It was, Deng acknowledged, a difficult balancing act, one at which successive ancient dynasties had spectacularly failed. The ancient Zhou had let everything drift apart; the First Qin Emperor had pulled everything too tightly together. The failures of the Zhou had been followed by a war of all against all, conducted over two hundred terrifying years. And while the collapse of Qin might have led to the glorious Han, it had also, ultimately, opened the way to the Taiping Great Peace rebellions, which had been followed by conquering barbarians tearing down from the steppes. These were lessons that had been repeated again and again across the last fifteen hundred years; it was time that China learnt them. What was required was a protection from overzealous local spirits and foot-draggers alike. And if the younger Party leaders were not up to it, then Deng himself would pick up the reins, and make the balance work. Fortunately, he reminded himself, in 1978, he had taken a very early step to protect against any risk of a return to the central madness of the Great Leap Forward by separating the country's provincial 'kitchens' from Beijing: allowing the governments of each province to collect their own taxes and balance their own budgets. If the East Winds were going to go on strike and insist on centralism, he would just have to go down to the provinces and get the kitchens on his side.

From 1990, Deng took himself off on repeated journeys to the south. Staying away from the capital for ever-longer periods of time, the less centrally opinionated and far more practical Shanghai became a particularly preferred retreat. Happy to have been left in planning charge of the Beijing headquarters, the East Winds thought that Deng was right to take account of his aging years and seek the solace of a quieter, and certainly warmer, provincial climate. They were all getting old. It was time to bring some younger spirits into Zhongnanhai: left-leaning ones, of course.

393

Once in Shanghai, though, Deng had no interest in wasting his time on rest. Turning quickly to a search for more emancipated minds, he soon found one in the person of a rehabilitated one-time rightist who had become the Mayor of Shanghai, by the name of Zhu Rongji. Keen to ensure that the wider body of provincial spirits across the country would also be able to grasp the urgent need to act, Deng had then picked up a pen – and a pen-name – and swept every willing journal with articles arguing for a clear-sighted understanding that whatever strengthened the productivity of the nation would naturally be socialist, and that capitalism did not have a monopoly on energy and imagination – unless of course socialism chose to bind its own feet. Zhongnanhai plugged its ears to the articles, and the lily-livered Jiang Zemin called for a 'great wall of steel' to defend China from America's dream of 'peaceful evolution'.

The provincial spirits, however, had heard Deng's clarion call and, picking up pens of their own, they argued that unless socialism was grounded on *provincial* production, both the Party and its people would remain in the trenches of the poor. In 1991, using his remaining Party powers, Deng then waved his Monkey King stick and '*bianned!*' Zhu Rongji up to Beijing as deputy premier of the nation at large. The East Winds regrouped, and launched an inky campaign against the dangerous rise of a 'one-voice hall' (Deng) and a return of the ancient fiefdoms of the Zhou state (the provinces) with their feudal lords (the provincial leaders) whose ambitions, they argued, would ultimately collapse heaven on everyone's heads.

With nothing less than the prize of socialism at stake, Deng decided to retreat to the past himself. Emulating the Crouching Dragon, Zhuge Liang, he meditated on the changes, and waited for the *dao* way to appear. When, in January 1992, the stars had seemed to be perfectly positioned, Deng decided to storm the pass of central Party opinion by climbing on to his special train and advancing under the cover of a holiday to the farthest fringe of the southern coast. Once in Guangdong, he swept off to the specially productive zone of Shenzhen, by now a forest of factories with an advancing line of skyscrapers, and declared it to be a beacon of the future. Addressing the whole of the country through the southern crowds, he then went on to explain that socialism was really three things: it was whatever promoted socialist forces of production; it was whatever strengthened the power of the socialist nation; and it was whatever raised the people's standard of life.

To this, he added the observation that in a country as big as China you could not always expect life to be calm and steady, and when a rare

Darwinian opportunity arrived to leap ahead in the bitter battle for the survival of the fittest, you had to seize the moment and '*jia you*' – speed up!

*　　*　　*

It would be more than two months before the East Winds unlocked the Party newspapers and allowed them to print not only the story of Deng's travels but also the headlines of what he had said. But before the end of the year – having marshalled the strongest of the provincial leaders and ensured that the biggest stars in the People's Liberation Army were on display – Deng finally recaptured the headquarters. It was 1992, a year in which the Party would open one of its five-yearly 'congresses'. Always the occasion for a review of what the state of the nation would be over the coming five years, this one, the fourteenth since the founding of the Party, had been especially designated for the announcement of a new, 'third generation', leadership (to follow after Mao and Deng). Once again, Deng rose to the pulpit. Having made sure that the pews were stocked with provincially-emancipated minds which were also clear that there was not an inch of space for any bourgeois liberal tendencies, he snatched a triumph from the winds of the left. Applauding his vision, the congregation congratulated him on the 'tremendous courage' that he had displayed in opening up both 'a new understanding of Marx' and 'an advanced way forward for the Party'.

As praise poured upon Deng's head, the Party acknowledged that socialism depended on developing the economy as fast as possible, and that productivity was indeed the measure of progress. Resolutions agreed that nine more coastal cities would be opened up, and productivity would be quadrupled by the year 2000. Guangdong was to be given the honour of catching up with the small fire-producing dragons of the Chinese influenced East (Taiwan, Singapore, Hong Kong and South Korea which, while technically not a Chinese outpost, had been loyally following the Chinese idea for over a thousand years). Even Jiang Zemin, hitherto a rather disappointing successor-in-waiting, agreed to board the train and push things forward faster. In fact, softening to the notion of a Party-led prosperity, Jiang even offered Deng a new mantra to smooth the difficult edges of socialism-as-riches: 'the socialist market economy'. Of course, as Deng knew better than anyone, the idea of a socialist market economy was, like all great goals (and Daoist visions), something of a contradiction: a river of rapids to be crossed in itself. Working out what it actually meant would take years of careful stone-studying. But surely that was what mantras were for – to keep you going. The important thing was that Jiang had finally boarded the train, with a grasp of the ancient wisdom that all journeys of ten thousand miles had to start with a single first step.

Bearing the enormity of the journey in mind, Deng also noted that, disappointing while this would be to many, even if they advanced at a relatively fast pace, the Party would have to accept that the primary stages of socialism would not be completed until 2050. Marxist-Leninist-Mao Zedong Thought had been secured, as had the Democratic Dictatorship of the Proletariat, led by the Party, with everyone firmly committed to the socialist road. But, as he had noted in the late 1980s, in their zeal to race ahead, the Chinese people had skipped one of the early stages on the road to socialism: the capitalist one that was necessary to pave the way for the final utopian triumph. Going back to cover the lost ground was going to take longer than he had originally thought. No one should worry, though. The winds had changed, the course was now clear. After Tiananmen, no one was in any doubt that while there would be 'relaxed controls on economic matters', on political matters, there would be 'tight controls'. *Liu si*, June Fourth, was a never-to-be-mentioned-again 'political incident'. And in order to ensure that it never returned, the memory of that Tiananmen day would be erased from everyone's minds. In its place would rise the story of 'one hundred years of national humiliation' overcome by decades of the patriotic Party sacrifice that had culminated in the triumph of the People's Republic: call it a 'Patriotic Education Campaign', suggested Deng. To be launched across the country, its texts would take the form of books for schools and children, with newspaper editorials for adults, and museums and monuments to remind everyone, young and old, of both the heroic battles which the Party had fought and of all the great humiliations suffered. Etched into the very rock of the country's architecture, the monuments would stand forever: just like the inscriptions with which the First Qin Emperor had announced his achievements to heaven, carved on the rocks of the great Mount Tai.

Listening to Deng's promises, not all of the East Winds buried their reservations about high-speed socialism. But everyone finally agreed to reach out across the river and at least look for the same kind of stones – socialist production, a strong socialist nation and higher standards for daily living – that would deliver the great dream of Marx and Mao. Suddenly, the dream that had been floundering only a year before, had, with Deng's indomitable spirit, and under Zhu Rongji's capable economic hands, found its feet. By the end of 1992, picture postcards of Deng's southern holiday were being printed in spreading newspapers, with many people pasting them on their walls. Productive spirits were rising once again. By 1994, there were even encouraging signs of speed.

* * *

The fastest-growing bamboo shoots (and those easiest to see) were in Shenzhen. Purpose-built for productivity, the special economic zone had become the immortalisation of Deng's productive ideas: full to bursting with factories, complete with special purpose dormitories so that everyone could sleep close to the job. Armed with Deng's calls for mind emancipation and speeding up, hundreds of thousands of eager hands had already flocked there by the end of the 1980s. And empowered with the Monkey King idea that the use of the people's land was really a right in itself – one which could be bought and sold without ever affecting actual ownership – the factories and dormitories had now swept across the flimsy fences which defined the special economic zone, and flooded the hinterland beyond. Villages had given up the ghosts of their ancestors; fields and fish ponds had fallen to bulldozers; and what had once been a fishing fringe of thousands had become a socialist landscape of four million newly productive people. Most of the new people were migrants who, with the special purpose powers granted by Deng, had managed to storm the *hukou* household registration barriers designed by Mao to keep the country cousins in the fields.

Throughout it all, the People's Liberation Army had been a powerful source of support. With the Party clear from the earliest days that socialism was not just about defending the nation but also strengthening it, their forces had long been volunteered to help with the task of socialist construction. Fresh from rebuilding the northern steel city of Tangshan (after the earthquake which had eerily shattered the city, six weeks before Mao's death), a crack corps of officers and soldiers had become an instant body of civil engineers and construction managers. Called down to Shenzhen, the army had then swiftly raised pavilions of production and power as far as the eye could see. The factories had then been furnished with automatic equipment capable of carrying out orders with optimal efficiency: no messy subjective thinking required. Dormitories had been raised in scientific rows, efficiently designed just to cover the sleeping hours of the workers, with no need for anyone to waste time or space in accommodating inconvenient families. Watching the speed of the army's progress – and always quick to see an opportunity – Hong Kong's land-hungry *da ban* big bosses (*taipans*, to those who spoke in Cantonese) had then put forward plans to develop vast areas in a single leap. When local planning bureaucrats pointed out that Shenzhen had reached its limits, Deng waved his magic stick to *swoosh!* the limits away.

By 1985, the army had raised up China's first skyscraper; by 1989 Shenzhen was beginning to look like a real city, which, in 1990, with a declaration from Beijing, it duly became. In 1994, refreshed by the bracing breeze of Deng's 1992 visit, and with the help of an eager Hong Kong Chinese engineer, Shenzhen then emancipated its own mind and launched a new urban revolution as well. Blazing a way through hills and mountains, leaping across rivers, new roads rushed out of the city like hungry dragons, stretching the city's limits far and wide.

Villages fortunate enough to find themselves licked by the dragons' flames, exploded like stars into industrial zones, each (just like the villages of Wenzhou) with their own particular productive idea: shoes, lights, or whatever else the outside world might want. Indeed, everything had all happened so quickly and over such a vast area, that many wondered what to call it: was it a city or a state? Or was it something else entirely? But revelling in the roaring socialism that it was producing, no one on the ground had any time to worry about the niceties of names. In the end, they settled for a description pulled out of the geography books: the Pearl River Delta.

* * *

Further up the coast, the once foreign emporium of Shanghai looked down with envy at Shenzhen's new socialist credentials. The most sparkling of imperial China's treaty ports, this was the old *Shanghailand* that had once observed no other laws but its own. From 1949, its decadent past had brought it nothing but shame. After forty years of distrust, however, Deng the crouching dragon had looked at the city with new eyes, and seen the possibility of something quite different. Refreshingly far from Beijing, it was already a port and a city that not only sat near to the sea but, spanning the wide Huangpu tributary river mouth of the Yangzi, had a spreading eastern area, Pudong, that had scarcely been touched. Like the southern lands around the Pearl River, this was a geography that had the power to transform not only its own productivity, but that of the entire Yangzi River delta as well.

By 1992, new construction enterprises (among them, many founded by army veterans from Shenzhen) were already advancing onto Pudong's mudflats. By 1994, a *Pearl of the Orient* television tower touched the skies, while bridges rose to reconnect the city under the sparkling banner of socialism. As with Shenzhen, more roads set off like dragons, carrying torches to light up not only the lands of surrounding fields, but those of whole cities and provinces which spread all around. Suddenly, ancient towns whose crafting treasures had once floated up the Grand Canal to the Ming and Qing heavens in Beijing found new fortunes of opportunity lapping at their feet – even as the villages of Wenzhou, now openly displaying their productive powers, found a vast port ready to hand.

Watching images of flashing dragons and rising skyscrapers on evening television, hundreds of other cities across the country, not to mention tens of thousands of towns, entreated the approving powers above to grant them the official chops required for special zones of their own. Some succeeded; others failed. But in the prevailing spirit of mind emancipation, even those who failed decided to go ahead just the same. And out in the fields, tens of millions of eager hearts picked up bundles of hopes and clothes, and decided to create their own opportunity by storming the passes to the cities. For many, *hukou* registrations came to be seen as nothing but a temporary inconvenience which would surely soon be 'disappeared'. The country cousins rolled into the new city world like a tide.

*　　　*　　　*

Upon reflection, it had all happened just in time. On 1 October 1995, television images of Deng Xiaoping observing the fireworks of the forty-seventh anniversary of the founding of the People's Republic of China showed everyone that, at ninety-one, his light was finally fading. But as Deng moved into the shadows, Jiang Zemin found that the waters of his own river were rising fast around him. Once again, prices were soaring to the skies, while state-owned factories were sitting on mountains of debts. It seemed that without Deng's personal power to keep them in check, the provincial energies had run away with themselves. But in the absence of anyone with Long March credentials, how was the Party going to calm them down without risking another sinking of the productive socialist ship? Fortunately for Jiang Zemin, Zhu Rongji, now premier, was there to take the blame.

Jiang Zemin was clear that finding the next stone to cross the river was going to take more than a holiday postcard – just as he was clear that the

East Winds which had been temporarily becalmed by Deng could easily gather themselves up into another gale: one which he might struggle to command. Already at the end of 1994, looking for a personal *pai banzi*, do the deal, strength, Jiang had invited loyal Shanghai powers to join him in the Politburo height of Party authority, in a bid to bolster his support in the rather frightening courtyards of central Party's families. Thus reinforced, Jiang had then managed to secure a Party resolution to reiterate the old Leninist principle that centralised decision-making was everything. With central power clarified, he followed it up with a confirmation that, as general secretary of the Party, chairman of the Central Military Commission, and president of the People's Republic of China, he was the *hexin* heart of everything.

With the full force of the Party's order now behind him, Jiang decided to make it clear that, while he had not had the privilege of standing shoulder to shoulder with Mao on the Long March himself, he was nonetheless a true inheritor of the ancient skills with which Yu the Great had tamed the lands. The Leninist institutions that he had inherited would not just be nourished, but strengthened. The Party's principles of Marxist-Leninist-Mao Zedong Thought would be tightened. Anyone likely to cause trouble would be asked to step outside. Looking back to the strategies deployed by rulers of the past, he also noted the virtues of campaigns against corruption – campaigns that provided a leader with a convenient whip with which to beat down any unruly weeds of critics, and also the power to sort out any self-strengthening excesses. As ever, it was simply a matter of whispering a troublesome name and then, not only would the individual weed disappear, but the waves of shock would ensure that any wider weeds would be quick to step into line – or leave the country. That should be enough to keep any awkward voices at bay.

Jiang, however, had forgotten that everyone had read the same history books, with many of them doing so at the far more frightening feet of Mao. As the fourteenth Party Congress neared the end of its five-year term, the East Winds leapt ahead of him. Presenting a carefully inked ten thousand character memorial, they declared that the socialist state was disappearing, and that a new bourgeoisie was advancing up the productive ranks. They also argued that, thanks to Deng's love of studying the treacherous West, a new insurgency of stubbornly subjective intellectuals had been gathering, all steeped in the technical aspects of Western wealth-creation, and very likely harbouring bourgeois liberal ideas as well. It was, they argued, nothing more nor less than another battle in that endless American campaign for 'peaceful evolution'. And with the intellectuals dedicating themselves to their own subjective opinions, China was at risk of being colonised by undisciplined Western ideas that had no concept of the pivotal importance of leadership by a Party.

Jiang bravely refused to listen. The East Winds then decided to pick up a trick from Deng, and step on to a train of their own. This time, though, the train was not bound for the south, but for the industrial heartlands of the north-east, where men who had once worked for the Party state were not only losing their jobs, but their iron rice bowl pensions as well.

With Deng's dream, and everybody's productive futures, at stake, it was not long before a countervailing force of right-leaning 'West Winds' rose up behind Jiang. Representatives of the more productive provinces, they were determined to continue their rise – and, over time, to secure their gains with the additional protections of democracy and the rule of law (protections which, they argued, even Marx himself had advised).

Jiang, carefully tutored by Deng in the critical necessity of avoiding any discussions of either democracy or the rule of law if productivity were to prevail, now found himself caught between an East Wind left (which wanted nothing to do with wealth-creating productivity), and a West Wind right (which wanted wealth-creating productivity, but insisted on having the twin demons of democracy and law as well). Like so many before him, Jiang turned back to the past for inspiration, and hit upon the old idea of a personal school of brushes. Finding a committee of supporting minds – sensible ones which understood the importance of having both productivity *and* a disciplined obedience to the Party – he armed them with a free flow of ink, and commanded them to come up with a definition of socialism that would defeat both of the storming winds: East and West alike. Take your time, he said – but not too much of it.

As Jiang's brush committee set to work on the definition that would square his circle, the ink-hurling continued. In early 1997 Deng Xiaoping finally died. The battling brushes paused for a moment's reflection and Jiang Zemin, still firmly at the helm, stood up to declare that he would work as hard as any of the 'Great Men' before him. As he spoke, the hands of a long-ticking clock moved towards the midnight hour when, on 1 July 1997, the imperial British rule of Hong Kong's island rocks would run out. This was the eagerly-awaited date when the magnificent market which sat off the shore of Guangdong would return to China, carrying some of the world's most potent capitalism in its bags (unfortunately, with some last-minute

British ideas about democracy smuggled in as well). With Deng departed, it was Jiang Zemin who rose to welcome the people of Hong Kong back to the heartlands of China and, in so doing, to herald the triumph of the Chinese nation over 'one hundred years of humiliation'.

By the time the Party came together at the end of 1997, for the fifteenth five-yearly Congress, Jiang and his committee of brushes thought they had finally found a definition of socialism that would knock the stuffing out of both of the battling winds. Its name was not exactly elegant – but this was, after all, the Communist Party, and not some salon of scholarly minds. The key was a new 'science of Deng Xiaoping Theory', complete with one 'centre' and 'two basic points'. The 'centre' was *jingji fazhan*, spreading economic development. As for the 'two basic points', the first was Deng's familiar Four Cardinal Principles' (keep to the order of the socialist road, uphold the dictatorship of the proletariat, uphold the supremacy of Marxist-Leninist-Mao Zedong Thought, and uphold the leadership of the Communist Party); the second was Deng's 'mind emancipation'. Armed with such scientific clarity, who could fail to distinguish between those ideas of Marxism that were truly Marxist, and those ideas of Marxism that were actually devilishly anti-Marxist ideas in disguise? In short, the central task was economic development, with every problem to be solved by the power of the Party, coupled with a heavy dose of more economic development (and, where necessary, a dose of Monkey King logic as well).

Standing tall in the Great Hall of the People, Jiang Zemin presented the new Deng Xiaoping Theory to the Party, with onward broadcast to the masses. Also charged with appointing a new Party leadership, he took the opportunity to strengthen his own revolutionary credentials. Always the late-coming engineer rather than a pioneering Long Marcher, he decided to polish his position with the appointment to the Politburo of some of the sons of the Party's greatest founders. While Deng had always insisted that the Party should on no account perpetuate its own 'aristocracy', the invited sons were only too happy to continue the family tradition. Others, remembering Deng's words, looked up at the skies in consternation. Casting their minds back to the early centuries of the Zhou dynasty and to the fiefdoms of families that had been spread across a land which had ultimately fallen to their battles, they lost no time in calling the sons 'princelings'.

When the new Politburo members rose to take their places in the Communist pantheon, the third generation leadership of the Communist dynasty was not only younger than its revolutionary forebears (and if the newspapers were to be believed, a lot better educated) but a sparkling combination of some of the country's most exceptional Party talents and the descendants of some of the Party's greatest family lineages. What the third generation leadership actually thought, however (about anything) was not much clearer than the scientific 'one centre and two basic points' of Deng Xiaoping Theory. Apparently, they had found an answer to the losses and debts of the state-owned enterprises – a solution which was supposed to sort out everything else as well. The biggest and most important of the state-owned enterprises were going to remain the property of the people: as Jiang Zemin had correctly observed, how could China be a socialist country if it did not own the core means of its production? The smaller and less important ones were to be allowed to emancipate their minds by experimenting with ideas which had once been seen as monopolies of the capitalists, but which, since the unveiling of Deng Xiaoping Theory, were now understood to be available for anyone and everyone to use under the helpful mantra of the 'socialist market economy'. Still not quite clear about how exactly a socialist market economy was supposed to work (no one really was), most cadres decided that it was time to transform whatever state assets they could into more productive 'companies', with themselves and their families as shareholders.

For those on the podium of the Party (and all of those, friends and relations, who stood behind them), the stones were clearly lining up for a heavenly crossing of the river. Outside the Party, though, a number of intellectuals saw the stones as something more like rapids. Intellectual minds divided, as they had been dividing since Deng had declared the Four Modernisations (as indeed they had been dividing since the time of the shamans). On one side were those who had chosen to follow a Party which they felt had made mistakes, but was learning its way to a better future. On the other side, were those who wanted the freedom to look for other answers, whatever they might be.

The divide had been particularly acute after the shock of 1989 had been followed by Deng Xiaoping's 'southern holiday'. Many of those who, in the 1980s, had dreamt of Wei Jingsheng's Fifth Modernisation, had begun to think that they (and everyone else) might be better off following Deng and his mind-emancipating economic development: it might take a little longer to get to the ultimate utopia, they had reasoned, but Deng seemed to be on a genuinely progressive track and perhaps such an ambitious revolution really did need both a strong nation, and time. But as economic development had come to be raised to the pantheon of the gods, with every problem supposed to be solved with more economic development, more Party power and, where necessary, a dose of Monkey King logic, a number of intellectuals had increasingly argued that the Party was building up the same kind of 'human portents' which had brought down the First Qin Emperor and had been rocking the Chinese world ever since. Hard though it might be to achieve, they argued, there was no getting around the fact that for a state to be strong, heaven had to be able to listen to its people. Western democracy was clearly flawed but it was not the only model; and heaven could not listen to its people if its laws had been hijacked by a gun.

The critical logic of the questioners was hard to fault: having watched the fields of the revolutionary past being so quickly concreted over for cities of glittering dragons and trains, those left in the mud naturally wanted to know what had happened to the socialist dream. Deng had not only brought back the bourgeois bureaucracy which Mao had fought so hard to resist, but in the process he had managed to recreate the age-old, 'never-left-out' class at the top – the one that always managed to appropriate the profits of any opportunity that ever opened up. You could dress it up as black and white cats if you wanted, they argued, but China was now repeating old imperial lessons that it surely should have learnt by now. The floods of peasants migrating to Shenzhen and Shanghai were simply Hankou all over again. And the currents of cadres pursuing their own personal modernisations were nothing but reincarnations of nineteenth-century self-strengtheners without a belief in anything or anyone other than themselves. And as for 'modernisation' – well, that was nothing but a euphemism for the fact that the people's property (the state-owned factories and the land) was once again disappearing into private pockets as fast as it had ever done in imperial times before.

*　　*　　*

One mind that was particularly shocked at the speed with which Deng Xiaoping Theory was converting the Communist revolution into a new age of imperial feudalism was that of a forthright intellectual by the name of He Qinglian. A historian-economist editor of a Shenzhen newspaper, in 1998 she decided that it was time to call the colour of the cats. 'The bureaucrats', He Qinglian observed, 'are using their official positions to enclose a people's property that has been won with blood, and then siphoning off everything worth having into their own personal accounts.' 'In the cities', she added 'the People's Republic is being left with the cost of supporting the loss-making carcasses of factories, not to mention paying off workers who have lost their jobs, while Party-appointed cadres are taking the productive assets off the public stage and walked away with the profits.' 'Meanwhile, in the countryside', she continued, 'a new bourgeoisie of self-strengthening peasants has emerged, turning once-fertile fields into factories, and, just like the old scholar-merchants, floating themselves off to the cities to enjoy their new-found fortunes.'

Gathering her thoughts into a book, He Qinglian went on to set out her view that it was all rather reminiscent of seventeeth-century England, only with the added Chinese characteristics that the feudal families and secret societies were of an industrial scale. Red leaders and bureaucrats got rich, and in order to keep the gains coming, they passed on new opportunities to their children – even as they declined to open up the Party to any further reforms that would enable outside eyes to check the size and origins of their wealth. Prices of state assets were being fixed low enough to ensure that property could be transferred into their hands, and once that was accomplished, the prices were then being allowed to soar, so that profits cascaded into their own accounts. This left those who had not managed to make the same self-strengthening leaps – anyone who was not an official or related to an official by birth, marriage or mutual bonds of blood – out in the cold. The piles of profit were then being thrown at more of the fields to convert them into cities. As if all that wasn't bad enough, given that the fastest growing possibilities were on the coast, cash from all over the country was pouring into the cities of the east. With such an imbalance, even the ancient Nüwa would have struggled to keep the pillars of the skies from crashing down and dangerously tilting the country off its axis. Industries that Mao had painstakingly tried to rebalance across the country's vast geography were now crumbling. Indeed, the whole of China was being deliberately marched backwards towards a so-called 'primitive stage of capitalism' that would have shocked both Marx and Mao. Meanwhile, the Party was a secret society all of its own. Not surprisingly, China's people were becoming more unequal by the day. If someone did not pull up the never-left-out class by its roots, and soon, it would take all of China down with it, just as it had always done before.

Keen to retain the talents of the scientific intellectuals, Jiang Zemin was willing to let a few flowers bloom. But in the face of He Qinglian's assault, he retreated to the firmer footing of Leninist discipline, and took the opportunity to remind everyone that China was still a revolutionary socialist state under the constant threat of peaceful evolution from an ever-imperialist West. The verdict of history (according to Jiang Zemin, and now supported by the textbooks of the Patriotic Education Campaign) was clear. The Republic's flirtation with a national assembly in 1912 had been a disaster: pointless arrows had been hurled in every direction, Sun Yatsen's protégé-premier (Song Jiaoren) had fallen to an assassin's bullet, Yuan Shikai had dressed himself up for an imperial role, the provincial fiefdoms had protested, warlords had stepped into the breach, and then a nationalist Guomindang party had turned itself into a bunch of industrial-militarists and nearly sold the country up the capitalist river. Conversely, the Party's founders had sacrificed life and limb to fight the Guomindang. And in the face of appalling odds, they had eventually applied Marxist principles of socialism and Leninist principles of organisation to rescue China, not only from capitalism but from the imperial foreign powers with which capitalism so regularly marched. Times had been tough, some of the Party's bravest hearts had fallen, the people had had to eat a lot of bitterness, but with the road so painstakingly prepared by Mao, Deng Xiaoping had been able to arrive on the horseback of mind emancipation, and the possibilities of a socialist market economy had been miraculously discovered – on which the Party was now building a strong and productive socialist future. It was as worthy a triumph as any of those of the Great Men of the ancient past.

Having summed it all up, Jiang went on to declare that, against all the odds, the Party had succeeded in creating nothing less than a 'socialist spiritual civilization'. This having been so miraculously achieved, the ink-splashing intellectuals had a collective duty to craft their characters in ways that would promote the people's 'socialist harmony' – just as Mao Zedong had put it so clearly in Yan'an. The hurling of subjective opinions was putting everyone's future at risk: it was time to stop. The recklessly intellectual brushes were banned; and those who refused to listen to words of warning were threatened with the prospect of a stay in Beijing's Qincheng jail. He Qinglian remained at liberty, but her works were cut down to a more acceptable size, and the question of her future acquired a clear black mark.

As the recklessly intellectual brushes were learning their lessons, Jiang suggested that it was time for all of China to reconsider and reflect upon the better traditions of its Confucian past. Specifically those Confucian values of an orderly and productive *jia* family, guided by *li* ritual and *yi* integrity: principles that meant that every individual kept to their particular place, with the fatherly heads of everyone always at the helm. What China needed was more *gao suzhi*, high quality, individuals – people who would be scientifically fit to man the fortress of a spreading economic development, and thus to accept the Party's leadership of everyone into a harmoniously unquestioning future. What the country did *not* need were selfish individuals of the low-quality kind who could not stop themselves from asking questions – a recklessness which was a risk to all. Confucius had been on the right track when he had suggested that man should cultivate himself. The First Qin Emperor had also not been wrong: left to his own devices, man was an unreliable creature at best. Fortunately, socialism, with its emphasis on scientific facts and objective thought, was able to light the way. With enough 'high quality' people, the revolution would be unassailable. But let the weeds of the 'low-quality' people creep in, and heaven would fall down on everyone's heads.

The text clear, every institute of learning, high and low, was instructed in the critical importance of the *gao suzhi*, high quality goals. To help everyone remember how they were supposed to be thinking, four new 'must haves' were announced: lofty ideals, a sound morality, immaculate discipline and the knowledge required for a new productive world. All four had the historic endorsement of 'what Confucius must have thought'. Sadly misunderstood at various points in the revolution, Confucius' towering ancient mind was now to be recognised as one of the greatest the world had ever known. The direction clearly (re)set, newspapers and television channels were commanded to take up the task of shaping a higher quality of popular views. Advertising billboards – now (once again) gracing every city and would-be city – were instructed to inspire the higher quality virtues. As one expert on the idea so helpfully explained it: 'If a factory strives to produce high standard products, how much more important for a state to ensure that its people should meet high standards too.'

To make the point crystal clear, when ten thousand 'meditators' assembled in front of the gates of Zhongnanhai in 1999, Jiang Zemin met them with the full force of the state's security. A new generation of Taiping Great Peace fanatics, now inspired by the combined dreams of Buddhism and Daoism, they were men and women who had taken up the banner of a dharma wheel in action, calling themselves the *Falun Gong*. With most of them retired – and all of them seemingly determined to use their time to make some kind of point about a power greater than the Party, Jiang followed up the security with arrests. Declaring that China was under the threat of a new form of 'spiritual pollution', he then outlawed any and all superstitious forces that dared to challenge the revolutionary Democratic Dictatorship of the People with such a threat to the *gao suzhi* high quality of the people. Every channel of education and information, from schools to newspapers, television channels to museums, was mobilised. No one was left in any doubt as to his or her duty to shun the Falun Gong as well as any other 'other world' idea. The hundreds of thousands who failed in their duty found their way to one of the many *laogai*, reform-through-labour, camps, situated at the harshest edges of the Communist empire, not least in the deserts of the north-west.

* * *

In 2001, the historian-economist He Qinglian stood up again: this time arguing that the state was not a god, and economics was about subjective human beings rather than objective science. With the forces of the Party now very clear about the risks of spiritual pollution, and with her own card clearly marked, He Qinglian found herself under the sharp chill of Mao's long shadow. Unable to keep her silence, she left her homeland for the 'lower quality' country of America, where she could safely speak her mind. Once again, the intellectuals divided. Some decided to follow her, if not out of the country then at least into the retreat of more academic studies. Some determined to keep up the battle, but to take a bit more care in what and how they wrote. The greater number, however, decided that, with the Party's position so clear, and with spreading economic development now beginning to look as if it could work, it might finally be time to take up Deng's ideas on mind emancipation and start to think about how productivity might be profitably pursued under the leadership of the Party.

Among those who decided to apply their talents to the market, many recalled the early days of Deng, when a seasoned Party veteran had compared the creatio of a socialist market economy to building a birdcage. Explaining that free market principles were the bird, and the socialist plan was the cage, the Party veteran had gone on to note that it was all about the physics of flight, and the structural engineering of cages. Build the cage too small, and the bird would not be able to fly at all. Make the bars of the cage too wide, and the bird would fly away and leave it empty. This was obviously a science that would require truly great minds. Ready to serve the people, the market intellectuals flocked to the side of Deng's shaman successor, Zhu Rongji, still premier, and to the Communist dynasty's formal resurrection of the ancient Hall of Light: the 'National Development and Reform Commission'.

Now reassuringly supported by a *gao suzhi* body of loyal intellectuals, Jiang Zemin and his Politburo were able to get back to the business of crossing the river by feeling for stones. But as Zhu Rongji and his new disciples tried to work out how the socialist market economy would function, it was soon as clear as ever that nothing was going to be easy. Comparing the sorry situation of the state-owned factories (iron rice bowls, mountains of unwanted production, towering debts, and now losing even more money than ever) with the rising energies of the newly independent enterprises, they decided that the only hope was to move forward faster: get on with splitting up the state-owned enterprises, sell the loss-makers to any buyers they could find, and rescue those which were too important to give away. Wherever possible, this should be achieved by learning from the Western science of markets that helpfully seemed to say that it was always better to use other people's money (with Hong Kong's stock markets offering an obvious pool of funds). While they were at it, they should also offer the best of the new private spirits an invitation to join the Party. 'Capitalists into the Communist Party?' a quick left-wing chorus shrilled. 'Not capitalists', explained Jiang Zemin patiently, 'entrepreneurs – who, just like the cats, can always be black or white'.

In 2001, the entrepreneurs were welcomed into the Party as 'advanced productive forces', to clapping applause. Whispering offstage, a muttering of low quality voices noted that it was not really much of a change: given that it was the officials and their families who had been buying up the people's assets and turning them to a profit, the Party was already awash with entrepreneurs. Oblivious to the humour, Jiang Zemin stood up to note that, with all of the complications involved in building a socialist market economy, the Party ought to extend Deng Xiaoping's estimate of how long it would take to get to socialism: add another fifty years, say 2100. After all, in the greater scheme of five thousand years of history, being becalmed in the capitalist stage for another half century was surely not too much of a price to pay for the ultimate utopian ideal. Other muttering voices (of the lowest quality) suggested that far from marching towards a Marxist utopia, the Party seemed to be privatising *itself*.

* * *

In October 2002, the third generation of the Communist dynasty gathered again, this time to launch the Party's sixteenth Congress. Once again, Jiang

Zemin advanced to the centre stage of the Great Hall of the People to announce the state of the nation for the next five years. After two terms of five years at the helm, he was also going to welcome a new 'fourth generation' of Communist dynasty leadership to the top.

Accepting the praise of a grateful Party – as much for his helpful clarification of Communism as for the powerful forces of production unleashed – Jiang then handed over the general secretaryship of the Party to his vice-president and fellow engineer, Hu Jintao.

Before leaving the podium, however, Jiang took the opportunity to declare that 'the strategic adjustment of the economic structure has been crowned with success'. Couched in such objective terms, it was not immediately obvious to everyone in the audience what he meant – certainly not to those watching from home. But the word 'success' was a clue, as was the uniform ripple of applause that seemed to confirm that this must be something good. Continuing, Jiang Zemin noted that there were still some problems: a countryside that had decoupled from the cities; a western hinterland that had somehow got separated from the coastal east; a few people who did not have a job; and some inconvenient 'climate events' that nature was inconsiderately throwing in everyone's way. The problems deftly filed into individual boxes, Jiang Zemin then went on to restate the *jingji fazhan* spreading economic development cornerstone of Deng Xiaoping Theory. To which he added, with a final revolutionary flourish worthy of Deng himself, that the Party would now proceed to deliver a quadrupling of socialist production by 2020. With obedient Party clapping ringing in his ears, Jiang then unveiled his own addition to the pantheon of Chinese Communist Party thought: the Party should 'represent advanced social productive forces; represent the progressive course of China's advanced culture; represent the fundamental interests of the majority'. With the artistic elegance of an engineer, he skilfully named his contribution the 'Three Represents'.

Those still watching on their televisions at home were, by now, scratching their heads – with most deciding that the 'quality' of their minds was obviously not high enough to keep up. Looking closely at the screen, though, it seemed that even those sitting on the highest-quality Party seats were struggling to see the point: Three Represents ? Representing who? And representing what? Some decided that it must be about representing everybody and everything. Others said it was particularly about representing new classes of entrepreneurs and intellectuals (those who understood that working with one's mind was not about asking dangerous metaphysical questions of 'why', but about responsibly focusing on the essential scientific point of 'how'). Yet others said that it was really all about creating that Western idea of a large middle-class of people who could hold everything together while the top was still feeling for the stones. 'Isn't class struggle a thing of the past?' asked some of the more confused minds. 'That's right', replied others who had been quicker to get the knack of the new: 'this is class without the struggle.'

*   *   *

When, in the spring of 2003, Hu Jintao joined Jiang Zemin on the podium of the annual meeting of the National People's Congress as the newly appointed general secretary of the Party and president of the country it was clear to all that something was missing. Jiang had passed on the leadership of Party and State – but kept the all-important command of the Central Military Commission under his own personal wing. With only the most tenuous of links to Deng Xiaoping, and none at all to the princelings, it was clear that Hu was going to have a struggle on his hands to wrest the final and most important piece of the Party's power from his predecessor. But observing Hu's relative youth, noting his engineering background and decades of work in some of China's toughest inland provinces (not least Tibet at the time of Tiananmen), and looking at the increasingly worrying state of the peasants, some thought that even though the withheld leadership of the military was a problem, there was a lot that Hu could do to get things on a smoother track – particularly in the countryside.

Over the previous few years, while the advanced forces of production had been speeding ahead in the rising cities of the coastal east, peasants in the listing landlocked west of the country had been floundering in the mud. Anyone who could, had smuggled their way through the border controls of *hukou*, and rushed to the coastal east. Willing to eat any bitterness in order to keep aged parents and young children afloat in village homes, the riskiest of jobs had been taken with the poorest of pay. In some provinces and districts, so many had left their homes that entire villages had been hollowed out, leaving an 'army' of the oldest and the youngest to keep the countryside going.

Not all of those in the countryside had left, however. Some (particularly those able to serve the local officials) had stayed to see what more might be done with Deng's Monkey King logic, transforming any remaining relics of the socialist landscape into an entrepreneurially personal profit. Rights which

411

the peasants had been given to 'use' the land for their individual household responsibility plots had been a particular object of interest: thirty years long, and with any underlying ownership being held by the Party state, they offered obvious opportunities to persuade village heads and their committees that the land which the peasants were 'using' should be redistributed to a more productive cause. Of course, the peasants were complaining. But as Deng had explained so carefully, and Jiang Zemin had confirmed, this was all for the far greater cause of an eventual (now 2100) socialist utopia for all. Meanwhile, the local officials had been making contributions to their own self-strengthening treasuries by raising taxes, levying fees, and looking for any other possibilities to convert the public assets of their neighbourhoods into a personally private wealth.

Transfers of land rose to the skies, and cash began to circulate on a scale not known since the rise of the self-strengtheners at the end of the nineteenth century – or the early trading fortunes of the Ming. As in the past, the circulation was largely limited to the hands of those whose official positions gave them the power to approve a transfer, including of course, those of the officials' families and friends. Obviously, one could not expect the peasants to understand the greater importance of the exchange, and heaven forbid that anyone should see bundles of cash changing hands and get the wrong idea. Scratching their heads for a way to trade land for cash without the risk of inconvenient questions, some suggested that a solution might be found in the popular game of *mah jong*: with everyone in China a skilled player, it was just a matter of a would-be buyer intentionally losing, and then showers of cash could be transferred from one playing hand to another.

As the officials, the self-strengtheners, the families and the friends pulled their chairs forward for the game, chill winds began to blow across the precarious fortunes of the fields. With the communes long gone, and modernisation racing ahead all around them, the peasants were struggling to survive. Lucky ones found themselves staring at a stubborn soil that, after decades, if not centuries, of exhaustion, was once again failing. Unlucky ones were evicted to make way for a factory or a town. Educating children had become an unaffordable dream: even if a school had been built in a neighbourhood, admission and attendance required a host of supplementary fees. The cost of admission to anything but the barest of hospitals was a crisis that would always plunge a family into debt. And whenever an official knocked on the door, everyone knew that it could only mean yet another demand for a tax. Poor, sick and desperate, once again, as in the imperial past, the peasants began to band together in brotherhoods. And, once again, they found themselves confronting the organised forces of the officials and self-strengtheners: battalions of thugs who had been deployed for centuries to keep the countryside under control. Now, however, the thugs were operating not under the name of an emperor, but under the banner of a Party order which Deng Xiaoping had called 'stability maintenance'. This was no imperial tyranny but a single heart, beating as one, with anyone whose heart wanted to think otherwise necessarily needing to be 'harmonised.' Any and all opposition was just an irresponsible splash of spiritually polluted minds. And, as in the Great Leap Forward, anyone who dreamt of smuggling a hopeful plea for help out to a higher authority would find that it was either buried or returned with a punishment.

By 1999, things had already become so bad that a rare good official, by the name of Li Changping, took his career into his hands and wrote a letter to the premier, Zhu Rongji. 'The peasants' life is so hard', wrote Li Changping, 'the countryside is so poor, the soil is in such a desperate state; the township governments have not only bankrupted themselves but the peasants; and the peasants are being held hostage to the rampant ambitions and buried debts of local officials who have modernised nothing but themselves.' 'It is', he declared, 'time to tell the truth.' Investigation teams were sent down to Li Changping's particular corner of the countryside, but the cats had scarpered, leaving only a few black rats of thugs to take the blame. Published by a brave southern newspaper, however, Li's letter began to circulate widely, and in 2002 it was converted into a wildly popular book entitled *Telling the Truth to the Premier*. As the countryside stayed in the mud, other reports began to rise: some so much blacker than Li Changping's that no one in the Party wanted them to see the light of day.

By the time that Jiang Zemin finally stepped down as general secretary and president in March 2003, the state of the peasants in the countryside was so desperate that hope was daring to spring. Surely the Party would do something to save the peasants who, after all, had been the ones who were supposed to have won the revolution in the first place. Like a loyal son, rising to the pinnacle of power, Hu Jintao rolled out Deng Xiaoping Theory in deference to the greatest of the recent ancestors, and the Three Represents in an act of filial piety to his 'godfather' Jiang Zemin. Hu lingered longest on the last of Jiang Zemin's trinity: 'the fundamental interests of the vast majority of the people'. Deng was right, declared Hu, to recommend the Four Modernisations; but everyone should always remember Mao's

413

two revolutionary musts: 'modesty and prudence without arrogance' and 'plain living, hard struggle'. Beside him on the podium, newly appointed as premier, was the kind face of Wen Jiabao: a geologist by profession, but far more striking as the man who looked like everyone's favourite grandfather. Once again, some began to dream of snow in summer.

No sooner had Hu and Wen taken the reins, than it was clear that heaven had already secretly struck its moral judgement on the events of the recent past. A mysterious and deadly virus had been spreading across the countryside; flagrantly disregarding the formalities of *hukou*, it was now jumping from the countryside directly into the cities. There had been whispers about a strange disease among the peasants for quite a while, but those in the higher-up towns and cities had been too busy burying facts to listen. Already in 2002, the virus had gripped the lungs of a number of southern peasants, squeezing them to an early death. While some brave hospital brushes had reported the cases, local officials had buried the news along with the bodies – worried about 'stability maintenance', in light of the fact that many of the dead had been turned away because they could not afford the deposits required for a bed.

In early 2003, quiet burials had become a little more difficult when visiting doctors from Hong Kong became infected with the virus, and carried it back to Hong Kong, where it had been given a name: SARS. Then in early April, less than a month after Hu Jintao had assumed the mantle of power, the virus suddenly jumped all boundaries of brush control when a reckless doctor of some seniority (retired, of course) informed the television networks of the capital and Hong Kong that the virus had taken hold of hospitals in Beijing. The origins of the infectious agent, it turned out, were to be found in an ever-expanding population of pigs and poultry reared on tiny plots of land by peasants who, looking for their own place on the self-strengthening bandwagon, had been trying to keep up with the cities' rising demand for ever-greater quantities of pork and duck. Having made the leap across the species, from there, the virus had jumped but a few inches to the peasants themselves who, rearing as much livestock as they could on tiny patches of land, had been living cheek-by-jowl alongside their charges. Whether or not SARS was a strike of heavenly anger, it was clearly a sharp rebuke to Deng Xiaoping Theory and its central idea of spreading economic development, supported by two basic points: one of which (mind emancipation) had encouraged everyone to do whatever they could to get rich; the other (the Four Cardinal Principles) had ensured that the Party's powers were beyond the questions of any human voice.

Shocked at a natural disaster that was clearly man-made, Hu Jintao and his premier, Wen Jiabao, immediately launched a 'People's War' against the latest heavenly disorder. Thousands were quarantined: whole villages in the countryside, and entire apartment blocks in the most affected cities. Everyone's productivity dropped. Some of the most advanced productive forces railed against the interruption to socialist growth, while a number of left-leaning intellectuals argued that it was obviously not only time to slow the pace down to something a little more human, but it was also time for the Party and its state to start listening to the people at large.

The war on SARS was eventually won. But when the (official) numbers were counted, five thousand Chinese had been infected, and three hundred and fifty lives had been lost (not including another two hundred and ninety-nine others who had died on the outlying rock of Hong Kong). The country's socialist civilisation had been humiliated. Hu and Wen stood up to say that Deng's *jingji fazhan* economic development remained the primary goal, but that the territory over which it was to be pursued would now be firmly expanded to include the countryside. Henceforward, the peasants were to be at the forefront of the Party's paternal concerns. At the end of 2003, Hu Jintao went one step further, quoting the words of one of Confucius' greatest disciples to say that 'the people are the root of any power'. Now seemingly reading a lot of the classical texts, a year later Hu Jintao went on to embrace Confucius outright. Once banned, the ancient scholar was now well on his way to becoming part of the Communist dynasty's pantheon. Quoting from the texts ascribed to the highest master of imperial thought, Hu declared that not only should society be ordered, but it should be a harmonious whole as well.

While Hu Jintao was reading his books, two recklessly intellectual brushes in the provinces decided to travel across the countryside and see for themselves what was going on. Gathering up their life savings, they travelled across fifty villages in one of China's poorest provinces (Anhui). Their social survey completed, they then wrote it up in a book entitled: *An Investigation into the Lives of Chinese Peasants*. The lines of their text described in painstaking detail the taxes and fees which were cannibalising the peasants; its pages bled with the stories of their miseries. Like sheep under the power of official wolves, the peasants were being ravaged by taxes, raped by transfers of their land, and whenever they dared to protest, they were being arrested so that the stability of the socialist order could remain undisturbed. Thoroughly grounded in objective research but outrageously subjective in spirit, the book spread like wildfire: initially openly, and then, when the organising principles of socialist harmony banned its polluting poison, in the underground market of ideas.

Over the next three years, Hu Jintao and Wen Jiabao applied their energies to improving the lot of the peasants. Seeing the obvious solution as more economic development, plans were announced for a 'new socialist countryside'. Roads were quickly forged in every direction, in the hope that blazing dragons would follow in their wake. Power stations were swiftly raised for everyone's electrification. Schools and hospitals were ordered to be built, immediately. Taxes on peasants were to be cut – with the costs of the cuts to be covered by the local governments. Meanwhile, 'stability maintenance' was to remain the order of the day. Commanded to deliver results in double-quick time (and not sure where to get the cash from), many of the village heads and their committees looked at the land use rights which were floating above the fields, and decided that their only choice was to sacrifice a few more peasant plots to generate money that could be used for the greater good of all. Others, with even more emancipated minds, decided that it was time not just to sell a few fields, but to jump right into the sea of the city, and get into the business of building towns. In terms of getting rich quick, it seemed a reasonable solution: with cities now treasures of industrial production, and comsumption over the last twenty years, the act of building offices and shopping malls had become an important source of high productive value – not to mention the added productive benefits of building roads and accompanying airports.

Before long, village heads and local mayors were becoming construction entrepreneurs, rewarded for city-raising success; the countryside was on the move. The more ambitious villages became small towns, and the more ambitious small towns set off on their way to becoming bigger towns (if not small cities). Every now and again, a growing village or town would find itself colliding with a bigger city. When that happened, the bigger city just expanded its boundaries – and the price of everyone's land went up.

But not everyone hit the jackpot. A lot of the small towns remained works in progress: sky-rising pavilions in the middle of nowhere, they hung, suspended, somewhere between a dream and a nightmare.

*   *   *

Meanwhile up in the capital city of all, Beijing had beaten the rest of the world in a bid to host the 2008 Olympics. A model for the rest of the country's cities since Mao, every possible productive energy was being harnessed to turn the luck of Beijing's Olympic draw into a socialist triumph that others could copy. With so much to do, and so little time in which to do it, the urban planning bureau, once preoccupied with protecting the flight paths of ancestral spirits and still stuck in a dusty corner, was easily overlooked. Greater men, clear about the need to build a lot of storeys, looked at the big old chequerboard squares of the old Inner and Imperial cities and offered them up to self-strengthening enterprises, state and private, who could develop them, one vast block at a time. Architects seemed an unnecessary complication: hard to find, they were easily replaced with a 'cut and paste' click of a mouse to reproduce the same building over and over again, with a thoughtful adjustment of the 'hat' on top, just so that everything didn't look *exactly* the same. Roads were raced into existence; and as more and more cars began to appear, rings of roads were wrapped around the city to try and speed things up. Meanwhile, water and power, essential for both production and consumption, were assumed to be as endless as the heaven that obviously supplied them: a heaven that would also naturally clean up the resulting waste as well.

Inconvenient planning and architectural voices silenced, clouds were now pierced on a regular basis, with any and all of the spirits' ancient flight paths permanently cancelled. The new ring roads notwithstanding, roads spread, and then jammed. While profits tantalisingly beckoned at every turn, tempers began to fray. Once-distant villages were swept into the city, ten at a time. Distances between everywhere got so big that bicycles could not possibly keep up. Still, new cars poured on to exhausted roads, ten thousand by the month – with each new ring road inconveniently creating a whole new city within the city, even as the original Beijing was still struggling to find itself. More productivity, and more people, needed more water and power. But the wells of the city had long ago run dry, and more power would require new power stations, with new power stations requiring a lot more coal.

As the capital grew like topsy, more and more hands were needed on deck. The most preferred were the revolutionary kind: those willing to work for the socialist dream, with only the most modest demands for cash. With everyone in the city jumping into the rushing sea of enterprise, though, such revolutionary hands were now in short supply. Out in the Communist countryside, though, there was still a seemingly endless reserve of peasants, all desperate for a city job. Equipped with their labour, any city would be able to rise without bounds. More *hukou* barriers were temporarily bent, and the dust and smoke of destruction and construction soon filled the air. Office blocks, residential compounds and shopping malls were anchored in every imaginable spot; pavements were dismissed as a waste of space; and the old willow trees that had wept across the past were liberated from their roots.

By 2006, hundreds of cities across the country, new and old, were racing to follow Beijing to the dizzying heights of a 'global city'. No one was very clear what exactly a 'global city' was but, copying Beijing, one couldn't go far wrong. Up and down the country, no matter how far away they were from the capital, ambitious mayors threw themselves across every imaginable river to get to the global city dream as quickly as they could. The people's air, land and water – not to mention the peasants – were all commandeered for the cause.

* * *

Watching the rise of the cities, and the spread of re-organised state-owned enterprises (many of which, now flushed with the cash of offshore markets, were expanding so fast that the Party's government departments were struggling to keep up with them) more reckless brushes began to protest. China was returning to the world of feudal lords that had collapsed the ancient state of Zhou. Whether they were the offices of city mayors or the towers of now-revived state-owned corporations (or indeed the palaces of those whose wealth had rocketed with the profits pocketed by sending public assets to market in Hong Kong), the headquarters had been commandeered by the same never-left-out class that always seemed to come out ahead. Pointing to the clutch of names at the top, a bunch of particularly irresponsible brushes splashed their ink at the rise of a red aristocracy whose families had captured the people's wealth.

The blackest of the brushes were harmonised with jail sentences; and a popular intellectual magazine that told a more subjective version of the Party's history found itself relegated to the bin. But it was not long before the ripples of anger repeated themselves within the Party itself. Left-leaning East Winds rose up again, shouting that the Party had gone so far and so fast that it had given up the hard-won revolutionary gains, and was handing the country back to the Western imperial capitalists. West Winds – now armed with the riches of socialist success, and anticipating the benefits of a continued national strengthening – rose up in even bigger gales to argue that the only way to solve any of the problems was to keep moving forward. Faster.

In October 2007, the Party gathered once again, this time to convene its seventeenth Congress. Like his ancestors before him, Hu Jintao faced the not uncommon revolutionary challenge of presenting a united Party front to the masses, even as war had broken out within the Party's own ranks. Having scoured the classics of the Party's texts, Hu delivered a report that was crafted in the most objective and harmonious of terms. Socialist culture was thriving, he reported; the people as a whole had a *xiaokang*, relatively comfortable, standard of living. To which he added that there were, of course, problems to be addressed. Carefully listed in the dull language of the Party's objective thought, the problems did not, however, seem to be so grave that they would stir up any human portents. 'Some' Party cadres were not quite straight – but Hu explained that they were only a 'small number'. All in all, socialism was still defined by Deng's ideas of 'productivity, nation-building and living standards'; the route to success was still Deng's central point of *jingji fazhan* economic development and his twin pillars of the Four Cardinal Principles (by now fairly easily summarised as 'leadership by a single top-down Party mind') and mind emancipation. And Jiang Zemin's Three Represents were still there to lead the way.

To these foundations, Hu Jintao added a new principle that ought to finally fix any residual theoretical problems with a great advance in Marxist-Leninist-Mao Zedong thinking. The new principle, Hu declared, would 'take development as its essence, put the people first as its core; take comprehensive, balanced and sustainable development as its basic requirement; and employ overall consideration as its fundamental approach'. Its name, Hu announced triumphantly, was 'scientific development'. While the trained minds in the Great Hall of the People managed to keep their eyes wide open, most of those sitting in the aisles of their television homes couldn't help but fall asleep.

Oblivious to the fading energies of his audience, Hu then went on to point out the revolutionary virtues of the new principle. Unwavering in its pursuit of a socialist society that would realise the full potential of man, 'scientific development' was quintessentially Marxist. Tightly managed, it was also a beacon of Leninism. Putting, as it obviously did, the revolutionary triumph of the Chinese people at the forefront, it was also pure Mao.

For those concerned with theory, the idea of 'scientific development' seemed to have successfully managed to say something, while leaving the disputed terrain of the past largely unchanged. For those concerned with the practical world (whether inside the Party or outside), its value depended on where they were sitting, in what, to quote the historian-economist He Qinglian, was rapidly becoming a 'runaway train'. In first class, the Party, flanked by its advanced productive forces of entrepreneurs and scientific economists, was settling down for a comfortable journey. In the soft seats, the supporting middle classes could take confidence in the fact that the train would keep going long enough to get them to their destinations. On the hard seats, the lower classes, struggling to make ends meet, were getting anxious about the rattling. And anyone who had lost their job, or who had smuggled themselves into a city with nothing to call their own, was either clinging on at the *hukou*-less edges, or (in the case of those whose land had been sold from under their feet) had already been thrown off the train.

*　　　*　　　*

On 12 May 2008, obviously frustrated, heaven expressed its loudest opinion yet. As Beijing sat down to an early afternoon, somewhere off in rural Sichuan an earthquake shook with such a tremor that even the capital's seats moved. For a cluster of remote rural Sichuan counties, the floors of their lives completely disappeared. Premier Wen Jiabao and the People's Liberation Army advanced to the front. Lei Feng-like heroes were filmed in action (even truer heroes appeared in their thousands, but not belonging to the army, they were missed by the cameras). Thousands of survivors were rescued; but many more thousands died. As the dust began to settle, it seemed that the greatest losses of life and limb had been in the buildings put up by those with official connections: the schools and the hospitals raised in the rush for the 'new socialist countryside' – the ones where the profits had been pocketed by local self-strengtheners. It was even rumoured that a stubborn and subjectively-minded geologist had sent a warning of an earthquake to the offices at the top; but as with so many other reckless letter-writers, his words had hit the dust. Once-tamed brushes began to dip themselves into the internet ink, posting daily updates of the names of the dead, and offering a voice to families whose children had been lost to the corruption of socialist speed. The people's *Xinhua*, New China, news agency reported over sixty-nine thousand dead, and the forces of socialist harmony began to roll into controlling action. Everywhere, heads were dipped in sorrow; hearts wept with grief.

As the months passed, Deng's glittering train picked up its speed once again, and attention returned to Beijing, where, at eight p.m. on the eighth day of the eighth month of 2008, the city exploded. Across the world, human breaths were whisked away as the Olympic Games opened with the words of Confucius, and the greatest man-made spectacle on earth unfolded. Fireworks put the footprints of mankind in the sky. Carefully choreographed dancers stepped out images of China's greatest inventions, from the Confucian ideal to paper. The planet appeared as a vast metal ball, covered with acrobats who, with a quick cloud-somersault tumbling, transformed the whole into a glowing Chinese lantern: red, of course. By the end of the Opening Ceremony, the Confucian principles of heavenly order had been displayed for all to see. Over the following weeks, almost every symbol of heaven-sent luck and Great Man-delivered triumph was unleashed; medals cascaded from the skies.

By the end of the games, the socialist market economy seemed to have delivered the kind of golden success which other countries could only dream of – with the point now deftly made that such successes were obviously built on the innate wisdom of a heavenly civilisation burnished over thousands of years.

Within a month, the truth of that point seemed to be spectacularly confirmed by the shock of an astonishing collapse in the capitalist numbers of the Western world. 'A global economic crisis' according to the headlines of the foreign papers, echoed by the shaking voices of Western bankers who seemed to be at the forefront of the crash. 'Global?' asked the Party – 'surely, what you really mean is just "the West".'

CHAPTER 2

NATURE'S TRAILS

The world is a holy vessel. Let him who
tampers with it, beware.

Dao De Jing, Laozi (sixth century BCE)

The wind and the rain had been pouring in all day. By the early August afternoon of 1975, the skies were so dark that it could have been dusk. At midnight, the heavens above seemed to have turned into a storm of so much water that it could have been day. But by then, no one in the old Henan district of *Yicheng* was thinking much beyond sandbags. Battered by winds, drenched by the rain, a place of desperate men, women and children stood shoulder to shoulder in a race against a tide of water that was lapping at the top of the local Banqiao dam. Higher and higher they piled their sandbags, but as high as they went, the water just kept rising. At one a.m., the sky suddenly cleared and the stars emerged. An excited spirit shouted that the waters were receding, Yicheng was saved! And then, within the time that it took for a head to turn, a flash of lightening struck from above, a stroke of thunder clapped, and another voice screamed the last words that Yicheng would ever hear: '*he long dao le!* the river dragon has come!' Rearing its head as high as the sky, a mountain of water roared across the dam, and flung itself down upon everyone's heads.

For eighty-five thousand souls, the world came to an end that night. The river dragon did not blink. Breaching banks without a pause, its heavy coils rolled like tides across the fields of the wider land. Surrounding towns and villages became instant islands in an ocean; lower-lying settlements were swiftly swallowed into watery graves. Finding themselves afloat, hundreds of thousands of surviving souls clung to passing branches and gripped the tips of roofs which had suddenly become rafts. Over the days that followed, marooned others clung to life by stripping trees of all their bark and chewing on the leaves, while those afloat snatched at passing pumpkins and floating pigs. Then, under the hot August sun, the watery fevers followed. When the river dragon finally departed two weeks later, he left the sacrifices of one hundred thousand corpses rotting in sodden fields now baking in the heat. Cut adrift from the rest of the earth, eleven million people lost their homes, with hundreds of thousands ravaged either by the following fevers or the poisons of the floating food.

Henan hearts never forgot the river dragon's rage, but the Party's Propaganda Department ensured that few others in the Yellow Emperor's lands would ever even know that it had happened. A miracle of socialist construction, the Banqiao dam had been built in 1951, to hold back the waters of even a one-in-a-thousand years appearance of the river dragon: an 'iron dam' which even the wildest forces of nature would not be able to move. But the dragon which appeared on the 'qi-ba-wu' seventh day of the eighth month of 1975, had been unmoved. Counting time by the cosmic calendar, he had been asleep for the last two thousand years.

*   *   *

Water: the first of the 'five elements'; the stuff of the rains and the rivers which had been the most constant threads in the twisting life and death fortunes of the Yellow River's people and their heartlands. When ancient dry days had turned to cloudless months, or when deluges of storms had washed the river over its banks, hunger had gnawed at the feet of the black-haired people, and anxious emperors had summoned their shamans. The shamans had then consulted the oracle bones for news of heaven's intentions, and raised sacrifices to the skies. And when the monstrous Gong Gong had reared the river up, flooding the fields beyond human endurance, the ancient Great Men, Yao and Shun, had not only carried on the sacrifices (including appeals to the ancestral Yellow Emperor) but also dyked and dammed as hard as they could to protect the heavenly lands. And then Yu the Great had spent thirteen years surveying the vast twists and turns of all of the rivers. Tracing their terrains right up to the spirits of their mountain sources, he not only charted every depth but classified the surrounding soils. The survey completed, Yu had then divided the lands into nine provinces (each with their own specific sets of commands for taming the disorders of nature) and turned the ordering of the Yellow River's heartlands into the heavenly duty of man.

Such was the determination of Yu the Great, that the Yellow River had indeed bided its banks for a while, as had the smaller rivers which washed across the expanding territories of the Yellow Emperor's people. But within a hundred years, river dragons were rearing their heads again, with those of the Yellow River being particularly troublesome. Hiding in the muddy waters from which the river took its 'yellow' name, they seemed to see its sandy banks as nothing more than an invitation to jump as high as they could. Looking more closely at the depths, though, and listening to travelling tales of higher mountain waters which flowed as clear as a mirror, later minds would wonder whether the dragons themselves might have been composed not of water but of silt: the silt of the rich yellow earth of the plains through whose plains the river flowed.

Certainly, grains of sandy soil had been swept along by the river's waters like a harvest, settling on to the bed of the Yellow River that simply rose and rose. And from time to time, the settled grains reached such a height that the river was forced to change its course completely. Oddly enough, this happened particularly in those places where a lot of trees had been cut down, or where the natural course of the river took a sharp turn. As successive emperors peered at the problem, some (particularly those of the shaman tradition that insisted on looking at the patterns of the earth, rather than serving the taming will of man) had wondered if it would not be better to let the rivers wander at their own will, possibly even letting the trees stay rooted in the ground as well. But the advising scholars of the emperors were of the opinion that dykes and dams were a better proposition – even though everyone agreed, among themselves and with the peasants, that it would take a Great Man Emperor indeed for the waters of the Yellow River ever to run clear.

Centuries, if not millennia, had passed; the people and their harvesting fields had grown and spread. Forests had fallen to timber, and the earth had dried. Some of the Yellow Emperor's people decided to push south into other lands, looking for more water (and more fields). By the time that the First Qin Emperor had unified the world of the Warring States in 221 BCE, the lands that barbarians were beginning to call 'China' had stretched to embrace many more rivers than the Yellow River alone. Some were simply tributary branches of bigger rivers. Others seemed to fall from the mountain heights of newly conquered central lands. One was a torrent of a force that seemed to roar out of mysterious mountain reaches in a higher west, before meandering across lands that had once been home to the once-independent states of Ba, Shu and Chu – renamed by Qin as the heavenly provinces of Sichuan and Hunan.

Almost as great as the Yellow River, this mighty torrential force had come to be known by two names. To those who lived their lives along the banks of its higher reaches, it was the *chang jiang*, eternal river. To those who lived in the fishing villages around its mouth on the eastern sea (including the early village of Shanghai), it was the Yangzi: said to have been so named after the glittering Yangzhou city under whose shadow those villages sat. While the lands through which the river passed were not composed of quite the same fine yellow soil as that of the northern heartlands, as forest after forest had been felled to make way for new fields, and as the roots of surrounding trees had shrivelled and died, the earth had begun to float like dust into its waters. Nobody called it 'yellow', but the mud was clear for all to see. And every now and then, just like the Yellow River, watery dragons would also leap out of their beds and change the course of its journey. Emperor after emperor would try to tame the Yangzi, as they would try to change the course of almost every other river that washed across their lands. And while they were taming, here and there, they added a few imperial refinements, in the form of canals carved into the conquered southern lands, so that the many smaller rivers of this new region could be joined up into rising tides of trade. Eventually, in the early 600s, the Sui had completed their Grand Canal, uniting the original farming north – now a little dry and unadventurous – to the newer south, a place where rain and rivers had always flowed like silver, and where quick hands readily turned the treasures of nature into a glittering cornucopia of crafts.

Hardly surprisingly, in both north and south, while emperors tamed and quick hands crafted, the building, repairing and re-building of dykes, dams, irrigating ditches and various riverine diversions became part of the labouring peasant life. As natural as tilling the fields, felling forests, and soldiering in wars, they were tasks like any others, requiring a back-breaking labour which depended on nothing more nor less than a *chi ku* ability to eat the bitterness of suffering and pain.

By the time Mao Zedong ascended to the eaves of the Gate of Heavenly Peace in 1949, nearly four thousand years of river-taming had passed. But after the more recent decades of ravaging warlords and civil war (not to mention a war with Japan fought on Chinese land), once-settled peasants had been transformed into desperate wandering refugees, and river dragons had been left not only in charge of their own destinies, but those of the surrounding fields as well. Dykes, dams and irrigating ditches had fallen into disarray; waterways had become clogged with the debris of everyone's battles; and rivers that had breached their banks were left to pursue new channels. The fields (heavily contested prizes of war endlessly trampled on by troops of varying colours) turned to mud. Wherever possible, peasants, dependent on the earth for their food, made attempts to make do and mend. But working on their own, against all the odds of warring man and nature, they often struggled in vain.

Looking at the Great Man task of taming nature, like every emperor before him, Mao was quick to see his duty. He was also quick to see how, in a wider world that followed the logic of Darwin's idea of the survival of the fittest, his responsibility for the land dovetailed neatly with his duty to build a nation which would not only *survive* but which would find its place at the top of the tree of the world's fittest states. Declaring that China would leap ahead of Britain's steel production in fifteen years, Mao announced that the tamed forces of nature would deliver the energy on which the productive triumph would rise. Washed with obedient waters, the fields were to yield vast harvests; fired by the torrential power of fast-descending rivers, electricity would fuel the furnaces from which the necessary steel would be produced to deliver a great industrial future: a Great Leap Forward.

Gathering his people together for what he saw as a new campaign in the war of orderly man against the *ziran* wilderness of nature, Mao had organised the peasants into armies of communes, each divided into companies, platoons and brigades. Then, in 1958, declaring that 'great courage brings forth great yields', he had unleashed the full force of his peasant troops against the combined challenge of the rivers and the fields. Looking at the rivers, his mind had then turned, like the minds of all Great Men, to the essential matter of dams.

The raising of electric power from water, along with the watering of fields and their protection from floods, was a critical pillar of the earliest

426

planning. To assist the Party in its cause, Mao had early on called upon the skills of the big Russian brother whose engineers had built a raft of dams across the rivers of its own (Russian) Far East, stretched across Siberia. In 1955, however, keen to show that the younger Communist brother could also raise an engineering triumph, Mao announced a proposal truly worthy of a Chinese Great Man: Sanmenxia, the Three Gate Gorge. A parade of forty-six cascading iron walls to be strung along the Yellow River, its mighty centrepiece was a damming of the 'three gates' of a mountain gorge that, legend had it, Yu the Great had once opened with an axe. Once completed, billions of kilowatts of electrical energy would be unleashed for productive purpose, and millions of Chinese lives would be protected from the periodic rages of the watery dragons. There was even a promise that the ancient prediction – that the waters of the Yellow River would run clear when a Great Man ruled China – would finally come true. In the process, one million mu (670 square kilometres) of fertile land would have to be flooded to create the reservoir necessary to underpin the dam, and two hundred and eighty thousand people would have to be relocated to another 'quarter' of the country. Nothing but the usual revolutionary sacrifices to be made for the greater good of all.

From the moment that the Sanmenxia dam was first proposed, though, one impossibly subjective mind insisted on advancing a less than helpful 'expert' opinion. A hydrological engineer by the name of Chen Xing, this was a man who had surveyed thousands of kilometres of the Yellow River and its surrounding lands. Having done his surveys, Chen advanced the view that while Russian engineering principles might work for rivers passing through Siberia, they could not possibly be applied to the Yellow River. Siberia was a land of clear waters that passed through untouched forests, with hardly any people to speak of. But the Yellow River was one of the muddiest rivers in the world, passing through a terrain which had not only been heavily deforested, but planted with millions of human beings instead. The risks of any dam getting silted up with mud were far too great. To which Chen Xing unhelpfully added that the costs of any failure would not only be counted in the loss of Mao's dream of leaping forward: they would be counted in a toll of millions of lost human lives.

Not to be defeated by a reckless expert opinion, the Party leaders who had commissioned Sanmenxia pointed to fine engineering designs which showed hundreds of thousands of silt checks, not to mention a set of plans for extensive reforestation. But the hydrological engineer was stubborn, and in 1957, he was despatched to a *laogai* labour camp where, like all of the other subjectively-opinionated intellectuals, he could reform himself through bitterly hard work. Inconveniently, at about that time, the Banqiao dam in Henan had begun to develop a few cracks. With the Russian engineers' assistance, the cracks were filled with concrete, and Banqiao was declared to be an iron fortress that no waters would be able to break. The news about the cracks was buried, and with the disruptive subjective opinion also out of the way, the Great Man project of Sanmenxia could begin.

*   *   *

Dams settled, Mao then turned his mind to the rice and grain that were to fuel the Great Leap Forward. Details of the agricultural plan having been forged in the garden of his own courtyard in Zhongnanhai, Mao convened a meeting of his lieutenants to explain the fundamentals of farming. Traditional principles, he explained, were little better than any other counter-revolutionary superstition that needed to yield to science: only seeds that promised the greatest yields should be planted; any and all planting was to be close and deep; and as many crops as possible were to be squeezed into the clearly lazy seasons.

The peasant army was a little surprised at the strange instructions, and some brave spirits dared to raise their hands in questions. But the majority of the questions, like the earth itself, were soon overturned. As the more stubborn questioners were swept off for struggle sessions, most of the peasants concluded that silence was the safest policy. Perhaps, dreamt some of the more hopeful minds, Mao's towering spirit had mastered the art of squeezing grain from a stone. Eventually, everybody had picked up their hoes, but it was not long before they struck the very kinds of problems they had expected. With soils already thin after centuries of toil, and with the earth of mountain slopes having never been very thick, in many places, the revolutionary hoes found themselves striking rock. And when the time came to harvest, it turned out that the lessons of their fathers and the ancestors had been correct: where too many seeds are planted too close together, everything gives up the ghost of life.

With an industrial revolution to deliver in fifteen years, and a Great Leap Forward to achieve, commune leaders were told that, whatever the problems, no prisoners were to be taken: nothing less than a total victory over nature was required. Commanding the peasants to redouble their efforts with revolutionary zeal, war was then declared on the tea bushes, orchards, and any surviving stands of forests and trees that were obviously occupying valuable places in the soil. Meanwhile, a supplementary campaign was introduced to address 'four pests' which had sprung up like foes. Rats and sparrows were eating the grain from under everybody's noses; while flies and mosquitoes were refusing to give up a war of their own which they had been waging against man for as long as anyone could remember. Armed with catapults, hungry children were unleashed into the fields of battle. Equipped with pots and pans as drums, their even hungrier parents and grandparents followed them. The catapults scored heavy victories over the rats; the pots and pans managed to force the sparrows into a perpetual flight that eventually (so the story was told) saw many of them dropping from the skies with exhaustion. And with workpoints offered as a reward for the flattened remains of the enemy flies and mosquitoes, even fingers and thumbs seemed to deliver a few victories of their own.

But somehow, by 1962 nature seemed to be winning the war. Apart from the messy matter of local leaders overstating their estimates of production, and the following havoc of a human hunger which had reaped harvests of peasant souls, it turned out that rice and grain really couldn't be grown on rock – and even where the rocks were clothed with a film of soil, the soil itself simply turned to dust. 'Plant as deep and as close as you like', the soil seemed to taunt them, 'but I have nothing more to give'. Successes on the front of the four pests notwithstanding, it seemed that nature was a trickier opponent than even Mao had reckoned: wherever the familiar foes were vanquished, nature simply replaced them with squadrons of cockroaches and locusts, all marching in to fill the vacuum created by the others' defeat.

Yet another inconvenient expert told Mao that even man himself was becoming a dangerous force of nature. From a challenging four hundred and sixty-five million people in 1949, by the early 1960s, China's population had reached six hundred and fifty million – with every indication that it would reach eight hundred million by the 1970s. Growling that 'no one had ever heard of there being too many people', Mao silenced the 'expert': not just a reckless rightist, but obviously a sympathiser with the bourgeois imperialist ideas of Ma-er-sai-se, the British Thomas Malthus. In his heart of hearts, though, Mao began to wonder. Obviously, the results of the imminent (1964) census would have to be suppressed; and a lot more grain and rice were going to have to come from somewhere. Either that, or the size of the people would have to be cut.

Scanning the socialist countryside for better news, in 1963, Mao's attention had been caught by the Dazhai commune in the northern province of Shanxi. Named Dazhai, Great Outpost, after its closest town, it was also a *da zhai*, great outpost, in terms of spirit as well. Set in the Shanxi heartlands of the country, the land had been hoed and ploughed since the earliest of Chinese time, with rolling hills losing their forests and a bumpy earth tilled until it had turned to dust. Long and cold winters (often without a hint of rain) had not helped, nor had the short summer heatwaves with deluges of monsoon rain which regularly swept the rich loess topsoil into the Yellow River, ushering in the floods which always carried destruction and famine in their wake. Into this natural nightmare had stepped a true revolutionary spirit: a once-peasant who had become the local commune's Party secretary. Determined to snatch victory from nature, he had marched his brigades out across the rebellious land – thousands of peasants at a time. Labouring day and night regardless of the seasons, supported by singing loudspeakers, and spurred on by the promise of work-points, within three years 'Dazhai man' finally seemed to have conquered the earth. Trees – with or without fruit – had been felled. Stubbly hills had become towering terraces of rice. The dusty earth had become sweeping fields of grain. Everything was being washed by man-made streams of water. And wherever a stubborn mountain had tried to stand in the way of newly irrigating waters, a man-made tunnel had pierced its heart.

Enchanted by the doughty Party secretary's spirit, Mao compared the triumph of his feats to the ancient story of *Yu Gong Yi Shan* (the foolish old man) which told of an old man who had insisted on moving two mountains which blocked his view, one shovel at a time. While his neighbours mocked, the old man, helped by his loyal family, just kept going until, one day, heaven itself took pity upon him and sent down a pair of immortals who moved the mountains out of his way. By the end of 1963, Mao had decided that everyone should be learning from Dazhai. Party Secretaries responsible for communes across China were told to march delegations from their own communes to the Shanxi heartlands, to witness the art of successfully waging a war against nature. Led to the top of Dazhai's Tiger Head Mountain, the results were clear for all to see. Revolutionary armies of men, women and even children, were spread out like ants; and vistas of rice and grain appeared in a breathtaking display. It was clear to the visiting delegations that the straggling efforts of their own muddled fields were nothing but a personal disgrace. With other communes eager to learn, Dazhai's triumph became

430

the stuff of everyone's dreams: how to move mountains with thousands of hands; how to turn selfish slopes into yielding terraces; how to carve dykes in every direction. And, most important of all, how to make sure that the peasant-soldiering troops kept their socialist productivity high.

Returning back to their very different quarters of the country – from flat plains to high mountains, from deep jungles to watery lakes and marshes – no one could forget the visions of Dazhai's terraces. Nor could they forget Mao's new mantra: 'learn from Dazhai'. Inspired and shamed, the Party Secretaries pushed their communes and their lands ever farther. In the north, more of the grasslands were set to the plough. In the western south, ancient forests were felled for rice. In some places, the earth was piled into mountains so that terraces could be created. In others, lakes were drained and filled in with rocks, sand and earth, so that key crops of grain and rice could be grown where self-indulgent fish had once swum. At the extreme edges of the empire – in the remotest deserts, forests and steppes, to which the worst of the rightists were typically sent – man and nature were pushed to the end of their endurance and beyond. Every inch of land was turned to productive purpose, and the very veins of the earth were plumbed in an effort to find more water with which to wash the fields. With wells being dug deeper and deeper into the water table below the ground, many of them ended up hitting rock. As Party Secretaries continued to bark their commands, the peasants watched as nature yielded: flocks gave up their sheep for grain, primeval forests burned like tinder, lakes made way for crops, and ancient oases were transformed into desert dust. Questions, and tears, were everywhere. But few dared to interrupt the objective advance of the revolution.

*   *   *

While the peasants wasted their tears on the smaller matters of life, Mao was soon required to turn his attention to a rising storm in the relationship with Russia. It was a storm that, on the face of things, seemed to have little to do with nature. In the end, however, it would be nature that would pay the price.

After Nikita Krushchev – with Stalin on his mind – had raised the uncomfortable matter of personality cults in the middle of the 1950s, Mao had increasingly seen Russia as an overbearing older brother who needed to be put in his place. The strain on the relationship had been complicated by the Russian brother's cold but rising war with the American imperialists – whose numerous theatres of battle included a number that touched on Chinese borders. Initially conducted through the battles of a divided Korea in the unfinished aftermath of the Second World War, Mao had been supportive. But with a vast border across the north that separated the country from Russia only by Mongolian lands whose loyalties had been lost to Moscow since the early 1920s, Mao's China was heavily exposed to the Russian bear. And with a completely open expanse of coasts all along the east and south, where most of the country's industry lay, it was even more exposed to American ambition from the Pacific.

Clear about his history and geography, Mao knew that the risks for China were accentuated by the complicated history of the south. From 1884, when the Vietnamese – occupying French had defeated the Manju Qing army, and destroyed the Fujian fleet in a single hour, Vietnam had become a hotly disputed territory with the West. In 1940, it had been invaded by Japan. By 1944, the Guomindang were supporting the American-led West in a mission to oust the imperialist Japanese from its lands. By 1950, Vietnam had divided into a north and a south – with the north supported by the Communist brothers of Russia and China, and the south supported by the American-led West. As Russia became an increasingly close friend of the North Vietnamese, Mao found himself looking at a Russian-influenced border not only to the Mongolian north but to his south, in Vietnam as well.

Foot-draggers that they were, it took Mao until 1961 to get his own Party comrades to declare the Russian Communist Party a gaggle of revisionists, traitors to the ideals of Marx and Lenin. Soviet Russian engineers and loans were withdrawn and Mongolia became a military buffer, increasingly stuffed with Soviet rockets. It was obvious to Mao that no one in the Party had understood the scale of the threat, but with China exposed to the north, the south, and along its coasts, he managed to secure some contingency planning for war. Then, in the summer of 1964, the United States collided with the Russian-supported North Vietnamese in the Gulf of Tonkin, and even the foot-draggers agreed that the forces of Russia and America might be spending too much time on China's south-west border. The fact that the Great Leap Forward had so far failed to catch China up with anyone, just made everything worse.

Looking closely at his maps, Mao decided that if China was to survive, let alone become the fittest state of all, more assaults on nature would be required. By the end of 1964, with the help of the surviving scientists, the first of China's atomic bombs was tested, at Lop Nur, on the edge of the

Taklamakan desert: remote, but close enough to Russia's Central Asian Republics for the impact to be felt. By 1965, having explored his own inner crouching dragon, Mao more quietly launched a 'Third Front' which would see every industry vital for the survival of the People's Republic carried to the sanctuary of the country's mountainous centre: Sichuan. *Kaoshan*, close to the mountains; *fensan*, dispersed; *yinbi*, hidden. The Third Front and its industries would be spread out across places where no boats could ever land and no planes would ever be able to see what was going on below. With plenty of mountains that could be pierced with tunnels, the movements of production could easily be hidden; surviving forests could screen the skies; and seams of locally abundant minerals and metals would be able to fuel both construction and production. Armed with such advantages, an entire new world of industry could be conjured up from the midst of the wildest nature.

Advancing to the new Third Front, the People's Liberation Army was given the task of building the roads, railways and bridges that would carry productive machines out of their industrial city homes – and of blasting open the tunnels that would hide the final destinations from any prying eyes in the sky. Workers and students were commanded to follow, so that new forests of chimneys could be raised within the mountains. Smoke-emitting funnels peeped out from places where no airborne bomber would think to look; rocky cliffs housed coal-powered generators. Perpendicular gorges became powerhouses producing steel, chemicals, tanks, cars and planes – all with the grey clouds of their energies hidden behind the mountains. River banks became hosts to furnaces of iron and steel, planted where chemical and metal waste could pour smoothly into the waters below, and so carefully located that if ever there were an accidental leak of a brightly-coloured substance, no enemy would never need to know.

The anticipated war with Russia never happened. But by the time that Mao died, the mountains of Sichuan had been tamed to host the industry of man. And when Deng Xiaoping resurrected the idea of the Four Modernisations in 1978, no one looked forward to increasing industrial production more than the invisible industrial-military powers of production scattered across the remote mountain areas of Sichuan. Equally enthusiastic were a number of self-strengthening individuals who, soon to be liberated from the mountainous communes, would be free to spread their own industrial possibilities in the heart of nature's silence.

*   *   *

Meanwhile, as Mao was devoting his energies to the possibilities of man at war, the old matter of dams raised its head again. The Sanmenxia dam had been ordered for construction, but by 1962 it was clear that things had not gone entirely to plan. Once raised, just as the hydrological engineer Chen Xing had so expertly predicted, vast quantities of Yellow River silt had not only built up against the dam itself but were backing up along the length of one of its tributary rivers. With the silt rising higher by the year, there was a risk that the tributary river might breach its banks and flood the once imperial city of Chang'an – now the industrial city of Xi'an. Battalions of hydraulic engineers were thrown at the problem, but the silt refused to retreat. At one point, with no Russian engineers to lend a helping hand (and with a number of other things on his mind), Mao suggested that if nothing could be done, the mighty dam would simply have to be dynamited into dust. Anxious engineers prevaricated, and the backed-up waters flooded the surrounding land with salt. In the event, the loss of Xi'an was averted by drilling silt-liberating holes into the walls of the dam: so many holes that while the great dam itself survived, by the late 1960s, it was good for neither power nor controlling floods. Meanwhile, the salt stayed in the soil, destroying crops for years to come.

Not to be defeated by a failure or two, Mao was keen to find an opportunity for a socialist success. With a steady flow of objectively minded hydraulic engineers always eager to please an emperor, new proposals were submitted. One was for a mighty dam at Gezhouba, on the Yangzi. Another was for an even greater dam, slightly higher up, at the Yangzi's Three Gorges. The idea of a dam at the Three Gorges was a great temptation. Sun Yatsen had first suggested it, and Mao had often dreamt of it – even immortalising his dreams in a poem that had been learnt by hearts up and down the People's Republic. In the event, it was reluctantly decided that Gezhouba would go first and pave the way. But the dream of a dam at the Three Gorges was simply biding its time.

Eventually, Mao followed all of the other Great Men up to the ancestors' skies. But the idea of a Three Gorges dam had acquired a life of its own. After years of reports and discussions within the inner recesses of the Party, by the beginning of 1989 a plan for the dam had finally, and rather quietly, been approved by Deng Xiaoping. All that was required was a final rubber stamp from the annual spring meeting of the National People's Congress – the representative body of the people that was designed to be a truly objective voice. With the Four Modernisations now underway, however, things had changed a little from the days of Mao. Not least, Chinese experts were travelling abroad to learn from foreigners, particularly those in America. And as the scientists travelled, they were often accompanied by journalists instructed to cover the story. At one point, one of the accompanying journalists – an engineer who had changed her trade – found herself passing through Hong Kong, where she read an anxious story in a local newspaper about a dam. Headline news in Hong Kong, the story had failed to make the back pages of the Party papers at home, even though the dam was in the heart of mainland China. The journalist's name was Dai Qing, and the fearful story was about the risks of a proposed Three Gorges dam.

Rumours that Mao's dream of a great dam at the Three Gorges might be resurrected had indeed been whispered at home for some time. Realising that the rumours had become fact – and realising that the outside world was highly informed about its risks – Dai Qing decided that she would investigate things on her own. When she returned to Beijing, she found her way to other Chinese who had heard the same news on their travels abroad. She also found her way to Chinese government officials and scientific experts who had been directly involved in the Party's preparations, and were themselves becoming increasingly concerned. Two kilometres wide, with a man-made reservoir whose watery dragon would soon swallow nineteen cities, three hundred-odd towns, a thousand villages, and vast swathes of farming land, not to mention the homes of over a million people, the scale of its imagination defied even the greatest of the First Qin Emperor's works.

Piecing together a picture of the risks, Dai Qing suggested to her new-found friends that they compile a set of expert opinions and factual documents which could check the Party's calls to 'conquer nature!' More importantly, she added, such a book of documents could clarify the precise technical and human problems of a Three Gorges Dam in words that the members of the National People's Congress could understand. True, the National People's Congress had always followed the objective order of the Party, but a lot had changed since the death of Mao. Perhaps it was time for the People's representatives, the men and a few women who technically had the power of a final say on everything (at least under the formal terms of the Chinese Constitution), to get a little homework.

Prepared and circulated to its intended readership, Dai Qing's book, entitled *Yangzi! Yangzi!*, found its mark. Discussions with the representatives arriving in Beijing for their annual meeting showed that they were beginning to echo the opinions of the book's contributors with questions of their own:

'What about the silting that builds up behind a dam and puts at risk the very lives which the dam is supposed to be saving?' 'What about the million people who would have to move their homes?' 'What about the already-disappearing *baiji*, white dolphin, that would have no waters left to swim in?' 'And what about the treasures of the old state of Chu on whose ancient lands the Three Gorges sit?' To all of these questions, yet another expert added the very inconvenient observation that the Yangzi River was perched upon a geological fault line that made every dam constructed on its saddle a risk. Not only a risk of provoking the very flooding which the dam was supposed to prevent, but a risk of triggering an earthquake as well.

When the formal report on the Three Gorges Dam was delivered for its anticipated approval, the harmonious ritual of the National People's Congress was interrupted with a host of unscripted questions. The microphones of the questioners were quickly cut. Answers to the most persistent questioners were then issued in the corridors – all grounded on the strengths of Party science. To these were added lectures on the objective decision-making that was required of all true supporters of the Party's continuing revolution. As far as the question of silting was concerned, that was clearly just a problem of cutting down too many trees: nothing that a quick planting of forests couldn't handle, and nothing to do with dam-building at all. The same went for the argument that the sewage of factory waste would get caught up in the dam: the factories would just have to be told to clean up. As for the now million-odd people who would have to move their homes, surely such self-sacrificing virtue had been displayed by China's people from the time of the Qin, if not the Shang: it was all part of what it meant to be Chinese. And as for the truly rightist arguments that the archaeological treasures of the ancient state of Chu would be washed away and the white *baiji* dolphin might disappear – well, relics of the past could always be put in a museum (or an aquarium). It was time to move on.

To those at the top, it was clear that the revolutionary discipline of the National People's Congress, like everything else in a 1989 spring of troublesome anniversaries, was experiencing a temporary lapse. It was ten years since the imprisonment of Wei Jingsheng (the dangerous spirit who had dared to call for a Fifth Modernisation); the astrophysicist Fang Lizhi had just had the audacity to send an open letter to Deng asking for Wei's release; and as if that was not enough, it was seventy years since the original May Fourth science and democracy protests had exploded in Beijing. With so much bourgeois baggage in the air, how could anyone hope to get anything done? By the time the National Congress of the People came to a close, it was clear that no vote was going to be taken – or at least, not one that could ever be officially recorded. Within a month, the streets of Beijing had become a river of banners: all asking why, after so many millennia, the truth about anything could still not be told. And then June Fourth silenced everyone. On 14 June, with *Yangzi! Yangzi!* now banned, Dai Qing was arrested. Like many of the other reckless intellectuals, some of China's greatest scientists began to make their way to a voluntary exile in the West.

It would take a little time for the Party's dam-building confidence to rise again. But Zhou Enlai's adopted son, Li Peng – a Moscow trained engineer who had specialised in hydroelectric – had recently been appointed premier; naturally, he was keen to ensure that the vision of the great dam did not die. In the spring of 1992, with the changes seeming a little more auspicious, Li Peng returned the dam designs to a chastened National People's Congress for a more obedient vote. This time, the rubber stamp was successfully secured, and armies of engineers were deployed to bring the dream to life. Five years later, in 1997, Jiang Zemin was able to rise to the Party's podium and announce the completion of the first stage of the Three Gorges dam. Declaring it to be a victory for the spirit of the 'foolish old man who moved mountains', he repeated the eternal Great Man cry: 'Man must conquer nature!' Four years later, with a successful bid for the Olympics under Beijing's belt, the schedule for the dam's completion was accelerated – so that it could be ready to demonstrate its revolutionary streams of energy for all the world to see.

*   *   *

Back in the countryside, after Deng's announcement of the Four Modernisations and his call for mind emancipation, few had been idle. As the communes had been transformed into township governments from the early 1980s, commune leaders had become mind-emancipating township officials with a host of useful powers. Among the earliest and more unusual of these powers was one that put them in charge of the reproductive possibilities of man. While Mao had chosen to ignore the problem of an expanding population, by the time that Deng returned to Beijing in 1976, the number of China's people had leapt to a shocking eight hundred million, with no sign of slowing down. In 1979, Deng had introduced a 'one-child' policy: one child in areas where there were more buildings than fields; two for those areas where there were more fields than buildings. Requiring an army of officials to enforce the policy, it had been obvious to those in local government that the townships and their new officials would be perfectly placed for a heavenly control of human reproduction.

The powers of the townships, though, went well beyond procreation. Indeed, the most officially appealing of the townships' powers was that of approval over which of the old pieces of industrial production went where. With everyone looking for pockets of profit, chimneys of all descriptions had begun to spread across the land. From coal washing and coking plants, zinc smelters and steel furnaces, to cement factories, sawmills and repair shops, the advance of the chimneys had been less like that of slow-growing forests and more like wildfire. With local cash reserves low or non-existent, and every penny needed for profits, the trick had been to get the furnaces of production firing on any and all of the rickety cylinders which were lying around. Engines that should rightly have died years before were resurrected to splutter into the future, regardless of their soot. And with roofs and insulation an unnecessary expense, plants and smelters were left to exhale in the freshness of the open air. It was not long before the fields of grain and rice were covered in soot – and not long at all before rivers were running with the sulphurous slurry of coal. When newly-enterprising villagers added peach trees and lettuces to their farming patches (not to mention water-drinking animals), the peaches, the lettuces and the animals ended up black as well. Busy withmind emancipation, though, the colour of nature was not considered to be the greatest of man's concerns. And while some of the villagers were unhappy about the changing taste of the air (and the water), everyone was encouraged to get on with the new art of making money.

Townships that were close to the booming coastal zones of the south offered some of the greatest opportunities. Observing the peasants struggling to farm their fields *and* work in the factories as well, local officials conjured up a mind-emancipating solution. With the old communes a fading memory, the chemical fertilisers that had been developed for their use could (for a fee of course) now be offered to a new generation of individual farming households. Indeed, with new, self-strengthened, fertilizer factories coming on local stream, the substances would be available in even greater volumes and strengths. Local officials became experts in the new magic: 'wealth just apply it in industrial quantities to make up for the loss of the nurturing human touch, and the fields can be left to farm themselves.'

Up in the north, the peasants were staring at quite a different challenge: a dry soil which had not only become so exhausted that it seemed to have no more nutrients left but which, in many areas, was now desperately struggling to hold the deserts back. Looking at the problem, local township officials saw the same solution as their southern peers: chemical supplements to give the dust a boost. Phosphorus, sulphur, zinc and other chemicals were swiftly ordered. Not everyone could read the instructions – and to the officials who could, they seemed unnecessarily complicated. Instant experts, the officials recommended that everyone just spread the powder in all directions, and let it do its work. And if it didn't work quickly enough – or if your fields had more rocks than soil on them – then, obviously, you needed to spread some more. Up and down the country, from the dry north to the watery south, fields (and rocks) were fed as they had never been fed before. And when it rained, the rain washed the chemicals into the rivers, and down into the tables under the earth. That way, everything got a shot.

Time passed, the Four Modernisations continued their promise of wealth, and by 2000, the countryside was reaping an industrial harvest – of sorts. Flush with hope and anticipation in the early years of Deng's productive revolution, after almost a decade of racing ahead, the peasants had found that fields sprayed with the new chemical fertilisers were struggling. More and more of the chemicals had been sprayed all over the place (with their compounds regularly strengthened) but the crops remained stubbornly in the dumps. Peasants looking for answers of their own began to look again at the countryside that had changed so quickly all around them. Many pointed to the forests of chimneys belching out oceans of smoke. Some (particularly those whose fields fronted onto rivers) pointed to sewage pipes which washed the waters with streaks of red, orange and yellow and which, from time to time, turned the rivers completely black – save for the layers of milky white froth that periodically appeared. Turning to their village leaders and township governments, some dared to suggest that it might be time to call a halt to the chemical destruction.

But by now, the factories of the town and village enterprises were also struggling. Constructed from the local tangles of pipes and smokestacks of the communal past, few had modernised themselves beyond the idea of getting rich. While the special economic zones of the eastern coasts had acquired more money, more science and technology, and more demanding Western markets, everywhere else in the countryside had fallen further behind. Local township officials had begun to worry. Since many townships and local officials had

439

(directly or indirectly) become owners of the factories, poor profits were a problem – not only for themselves but for the local government funds which were buoyed up by the revenues of their production. Looking anxiously at the performances of next-door neighbours, township and village leaders decided they would need to do whatever it took to keep their own local income rising. Sooty opportunities and mines relocating from places that did not want them (whether from China or anywhere else) were accepted with alacrity. And if ever a gaggle of villagers had 'an opinion', the leaders were always quick to point out that one village's loss was always another's gain.

While soot-covered fields and black rivers running with sludge had once seemed to be a mild inconvenience, as time went on, some of the peasants began to wonder whether there wasn't more to the darker colours than met the eye. Hacking coughs and unseasonal colds seemed to have taken up permanent rural occupation. In some parts of the country, the problem went well beyond coughs and colds. Here, a number of infants began to be born blue; there, other babies arrived with twisted hands and feet, not to mention minds that seemed to struggle to keep up. In many places, older adults, instead of living longer, seemed to fade well before their time: breath shortened to a wheeze, they were also wracked by pains which no one had ever had before. Those who could afford a trip to a county town clinic (or whose families were brave enough to take out a loan for something higher up), came back with faces longer than a pole. Lungs riddled with sulphurous water, and kidneys, stomachs and throats attacked by arsenic and mercury, their bodies were now being ravaged by cancerous cells. Treatments, they were informed, might be possible – but they would require levels of modernisation and cash that the countryside had yet to achieve.

In the early days, dismissed by local officials but still hoping for some sort of a solution, the peasants covered their sleeping faces with wet cloths to keep out the worst of the fumes. They also saved up their money for shop-bought bottles of water, trusting that it came from cleaner rivers than their own. With many worried that no one in the outside world would speak to them if they understood what cauldrons of death and destruction their villages had become, everyone did their level best to bury their fears. Some tried to appeal to the local factory workers and miners to stop the destructive production. But many of the labouring hands were migrants from other, even more desperate, corners of the countryside. And the migrants replied that if they had any hope of earning the cash of life anywhere else, they would surely carry themselves off to eke out an existence in another part of the land, but survival was a battle for everyone, everywhere. Listlessly lying down to die, desperate wives, husbands and children turned their gaze to the smoke stacks and the sewage pipes, and remembered that it had not always been this way.

As more of the death sentences were confirmed, relatives and friends inked brave appealing letters to township officials, begging them to close the factories. Clear, however, about their duty to follow Deng's exhortation to spread economic development under the leadership of the Party (and to emancipate everyone's minds), the officials replied with denials and disdain. To which, they added scientific questions so difficult that there was probably not anyone, even in a city, who could possibly find an answer, let alone a peasant. 'You say that this particular chimney or sewage pipe is killing your father', the officials challenged, 'but where is the link between the two? The hills and the plains are full of factories, and the air which passes over your heads has come through a lot of other places before it has got to here, not least the state-owned industrial plants in neighbouring townships and counties. How do you know the problem is not coming from them?'

Anyone who could, left. And as those who stayed behind watched their hopes vanish in puffs of red, orange and yellow dust, some decided that perhaps their only chance was to speak their own truth and call their homes by a more appropriate name: cancer villages. The township government might not like it – it certainly wouldn't help in attracting new money for enterprising investment; and ambitious careers would be bound to suffer. But the speakers of the names were too far advanced on their way to another world to care. And, anyway, if the god of war and great protector of the weak, Guan Yu, was on the peasants' side, the officials would eventually be going down to the hells below. Up in Beijing, a few brave voices tried to spread the truth of the peasants' misery, but somehow the airwaves were always stuffed with happier stories.

*   *   *

With the countryside collapsing under the weight of its many miseries, floating men, now increasingly with women and children in tow, flocked to the towns. Those who had the courage to try struggled their way into the bigger cities beyond. Schooled only in the socialist basics, few had any employer-pleasing certificates to show for their years in muddy classrooms; even fewer could find the *hukou* passport that provided an official passage

441

into city life. However naturally bright their minds and energies might be, without the necessary papers their horizons sank to the lowest '3D' jobs: dirty, dangerous and demanding. It didn't matter: anything was better than the black fields and the crows of the township towers. Pleased to have a labouring opportunity, even for the price of a song, the migrants then accepted the offers of rapacious landlords in the grey edges of cities where black rents hit the roof for a simple dwelling: temporary shelters from the weather, hopefully with few questions asked.

It was not only the peasants who went to the city in search of a better life. With their families' fortunes raised by early factory acquisitions, and tiring of the complications of the countryside, retired officials and their friends soon started to board the softer seats of the country's trains and make their way to the cities. Settling in the comforting compounds of suburban villas, they looked around at their new surroundings and congratulated themselves on having left the choking chimneys behind them and joining a modernised world where everyone's water was clean. Keen to explore the treasures of their new home – and to emulate the 'high quality' of the city's middle classes – they then climbed into newly-purchased cars, and took themselves off to the rising temples of consumption, where fountains of water (redirected from the fields) played like music, and every luxury in the world could be found.

New homes acquired air conditioners; televisions and washing machines were added. And when winter came, coal by the cartload was burned in someone else's backyard to power the electricity that would keep them invisibly warm. With so many people flocking to the urban dream, more coal and more cities were obviously needed – it was only a question of finding the space. Here, there, and everywhere, new citadels rose. Even up in the spreading Gobi desert of Inner Mongolia (now home to some of the fastest money-making speed in the country), someone stretched their imagination, and within the blink of an eye, a shimmering city appeared: Ordos, in an area dedicated to the production of coal and named after the spreading palaces of Chinggis Khan which had graced it in less sandy times. In the rest of the country, township officials looked again at the peasants' 'land use rights' to see which fields could be liberated for yet more productive urban purpose.

For a while, the cities seemed to sparkle like magic, certainly for the 'higher quality' middle classes: safe-to-drink water on tap, food wrapped up in shiny plastic packages, cool cars to smooth even the shortest journey. But as always, the superstitious rumours were quick to catch up, particularly in the dry and dusty north. Hundreds of cities were said to be sinking because people had dug too many wells. Others were falling victim to dust storms, unleashed by the rages of fallen forests. Those already full of industrial factories had also become home to plants which were burning coal at tonnes a minute in a bid to keep up with local demands. The countryside's clouds might have been left behind, but it seemed that the cities had clouds of their own – stealing all the bright blue skies and blocking the rays of the sun. Looking with sharper eyes at their new urban habitats, some even began to whisper that the vegetables which were wrapped up in such shiny plastic came from the same black fields, washed by the same black waters, which everyone from the countryside thought they had safely left behind. Others replied that there was always someone wanting to rain on a fortunate person's parade – chatterboxing gossips who just couldn't appreciate the value of the *gao suzhi*, high-quality, city life.

As time went on, though, more began to wonder. Measured in square metres of housing, television sets and washing machines, life in the city was certainly much better than it had been in the countryside. Schools, roads, buses, even metros, were bustling; shops sparkled, restaurants were full to the brim, and the cracking sound of celebrating fireworks was never far away. According to the newspapers, even life itself had got longer. But here and there, it seemed that not everything was quite right. Shining new industrial plants regularly appeared out of nowhere, stuffed full of modernising chemicals – and before one knew it, suddenly everyone in the neighbourhood knew of a child who was struggling to breathe. Everywhere, the rain began to take on a special metallic quality: washed with the acid of production, some said. Even the meat and the vegetables which appeared so temptingly on city plates turned out to have a poisonous sting, turning stomachs and sending people rushing to a hospital for help – where questions about the food led to a rather resigned shrug of doctoring shoulders and a new medical mantra: 'we get a lot of that, these days'. Meanwhile, as the cities continued to spread, once-smooth roads began to slow to little more than mobile parking lots, belching out yet more clouds of smoke.

Certainly, there didn't seem to be much sun anymore – and what sun there was looked dimmer than the moon. Even the clouds had changed: now harder to see in the grey cloak which shrouded everything, they were no longer soft balls of floating cotton, but menaces which concealed the grit of production in their misleadingly soft folds. Coughs and colds were everywhere; and few could escape the nagging doubt that something worse might be lurking within. For the young, the old, and the un-revolutionary weak, even the breath of life was becoming a bit of a struggle. One way or another, Mao had got his forests of chimneys – but unless there was a good stiff wind to blow away the fog, it was getting harder to see them.

*　　　*　　　*

On 12 May 2008, as Beijing counted down the last days to the Great Man spectacle of the grandest Olympics the planet had ever witnessed, eleven miles below its surface, the earth quaked. Spreading across 155 miles of a geological fault line under the province of Sichuan, the epicentre of the quake was a world of villages and county towns spread across the hills and valleys of the remote Ngawa region: once part of Tibet, and still scattered with people who traced their ancestry to the Buddha-jewelled mountains of the gods.

As broken hearts asked the skies why loved ones had been taken from them, a few expert voices ventured to ask a question with a past: why had the Three Gorges dam been built across a Sichuan land which was threaded with a fault?

THE EDGES OF ORDER

*In the Great Unity ... there is no division into national states
and no difference between the races. There will be no war.*

Da Tong, *The Great Unity*, Kang Youwei (1858–1927)

As an early March sun separated night from day, the jewelled peaks of the
Himalayan Mountains pierced the early morning mist. Waking to the dawn,
the snow lions of the Potala palace roared their *sunyata* silence of emptiness,
courage and truth – a roar so quietly powerful that it promised a freedom
from the *samsara* cycle of deeds and consequences. The palace itself, perched
on the red Marpori mountain, gazed out across the *Kyi* River, towards the
Che-la mountain pass: the path by which the Dalai Lama had walked his
way to freedom. Nearby, as the glint of the early light spread, two golden
deer appeared, kneeling on the roof of the Jokhang Palace. Soft noses raised
towards the *dharma chakra* wheel of the Buddha's searing sight, gentle ears
silently listening, they were a reminder to all that the Buddha-nature lives
within the meekest of human forms.

The sun rising a little higher, now dusting the sky with the soft red of a
rose, the world below awoke. Monks wrapped in saffron-coloured robes
began to hum their meditating mantras, filling the icy air with the warm

445

breath of a thousand searching souls. Crawling pilgrims added their own peregrinations, touching prayer wheels as they passed. As the prayer wheels turned, each searching centre added its own softly muffled mantra to the wider air: 'om mani padme hum'. Six syllables which any mind could translate as 'behold the jewel in the lotus' or some such simplicity, but which for deeper minds, with the humility and self-discipline to search, held ideas as big as oceans: the jewel as the enlightenment which comes from the heartfelt pursuit of wisdom; the lotus as the flower which blossoms in the muddy waters of life; and all real meaning to be found in the dedicated pursuit of an understanding which can never be captured in the simple language of a mantra's spoken words.

With the day now gathering its energies, a wide blue sky ushered in a caravan of clouds. Soon a forest of advertising boards caught the light for all to see. The biggest of the boards declared the power of a rising China Telecom across the once-medieval Barkhor Square, and (at 11,500 feet above the sea) the highest service in the world. Shops began to lift up their shutters, and in the Chinese characters of the Yellow River heartlands that had always insisted on a greater unity, goods were proclaimed for sale. Within the lanes around the square, thick white walls caught shadows of light, prayer flags flapped in a breeze, and busy stalls began to come to life. Miniature Buddhas vied with tempting trinkets, all carried up to the meditating heights from the productive energies of southern Wenzhou. Incense, rising from humble burners, spread in every direction; pool tables, recovered from their late night entertainment, were brushed off for a new day of play. Street cleaners, gathered in battalions, stepped around the clutter of construction, meditating on the dust to be swept from all around. The sun now higher, the whitest of clouds drifted across the clearest of skies, and clutches of southern tourists began to appear, rushed to the summit by the highest of trains. Stepping into the Lhasa city of the gods, they clicked the lenses of their third eyes across a feast of sights, advancing through the streets as fast as their mobile phones could carry them.

Deep in the Potala palace, the blue Akshobhya Buddha stared into the emptiness of eternal space, with the light of understanding. Blue, like the colour of water that carves through solid rock without violence, which hardens like the sharpest of intellects when frozen, and then softens to a free flow when it realises the liberating wonder of wisdom. A few miles away, at the foot of the Gambo Utse Mountain, the doors of the Drepung Monastery stood open, and hundreds of monks began to walk to the heart of Lhasa.

Hearts burning, their minds were meditating on the memory of the time – forty-nine years ago to the day – when the Dalai Lama vanished into an exile from which he had never returned.

In a few days, the old Barkhor Square, once home to the gods, now home to the Wenzhou trinkets, would explode into balls of fire. Soldiers would march in pairs; knives would appear; batons would strike; and an acrid smoke would fill the air. Below the Potala Palace, 'Beijing Street' would flood with tears of gas and screams of anger. And the *Kyi* River would continue to flow – along with the blood of days that would stretch into a seemingly eternal night.

It was not meant to be this way.

*   *   *

When Yu the Great had divided the heavenly heartlands, the order of China's settled world had been painted everywhere. It was greatest, of course, at its central heart: the place from which the patterns of nature had first been observed. The patterns transformed into a plan for heaven, earth and man, the ordering plan had then been stretched out towards the edges, where, separated from the centre, it had naturally dissipated. Walls had been raised to mark the boundaries of human civilisation. But, like so much else in the cosmos, they had been subjected to the energies of chaos, particularly the chaos of the barbarian world. Observing the wonders of the settled world, though, some of the barbarians had come to see the order of the heavenly plan as a model for all. Taming themselves into *ren*, human beings, they had learnt that it is only by cultivating himself that man can transform chaos into order. And they had learnt that, where an individual barbarian ruler could tame not only his own heart and mind but those of his people, he could even become a descendant of the Yellow Emperor himself.

With a number of barbarian rulers attempting to emulate the civilisation of the settled lands, and others being persuaded, the borders of the heavenly heartlands had gradually extended until they covered what seemed to be almost all the world. And with the best of climates and soil – best not only for producing harvests, but also for cultivating the orderly qualities of man – it had become clear to the Yellow Emperor's descendants that the civilising splendour of the settled lands was a gift to those with the misfortune to have been born outside.

Of course, there had always been stubborn spirits: wolves and dogs who preferred the wild. Far too primitive to understand the responsibility of man to order nature, these were people who had naturally kept to their chaos. But not all barbarians were the same: while starting as wolves and dogs, some were eventually able to appreciate the wisdom of the civilised settled ways. Just as not all of those born in the Chinese lands were civilised: even some of the purest descendants of the Yellow Emperor behaved in such an animal manner that they could really only be barbarians at heart. As with everything else in the settled, ordered, world, the important thing was to name a thing after its nature: call a dog a dog, and a wolf a wolf. Just as you would call a true father, a father; a true son, a son; a civilised man who had mastered the written word and the Confucian virtues, a *junzi* gentleman; and the man responsible for conducting the harmonies of heaven and earth, the Son of Heaven, ruler of all. Indeed, just as you would call all those who failed to understand the secrets of an orderly society, barbarians. And in a world where natures and names were plain for all to see, but where stubborn wolves and dogs could not be trained to see the importance of their order, a Son of Heaven ruler should not hesitate to take the sterner measures required for everyone's all-under-heaven-harmony – whether the measures took the shape of a wall or a war.

It had not been easy, even within the heavenly lands. While the Yellow Emperor's true descendants had settled to order, many others had insisted on carrying on with their tribal ways. They had not only tramped around with their muddy feet, but addressed themselves directly to heaven whenever they felt like a conversation. And beyond the boundaries of the heavenly civilisation, there were hosts of uncivilised lands where people never stopped chattering to heaven, whether or not heaven was interested in what they had to say. From the north, they appeared as wolves on horseback, descending like raging winds to sweep away the precious treasures of harvests, iron and silk that the settled world produced. To the south, a myriad of others kept to their forests and mountains, joined from time to time by wilful hearts who, born into the ordering reach of the heavenly cities and fields, inexplicably insisted on looking for heaven somewhere else.

Time passed, and the iron will of Qin pushed down into the south: imperial armies mustered, the stubborn spirits were pushed over mountains, across rivers, into remote rain-filled forests, and off to the south-western edges of the land. But just like the unruly elements of nature, these barbarians were tricky beasts. Across the next millennia, every time successive emperors followed Qin's steps to the south, they found yet more of them: hidden, and always muddy. More armies had been advanced, more forests felled, and as each forest was felled, the armies raised fields across lands that were obviously not occupied by any being that could possibly be described as a *ren*, human. From time to time, progress was made: finally seeing sense, some of the tribes had settled down beside the Chinese peasant armies. For every tribe that settled, though, there were many others that ducked and dived: looking for pockets of wild freedom, whether in the darkest depths of the wettest forests, or in the nooks and crannies of mountains whose stern and rocky faces would challenge any standing army. Even when confronted by the clearly superior forces of order, some of the tribes had astonishingly fought back. Battles were fought, seemingly to the death, only for others to appear from the midst of nature's chaos to take up the fight.

Eventually, the officials of the Ming dynasty hit upon a solution: 'train the tribes to manage themselves'. Casting around for individual tribal men who could learn to appreciate the power of the brush, and the value of the settled field, the officials made their selections. Individual tribal leaders were appointed as *tu di*, local chiefs, and rewarded with heavenly titles to note their evolution to the civilisation of man. The only price of the title was a dedication to unity.

Looking at the Ming solution (and initially encountering the southern tribes as they swept the land looking for Ming loyalists), the Manju Qing made a few improvements. Local chiefs were replaced with imperial officials, and the Kangxi Emperor issued a Sacred Edict that proclaimed sixteen virtues of settled Confucian values to the remotest corners of the conquered world. 'Esteem filial piety' had been the most obvious of the virtues, with others including 'respect farming, wipe out strange beliefs, embrace the correct doctrine, elevate customs and manners', and, naturally, 'guard against sheltering those who dare to disobey'.

In the northern lands, Kangxi then took tactical advantage of the split among the Mongols to create a biddable 'Inner' east, whose Mongols would be able to bend to the settled idea, and a wilder 'Outer' west, whose Mongols might take a little longer to turn. When the Tibetans had asked Kangxi to help them rid themselves of the tribe of Zungar Mongols from the 'Outer' west, Kangxi generously left a pair of *amban*, imperial residents, to keep a protective eye on the city of the gods – and on the peace of the most important of the Buddhist teachers: the Dalai Lama. As a faithful Manju, whose rulers had followed the Mongols in their centuries of Buddhist dedication, it was the least he could do.

With Tibet seemingly at peace, Kangxi's son (Yongzheng) had then been able to turn the army back to the south and spread Confucian schools across the tribal areas of the surviving forests. Yongzheng called it 'pacification': the taming of the tribes not just to the order of man, but to the discipline of the Manju hunt.

When Kangxi's grandson, Qianlong, took up the reins, the task of 'pacification' had still not yet been completely achieved – and there were a lot of lands that had not, yet, been embraced within the nurturing grounds of the Manju Qing. Following his grandfather's brave heart, Qianlong launched Ten Great Campaigns. At the north-west edges of order, he finally defeated the Outer Mongols. And with that success under his belt, in 1768, he marched his troops on to bring the Turkic lands of the Uighurs (those barbarian warriors who had once held the Tang dynasty's Chang'an to ransom) into the empire of the Great Manju Qing, adding a few oasis states for good measure. As Qianlong conquered, he settled the new lands with garrisons of soldiers, each charged with covering their costs by farming the oases of the fragile new frontier. Turning to the south, he then swept up the remaining unruly tribes across the south-west, pausing to pick up a few neighbours as well.

It was a shock, therefore, when, in 1855, Qianlong's descendants found that a band of Chinese Muslims had risen up in the south-west provinces. At the height of the Taiping rebellion, and with the barbarian Western devils pounding the ports, it could not have happened at a worse time. Astonishingly, the Chinese Muslims had not only dared to raise a 'Panthay' rebellion, but had gone on to declare an independent sultanate in the Dali city of Yunnan province as well: who on earth did these upstarts think they were? Investigating things, the Qing found that the rebels were descendants of Muslim traders who had arrived on caravans of trade from the lands of the tribute-paying Miandian, Burma, and that their leader was a Chinese-born man, once known by the civilised name of Du Wenxiu, who had then transformed himself into a sultan – and assumed the obviously barbarian name of Sulayman ibn Abd ar-Rahman. Battles followed across towns and villages. The rebels even besieged the capital of Yunnan province, Kunming. Eventually, a peace of sorts was restored: but not before a million Muslims had been despatched to another world, a host of survivors had fled across the barbarian Burmese border, and a pacifying passage of twenty years had had time to work its charms.

Unfortunately, as the nineteenth century advanced, the Muslim problems had not been limited to the south-west. In 1865, up in the Kokhand north-west (present-day Tajikistan), a Tajik leader snatched away the Kashgar oasis-state that Qianlong had captured, and declared it to be an independent Islamic kingdom of Kashgaria. Qianlong's descendants managed to get it back. But it took twelve long years, during which the greed of the barbarian Russians started to fray yet more of the north-western edges into states of unrest. Eventually, a treaty got the Russians under control (the Ili Valley secured in return for a pile of silver and a right to trade). The rebellions were then successfully silenced by converting the frontier garrisons, farmed by the army, into the clear black lines of a more governable territory whose name corresponded perfectly with the change of facts on the ground: *Xinjiang*, the new frontier.

By then, however, it had not just been the barbarians in bordering lands who were causing trouble – the far-off European and American West, as well as the nearby Japanese, had become a problem too. Wherever they could, the Westerners and their Japanese lapdogs used the bordering lands, of barbarians and neighbouring tribute-payers alike, as channels for attacks of their own.

In 1884, down in the deepest western south, *Faguo*, France, occupied the tribute-paying Vietnam; and when the Manju Qing's army responded to Vietnam's calls for a rescue, the French smashed the Fujian fleet to bits. Ten years later, the sea-neighbouring Japanese stepped in to the north: gunning the re-built Beiyang navy to pieces off the Yellow Sea coast of Shandong's Weihaiwei. With that victory under their imperial belts, they then moved on to take the ancient tribute-paying Korea – and snatched the island of Taiwan as well. By 1890, the north of the Manju Qing's lands had become a giant feast being carved up by everyone, with once-tribute-paying states having floated off to follow newer powers.

And then the Qing found themselves caught in a Great Game war between the British lion-in-India and the Russian bear-in-the-East, with the Himalayas in both of their imperial sights. In 1903, a British madman by the name of Francis Younghusband had advanced the Union Jack, with its maxim guns, into the lama lands of Tibet, wrapping the Buddhist kingdom in a 'protective' British embrace. Fortunately, the heavenly province of Sichuan had been able to pull the eastern edges of Tibet into its own embrace. Confronted with so much meddling in so many directions, however, the now-crumbling Manju Qing decided that it would be a good idea to make it clear that all of the Mongol lands (Outer as well as Inner) were theirs.

*   *   *

Heaven, however, still had some unsettled questions. When the intellectual rebels of the late nineteenth century had argued for revolution, much of their energy had been focused on the fact that the Manju Qing had been barbarian conquerors, unfit and unable to rule. Discovering the old Hunanese text, the *Treasures of Chu*, and seeing the Manju conquerors as a latter-day Qin, the Hunanese Tan Sitong had urged 'true' human hearts to rise against the conquerors Manju Qing. Tan had been followed by a Hunanese friend who argued that, in the battle for independence, origin was all. Pointing to the West's new science of anthropology, the friend, a young man by the name of Tang Caichang, declared that the world was divided into races, and while Westerners concentrated on the colour of someone's skin, it was obvious to any Chinese that race was not just a matter of colour but of civilisation as well. The barbarian Manju Qing were clearly not civilised Chinese; not only was their skin a darker colour, but no amount of Confucian learning could disguise the barbarian origins of the hunt-on-horseback idea with which they ruled.

True, Tang Caichang had continued, the West placed themselves, as 'white' Caucasians, at the top of the racial tree. But this was just a historical error on the part of a people who lived too far away from the civilised lands of China to know any better. Any 'top' should naturally include the Chinese (who the West had unfortunately labelled 'yellow'). And, being at the top, the Chinese should obviously be distinguished from the lower levels of darker brown and black who (as the West had so scientifically proven) were a lesser human race. Of course, being near-sightedly focused on their own 'brown' Indians and 'black' Africans, the Western scientists had not noticed that the inferior 'brown' races also included the 'brown' Manju-Mongols too. But it was really all just as the descendants of the Yellow Emperor had always known: the world was divided between the forces of civilisation in the heavenly lands, and the barbarians in the bestial wilderness beyond. The colour of a people's skin was just nature's way of illustrating this obvious and universal fact.

Tang Caichang having made his points, when Sun Yatsen invited the student rebels to join him, he had been quick to see the importance of the racial question – not just in terms of the barbarian status of the Manju, but in terms of the inevitable havoc that confused Western minds would wreak if they became involved. Referring people to the opinions of a returned scholar,

Yan Fu, who had translated many of the foreign works, Sun Yatsen noted Yan's warnings on the lessons to be drawn from the devastation of the brown and black races in India and Africa. 'They will enslave us', Yan declared, 'and hinder the development of our spirit and body ... [If] the brown and black races constantly waver between life and death, why not the four hundred million yellows?' Yan Fu was right, Sun declared: what if those Westerners, in their barbarian ignorance, mistakenly applied the same kind of treatment to the 'yellow' Chinese people who been hijacked by the brown Manju, as they would naturally apply to the inferior Manju themselves?

Listening to Sun Yatsen, anxious Chinese minds began to contemplate the dreadful possibilities of extinction. But Sun had a solution. It would all be fine, he argued, if the true descendants of the Yellow Emperor explained that they were not just an amorphous mass of black-haired people living under the Manju Qing, but a single, pure race with a common blood as well as distinctive common languages and beliefs: four hundred million men and women who, originating from a Great Man Yellow Emperor thousands of years ago, had devoted millenia to developing and personifying the civilised idea of a *ren* humanity. Yes, Sun conceded, they had failed to take the superficial step of proclaiming themselves a nation state – but this was just a sign of their higher evolution: any patch of land could call itself a state, but only the people of truly Great Men could be called a civilisation.

To all of which, Sun added that it was also important to remember that, one way or another, and over the great stretch of Chinese time, a number of other mingling races had found their way into the Chinese lands: a few million Mongols, a million Manjus, a few million Tibetans, and over a million Mohammedan Turks. These were to be distinguished from the 'Han' descendants of the Yellow Emperor. The Han were the people who had gone on to transform the original wisdom of the settled idea into a towering Confucian culture, predicated on the idea of a 'cultivated' people. And, with the transformation having been accomplished under the Han dynasty, naturally the people had taken the name of 'Han' to describe their race. It was now time, Sun declared, for the 'Han people' to rise up as the race they were and throw the brown Manju barbarians off their perch. When, in 1911, an accidental bomb had gone off in Wuchang, it seemed that was exactly what they had done.

When the Manju Qing empire was brought to an abrupt end, the various barbarians at the edges of the empire assumed that they were as free as the Han. High up in the Himalayan mountains – and with the eastern edges of the Tibetan empire having already been eaten away by China's neighbouring Sichuan province – the thirteenth Dalai Lama declared that his people should assert their freedom not only in the next life but in this one too. Chinese troops, not yet sure what the shape of the new Republican China was to be, stood up to hold the Tibetan territories that had surely come to be under the authority of the Qing. But in the confusion of the moment, loyalties wavered, and the battle was lost.

Similarly, when news of the accidental revolution reached the tribute-paying Ulaanbaatar, capital of (Outer) Mongolia, its Buddhist leader was declared Great Khan of the Mongol nation, and a statement was issued to the effect that any submissions of the past had been nothing more than the repayment of old debts to the Manju cousins – debts which were on no account transferable to any Han Chinese. Looking at the declared independence of the Outer Mongol cousin, Inner Mongolia was then torn between Buddhists who were keen to return to a great Mongolian Khanate, and the ambitions of a group of Inner Mongol princes who hoped, like many of their predecessors, to find a better future for themselves in a stronger China. To which was added the complicating detail that the Inner Mongol lands were already home to a large number of Han Chinese who had been flocking north for decades (if not centuries): escaping the collapse of their own overburdened soil, they had settled new fields and trading towns on what had once been pure Mongol grasslands.

There had been just as much chaos and confusion within the heavenly lands themselves. When Hunan province (the old state of Chu) had declared its independence, other provinces had followed suit, each rising up to throw off the Manju Qing. They were not alone. Seeing an opportunity to secure their own independence, a host of barbarian tribes also rose up to claim states of their own: in the lower south-west, a tribe to the south of Yunnan declared a kingdom of Sipsong Panna (Xishuangbanna, to the Han Chinese). Meanwhile, watching the Tibetans and the Mongols, individual groups of Turkic people in the north-west (including, but by no means only, the Uighurs) tried to shake the soldiers of Qianlong's garrisons out of what had become Xinjiang province. Fortunately for the young Republic, a wily once-imperial official with military ambitions of his own had been quick to turn his coat from the ousted Qing to the new Republic and hold the Uighurs in their place – but it had been touch and go.

Within a year of its revolution, the fledgling Republic was split. Newspapers exploded with opinions: divided between those who wanted a 'China proper' and those who wanted something 'greater'. Given the recent revolution of their own, and given Confucius' exhortation to always put oneself in other people's shoes, for those who wanted a China proper (seemingly, a minority) the situation was simple: just ask the Mongolians, the Tibetans, and everybody else, what they want. But those in favour of the 'greater' idea (far more in number, or at least far more vociferous) argued that any idea about simplicity was dangerously misplaced. The Han, with their greater civilisation, were obviously capable of developing the requisite national consciousness and political understanding required to survive in the new twentieth-century world of sovereign states. But the Mongols, the Muslims and all the other rag-tag barbarians who had ended up in the heavenly lands were nothing but simple animals, with no idea at all about the stakes and risks involved. And while these particular animals might be simple, there were greater beasts prowling around on the outside – Russia, Japan, Britain and the rest of Europe, not to mention America – which were extremely dangerous. The lesson of the past sixty years had been clear: the territories of any lesser races not held with an iron will would not only be lost, but would be used by the greater Western barbarian beasts as a springboard from which to try and capture the Chinese heartlands as well. As for Confucius and the old *ren* idea of putting oneself in other people's shoes, well that belonged to another time; obviously, the world had changed.

Once again, Sun Yatsen came up with a reconciling suggestion. If the survival of China as a country depended on the holding of the greatest possible land mass, then the idea of a single Han Chinese state would need to be adapted in order to embrace the other buffering races (and their territories) as well. Not one Han race alone, but five races, as one great *guojia*, state family, led by the superior Han, whose civilised sense of responsibility would ensure the essential unity upon which, as the earliest emperors had understood, the security of all depended.

With things a little clearer, the new Republic of China reached out to the edges of the old Manju empire and read them a series of revisions to their independent dreams. Tibet would just have to remain divided, with the eastern part of its Kham province now obviously a part of Sichuan. Mongolia would also have to stay in two pieces – at least until Outer Mongolia could be persuaded to change its independent mind. And if the Inner Mongolians were stupid enough to keep raising objections about independence, someone could explain to them that under the new Republic of China, any one of the five races could become President – as long, of course, as the individual had the right qualifications. As for Xinjiang, well, fortunately it was already in the hands of a loyal militarist, so there was no need to have a conversation at all. And as for the southern tribes, without any armies of their own, and not much of a voice, they would just have to accept the fact that they were a people whose time had long gone. Unfortunately, they had missed out on a lot of the civilisation, but they would be welcome to join the unity of all.

*　　*　　*

The security of China's borders, however, was not the only battleground of opinion. At the turning century's troubling time of change, many of the Han Chinese were concerned to find a common purpose and identity that could pull everyone together. 'What did it mean to be Chinese?' had been a hard enough question to answer in 1279 when the Song had fallen to the Mongol Yuan; but after the rise and fall of the Ming, after the hunts of the Manju Qing, after the ravages of the Western barbarians, and with the accidental, 1911, revolution lost to warlords, it was a question which had only got harder. Some, a little vague on the present as well as the past, suggested that Buddhism was the obvious glue. They were soon set straight with the observation that sprinkling holy water over a people who had long ago set aside the idea of the Buddha for the strength of the family could only be a remedy of the desperate. Others suggested that the common thread was origin: a common ancestor in the Yellow Emperor who had not only sired the people who became the Han but had probably sired many of those who, after five thousand years of migration and commingling, had not only got a little darker, but also lost. Yet others pointed out that, while the idea of a common Yellow Emperor ancestor might cover the tribes who had been pushed from north to south (even, at a pinch, covering some of the Manjus who had been sitting quite close to the heartlands before they had advanced on Beijing), it would be extremely difficult to stretch his progeny to include the Tibetans, the Mongols and the Turkic Uighurs. Others, digging deeper into history, pulled out stories of princesses offered up for tribute-generating alliances, and argued that the Yellow Emperor's blood was probably running through the veins of even these unlikely barbarians as well.

Some were convinced; others were concerned. 'Yellow river, yellow emperor, yellow people', the great reformer Liang Qichao observed, 'it all seems to add up to some idea that yellow is our operative identity, with a serious risk that the rest of the world will simply laugh.' After a long time arguing, however, someone else suggested that these kinds of questions were natural for a new nation. To which, Li Dazhao (Peking University's chief librarian, and the political economist who had been driven by the question of what it meant to be Chinese) observed that the questions which were being debated were really part of the wider challenge of 'imagining a people'. Scattered like sand, and with an illiterate majority of peasants cut loose from the written civilisation of the intellectual scholars and imperial classes, the question of precisely what it was that united even the pure Han had obviously yet to be answered. If the Republic was to be known as China, then it was time to go out of the city and down to the countryside to find the real 'Chinese people' – including *all* of the various races.

While they were at it, Li Dazhao added, they should take the time to find everybody's stories – those of the pure Han *and* the tribes – and weave them together into the colourful fabric of a new and greater whole.

The early Peking University students had indeed gone down to the countryside – in the company of many 'rural reconstructing' others. Waves of warlords had also spread out, as had some of the barbarian foreigners, particularly the Japanese. By the late 1920s many were suggesting that if one were going to weave everybody's stories together, it might be an idea to include an extra strong thread for the fierce tribal spirit of the Mongols and the Manju – a spirit which the Chinese 'sheep' had either never had, or, if they had ever had it, had obviously lost. Having been held in the noose of a Manju hunt for so many centuries, it was high time they learnt the value of an inner barbarian nature: clearly a strength which the imperialist West and the Japanese had managed to retain. When Mao and his fellow Communists slipped out of the Guomindang's net and set off on their Long March in 1934, it was a thought that many had carried in their hearts.

*　　*　　*

Leaving southern Jiangxi province in October 1934, the eighty-six thousand Long Marchers had initially walked west. Keeping to the shadows of the wilder world, they had first crossed the southern bottom of Hunan, and then continued on across the upper tip of Guangxi, into Guizhou, and then through the eastern edges of Yunnan, from where they turned north, to Sichuan. Walking across the mountains of Sichuan and further west on to the grasslands of Tibet and then into the deserts of the north-west, they had traversed some of the wildest lands in China's world, and met tribes of people who had only been seen as strange creatures in imperial picture-books. In Guangxi, a land dotted with strange hills like spires, they encountered groups of people known as the 'Miao' who, through their own many different languages, claimed to have been anciently ousted from their original home in the Yellow River north. In the tropical rainforests of Yunnan, they encountered the Yi, another group of people with many different languages who prided themselves on having ancestors who had battled against the ancient Zhou. Proceeding across the Jade Dragon Snow Mountain – and shivering through the vast and empty Tibetan highlands – they occasionally met wandering pockets of nomadic Buddhists who had little or nothing to share, but far more frequently found themselves victims of the hostile arrows of invisible Tibetan warriors, who were keen for them to leave. Entering the wastelands of the deserts, they then found themselves at the mercy of quite another nature, punctuated by Islamic oases shot with the divided loyalties of far-off central Asian lands.

Often desperate, and dependent at every step on the refuge and shared food offered by people who had no wish to be part of the 'five races, one family' idea, the Long Marchers discovered an entirely new world. Freed from the flatness of the picture-books, the 'tribes' suddenly appeared as real human beings. Some were inclined to be friendly; others not. Lives hanging on the hospitality and local knowledge of those who were helpful (and shocked at the encounters with those who were not), this encounter with other races led some to imagine a truly new China, one which would live at peace with the tribes which the imperial dynasties had wrongly tried to bury. Others, however, saw nothing but a world of uncivilised races simply waiting to be tamed. For his part, Mao, with a weather eye on victory, however it might be achieved, promised that old injustices would be redressed and the tribal brothers – to be described as *minzu*, minority peoples – would be given the right to choose exactly what and whose people they were.

The tribes were not, though, the only different people the Long Marchers encountered. Others were pockets of people whose voices seemed to be Chinese but who owed their greatest allegiance not to Confucius but to Mohammed. They called themselves the Hui. Long Marchers who had read their schoolbooks remembered that some of them were the descendants of early Arab traders who had arrived in the southern coastal ports of China from the later times of the Tang dynasty, while others were descendants of the *semu*, the coloured-eyes, brought by Kublai Kan from the Persian end of his cousins' Mongol empire, to supervise the conquered, and not-quite trusted, scholar-officials of the Song. Whether their ancestors had arrived from the south or the north, the men had married Chinese women and, insisting on living in Quran-reading communities, had followed the river routes of trade, looking for places to settle. Some had made their homes in the south-west, where markets spread along the soft borders with Burma and Vietnam; others had made their homes up in the north and west which were home to people who traced their origins to the steppes. The Hui were not a people in the sense of having their own independent language and geography, but they certainly had a different idea about life in both this world and the next. Accepting their hospitality and listening to their dreams, Mao made them the same promises of a truly new China: a People's Republic that would live at peace with any and all other people, all of whom would be free to choose their futures.

By the time the Long Marchers came across the last groups of Hui, however, in the Ningxia north-west, Mao was also floating another idea as well. Tales had reached his ears of Hui warlords who had allied themselves with units of the Guomindang, themselves allied with renegade forces of loyalist White Russians, all intent on smashing an 'East Turkestan Republic' raised in Kashgar by Uighurs – with Moscow's support. Contemplating the invisible currents of energy sparking in the Muslim world, Mao cast his mind back to his own studies of history, and remembered a man called Ataturk who had recaptured the Turkic remnants of the lost Ottoman empire from the Western imperialists. Once in Yan'an, and struck by the possibility of strengthening the Party's army with Muslim forces, Mao had invited other groups of Hui to raise a 'Mohammedan Red Army' – and then gone on to think about what other pockets of desperate people might be willing to stand beside the Communists in the hope of a future independence. The Inner Mongols were one possibility: now caught between Chiang Kai-shek's Republican China and the new Japanese 'Manchuria' which, established in 1931, was increasingly devouring neighbouring lands. The Xinjiang Uighurs, whose attempts at raising an independent East Turkestan had been smashed by the Guomindang, were another.

The right of a people to choose their destiny became a Party principle. Mao assured the most loyal of the *minzu* minority groups that, in the event of a Communist victory, a successful, and grateful, Party would reward them with autonomous areas of their own, named after their people, and united with the Communists by the common battling desire to be free. In 1944, the Uighurs lost a second attempt at an independent East Turkestan to the superior forces of the Guomindang and their allied warlords. But in 1945, the Russian brothers snatched both Manchuria and the neighbouring east of Inner Mongolia from Japan, and, two years later, in 1947, offered the lands to the younger Chinese brothers. Mao declared that the people of Inner Mongolia should have the first of the promised self-governing areas: the Autonomous Region of Inner Mongolia.

*   *   *

The idea of groups of independent *minzu* people was as intoxicating for some Party members as for the various minzu themselves. But as revolutionary victory approached, other senior Party minds began to wonder what exactly a future Communist government would do with pockets of minzu freedom. In an ideal world, promising them the power to choose what they wanted to be was laudable. But in the real world, where only the fittest survived, and in the lands of China, where any new Communist state would be immediately faced with just the same kinds of foreign imperial threats that the Qing and the Republicans had had to battle before them, was such a promise really practical? 'If we offer them a choice, won't we be encouraging them to accept?' asked some. 'And if they accept', asked others, 'won't we find that our borders have suddenly frayed into nothing but an open invitation to anyone to invade?'

Other Party leaders, less sympathetic to the minzu dream went even further: 'Who on earth are these *minzu* peoples anyway?' 'And why shouldn't they be evolving like everybody else, to the higher level of socialist man?' When the questions were answered with the point that promises made would have to be kept, the questioners responded with the sharpness of a people who had battled bitterly for their own survival. Having been so long in the grip of the Manju Qing's hunt, not to mention having become part of the board of a Great Game played by the imperial powers of Russia and the West, surely they had been hoodwinked too many times by other people to treat a promise with care.

Unaware of the inner battles of the Party's leadership, the wider body of the Party membership noted that when a provisional Constitution (entitled the Common Programme) was announced in late September 1949, it declared everyone to be equal, with each group destined to govern themselves within the wider embrace of a bigger, united family. The idea of equality still seemed to be standing firm when Mao Zedong rose to the eaves of the Tiananmen

Gate of Heavenly Peace two days later on 1 October 1949, to declare the founding of the People's Republic of China.

But behind the scenes, stronger winds of ruling reality had already taken charge. 'Minzu choice', they had successfully argued, 'was nothing but a slogan for a fractured past – not at all a principle on which a unifying present could be built.' To which they had added that it would be better not to make a public announcement on the point: the truth could always be hidden in the detail. It was clear, however, at least to everyone who counted at the top, that it was the Han Chinese who had sweated blood and tears to deliver a successful revolution, and it would be under the Han Chinese that everyone's future would be found.

Well before 1949 was out, the Party, learning from the past, began to tighten a grip around the difficult edges of the old Qing empire that would have been worthy of a Manju hunt. In the summer of 1949, the First Field Army of the People's Liberation Army advanced to Xinjiang to relieve the Guomindang of their posts, and liberate the people. In late August, the leaders of the (failed) Second East Turkestan Republic were invited to a conference in Beijing. Thanked for their great service to the people of Xinjiang and China, three days later, they boarded a plane to return home. Neither they nor the plane ever arrived. In December, three months after replacements accepted an invitation for Xinjiang to join the People's Republic of China, Beijing announced that the original plane had crashed 'somewhere over Lake Baikal'. It was one of those twists which, as everyone living at the north-western edge of China's lands knew, was rarely a matter of fate.

And then, in the early months of 1950, the People's Liberation Army marched on from Xinjiang to the Tibetan Plateau, across Himalayan lands that cut through a corner of a newly independent India. Severing the Lhasa capital from the entire Tibetan east, the army declared that the Tibetan people had returned to the motherland of the People's Republic of China. Setting off to build a hidden Himalayan highway between Xinjiang and Tibet – through India's Aksai Chin – the highest ranking military officer left instructions for the young Fourteenth Dalai Lama to send an envoy to Beijing to sign a seventeen-point agreement for peace. All typed up, and not open to negotiation, the 'agreement' stated that Tibet would be given a right to 'exercise autonomy' and that 'nothing would change in the political system' of the Tibetan lands. Advised by the Commander of Tibet's tiny army – and remembering a desperate prophecy of death and torture left by his predecessor – the sixteen-year-old Dalai Lama signed. Within months, the streets of Lhasa were overwhelmed with thousands of soldiers from the People's Liberation Army, all waving images of Mao and proclaiming the liberation of Tibet. Dazed, Tibetan monks and people had asked: *liberation from what?*

Back in Beijing, with the Party's provisional constitution having announced that the *minzu* people would not only be equal but would be able to govern themselves, attention now turned to three longstanding *minzu* questions which had not yet been answered. The first was how the *minzu* were going to govern themselves while also sitting under the Han Chinese. The second, a much older question, was who the *minzu* people were. And the third, which would probably need to be answered before the second and the first, was where exactly the various *minzu* were to be found.

In 1951, a Central Institute for Nationalities was established, populated by anthropologists and sociologists who had chosen to stay in the mainland under the new People's Republic. In 1954, they were secretly set to the task of finally working out the answers to the minzu questions – as quickly as possible. A little at sea, given the enormity of the task and the short timetable, the social scientists turned to the Russian big brother for ideas, and to their own books for facts. From Russia, they took their lead from a set of 'nationality principles' that Stalin had applied to the vast central Asian and Far Eastern empire of the Russias when it had been reconfigured into a 'Soviet Union'. For books from home, they buried themselves in the surviving imperial libraries of Song, Ming and Manju Qing picture-books – all compiled by successive emperors, each keen to compliment themselves on the many and varied colours of their lands.

Typically intellectual, however, the anthropologists and sociologists were just too slow. With a new People's Republic to run, and promised *minzu* autonomies to be created in some form or another, the Party had no time to wait for a scholarly text. A snapped census was suggested: if the imperial picture-books couldn't provide easy answers as to who was who, why not ask the *minzu* people themselves? Unfortunately, when the results of the snap census were compiled, it became clear that the people were no clearer than the picture-books. Most of the respondents had struggled to even understand the questions, and four hundred different groups (two hundred and fifty in Yunnan province alone) had popped up with a claim to be some kind of *minzu* or other. Obviously, the respondents hadn't studied politics or any other of the social sciences. With the respondents lacking the education necessary to produce responsible answers, the researchers were instructed to go out across the country and find out the answers themselves. 'Learn the languages, pick up the history and deliver your considered scientific opinion', they were told. 'And no need to worry about how long you will be away – a few months should be enough.'

The researchers did their best but, however bright they were, and however hard they worked, they could never have done enough. There was not one neat migration but layers of migrations over thousands of years. And the tribes had not just moved from north to south, but from east to west, and often back again. To make things worse, as far as the researchers could see, the idea of four hundred different groups was, if anything, a gross over-simplification. 'Local chiefs' had regularly simplified complicated tribal origins in a bid to get and keep imperial titles. And when the Manju Qing had sent central officials to replace them, the new officials (observing at first hand the more natural lives and beliefs of the tribes, acclimatising themselves to the softer life, and concluding that the less the centre knew, the easier things would remain) had insisted that, in the interests of imperial comprehension, the facts of origin should be simplified even more.

As the scholarly researchers researched, the fact that the origins were complicated soon became clear. But from what they could see on the ground, sorting them out in anything less than a lifetime would be impossible. Even the languages couldn't help: far from being able to identify a handful of common and learnable tongues, the scholars were struggling to come across any common chatter at all. Thrust into the fog of five thousand years of complicated tribal histories across one of the biggest geographies in the world, and with only months to find their way, they were close to drowning, when an impatient Beijing recalled them. Having taken far too long, the fussing intellectuals were told that the messy matter of who was who was being transferred back to the Beijing bureaucrats. Far from the field, they would have the objectivity that only official training, and distance, could provide.

Poring over their tea leaves, the Beijing bureaucrats came to the conclusion that, rather than worrying about reading everything, labours could be saved if they availed themselves of the practical assistance of a nineteenth-century British cartographer (and Major General) by the name of Henry Rodolph Davies. Having been charged with charting the boundary between British imperial Burma and Qing China in the early 1890s, the Major General had helpfully left his maps and definitions behind for Chinese posterity. With colonial clarity at their fingertips, the bureaucrats were able to deliver their verdict on the *minzu* situation in the commendably efficient space of only six months: fifty-six identifiably different groups in the Chinese lands, including the pure race of the Han. True, there were a lot of others who *claimed* to have more of a tribal difference. But they were obviously victims of a 'false consciousness': after so much time in the trees, they had obviously lost track of the links that related them to other tribal cousins. So what if their ancestors had always argued that they weren't the same? Ancestors could be just as mistaken as descendants. And as for those who argued that they had to be different because they spoke a different language, that was neither here nor there. Obviously the past had created a terrible mess; and while some might find it difficult to understand the languages of the long lost relatives with whom they would now be reunited, that was nothing that a little language training – and a lot of political education – couldn't cure.

Names were named, and by squeezing thousands of strands of difference into a manageable fifty-six, everyone was put in their places, and named. Even at this dramatically pared-down number, however, there were clearly far too many *minzu* for each to be given its own autonomous region. Which ones to choose? How to make sure that the chosen few were clear both about the meaning of autonomy within the greater Chinese family, and about their own responsibilities for unity? And how, given the essential importance of unity, were 'autonomous' decisions to be made? In 1954, a new Constitution had helpfully made a start by declaring that national autonomous areas would – as and when they were established – be inalienable parts of the People's Republic of China. Behind the scenes, desperate bureaucrats tried to work out the devilish details.

Eventually, it was decided that a small number of very big groups would be rewarded with a region – roughly the size and status of a province. Beyond these fortunate few, the majority of the minzu groups would receive smaller privileges of autonomous prefectures (cities, towns and surrounding areas) or autonomous counties (villages, smaller towns and surrounding areas). At the same time, everyone would have to recognise that some of the areas (particularly in the messy south-west) would have so many different *minzu* that it would be better just to call them 'autonomous', rather than give them a particular name. China might be a big country, but if one took out the mountains and the deserts, and factored in the number of people, everyone was really rather squashed in. That and the fact that, with the Han people being far more numerous than any of the other races across the heavenly lands as a whole, many of the autonomous areas would, in any event, naturally be home to much bigger numbers of Han.

Turning to the question of the meaning and responsibilities of autonomy, it was obvious that these would need to be understood in the bigger picture of the wider Chinese family – with the usual ordering 'unity' as the fundamental principle of all.

As for how decisions would be made *within* the autonomous areas, well naturally the minzu should benefit from the broader principles of socialist democracy, including the leadership of the Chinese Communist Party, under the Democratic Dictatorship of the People. Just as in other areas of the country, local people's congresses would be created, with locally elected members proportionately reflecting the colours of the (recognised) *minzu* groups living in the relevant area (including the local Han). Not everyone was happy and quite a few had their questions: 'Won't there be a risk that in some places the numerically greater Han Chinese will actually be running the autonomous regions?' 'Well', answered those in charge, 'with so many different *minzu* people and with so many Han, some of the *minzu* colour is naturally bound to fade – but, as man moves towards the realisation of both a socialist and Chinese unity, surely this is only to be desired.'

Returning to the more difficult question of exactly which others, beyond the Inner Mongols, would get the rewards of the big autonomous regions, in the end, it was events which settled the selection. In 1955, anxious about tempers raging across the wild Xinjiang north-west, Mao decided that things might be easier if the various groups could be divided even further. Separating out the biggest group (the Uighurs) from the many, generally Turkic, others (Kazakhs, Kirghiz, Tatars, Salar, Uzbeks, not to forget some lost remnants of the Cossacks), he created a Xinjiang Uighur Autonomous Region. Three years later, it seemed appropriate to give the better-behaved Hui a place of their own, as well. That was a little hard to do, given that they were scattered everywhere across the nation. But the Hui of Ningxia Province (sitting below the western stretches of Inner Mongolia, and at the entrance to the corridor which led to Xinjiang) seemed to be as good a candidate as any: being one of the people who had supported Mao and the Long Marchers on the latter legs of their journey, it seemed quite right that they should get an Autonomous Region of their own. With two autonomous regions now settled in the north, Party thoughts then turned to something that would balance things in the south. Looking at the map, the obvious answer was the biggest of the southern minzu groups, the Zhuang. Notifying them of their selection, an autonomous region was created for them in the misty mountains of Guangxi.

With all of that settled, each autonomous region was to be given a 'chairman' (just as each of the Han provinces had their 'governors'), selected from the relevant minzu minority and invited to sit visibly at the top. And just to make sure that the minzu remained clear about the importance of unity, Mao applied the same principle to them as he applied to every province in the country: behind every 'chairman' (as behind every provincial governor) would sit a Communist Party secretary. Selected from Beijing, and almost without exception Han Chinese, it would be the Party secretary who would hold the 'unifying' power.

*   *   *

With the first four autonomous regions now appointed, as well as a host of smaller autonomous prefectures and counties, attention then turned to the unifying principles of socialism under which everyone would live. The most fundamental was ownership of the land. Begun in earnest in the early 1950s, the reforms which gave every individual peasant a pocket of his own land were already hitting trouble among the most backward kinds of *minzu* – stubborn people who insisted that their lands had always been held by all of them together and could not possibly be divided. Moving on to the collectives and the communes should have been easier (after all, wasn't a collective just another kind of common land?). But the minzu had fussed again, this time arguing that if the land was asked to do too much, and if the people who farmed it were forced to follow the ideas of a single top-down mind, it would not be able to support anybody. Then there was the question of Tibet: with so much of its land owned by the monasteries, someone was going to have to talk to the monks.

Mao had originally been willing to give the Tibetan people the time they needed to adapt to the new state of affairs. But by 1957, the revolutionary transformations in the Sichuan-bordering east of Tibet had gone a little faster than planned. Local Party officials, first keen to divide the land, then just as keen to put it into collectives, had whipped up storms of local zeal. The monasteries and their lands had been folded into the people's property; monks had been returned to a lay way of life; herders arguing for nature had been trampled underfoot; and any and all other inconvenient Tibetan minds were now being denounced as feudal rightists and swept into jail.

Uneasy at the news that was reaching Lhasa, but without any idea of how to deal with the Chinese – and with no help from any other barbarians near or far – the young Dalai Lama pinned his hopes on a rather surprising declaration by Mao that he was an ardent admirer of Guan Yin. Given that the goddess Guan Yin was not just the goddess of compassion but had been inspired by the greatest of the Buddhist bodhisattvas, Avalokitesvara (the bodhisattva of which every Dalai Lama is a re-incarnation), this seemed to offer some grounds for optimism. But while the young Dalai Lama hoped for a meeting of minds, the eastern monasteries and temples were falling to the Party's land reform, and the tempers of the eastern Tibetans were exploding.

In 1958, Buddhist scholars tried to calm the rage by encouraging monks to rebuild their temples in their hearts, rather than on what were now heavily contested lands. Clear that what was at stake was the future of Tibet, the monks were unwilling to yield. By 1959, the news reaching the Dalai Lama was even more worrying. The Great Leap Forward, declared in China the year before, was now not only leading to famines in Sichuan but had taken a grip on the eastern Tibetan province of Kham as well. Waves of eastern Tibetans began to flock to Lhasa; saffron furies erupted in the city of the gods; and Chinese guns trained themselves on the people on the streets. Skies darkening for a storm, the Dalai Lama's advisers persuaded him to gather himself up as the hope of his people, and find his way to the sheltering slopes of Himalayan India. Meanwhile, fearful that the Dalai Lama was in danger, in the days around his departure, thousands of Tibetans gathered to protect him. In the ensuing encounters with the People's Liberation Army, two thousand Tibetans died. When news spread that the Dalai Lama had left, remaining Tibetans found themselves adrift in a world that had lost the beating heart of its Buddha: eighty-seven thousand others had set out across the mountains to follow him to the Himalayan west.

With the Dalai Lama gone, and the seventeen-point agreement obviously broken, as far as Mao could see there was no reason why the Himalayan kingdom of the gods could not now bow to the unity of the Chinese family. And with India having treacherously offered the Dalai Lama refuge, it also seemed appropriate to rename sixty-five thousand square kilometres of neighbouring territory that the imperial British had once marked off as Indian, as a new 'Southern Tibet'. Meanwhile, with the People's Liberation Army now firmly in command, the Great Leap Forward began to jump across all the Tibetan lands. And as the Great Leap Forward jumped, Tibet exploded. Rebel monks fell in their thousands to the new military power, condemned like so many other subjective spirits to *laogai* camps of labour. Eventually, as in the other minzu regions, a Democratic Dictatorship of the

People was declared – and a war of the classes was unleashed to set anyone who tilled the land against the 'landlord lamas'.

In 1962, having stayed behind to steady the rages of Tibet as best he could, the Panchen, Great Scholar, Lama (the highest ranking Buddhist teacher after the Dalai, Ocean of Learning, Lama) bravely stroked a secret memorandum to Mao: 'Two thousand five hundred monasteries have been reduced to a pool of seventy, and the army has declared war on the people of Tibet.' 'When', he asked, 'will it ever end?' Describing the memorandum as the 'poisoned arrow' of a separatist enemy, Mao despatched the Panchen Lama to Beijing's Qincheng jail. In the same year the People's Liberation Army was sent to insist upon the borders of the new 'Southern Tibet', pushing into the lands of India's Arunachal Pradesh and battling across the region of Aksai Chin. The ensuing war between China and India lasted only a single wintery month, at the close of which Aksai Chin had been firmly embraced within the People's Republic of China.

In 1965, with the border fixed and the Great Leap Forward having run out of steam, Tibet became the fifth, and last, autonomous region. Led by a Beijing-educated Tibetan chairman, it was naturally ruled by a Han Chinese Party secretary (a general in the People's Liberation Army). Not long after that, the battle against the 'Four Olds' was carried up to Tibet, and a Tibetan Red Guard was created, charged with ushering in a Cultural Revolution of its own. A thousand years of Tibetan Buddhist relics – monasteries, images, prayer wheels, bells and books – all went up in flames. Every religious observation was abolished. The Tibetan language was 'simplified' to the point that many no longer recognised it. Posters of Mao were placed in every household. Rebellious hearts were exposed to the cleansing education of struggle sessions. And, as elsewhere (although a little later), communes followed. Asking why Mao could not be satisfied with the secular world and leave their Buddhist hearts alone, thousands of Tibetans threw themselves into yet more uprisings. Their question answered with the bullet of unity, they were buried in graves that they had been forced to dig themselves.

By the time the furies of the Cultural Revolution had blown themselves out, the *laogai* labour camps had become a feature of the Tibetan landscape, even as the landscape had fallen under the familiar taming order of the heavenly Great Man. Treasured for the glittering minerals hidden within the veins of its earth, even before Deng announced his Four Modernisations, Tibet was being excavated for its temporal wealth. Uranium discovered, its distant plateaux then became natural sites for exploding tests of nuclear power. Above the ground, forests had been flattened and rivers had begun to dry; across the grasslands, soil had turned to dust. Mines were becoming towns, rivers were charged with radioactive energy, and the detritus of nuclear experiments was being buried underground. By the time that Deng departed to the next world, the taming of Tibet's nature had become an industry all of its own.

*   *   *

As the socialist dream set Tibet alight in the west, across the arc of the north, the Inner Mongols found themselves battling against similar storms of change. Guided by shamans, and raised with Buddhism, the Mongols also saw themselves as the children of a Tengr sky and a grassland mother – led by the essential totem of the wolf. Vast, and swept with oceans of grass, the steppe might seem to offer life to endless numbers of hungry mouths, but every Mongol knew that wild winds, poor rains and heavy snows made the grass a fragile support. Stewardship was everything. Storming horses, grazing gazelles, wandering yaks, greedy goats and sheep (even ravenous marmots and rabbits), all had their place, but only if each group of creatures kept to their individual limits within the 'bigger life' of nature. Hunting in cunning packs, culling the greediest of mouths, it was the wolves who kept the natural world in order. And man? Well, trained to see himself as answerable to the Tengr sky and the grassland mother, and tutored by the wolf, man could perform a similar role. Indeed, learning from the wolves, man and horse combined could even become a worthy opponent, ensuring that the hunting packs would, like the groups of every other species, keep themselves within the limits of the land. But to earn his place at the top, man-on-horseback had to keep himself and everyone else on a constant move, ensuring that no heavy herds of anything were ever able to stay so long on any patch of grass that it could be trampled into deadening clutches of mud.

To the Mongols, this was all a simple 'grassland logic'. But while the logic was something that even a Mongol child could grasp, it took a true man to master the actual forces of mind and body required to keep up with the wolf. Even after thousands of years of living at the edges of the Mongol world, few Han Chinese had managed to understand it. At home in a world where forests were flattened for fields, where nature was ordered for bumper harvests, and everyone was part of a family within which they were constantly told not only what to do, but exactly how to do it, how could they ever understand? Chinese scholars might sing the praises of nature in their books and paintings, but the nature they praised was an abstract idea of an ancient golden idyll that had very little to do with the reality of the natural world. Keeping to their studies, the scholarly Chinese had turned themselves into a herd of highly educated sheep. Perhaps it had been different thousands of years before: perhaps everyone had even come from a single sky. But if that was the case, the Chinese had clearly lost that early wisdom: settling on their fields, they had come to hear the cry of a wolf as the wail of a hungry ghost. Scratching at their yellow earth, they had become a people who grasped at patches of land, without ever understanding the bigger sweeps of life. And ordered in their families, imperial rulers had come to see them as little more than units of production – an idea that they had (largely) followed. Obviously it had not worked: when things had really begun to unravel in the nineteenth century, the northern Chinese had flocked to the Mongol grasslands. But even then, they had not come in search of the lessons of the wolf: having exhausted their fields, they were simply looking for fresh lands to farm.

Then Stalin had swept up the Inner Mongol lands in his iron fist and, eventually, turned them over to Mao; at which point the trickle of Chinese sheep had become more of a trampling herd. As in Tibet, land reform and the collectivisation of everything had been conducted under the unifying guidance of the Han big brother. Beneficiaries of the first of the autonomous regions, with a clear promise of a land of their own, the Inner Mongols had been shocked to find themselves first forced to divide up their grasslands with fences, and then ordered to plant sheds on the grasslands, and then settle everything under the command of commune leaders who had never even seen a wolf, let alone dreamt of one.

But that was only the beginning. The ravages of the Han's Great Leap Forward not only turned the grasslands into communes – complete with militarised brigades of work – but transformed the trampling herd of Chinese sheep into a flood that threatened not only the Mongols, but the very force of nature itself. This time, a torrent of people in pursuit of lands that could be turned to grain. Desperate descendants of that misguided ancestor they called Yu the Great, the migrants put up more fences and sheds, diverted rivers, felled trees, and pierced the ground with wells. And as their madness reconfigured the landscape of the wolf, their Great Man attention turned to the wandering yurt-like *gers* in which the Mongols carried their nomadic lives. Declared to be barbarian, the *gers* were replaced with immovable

470

boxes built from bricks and tiles, each adorned with one of the chimneys that seemed to follow the Chinese wherever they went.

As any wolf-child could have told them, it was not long before the horses got tangled up in the wire fences, and the sheep spread like clouds. Before much longer, the grass, on which everyone's survival depended, turned to mud. But, freshly arrived from southern fields to teach the Mongol brothers how to farm, the Han leaders of the production brigades dismissed any and all protests as the dying gasps of a backward world. And when the Mongols continued to complain, their (Inner Mongol) chairman was denounced as a rightist: no matter that he had been a member of the Chinese Communist Party since 1925. Complaints turned to protests, and more Mongols, monks herders and all – were denounced, this time as criminal 'separatists'. Time and again, the Inner Mongol chairman begged Beijing to remember Mao's promises of autonomy; and each time, Beijing replied that autonomy was only autonomy within the greater unity of the Chinese family.

When, in 1966, the Inner Mongol chairman finally realised that the idea of 'autonomy' was nothing but a trick of the text, the Party brothers rounded on the Inner Mongols as ungrateful dogs, unworthy to call themselves even cousins of the Chinese. At which point, a special force of the Cultural Revolution was unleashed to root out the dangerous separatist enemies looking for an independent state. With Soviet Russia now an enemy – stuffing missiles into Outer Mongolia, now known as the Mongolian People's Republic – Beijing unleashed the terror of its Cultural Revolution upon Inner Mongolia's two million heads: excruciating tortures that left hundreds of thousands crippled and maimed, deaths beyond anyone's imagination, and a toll of the disappeared which was almost as great as the dead.

The principles of unity now clearly established, a flood of Han students was sent to the grassland 'countryside', charged not with learning from the nomads but with learning from the commune leaders who were settling the nomads on the fields. Meanwhile, the borders of the Inner Mongolian Autonomous Region were redrawn to ensure that the surviving Mongol voices were in a more harmonious balance with the surrounding provinces of Han. Exhausted by its own rage, Inner Mongolia's Cultural Revolution eventually died out, although it would be a long time before the students went home.

No sooner had the Cultural Revolution died away though, than another Great Man idea appeared: the Four Modernisations. Large areas of grassland were set aside for mines, cities and their attendant industries. And in the race to get rich quickly, war was declared on the wolf. The bravest of all defenders of the big grasslands life, the very totem of the Mongols, there were few things that the wolves feared, but one of them was the explosion of gunpowder. Seizing on this useful fact, the Han modernisers armed themselves to the hilt. Realising that few of their number were very good shots, they also recruited dead sheep to their cause: wiring them up with explosives so that hungry wolves would be blasted to death, without anyone needing to raise a gun.

By 1989, Inner Mongolia was on its way to a modern future: the wolves had been defeated, and the big life of Inner Mongolia's grasslands was almost dead. With so many Han migrants, the Mongols could no longer be described as the majority of Inner Mongolia's people. Cities rose, and memories of a very different past were buried. Secretly, broken Mongol hearts wondered whether their world might have been saved if the wolves could somehow have become masters of the brush. Out on the steppes, however, men who had once ridden with the wolves wiped away their tears and remarked that, without the grasslands, Beijing would soon be feeling the dusting sting of sandstorms. But by then, of course, it would be too late for everyone: wolves and man alike.

*　　　*　　　*

As the Tibetans and the Mongols had battled, the changes of the People's Republic had also reached into the north-west lands of the Turkic tribes, including the 'new frontier' of Xinjiang province. A world of mountains whose white glaciers dropped into oasis valleys, Han adventurers had long been tantalised by its surprising green pastures. To those whose ancestors had lived there, however, this was a world where everything sat on the edge of a vast and hungry desert: seed too many fields and the soil would turn to sand.

From 1950, Xinjiang people were offered the supporting hands to help them build the socialist dream. Engineers from the big Soviet brother arrived to help open up the seams of the earth. A Xinjiang *Bingtuan* Production and Construction Corps, a military-led division of Han settlers, was put in charge of almost all farming (including a thirsty cotton spread across the valleys) and given responsibility for planting factories as well. Schools taught children that the heroes of the Uighur past were no better than bandits. Scarves of Islamic modesty were banished. And then, as everywhere else in the great

Chinese family, land reforms first swept out landlords and subsequently pushed the 'liberated lands' into collectives. In the accompanying class wars, landowners, moneylenders, mullahs and traders across the roof of the world were all renamed as 'sheep' and 'goats'.

Few, if any, Uighurs believed that the socialist future was going to be any different from the imperial past. In 1957, Beijing's Anti-Rightist campaign reached up to Xinjiang: Uighur homes were stripped for searches; Uighur men disappeared into the night. Then, as the Great Leap Forward loomed, the fragile lands were put under more ploughs than anyone could ever have imagined, and more seams of the earth were opened up for yet more mineral prospects. As Uighur hearts cried, loudspeakers, installed on every corner, rejoiced in the fact that the Chinese and the Uighurs were now one very big family: as if anyone needed reminding.

Up in the Altai north, stronghold of previously attempted East Turkestan Republics, anger had grown to rage and, in 1959, the rage exploded into rebellion. When the rebellion was successfully flattened by the People's Liberation Army, floating rumours whispered that Mao had expressed his gratitude for a mountain of dead Uighur bodies which could be used to fertilise a hungry soil. As elsewhere in the minzu world, rebels who survived were sent to *laogai* labour camps – and anyone suspected of any sympathy whatsoever was 'migrated' to the south of Xinjiang.

With Uighur history officially condemned as a counter-revolutionary force, Uighur parents whispered the stories of their heroes into their children's hearts. Tales were told of lions who had once swept across the roof of the world, carrying the trades of all; and of men who had offered their fighting courage to the sheep-like Tang, and who, even in their own conquest, had never given up the fight. Brave rebels across the ages, their numbers included not only hardened warriors, but women with a beauty and courage which matched the land. Of these, none was braver or more beautiful than the great Iparhan. Captured by a Manju Qing general, she had been given to the Qianlong emperor as a 'fragrant' concubine. Captivated, the Qianlong emperor had offered to recreate her lost Uighur world at the gate of the Imperial City in Beijing. Chinese schools taught of her returning Qianlong's love, but every Uighur heart knew that she had never yielded: threatening to starve herself to death, she had spurned the counterfeit paradise; reluctantly agreeing to live on, she had insisted that her corpse be buried in her homeland. Smitten, Qianlong agreed – and kept his word.

When the Cultural Revolution arrived, its furies were trained to find every treacherous Uighur heart suspected of harbouring a separatist sentiment. In Xinjiang as elsewhere, the 'Four Olds' were set to flames, with any surviving scarves of Islamic modesty added to the fire, followed by books of prayer. Enemies of the Han people were burned in hells of oil; and more and more of the fragile valleys were set to crops of cotton. An already steady flow of Han migrants (one that included shocked waves of exiled Chinese intellectuals, sent to reform themselves by smashing up Xinjiang's rocks) was followed by a tide of city students despatched to man the fields.

Nature collapsing, smoke rising, coughs hacking, hearts breaking, few Uighurs noticed when Mao exploded his first atomic bomb in 1964, on the Lop Nur edge of the Taklamakan desert. Being a land of barbarians, it had not occurred to him to put up a protective fence or tell the Uighurs of the risks. Before long, though, wandering camels and Uighur shepherds found themselves scorched with cosmic dust – and over the years that followed, thousands (perhaps two hundred thousand) were kissed to death and destruction by the spread of the radiating power. In 1968 (with Russia and China now in a cold war of their own), Moscow helped the Uighurs rise again in a struggle for an independent East Turkestan; again, they lost.

Across the next twenty-five years, and with the rise of Deng's Four Modernisations, the Xinjiang Production and Construction Corps continued to tame the lands, expanding its industrial activities, and raising new cities as it went. Rebellions were met with arrests and executions; suspicions of separatist sentiment were followed with torture. And when, in 1991, the collapse of the Soviet Union relaxed Russia's grip on the wider Turkic people at the edges of Xinjiang's borders, instead of thinking again, Beijing simply tightened the noose within which the Uighurs were held.

*   *   *

And then there was the south. With waving coconut palms and tropical rainforests, all watered with mists and washed with torrential rains, these were very different lands. Unified for harmony, however, the same taming forces were unleashed.

Stands of coconut trees were first divided for land reform, and then reunited for a collectively greater productive power. Superstitious spirits who dared to argue that the trees had a life of their own were despatched to another world, or a *laogai* labour camp, before they could do any real harm. The Great Leap Forward brought neighbouring brigades of Chinese communes, in search of the tropical possibilities of a jungle – although eventually they had been obliged to admit that growing grain and herding sheep was really not a possibility in the tropics. Surviving coconut trees, seen as far too idle, were replaced with a more productive rubber; mountains were terraced with rice.

As once-magical rainforests fell to make way for greater production, hanging gardens and sacred groves followed suit. Without their ancient homes, eagles and tigers scattered in all directions, peacocks and pheasants disappeared, and any of the shy snub-nosed monkeys who had managed to hang on to their branches quickly found their heads on the plates of hungry men. And the descendants of the elephants that had fled from the Chinese north thousands of years before lost their final sanctuary.

The people who had survived the Great Leap Forward lived to find themselves beaten down in the bitter battles of the Cultural Revolution. Ancient spirit-gods who had watched over the fortunes of animals and humans alike since time began were pulled from the skies and trampled on the ground. While the silenced tribes watched open-mouthed as their world died, Mao observed that 'battling with nature was a boundless joy'. The tribes themselves would come to call it the 'age of wild ghosts': a time when the fragile boundaries between the living and the dead all but disappeared.

When the Cultural Revolution eventually blew itself out, and Deng Xiaoping ushered in the Four Modernisations, even the Communist Party had to admit that something precious had been lost. Soils struggled to death in a land that had once seemed boundlessly fertile; climbing wisteria and tropical orchids were giving up their ghosts; and groundwater was being sucked into the greediest tree that anyone in the rainforest had ever seen: rubber. Not only had much of the ancient forest fallen – and much of the newly planted forest failed to thrive – but even the once abundant torrents of rain, and the watery mists, had begun to fade away in protest.

Then, on a summer's night in 1975, a Yunnan village exploded. Hard on the edge of Vietnam, and flat on a route that had once carried traders across a southern Asian sweep from Bengal to Malaya, its name was Shadian. The explosion was triggered by a simple misunderstanding: with the Cultural Revolution having faded, a gentle population of Muslims had assumed that it would now be safe to revive a mosque that had been smashed by the Red Guards. But while the Cultural Revolution had come to an end, no official had been willing to approve a resurrection of the old superstitions. The Muslims had become rebels, and fighting broke out on the village square.

Remembering the Yunnan troubles of the Manju Qing, the Party rushed heavy cannon and artillery to the scene – and then commanded MiG jets to sweep the streets with rockets. Before anyone had time to say their prayers, Shadian had been reduced to rubble, a thousand people had lost their lives, and a small pocket of the Muslim world had been shot to kingdom come. A few years later, in 1979, apologies were made, and a number of new mosques were offered in a bid to make amends. But in many parts of the country, Muslims quietly observed that, whatever was going on in Beijing, they would stick to Islam: whichever way the Chinese winds blew the Quran never changed its mind.

* * *

When Deng Xiaoping arrived at the head of the Chinese Communist Party's family, it was clear that if the Four Modernisations were ever going to flourish beyond the Han heartlands, a lot of damage would need to be repaired. Privately acknowledging that thirty years of socialism had delivered more feudalism than progress, the Party offered to loosen the noose of unity, and give autonomy a bit of space to breathe. Here and there, in the corner of a corridor, some senior Party members even whispered that it might be time to face up to the fact that it might not actually be possible to get the *minzu* minorities to relinquish their foolish dreams of gods, wolves, spirits and Islam – at least not in this life.

Talks were offered to the still-exiled Dalai Lama, on condition that he return to Tibet. Declining, the Dalai Lama, nonetheless, sent a delegation of his own to explore the facts on the ground. Arriving in Tibet, his 'eyes and ears' saw a shattered landscape and a desperate people. The worst of their fears had been confirmed.

Rising to an American podium some years later, on 21 September 1987, the Dalai Lama gently reminded his audience (including the distant but acute ears of the Chinese Communist Party) of a thousand year old pillar which, still standing in Lhasa, had been inscribed with the words of a treaty between the Manju Qing and the Tibetans: 'Tibetans will live happily in the great land of Tibet, and the Chinese will live happily in the great land of China'. The Dalai Lama then went on to ask the powers of the mortal world to embrace the land of the gods as a zone of peace.

Within weeks, Buddhist monks were recklessly chanting dreams of an independent Tibet. The chants turned to protests, the protests turned to arrests, beatings and spectacles of trials – all of which fuelled further furies, not only in Tibet but across the neighbouring lands of Xinjiang.

By early 1989, the protests began to wash into a wider Beijing spring that was marked not only with marches in the capital of the country but in the Urumqi capital of Xinjiang as well. For a moment, Tibetan and Uighur hearts dared to hope that Wei Jingsheng's dream of a Fifth Modernisation – the voice of the people – might be possible for all. But even before Beijing's students had settled down for their hunger strike in Tiananmen Square, in Tibet and Xinjiang alike, the protests had been followed by yet more arrests, more beatings and more spectacles of trials.

By the time that Deng Xiaoping boarded his train in 1992, China's edges of order were fraying, badly. Minzu hopes dashed across the land, once again heaven was offering its opinion through ravages of nature that confirmed the worst of the minzu fears. Up on the now-muddy grasslands, it was not only wolves that had become hard to find but even the gazelle (although in the rising dust, some argued that it was difficult to tell). Tractors, motorbikes and chain-link fences had killed off the horse-borne herders, and with them had gone the strength of the Mongols' once-legendary horses. Green grass had been replaced with a yellow stubble and, as the herders had predicted, sand storms had risen up and raced down to Beijing. Meanwhile, across in Xinjiang, while the Xinjiang Production and Construction Corps expanded its industrial and agricultural empire, cancers were eating into the lives of the Uighurs, even as the desert stretched its sandy fingers ever further into once-green valleys. Up in Tibet, the white glaciers of the Himalayas were melting, and the Tibetan grasslands were, like the grasslands in the Mongol north, turning to dust.

Down in the tropical south-west, rubber having failed to meet its quotas, anxious officials were redirecting production to the pleasing of tourists, with Miao minority dances. Sun-kissed girls sparkled to order in headdresses of silver, and colourful skirts swirled with twinkling bells, all reminiscent of the romantic pages of the old imperial picture-books. But a few surviving older minzu stubbornly refused to give up stories of an ancient past which they had tried to describe to the ethnographers so many decades ago. 'There was an epic flight', they insisted, 'from ancient lands of ice and snow which had once been ours'. Full of fantasy, their tales told of brave journeys across treacherous mountains, of leaps across rivers, and of the discovery of a cinnamon sea that, even with all its beauty, had been only a shadow of the wonderful world they had been forced to leave behind. Recounting their tale, some even pointed stubbornly to poems etched on the cliffs of Sichuan: the desperate words of other fleeing tribes who had made it that far but not beyond, standing like cries across the ages.

Declining to accept the Party's account of their people as one of many tribes who had been civilised by the Han, the descendants followed up with an ancient story that explained it all. A long, long time ago – almost as long ago as the days of the Yellow Emperor – two brothers had set off on a journey, each one carrying a book. Sleeping in the wild one evening, the brothers' makeshift camp had been attacked: possessions scattered, the older brother had lost half of his book; the younger brother lost his book completely. For some time, the brothers had continued on their journey, but eventually they had gone their separate ways. Armed with half of the book, the descendants of the older brother had raised an empire on the power of the written language, and eventually become the Han. Without a book at all, the descendants of the younger brother had kept the power of their own ideas and speech but lost the key to a written language: they had come to be known as the Miao. Most scholarly minds sniffed at what was obviously a foolish fabrication. In the 1990s, however, a Chinese scientific researcher announced that the earliest inhabitants of the Yellow River (five thousand years ago) were, in fact, the ancestors of the Yunnan Miao. While the Han Chinese were astonished, the Miao themselves were not surprised at all – they had been telling the Han that the heavenly lands had originally been theirs for as long as they could remember. By then, however, there was little to be done: the past was gone, and what did it matter who had originally been who?

While the foolish minzu minorities kept clucking about their pasts, the Great Men of the Party were looking to the future. In 1997, with Jiang Zemin now at the helm, a grand plan was unveiled to unleash the true productive potential of the failing edges of order, and, in so doing, to finally bring their superstitious people into the rising triumph of the modern world. The name of the plan? 'Develop the West'. Up in the north, across the arc of Inner Mongolia, Ningxia and Xinjiang, a necklace of new industrial parks-cum-cities was promised: a 'Northern Shenzhen'. And for Tibet, a high-speed train was announced, one that would whisk productively touring Han Chinese right up to the dizzying heights of the new market of the gods.

By the year 2000, Develop the West was spreading its civilising energies as fast as Deng Xiaoping's train had sped south. Modernising eyes, Chinese and foreign alike, lit up at the prospects, even as many of the hearts at the edges of China's order sank. Looking at the speed at which the fragile Tibetan world was unravelling – and meditating on the Party's anxious concerns about the security of China's borders in that constant battle to survive – the Dalai Lama suggested a 'middle way': one where Tibet would remain within the iron borders of China, but would be given the freedom to pursue its own dreams. To many who heard his words, it didn't seem so different from Mao's original promise of 'autonomy'. But His Holiness was dismissed as an incorrigible separatist and a danger to all. Tibet was wrapped even tighter into the Chinese family, and foreigners hoping to trade with the bigger empire were reminded that unity was everything.

The Tibetans, however, were not the only barbarian people to speak out; and the Dalai Lama was not the only voice. In the lands of Xinjiang, a stubborn woman had emerged from the desert on the back of Deng Xiaoping's Four Modernisations: her name was Rebiya Kadeer. A picture-poster of what a Uighur with a high quality productive mind could do, Rebiya had built a trading empire of such success that in 1992 she had even been invited to join the National People's Congress. Now officially responsible for representing her people, she decided that it was time to tell the tales of what had been happening to them in recent years. Rebiya's stories included the tale of a 1997 rebellion that had become a massacre in Yining, a city known by the Uighurs as Ghulja. They also included the hitherto unreported tragedy of an earthquake that had struck the village edges of Kashgar in the same 1997 year, burying thousands of Uighurs. In 1999, having chosen to put truth above unity, Rebiya and her tales were relegated to the dark corner of a prison – yet another incorrigible separatist who had abused the generosity of the Party, and whose freedom could only spell a danger for all.

Certainly, there was danger. As the Uighurs found themselves in an ever-tightening noose, they fought with every ounce of Quranic conviction for the independence which they believed should be theirs. Already in 1997, a 'strike hard' campaign had been launched against Xinjiang and Tibet, charged with smashing anyone and everyone who insisted on 'telling truths from the past.' But 'strike hard' notwithstanding, in Xinjiang, explosions on buses – rarely reported and largely buried – became regular occurrences, as did a number of equally buried assassinations and plottings, disturbances and riots, poisonings and carefully placed bombs. More 'strike hard' campaigns followed. In 2005, Rebiya was eventually released into the custody of a complaining America. As she departed, Hu Jintao, the new head of the Communist dynasty, once Party secretary of Tibet, stood up to remind everyone about the importance of unity: the Han were not to be separated from the minzu minorities, and the minzu minorities were not to be separated from the Han.

By the time the Chinese family prepared to welcome the world to the Olympics in the early months of 2008, hearts from the most stubborn edges of order were mustering whatever voices they could. From the desperate lands of the Uighurs came a host of plots, imagined and real.

And from Lhasa, the city of the gods, came the chants of a swelling tide of Tibetan monks that gradually rose to a crescendo of *Bo Rangzen!*, Free Tibet! By 14 March 2008, the streets of the city of the gods were burning with anger and pain.

It was not meant to be this way.

PART 7

HOW MANY SUNS?

In the era of Yao, ten suns rose all at once;
Yao ordered Yi to shoot nine down.

The Classic of Mountains and Seas (fourth century BCE)

CHAPTER 1

THE HEAVENLY PARTY

He who wished to bring order to the state first harmonised
his family, and wishing to harmonise his family, he
cultivated his person.

The Great Learning, Confucius (551 – 479 BCE)

Dusk fell early on the mid-November evening of 2012. Streets cleansed of all but the most important of passages, a muffled silence had descended. Mao Zedong's spirit peered out from his portrait, still suspended from the Gate of Heavenly Peace. Calm though his features were, however, an air of nervous anticipation seemed to hang in the late autumn chill. With all thoughts, near and far, fixed on the outcome of the Party's eighteenth Congress, the attentions of those nearby were set on the blazing lights of the Great Hall of the People and the movements of the heavenly Party within. After a year of carefully negotiating the parting script, the moment had come for Hu Jintao, leader of the fourth generation of the Communist dynasty, to stand at the Party's podium and make way for a younger brother: Xi Jinping. The ascent of a new star was never easy, and the vermilion walls of Zhongnanhai had tried to keep the rising squabbles secret. But as with imperial families across China's ages, there had been so many squabbles, and some had been so loud, that whispers of disharmony had eventually floated out on somebody's vapours; and floating out, they had naturally landed in earthly ears. So many squabbles, it was a miracle that it had not all ended in a war. And so many factions, each with so many different strands, that whispers alone made it difficult to work out what was really going on. Certainly, some of the tales were so shocking that it seemed to some as if the Monkey King himself was in charge.

At one point, Xi Jinping had disappeared from sight. Rumour-mongers suggested that he had locked himself up with his Party godfather, Jiang Zemin, refusing to budge unless and until he was given all three of the highest Party powers (not just general secretaryship of the Party and presidency of the country, but chairmanship of the Central Military Commission as well). Others, closer to the central stage, said that he was simply recovering from taking a heavenly chair in the back – wielded, like a cudgel, by a competing contender in a rage. It was all just as the Jade Emperor had once observed: 'Made up of the essence of both heaven and earth, nothing that goes on among these creatures in the world below should surprise us'. Calmed with honeyed promises, tempers had finally been contained and on an early November day, the Zhongnanhai squabblers had been coaxed underground, into the passage that would sweep them under the Avenue of Eternal Peace and up to the bright lights of the Great Hall of the People. Above-ground, black-winged saloon cars would glide across Tiananmen Square, revealing a movement in the ordering will of heaven to the waiting hearts of earth.

Emerging on to the star-lit stage of the Great Hall itself, the sequence of the squabblers' appearance had been all that any Party eye, or even the televisions at home, had needed to understand the ranks: first came Xi Jinping – obviously the new son of the Party's heaven; next, Li Keqiang, the man who would clearly be premier; then the five other successful squabblers who would serve along their side. The unity of heaven and earth now clearly displayed through the highest levels of the Party's Politburo, the seven men then left the stage. As the men made their way back through the underground passage, on the earth above, the same black-winged saloons ignited their engines, and traced the path of the celestial rulers back to the velvet portals of Zhongnanhai – with only a tail light to hint that heaven had truly touched the earth.

*   *   *

It had certainly been a long march for everyone. Not just for those who had reached the top, but for all of the other Party members who had taken part in a journey that, one way or another, had taken much of the last thirty years. Thirty years in which the lectures of the Party's founding ancestors had never been far from their side. Thirty years of inner Party battles; years in which everyone had had ample opportunity to contemplate the extraordinary relevance of the lessons of China's ancient past. Some said that one could trace the text of those years across the rhyming lines of an epic Song dynasty poem about the *weiqi* game of 'Go' – that wooden board of squares on which two players, armed with opposing piles of black and white stones, set down their pieces one by one, in a bid to encircle the other and win.

They seemed to have a point. In its opening words, the poem described the early years of the recent succession to perfection: 'While the etiquette of guest and host had been thoroughly observed, facing each other, the opponents had become like barbarians and savages'. Warming up to the ambitions aroused by the game, the Song dynasty poet had then uncannily described exactly what had been happening over the past five years: 'Dragons and snakes had raced, ghosts and spirits had laboured, fire and smoke had risen'. Even the observation that 'Palaces had been plotted, tigers had been ridden, and flags of armies had been raised' had been faultless. And the description of calculating hearts could not have been closer to the mark: 'Truth and deceit had been blended together, slandering and cheating had been woven through speech, rotting bones had been called oracles, righteousness had been squeezed by profit'.

Across it all, precisely as the poem had observed: 'The past had been used to observe the present'. And just as today: 'Family and state had advanced together, in the extreme'. Nor was it just the past and the present in terms of human ambition. Threaded across the past was that impossible conundrum of reconciling the contradictions of Laozi and Confucius. Laozi, who had cryptically observed that the 'Way is great'; and Confucius, who had offered a guiding set of principles, and had then unhelpfully added that 'Talent is difficult to come by'. Hardly surprising that the journey from the past to the present had been such a challenge. Indeed, one could scarcely believe that the poem's author had not been writing about the facts of the last few months when he had observed: 'About to rise, plunging falls had followed; everyone had known that when one meets the blade of a knife, not a single hair of an error can be tolerated'. Written in the eleventh century, who could tell how many times the truths of the poem had been repeated in the thousand years that had passed since then. And who on earth could have imagined, back in the revolutionary ranks of 1949, that in 2012, the Party's very own spirits would be reading its lines again.

The latest Son of Heaven, Xi Jinping, was born in 1953: the son of a man who had thrown his heart into the earliest heroic years of the Communist Party. Xi had been raised on the battleground of Mao's Zhongnanhai, and his father, like the fathers of a number of his peers, had been despatched to a tractor factory, not far from the ancient Zhou capital at Luoyang, in present-day Henan. As the Cultural Revolution wreaked its havoc, the young Xi's father had been swept off to jail – and Xi had stepped into the angry tide of Red Guard youth, deftly navigating the raging battles until he was leading a production team of his own. When the Cultural Revolution had blown itself out, Xi found his way to the newly re-opened 'red and expert' doors of Beijing's Tsinghua University. By the time he graduated, Deng was blowing the Four Modernisations in, and Xi's father had been resurrected to the constellation of Party leaders: placed in charge of the southern province of Guangdong, far from the smouldering factions of the Party family in Beijing.

Setting his sights far into the future and firmly on the top of the heavenly Party, the young Xi Jinping decided to place himself first at the feet of a Party general. Gaining experience (and brotherly connections) at the military wing of the centre, Xi had then consulted the past, looked at the seasons, and remembering the words of an old Tang dynasty maxim, 'No experience at the local level, no nomination for the centre', had declined the spoiling comfort of a princeling's desk in Beijing in favour of a lowly official post in a county town that few of his peers had ever heard of, and to which none had any desire to go. The lowly post had its fair share of local dragons and snakes, from which Xi learnt his lessons; it also had a number of ghosts and spirits, who were more than willing to offer their wisdom.

More experience gained, Xi then consulted the winds of change – which, in the 1980s, were blowing firmly south. His father having persuaded Deng to look more closely at the special economic zone possibilities of Guangdong, Xi found himself a position in the nearby province of Fujian. Still learning, Xi had watched as Deng struggled to tame the Four Modernisations. On the Fujian coast of Xiamen (once known as Amoy), a sparkling special economic zone had been raised – only to find that a smuggling nest of official vipers had reared its ugly head. And when, in 1966, the Guomindang, still ruling on the renegade island of Taiwan, had announced that they were going to launch themselves into a sea of democracy, Xi, now higher up in Fujian's government, watched, in 1966, as his olders and betters launched a volley of angry missiles across the Taiwan straits – and as a prowl of American aircraft carriers nosed their way through the separating waters, in an imperial show of silent warning.

Painstaking in his attention to detail, exercising the utmost care when feeling for river-crossing stones, Xi's advances eventually attracted the approving attention of the then Party secretary and President Jiang Zemin. In 2002, he was welcomed on to the first of the banks of the Party's promoting rivers, with an invitation to become governor (and soon afterwards Party secretary) of the neighbouring province of Zhejiang. A rollercoaster of a province – home to Wenzhou, close to Shanghai, and never far away from a typhoon – Zhejiang was already one of the fastest, and loosest, of China's dragons. Xi took care to watch his step. With Hu Jintao and the third generation of leadership moving into a ten-year period of office, and with new retirement limits set by Deng, it was now clear that he had ten years, and ten years only, to reach the top. Hu Jintao had already gained the summit of power in 2002. If Xi failed to take the prize in 2012, by 2022 he would have passed the sixty-eight-year limit on the age at which leaders could take up a post.

Looking at the *weiqi* game-board, consulting the past and its lessons, and the present with its changes, Xi watched for possible steps. Once again, 'racing dragons and snakes' were meticulously observed. And once again 'ghosts and spirits' were approached for their advice. In 2007, after the Party secretary of Shanghai had tripped over his own corrupting ambitions, Xi's diligence was rewarded: Party secretary (far more important than the governorship of anywhere) of the great Shanghai municipality that reported directly to Beijing. It was a position that offered a direct route to the Politburo, at the Beijing top of everything. Within a year, Xi Jinping was in pole position: not only admitted to the highest, Standing Committee, level of the Politburo, but vice-president of the country itself – with the added honour of leading the Central Party School, which since the time of Yan'an had always trained the Party's highest minds.

Xi Jinping was not, however, the only tiger clawing his way to the top – nor even the only prince. As Deng had rebuilt the Party, and as wealth had become a productive possibility, many a red heart – Party princes and commoners alike – was looking up at the promise of the socialist sky, and fixing their sights upon the heavenly ladder. With their mettle forged in the hottest furnaces of the Cultural Revolution, the toughest were always likely to be those cubs who had learnt their lessons in the brutal heart of the Party's family factions – and the toughest of those would be the ones who had learnt alongside their fathers in the *laogai* camps of labour. Indeed, in 1976, when Deng had tried to repair the damage of the Cultural Revolution's storms by rehabilitating parents with positions of power, many had felt that the young cubs had paid a high enough price for the terrors of the past.

While Xi had guided himself by the proverbs of the imperial past (particularly the one about gaining local experience), most of the other young cubs had been more than happy to accept the soft seats which would keep them in the comforts of Beijing – close to the pulse of Party power. It was a simple mistake: with so much change in the air, most assumed that the old imperial ideas had ceased to apply in what would surely be a new socialist world.

Most, but not all. Four years Xi Jinping's elder (born in 1949), Bo Xilai had been born to a man who had swum with Mao in the waters of the Yangzi River, and later became one of the 'eight great immortals' (the early Party leaders who fell foul of the Cultural Revolution and had been rehabilitated by Deng in the late 1970s). Imprisoned at seventeen for nothing more than being the son of his father, when Bo Xilai returned to Beijing in his mid-twenties, he was offered the solace of a research position in Zhongnanhai. But, like Xi Jinping, Bo sensed that the battle for the top would require a greater grasp of the country at large.

Springing himself from the gilded cage of the capital, Bo Xilai also went to a dusty county town that no one had ever heard of. Unlike Xi, however, from there he turned north, making his way, in 1990, to the port-city of Dalian, part of the old Manju lands that had become the present-day province of Liaoning.

Dalian was a place that had been at the heart of so many of the ravages of the past. Pushed and pulled between tugging imperial powers at the end of the Qing, in 1931 it had been wrapped up by the Japanese into the new Manjuguo (Manchuria), and transformed into an industrial powerhouse. Returned to Republican China at the end of the Second World War, it had then changed its industrial colours to serve the Communist Party's state-owned enterprises, SOEs, only to fall to Deng's modernisations with the collapse of the SOEs and the rise of a more enterprising south. Many, observing its tattered glory, would have seen a bedraggled city best left alone. But Bo Xilai, and his father, saw the possibilities of applying the same kind of Monkey King magic that Deng was launching in the softer south, only this time for the popular benefit of a neglected industrial north.

While Xi was carefully feeling for stones in Fujian, Bo Xilai became mayor of the city and, in so doing, found himself a magic stick of his own. Waving the stick to trade favours across family, friends and Party, he strengthened the forlorn Dalian like no other Chinese city of its size. *Flash!* and an expressway leapt up to link the city to the future. *Swoosh!* and spreading boulevards appeared, washed with colour-changing fountains, and serenaded with musical notes broadcast from the controls of his very own office. Over the next ten years, while Xi Jinping scoured the lessons of the past to avoid the errors of the ancestors, Bo Xilai repeated the races of the dragons and the snakes. Riding tigers, plotting palaces, raising questionable bones as oracles, he had 'advanced the family and the state together – in the extreme'. Dalian was transformed, but those outside his family began to wonder whether virtue had not been squeezed by profit.

Bo Xilai expected his northern magic to result in a shower of promotions. But enemies had been made, with some even repeating Confucius' observation that 'true talent is difficult to come by'. Bo, the father, however, was standing by, and the Party's propaganda resources – very sympathetic to Bo Xilai's past – had been commandeered to change opinion. In 2001, when the Governor of Liaoning province fell to a sudden scandal, Bo Xilai was ushered into the post. From there, in 2004, he was able to leap back to Beijing, as the head of a ministry. With another leap in 2007, he found himself in the wider ranks of the Politburo. But the leaps fell short of Xi Jinping's attaining bounds, and without a coveted seat on the Standing Committee of the Politburo, the two were not quite neck-and-neck. Casting around for catching-up possibilities, by the end of 2007, Bo Xilai found himself denied the coveted vice-premiership and offered the snub of a position as Party secretary of Chongqing instead. Not at all the *pai banzi*, do the deal, leap which would carry him to the top position in 2012. But perhaps a platform from which he could muster up a set of changes which might, just possibly, cloud somersault him to the front.

Chongqing, once the capital of Sichuan province (once, indeed, Guomindang capital of all), had recently been expanded and raised to become one of four great municipalities reporting directly to Beijing, acquiring a 'greater' population of thirty-three million Chinese heads. It was also a city of debilitating heat, monsoon rain and organised brotherhoods of crime, with so many waves of unemployed refugees from the Three Gorges dam that it would make even a black heart weep. In many ways, it was yet another of China's lost souls of cities.

Looking at the *weiqi* game-board, and facing his opponent with as much grace as he could muster, Bo knew that every advance would now require a savage battle. Given the scale of the challenge before him – the terrain to be covered and the short time to hand – the only obvious spirit with which he could conduct his campaign was the ghost of Mao Zedong. Not just Mao, the master tactician who had wrought endless victories from the jaws of defeat, (although those were obviously useful lessons), but Mao the great glowing sun who, when challenged by the Party as a 'cult that had gone too far', had risen above the factional fray to directly command the hearts of the people at large. True, it had taken a Cultural Revolution, but hopefully it would not come to that.

With the clock now ticking, and only five years to go before the career-defining 2012, Chongqing was launched into an eye-catching extravaganza which would not only capture the attention of the Party's greatest leaders (those who would decide which contender would be invited to take the helm) but also the hearts of the people as well. Drawing on the family favours and princeling confidence which had stood him so well in the past, once again Bo picked up his magic stick, and as he had done with Dalian, 'swooshed' Chongqing into the future. Ignoring the shrouds of almost perpetual fog, and the cauldron of heat, he poured so much concrete into the Jiangbei city centre that it began to look like New York. And aware that only the strongest of headlines would capture Beijing's attention, he pulled his toughest Dalian policeman to his new Chongqing side, declaring a war on anyone whose money insisted on having a mind of its own. The rich found their assets redirected to Chongqing purpose. Complaining officials were despatched to the countryside. And any lawyers contemplating taking up a cause were reminded that the font of all justice lay with the Party secretary (with any disagreements to be settled in jail).

Chongqing advanced to become the fastest growing city in the world, with further medals acquired when Party generals were invited to take part in local military games. Headlines glowing, Bo then announced some improvements for the benefit of the masses at large (particularly those hanging on for dear life to the hardest seats of Deng's runaway train): a 'red gdp' to give everyone a share in the municipality's SOEs, and a nostalgic return to the sound of songs which had once put a spring in the step of revolutionary hearts. 'Sing red!' Bo declared. And with no need for any further encouragement, the men and women in the hardest seats joined in a chorus whose high notes could be heard even in the gardens of Zhongnanhai.

After only three years of Bo's magic, by 2011 Chongqing had leapt to become the greatest model of China's cities, and Bo's Monkey King magic had captured a number of imaginations. With only a year to go before the leaders of the heavenly Party announced their successors, Bo Xilai confidently expected a reward. But the Party was divided. Some were mesmerised; others refused to be fooled. Hu Jintao, no scion of a princely family and shocked at all of the heavenly havoc in Chongqing, watched in stony silence. Having spent so many of the last few years proclaiming the ancient principle that 'the people are the root of any power' and insisting that 'society should be harmonious', it was hard for him to argue that Bo and his red songs were anything other than a *tianbao* treasure sent directly down from heaven. Equally, it was hard to avoid the fact that Bo Xilai had created a personal fiefdom as challenging as anything in the ancient Zhou past. It was even harder to ignore the military games that Bo personally hosted in Chongqing – and with them, the nagging fear that he was preparing the way for another Cultural Revolution if he did not make it to the top.

Xi Jinping began to wonder if he had been outfoxed. 'Observing the etiquette of guest and host', in late 2011, he decided to pay a visit to the reddest-hearted and fastest growing city in the world (and the personal fiefdom of his would-be rival) to see for himself what was going on. As shocked as Hu Jintao, but with a far greater personal stake in the game, Xi Jinping quietly complimented his opponent on the wonders of Chongqing and the joy of being so red.

*   *   *

As 2012 appeared on the horizon, and as the tigers faced each other on the mountain of power, the wider ranks of the Party were also getting ready for a change. After years of trying to tidy itself up after the disasters of the Great Leap Forward, the Cultural Revolution, and the Gang of Four (not to mention the Tiananmen events of June Fourth), the Party had finally organised itself to a point where everyone accepted that they would not be eligible for a new position after the age of sixty-eight. Accordingly, 2012 was not only a year which would usher in a new son of the Party's heaven, it was also a year when there would be an unprecedented exodus of older leaders – with the ranks opening up for an almost entirely new sweep of Communist Party officials as well.

The oracle bones having been clear about the change for a few years, as Xi Jinping and Bo Xilai had been plotting their final triumphal moves, everyone else in the Communist Party had also been playing their own personal games of *weiqi*. With an official office now worth its weight in gold, every platform of promoting possibility had been explored, both inside and out. And in the exploring, everyone's attentions naturally turned to the palace of all promotions: the outwardly invisible department of the Party that was responsible for organising everyone's appointments and which, unsurprisingly in the earthy language of the Party, was simply called the 'Organisation Department'. Rising from a horde of personal files painstakingly compiled since the time of Yan'an, over the previous decade, the Organisation Department had been transformed into a powerhouse of personnel intelligence unmatched in any of the four quarters of the world. In the process, it had become so big that it now commanded a vast Beijing building of its own. Such was its power over each Party position, and over the files of everyone's past, that every official aspired to have a friend or a relation who worked there – and no one whose future it governed ever needed to ask for its address.

Some said that the Organisation Department was, like so many other institutions of the Party, entirely Lenin's idea, born of the scientific need for an all-powerful Communist machine which could direct the many strings of its own orchestra without a single stumbling fault. Others said that Lenin had simply copied the idea from his Moscow ancestors, who had got it from Chinggis Khan and his conquering Mongols. Yet others argued that the Mongols had got it from the Song dynasty Chinese whose officials had been commandeered along with the conquest of the empire in the thirteenth century. How had the Song dynasty Chinese got it? From their own ancestors, of course – right back to the Qin and that idea of cloaking the country in a grid of iron. Where had the Qin got it? Probably from being a dust bowl in the western back of the sparkling Zhou's beyond. Wherever it might have come from, in the years after the Tiananmen 'incident' in 1989, the Organisation Department was an institution that had been tightened and polished like never before.

With so many careering fortunes at stake, when the soft 2011 Year of the Rabbit jumped into the 2012 celebrations of a new Year of the Dragon, it was not only the families and friends of Xi Jinping and Bo Xilai who were concentrated on the upcoming eighteenth Party Congress. Nor was it only those who had dreams of serving from the centre. Out across the country, with thousands of Party-powered jobs about to open up within the provinces and the counties, everyone who was anyone was in hot pursuit of a heaven-sent fortune. And, just as in the capital, it was clear to all that the beneficiaries would not only be those who got the jobs – and, of course, their extended families – but also those who were able to ease a personal protégé into the kind of position that could provide a lifetime of reciprocating favours. In a land where every Party official, high or low, was some sort of emperor, everyone was looking for a horse to back.

With no one in any doubt about the stakes, and with winter now yielding to spring, for those in the Party's Organisation Department, heaven seemed to have already arrived. Filing cabinets were groaning so heavily under the weight of highly qualified candidates that it was plain to all that for most positions there was an embarrassment of choice: obviously, it was just a question of listening to the finer qualities of persuasion. Clear about their orders for years, suddenly godfathers, fathers, grandfathers, blood-brothers and every other qualifying kin from across the realms of heaven and earth, were all sent into a final frenzy of competitive action. Private rooms in restaurants were discreetly booked (with restaurants now filling to the rafters); flattering gifts were offered with the delicacy of afterthoughts; flowers were ordered to perfection; telephone lines were stroked with assiduous attention. And in the race to accumulate the mountain of favours necessary to swing a heavenly Party mind, there was no possible official desire on earth that would be too hard for the most determined candidate to fulfill.

Of course, it was not quite that simple. True, there was an embarrassment of technically qualified candidates; and, true, the favours on offer were extremely appealing. But there were other matters – and pressures – to consider. With the battle for heaven raging above, few were in any doubt that the future of the Party was also at stake: Left or Right? With the glittering train racing full speed ahead to a socialist future which now included the creation of a missed capitalist past, not everyone could tell the difference anymore. But across the years of Hu Jintao's leadership, it had also become increasingly clear that the fuzziness of the past might not be able to continue into the future.

The importance of the question was felt well beyond the Communist Party. As the business of business (private and state-owned) had come to depend on the Party, it was not only the future of the Party that was at stake but everybody's economy as well. Indeed, while Xi Jinping and Bo Xilai had been battling it out for the top job, businesses across the country (and from abroad) had been reaching deep into their pockets to entice the princelings and other well-connected Party spirits to join their corporate ranks. And with the positions of the princelings and the well-connected Party spirits dependent on the politics of the Party, there was barely a business in the land that did not have some kind of stake in the game. If the Party lurched towards Bo Xilai and his Maoist left, while Bo and his family might reap a giant harvest, would the wider princelings and well-connected Party spirits still be able to hold their value, or would some sort of avenging 'Cultural Revolution' be unleashed to show everyone that Bo was in charge? What if the Party veered towards Xi Jinping? Would he be able to hold the levers of the glittering train steady or would he tilt them to one side? With so little known about the personal opinions of a man who had always upheld the highest Party etiquette of secrecy, who could know which way he would go if he tilted: Left or Right? And whichever way he went, what sort of a reckoning might follow? To this, some replied that change would have to come at some point or another – and if blood were not to be spilt on the streets, the sooner it came, the better.

Others pointed to the diamond-studded skeletons in everybody's closets and said that change of any kind was the last thing anybody needed. What if Xi Jinping tried to hold the tiller steady, but Bo Xilai decided to throw a monkey king's temper tantrum and unleash the disgruntled 'sing red' populace to tip everything upside down? Those who remembered the Cultural Revolution, shuddered.

*　　*　　*

Braced for the usual rollercoaster of a dragon year, few, however, were prepared for the rocket that February 2012 would explode in the fiefdom of Chongqing. Xi Jinping seemed to be best prepared for the pole star position, but with red hearts loudly singing Maoist choruses, some were expecting Bo Xilai to make a last minute cloud-leaping sprint for some kind of Party pinnacle. Others, well ahead on the *weiqi* board, wondered whether the whole game might not change completely if Bo got his way. Impatient eyes turned to the advancing March meeting of the National People's Congress. This was not the formidable heavenly eighteenth congress of the Party which would (as always) follow in late autumn, but the annual spring grandstand of three thousand carefully (s)elected delegates, which the flamboyant Bo might well try to turn to some Monkey King advantage.

493

Chinese New Year banquets only just digested, Party mouths dropped in shock when on 6 February, the internet flashed out a story which even the Jade Emperor might have found difficult to believe. Fleeing from the Chongqing court of his master, Bo Xilai's Dalian policeman had apparently appeared at the guarded gates of the American consulate in nearby Chengdu begging for protection – and chased by a host of armoured vehicles with Chongqing registration plates. Bo Xilai's offices had made a quiet announcement to the effect that every valued employee needs a 'vacation-style therapy'. Meanwhile, the internet followed up with yet another explosive story: after a brief spell of American hospitality, the Dalian policeman had been returned to the Chinese world and was being escorted to the Beijing capital by Party powers – in the security of a commercial airline, for fear that Bo Xilai's dark Chongqing forces might shoot a rocket at any private plane.

As the masses struggled to keep up with the pace of the story, Bo Xilai quietly boarded a flight of his own, and paid a personal visit to the 14th Group Army, whose earliest roots had been nurtured by his father at the time of the Long March. 'Cherish the memory of the revolutionary ancestors', he was said to have remarked. A few weeks later, a host of Chinese whispers fluttered across the sharper ears of the country, murmuring that the army had contemplated a coup.

Curiouser and curiouser. Minds now turned with even greater excitement to the looming date of the National People's Congress. Although technically the highest power in the land, no one was under any delusion that its rubber-stamping delegates would be dealing with any of the important matters of Party succession. But after the events of the previous few weeks, hopes were high that Bo Xilai might make a pulse-raising appearance; and many wondered whether Hu Jintao might take the opportunity to pass a judgement.

For two weeks, the delegates shuffled dutifully in and out of the Great Hall of the People: work reports were chanted, duty-bound votes were counted; and no one said anything so interesting that microphone communications needed to be cut. There was a moment of excitement when Bo Xilai met the Press to explain that even heavenly heroes could not always be sure that their friends could be trusted – and went on to call for an assault on the capitalist devils who had captured the high ground. Then, just as the short grandstand seemed to be over, Wen Jiabao, the outgoing premier, popped his head above the parapet and quietly unleashed an observation that stopped almost everyone in their tracks. 'China is facing unprecedented problems',

Wen declared. 'And unless deep and widespread change takes place within the Party, the Cultural Revolution could easily happen all over again.'

The following day, Bo Xilai was dismissed as Party secretary of Chongqing. A month later, he was suspended from the Politburo. But long before that, he had disappeared, and would not appear again until well into the following Year of the Snake. By which time his wife would have astonishingly confessed to the murder of an unknown foreign-devil businessman who had become a family friend – and Bo himself would have been charged with a dazzling display of corrupting crimes.

* * *

Back at the frontline of the Party's succession, as spring turned to summer, the myriad of interlocking races for the heavenly positions moved into their final laps. Long-distance runners worked overtime to make sure that promised positions stayed on track. Outliers who faced the bitter prospect of being an 'also-ran' pulled on every favour-fuelled lever in reach. Godfathers were kicked into overtime, fathers and grandfathers were told to dig deeper into the webs of their relationships; and in desperate cases, they were instructed to wake up the near-dead, if that was what it would take. As hopeful candidates put the final touches to long campaigns, the provinces began to arrive in Beijing. Hotels were stuffed to the gunnels; and patient officials in the Organisation Department waited for the prices of their favours to go up. Gifts rose to the skies: from fortunes of apartments at the higher levels, to overseas school fees, must-have watches and vacations in the lower ranks. Promises flowed like fountains, and even the smallest of favours, embellished and amplified to keep up with the times, were dredged up from the past. And in every corner of the capital, the personal assistants to everyone-who-wanted-to-be-anyone were keeping minute-by-minute mobile tallies of where their own particular player was standing, and whether or not any other horse had somehow managed to storm ahead.

With all eyes on the race, summer arrived. Bo Xilai's wife suddenly appeared in a court, calmly admitting to a cold-blooded cyanide poisoning – even though a quietly spoken forensic expert had dared to make an off-the-record observation that the evidence did not fit. A death sentence, suspended for life, was gratefully accepted by the penitent confessor. Once again, China's internet ignited with speculation. Most of the microblogs were of the opinion that if the Party ever presented something as fact, it could be reliably assumed to be untrue. Some suggested that the softly spoken woman who had made the court appearance was nothing but a body-double. Conspicuous in his absence, Bo Xilai was assumed to be in the bowels of the Party's prisons, while the Party's tigers were battling over what to do.

Up in the inner sanctum of Zhongnanhai, however, with nothing short of the heavenly future of everything at stake, everyone's tempers were exploding. What had started as a fundamentally family affair, had now managed to mix up the next generation of Party leadership with the perilous question of what kind of a Party it was. Given that Xi Jinping and Bo Xilai were princelings, neither the question of the succession nor the matter of the madness in Chongqing could be separated from the Party's battles of the past. And the Party's battles of the past could not be settled without slandering someone else's parents – and bringing in all of the politics of power. In the light of the treacherous shoals of Party history, was Bo Xilai a hero, a traitor, or a victim of a Cultural Revolution that had torn up everyone's sense of right and wrong? If Bo was indeed a traitor, could the Party really sacrifice the son of a man who was one of its 'eight immortals' – and what, given the popularity of his 'sing red' campaign, would happen if it did? Underneath these family dramas, sat the question that had haunted the Party since Tiananmen, and arguably since the caves of Yan'an: what kind of a Party should it be? After the travails of the last thirty years, was it really practical to retain the fig leaf that the Party was the guarantor of a Democratic Dictatorship of the People? And if it was not, could the Party become accountable to the people without bringing heaven crashing down on earth? Of course, these were questions for cosmic time, rather than the season of a Party congress. But, just like the Monkey King, Bo Xilai had wreaked havoc in heaven and now even cosmic time was running out.

As the opinions battled back and forth, it was clear that it had become impossible to separate 'the Party' from its battling families. With every opinion came a memory, and with every memory came a flash of the Party's savage past: backs stabbed for a quick advantage, innocent children sacrificed like lambs, blacker sheep protected with lies. Power-grabbing wrongs had been buried to keep the truth from rising, feuds had been fuelled from generation to generation; and almost every friendship, sooner or later, had been betrayed for somebody's gain. Everybody had a family tree of friends and foes inked deep into their hearts. As the claims and counter-claims were hurled across Zhongnanhai's courtyards, few could fail to notice the indelible legacy of the bigger past: Mao's blood red betrayals, the sacrifices of the questioning intellectuals, the buried bodies of the Great Leap Forward, the assassinations of the Cultural Revolution, the betrayal of Tiananmen, and the bonfire of state-ownership followed by the phoenix-like rise of the Party leaders' wealth. As each troubling trough of the Party's past was once again revealed to be just a matter of someone's private store of family secrets, Hu Jintao and the other Party members who had risen through the ranks outside the Zhongnanhai family ring could only watch as bystanders. They had plenty of time to reflect upon the fact that Deng Xiaoping had warned everyone to keep the princelings in a box. Jiang Zemin had disobeyed him. And now they were all paying the price.

*   *   *

Time turned. High summer dimmed, and autumn began to whisper in the wind. Within the portals of Zhongnanhai, the battles continued to blaze. Outside, the lights of the internet struggled to keep up. By the end of September, however, a fragile truce seemed to break out and Zhongnanhai opened its gates to make an announcement: Bo Xilai had been expelled from the Party. Returning to battle out the finer details of the families' fires, the internet was left to its own devices, and the restaurants kept on chattering. Few days passed without some rumour or other of a lost temper – and when Xi Jinping had disappeared from his vice-presidential functions for a couple of weeks, some had begun to fear for more than just his health. By November, however, when the Great Hall of the People opened its doors to the Party Congress, the heavenly battles seemed to have all been settled: well, perhaps not settled, but at least momentarily set aside. Xi Jinping had finally been clapped to the clouds.

Anointed as general secretary of the Party, chairman of the Central Military Commission, and president of the People's Republic of China (in that order of importance), Xi Jinping was nothing if not prepared. Head of the Central Party School for the past five years, it had long been clear to him that there was a backlog of heavenly questions about every kind of order to be addressed – from the order of the people, to the order of nature, to the disorder of the rest of the world. It was also clear to others that, after such a long time at the head of the Party School, Xi was in a strong position to address the questions (although what he would be able to do with the feuding Party family was still anybody's guess).

Successor to a Communist School that had been created as a substitute for the Moscow original, the Central Party School was a Party institution that had been forged in the caves of Yan'an. Ding Ling had been one of its many early students – taught by Liu Shaoqi, the then-rising star whose 1930s thoughts on the importance of Communist self-cultivation (*How to be a Good Communist*) had become one of the Party's classical texts. And while the idea of a Party school might have come from the Russian big brother, the idea of a Party bureaucracy that prided itself on scholarly credentials had been grounded in the Chinese lands since the time of the Duke of Zhou and his Hall of Light. As Confucius himself had once observed: 'Thinking without studying is a dangerous occupation'. Education was everything. How could anyone be Chinese without it?

In the early years, as revolution had turned to power, the Central Party School, with its rapidly expanding branches, had become the pivot of the Party's future – training millions of new recruits for a Communist Party which had come to rule from nowhere. With every single position of power (central and local) under their command, Party membership had leapt by millions in the first ten years of its rule. By the time Deng Xiaoping had taken the helm, Party membership had reached sixty million. And although enthusiasm had waned a little across the 1980s and 1990s, when the Party had opened itself up to privately enterprising members in 2001, the number had leapt forward again: more than eighty million members by the time Xi Jinping arrived at the Party School in 2008 – all needing to be trained.

With branches spread across the country, the Party School had a formidable reach. And with every branch not only teaching the essential theories of Communism with Chinese characteristics, but also giving lessons in both the practical skills and the knowledge of current affairs required for rule, it had a formidable understanding of what its members needed to learn. For the very highest Party members, and faithful to its scholarly tradition, the Central Party School in Beijing gathered together the greatest minds from home and abroad to stretch everyone's ideas. Refreshing courses were offered on the latest developments in Marxist-Leninist-Mao Zedong Thought, together with updating programs on current world affairs, and a constant exploration of both the essential challenges facing the Party itself, and the comparative qualities of political parties around the world – particularly the most successful parties. Compulsory courses included investigations into how to make sure that the Party was always the greatest interpreter of the classical Communist texts (including the newer classics of Deng Xiaoping Theory, Jiang Zemin's Three Represents and Hu Jintao's

Scientific Development). But the most important course of all – a course which was not only compulsory but which no Party power would ever want to miss – was the one which explored the questions that had occupied the minds of every ruler since the beginning of China's imperial time: how does a Son of Heaven maintain the order of heaven and earth? And while the Son of Heaven is working out the answer to that cosmic question: how can he keep the foreign barbarians at bay?

When the wealth of the Western capitalist world had gone up in smoke in the late summer of 2008 (just as the Olympic fireworks exploded above Beijing), the first of these two questions had been at the forefront of leading Party minds – with suggested answers splashed across almost all of the Party school's curricula. The Olympic applause of visiting foreign titans (suddenly paupers) had been reassuring music to Zhongnanhai's ears – a long-awaited recognition of the value of the Party's wisdom. But as 2008 had turned into 2009, it had also become clear to everyone in the Party School (and pretty much everyone else in China) that the rapid rise in Chinese fortunes had become a rollercoaster of a ride, with everyone rattling in their seats. As He Qinglian (the historian-economist now in the US) had pointed out, those in the lowest classes were having the toughest time – so tough that some of them had been thrown off the train. And while there were certainly more people now sitting on the softer seats and in first class, the problem was that most of them were either members of the Party or people who (whether as relatives or friends) had managed to find their way into a Party pocket or two. Meanwhile, the natural landscape through which the train was passing seemed to be rebelling – even as the 'high quality' people were losing their tempers; not to mention the selfish separatists at the edges of order who were insisting on their bombs. Of course, the Party had realized that unless and until the minds of the people reached the necessary *gao suzhi*, high quality, thinking, protests were to be expected, with any resolution of the problems certainly taking all of the hundred additional years of revolution that Deng had declared. In the interim, however, the problems would have to be managed – and managed in a modernised state, where the control of communications had been undermined by the availability of the internet to anyone with a mobile phone. Fortunately, the Patriotic Education Campaign was now well underway: explaining to everyone that without the Party there would not only not be any 'new China', but there would also not have been any 'China' at all. But there were always those stubborn low quality spirits who just refused to learn. Maintaining the order of China was not getting any easier.

The heart of the problem was really the old question of whether heaven was a single-top down ordering mind or some muddled up idea of reflecting the people. The latter had been expressed in that Fifth Modernisation (the voices of the people) that the electrician Wei Jingsheng had conjured up. Not content with advanced industry, science and technology, agriculture and national defence, everyone had to be able to have their say as well – all one point four billion of them. Of course, Wei Jingsheng was long gone: eighteen years in jail, then off to America, far out of anyone's Chinese sight and increasingly out of their minds. But as the Party had produced economic miracle after miracle, other inconvenient voices seemed to have leapt, one after another, into Wei Jingsheng's stead. Waving the most simplistic interpretations of Marx like magic talismans, these voices were not only protesting but suggesting that even a hundred years of Party-driven socialism would not lead the people to a Taiping world of a great and comforting peace. Some had even taken to twittering that it was time for the Communist Party to open up its mandate of heaven to the chaos of a competition for all. After everything the Party had done for everyone, the ingratitude beggared belief.

Looking at the scale and complexity of the problems, Xi Jinping turned the Central Party School into a glittering Hall of Light. Gathering his scholars together, they were instructed to scour heaven and earth for any and every idea that might help. Digging deep into the past, they 'investigated everything'. Advancing through the history books, they found themselves in the reassuring presence of ancient minds: minds which had argued with astonishing perspicacity that the legitimacy of a ruler's power depended on everybody's satisfaction – but that the people themselves were very unlikely to be the best judges of how they might be satisfied. That things are unequal had been acknowledged as a matter of fact for the last two thousand years – as had the sad fact that, while the highest quality minds can understand the complexities, one cannot do much about the level of understanding of those below. For this, there was no alternative but for a ruler to accept that his responsibility was to *rule*.

Wading on through the history books, the apocalyptic nightmare of the decline of the Zhou and the battles of the Warring States leapt out at them – a tale, if ever there was one, for a world where the bright star of America was dimming fast. Fortunately, that terrible time had been followed by the triumph of the First Qin Emperor who had unified everything. Helpfully, the scholars who had shaped his thinking, had also left behind their precepts, from which everyone could learn. 'Loving mothers are the ruin of their children', was the most obvious one. 'Swords are sharpened on whetstones', was another. There was also the one that helpfully explained that 'wood is straightened with a tight rope, and turned into a wheel by aligning it with a compass'. And then there was the wise observation that 'a household with clear rules and punishments runs as smoothly as water'. Contemplating the clockwork efficiency of the Qin realm, it was clear why Mao had been so devoted to the memory of the First Qin Emperor: castigated by lily-livered scholars across the ages, he was a man who had been much misunderstood. Those who rule are supported by those who are ruled. All that matters is that the ruler is fit for the task. Such an obvious and simple proposition – but one those lower quality minds had always found so difficult to understand. The task of a ruler is hard indeed.

Turning then to the second question of 'how to keep the foreign barbarians at bay?' Xi Jinping and his Party School scholars found some surprising treasures of wisdom in the Western world of thought – although being barbarians, it seemed that the foreigners were incapable of understanding and acting upon their own good ideas. There was the Greek idea that only qualified men should have a voice: clearly a world that had understood the importance of high quality people. Then there was that nineteenth-century perception – so familiar to everyone in China – that the world was engaged in a bitter struggle for the survival of the fittest. But, having failed to follow Confucius' model of *zhi* knowledge, and being infants in the art of order, the foreigners had not only been unable to learn from their own past but incapable of even remembering it. The problem was that in their ignorance, they were getting the people in the heavenly lands confused as well. Instead of concentrating on the *qualities* of the ruler, they had tangled themselves, and everyone else, up in questions about *who got to choose* the ruler. And with more than their own fair share of low quality minds (what do you expect if you don't give education a truly Confucian respect?) they had clucked around like a bunch of women in skirts, fussing about the importance of 'one man, one vote'. No consideration at all had been given to either the quality of the vote, or to the fact that unless everyone is equal to start off with, the poorest voices inevitably get bought up by the rich. What had they ended up with? A gaggle of rulers currying favour with claptrap, and democracies of voters who could not tell chalk from cheese. No wonder the West had got itself and so much of the rest of the world into such a mess.

Investigating everything, Xi Jinping then directed Party School attention to the question of Russia's Soviet Union and the lessons that Deng had urged everyone to learn. Lenin had given his comrades a model of ordering discipline, complete with the necessary understanding of the critical importance of unity, on which all order rests. With the chaos of imperial capitalism all around, it was Lenin who had hit upon the idea of an advanced guard of Party members to get the revolutionary show on the road. And it was Lenin who had understood that democracy is a treacherous shoal, with more than one false meaning. There was only one *real* democracy which would save the world, and that was the Democratic Dictatorship of the People ('democratic centralism', for short). Once a revolution had been carried out and a new order battled into power (the democratic part), decisions should be made by whoever had won the revolution (the centralism). Let the people's voices sing as much as they liked, but one had to put them in a hierarchy of order, and make sure that they were guided at every step of the way. Those at the bottom could elect local representatives to sing for them at a higher level – as long as those local representatives had been properly qualified by the ruler. Those so (s)elected could go on to elect representatives to sing for them at the next level up – as long as they were only choosing from those who had already been elected (and of course pre-qualified by the ruler before that). Proceeding on up the hierarchy, by the time one got to the central top, there would be a manageably small number of representatives who would also be sufficiently well educated to see that only a Son of Heaven who has carefully studied everything can be in any position to rule. As Lenin himself put it: 'You can have as much voice as you like, as long as you don't disturb the unity required for definite action'.

Russia, of course, had collapsed. Or rather, the Soviet Union had collapsed, and in letting this happen the Russians had also abandoned their Communist Party. It was as clear to Xi as it had been to Deng that the reasons for, and consequences of, the Russian Party's failures were probably the most helpful of all the lessons for the Party to learn. Without a deeply rooted appreciation of the importance of investigating things, once Lenin had gone it had probably just been a matter of time before the Russian brothers tripped and fell. If they had just kept the faith with Lenin's architecture of order (and listened to their more educated Chinese brothers) they might have been able to keep their Party going. But that amateur Gorbachev had been seduced by the bright lights of America and its cacophony of opinionated voices. In 1991, when the Soviet Union and the Communist Party had both been cancelled, and before anyone could say *glasnost*, the Soviet satellite states –

as many of them in China's backyard as in that of the European West – had rushed off to an impatient independence, leaving China to deal with a host of rebellious central Asian dreams in the neighbouring province of Xinjiang.

With the vast territories of the Soviet Union floating away like clouds, up in Moscow, Russia's waiting-in-the-wings capitalists, the oligarchs, had then not only occupied the state's assets but stuffed them into their own private banks. Meanwhile, the dreaming Gorbachev had been replaced with the drunkard Yeltsin who, predictably, had soon begun to fall off his drunken stage. Presenting Putin as a puppet had been a rather astute step by the oligarchs: with his KGB discipline, he had certainly had the best chance of digging in his heels and stemming the rot.

But it had all been far too late. Even Putin couldn't conjure up the towering majesty of a Leninist Party: it would take another revolution for that. By then, Russia had all found itself in the same position as China in the time before the Zhuanxu Emperor, over four thousand years ago, with the people allowed to think whatever they wanted, and to shout it even louder. Talk about cutting yourself off at the knees. Vodka at the ready, a twentieth-century nuclear power, and master of one of the world's biggest piles of arms, had been reduced to a drunken fighting spirit (no doubt the influence of the Mongols who had occupied them for so long). The nuclear weapons and the arms were a worry: admittedly increasingly rusty, but far too close to Xinjiang and Mongolia to be of comfort. And, with such cracks in the stately order, there was clearly going to be a need for some careful Chinese footwork in central Asia and neighbouring India, not to mention some sharp management of the tricky Japanese whose islands flanked the Siberian coast of the Russian Far East.

But the truly salutary tale for the Party School to teach was that, with no understanding of the need for learning, the Russians had managed to lose both their Party and their empire – and in so doing, they had put any *suzhi* quality of their people into reverse as well.

As Xi Jinping and the Party School looked back across the stories, the lessons were clear. That order and unity were everything had been proven as much from the recent collapse of Russia as from the ancient triumph of Qin; while 'democracy', as 'one man, one vote', was simply the hallmark of the uneducated and uncivilised barbarian. But, how to get the stubborn internet voices that the Westerners had unleashed, to understand?

On these thorny questions, though, the Western barbarians seemed to have come up with some useful ideas. Digging deep into the American past,

Party School scholars came across the observations of Thomas Jefferson and his successor Andrew Jackson. Jefferson had noted that any democracy would need a reasonably intelligent public that could keep itself informed. Jackson had then followed up with a warning that, in a rising world of corporations, everyone would end up a slave unless someone found a way to keep minds free – to which end, America had decided to give investigating journalists the freedom of the land. By the 1920s, with the journalists' reckless questions wreaking havoc in all directions, stronger American spirits had realised that the public mind was going to have to be managed if their 'civilisation' was going to survive. Attention had then shifted to the importance of protecting the people and the state from the irresponsibility of untamed opinions. Soon after that, the Europeans barbarians had, once again, tangled themselves up in a world of war – and, in the process, had stumbled upon the useful lessons that propaganda could be as powerful as a military weapon, and that 'advertising' might be one of the most powerful tools of all.

Looking deeper into the history, Xi and the Party School found that it had been the German Nazis who had first grasped the possibilities of propaganda. But the British and their American allies had not been slow to follow suit. Realising that difficult times required backbone, they had recognised the need to help low quality human minds come to grips with facts that they might not otherwise understand. Fear had been grasped as the most powerful tool: whenever an important point of principle had seemed to be at risk of getting lost, pure animal anxiety had been spread among the people. And wherever there had been individuals or countries who were obviously enemies, but the people had not yet understood their threat, rabid names had been launched at them like rockets to emphasise the risk. At the end of the war, being well ahead in their science, and with advertising cheaper than violence or bribery, the American government and its corporations had then raised an armoury of technological tools designed to make sure that the minds of the public stayed in order. To which, the wisdom of a new science of psychology had been added, offering new opportunities to get deep inside the people's heads. As the science of the mind had advanced, the electronic pulses of television and radio had been switched on to amplify the effect. It turned out that even the internet had not been a problem – or if it had, the West had quickly overcome it. At the turn of the twenty-first century, with Britain lagging in so many other scientific ways, its prime minister Blair had apparently even applied the sum of the new scientific know-how to propel a New Labour party to power. And helpfully (like all foreigners keen to crow about their discoveries), he had been more than happy to share the knowledge with the Central Party School. Invited to listen, the Party's Propaganda Department had been very keen to learn.

* * *

Charged with teaching the highest leaders in the land, Xi Jinping had gathered plenty of knowledge about the present and the past. With China's star now shining so brightly, he had also had the opportunity to explore various ideas with some very powerful minds. The all-important first question of 'how to maintain the order of heaven and earth' had been particularly carefully looked at (behind closed doors of course) in terms of how to keep the Party in power. Studies of almost every success and failure – across time and around the world – had been delivered, and then pushed and prodded until every ounce of learning had been extracted. All of it had been tested with the help of visiting Westerners whose lecturing ideas could ensure that China remained the fittest survivor of them all. Which was, of course, also the key to the second question, of 'how to keep the foreign barbarians at bay'. With every study done, and every lecture learnt, the fundamental wisdom of Deng Xiaoping had been proven, both on maintaining the order of heaven and earth through the principle of a highly disciplined Party power, and on dealing with the barbarians.

Ai guo, love the country, was what it was all about. Or rather, as Deng Xiaoping had understood so well, it was really ai dang, love the Party, first, of course. After sixty years of the Party having built a new China, and after thirty years of a Patriotic Education Campaign, the two were, quite rightly, becoming impossible to tell apart. Of course, that was not always obvious to everyone, particularly with those pesky Westerners constantly banging on about freedom and independence: as if that were ever truly real, or even possible. It had not been easy. After the Tiananmen 'incident', the Party's Propaganda Department had had to work hard to get the people to understand that, without the Party, everyone would have been back in the opium dens of imperial Hankou. But with Deng firmly at the helm, the minds of the Party's members had been swept root and branch for even the smallest sign of a failing heart; interrogations had been conducted and, naturally, the Party School had stepped forward with a training programme for all.

It had been the mantras of the Patriotic Education Campaign (the triumph of the Party over the terrors of the past) that had slowly guided the people to an understanding of the fact that it was the pillar of Party patriotism that really defined what it meant to 'be Chinese'. Plastered in every possible place of learning and knowledge, stories and images of the Party's sacrifices had also been splashed across every possible site: from schools and universities, to museums and parks, not to mention television and radio stations, newspapers, public broadcasts, billboards and even films. History books had been rewritten to tell the tale more clearly, and new museums had been raised to make sure that the wider public could see and understand.

Some thought the campaign had gone into overdrive, but given the challenges of the last few years, it was becoming clear that it had not gone far enough. 'A hundred years of humiliation' at the hands of barbarians had been overturned in fifty years of Communist Party rule – what an astonishing achievement. But after thirty years of rising fortunes, there were a number of overstuffed people who had taken the sacrifices of the Party's revolutionary heroes for granted, or worse. Without the Party there would have been no new China: it could not be repeated enough. 'Get it into their heads, get it into their ears, and get it into their hearts', the leader of the Propaganda Department had pounded. And he had been quite right. Anyone could come up with bad news; and with a Party of eighty million official adherents, any fool could come up with a member who looked like a monkey. But the real challenge, as every Great Man ruler across the past five thousand years of Chinese history had shown, was to live up to the responsibilities which heaven had sent. Rule: and in your ruling, concentrate everyone's minds on the positive possibilities of everything.

Which brought one back to the question of the foreigners: a problem which, as China's fortunes had risen so far and so fast, had only got worse. Of course, as China had risen, the Western barbarians had turned more and more to their phoney war of 'peaceful evolution' – that conspiracy of words with which a 1950s America had imagined that China could be seduced out of her revolutionary conviction. After 2008, with the once-glittering palaces of the West dimming, it had become a little more difficult for the barbarians to persuade the Chinese people that the West was a better world. But, never content to keep to their own channels, the Westerners had crept ever closer to the East, encouraging everyone in the Asian neighbourhood to forget the lessons of the past hundred years. Not, of course, that the tricky Japanese had needed much persuading.

Deng Xiaoping had been right that China and the Party should bide their time: let China first quietly rise. But as Xi Jinping looked at the landscape, it was clear that the facts had changed. China's light had been hidden for so long that the Westerners had not only forgotten their barbarian name and nature – they had also forgotten their proper place. It was time for them and the rest of the world to get an education. And if they were not capable of educating themselves, it was obviously going to have to be the next Party Son of Heaven who would have to do it for them. Geography and history would be good places to start. After hundreds of years of sailing around the planet, armed only with their own misguided maps, and without a history book of the real world to rub between them, the Western adventurers had completely failed to understand not just the facts on the ground, but the very principles of heaven on which everything was based. Poor old Lin Zexu, that nineteenth-century Confucian who had tried so hard to get the opium pedlars to see the errors of their ways. He had certainly tried to explain the principles of heaven to the barbarians, but he might as well have been (as Confucius had once put it) 'playing the zither to an ox'. One spreading sky, ruled by a single Son of Heaven, and guided only by the pole star idea of *ren* benevolence and humanity (putting oneself in other people's shoes): how hard was that to understand?

But the foreigners had insisted on their idea of sovereign states – and stuffed it in their steamboats, gunning up the eastern coast along with their self-righteous rages. As, indeed, they had insisted on the old chestnuts of sovereign self-interest and invisible hands – shot straight from the barrel of Adam Smith's British mouth. Once they had dumped their ideas on Chinese lands, it had not been long before the foreign rot had set in. Treaty ports had been taken up and down the nineteeth-century coast, as if heaven had never existed; Hong Kong and Macau had been pocketed. Edges of Qing-protected Tibet had been snatched away, as if they were nothing but clouds. And northern lands had been traded under the far-off tables of early twentieth-century Versailles. Of course, when one understood what Charles Darwin and Herbert Spencer had written, it was all crystal clear: the 'sovereign state' and the 'invisible hand' were not principles, but weapons in a battle for the survival of the fittest people on earth. Mao had seen them for what they were – barbarian imperialists – and packed them off, back to their own borders. But when Deng had opened the door to their science and technology, they had simply picked up again, whispering 'peaceful evolution' as if the celestial kingdom were just a historical aberration in need of a change.

And then, of course, one had to remember the Japanese. After a hundred and fifty years of imperial dreaming, it was about time they too began to read a few more history books – and take a closer look at their geography as well. The history was certainly clear: a heavenly navy wiped out in 1895; Taiwan pocketed like a stone in a game of *weiqi*; a battle with Russia (in China) over who was going to own which bits of the northern heartlands; a dastardly deal with a two-timing Republican politician to appropriate Germany's stolen Chinese lands; the raising of a puppet state of Manchuria; and then a full-scale assault launched across the country, north and south. (True, Mao had thanked them for distracting Chiang Kai-shek in the 1930s and clearing the northern fields for the eventual Communist victory; but everyone knew that he had always had his Monkeyish side.) Looking at the geographic facts, Japan was nothing but an upstart scattering of islands which, two thousand years ago, the First Qin Emperor had mistakenly imagined to be the Penglai home of the immortals (well, we all make our mistakes). In reality, they were nothing more than a group of stunted orphans – a flotsam and jetsam of a people who had probably first been born in the Yellow Emperor's lands and then, floating off on the waves, had not only forgotten their history, but their manners as well.

Deng Xiaoping had, indeed, been wise to counsel the Party to hide its martial light under a bushel and bide its time. It was just the kind of advice that the Crouching Dragon, Zhuge Liang, would have given – a man whose instinct for the less visible tracks of the *dao* had been faultless. But China's rise had been faster than Deng could have predicted, and the foreigners' fall had been faster and more spectacular than anyone could ever have dreamt. The facts had changed, and the foreigners had become more cunning. That war of 'peaceful evolution' had been carried on as if butter wouldn't melt in their mouths: the internet and its so-called 'freedoms'; free speech, as if anything ever came without a price; and 'non-governmental' organisations, as if they existed without the will of the state, and all flooded with reckless voices, complete with piles of free Western cash. Irresponsibly carping Chinese intellectuals had been welcomed to their foreign capitals for feasts; the Dalai Lama – the greatest traitor of them all – had even been invited to express his opinions on Tibetan lands that were clearly an essential part of China's unity. Even the obvious terrorist Rebiya Kadeer had been offered safe harbour in America, following Wei Jingsheng and his Fifth Modernisation, and countless other subversive enemies of the state. Did these barbarians have no shame?

Deng Xiaoping's wisdom had been right for the conditions of his day, but now it was time for everyone to face facts and name names. Near or far, the barbarians needed to decide where they stood in the world – on the side of a heavenly order, or against? It was a pretty simple question: no room for sitting on the fence.

*   *   *

After five years at the helm of the Central Party's School, and decades of his own diligent observations on the ground, when Xi Jinping finally reached the top of the Party, his thoughts on affairs at home and abroad were as clear as crystal. With the quiet confidence of a prince who had trained himself to be a sage, he had planned every step of his new power with care. And having studied the past and consulted the present, he was clear, like every ruler before him since the Duke of Zhou, that the best way for the people to learn was to watch, or better still, take part in, a choreographed performance of words and movements (a ritual) that everyone could follow, and remember.

Flanked by his six highest Politburo peers, in November 2012, Xi Jinping demonstrated the principles of unity and *ai guo* patriotism in an appearance at the country's National Museum. Illustrating the points for even the lowest quality minds, colourful images showed him inspecting an exhibition which traced the ups and downs of the more turbulent recent past – from the floating boxes of opium in the 1840s, through the revolutionary sacrifices of the Party's heroes, to the triumphs of the present day.

At the end of the visit, and rather unusually for Chinese leaders accustomed to a more invisible pursuit of the *dao* way, he paused to share a dream. 'With so much already achieved by the Party', observed Xi, 'it is now time for the Chinese nation to stand tall'. The dream declared, in the first week of December, he went on to Shenzhen, to stand before a statue of Deng Xiaoping that celebrated the aged warrior's southern vacation – the vacation which had set off a revolution all of its own. By the end of the year, Xi had stood up and declared his dream in the army strongholds of all seven of China's military regions: with the two million soldiers of the People's Liberation Army as an audience who were also part of the choreographed cast.

Message clear to those at home – and as clear as he could possibly make it to those abroad – by the start of the 2013 new year, Xi Jinping was beginning to light a few necessary fires, starting with a campaign against the tigers and flies of corruption. Bearing in mind the acrobatics of Bo Xilai, it seemed appropriate to conduct himself in the popular homespun image of Mao. At the front of the house, flowers were stood down, and bottles

509

of *mou tai*, every official's favourite white spirit, were dismissed. Behind the scenes, the Party's Central Commission for Discipline Inspection was set off on a silent hunt for piles of hidden cash. Having sharply observed that corruption was the greatest threat to the survival of the Party and the State, it was reasonable to think that the hunted would include every tiger and fly that could be found. But with so many tigers and flies at large, few were surprised when Xi seemed to concentrate on the monkeys who were causing the greatest havoc in the Party family's heaven.

Son of Heaven ruler that he was, however, Xi Jinping was still human. Not beyond making a mistake, a small slip in the spring of 2013 caused an unfortunate confusion. Keen to emphasise the democratic credentials of the Party, Xi had pointed to the paramount importance of the People's Constitution, and to its rule of law. His words picked up by a gaggle of tricky intellectuals, he found them twisted into rumours that the freedom to ask and answer questions was now to be permitted, with a flurry of ordinary individuals also taking it upon themselves to blow whistles on errant Party officials across the land.

Xi chided himself for jumping ahead of the people, who clearly still had a lot to learn. While any truly red heart would understand the meaning of the Party's constitutional text and its rule of law, as ever, the intellectuals were always the last to grasp any important point – just as they were always the first to shout about whatever it was they mistakenly thought they had learnt. When he had mentioned the constitution, he should also have pointed, plainly, to the finer print: to the single operative sentence under which its pages were obviously to be interpreted; the one in the preamble which put everything under the unifying leadership of the Party and its mind. And when he had mentioned the rule of law, he should have been clear that this was the 'socialist' rule of law – the one where the harmony of Party wisdom was far more important than any black and white rules. Realising that there was a lot more work to be done if the intellectuals were to understand the true meaning of order, Xi decided to spell it out with a clarifying statement of 'seven not-to-be-mentioned things': things not to be mentioned by anyone in the public eye. Obvious to anyone who had read the Party classics (or their history), the seven things included most of the armoury of the West's 'peaceful evolution' campaign: so-called 'universal' values, freedom of speech, civil rights, judicial independence – and, naturally, any historical mistakes which the Party might accidentally have made.

In August 2013, with the script now surely plain enough for the people to follow, Bo Xilai was presented to a Shandong court, flanked by the people's guards. Accused of bribery, corruption and abuse of power, he seemed to be 'number one' of the tigers that Xi Jinping's corruption campaign had in mind. As Bo stood in court, the Party's Propaganda Department, in no doubt about their critical role in choreographing the Party's celestial constellation, furnished the covering journalists with sufficient tales of jets and lavish lifestyles to kill any rising Maoist sun. Some, reading the stories, were as shocked as the Party wanted them to be. But while the Propaganda Department had done its best, it had not been quite enough: many of the readers saw the stories as confirmation that everyone in the Party was awash with the ill-gotten riches of power.

Out on the wider streets, however, there was an even bigger challenge. Devoted to the Monkey King who had lit up their lives with the promise of some truly revolutionary change, those who had sung Bo's revolutionary chorus so faithfully when he had been in the seat of Chongqing power were now taking up their song sheets and singing again. On that point, though, the Propaganda Department was better prepared. Laptops at the ready, and with the handy tool of fear to hand, the Party's papers spread a host of editorials asking the people if they *really* wanted the ravages of the Cultural Revolution to return? At the end of it all, after five days of listening to a pack of Bo Xilai's lies, the socialist court of law discharged its duty, and (as instructed) declared Bo Xilai to be guilty of the bribery, embezzlement and abuse of power with which he had been charged. Sentenced to life imprisonment in Beijing's elite Qincheng jail, if Xi Jinping had anything to do with it, it was unlikely that he would appear in public again.

With Bo Xilai despatched from the public stage, Xi could breathe a little more easily – although there were still a lot of Bo's friends and relations to deal with. If the unity of the Party was to be truly maintained, that pack of tigers would have to be painstakingly hunted to the end – with any surrounding flies firmly swatted, and probably quite a few monkeys too.

As the Party's Central Commission for Discipline Inspection spread the exercise of its terrifying powers across the land, though, it seemed that the People's security forces had been a little less well schooled in their own responsibility for maintaining unity. At the end of October 2013, just days before the grand meeting of the Party's annual plenum in Beijing, a 4x4 following an everyday route of traffic across Tiananmen Square suddenly wheeled off its course: gunning its engine for the portrait of Mao Zedong, it had exploded into a ball of flames. Clear about his history and geography, from behind the vermilion walls of nearby Zhongnanhai, Xi saw the desert prints of Xinjiang's Uighurs stamped across the shocking scene.

Remembering the words of his hero Deng Xiaoping, Xi Jinping observed the situation all around him, coolly held his ground, and, sending the security forces off for better training, calmly moved on. Thinking about the struggle to improve the *suzhi* quality of the people, and the on-going battle for the survival of the fittest state, he returned his own attention to the heavenly Party and its Propaganda Department.

And then, reminding everyone of the critical importance of a heavenly order, he repeated his dream: a great Chinese nation, united at home and abroad.

CHAPTER 2

EARTH BELOW

In the book of history, it is said: heaven having
produced the people in the lower earth, it appointed
for them rulers and teachers.

Mencius (372 – 289 BCE)

It was early in December 2011, when the coastal village of Wukan found itself cut off from heaven. Waking up one morning, the villagers looked out to see their roads to everywhere blocked by walls of bullet-resistant shields, held in place by men clad in rubber-black. Visors down, it was impossible to tell whether the faces had come from near or far: but there were so many of them that it seemed unlikely they had been mustered from the minor stables of the local Lufeng county alone.

When the villagers had first decided to fight for the land which had been stolen by a Party secretary, no one had thought much beyond some brave petitioning trips to the seats of higher government, and perhaps a banner or two. Just along the coast from the Haifeng county where Peng Pai had raised his Peasant Union, they had thought that once the early memories of his band of landless peasant brothers had been revived, the superior spirits of the Party would soon stand along their side. But when the villagers had

513

sent their representatives to Lufeng's county-town, its officials had become as scarce as snow. Warned by their county cousins, higher-up officials in the superior prefectural city of Shanwei had similarly melted away. Even petitioning letters, sent to the governing heights of Guangdong province, had failed to find an audience. And when the villagers had decided to deliver their petition by hand – printed in large letters on a six-foot board of card – Lufeng had sent its county cats to lie in wait at the entrance to the provincial government's buildings, determined to keep the mice of Wukan at bay.

After two years of playing 'stability maintenance' some of the villagers had exploded in anger. But wiser heads had asked an older villager – one who had survived the pitched battles of the Cultural Revolution – for advice. Reflecting on those past years of anger and bitterness, the once-cultural-revolutionary had offered up three lessons: don't hurt anyone, don't destroy anything, and make sure you have black and white evidence to support your cause. The villagers had found their evidence: papers showing that it was not only their own Party secretary and Village Committee who had profited from the sale of the land, but renegade Party powers in Lufeng as well.

Armed with nothing but the truth, four thousand of Wukan's villagers had peacefully marched to Lufeng's county town, asking for the return of their land. The mayor had made a promise, hearts had rejoiced, and the villagers had marched back home. But like the land rights that the villagers had once owned, the mayor's promise had quickly turned to dust. Resisting the temptations of violence, Wukan had followed up with a strike: fishing boats stayed in their harbour, and the market stood down for a rest. Shocked at the interruption of local productivity, the superior Shanwei prefecture had retaliated with a warning force of police, beating up every villager who could be caught, and issuing a 'most wanted' list for all of the ringleading state-subverters the police had been unable to catch.

As the villagers were plastering pictures of wounded brothers on their walls, one of the arrested heroes reappeared – offered up on the slab of Lufeng county's mortuary. Bruised from head to foot, a ring of black around his neck, the county claimed he was the victim of an 'it-could-happen-to-anyone' heart attack. By the time the rubber-black battalions had cut the village off, the younger inhabitants of the village had bonded together in a Wukan Blood Youth League with which to provide a security of their own: twenty-four hour walkie-talkie protection for every villager on the 'most wanted' list, bamboo poles and steel pipes for every able-bodied resident and, most importantly of all, a secret motorbike shuttle for journalists to come and write Wukan's side of the story.

Laptops set up in a makeshift news centre, stories began to flow: of how Wukan's Village Committee had shared in the spoils of stolen land with the Party secretary; of how the Party powers of Lufeng had been part of the game; and of how not even the memories of Peng Pai and his truly peasant union, had been able to make a dent in the Party wall. The internet plugged in, the plight of Wukan began to fly across the country and around the world. Days passed, food began to run low, and the remaining grains of rice were counted out and passed to the poor. More days passed, and with red flags of defiance still flying, the villagers prepared to make a last stand: a desperate dash to bring back the body of their fallen hero, so that he might be allowed to float in peace to another world.

Hours before the breakout, a message arrived: Guangdong's heavenly Party secretary had finally read their letters. If Wukan promised to go back to work, the villagers could set about electing their own honest men as leaders, and start on the job of getting back their land. Heaven seemed to have heard their prayers. Hope could rise again.

*   *   *

The dream of a more popular voice for the countryside had first revived during those 'thinking again' years in the early 1980s – the time when Deng Xiaoping had made it clear that the five winds of the communes, particularly the winds of commandism, chaotic directives and cadre privilege – needed to yield to something more productive. With peasants permitted to pursue individual incomes on farming patches of household responsibility, it had seemed only sensible to recognise that, however the city chose to see the facts, most of China lived in one of its nine hundred thousand villages.

With a sharp eye to government order, Beijing had looked at its maps, and consulted the geometry of rule: one heavenly centre, thirty-one provinces reporting to the centre, three thousand counties reporting to the provinces, and all of the villages under the official care of a county. Looking at the gap between the counties and the villages, it was decided that a new layer of 'townships' would be inserted: designed to absorb the energies of the now-redundant commune leaders, redirecting them away from mass production and more towards a general management of everything, with a regular report up to the counties above. The villages themselves had also been re-organised:

no longer the messy hamlets of 'natural' villages which had sprouted like tumbleweed over the millennia, but 'administrative' villages which could gather the hamlets of the older villages into something a bit bigger and easier to order.

With the map of order a little clearer, attention had then turned to the knottier roots of decision-making and action on the ground. Under the old communes and production brigades, questions about which crops should be planted, and where and when, had been decided by the Party, on behalf of the people. The peasants, of course, had had a say, of sorts, in keeping with the pyramid principles of the Democratic Dictatorship of the People. Like everyone else at the productive bottom, they had been allowed to elect representatives for their production brigades, who had then elected representatives for the commune; and so on up the chain until a manageable number of representatives had been selected to represent the people at large in the National People's Congress. Of course, given the importance of unity under the Party, even this pyramid of elections had had to be carefully managed, with only Party-qualified candidates standing. Up and down the country, obeying orders from the centre, Party Secretaries at every level (from brigades and communes to counties and provinces) had appointed election committees to manage the process, with each committee choosing the local Party members who would be qualified to stand.

It had not been easy. The first and most important task had been to decide who the candidates were going to be. Meetings had then been convened where everyone could express whatever views they wanted – as long as they observed the all-important principle of unity (which, under the highly changeable conditions of the Great Leap Forward and the years which had followed it, obviously meant agreeing with whoever was in power at the top). With everything clarified in advance, when elections had been held, they had been models of heavenly order. And if ever, for some unaccountable local reason, they were not so orderly, Party men from higher levels had always been ready to come and fix the problem on the ground. True, things had taken a bit of a battering under the Cultural Revolution – when competing claims of heavenly authority had battled for revolutionary power, and everyone had been fighting for the all-important seals of authority with which heaven stamped its decisions. But such unruly changes had obviously been undesirable. In fact, the one good thing one could say about the Cultural Revolution was that it had provided an excellent lesson to everyone in the dangers of unbridled democracy: too many voices, and no one in charge.

When the new peasant world of household responsibility had been launched, some had argued that the old Democratic Dictatorship of the People also needed a change. Up in the cities, in 1978, Wei Jingsheng had argued for his Fifth Modernisation – democracy as a voice of the people. Although Wei had been swept off to jail – and a following campaign of spiritual civilisation had been launched to make sure that everyone else's minds stayed pure – many of the peasants thought he had a point. When Deng Xiaoping had then announced that individual households could decide how to farm their own patches of earth, a number of peasants had begun to argue that perhaps it was time for the Democratic Dictatorship of the People to be modernised as well. How could fields be individually farmed if decision-making was always subject to Party-driven unity? It had all been very well when the Party had been an army of donkey drivers and snow really had fallen in summer. But as Party membership had mushroomed in the decades after 1949, it had been hijacked by a pack of rats who had progressively hollowed out the people's prosperity. If Deng truly wanted to change production, he would need to change the way in which decisions were made – and the people who made them.

Deng had been advised of the peasants' arguments, and had even seen their logic. But it seemed to him to be wholly unfeasible. If the principles of the Democratic Dictatorship of the People were ever dislodged, how on earth could the Party conduct the orchestra of the country at large? Things had been left as they were, and the villages had remained under the charge of the townships, albeit with committees of their own which (headed by village men appointed by the Party) were really there just to save the townships' time by making sure the villagers were kept as quiet as mice.

By the time the people of Wukan had discovered that their land had been written off the village books, things had moved on a little. From 1999, villages across China had been allowed to 'elect' their village committees. The kind of elections the villages got depended on their location, and the patterns of the past. In areas where the spreading promise of socialist wealth was unlikely to be much more than a pipe dream – and where taxes were accordingly not likely to amount to much either – most people were too busy struggling to survive to worry much about the details of elections. Conversely, in places where accidents of fate meant that there were some brave local individuals who still insisted on asking questions, there was a chance that the peasants might be able to make their own choices, and cast their votes accordingly. Everywhere else, however, individual Party powers had dug themselves in so deeply that very few peasants dared to question their suggestions as to who to vote for. As a general rule, the closer one got to the fringes of any fortunes to be made, the more likely it was that the villagers' votes would be bent to the superior order of the township's Party minds: those quickest to see the possibilities of profit, and with the sharpest understanding of how to work the levers of power.

As in the communal past, election committees organised by the township told the villagers who their candidates could be, with the election committees headed by the Party's appointed secretary for the village, and manned by men who he could trust. Anyone attending an election committee meeting was advised to remember that unity was everything. If anyone seemed tempted to forget their place in the orchestra, and try to ask a question, a helpful reminder could easily be delivered by 'a friend'. If anyone seemed to have gone tone deaf, stronger voices (and rougher hands) could always be found.

Heaven forbid that anyone should think of standing for election without an invitation; but if they did, there were plenty of persuasive means available to change their mind. Rules were an obvious place to start: young candidates were told that they did not meet the qualifications of experience; more experienced ones were told that they were too old. Whenever any independent candidates asked to see the rules for themselves, there was always a local lock-up, where they could be given time to reconsider their request. Of course, some stubborn candidates would keep on asking, but the local Party war-chest was full of clever ideas: an independent candidate inviting villagers for a conversation over a bowl of noodles was a clear case of vote rigging; insisting on standing for election even when patient Party minds had set out the facts was an obvious indication that the candidate was a criminal in disguise, responsible for a recent spate of unsolved thefts. As for anyone who wanted to make electioneering claims that peasants still owned land that had already been sold, that was plainly a subversion of the power of the state.

* * *

As the glittering train had sped up across the 1990s, the peasants' anger had risen almost as fast as the speed of the train. Farmland had been sold from under their noses, and then concreted over to reappear as a local government-blessed factory; taxes had been collected and then buried under someone's Party garden. By the year 2000, it seemed to the population of the countryside that the 'elected' village chiefs and local Party Secretaries (very often one and the same), had turned into rich and powerful *tu di*, local emperors. So rich and powerful were they that even their chickens and dogs were living in heaven, with their wealth stored so wisely that the *tu baozi*, country bumpkins who lived alongside them could scarcely find a wholesome meal, let alone afford a waterproof roof to put above their heads. In some cases, the local emperors were new brooms – nominated by someone above, whether for the value of their money or their willingness to do what they were told. In others, they were old hands who had navigated the raging tides of the Cultural Revolution and managed to come sailing out on top. Either way, the faster the train had travelled, the tighter the Party's local officials had closed their grip on the profitable village worlds – and the faster those worlds had begun to crumble. Land won by the revolutionary sacrifices of parents and grandparents had been sold beneath the peasants' feet, fields had turned black with soot, rivers had taken to running red, and a lot of children had been born blue.

The countryside possibilities of the glittering train had not been limited to the land. From the 1990s onwards, local Party secretaries and government officials had plumbed every imaginable depth in their eagerness to find a profit. Deng Xiaoping's one-child policy had been one opportunity – providing an excellent stick with which to force stubborn village minds with too many children to cough up the heavenly fines. In Henan province, local officials had found an even better idea. With peasants living on pennies, the officials offered them the chance to make a few bucks in return for letting them milk their blood for onward sale to hospitals. Ever keen to boost productivity, the blood had been pooled in blood banks, stripped of its red cells and then reinjected back into the peasants so they could be quickly milked again; but while the red cells had been removed, in many cases, a dose of HIV had inconveniently found its way into the blood banks, and AIDS swept across the fields. Of course, those villages most infected had soon lost their value and had had to be buried in silence. But there were always other ideas. A popular one in many provinces was children: snatched up by snakehead brothers who smuggled them in to brick kilns, the profits of their labour was shared with the local Party secretaries and officials, who turned the necessary blind eyes.

Nor were the possibilities limited to immediate profit: careers, with their potential for longer-term gains, were important too. So essential to the natural ordering of things, they were all dependent upon keeping in the good books of any superior supervision (particularly in terms of the measurable indicators of productivity and wealth created, and births avoided, by which every local Party career was judged). Up and down the country, village lands were transformed into job-creating factories (or, better still, hopeful cities-in-progress). And whenever the central government inconveniently asked to check the numbers of births, local officials rounded up any women who might have slipped the educating net, and pushed them into steel-rimmed surgeries to cut the cord of life. If anyone threatened to raise an alarm to a higher-level authority, it was easy to shut them up in jail – just put it down to 'stability maintenance'. And if a spell in jail didn't do it, it might just be worth an official's while to have the inconvenient would-be whistleblower removed.

* * *

For a long time, many villagers continued to believe that the Party's heaven was still up there: it was just that a few bad clouds had got in the way. Disregarding those who insisted that, after thousands of years of communications having been cut between heaven and earth, one shouldn't have any expectations of change, these more trusting spirits had argued that the Party had started out as a heroic band of brothers – and that leopards did not change their spots. The problem, they insisted, must just be in the lower ranks who had obviously lost their way (or, come to think of it, who should not have been in the Party at all). All they had to do, the loyal peasants argued, was to find a way to get their messages past the local snakes, and up to the heavenly skies. Willing to give anything a try, and aware that the Party's government (like all imperial dynasties before it) had set up 'letters and petitions' offices precisely for this purpose, petitions had been prepared by the bucketload, inked in the best hands that the villagers could muster.

Writing petitions was one thing. Getting them through the guarded portals of the letters and petitions offices, however, was quite another. Charged with stability maintenance, lower level officials became masters of the art of keeping uncomfortable messages from getting anywhere close to the higher echelons of power. Once alerted to the fact that a village was thinking about writing anything on paper (there were always spying eyes and ears happy to pass on such news for a favour or a fee), the misguided letter-writers would be invited to 'have a cup of tea' at the welcoming offices of the local Public Security Bureau. If that didn't work, the same spying eyes and ears could usually be relied upon to give the township or the county an advance warning on what the villagers were planning next. Any village mice thinking of making a personal visit to the provincial government could usually be headed off at the local bus or train station. But, just to be sure, guarding cats could also be sent to keep watch over the higher gates of power themselves. And if any mice looked as if they might jump all the way up to Beijing, all available stability-maintaining energy would be deployed to head them off. Hired hands in plain clothing would stake out the railway stations and every possible train. If that failed, the same hands would be sent to the intended petitioning destination, and told to use every crafting wit they could muster to hunt the devilish mice down. The most obvious destinations, other than the letters and petitions offices, were the television stations. With both placed under a 24-hour cat surveillance, the face of any mouse which appeared to match any 'wanted' images would be whisked off the streets and into one of the special 'black jails', which every province kept in the capital, ready for a bumpy ride home.

By 2008, though, so many people were falling off the glittering train that it was getting hard to find villagers who still believed in the dream of a Party heaven. Driven to desperation by the deception of the Democratic Dictatorship of the People, many villagers forgot the trains and simply went on local rampages. White-tiled pavilions of township and county power started to explode in flames; sleeping police cars shot up like fireworks. With villagers now convinced that there was no difference between local Party officials and the gangster criminals who served them, the heavenly Party's representatives increasingly found themselves at the pointed end of pitchforks and hoes. Fear of Party power now trumped by the loss of almost everything, villagers began to argue that if one wanted to talk about patriotism, the 'people', who had fought and won the revolution, had not been an abstract collective, but their very own ancestral fathers and grandfathers. Whatever 'heaven' the thieving official thugs might claim to be representing, the land that the peasants stood on was theirs.

With the thousand year old tale of Song Jiang and his fellow marsh outlaws carried deep in their hearts, many peasants had vowed, like their forefathers, to stand together, or die. Fortified with the memory of the hero Guan Yu, the god of war who always protected the weak, they had stood up in their hundreds of thousands to protect their earth. Just as inspired by the stories of the Monkey King as Mao Zedong (not to mention Bo Xilai), they refused to be dazzled by any of the claptrap references to the 'socialist rule

521

of law'. And, masters of the story of the *Outlaws of the Marsh*, they began to occupy even the land that had already been snatched away.

Although China's villages had been carefully corralled into isolation by the Party's Leninist principles of administrative organisation (every village under an administrative order of its own), and although each was a tiny pocket, scattered across the vast expanse of the country, all of them had drawn on the same common store of strategies and courage which had served their ancestors across thousands of years. Threats raining down upon their heads from the townships and the counties above, the villagers simply wrapped themselves more closely together – and shut their ears. Of course, the villagers were not the only ones to have read the story of the *Outlaws of the Marsh*: local government-hired hands in plain clothes, having also grown up with the familiar tale, had smuggled themselves into the villages, and picked off the weakest villagers, throwing them into jail. Sworn to the brotherhoods, however, the families of the fallen had been clutched to the hearts of surviving brothers, and protective timbers had been cut from trees and rolled across village roads to keep the evil interlopers out.

With so many parts of Hu Jintao's, new socialist countryside, struggling, and with Beijing getting more and more anxious about unity, more of the local governments began to hit back in greater force. Equipping themselves with great new armies of bulldozers, rubber batons and shields, village by village, they had beaten the villagers down. Blood and tears washed the streets; jails filled to overflowing. Within their midst, though, a new generation of men were becoming local heroes, with some of them well on their way to the local pantheons of the gods.

* * *

As the peasants watched the tragedy of the countryside unfold, some sharp eyes observed that the 'socialist market economy' was issuing an increasing number of laws to support its new ideas of order. Indeed, from the end of the 1990s, a few peasant minds had begun to wonder if salvation might not in fact lie in the law. Not the 'socialist law', which put the Party above everything: that had obviously not been designed to help. But with the crafting of so many new laws to support the glittering train and its markets, there were a few which seemed to be giving the peasants a bit of a chance against the local rats who ruled their world. One of them even granted a right to sue local government officials. Of course, that right did not extend to suing local Party secretaries (in the socialist legal system, anyone in the fold of the Party would always be above the law). But it was a beginning. Certainly, given the desperate state of affairs, anything was worth a try.

Where to start? Full of peasants, few villages had ever seen a lawyer, let alone raised one in their midst. For most of China's peasant children, schooled on rough benches, the very idea of mastering the endless strokes of black rules inked on white, would have been dizzying enough, without the discouraging observations of teachers who knew that their pupils would struggle to find a job in a factory, let alone anything more. But with every peasant's child trained in the art of 'eating bitterness', as some got older and left school they decided that they would just apply that art to swallowing textbooks on law. The most dedicated were those who had found themselves tested by local government and Party forces far more frightening than any ink that might jump off a page.

Almost all of the would-be lawyers were stubborn minds chasing a stolen justice. Prepared to apply themselves to endless homework at the end of their daily labours, they buried their eyes in the pages of government regulations that might be able to save the day. The most difficult job was getting hold of the relevant texts. Most of the basic regulations that governed the rights and duties of the countryside could be bought for pennies on an open market. Covering a host of issues – from land use rights, tax collections and local elections, to procedures for imprisonment, administrative actions against government officials and appeals – they were a treasure-trove of information. But in the socialist world of law, any local court would read the regulations in the context of Party principles of unity, and firmly beneath the many 'local notices' issued for guidance in applying central government regulations to conditions on the ground. Which, of course, was another problem: the most important of the local notices – the inconvenient ones most likely to help a peasant, or those which were themselves a flagrant breach of higher laws – were often kept under lock and key, lest anyone should ever try to send a copy up to Beijing.

It seemed that the skills required for studying the law were not much different to the tactics of cunning and stealth that the villagers had learnt from the Cultural Revolution, or the *Outlaws of the Marsh*. Thanks to Mao, though, if one bought the basic regulations at a market stall – and one was able to liberate the relevant pages of the local notices from their filing cabinets (usually only a matter of greasing someone's palm, or calling in a family favour), mastering the basic rules was surprisingly easy. Converted early on to the First Qin Emperor's school of law, Mao's view of the law was that it was only a matter of stating rules plainly – and ensuring that the punishments were clear. Deng had agreed, so that even when the socialist market economy demanded more laws with more details, the bureaucrats had been told to write them in simple words that anyone could understand.

With such an earthy approach to the law, one would have thought that even the least educated of the officials would have been able to keep their local notices broadly in line with the rules at the top. But as more and more of the peasant lawyers managed to liberate more and more of the notices, they noticed that not only were the grubby characters of the texts often at obvious odds with central regulations issued by Beijing, but many of them were also at odds with themselves. Notices purporting to give official approval to the expulsion of families from their fields were found to be nothing but local lies. Other notices approving peasant arrests were found to have no more legal authority than an inkpot. It was not long before the peasant lawyers were turning the tables and waving the fine print of the local notices before the very noses of those who had written them.

Consoling themselves with tea and cigarettes, the local officials cast their thoughts back to the socialist basics. No wonder Mao had beaten the intellectual lawyers to within an inch of their lives: if spiritually polluted rightists like these self-taught peasants were allowed to poke their opinions into everyone's business, it would not be long before heaven collapsed. Skip the rules, they concluded; go straight to the punishments – and, given the ease with which these peasants communicate with their brothers, make sure you capture their mobile phones before you carry them off to jail.

Many peasant lawyers disappeared: some into jail, some shut up for an educational spell of house arrest, some never to be seen again. Despite this, few gave up. Doors open to anyone with a problem, willing to work for nothing in order to defend a fellow man, they did whatever they could to steel themselves against the inevitable storms of official fury. Clear that the key to survival was less about the letter of the law and more about the number of brothers who could be mustered, they looked for (and gave each other) plenty of *hu zhu*, mutual assistance. Sweeping the internet, they were quick to spot their fellow travellers: a journalist here, a blogger there, other peasants-at-law in nearby villages and counties, even academic law professors in far-off cities, whose sympathetic city pockets would, from time to time, also send supporting cash when the peasants' own meagre resources ran dry. And whenever there was a case to lodge, others with similar claims were invited to join their applications.

Learning quickly, the wisdom of every lesson was shared, posted up or printed off for others to see. And if ever the peasants thought that one of their number was about to be 'disappeared', they made sure that their defences were strengthened – notifying brothers in law who could be relied upon to try and come to their rescue, particularly, the city bloggers and law professors who would be ready to splash the black text of truth across the four quarters of the internet.

It was not always enough to keep a peasant lawyer out of jail, but the knowledge that no one would be forgotten enabled everyone to cling on in hope.

*　　*　　*

While peasant lawyers were going into battle for the people of the lower earth, many of the peasants were calling the countryside quits. It was hard enough to make the price of a meal in the middle of nowhere, let alone battle against forces of heaven that had clearly got out of control. Some peasants packed their bags and took their chances, counting on finding a job in one the factories that had now spread like new-generation forests around the southern coast. Others paid a fee to the snakeheads to fix them up with a position in advance. Floating or pre-paid, squashed into crowded trains heading east and south, the warmth of fellow companions, all travelling in the same direction, gave their hearts a lift. The green-eyed demons of the village officials left behind, the peasant migrants shared their stories with the black humour which only a bleeding human heart can understand. Windows open to softer winds, hopes began to rise.

Unfortunately, once through the factory gates, most of their hearts had fallen. Assembly lines and systems scientifically primed for socialist efficiency, the migrants found that the days were long, the rules were longer, and the cost of disobedience was more than most could afford. The basic day was thirteen hours; the basic week forgot about weekends. Talking on the job was punishable with a five yuan fine; packets of pay were docked for every minute wasted; and the first two months of everyone's wages were held as a deposit against reliable time-keeping. Pleading tales of children left behind who needed the money for food and school were ignored – with those responsible for docking their pay informing them that they themselves were only doing their jobs, and if anyone didn't want to work like a machine, they should not have turned up in the first place. After a while, though, the peasant workers found that the hours and the pay were the least of their worries: with profits to make and fees to pay to local government and Party officials, factory owners were cutting every safety corner in sight. Accidents were a fact of life; compensation was a dream.

At night, packed into dormitories like sacks of rice, young hearts would remember their hopes of freedom and whisper to each other in the dark. Some would suggest that they band together and walk off the factory floor. Older heads, who had already been on the job for a while, would explain that the last time they had tried that, the factory bosses had cut the lights, and then unleashed their thugs to drag them out and beat them up, docking their pay to boot. Refusing to give up, some of the younger ones would suggest that they follow their peasant lawyer brothers back home and look at the law: surely even the socialist legal system didn't allow factory owners to treat their workers like beasts. At which point, one or two eager voices would pipe up, saying that they had heard about lawyers in nearby cities who might be willing to help. Hopes rising, communication with the lawyers would then be made on someone's mobile phone.

Whenever the lawyers were contacted, the answer would always come as a shock. First, the rules would be outlined: always painful for trusting hearts looking for threads of red justice in a world where everything was so black. Apparently anyone could join a union, as long as it was a branch of the Party's mass labour organisation – that All China Federation of Trade Unions, ACTFU, into which every union had been bundled up just after the 1949 revolution. But although ACFTU was grounded on the Democratic Dictatorship of the People, this did not quite mean what it said. The democratic part was limited to having chosen the Party in the first place. And, with the Party having become the revolutionary representative of 'the people', it was the Party that exercised the 'dictatorship', rather than any upstart workers. As ever, explained the lawyers, in the Party's legal system, unity was all. To which they would add wistfully that the constitution used to have a right to strike – not that many had dared to use it. But once the glittering train of the socialist market economy had left the station, the drafters had had a change of heart, and struck it out of sight.

Hope sinking in the ears of the listeners, the lawyers would note that it did not necessarily mean that one had to give up: there was still a labour law, with rules that any employee could use. The only problem with relying on the labour law was that it would probably cost the petitioner his job: that and any held-over pay that had not yet made it into his hands. To which one had to add the fact that the socialist judges of justice were also charged with applying the principle of heavenly unity, so that in any case involving labour, the local officials would need to be consulted. And given that the local officials were likely to be on the payroll of the factory bosses (just to make sure that they were always in the factory loop), the ultimate decision would probably lie with the factory head.

After so much bad news, a number of hearts would falter. Many – particularly those with children in schools, or parents expensively sick at home – would go off to find the snakeheads who were always prowling the factories, looking to profit from a migrant's pile of debt. But, others, desperate to find a way out of their nightmare, would decide to brave a strike in the hope that some good Party official in heaven could, somehow, be touched: you never know, it had happened before; maybe snow could fall again in summer. The lawyers would then be asked to do whatever they could to help; although neither lawyer nor client had any idea of whether, or how, the cost of their services was ever going to be met.

*   *   *

Having heard the stories of the factory floors, not all of the villagers who left the countryside went to the production lines of the coast. Many decided to try their luck in the cities instead, eyes caught by the sparkle of a Beijing or Shanghai. Apart from the price of the train fare, though, there was that difficult question of storming the city's *hukou* passes in order to get in. Born in a village, the essential household registration papers of every peasant were stamped with the name of the village from which they came, and in which they were expected to spend their lives. When Deng Xiaoping had called for a faster socialist market economy, millions had been given the special red chop which opened the gates to one or other of the new factory towns: free to stand at the assembly lines for as long as they wanted. For a fee, smaller cities could even be persuaded to overlook the dirty question of birth, and change the chop. Getting a chop to go to a real city, however, was quite another matter. Of course, there was not a building site or a restaurant in the country that did not want the cheap souls of the countryside to come and lend a temporary hand. But living wages were another matter, and storming the big city passes without paying a king's ransom was the hardest trick in the land. Steeped in a history of brave adventurers, though, many peasants decided to try. The price of their efforts would be high.

With city officials under orders to limit the size of their own populations, and equipped with the powers to check everyone's *hukou* papers day or night, any migrant who smuggled themselves into the bright city lights either needed to keep in the dark or find the money to persuade an official to turn a blind eye. Most of the migrants found it easier and cheaper to keep to the dark. Making their way to the rough-and-tumble edges of the city world, they did everything they could to avoid the searching lights of detection, whatever the price. Squeezing into 'urban villages' – older villages around the cities, whose land had not yet been sold to a high rise – the migrants paid through the nose for every inch of electricity, and for every drop of water too. Try as hard as they might to hide, only a few succeeded. Most found themselves stung for a honeyed bribe to keep someone's lips sweet. Those unable to afford the bribe were packed off on a slow train back to the countryside, with any wages they were owed lost as a lesson in order. Those who succeeded soon realised that, however many lips they sweetened, life in the city could only ever be a temporary arrangement. Once their limbs hit thirty, they would be replaced with younger models. Meanwhile, for as long as they were in the city, no hospital would open an affordable door to their illnesses and injuries; and no school would contemplate taking on the clutter of their children's muddy feet.

Some of the more confident would-be migrants tried to persuade the forces of order that they were really city people just waiting for a chance. It was an argument for which they had been well prepared. Schooled in the struggling countryside, they and their parents had always been clear that getting into a city would be the greatest 'survival of the fittest' battle of their lives. Digging deep into threadbare pockets, parents put every possible penny into the education of the single child who, given the current state of the glittering train, would one day have to be their pension. Mindful of the hurdles ahead, rural schools tried to even out the odds by extending the hours at school. By the end of the 1990s, most were opening seven days a week, with lessons of up to fifteen hours a day. Given the hours and the distances – many children would walk hours to get to school and back – dormitories were usually made available. Aware that peasant children would be unable to compete with the textbooks of the city (let alone their computers), they were taught to swallow every possible bitterness – with a stiff dose of physical training added, to give them an extra edge. Hard wooden desks doubled up as beds to toughen up the body; blackboards kept a constant rallying tally of which children were ahead. The *shudaizi*, bookworms, of the city might have their libraries and laptops, but the children of the countryside would have their age-old power to eat the bitterness of hardship, taught from the youngest age. Those who managed to stay the course would then battle with each other and everyone else in China to pass the exams which could win the dream of a place in a city university – and the promise of a job which would be something other than the '3D' dangerous, dirty and demanding labour that was the usual peasant's lot.

These, of course, were not the only hurdles. In the world of the survival of the fittest, with so many students looking for results, and with peasant children so obviously lacking the *gao suzhi* higher qualities of the mind, just getting to a university did not guarantee a degree. Those who failed to secure the life-changing certificates then found themselves back in the pool of all the other would-be-migrants and its general luck of the draw. Chasing whatever paper certificates might be on offer – English lessons, computer training, hospitality – every possibly affordable course was swallowed like the sky. Then they would put their best feet forward, bravely presenting themselves for the formal approval of city officials who had the gift of a limited number of urban places for candidates with the appropriate skilled qualifications. Either that, or find the money required to help an official tick the right box. Even then, while their parents' labour, or the bribes, might squeeze them through the extra years of study, no certificate could disguise their low quality earthy accents, just as no amount of peasant savings could cover up their clumsy clothes. For most, the best hope was a job at the bottom of someone's city dump, or in the back rooms of something better: somewhere they could not sully with their low quality country ways.

*   *   *

While the peasants were fixing their eyes on the possibilities of the bright city lights, those born with a city *hukou* were struggling to keep up with the demands of the high quality life. With television sets now broadcasting the virtues of refined consumption, some in the smaller cities imagined that the greatest demonstration of high quality was to have enough money to buy a foothold in the sparkling metropolises of Beijing or Shanghai. And with billboards in Beijing and Shanghai smiling most brightly on the *gao suzhi*, high quality, consumer, the residents of these cities were clear that only a sweeping apartment at the height of a newly rising tower, or a spreading villa in a gated and guarded suburban compound, would do. At the end of the day, wherever one came from, everyone knew that high quality was a question of money, and that unless one had a village or a Party official on tap, money was a matter of finding or creating the most rewarding kind of position.

Crystal clear about the calculus, those born to the cities climbed their careers with the dedication of mountaineers. By the early years of the twenty-first century, ordinary hours in the office were simply badges of honour, with any failure to stay late considered a matter of personal shame. As everyone battled their way up the same narrow paths, with the same sparkling credentials, it was obvious that what really made the difference was the quality of one's relationships. Given the all-important powers of the Party over everything, the best quality relationships would naturally be with Party people who could either provide a promoting approval themselves, or offer an introduction to another Party power who would be able to help. And as relationships always needed delicate nurturing, restaurants became essential institutions for the promotion of one's career. Indeed, as the years passed, and as the glittering train got faster, the line between the office and the restaurant got thinner and thinner, until few could tell the difference. Not that dining out in restaurants offered any kind of rest for the career-builders. Given the number of favours on which every relationship depended, time spent at the table usually created an ocean of extra work. And however high anyone climbed, with prices rising and everyone else climbing up as well, it was not only clear that one could never be high enough, but that any heights reached just made it frighteningly further to fall.

As the first decade of the new millennium advanced, insomnia had become a ticking time-bomb, depression stalked the streets, and every now and again, and more than in the two decades before, the peace of another world would be found at the end of a rope. The city was just like everywhere else in the heavenly lands: a tooth and claw struggle for survival.

No one understood the nature of the struggle better than city parents. Sights fixed on the education that would determine the quality of their children, fathers and mothers (and particularly mothers) scoured every inch of the school curriculum looking for space to squeeze in yet another lesson, while reading every quality raising self-help book available. Many decided to use the pre-birth months for extra advantage: Tang dynasty poetry was popularly intoned for the womb. And with Confucius having made an official comeback, flocks of parents turned to the now rediscovered ancient classics. *The Great Learning* was the most popular text: the one with which Confucius (possibly with the help of someone in the later Han dynasty) had set everyone off on a two and a half thousand year journey of cultivating themselves, even as they strengthened the family and the state beyond. Another popular light from the past was the *Yi Jing, The Book of Changes*, from the time of the Duke of Zhou.

Fretting about the limited number of hours in a day, city schools found themselves transformed into places where everyone could test themselves, with the real front-line of advantage moved to after-school tuition and self-cultivating activities. Exams were set like races, races were timed like the Olympics, and evenings and weekends were requisitioned for yet more reading and writing, with punctuating lessons in tennis and swimming taught as master classes. If the ancestors had been able to eat the bitterness necessary to pass the imperial exams, there was no reason why their descendants should not be able to match up. At home as well as at school, children were taught to keep self-evaluating records, charting both how well they completed a given task, and the quality of the thoughts with which they worked. Meanwhile, everyone was exhorted to emulate the physical prowess that had kept the Long Marchers on their road to victory-against-the-odds.

Being children, many tried to launch rebellions. Although, as the years passed, as exams piled upon exams, and as the stories of their parents' and their grandparents' sacrifices were constantly heaped upon their heads, most eventually accepted their lessons. But as the time drew nearer for the exams that would decide which children would go to a university, and which university they would go to, some turned to the windows of their high-rise, homework-filled, bedrooms and saw the promise of another world.

Counting the increasing number of suicides, many teachers and onlookers said that it just confirmed what they had been saying all along: the children of today were not tough enough to win the battle for the survival of the fittest. Others looked up at the skies and wondered why such young lives had to die.

*   *   *

By 2005, looking at the more human quality of their citadels, many of the city people were beginning to wonder if the price they were paying for a high quality life had not become a little too expensive. Forests of chimneys had spread in all directions; city roads had become mobile car parks. Taps were pouring out water tinged with the chemical waste of over-enthusiastic production; and more and more food was being packaged with poison for somebody's profitable gain. In Beijing, *hutong* lanes of houses were demolished under the feet of their occupants, while spreading pavilions that had survived the past were falling ever faster to the demolitions of a runaway present. And in every older city, inconvenient residents were redirected to new homes outside the city limits. New and old, city neighbourhoods found themselves exposed to polluting power plants. The dust of destruction for construction was in everyone's eyes, even as the pursuit of profit prowled across everybody's lives. Sparkling malls offered compensating fountains of consumption for those who could afford them, but the ticking minutes of every waking day had become nothing more than a race, whose only end was not to fall behind.

Spirits already exhausted by a lack of sleep, many began to lose their tempers. Angry voices rose on overcrowded buses, in the streets of neighbourhood communities, and even in the clubhouses of the gated compounds and the towering apartments.

Thinking on the stresses that were driving the rage, those who lived along the streets turned to the neighbourhood committees whose job was supposed to be looking after the local households. Turning up at the meetings, however, most found that the committees were governed by the same Democratic Dictatorship of the People which ruled everything else. They also found that the local powers were repeating the same heavenly mantra of unity that everyone could read, whether in the daily papers or in solicitous government messages now regularly sent directly to mobile phones: 'build a harmonious society'.

Life in the gated compounds was not much easier. True, the more privileged, higher quality, people who owned such homes were able to call meetings of themselves as 'residents committees'. But it was not long before they learned that the same Party powers which plagued the countryside and the city's neighbourhood committees had found their way into the richer city compounds as well. As owners with a paper title to their property, and contracts with developer-managers, they might have expected their voices to carry the day. But any well-organised management would have local officials on a payroll of some sort. And with most of those who could afford the gated compounds working every available hour of the day, few had the time or energy to do battle. Many resorted to crossing their fingers – hoping that heaven would eventually get around to solving their problems one day.

Exasperated by the deceptions of the Democratic Dictatorship of the People, some, with the same idea as the peasants in the countryside, decided that the only way a harmonious society was going to be built was if they created the harmony themselves. Having read the same books as the peasants (and far more), up and down the country, a number of city-dwellers began to organise themselves into their own bands of brothers, determined to fix what was going wrong. A chemical factory to be built in a southern city? Residents collectively pulled out their mobile phones and organised a million-strong 'stroll'. *Hutong* lanes to be swept away, along with the last memories of Beijing's past? City spirits launched themselves across the internet and bombarded the district mayors' headquarters with copies of rules and regulations, accompanied by logical arguments which tore any local notices to shreds.

Seeing strength in their own numbers and abilities, many of the city-dwellers proceeded to create *hu zhu* mutual self-help societies of their own. Digging deeper into problems than any official ever had, and reaching out across the crowds, the organisations not only came up with smart solutions that took the officials by surprise – but also offered to muster whatever manpower might be required to make the solution happen. As fixed as ever on unity, the Party and its government insisted that every one of these 'non-governmental' organisations should register itself under the tutelage of a superior government institution. Many thought this might not be such a bad idea – it was always easier to win a war with an official at your side.

For a while, it seemed as if the self-helping societies were making progress, and that even the Party might begin to appreciate some of the helping hands from below. Journalists began to float supportive stories; and while technically bound to the Party, editors began to print them – turning a blind eye to the idea that the principle of unity meant that the Party had to do, and to be seen to be doing, everything that the people could ever want or need. But as time turned, and as it seemed that everyone wanted to have their own 'conversation with heaven', the Party began to tighten the lines. Many of the organisations found that government institutions that had once offered tutelage suddenly withdrew their support. Others woke up to find that someone had manufactured a charge against their leaders – droppable after a clarifying 'cup of tea' and an agreement that the organisation would give up whatever solution it thought it was providing (with the alternative being a socialist court of law and a sentence in jail). As the people's self-help was forced into retreat, editors of newspapers found themselves under pressure to call in their journalists and remind them to 'harmonise' their words.

Unwilling to give up, some tried to work within the stricter rules – faithfully believing that heaven would *eventually* come to its senses. Others were less sure. Believers or not, almost everyone began to look to the internet for assistance. The *hu zhu* self-help groups began to recreate themselves in the virtual world: assembling together in whatever numbers they wanted, and communicating with anyone and everyone they wanted to, at any time of the night or day. True, there were 'firewalls'. Installed before the internet had ever been allowed to spread in China, and significantly strengthened with the benefit of experience since then, these virtual fortresses had created a 'Chinese internet garden', in which every site and user in the country was subject to the harmonies of the state – and where inconvenient words triggered alarms. There was even a special internet police to guard the electronic borders.

Given the pedestrian nature of so many of the issues which the people were dealing with, in the early days, few of the alarms which the Party had put into the system rang – and many of the organisations had flourished. Quick to learn, though, as the online organisations flourished, the Party and its state responded with a more revolutionary zeal. The number of words (and names) which triggered the alarms was substantially expanded – ambitiously attempting to include anything which might conceivably be interpreted as threatening the principle of unity, or as somehow suggesting that the state was failing to meet its heavenly obligation to delivery harmony for all. More eyes were also added to the force of the internet police, with more technology to help: more eyes to find more words, and more technology to automatically shut down the sites which threatened everyone's unity. A *wu mao dang*, fifty-cent party, was also raised, deploying hundreds of thousands of cyber-surfers, each paid in units of 'fifty cents' to scan the internet for 'inharmonious' sites and posts, and redirect the online chat with more appropriate views. To these resources were added new, Western, technologies that could freeze a disobedient computer, and issue an electronic warning of worse to come.

But the Party had underestimated its people, and the power of the past. The old stories of the *Outlaws of the Marsh*, not to mention the legends of the Crouching Dragon, Zhuge Liang, were all as fresh today as they had been in the times when the stories were first told; and all as applicable to the corrupted power of the Party as they had been to that of imperial officials of old. Proxy servers were used to leap across electronic borders, and the expanded lexicon of alarm-triggering words was quickly learnt, and shared, so that everyone could simply type around them. Of course, the Party ordered a crackdown: widen the lexicon (again), strengthen the internet police, lock up offending computers. But the online spirits just jumped higher, and learnt more words. In the end, the Party resorted to the socialist rule of law. Deciding to kill a few monkeys to scare the chickens, it began to cart the most annoying offenders off to jail.

It was not long before the internet became yet another game of Party cat and people's mouse. And as the stakes of jail grew higher, some of the internet users decided to follow the peasants, and turn their attention to the law. With cities being close to universities, and with a number of university professors being not just the high quality city residents which the modernising Party wanted to embrace, but accomplished internet users as well, many assumed that the prospects of success would be much brighter. Like their peasant peers (and often helping them), many lawyer-professors were willing to take up cases for the values of truth and justice alone. Laws were read, documents were prepared, applications for hearings to adjudicate government actions were made.

In the beginning, a number of measured judgements seemed to offer hope. But as the volume of petitions rose, the lawyers found themselves bumping up against the model of a socialist judge. Unveiled by the Party in the same revolutionary spirit with which it had once conjured up the diaries of Lei Feng, one of the model judges was named Chen Yanping. Suddenly appearing online, Judge Chen reminded everyone about the judicial principles of a 'harmonious society'. With her judgements directed to setting any wavering courts straight – and to redirecting any misguided litigants – the model mudge reminded any and all courtroom adventurers that the fine print beloved of Western lawyers was only fit for barbarians. The black and white texts and the mechanical procedures of the West were nothing but the desperate refuge of bourgeois states who had lost the hearts of their people. In any and every case, the facts of a matter should always be explored in the softer light of harmony – ideally, out of the glare of a court, and over a cup of tea.

The lawyers did not give up, but some of them began to disappear. And over time, some, seeing the dark judicial winds blowing across the internet, packed their bags and left the country, continuing to offer their help, but henceforward from afar.

*   *   *

535

By 2010, it was not only the internet and the courts that were getting darker. Overwhelmed with chimneys and cars, city skies had got a lot darker too, particularly in Beijing. Blue had been on the retreat for a number of years, with its appearances now limited to an exceptionally strong breeze, or a Party-convened meeting which had the power to close down production. True, a number of power plants and factories had been moved to other less visible places (smaller cities, or better still, the countryside) in an attempt to clear the air. But with the glittering train speeding ahead, not everything could move: and whatever stayed just had to work harder, belching out galaxies of smoke.

Meanwhile, the city's roads had become so congested that they were more like car-parks, with fuel tanks overflowing into fuming clouds. What had once been an imperially bright ether had not only been transformed into a productive grey, but was also getting worryingly clogged up with dust: *xi-ke-li-wu*, fine particulate matter, as it was called by the scientists who understood these things; 'gdp particles' to the coughing people on the ground. Across the (now very mobile) internet – and particularly on the twittering *Weixin*, Wechat, microblogs (with features of Facebook), which were becoming increasingly popular among the city's twenty-odd million residents – the people loaded up images of a city that was racing out of control. To which they added scores of the blackly humorous jokes which Beijingers had always conjured up whenever heaven lost the plot: 'Want a cigarette?' they asked each other. 'Just open a window and take a smoke.'

Then, in the late summer of 2012, at the height of the squabbling months before Xi Jinping had risen to the head of the Party, the city itself was washed into a flood – swept by rains which had tried to fall on a once-soft land, only to find hard concrete instead. Motorists caught on the streets turned their mobile phones to the radio stations of the People's Republic for news and guidance, but found themselves serenaded by nothing more than the music of uninterrupted harmony broadcast across the waves. Before long, cars were cut off by lakes which had once been intersections, and engines were drowning in rivers which had once been roads. Desperate drivers looking for news had then turned to the microblogging *Weixin*, Wechat, world that held the twittering chatter of their friends. And news there was. Where the broadcasting stations of the Party-state had been silent, the people had rolled up their sleeves and got down to the job of serving themselves. Posting up maps and bulletins to guide their fellow men through the washed-away land, they had even proceeded to organise 'the people's' cars to pick up anyone in need of a ride.

Seventy-nine Beijingers died in the days of the flood, many of them drowned. For a short while, Beijing shed its sparkle, looking more like Bangladesh. In the days and weeks that followed, even more of Beijing's people poured into the *Weixin* world, trying to make sense of a city that had sunk. Immersing themselves in a wild virtual society where questions could not only be asked but would almost certainly be answered, they posted not just questions, but opinions, images, and jokes. Most of the posts raised the obvious simple queries: 'How could a city that had spent so much on the Olympics forget about its drains?' and 'How could a Party so proud of its propaganda fail to master the practical news that could have saved lives? One of the jokes even thanked the Party for giving everyone a wash.

In the months that followed, and as the Party carried on with its squabbling, things seemed to go from bad to worse – not only in Beijing but across the country at large. Hardly an hour passed without an image of some chaos or other appearing on the internet. Pictures of buildings and roads collapsing under the weight of the socialist market economy were two-a-penny. Just as common were pictures of people exploding with rage. Many were the victims of 'stability maintenance', and of a 'harmonious society' that had left them with nowhere to turn. A number were peasants who had been pushed beyond the limits of endurance, in villages that had once been invisible pockets of countryside and were now beginning to appear online. Pushed beyond despair, peasants were now turning the tables on local officials, killing them with knives, pipes and hoes. Others were the raging casualties of city dreams that had vanished in the puffs of other people's profit: parents who had lost their children to poisoned food; husbands and wives who had lost each other to hospitals which had taken large deposits and then failed to deliver a cure. Yet others were the simple explosions of the ticking timebombs of people who could not keep up: one was a Party official who, delayed at an airport, had smashed his rage on terminals of computers – with the help of a nearby chair.

When Xi Jinping was clapped to the clouds in November 2012, the people certainly watched with interest. If nothing else, the twisting tales of Bo Xilai's adventures, and of Xi Jinping's mysterious disappearance, offered a whole new novel to the classics of the time. With things so clearly out of the harmonious order that the Party liked to insist upon, it seemed obvious that any new ruler was going to have to introduce some kind of change. The only question seemed to be what, how and when? Some thought that Xi Jinping's dream offered interesting possibilities. But it had not been long before the microbloggers replied with dreams and observations of their own:

'Fresh air, clean water and vegetables that are safe to eat', was a popular one. 'If I were an official, I wouldn't need to dream', was another.

Meanwhile, life in the People's Republic continued: local officials raked in their profits, roads collapsed, trains crashed, and more and more of the people decided to pursue a rough justice of their own. The internet was flooded with more images, and more posts piled up on *Weixin*, as did the blackly humorous comments of a people who had come to the conclusion that China's history was doomed to repeat itself. 'Anyone in government arrested for siphoning off a million or less should be lauded as a clean official, and released immediately', cracked one microblogger. 'After chemical hotpots and poisonous rice, the Chinese people are now fit to survive any biological warfare', joked another. When ten thousand pigs floated up Shanghai's Huangpu river, lighter hearts suggested that everyone should just turn on their taps, add a bit of sesame oil, and enjoy a heaven-sent bowl of soup. And when Xi Jinping announced a crackdown on corruption, the internet had been flooded with pure derision: 'tigers would make their reports, foxes would clap with laughter, flies would hum along happily, and only the mice would run scared in the streets'.

       *   *   *

As the cities wrapped themselves up in clouds of humour, Xi Jinping and the Party family became less and less amused. And when battalions of high quality city-dwellers started blowing *Weixin* whistles on corrupt officials, the Party's propaganda troops were put on full alert. Anyone who stepped across the boundaries of harmony found their *Weixin* accounts cancelled. And those who had more than a handful of followers were reminded that the crime of counter-revolution had been replaced with the new, but equally treacherous, offence of 'subversion of the state' – and that subversion of the state took place every time the unwelcome opinions of a reckless twitterer were re-posted by five hundred people or more. Meanwhile, journalists who tried to jump on the bandwagon of telling the truth were instructed to remember that their revolutionary duty was to deliver positive news.

In the early months of Xi Jinping's reign, as 2012 turned to 2013, a Guangdong newspaper, inspired by the idea of the President's dream, decided to prepare a front page story to explore the possibilities. 'What exactly is the dream of the Chinese people?' the story asked, following up with 'How did China come to have this dream?' and 'If this is truly a dream of the

Chinese people, how can everyone help to make it come true?' Presented to Guangdong's Propaganda Commission for editorial review, the story was swiftly spiked. Telling the journalists to work overnight to prepare a more acceptable alternative, the official in charge of the harmonies of the printed page suggested that they try a more appropriately worded tribute to the Party's unifying powers.

Shocked that even the dream of a dream was going to be hijacked by the Party, the paper's pens argued back. No one could possibly be a journalist, they pointed out, if every word was unified from the top. Encountering a familiar silence, they then crafted an open letter to the Party asking what they had done wrong – and went on strike. The presses of the paper fell silent; flowers and banners of popular sympathy piled up outside the newspaper's doors. But it was not long before the superior forces of harmony put the paper quietly and obediently back on the stands.

Meanwhile, as a cool winter wind blew across the Guangdong south, a little up the coast – not far from the old Haifeng home of the long dead local hero Peng Pai – Wukan's villagers were still looking out to sea. After two years of chasing the tigers and flies who had stolen their land, they had been outfoxed at almost every turn. Once made, heaven's promises had, yet again, been snatched away by a local wind. Who on earth could tell whether and when they would ever come true?

CHAPTER 3

BEING CHINESE

*You cannot write my poems; just as I cannot
dream your dreams.*

Dreams and Poetry, Hu Shi (1921)

Up on the edge of Beijing's city, the black of winter had hardened the concrete of a cold confinement; ice had chilled its steel. Outside, warmer bodies would be chasing the pleasures of the glittering train. Inside, evening drawing to a close, time turned like the seconds of a century, or a millennium: an endless night. Clouds passing across a small window above, the solitary heart of a man who had told his truth too often and too loud looked out and floated up towards the moon. The walls of the prison might be thick but the freedom to fly depended only on the mind, even as a mind depended wholly on being able to tell the truths that really connect heaven and earth through man.

The raw coughs of fellow prisoners a distant echo, the spirits of the ancient past swept across the captive's thoughts with the full force of the present. That old poet-prince Qu Yuan, dismayed by the treacheries of Qin, and asking heaven's porter to open the gates to another world, was one such spirit. The brave Song dynasty brush that had insisted on painting the

540

miseries of the 'floating people' to an emperor-in-denial, was another. But for the man behind the bars of steel, the loudest of the voices were the young ghosts of a summer-spring in the not-so-distant past: a summer which had turned to the death of autumn; a spring which had changed every life that it had touched – including his own.

Some of the ghosts appeared as struggling screams, smashed bones and blood-soaked bodies; many wrapped with fallen bicycles in a dying embrace. Others surfaced like the surge of a great river, an ocean, that had washed into and across the heavenly city over weeks of softening days. Youthful spirits rising like sap, banners floating on high, they had picked up the rocking chords of a popular Taiwanese voice and sung themselves as children of a dragon whose fate had become intertwined with their own. 'In the ancient East there is a people', they had cho_sed: 'They are all the heirs of the dragon'. Hope flushing through their veins, the 'heirs of the dragon' had then looked at Zhongnanhai and asked a question: 'Why is it that the heavenly dynasties have never thought that the people were worth the candle of a conversation?' Standing before its vermilion walls, the dragon's heirs had then begun to sway to the beat of a Beijing guitar, singing the words of another star whose song everyone knew by heart: 'I want to give you my dreams, but you always laugh at me; me with nothing to my name; just get it together, and come with me'. As the young voices had rounded on the 'nothing to my name' refrain, they had not been alone. Beijing had poured out to join them: workers and street vendors, imagining that the people might have a part in the future; old men and women, crying at the possibility that a three thousand year old dream might finally come true. Even the police had whistled along to a tune that warmed the hearts of every Chinese.

Behind the vermilion walls, a world away from the floating people across the land, and after months of a messy chaos gathering on the streets of Beijing, the stubborn East Winds had whipped themselves up into such a fury that even heaven could not make itself heard. When, on 2 June, a group of four older spirits, *junzi* gentlemen, had joined them in a strike of hunger, the sun had carried on shining, but tanks had begun to gather, growling like dark clouds across the far-flung street. Loudspeakers announced that a storm of troops was coming. No one in their wildest dreams thought that they would fire, although some imagined that a rubber bullet or two – the price of a voice, they reasoned – might come their way. As the heat of that early June evening turned to dusk, many Beijing spirits, young and old, ran onto the streets asking the tanks and their following trucks of soldiers to think again. Subjectively remembering the art of being human, some of the troops stopped in their tracks. Others, obeying the commands of the last five thousand years, paused, blindly loaded their guns with live ammunition, and shot to kill. A boy here, a mother there, a father, a daughter, a husband, a wife; by midnight, all across the streets surrounding the square, they had fallen in their hundreds or more.

By the earliest hours of the morning of 4 June 1989, Tiananmen was surrounded by soldiers and tanks crawling in for the kill. The small band of older hunger-striking friends had looked at the thousands of students marooned within and decided that someone needed to ask heaven's troops to give them a safe passage home. One of the friends who volunteered was the 'Taiwanese voice' who had written *Heirs of a Dragon* from his home in Taipei; his name was Hou Dejian. Jumping the straits, Hou had defied the enmity of a divided nation to come to Beijing in search of what it meant to be Chinese. By 1989 he was not only famous (and infamous) in Taiwan, he was a rare and shining musical star in the still-grey mainland Chinese world. Looking across the vast expanse of the now-black square, Hou hitched a lift to the frontline in an ambulance full of doctors, and stunned a troop of battle-ready soldiers when they saw their idol appear like a dream in the midst of a nightmare. Begging a colonel for the crack of a corridor through which to march the students free, he was offered the last ticking minutes of the moon: just until dawn.

Snatching a loudspeaker, Hou and his band of hunger-striking brothers implored the students to leave. With comrades fallen in the streets all around, many wanted to make a stand and die where they stood. One hand at a time, the band of hunger-striking brothers pulled them to their feet, persuading them to live for their future, rather than die for a dream. As the first rays of the sun appeared, the impatient troops began to step forward, tanks advancing into the early twitches of light, warning bullets shot to the sky. Just in time, the last straggling souls were swept from the square, and shepherded to safety.

Protected by the hunger-striking friends, no one died that night in Tiananmen Square. But as the spirits of the dead of the streets around had flown to another world, the earth-bound ghosts of the departed had swirled with the questions which now haunted the heart imprisoned in a Beijing jail, just as they had haunted every human heart from the beginning of China's time: '*What is heaven?*' '*Who are the people?*' and '*How, on earth, are they ever going to be able to talk to each other?*'

*   *   *

It had all begun with the cutting off of communications by the Yellow Emperor's grandson, Zhuanxu. Beside himself with worry about the flooding waters, he had become convinced that everything would work much better if heaven had only one earthly voice to listen to. Time had passed, and while many of the surviving shamans had tried to explain that the idea of order was as ephemeral as the dream of a butterfly (and that trying to catch such a dream was more likely to end in disaster than any amount of unruly voices), successive emperors had found themselves unable to change course.

The ancient Zhou had tried to adjust a little, influenced by the text of an even older history that told of a heaven that 'hears as the people hear and sees as the people see'. But what was it that the people heard and saw? Without being able to ask them, no ruler could possibly know. Meanwhile, fixed on the importance of order, the strongest men had raised city-states of glittering splendour. And while Confucius had urged them to moderate their greed and ambition with a *ren* humanity, an *yi* integrity, a *li* ritual (to prompt forgetful minds), and a *zhi* regard for the pursuit of knowledge, it had not worked. Before long, the city-states had been at war with themselves, a war which had been resolved by a state which, following the logic of Zhuanxu, had gripped the people together in a single heart, and then proceeded to forge the Warring States into the unity of one – Qin – world.

Of course, it had not lasted. As Laozi had explained, any iron will that tries to grasp the world in its hands will ultimately fail. But the dynasties that had followed Qin had found it impossible to set the dream of unity aside. The learning of the past having been burnt to a cinder by the First Qin Emperor, the following Han dynasty had raised a new library of books, with a special place for a train of Confucian thought which seemed to embrace the *ren* humanity, the *yi* integrity, the *li* ritual and the *zhi* knowledge, but in fact placed all of those virtues under the unity of an iron fist. Unity had then been pursued beyond the edges of the Chinese world, bringing chaos down on Chinese heads – not only from barbarians outside, but from the human portents of Chinese peasants pushed beyond endurance.

New emperors had risen; and raising schools of well-trained scholars, they had repeated their insistence on the single order of a Son of Heaven, underpinned with scholarly interpretations of Confucian texts that insisted on unity above all. From time to time (whenever an emperor had failed), packs of wolves had descended from the steppes above the Chinese lands.

543

Eventually, the Manju Qing had appeared, wrapping up the Confucian ideas in the discipline of a barbarian hunt. Which only seemed to prove the point: unity was all. In 1850, Taiping rebels had then risen up against the alien Manju Qing, only to be put down by a new, strengthened, Confucian army. And then, different, Western, barbarians had arrived from the sea, insisting on an idea of sovereign states, and demanding a right to occupy Chinese ports.

At that point, some of the scholars had stepped outside their training and questioned the very foundations of everything. Kang Youwei, the late nineteenth-century scholar whose ideas had inspired the hundred day reforms, had smashed the travesty of an imperial heaven while retrieving an ancient dream of *Da Tong* unity: not unity under the single iron-fisted rule of an emperor, but unity under a heaven of self-cultivated people at large. As foreign imperial powers snatched away at more of the weakening empire of the Qing, the young Tan Sitong, the Hunanese who had been so inspired by the *Treasures of Chu* and the story of the poet-prince Qu Yuan, had argued that the only truly independent state was one whose people had the freedom to have independent minds as well. Abraham Lincoln's promise of a 'government of the people, for the people, and by the people' had struck a particular chord, as had Darwinian theories of a tooth and claw nature in which only the fittest survive. Young hearts had then turned to the dream of a new people whose independent minds at home would make them fit enough to ensure the survival of the Chinese nation, even if it would take a revolution to achieve.

For a brief moment, from 1911, a dream of a Republic seemed to be within the people's grasp, with a promise of science and democracy as guarantors against the blind imperialism of old. And while Yuan Shikai's hijacking of the National Assembly had given way to corruption and warlords, within the corridors of Peking University, more dreams rose: of finally wiping away not just the emperors of the past, but the imperial deceptions; and of raising a people who could think for themselves, not only in the cities but in the countryside as well. In the turmoil of wars between self-strengtheners and a young Communist Party, and between China and Japan, the dreamers had scattered. Many went to other cities across China, some to the caves of the new Communist city-state in Yan'an. Eventually, Mao had proclaimed a new truth for a new age, and in 1949, declared the country to be a People's Republic of China, under the Democratic Dictatorship of its people. Not everyone had been convinced: families had divided, and many left the mainland to find a way of being Chinese in other parts of the world. By 1957, those who had stayed realised that the Democratic Dictatorship of the People was about the same kind of iron-fisted single mind with which the First Qin Emperor had once 'unified' everything. Over the next fifteen years, as the Communist Party subjected both science and human voices to the 'greater truth' of a perpetual revolution, China's very human beings found their dreams transformed into a nightmare of lies, in which tens of millions died.

By 1978, a calmer Deng Xiaoping had taken the helm, raising a banner of Four Modernisations, but dismissing any question of China's people having a voice to the silence of a prison cell. Party members who had been despatched to *laogai* labour camps, whether in the countryside or at the brutal edges of empire, were quietly returned. But while many had been happy to join Deng's glittering train, some had raised their voices. Ai Qing, a favourite Party poet, had dreamt of the possibility that 'a time will come when we, this ancient nation ... will accept Light's invitation to knock at gates now firmly closed'. When Tiananmen Square had been lit with human songs and opinions, the Party had made it clear that that time was not yet. 'On economic matters, relaxed controls; for political matters, tight controls' had been swiftly adopted as the appropriate slogan for the Party – with a shorter version of 'stability must crush all else', for the benefit of the wider public.

Within hours of the sun's rise on 4 June 1989, television signals had broadcast the names of the 'most wanted' individuals, in a bid to keep them from smuggling themselves underground. Some six thousand people were swept up in the grid of steel that was flung across the land; thirty or more were executed as counter-revolutionary enemies of the state. With the lesson of the 1911 revolution still ringing in its revolutionary ears (that a heavenly empire could be riddled with invisible rebels) the Party began a spring-clean. A needle-fine investigation was launched across five million of its own members; every imaginable organisation of anything was put under the careful eye of a watchful Party cell; and 'intellectuals' – anyone who read a book and dared to express a contrarian opinion – were hounded into the ground. When the rock musician Cui Jian (the star whose guitar had called out to the Party to join the people) emerged from temporary cover, the Party told him to cut the offending track, and any others likely to pollute the spiritual civilisation of the people. When Cui's strings kept strumming, the stages were removed. Within a year, Hou Dejian, the Taiwan-born voice, had been rounded up from a sound studio and smuggled on to a fishing boat: pushed across the straits in the dead of night, he had been summarily dispatched back to the renegade island from which he had sprung.

Concerned to ensure that the people understood how much the top was doing for the bottom, the Party's Propaganda Department and its Patriotic Education Campaign had then advanced to the front line of thought. Exhibitions were raised to make sure that everyone could see the true face of the counter-revolutionary rebellion, and understand that it was only through the sacrifices of the Party that the land had been cleansed of its humiliations of the past. Re-educated minds had then been redirected to the single patriotic idea of the Party's order.

Time had continued to turn, Deng's modernising train set off for the south, and the intellectuals divided. After the shock of Tiananmen, many of the intellectuals had buried themselves deep in whatever and wherever it was they were studying, trying as hard as possible not to come out. But as the train began to gather speed, they divided: some choosing to remain in the silent protests of their studies, others deciding to contribute their hard-won knowledge to Deng's new idea. When it became clear that the collapse of the Russian big brother had ushered in a decade of such economic disaster that the Russian people had struggled to eat, more had joined those flocking to Deng's dream. Others, however, not least the outspoken economist-historian He Qinglian, had refused to give up the ghost of being human – even for a temporary hundred years. Investigating the roots of everything with their own hearts and minds, the stubborn intellectuals had insisted that the relationship between heaven, earth and man was a question for everyone – and that as the enquiring descendants of the shamans, they had a five thousand year old duty to question the ideas of anyone who declared that a single mind knew everything: a duty to ensure that heaven heard as the people heard, and saw as the people saw.

The price had been high: many of the questioning intellectuals found themselves out of jobs; some found themselves in and out of jail. More than a few, including He Qinglian, took themselves into a self-imposed exile so that they could continue to tell the Chinese truth. One of them set up a Democracy Party for China in the other world of America, which a number of followers joined. Others decided that the best way to be Chinese was to stay where they were and to dedicate themselves, as best they could under the circumstances, to being not just the ears and eyes of the people, but also their voice.

Those who stayed behind to keep up the questions were united in their belief that heaven was not a single mind but the art of being human. Whether from the city or the countryside, the brush became an increasingly valued tool. In a country where only twenty years before, the educated youth of the city had been despatched to the countryside in their millions, and where rural rebels were among China's most popular ancient heroes, intellectuals were not only to be found in the cities. Wherever they came from, some, like the artists of the past, chose to make their points in carefully calculated novels and paintings: portraying the misery of the present in coded terms of art. Others dared to write the truth for all to see. With the Patriotic Education Campaign rising, and with younger minds being directed towards a Party history that disguised the facts, many begged the people to open their eyes and look again at the country's calendars, not least 4 May 1919. Not an anniversary of Communist Party sacrifice (the Party had not even been founded in 1919 – and its founding had had more to do with Moscow than Beijing), but a monument to a Chinese youth whose greatest dream had been of an order grounded in a people who could think for themselves.

One man, a wandering soul rather than a battling intellectual, had been so shocked by what had happened at Tiananmen that he wrote a poem about a Party which had smashed the skulls of its own people, and 'blasted a hole in the stars'. Sent to prison for his art, Liao Yiwu then spent his time in jail gathering together the stories of his fellow *leifan* jailbirds into a book which he titled: *Interviews with People from the Bottom of Society*. Many of those who managed to read it called it a true history of the people, written from the raw stuff of life which any history should take as its source: beggars, human traffickers, murderers, grave robbers, migrant workers, teachers, *Falun Gong* spirits, and all of the other 'mad men and women' who made up both the brutal cruelties and the heart-breaking kindnesses of life in the Chinese lands. Published in renegade Taiwan, the Party had not considered it suitably harmonious reading for the Chinese people at large. After more time in jail, Liao Yiwu, like so many others, would eventually find that the only way that he could keep the idea of being Chinese in his heart was to leave the country and the Party behind.

It was not only the hungry ghosts of Tiananmen that haunted the minds of the stubborn intellectuals. For older men and women, it was also the memories of the great Party campaigns of the past. From the Anti-Rightist purges of 1957, through the Great Leap Forward and the Cultural Revolution, lesson after brutal lesson had been learnt about the dangers of a top-down order executed in the silence of a heavenly night. Or rather, the lessons had been taught, but it was not at all clear that the Party had learnt them. One man whose mind was haunted by the lost lessons of the past was Yang Jisheng. Like so many others, Yang was the son of a father whose life had been shrunk to the skin and bones of a Great Leap Forward death. Loyally writing off his parent as a casualty of socialist progress, the young Yang had become a journalist with the Party's Xinhua News Agency. But when living Chinese bodies had been smashed on the streets around Tiananmen, his mind had returned to the memory of his father's sunken eyes, and he found that his head had been cleared of a mist. Having become one of Xinhua's most senior journalists, in 1990, he decided to use his rank to reveal the human story of what had happened in the Great Leap Forward – and in so doing, raise a tombstone to the memory of his father.

Travelling up and down the country, Yang used his senior cover to scour the caves of local archives, looking for the traces of deaths that, whether for fear or shame or both, everyone – Party members, government officials and the people at large – had buried. As clear as everyone else that the Party had declared the Great Leap Forward a lesson that was never to be named, Yang was aware that, in the process, he might well be digging not only his own grave but those of any helpers. Across the country's county towns, though, secretly sympathetic men and women quietly directed him to where the answers were buried: in the dusty records of population statistics, and in the reports of weather and grain production with which the Party's bureaucracy had recorded the acceptable past. Line by buried line, over the next ten years, Yang painstakingly pieced together the fragments of local facts across each of China's thousands of counties. As he did so, he began to see a monumental historical truth: not one or two million dead, but thirty-six million Chinese people starved to an excruciating extinction by a single top-down mind. And the voices of their surviving family and friends silenced with a rule.

In 2008, Yang published his work – entitled 'Tombstone' – across a thousand pages, all (necessarily) printed in Hong Kong. As he did so, he respectfully suggested that it was time for the Party to come to terms with heaven, the people and the past. A 'truth and reconciliation commission' seemed to him to be the answer. Not one of those clumsy commissions of the West which seemed to make nothing but a mess – and certainly not an 'investigation of things' which limited any questions to a set of approved textbooks – but the kind of investigation of things which Confucius must surely have originally had in mind, and for which, two thousand years later, that senior Ming dynasty minister, Wang Yangming, had argued: an actual enquiry into the real world, guided by the human conscience. Yang also suggested that it was time for the Party to step aside from the heavenly illusion that a single Great Man at the top could ever be relied upon to know the everything on which the security of human beings relied. 'Scattered across a people', he declared, 'human memories might seem messy, but they are our only ladders to the future.' Or, to put it another way: it was not bad people who had caused the deaths (although plenty of those could be found), but a top-down way of heavenly thinking which had been haunting the lands of the Yellow Emperor for far too long.

Yang was not alone. Other brave hearts had also been digging into the past: from the children of parents who had been terrorised to death in the Cultural Revolution, to the mothers of children who had died or disappeared more recently in the streets around Tiananmen. These others went a step further, arguing that it was time for the Party to live up to the promises of the constitution which it had written: promises which included the right of everyone on earth to speak to heaven, including all of those whose pasts had been consigned to hell.

It was not, however, just the terrors of the Great Leap Forward, or any of the other individual campaigns, that were on the stubborn intellectuals' minds. There was also the bigger question of the whole of China's story. When Deng Xiaoping had introduced the Patriotic Education Campaign to replace any memory of Tiananmen with the greater story of the sacrifices of the Party and its triumphal successes, the Propaganda Department had embarked on its own long march – this one for the rewriting of history. Raising a new revolutionary banner of *wu wang guo chi*, never forget the national humiliation, immediate attention was centred on the 'hundred years of humiliation' inflicted by the foreign barbarians. From the opium spat in 1839, with its following British gunboats, across the division of China's northern lands by the wider imperial powers, to Japan's invasions (and the Japanese massacre of Nanjing at the end of the 1930s): a string of national humiliations which had nearly lost not only China, the state, but China, the people, as well.

Setting aside the inconvenient details of the homegrown poppy fields – and not mentioning the Taiping rebellion and the following decades of self-strengthening feudalism which had followed – the Party had directed popular attention to the conspiracy of opium which the foreigners had dumped on the docks of Guangdong, and to the Western gunboats which had then sailed up and down the coast, forcing open 'treaty ports' at every profitable point of call. The burning of the *Yuanming Yuan* Summer Palace (the alien Manju Qing's Jesuit-designed fantasy that, raised for a conquering emperor and never open to the Chinese people, had been selected by the British for retaliation after a murder of some of their negotiators during the 'opium wars') was claimed as a particular affront.

Rather improbably, to anyone who *did* remember their history, Zeng Guofan, the nineteenth-century capitalist self-strengthener and defeater of the Taiping peasant rebels, reappeared as a national hero. And the Boxer rebels, who had so terrified the Dowager Empress that she turned them on the foreigners, were resurrected as patriots. The battles that the Guomindang and their Chinese soldiers fought against the Japanese were also swept under the carpet. As were the young voices of the Communist Party who had been silenced by Mao, not to mention the earlier factional fighting between Mao and other Communist leaders that had led to so many deaths. And as was the leading role of Moscow in the revolution's success. The fact that many of the lands which the new Republic had claimed in 1912, and which the Party had insisted upon at the point of its 1949 victory, were the conquests of the 'barbarian' empire of the Manju Qing, was a detail of the past best forgotten. The Tiananmen 'incident' was recast as a dream (or a nightmare) that had happened in someone else's land.

By 2005, as the Party's Propaganda Department was congratulating itself on the fact that anyone under twenty-five was now patriotically clear that stories of a June Fourth massacre in Beijing were either a foreign lie or a Western conspiracy, older heads began to worry about the truth. Alarmed at the risks the Party was taking with lessons from the past which were essential to everyone's future security, a professor of philosophy, Yuan Weishi, put pen to paper and tore into the textbooks that schools and universities were being told to teach. 'China's children', he railed, 'are being fed on a wolf's milk of whipped up patriotism liberated from the truth.' Turning to the past, Yuan pointed to the Anti-Rightist campaign of 1957, when the Party had attacked every expert opinion other than its own, claiming that their truths were lies. 'Look where that had got everyone', urged Yuan: 'A nation of people too timid to tell the truth, and with black universally accepted as white'. Then he had turned to the manufactured anger of the Cultural Revolution that had produced a generation of people so badly damaged that they no longer believed in anything or anyone. Was the next generation to be transformed into blind nationalists and bitter xenophobes – the kind of 'human portents' who would almost inevitably (and, remembering the Boxer rebellion, not for the first time), bring heaven down on everybody's heads?

Within two weeks, the Party magazine that had published Yuan Weishi's 'opinion' was suspended. Noting that his stinging words had 'gravely violated historical facts' and 'hurt the feelings of the Chinese nation', any future reference to the article in which Yuan had expressed his opinions was promptly banned. Privately, the Party repeated its position to itself: Mao had been thirty per cent mistaken and seventy per cent right; the Great Leap Forward and the Cultural Revolution had been regrettable errors but, as Mao had always said, truth was always discovered from facts. Guided by history, the Party was crossing a river by feeling for the stones; and without the learning, the new China could never have found its feet.

Officially out of bounds for the public at large, Yuan's article and the Party's private views then circulated in the depths of the underground. As they circulated, the public added questions of their own: 'If the lessons were so important', many whispered, 'why wasn't everyone allowed to learn them?', and 'Given that the deaths had been those of the people at large, why is it always the sacrifices of the Party that are celebrated, rather than those of the tens of millions of Chinese who paid for the lessons with their lives?' Others went on to wonder whether the Chinese people would *ever* be anything more than stones to support the river-crossing steps of whichever imperial dynasty had most recently hijacked heaven.

*   *   *

As Yang Jisheng and Yuan Weishi had been battling for the truths of the past, another intellectual was looking at the landscape of the natural world, and wondering how heaven had ever allowed the emperors to insist on a unity that struck at the security of all.

Wang Lixiong started out as a truck mechanic who had once posted an idea – for a slow and carefully considered drive towards elections – on the Democracy Wall of 1978 Beijing. In 1984, as Deng Xiaoping was battling against the treacherous Fifth (voice of the people) Modernisation, Wang decided to launch himself into the heart of China's natural world to listen to the stories it might tell. Lashing a raft of tires together, he had hurled himself down eight hundred miles of the upper reaches of the Yellow River. Observing crystal clear waters running at the old Tibetan top of the Qinghai plateau, as he journeyed downstream, he noticed that the closer the river flowed to the Chinese east, the muddier (and yellower) it became. Floating through a landscape that had been so deeply intertwined with China's dreams of order,

Wang's heart had been tugged by the haunting and disappearing beauty. It was a tug that would only get stronger when the Party fired on Beijing five years later, and again when Deng's glittering train took off.

Returning, over the years, to the haunting plains of Tibet, and even venturing into the neighbouring lands of Xinjiang, Wang Lixiong eventually came to the same conclusions as Tan Sitong and the earliest revolutionaries. 'Heaven', in his intellectual opinion, was indeed composed of the eyes and ears of the people, rather than the self-strengthening plans of rulers at the top. And the guiding principles of earth were nothing less than the *ren* art of being human, the *yi* responsibility that everyone had for their own integrity, and the *zhi* need for everyone to absorb knowledge in order to understand. If, reasoned Wang Lixiong, all of that was too difficult to imagine across a land that had grown to the great size of China, then maybe one should start with individual counties and communities, and help them to find their feet first. And, given the great differences between the many very different people of China, if one were to do that, then one would also need to reconsider the towering importance which the Party, and every previous imperial dynasty, attached to the idea of forcing unity across the very different races of the Chinese lands.

Thinking on the matter of unity, Wang also asked himself why Mao had raised up the illusory idea of autonomous regions in the first place: had he really wanted to create a cauldron of rage? Consulting the records of the Long March and the promises that had been made, Wang found it hard to find an answer – other than the ancient idea that a single heaven always seemed to demand a single earth.

And as to why the Party had raised up hundreds of individual *minzu* dreams only to rework them into fifty-six artificially manufactured compounds of a very complicated past – who could tell? Pondering the mysteries of the Party's minds, Wang wondered whether it was just because they liked the imperial picture-books? Or was it just the fact that 'big brother' Stalin had created a colourful cast of 'nationalities'?

But things were as they were: Xinjiang and Tibet had been forcibly wrapped into China's borders, with a once-hesitating Inner Mongolia gathered up as well. Meanwhile, the other *minzu*, once part of a woven fabric, had been pulled out and put into artificial parks of their own. The question now was how to manage the future.

Trying to imagine solutions, Wang Lixiong began to sketch a set of ideas with which a mutual respect might be coaxed, rather than a unity forced from the barrel of a gun. His ideas had a lot in common with those which he and others considered that the Han Chinese *themselves* would need if they were ever to be free: the power of different people in different places to think for themselves; local elections with which the people could protect themselves from official wolves; and a rule of law that would guarantee both independence and a voice. With these three fundamentals, surely the many different people could be woven together into a wider tapestry which, given a fair competition of qualified hearts and minds, could elect a nationally governing party. And if such a wider tapestry could be woven, surely it would be able to raise the necessary security required to protect everyone from any hungry foreign wolves outside.

As far as Wang Lixiong could see, with every year which passed, however, the obstacles to unity were only getting bigger – particularly in the lands of Xinjiang and Tibet, where the anger of the people was now getting out of control. The military trucks of Han settlement (the *Bingtuan* Production and Construction Corps of the People's Liberation Army) had already spread across the oases of Xinjiang. And as Wang was writing, the glittering train was sweeping carriages of Han Chinese up to Lhasa, and setting them down to work their productive magic in the city-sanctuary of the gods. It would not be long before Tibetans followed the Inner Mongols into being a rare species in their own lands. Not that they would go quietly into that dark night: after sixty years of violent occupation, the monks were clearly going to continue to chant 'Free Tibet!' to the end. Just as the angry Uighurs were going to carry on reciting the truth of their Quran until their last dying breath – not to mention building every possible bridge with those outside spirits (Islamic, Russian or anything else) which might offer a helping hand.

After more than two thousand years of pursuing unity, Wang, like so many others before him, wondered whether anything at all had been learned from the past. The Patriotic Education Campaign had unleashed a generation of young Chinese whose only idea of history was a sense of a trampled-upon people, betrayed not only by the West but by the Xinjiang and Tibetan edges of their own order. When, in March 2008, blood and flames had swept out of Lhasa to haunt the Chinese torch of Olympic harmony as it made its way around the world – and as the Party's patriotically educated populace had exploded with rage at an ungrateful Tibet – Wang Lixiong bravely tapped out an open letter with *Twelve Suggestions* for resolving Tibet's questions. Asking his friends to join him, three hundred and seventy dared to sign their names.

One of the intellectuals who Wang Lixiong approached was in no doubt about the risks that he was taking. As a university lecturer who specialised in human freedom – and as one of the four hunger-striking friends who had urged the students to leave Tiananmen Square in the early hours of 4 June – he had long ago decided that he had a duty to serve the people. His name was Liu Xiaobo. Originally going to the square to talk to the students about the art of being Chinese (and the importance of not getting carried away by the anger of the day), Liu had shouted his words for all to hear: 'There is no enemy other than hatred and violence'. It was Liu who had realised that someone needed to talk to heaven's troops on the square. And as Hou Dejian, the 'Taiwanese voice' and a close friend, had raced to the front line, it was Liu Xiaobo who had stayed in the students' midst, persuading them to let go of the guns which they had 'liberated' from soldiers in the surrounding streets. Bullets exploding, sirens blaring, messengers arriving with reports of the injured and dead from the streets around, it was also Liu and his friends who had urged the desperate students to set aside their anger. Eventually, having walked the students safely out of the square, while others had scrambled underground, Liu Xiaobo had chosen to walk home in the bright light of the dawn. Two days later, he was bundled into a van and despatched to Qincheng jail – three dark years of being haunted by the searing memories of the dead.

Released in 1991, detained again in 1995, and again in 1996, in the years that he was free to be at home Liu Xiaobo used his time to write. He was as shocked as the historian-economist He Qinglian at the speed with which the Party was throwing the peasants off the glittering train, even as their labour was being used to fuel it. He was also incredulous at the seemingly eternal silence of so many Chinese intellectuals across thousands of years of a hijacked heaven. Why had so many of the country's scholars always limited their battles to their private inkpots? Why had it not been until after the end of the Manju Qing that they had thought about rolling up their silken sleeves and fighting with the people on the ground? And why had so many of them allowed themselves to be corralled back into their libraries again after 1989? Whether it had been studying in their own pavilions or jumping on Deng's glittering train to find fortunes of their own, so many minds seemed to have left the true search for heaven to rough bands of peasants – men who had not hesitated to stand up for their brothers.

Returning home in 1999, from a three-year spell of *laogai* labour, Liu Xiaobo had found the gift of a computer waiting for him. Taking to its keys like a mind to a book, Liu had flown off into the clouds of the web, revelling in the power of the internet to give virtual substance to the idea that heaven was a people rather than a single top-down mind. Recalling the silenced voices of the ancient past, remembering the First Qin Emperor's burning of the books and burials of scholars alive, Liu watched the internet light up China as if it were a magic engine sent directly from heaven above. And as he watched, stars of other minds began to join him, exploding new light into the darkness: peasant brothers banding together to find and tell the truth; migrant workers organising for a strike; and brave lawyers advancing to the front line in an attempt to defeat the false logic of the Democratic Dictatorship of the People.

As the internet ignited, however, so did the powers charged with maintaining a harmonious order. Liu found that the Party had provided a personal online guard to keep an orderly eye on his conversations. And in 2004, when his tapping keys tripped over a forbidden word, the computer and all of his files found themselves under arrest. Another computer was soon acquired. As the censoring eyes carried on reading and blocking, Liu's fingers kept on typing. With true believers in Communism now as rare as unicorns, and with those in the front carriages of the glittering train seemingly oblivious to the dangers of its speed, Liu pounded out a steady stream of posts and articles to try and wake everybody up. 'The people are not a bunch of precious animals to be raised like prey for a hunt', he argued: 'A single hijacked heaven has not only corrupted itself, but eroded the power of millions of China's most educated minds to think for themselves'. To which he added that everyone's security lay in the ability of 1.4 billion Chinese to work out not only how to talk to heaven, but also how to talk to each other, without a black cloud of officials getting in their way.

When Wang Lixiong asked Liu Xiaobo if he would add his name to the *Twelve Suggestions for Tibet*, Liu had agreed. Both knew that nothing could come of any call for resolving Tibet's problems unless and until the Chinese people had a voice of their own. And for that voice to be found, the very meaning of 'being Chinese' would have to be constantly repeated, again and again: the *ren* humanity of putting yourself in other people's shoes; the *yi* integrity of telling the truth; the *zhi* knowledge that included investigating facts with your own heart and mind. The dangers of not doing so were getting clearer by the year. If someone did not start listening to Tibet and Xinjiang soon, any dream of unity would be swept away in the kind of nightmare which had brought heaven down on the adventuring heads of the

Han and successive dynasties ever since.

Conscious that every journey of ten thousand miles starts with a single step, Liu signed. A few months later, he was asked by another band of internet brothers to sign another open letter; he agreed again. This one, a Charter known by its year, 2008, got closer to the point. Setting out an argument for a change in the relationship between heaven and earth, it included some practical suggestions on how China could start a responsibly slow but steady march towards a heaven that would be based on the voices of China's many people, rather than on a single top-down idea. Liu Xiaobo not only agreed to sign but helped the drafters make sure that their ideas were carefully and calmly presented as an invitation extended to the Party for a conversation – rather than a threat.

Casting minds back over the same hundred years covered by the Party's Patriotic Education Campaign, the final draft of Charter 08 set out its own version of the milestones of China's history that had created the disasters of the past. The devils, explained the text, were not foreign gunboats and opium, but homemade self-strengtheners who had sold the people up their own treacherous rivers of fortune. There were certainly heroes – but they began with Kang Youwei, the originator of the hundred day reforms, and Liang Qichao, the man who had set such store on 'imagining a people', and whose ideas had spread across the decades to the lawns of Peking University, to the dreams of a Mr *Sai* Science and a Mr *De* Democracy, and to the first-ever practical expeditions of city minds to find the peasants in the countryside, and in so doing to try to bridge the gap between the city and the village worlds. To this, the draft added a note on the guns of Chinese warlords who had split the country, and the squabbles between the Guomindang and the Communist Party that had opened the country's doors to a waiting Japan.

Also described in the text of the Charter was the rise of a Communist Party that had promised the treasured dream of a People's Republic, and delivered the nightmare of a Democratic Dictatorship of the People. Intelligent men and women had been attacked and buried for questioning facts; a Great Leap Forward, the Cultural Revolution, a Tiananmen massacre, and the glittering train had carried off countless lives – not to mention dreams, and let alone nature – and dumped them all in a ditch.

The miracle of the 'New China', noted the text, was only a miracle if one didn't count the cost. And as for those who wanted to pin their hopes on a benevolent celestial emperor at the top, no one should imagine that that would fix the problem: China's true problems were not the result of messy conversations on the ground, they were the trouble that naturally arises when a single mind insists on doing everything. Some might argue that the Chinese people were still nothing but a loose tray of sand; they might even point to the failures of the 1911 revolution, and the brutality of the Cultural Revolution, as evidence that this was a people who would never be able to govern themselves, a people for whom democracy would always be a danger. But, urged the Charter, just look at the patient ladder of peasants trying, against extraordinary odds, to teach the lower levels of the Party how a simple human being should behave. And while the foreigners were not always clear about its meaning or possibilities, democracy was not an all or nothing idea: what might be a reckless cacophony in some wild places, could, in others, be a natural harmony of many different human voices, underpinned by a principle that a self-cultivated reason should guide all. What mattered was the quality of the relationship between heaven and the people: and after thousands of years of thinking about order, the Chinese people had surely learned more than enough lessons to be able to make it work.

Clearly, patiently, and in simple words of black and white, the drafters of the Charter set out a pattern under which heaven and earth could come together, safely conducted by the *ren*, human being. A constitution which meant what it actually said – not only in a few words buried in a preamble which slyly put everything under the unity of the Party, but across every following 'right'. Constitutional freedoms that went beyond a splash of black on white, to genuinely protect the right of the people to be human: a judiciary that reached its judgements independently of a Party phone call; and an elected government (and a military) that was independent of this or any other political party; officials accountable to the people. For all of which, China would need cities that did not see themselves as protected palaces, and a people – in both the city *and* the countryside – who accepted the responsibilities of knowledge, but were also free to speak their minds.

Caught within the garden of the Chinese internet as much as any beast corralled in the grounds of a hunt, the draft text of the Charter was read by censoring eyes before it was even finished. On 8 December 2008, two days before it was published online, Liu Xiaobo was detained on suspicion of rumour-mongering, slander, subversion of the state and plotting to overthrow the socialist system. One year later he stood in a Beijing court, charged with inciting state subversion.

Knowing that his guilt had already been determined by the fact of his arrest, and aware that any defence would only inflate his sentence, Liu

Xiaobo stood up to make a statement for the benefit of future generations: 'Criticism is not rumour-mongering. Opposition is not slander. Changes in the relationship between the Party and the people should be gradual, peaceful, and orderly – precisely for the purpose of avoiding the sudden leaps which have caused such chaos across China's past.' And, quoting from a Chinese text passed down by questioning minds across hundreds of years, he reminded everyone that, in a land where people can think for themselves, there is no danger in speaking the truth: 'Say all you know in every detail: a speaker is blameless because listeners can think. If the words are true, make your corrections; if they are not, just take note.'

Cutting Liu Xiaobo's speech short, the judges of the Democratic Dictatorship of the People noted that a Defendant was allowed no more time to make a statement than that taken by a Prosecutor to make his case. Moving swiftly through their judgement (guilty), they announced the sentence: eleven years in the dark and silent prison of the single top-down mind. Liu Xiaobo was returned, once again, to the cold confinement of a jail, with the souls of the dead still echoing in his ears.

* * *

On 12 May 2008, when a dragon of an earthquake struck at the dreaming hills and valleys of remoter Sichuan, questions of life and death had again crashed into every Chinese mind. The first hundred dead had quickly become tens of thousands. China quivered with shock and anyone who could, rushed to the scene. Visiting the wreckage of lives lost, the then premier, Wen Jiabao, declared the sorrow of a nation – but suggested that the rescue and recovery should be left to the single mind of the state.

Watching Chinese soldiers bravely pulling children from the wreckage of nature's wrath, many agreed. But as the days passed, and as the toll of the dead rose and bodies were buried in a collective mass, an official mist seemed to descend on the land. Surviving villagers began to look at the landscape and ask some questions of their own: 'Why is it that some buildings had stood their ground while others had crashed? Why did the worst of the crashes attack the classrooms of the schools?' Reminding people of the unpredictable changes of nature, officials had offered devastated parents a handful of money, and the chance to have a second child. Rocked with grief, the villagers had rubbed their eyes in disbelief: surely after the highest heavenly hearts had expressed such sympathy, the story of what had caused so many deaths was not going to be buried as well? It was not long before local spirits were digging into the rubble and asking stubborn questions; and it was not much longer before policing officials were reminding the questioners that rumour-mongering and defaming the state were serious offences, and that inconvenient enquirers would find themselves disqualified from receiving any cash.

It was not long after that a Beijing artist with a reputation decided to do some digging of his own. The son of Ai Qing (the Party's favourite poet who, like so many truth-telling revolutionaries had been despatched by his closest comrades to the bitterest wastelands at the edges of the empire), Ai Weiwei had grown up in brutal camps of labour. Returning to Beijing in the rehabilitating 1970s, he had encountered a bickering chorus of Zhongnanhai 'aunts and uncles', each blaming the other for the collective shame of the Cultural Revolution. They had seemed like a family from hell, and Ai Weiwei had given them as wide a berth as he could. Time had passed, Ai Weiwei had dabbled in ink and sculpture. He had even added artistic touches to a Bird's Nest stadium for the Olympics, before sensing that the games had become a grand stage for the Patriotic Education Campaign. Noting that, as the Bird's Nest had risen, much of old Beijing had been bulldozed to the ground, Ai Weiwei had stood aside from his work, and declared that, mesmerised by the glittering train, the choreographers of the games had forgotten the art of being human.

The Party's shock was palpable. Being part (albeit an eccentric part) of the Party family, Ai Weiwei's words were initially brushed under the red carpet. The artist himself was left to the madness of his studio, with a hope that he would stay there in that cloud of 'art' that, as Mao had always said so clearly, was nothing to do with the people. For Ai Weiwei, however, art was at the forefront of any revolution: no artist was worth anyone's salt if he did not speak for the people at large.

And so it was, that when Sichuan's people fell into the nightmare of both the earthquake and the concealing official mist, Ai Weiwei gathered together some volunteering energies, and took it upon himself to make a few enquiries of his own. Dialling directly into the offices of the local officials responsible for the hundreds of grieving villages and towns, he framed his questions with the experience of a man who knew his way around the Party, with the confidence of an artistic voice that was used to being heard, and with the plain-speaking bluntness of a revolutionary spirit. 'What sort of condition was your local school in when it fell through the floor?' he enquired: 'And while you are checking your reports, perhaps you could give me a list of the children who are dead and missing as well.' Across every line, the answers were short, and astonishingly uniform: 'Any question about the condition of the buildings is a matter for the government alone. And, as every true Chinese ought to know, the lists of the missing and the dead are secrets of the state'.

Determined that the people should be served with the art of being human, Ai Weiwei and his team of volunteers spread out across the settlements that had been struck by the earthquake and, together with a number of brave and equally stubborn people on the ground, pieced together the fragments of a disaster that had been anything but natural. They found that the answer to the question of the condition of the buildings was relatively simple. When, in 2006, Hu Jintao had tried to replace the nightmare of SARS with the dream of a new 'socialist countryside', counties and towns across the country had been commanded to roll out the schools necessary for a promised nine years of compulsory education, while cutting the burden of taxes on peasant heads – all to be achieved within two years. Pinching and pocketing pennies by the billions, the services of surveyors and architects had been dispensed with. Concrete had been mixed with sand; steel had been set aside as an unnecessary expense. Hu Jintao's heavenly deadline had been met. But the youngest and smallest of the people's voices had been set to study in the least safe of all places: classes of rooms which had been made from little more than the *doufu* curd of beans.

The answer to the question of the names of the dead and missing took a little more time, and a lot more work. Over the course of the next twelve months, patiently and painstakingly, the investigating volunteers covered the heart-breaking ground of the villages and towns shaken by the earthquake, and patched together a list of the names of those children who had disappeared or died. Forty-five names here, ninety-four names there: village by village, town by town, the numbers mounted up. In the end, they found 5,385 small souls enrolled in ninety-six shattered schools. All of the shattered schools had been built with sand.

Determined to keep the memories of the children alive, when the list of the dead and the missing was complete, Ai Weiwei and his team invited 5,385 living voices each to speak a single name out loud – and then spread them across the internet for the ears of the wider world to hear. As the voices were reading out the names, Ai Weiwei went to open an exhibition in Munich. While he was there, he raised a 'remembering' wall of bright blue children's backpacks. Across the backpacks, he painted the words of one of the thousands of messages that his investigating volunteers had received from Sichuan: 'She lived happily on this earth for seven years'. They were the words of a mother who had wanted only one thing for the death of her daughter – that her memory should survive.

While Ai Weiwei had been preparing the lists and the backpacks, however, an inconvenient questioner on the ground had been bundled away to a prison in the Chengdu capital of Sichuan. His name was Tan Zuoren. A local writer and lover of nature, he had started an investigation of his own into who was dead and missing, and why. Tan was not the only one to be arrested: there had been a steady stream of parents and teachers who, insisting on rumour-mongering, were obviously begging to be carried away. In Tan's case, a charge of 'subverting the state' had been added as a twist. Early on in his investigations, and as aware as everyone else of the risks he was taking, Tan had wrapped a white scarf of truth around his neck, and spoken to a camera before he could be swept out of sight. 'Better to spend years in another world', he had declared, 'than to live among a people who have lost the power of speech – years which one could pass in the hope that, at some time in the future, China's people will have reflected on what has happened and on what has been learnt about how to be Chinese.'

Hearing of Tan's arrest and impending trial, Ai Weiwei decided that he would attend the Chengdu hearing, and give his own evidence of the truth. No one was in any doubt that Tan would go to jail, but if the Party was going to imprison him for subverting a state which was supposed to be a 'People's' Republic, Ai Weiwei could testify to the fact that Tan had not only been working *for* the people, but *with* them as well. As Tan's lawyers confirmed: while it certainly would not help Tan to secure an easier sentence, when the judges passed their judgement, it would be clear to every independent mind, and to the judges themselves, that any sentence passed could not be truthfully said to be in the name of the people. It was not much. But with a journey of ten thousand miles stretching out before everyone who believed in the art of being human, it was one of those important first steps.

The Party, however, was equally decided that Ai Weiwei should keep his peace. The night before the trial, hired thugs (or plainclothes policemen: it had never in all of China's history been easy to tell the difference) exploded into his hotel room. Beating him heavily about the head for his stubborn questions, they then kept him under the wrap of a blanket until the court had delivered Tan's sentence. Ai Weiwei responded with an under-the-blanket recording of the hotel proceedings – for later launch as a made-for-the-internet movie, with the thugs appearing as themselves. The following morning in the courtroom, Tan's lawyer gathered a courage of his own, and rose to defend his client in the face of what Tan, and all the families who had lost their children, believed to be a lie. Quoting from a command engraved above the gate to one of Chengdu's oldest and best loved temples, he read the following words aloud: 'It is those who understand the people's hearts who are fit to rule; all you who come to govern these lands of Sichuan, think on this.' The temple in question was not just any temple, and the words were not just any words. Raised to the memory of the Crouching Dragon, Zhuge Liang, the temple had been standing for almost two thousand years of Chinese history. And the words had stood above it as an enduring testament to the very essence of what it meant to be Chinese. With judicial eyes aware of the meaning but reading from the Party's script, the adjudicators of the socialist rule of law sentenced Tan Zuoren to five years in the prison of the single top-down mind.

*   *   *

Within two years Ai Weiwei found himself in a prison of his own. Although, being part of the Party's extended family, the events of his imprisonment were not only touched with strokes of heavenly opera, but also shot with the mind-leaping logic of the Monkey King.

It had probably all begun with the rather clumsy surveillance that the Party had arranged since Ai Weiwei had begun his personal investigation of things – starting with the succession of undercover thugs who were pretending to be on holiday outside his Beijing home. Insisting that everyone practise the art of being human, Ai Weiwei had consistently made a point of politely asking the suburban tourists to assume responsibility for their own *yi* integrity, and give him their names. When the names were refused, Ai Weiwei took photographs for the people's 'family album', and posted them on the internet.

Later, returning to China after his 'backpack memorial', and recovering from an operation for a brain haemorrhage brought on by the hotel beating in Chengdu, Ai Weiwei had decided to demonstrate his own *yi* integrity, and make an official complaint: the Chengdu police force was respectfully requested to acknowledge the unjustified violence of their actions. Long months of idle inquisition made it clear that Ai's case was unlikely to get very far. On one of his many visits to the police station, though, Ai Weiwei accidentally happened upon one of the hotel thugs – comfortably installed behind a supervising desk. The official 'thug' refused to give his name. Ai Weiwei, the artist insisting on the truth of responsibility, removed the man's dark glasses and took his photograph instead. The colour of the photograph was not enough to make a difference to the legal process; and no one, least of all Ai Weiwei, was surprised when his case was summarily dismissed. But up and down the country, the people saw the image of the thug-official shining across the internet; and many felt that at least a certain kind of justice had been done.

Time turned to 2010. Ai Weiwei had continued his 'art of being human' campaign; the Party continued its insistence on stability maintenance at all costs. A battle of wills was clearly underway. Pressing his point a little further, Ai Weiwei gathered up a hundred million hand-painted sunflower seeds, and took them to London to show the Western world what it meant to be an individual in a Chinese crowd. Meanwhile, raising the banner of a *hexie*, harmonious society, at home, Hu Jintao's forces of stability maintenance demolished Ai Weiwei's studio in Shanghai. Ai Weiwei responded with a lesson in literature. With the pronunciation of the two written characters for *he* and *xie* (*hexie*, harmonious society) sounding like the two written characters for the 'river crab' which the Shanghainese love to eat, he announced a Shanghai crab banquet to which everyone was invited to come and eat the President's '*hexie*' harmony words.

As 2010 turned to 2011, and as spring began to foment in the deserts of the Arab world, the Party had become ever-more anxious about unity. The Democratic Dictatorship of the People launched an attack on harmony-disrupting bloggers and put a number of them in jail. Long expelled from the walls of China's internet garden, Ai Weiwei had carried on twittering as freely as a bird. Worried friends tried to warn him that there was a time and a place for being human, and that the time and place was not now, and not in Beijing. The artist did not stop. 'To be human or not to be human? It's a simple question', twittered Ai Weiwei, 'and in case you haven't noticed, you get the chance to answer it a million times a day.'

And then, in April 2011, Party patience had finally snapped and Ai Weiwei was snatched from sight under the bright lights of Beijing's airport. Bundled into a van, he was carried off to a shady hotel for a 'chat' about the Party's policies on art. Meanwhile in the Zhongnanhai garden, the Party family squabbled about what to do with the Monkey in their midst.

Confined to yet another hotel room, as the Party family squabbled, the artist found himself under the constant guard of a pair of uniformed teenagers, with regular interrogating visits from older minds who were struggling to understand their instructions from above. Interrogating an artist was not a problem – but what exactly had this particular one done wrong? With heaven in confusion, the young guards ended up telling Ai Weiwei the story of their own imprisoned lives: peasants who had joined up for the uniforms, only to find their days spent inside airless rooms, they longed to be free. The older interrogators – at a loss to know what to talk about in the absence of any clear instructions – first found themselves engaged in a little light conversation about Marx and Engels' dialectical materialism, and then in a rather exhausting exchange of quotes from Mao's *Little Red Book* (everyone present knew the quotes by heart). Added time was strung out on a debate about the comparative virtues of Beijing noodles: with spring onions or without? After eighty-one days in which everyone had ended up banging their heads against the brick walls of the prison, Ai Weiwei was released to a pinching pair of propaganda shoes, and an un-free kind of freedom.

On the airwaves of the outside world, broadcasts scripted by the Propaganda Department denounced him as a bigamist, a pornographer and a tax dodger. On the ground in Beijing, he was told in no uncertain terms that his liberty depended on shutting up, not only about the circumstances of his arrest, but about any other matter on which he might have an artistic opinion. Some months later, a bill for a fifteen million *renminbi* fine (two million US dollars) was delivered to his studio, payable in fifteen days. As the Propaganda Department published the opinion of the Democratic Dictatorship of the People that no artist on earth had the right to tell the people what the difference was between right and wrong, tens of thousands of hundred *renminbi* notes began to flutter over the wall of Ai Weiwei's studio and into the garden of his truth beyond. With the image of Mao Zedong beaming out from the face of each and every one of them, they seemed to carry the words of voices who had fought for the earlier, 1911, revolution, not to mention the banners of May Fourth: 'not in my name'.

*　　*　　*

While Ai Weiwei was pushing the boundaries of the art of being human, the advancing Arab Spring was putting the Party and its police on to an ever-higher state of alert. Troublemaking questioners – journalists, documentary film makers, actors, writers and professors – were whisked away. Arrested? It was hard to say; most of them simply dropped out of sight.

By the end of 2011, increasing numbers of city lawyers were bravely stepping into court. Not many dreamt that they could get their clients out of jail, but they were beginning to believe that, with heaven changing its son in 2012, the time had come to stand up not only for the Chinese ideal of *ren* humanity, but for the ideals of *yi* integrity and *zhi* knowledge as well. Pointing to the Constitution of the People's Republic of China, as promulgated by the Party itself, the lawyers noted that, apart from helpfully describing heaven as a Democratic Dictatorship of the People, it also clearly guaranteed all of the necessary freedoms – of speech, the press, assembly – which enabled individuals to act as human beings. But as the Party so often pointed out, every freedom in the constitution was hostage to that single phrase in the preamble that put everything and everyone under the unified leadership of the Chinese Communist Party, and its guns. With every one of the people as much a prisoner of the Leninist Party as any defendant in a dock, the lawyers harboured no illusions: judges had no choice but to apply Party instructions, just as the police had no alternative but to make up whatever twists and turns would keep stability maintenance on the ground. But each time a lawyer advanced into the courtroom – and each time a defendant dared to question his sentence – they were making a statement that the people had been trying to make for thousands of years: heaven is heaven when it listens to the people, not when it conducts itself like a single top-down mind. The Party might have used the power of the gun to paint itself the façade of a courtroom but, like the peasants in the countryside and the secret supporters of Ai Weiwei, the lawyers in the cities were increasingly saying: 'not in my name'.

As 2011 moved towards 2012, and as more and more of the high quality population began to ask themselves what was going on, even the forward carriages of the glittering train began to blaze with questions. Some of them had heard the arguments of the city lawyers, and thought they had an obvious point. Others had been shocked into their questions by a book that had spread from Hong Kong.

Published in 2009, set in the near future of 2013, and entitled *The Fat Years*, the book was a fictional fantasy about the miracle of the glittering train. Painting a picture of a golden age of China's ascendancy where (almost) everyone is happy, the author, Chan Koonchung, told the story of a handful of misfit friends who found themselves mysteriously unable to share in the universal joy of the People's Republic. Where once their microblogging friends and acquaintances had joined them in lambasting the Party for being a single top-down mind which stopped the people from being human, they now seemed to be marvelling at the fact that the Party's hard work and wisdom had not only spared China from the scourge of a global economic recession, but had saved the rest of the world as well. The microblogging friends and acquaintances were even arguing that the Party had been right all along: it was indeed only a Democratic Dictatorship of the People, under the leadership of the Party, which could deliver the kind of prosperity and satisfaction that the Chinese people now enjoyed. If anyone ever mentioned the Cultural Revolution, it was only to remark on what fun those years in the countryside had been. And if any of the misfit friends made a reference to Tiananmen, almost everybody else's faces just went blank; unless the friends or acquaintances were under thirty, in which case they insisted that it was all a Western imperial lie.

Even more worryingly for the novel's misfit friends was the fact no one seemed to be aware that the month of February 2011, had gone missing, nor did they seem to remember the events which had led up to it. The terrifying unravelling of the global economy which had spread fear in every direction and pushed rumour into overdrive; a Party crackdown which had sent even the monkeys running scared; the return of the People's Liberation Army to the streets of Beijing; and an all-China bird flu vaccination which everyone was supposed to have had. The Party insisted that February 11 had been a calendar day, just like any other. And with everyone else bathing so blissfully in the harmony of everything, when the misfits tried to share their concerns about the missing month, nobody else seemed to care.

The misfits become convinced of a link between their inability to join in the general joy and the fact that February has been forgotten. And they agree that the only way they will ever be able to get to the bottom of what has happened will be to ask a senior Party member. Given, of course, that no senior Party member would ever talk to the likes of them, they realise that the only way to have such a conversation would be to kidnap one of them, and squeeze him until he talked. Through a friend of a friend, they manage to catch a member of the Politburo and tie him up for a night of frank questions and answers.

Eventually, the Politburo member admits that the month of February 2011 had indeed been disappeared. But he insists that there had been no other way. 'You think it's easy to look after 1.4 billion people?' he snaps:

'We had to do it'. And with that, he proceeds to describe what had actually happened. With the rest of the world in the grip of its economic crisis, and spiralling out of control, China had been on a knife-edge. Western demand flattened, the factories were slowing down, and the Chinese people were up in arms about everything; the Party family was squabbling; and Tibet and Xinjiang were poised like tinderboxes, waiting to explode. The Politburo had wracked its brains to find a solution. Finally, it had realised that the only way to avoid the end of everything was to create an opportunity out of the crisis. It had not been easy, but eventually they had come up with an 'Action Plan for Ruling the Nation and Pacifying the World'.

The idea behind the 'Action Plan' had been to let the people work themselves up into such a frenzy of rioting chaos and fear that they would rejoice at the comforting sounds of the steps of the People's Liberation Army. With the army firmly on the streets, the Party could then set about changing facts on the ground. *Bian!* they had turned a quarter of the people's savings into vouchers which could only buy things made in China, and had to be spent within six months. *Flash!* they had ripped away the red tape which tangled up production, and let the factories produce like pistons to satisfy the waves of demand. *Swoosh!* and the land of the peasants had been privatised so they could turn their attention to making some money for themselves. Another quick *flash!* and the Chinese internet had been commandeered to create an automated system of price controls to keep everyone happy. After which, a string of *cloud somersaults* had been undertaken to wrap up the messy corners of the rest of the world. With China rising, and everywhere else collapsing, it had not been very difficult. Japan was embraced as a most-favoured-forever partner – which meant that the interfering Americans could be sent back to their barbarian corner of the world. At the same time, the People's Liberation Army rattled its rockets and made it clear to everyone, especially the Americans, that if anyone started muttering about an over-confident China, China itself would be the first to attack. Those feats achieved, the Party had been left with the question of the people themselves and their inconvenient memories. For that, they had just added a mild 'ecstasy-like' substance to everything the people drank, and *bian!* everyone had forgotten everything. As a final touch, they had then added a jab of a bird flu vaccination, and a quick clean of the Chinese internet, and, with the Great Man mission accomplished, everyone in the Party and the population had been able to get on with the harmonies of their lives.

At the end of the Politburo member's account of events, the misfit friends blast him with anger. 'What sort of a Party do you think you are? Hijacking heaven and the people just like the emperors of old, but this time with the added twist of technology to turn truth into lies'. To which, the Politburo member suggests that they just look at the harmony spreading all round them, and at the peace which has settled across the world. Could they really, he asks, believe that truth is better than lies? And while they were thinking, he suggests that they also look at the mess which the foreigners have created with all of their crashing around the world as if they owned everything, not to mention their total disregard for history, geography, and anything else that didn't fit into the simple fixes of their tiny, irresponsible worlds. 'If you have any better ideas', he concludes, 'the Party would be delighted to hear them. But you might just want to give us some credit for swooshing a paradise up out of nowhere, while the rest of the world has been scrabbling around in the dark.'

The friends look at the Politburo member in disbelief, and remember the question, familiar to all Chinese, posed by the works of the towering, and Party-favoured, early twentieth-century writer, Lu Xun: 'Which would you prefer: a counterfeit paradise or a good hell?' It was obviously not a pleasant choice, but now it seemed that it was not even theirs to make. A single top-down mind had decided the matter for one and all, and done it in such a way that no one would ever again be able to tell the difference between black and white. True, the boundaries between the real and the not real had been a question since the time of Zhuangzi's butterfly dream. And true, history could be a bit painful and the world is a complicated place. But to lose the power of your own mind and memory, and to be turned into a character in someone else's dream: it was a hell of a leap of faith.

Circulating under intellectual tables – banned in China, but smuggled in from Hong Kong – Chan's book might not have lit the kind of prairie fire that brought everything down in its wake, but it was certainly a significant spark. Many in the Party read it in the privacy of their studies, and thought that it pretty much summed up something they had been trying to say for years: 'We may not be perfect, but this is a difficult world'. A few were pleasantly surprised that an intellectual could have come up with such a clear understanding of how hard the Party had to work. Some outside the Party sighed with regret, but wondered what one could do: 'It was all a little bit sad, but the world had changed, and if one could manage to make it as painless as the author had imagined, perhaps it would be all for the best.'

Piling on to China's glittering train as fast as their feet could carry them, even the foreigners seemed to be agreeing that a counterfeit paradise was preferable to a good hell. Who needed to tell the difference between black and white, as long as you could keep on shopping?

Many others, however, reeling in shock at how close the future had become, began to think again. As Zhongnanhai squabbled its way to a new Son of Heaven, some of those others began to play a game of 'what if'. 'What if' being Chinese meant that you actually saw heaven as the voice of real human beings, rather than the choreographed broadcasts of a Leninist symphony? It might seem fantastical but, frankly speaking, Chan Koonchung's book seemed a bit fantastical too. Yet everyone knew, in their heart of hearts, that so much of the spirit of what it described was already true. 'Could China ever be a country where the people themselves could be trusted with a voice?'

Thinking again, many reflected on the fact that in another, admittedly much smaller, Chinese world, a group of Chinese people had been given a voice only fifteen years before. From 1949, schooled in the same ancient ideas of order, the Guomindang had ruled the renegade island of Taiwan as a single top-down mind, supported by the barrel of the gun. But then, in the 1980s, Chiang Kai-shek's son and heir had experienced a sudden and surprising *snow-in-summer* change of heart. By the end of the 1990s, having defied the rockets of rage that the Party had flung across the Taiwan straits in 1996, heaven (at least in Taiwan) had been liberated, and communications had been handed over to the people without a single muzzle of a gun. Could the next leader of the Chinese Communist Party possibly be another snow-in-summer ruler who would finally open communications between heaven and earth for the mainland of the country as well? It was hard to believe, but given that every Son of Heaven since the beginning of time had been taught to keep his counsel silent, could anyone really tell?

*   *   *

As 2012 began to change into 2013, Xi Jinping – the new general secretary of the Party, chairman of the Central Military Commission, and president of the People's Republic – had stood up and repeated the traditional announcement of the Party's historic sacrifices and successes. He had then, in something of a departure from the usual practice, gone on to declare a dream, imagining China as 'a strong and prosperous nation', and the Chinese people as 'happy and free'. While the idea of a dream was new – and a lot more interesting than 'One centre, Two points', 'the Three Represents' or 'Scientific Development' – with peasants manning the barricades in the countryside, cities spluttering in smoke, and the Party continuing to insist on unity at the expense of human lives, the words had seemed to be a little hard to reconcile with the facts. Within days, the twittering *Weixin* had been awash with humour. Some suggested that the Party state was working way too hard. All of that building and demolishing, surveilling and policing; and all of that exhausting worrying about the state of everyone's hearts and minds: grateful though the people were for its attentiveness, the Party was clearly well overdue for a long-earned break. Others had noted that if only the internet police could swap places with the government's food administration, everyone's dream of being able to eat safe food would be realised, with the added advantage that they would also be able to talk to anyone they liked.

Sensing a danger to the Democratic Dictatorship of the People, the Party's Propaganda Department had quickly come to the defence of Xi Jinping's dream, and rafts of twittering *Weixin* users had been thrown off their accounts. Familiar with the game of cat and mouse, the users had simply assumed the names of ancient heroes – characters from the *Outlaws of the Marsh* were particularly popular – and reincarnated themselves with new accounts. Almost as adept at the game as the users, the Propaganda Department had hit back with a rule that anyone who reposted a 'rumour' more than five hundred times would be committing a serious crime. Up and down the country, the internet police, supported by the *wu mao dang* fifty cent party of cleansing cybersurfers, had flown into overtime. The most irreverent (and popular) bloggers had been invited for a cup of tea and a chat at their local police station. Those who were slow to get the point had been invited to stay the night.

Some of the bloggers fell by the wayside, but others just kept blogging. Where inconvenient posts were harmonised with a deletion, the deleted posts were quickly reposted. As more and more inconvenient words and names were banned, the blogosphere searched through dictionaries to find harmless alternatives of characters which looked completely different when written down, but when pronounced sounded exactly the same. As it had always been, in the battle between the single top-down mind and being human, the Chinese language had been requisitioned for a war of words. One writer suggested that it would save a lot of time – and a lot of 'character' crimes – if the Party could just publish a glossary of 'sensitive strokes'. Others noted that, at the rate at which words were hitting the dust, it might be hard for any glossary to keep up. Some just wanted to announce to whoever was reading their private email, that they were not class enemies, troublemakers, or overthrowers of governments: they were, just like Xi Jinping, dreaming of a better world. But unlike Xi Jinping, they could see what was going on in their very local corners of the Chinese world, and they wanted to report some seriously corrupted Party officials in the hope that everyone's dreams might come true. The Party struck back with a call for ever-greater harmony – and a crackdown not only on corruption but on the whistle-blowers as well.

Across 2013, peasant protests carried on rising, and arrests of city intellectuals were becoming harder for anyone to ignore. For many, dreams of freedom and happiness seemed to be in recession. A number of the intellectuals who had once trustingly offered their mind-emancipating services to the Party began to worry that the glittering train might come off its tracks. Xi Jinping moved swiftly to reassure. With many eminently qualified minds to hand, policy after policy flew over the walls of Zhongnanhai and the wider government, all designed to steady the rails. Consummately skilled in the art of investigating everything, the Party also floated policies to address some of the knottier questions of the time: peasant land, single children, *hukou* passes, and the *laogai* labour camps in which oceans of stubborn minds were still being held. Soon it was announced that peasant land would be reformed (once again), more people would be able to have two children instead of one, more migrants would be able to get a *hukou* passport to live in a city, and the *laogai* labour camps would disappear.

Meanwhile the anti-corruption campaign rolled on with such thunder that even the doubters began to wonder if this time it might be real. Across the restaurants of the capital, and every other city, concerned minds tried to fathom the direction of Xi Jinping's new order. Was he possibly drawing the reins of power closer to himself so that he could first defeat the Party's factions, and then give the people a voice? Or was he just another Party man, dressing up the Leninist-imperial order with a propaganda trick?

Some hopeful chopsticks pointed not only to the new policies but to a host of lower Party officials who were having to give up their Swiss watches as well as some of their numerous homes. Others pointed back to the past: corruption campaigns had always thundered in their early stages, before gradually dying out; and they were always a cover for targeting some inconvenient mind or other, rather than the mass of corruption at large. And as far as Party policies were concerned, they added, one should always read the fine print. Land reform without giving the peasants a voice was, as the whole of history could testify, tantamount to handing any newly acquired gains straight into the waiting arms of Party wolves on the ground: any land given to the peasants would soon be consumed in taxes and fees, with the land itself eventually being picked up by a local power for a song. As for child births and *hukou* passes, the Party state was not proposing to give up its controls, only to adjust the settings. While the loss of the *laogai* labour camps was to be welcomed, what about the black jails, the hotels, and the psychiatric asylums that were always ready to accommodate the subjectively subversive mind?

Back and forth the chopsticks went, until someone would eventually sigh and remind everyone at the table that the members of the Party's family were a law unto themselves: hidden behind their screens, who could ever really know what they thought. And even if Xi Jinping wanted to change the heavenly order, one 'good official' on his own would never be able to make a black system white.

Some, however, looked at Xi Jinping and wondered. Maybe he was not intending to fundamentally change the relationship between heaven and earth, but perhaps with a bit of popular encouragement, he might come around.

Going back to their *Weixin* microblogs, believers and doubters alike began to exchange some thoughts on what would really be required to make 'the dream' come true. As their suggestions were noted by the Party's Propaganda Department, more *Weixin* accounts were closed, and heaven began to look for a few monkeys with which to scare the rest of the chickens on earth. A highly respected businessman who had become a popular blogger was arrested. Having suggested that business would struggle to thrive if the Party wasn't put under some kind of law, he was given even tighter shoes than Ai Weiwei: accused of prostitution, he appeared on television to make his self-criticism in chains. Another popular blogger, the founder of a company that had designed and built much of new Beijing, was invited to denounce the rumour-mongering blogosphere on prime-time television, explaining to the people at large, and with obvious discomfort, that harmony was everything, and blogs were nothing but troublemaking chat.

Those who continued to openly and publicly argue that it was time for communications between heaven and earth to be improved, soon found themselves picked up and deposited in the single-minded top-down jail. Some used the time to reflect on the truth of an observation made by Confucius two and a half milllenia ago: 'whenever heaven invests a person with great responsibility, it tests his resolve, exhausts his body, starves his person, leaves him destitute, and confounds his every endeavour: thus are patience and endurance developed, and weaknesses overcome'. Others decided that it was time to take themselves off to other worlds: to quiet studies where they could dream of misty mountains, or to real lands abroad. Yet others decided that there was no alternative to staying at home and being the best Chinese they could. One of these was another lawyer, by the name of Xu Zhiyong. Like the drafters of Charter 08, he had raised a banner arguing for a constitution whose rules would govern the Party as well as everyone else. And, like the late nineteenth-century Liang Qichao so long before him, he had gone on to create a *xinmin*, new citizens, movement of people who would gather together peacefully, perhaps over dinner, to find the myriad local and practical ways through which the people could give heaven a helping hand.

In 2013, Xu Zhiyong was arrested and charged with disrupting public order by gathering a crowd. At his trial, in the first wintry month of 2014, Xu stood up and made a statement of his own. 'Being human is about more than having a full stomach', he observed. 'And any investigation of things can only work if the people can apply their own judgement to what they see and hear – and if the people themselves can be heard'. Guided by a Party telephone, and applying the socialist rule of law, the judges sentenced him to four years in the jail of the single top-down mind.

As Xu Zhiyong departed, other wilful hearts thought on a world where anyone could talk to heaven and say whatever they wanted to say. Some thought that it was just a foolish dream. A world without a single top-down order: how could that be real? Others cast their minds back across everything which had happened in the Chinese lands since the beginning of time: on the dynasties which had risen and fallen; on the brave men who had stood together as bands of blood brothers; on the irrepressible spirits who had dared to tell the truth as they saw it; and on the memory of an ancient time when anyone had been able to talk to heaven whenever they wanted, and say whatever they wanted to say. Remembering, they whispered ...

You may be a Party. But we are all Chinese.

CONCLUSION

DREAMING

Let us start from the earth – and soar towards the sun.

In Praise of Light, Ai Qing (1978)

Blazing from the newsstands, the headlines of the *People's Daily* said it all: '*Da Tong!* The Great Unity!' Not that anyone needed a newspaper to know the news. Fireworks had been exploding all night, televisions had not stopped chattering, the internet had ignited, and when they were not pinching themselves or hugging their neighbours, most people's eyes were glued to their phones. Lit up brighter than the brightest of stars, Tiananmen Square looked like heaven itself. Warm from the heat of an early June day, blessed with the soft breeze of evening, it even *felt* like heaven. So many cars had flocked there that the square and its surrounding streets had become a car park. Nobody minded: drivers got out and talked to whoever they wanted to, and those they talked to were only too happy to share the pleasure of being Chinese. As thousands more poured out of the metro, there was certainly no shortage of people: men in suits and women in high heels; youths in T-shirts and jeans; migrants still pinching each other to see if they might wake up from the dream; children sitting aloft on their fathers' shoulders; grandparents giggling with a joy they had thought they would

575

never feel. Beijing was not alone: Hong Kong's Victoria Park was an ocean of light, as was Taibei's Freedom Square, not to mention the centres of Kuala Lumpur, Vancouver, San Francisco, London, New York – and everywhere else that Chinese hearts beat.

The first picture, of course, told the story. Arrayed before a yellow-red sun at the dawning moment when night becomes day, the image of those five men standing before the camera at the peak of Mount Tai must have given even the Jade Emperor a surprise. A sea of clouds rolling across a wider range of peaks behind them, the earth at their feet, hands gripped in unity, it was a vision no one could forget: Xi Jinping standing side by side with the Dalai Lama, Liu Xiaobo, Xu Zhiyong and Ma Yun (known better to the foreigners as Alibaba's Jack Ma). It told everyone that heaven and earth had moved. And the fact that they were all appearing together at the dawn of 4 June 2019 was enough to tell every Chinese on earth that snow had, finally, fallen in summer. The hundredth anniversary of 1919, the year in which China's youth had first stood up to the state, and the thirtieth anniversary of the June 1989 day on which another generation of young Chinese had stood up to the Party's guns with a request that the heavenly state should listen to its people.

Those who had ever made the journey to the top of Mount Tai knew what it had taken for the five men to get there: 7,200 stone steps to the point that had been holding up the sky since the time of Nüwa all those thousands of years ago. A point from which the earliest shamans had stared at the stars and spoken to heaven; and the point from which every great following Son of Heaven had offered the sacrifices that brought heaven and earth together. Spread with the 'three friends' of pine, bamboo and plum trees, its landscape had become a symbol of Chinese endurance: defying the coldest of winters with a steadfastness akin to that of the true man who stands for what he knows to be right. But anyone born in the lands of China, or who knew their Chinese history, was thinking less about the 7,200 steps of the early-morning climb, and more about the five thousand years it had taken to get there – and, of course, the question of how on earth those five thousand years had finally been crossed in what can only have been a short period of time. That was something that only the five men on the mountain could explain.

Video streaming, the five could be seen moving on to the terrace from which Confucius had once looked out and humbly made what had become a famous observation: 'The world is small'. There, they stopped again so that the cameras could catch their light. Moving down to the foothills of the mountain, to the spreading courtyards of the Dai Temple: they reached the altar from which the Han dynasty's Wudi (Martial) Emperor had raised his great sacrifices in 110 BCE. Standing before two characters whose meaning had expanded over the millennia to embrace something deeper than anything a simple sentence could explain, the message they conveyed was full of a greater weight. 'Tai'an', Great Security, the two characters stated. 'When Mount Tai is stable, the world and its people are at peace,' added every knowing Chinese heart.

Camera shots now showing the sun a little higher in the sky, Xi Jinping advanced to a microphone, and made a statement that no heaven could fail to hear. Explaining that he was speaking for his brothers, and that each of them – himself, the Dalai Lama, Liu Xiaobo, Xu Zhiyong and Ma Yun (Jack Ma) – would be answering questions later in the day, he went on to tell a story, and to set out a plan. Delivered to a hushed press, and appearing within seconds on everyone's handheld screens in China, his words swept swiftly across every corner of the earth.

'Nushimen, xianshengmen, dajia hao (Ladies and gentlemen, greetings).

'The Way of the Chinese people has been the longest unbroken journey in the world.

'Starting thousands of years before time was even counted, our earliest known ancestors advanced to the peak above me to talk to the sky. Since that time, Chinese hearts and minds have struggled to understand how man can deliver the order of heaven on earth. From the time of the Yellow Emperor, finding the answer to that question has been a responsibility that has weighed as heavily on Chinese shoulders as the mountain on which we stand today, Mount Tai. Clear that our duty could only be discharged with the most thorough investigation of things, we have scoured the present and the past to understand not only the facts of heaven and earth, but the precepts by which they change.

'Great men have guided us. But it has not been easy. Laozi's observation that the"way is great" set us on an eternal quest. Ringing in our ears, Confucius' observation that "talent is difficult to come by" has been a constant challenge. We have made mistakes. We have tried to learn from them. And in trying to learn from them, we have never shied from taking the first of the steps with which every journey of ten thousand miles must always begin. We have long understood that the world is composed of the constant changes of yin and yang, but as to understanding how man should conduct himself so that heaven and earth are in harmony across those changes, and within what so often seem to be irreconcilable contradictions, that remains a journey.

'Today, we stand before you on this mountain to tell you that it is time to start a new stage in that journey. This time, we ask you to come with us.

'The last seven years have been a challenge for us all. Within our lands, terror has become a part of our lives. While the Party has done its best to harmonise the news, few corners of our country have not experienced the violence of anger. We have managed to stop many of our own tigers fighting in their factions, but only at an extreme cost to our economy. We have battled – with some success – against the tigers and flies that have eaten away at our achievements, but we are also aware that the roots of the corruption that plagues us are buried deeply. We know that, unchecked, many of our own officials remain tyrants on the ground. Even our efforts to cleanse the environment have been challenged: we have worked as hard as the ancient Yao and Shun to restore our blue skies but the battles among our tigers have made progress hard. And as our desire to keep the bird of our economy alive in its cage has led us to stretch our production and construction across "one belt" of roads and railways and "one road" of maritime routes, other people's skies have clouded with the smoke of our past, even as the oceans have been turned to a productivity of their own.

'Around us, Asian seas and skies, shot with the faultlines of an imperial past, have gone to the brink of war a number of times. Beyond us, foreign dreams have fallen. Dreams of democracy have become victims of exactly the same kind of unprepared assembly that we ourselves experienced after our 1911 revolution. While the fragile unity of once battling nations has foundered in a failure to accept the responsibilities of power. To which has been added a rising violence as individual governments lack the courage to rule, and as individual citizens have not understood the importance of cultivating themselves.

'In the heartlands of the West, the rising chaos accompanying America's inevitable decline reminds us, every day more sharply, of the early period of our own Warring States, which went on to ravage the last centuries of the failing dynasty of the Zhou. America's latest, bitter, election having divided its people as they have never been divided before, the responsibility of government has been lost to competing interests, while the people have failed to understand the responsibility of the ruled. Within their homelands, guns roam the streets without control, while in the world at large, their rulers seek to insist upon a power that has already been lost. The "colour revolutions" that followed the end of the first decade of the new millennium have long since replaced hope with despair: dreams of freedom have been shot with danger. The Middle East has become a land of darkness where no one dares to go. And the pillars of Western globalisation – the global companies and the world's great cities – have become targets of a rage borne of a deep sense of betrayal and distrust. Meanwhile, as temperatures increase everywhere, even the seas are rising and the seasons have lost their direction.

'Within our own lands, we have done our best to deliver great peace through great order. Our Party's power has been devoted to delivering stability. Our people continue to prove that they are capable of eating the greatest bitterness. We have delivered as much order as others and, frankly, more than most. But the countries that have followed us have struggled. Those who looked to our once-glittering train for an economic order have found that, in the absence of their own Party dedicated to harmony, and without a people who can eat bitterness, the result is nothing but a chaos of unrealised dreams. Those who have followed our "one belt, one road" have also come to have their questions, not least about the nature of our economic bird, and the expanding size of its cage.

'Of course, we have delivered considerable wealth to many. We have also contributed extensive knowledge. But we must accept that the contradictions have been great. It is clear that even the most diligent dedication to hard work cannot, alone, deliver the order of heaven and earth. And it is equally clear that being human is, as the lawyer Xu Zhiyong once pointed out, about more than having a full stomach.

'While the world has not yet returned to the darkest times of the Warring States, we know that that time may not be far off. Certainly, we have left the golden age of the early Zhou long behind.

'When I first appeared before you in November 2012, I talked of a dream. In the clouds of speculation that arose at the time some of you, imagining that, like the Monkey King, I could wave a magic stick and change the world, were disappointed when I tightened my grip on the order of everything. It is easy to underestimate the responsibilities of a ruler. It is difficult to imagine how hard it is to rule. With corruption eating away at everything, with factions at every level and in every direction, and with a people who were not only angry but had good reason to be so, I did what every responsible ruler would do. I tried to make corrections by holding firm to the tiller of the only obvious strengths we had: the Party and its dedication to a new order of man and state. But the costs were high, and some of the highest costs fell on those least able to bear them – and on those who wanted only to lend their energies to help.

'As I have said, it is not easy to be a ruler. And no ruler can afford the luxury of making popular changes without preparing the way.

'Standing before you today, though, I can say that even as our problems have been great, across the past seven years, we have managed to nurture a small but strong group of men and women who understand both the importance of order and unity, and the imperative of orderly change. To these men and women who promised to keep the true depth of my dream secret, and who have done everything within their power to make it come true, I say that heaven – whatever you may believe that to be – would be proud.

'Those seven years ago, I gathered together the work of the Central Party School – which some of you may be surprised to know includes not just the texts of Marx, Mao and Deng, but also the thoughts of each of the gentlemen to my left, and indeed a strange novel about a missing month of February that everyone seems to have read. You are right that it was not long after this that the Party banned a large number of books, not only here in the heartlands of China but in Hong Kong as well. And not long after that that we ignored the calls of Hong Kong's students for an election that would give the Hong Kong people the freedom to choose a ruler from a list prepared entirely by themselves. Not long, indeed, before we took the necessary steps on the mainland to return any idea of the rule of law back to the ordering rules of Qin. As I said, it is not easy to be a ruler, and all change needs its time and seasons.

'Five years ago, I quietly upgraded our longstanding conversations with our brothers in Taibei: the Guomindang who were forged from a similar metal to our own, and the opposition parties. Their ideas about democracy seemed to suffer from a number of the simple errors that the West has always made, but they had set off on a journey, and from that journey there was a lot to learn. As pitched battles erupted on Hong Kong's streets, it was not an easy conversation to maintain.

'At about the same time, I also opened an even quieter conversation with His Holiness the Dalai Lama – a man whose own journey has, I know, inspired so many people not only in Tibet but around the world, and whose Buddhism continues to touch the hearts of many Chinese. As you might imagine, finding a retreat where we could talk without throwing the world into a chaos of speculation was a challenge of its own.

'One year ago, I opened an equally quiet conversation with Liu Xiaobo and Xu Zhiyong, both of whom had recently been released from jail. While the Chinese people's great respect for secrecy has brought us many problems, I must say that I am grateful for the integrity that these two men exemplified in keeping those conversations to themselves.

'Six months ago, I met with Ma Yun (Jack Ma). In a world of economics, finding a reason to talk to a businessman was, of course, easy. But Ma Yun's commitment to serving his country with a secret as weighty as Mount Tai was yet another reminder of what a truly great people we are.

'Beyond these conversations, there have been many others: too numerous to describe today, but at home and across the wider world, there are scores of Chinese brothers and sisters who have proven that the virtues of our earliest ancestors – particularly those of *ren* humanity, *yi* integrity and *zhi* knowledge – have not been lost, even as they have travelled far and wide.

'Across these conversations, and supported by the deep and wide-ranging studies undertaken by the Central Party School, the idea that started as a dream began to take shape as the possibility of a plan. A *Da Tong* Great Unity, which would both restore the unity of our Chinese hearts on the mainland, and revive the integrity of the greater Chinese family that now lives across the earth.

'It is this *Da Tong* Great Unity that I announce to you today.

'Details will follow over the coming days, weeks and months, but I would like, this morning, as the sun of a new day rises behind us, to set out a description of the Five Advances and Five Commissions with which we expect to make our *Da Tong* dream come true. The path to our *Da Tong* Great Unity will be neither short nor easy. We will have to navigate both the path that we can see right now, and all of the yin and yang changes that we will encounter on our journey. Our success will depend both on the qualities of those responsible for ruling and on the qualities of you, the people, as well.

'The First Advance is that, from today, the name of the Chinese Communist Party will change. Henceforward, it will be known as the Chinese Unity Party. Membership will be open to all. All members, existing and new, will be required to pass an examination in citizenship.

'As our Second Advance, and the foundation of our journey, we will take up a task begun by our predecessors over a hundred years ago: to "imagine a people", and in so doing, to build a new relationship between the people and the state. To achieve our goal, we will establish the following Five Commissions:

a Constitution and Law Commission, an Election Commission, a *Xinmin* New Citizens Commission, a Press and Communications Commission, and a Commission that will be charged with creating a *Da Tong* Great Unity Charter for the Chinese people at large. All of these commissions will be given one year to formulate their recommendations and to prepare an educational programme designed to ensure that every Chinese will be able to understand the recommendations that each commission makes, and the way in which all of the recommendations fit together. Each commission will then be responsible for delivering its educational programme across the following year, and for evaluating the results, with feedback from the public at large. Based on those evaluations, the recommendations of all the Commissions will be finalised. All recommendations will include proposals for ongoing educational programmes to support us as we move forward on what may be a long, but hopefully steady, journey towards our goal.

'The Constitutional and Law Commission will be headed by myself, with a working group that will include the heads of the Central Party School and the Ministry of Justice, as well as Liu Xiaobo and Xu Zhiyong, two of the gentlemen standing here with me today. Our work will include the drafting of a new constitution that will place every Chinese individual and organisation (including the Chinese Unity Party, the People's Liberation Army and the People's Courts) under its rules. It will also include a framework for the transformation of the People's Republic of China into a federation of states that share the common ideals of Chinese civilisation – including the *ren* empathetic humanity with which we each put ourselves in others' shoes, the *yi* integrity that ensures that words and meanings come together as truth, and the *zhi* knowledge on which all right action is grounded. We have reason to hope that this will strengthen our nation and help to reunite our divided Chinese family across the Taiwan straits, while restoring the bonds of trust with our brothers in Hong Kong. Our federation will also include those regions within the People's Republic, which, although sharing many of our ideals, wish to emphasise peaceful ideas of their own. In this respect our Constitutional and Law Commission will include a working group on Tibet, Xinjiang, Inner Mongolia and the south-western minorities. His Holiness the Dalai Lama has agreed to return to Tibet, and from Tibet to co-chair that working group. We will be exploring how his idea of 'zones of peace' may help us to find a unity of hearts – and how it may also help us to find a way to restore our lost natural worlds.

'The Election Commission will be charged with creating a framework for local elections, by village and city neighbourhood. Its members will include an older brother from the village of Wukan who, you may remember, has had a lot of experience on the ground. We have not changed our deep belief that the voice of all our people should be predicated on an individual and collective responsibility for the order and well-being of all. We have also not changed our belief that, without a profound dedication to education, elections raise significant risks not only of self-interested electioneering but of distorted results. As one of our intellectuals once so astutely observed: "Democracy is a good thing, but that does not mean that everything about democracy is good". Democracy is not a good thing if self-strengtheners see themselves as being in a race to make the biggest promises, and then fail to deliver. Democracy is not a good thing if individual groups can lobby the state to do their will. Democracy is not a good thing if the state cannot manage its own responsibilities. Democracy is not a good thing if the people do not understand that it is a responsibility as much as a right.

'We do not at present propose to introduce multiple political parties to compete in national elections, although we expect the Election Commission to offer a proposal on how such a stage could be reached within the next five years. The immediate attention of the Election Commission will be on creating a framework of elections to capture the responsible voices of our people, and to release them from the arbitrary power of local officials. We expect that this will take the form of local elections on the basis of a one person, one vote system. But every voter will be required to complete a Citizenship Programme and to commit to an ongoing education in the same. This will include the study of fiscal management, science and technology, and current and global affairs. We believe that democracy without education is a danger rooted in a blindness to the essential importance of the human quality of empathy that *ren* humanity without which the order of all is at risk. The world changes constantly, and fast. A responsible people needs to have a responsible understanding of that change. At the same time, democracy is not just a matter of a competitive election, it is a way of life for all. Order cannot be guaranteed by the simple process of an election: it requires rulers who are equipped to rule, and for such qualified rulers to be elected, it is essential that voters achieve and maintain the highest quality of understanding.

'Together, the Election Commission and the Constitutional Commission will also work on recommendations for a new National People's Congress to reflect the many different constituencies of our country. The obvious constituencies will be the young, the old, the rich, the poor, the migrants and the minorities. To these will be added constituencies formed by think-tanks and civil society organisations representing the natural world, the city, the future, and the learnings from the distant past.

'The Third Commission – the *Xinmin*, New Citizens, Commission – will be charged with opening up the public space required for our people to provide the *hu zhu*, mutual assistance, that so many of you have wanted to do for so long. We have learnt from our own experience and from studying the experience of others, that no ruler can do everything – even democratically elected ones. Being closer to the ground, responsible people can see both risks and practical solutions more clearly; they are also better able to turn dreams into reality. We do not underestimate the challenges of opening up such a public space, but we understand that we will need to rise to meet them, as they indeed will rise to meet us. The New Citizens Commission will be responsible for the crafting of the Citizenship Programme – a programme that will not only underpin our elections but will ensure that in building a land where the people can mutually assist themselves, all of the people's societies are run by individuals who are qualified. Qualifications will not be purely defined by the shallow pages of textbooks but also by the practical experience which truly forges the *ren* quality of man. The Commission will also ensure that the state and the people's societies are able to support each other where appropriate. Across all of its activities, knowledge and education will be key: for the tens of millions of volunteers who we expect will work with the people's societies; for government officials in society; for society working with government. Armed with such knowledge, and with a clear understanding of everyone's responsibility both for their own activities and for the wider order of all, a significant number of the services of our state will be delivered by our people, for our people.

'The work of the New Citizens Commission will also include the creation of a working group on truth and reconciliation. We accept that there is much anger in our lands. Mistakes have been made and trust has been lost – not only between the Party and the people, but among the people themselves. Great wealth has been created, but in the process much has been lost, destroyed or stolen. We recognize that trust is the single most important requirement for a secure future and that without it no order can truly prevail. At a practical state level, we will distribute all shares in our state-owned enterprises to the public at large. We will also expand the twinning of cities and villages and the reciprocal exchanges of students and youth between the city and the countryside. We expect these measures to see the launching of many of the kinds of societies with which, once upon a time, Peking University's students set out to find the people. We do not imagine it will be easy. But after five thousand years of thinking deeply about the idea of order, guided by the principles of *ren* humanity, yi integrity and *zhi* knowledge – and given the alternatives that face us – we are hopeful that we will all be able to draw deeply on our love of our country, and to restore respect for our fellow man.

'The Fourth – Press and Communications – Commission will be charged with creating an order for the expression of everyone's voices in whatever form those voices take. We understand that, in our lands, "harmony" has become a byword for censorship, if not tyranny. We also understand that nothing cleanses more than truth – although we believe, deeply, that the experiences of our past teach us that, to be positively effective, the freedom to tell the truth must come with a reciprocal responsibility, on the part of both speaker and listener, for the order of all: this world is full of contradictions. We appreciate the people's great sense of humour and we have come to understand its strength. We repeat our deep belief that every citizen needs to take responsibility for what they say. We also acknowledge, as our ancient thinkers acknowledged, that both the state and every citizen needs to take responsibility not just for what they say but for their understanding of what they hear, including the ability to tell the difference between truth and lies, and to understand a joke. Again, education is essential: for the state and its officials as well as for the people. The Press Commission will have the challenging task of creating a code of conduct for our people, including the officials, that reflects the level of self-cultivation that, as a people, we acknowledge as necessary for the greater good of all. The code of conduct will be placed in the hands of every media organisation and every citizen alike; it will include a description of our values of self-cultivation as a reminder to all of us of our greater goal of an eventual Da Tong Great Unity.

'Last, but not least, our Fifth Commission will raise a *Da Tong* Great Unity charter. We have long understood that being Chinese is about something more than having been born in the mainland of China. At its best, being Chinese is nothing more nor less than being human: being an individual within a greater natural cosmos and within the greater society of man. The idea of being an individual within a greater whole is, of course, another contradiction. But, like all contradictions, it is one with which we must learn to live. The challenge – indeed the challenge of our whole *Da Tong* journey – is to find that balance: the point at which order can be found between heaven and earth; between the individual and the group. Our earliest ancestors understood this and while only a fool would imagine that China was not a land of over a billion individuals, it is true that, more than many others and after a lot of pain, we have learnt the wisdom of understanding ourselves as individuals in a wider community of others. We have disagreed about the balance between the state and the individual. We acknowledge that the answers are not easy. But we have always been a land of brothers. And we have always been a people who love the idea of China more than life itself. We have a long journey ahead of us. We would like to take that journey with our brothers and sisters abroad. They may have been born to Chinese parents, they may have been born to parents abroad, or to foreign parents, and they may or may not have have visited China, but they are people who share our ideas of *ren* humanity, *yi* integrity and *zhi* knowledge. To these brothers and sisters I say: wherever you come from, in the spirit of the nineteenth-century Kang Youwei, we invite you to join us in building a *Da Tong* Great Unity that goes beyond our Chinese lands to include the civilisation of man.

'These are the Five Commissions on which we will build our *Da Tong* future. Having already described the first two of our Five Advances (opening up our Party to become a Chinese Unity Party, and embarking on the long journey of rebuilding the relationship between the people and the state) I would like to present the three further Advances that will be important to the achievement of our goal.

'The first of these is the creation and sharing of knowledge. Creating knowledge is one thing; sharing it across the people is another. Progress in this area is critical, not just in China but around the world. Under our Third Advance, we will apply the power of technology to ensure that our people have access to the information and insight that will enable them to become responsible citizens both of our state and of this planet. This will include not only education and information but the tools necessary for the people to share knowledge and, in so doing, to communicate with the state and with each other. We believe that our lands and our people have already made great progress in developing the *technology* of communication: the *human aspect*, however, will require a lot more work.

'From henceforth, all public knowledge will be available to everyone, wherever and whoever they may be. In so doing, we will expand the range of public knowledge to include all knowledge essential for citizenship. As part of their commitment to education, each of the Five Commissions will also be charged with developing mobile technologies and applications that will enable us to have informed conversations by village, by county, by province, by country, by issue, and by idea – and across them all. To this end, we will develop the necessary technology to ensure that whenever a question is asked of anything other than a human being – whether it be a company, an organisation, or the state – it will be answered by a human being. Observing the difficulties that the West has had in this respect, we do not underestimate the challenge. Indeed, as we look towards a planetary population of nine billion people, this may be one of the greatest challenges that the world as a whole will face. But without strengthening our ability to engage with each other as human beings, all other steps towards our Great *Da Tong* Unity will fail. Ma Yun (Jack Ma) will be creating a working group of peers across the technology industries to take this forward. Guided as we have always been by our Halls of Light, committed as we have been since the earliest of our time to investigating things, I am in no doubt that Ma Yun and his peers will achieve this goal.

'While knowledge of this world is essential to creating the peace and stability required for a people to live together in harmony, we acknowledge that, on its own, knowledge is not enough. The hearts of men and women are governed by ideas of love, of courage, and of loyalty; ideas that are at the heart of being human, and which experience has shown us are essential to human achievement. Some may describe them as spiritual qualities, others as simple tools for survival that have been honed and passed down across the millennia of our past. Looking at the long and hard road ahead, however one chooses to see them, we consider it essential that our people are equipped with every possible human resource required to make that journey seem as light as a feather. To this end, and as part of our broad emphasis on education, our Fourth Advance will be the introduction of practical studies in the calming of the restless human mind, including the meditation from which many of our greatest ideas of order have come. It is a course of study that will be undertaken not only by our people but by every man and woman who becomes an official of our land – including myself. His Holiness the Dalai Lama has kindly offered to take personal responsibility for this journey.

'Our Fifth Advance will require great understanding – at home and abroad. You may remember Confucius' observation two thousand five hundred years ago, that 'things have their roots and branches'. Clearly, the way to find peace and unity is to begin at the beginning. With the points that I have outlined above, we will put our great state in order, not just by

587

ordering the state but by ordering our hearts and persons, with empathy and knowledge at the core. With our hearts, our persons and our state ordered, we will have created a strong root for peace.

'Supported by this root, our Fifth Advance is a commitment to reach out to the Asian lands around us to create a border commission that will help us resolve the fault-lines of the past. I have already held preliminary conversations with our many neighbours: the fourteen countries whose lands border ours, as well as those (including Japan, Vietnam, Malaysia, Singapore, Thailand, the Philippines and Indonesia) who, while not directly contiguous, touch our immediate seas. Our disputes have become bitter, particularly with Japan and particularly around the South China Sea. But we recognise that with our great size comes great responsibility. Over one hundred and fifty years ago, our respective borders became confused by the rise of a Western idea of sovereign states for which none of us was prepared. Over seventy years ago, the treaties forged at the end of the Second World War were of little help and, indeed, added to the confusion: drafted by the old powers of the Western world, they had little understanding of our geography and even less of our history. It will be hard to unravel the tangled past, and hard to imagine a different future. The Dalai Lama's idea of "zones of peace" may be of some assistance.

'We understand that other countries and other peoples have different ideas about the level of individuality which is compatible with a strong society. We acknowledge that we are all learning. But we respectfully submit that the raw individuality that has roamed the world for so long is now a danger to us all. Two thousand five hundred years ago, China lived through an experience from which the world has much to learn. A land of family fiefdoms became a competition of city-states that forgot their mutual bonds and battled against each other for power. And as a landscape of walls divided the wealth of the city rich from the misery of the fields of the poor, the *ren* compassion of human empathy was lost. *Yi* integrity was reduced to promises sold for a price; *zhi* knowledge became a matter of knowing whatever was needed to stay on top. In the end, our land became a war of all against all. We know it as the time of the Warring States. The experience of those wars – the descent into centuries of battles of all against all – transformed how we saw the world in ways that few other people and states have ever understood.

'To our fellow states, near and far, we say this. We have all made our mistakes; we have all been blinded by our empires and by our fears. But at its heart, being Chinese has always been about being human enough to have the humility to search for knowledge and understanding, about matching words and actions in truth, and about pursuing wisdom as light. We do not believe in the peaceful evolution proposed by America – because we do not believe that America, any more than any other state, has yet found the *dao* Way. But we do believe in peace. And to our brothers in America and indeed across the world, as we set off on our journey to a *Da Tong* Great Unity, we offer everything that we will learn, to all of you. We are a people of 1.4 billion in a world that has now reached a population of eight billion. By 2050, we expect the world's population to have leapt to nine billion; by 2100, it could reach eleven billion. While we may all sometimes wish that it were otherwise, we are one world, even though we are so different. Our future depends upon us finding a way to live together in our differences, for the greater good of all – and on a planet that will have become truly small. Remembering a time over a hundred years ago, when we set out to imagine a people and ended up as a land upon which other countries feasted, we ask only that you respect our immediate territorial integrity and in so doing, give us the space and time to take what we believe will be one of the great journeys of man. It is a journey that can be undertaken only, as that twentieth-century philosopher Hu Shi once said: 'Bit by bit, and drop by drop'. It is a journey that will take time.

'Friends, we have a long way ahead of us. We may have utopian dreams but we are still men. We cannot realise our dream in a day. And as we walk towards our dream, we will not be able to divorce ourselves from the reality of conditions in the world around us and at home. We once thought that some of us would first lead the way as a Communist Party, gradually teaching others who would follow in our path. As a Party and as a people, we have learnt a lot from that experience, much of which has been painful. But even the pain has taught us. After seventy years of Communist Party rule, it is now clear that the next steps can be taken only by all of us together, as a people; as Chinese. From this day on, 4 June will become a day for all of us to reflect on what it means to be Chinese. I hope that you will continue to light your candles around the world – in memory of those whose courage and conviction kept that flame alight, and as a reminder to us all that, without the empathy of our human hearts, there can be no heaven or earth within which we will be able to find our order.'

*   *   *

Waking up, some of you will no doubt think that this is just a foolish dream. A China without a single top-down order – how could that be real? And a people without an unconditional right to vote – how could that be a dream? But some of you might remember the stories of China's ancient and recent past, and wonder. Whether unconvinced or wondering, pondering on this dream, I think there are two questions which we could ask ourselves. The first is: what would we do if the dream came true? The second is: what would we do if it did not?

What if this dream came true? What if the Party and the people found a way to talk to each other?

Like everyone else who has spent a lot of time in China, I have often been asked for my 'predictions' on what will happen – often by questioners who have insisted that the answer be either a black or a white, a rise or a collapse. For a long time the 'rise' was generally expected to be a conversion to the Western ideal of democracy as a simple 'one person, one vote', complete with the continued acceleration of the glittering train – and without any of that train's inconvenient consequences. More recently there has been a sense that the 'rise' is unlikely to include a conversion to the Western democratic ideal and that, as such, any Chinese 'rise' represents a threat to all. The 'collapse' was generally expected to be some variation or other on a revolution. So much attention has been focused on these binary alternatives that little thought has been given to what might happen if a dream of the Chinese people were to come true.

As the *All Under Heaven* stories have shown us, such a dream would not be of a future like the West – but that does not mean that it may not be a dream, not just for China but for others as well. And while many people around the world risk their lives to chase the dream of a Western utopia, those who are living in the utopias of America and Europe are becoming increasingly worried about where their dreams are going. Few feel that it is realistic to imagine that the costs of that utopia are costs that the world as a whole can bear: electioneering pacts that offer prizes without responsibility, an anger that is increasingly met with batons and men clad in a rubber-black, and so many walls created to keep others out that one has to wonder whether the world and its cities are global for anyone other than the richest, and for anything more than the trade of money and goods.

Many wonder whether the order of human beings can really be as simple as the Western 'one person, one vote' ideal.

Certainly, few people in China (and none of those you met in the last

590

chapter) believe that simply 'being like the West' would be a dream come true. Theirs is a dream in which the heavenly state listens to its people, and both the state and the people take responsibility for their future, including a responsibility for reconciling the often seemingly contradictory claims of the individual and the group, and between different groups. Heaven is not a black and white choice between a single-minded top and a wildly chattering bottom.

If the dream which I have described came true and the Party and the people were able to find a way to talk to each other, I suspect that, while it might not match up to an individualistic idea of utopia, the Chinese people would be able both to build a trust in the state and to rebuild a long-lost trust in each other. I also suspect that the people of the greater Chinese world – of Hong Kong, Taiwan and all of the many other places where Chinese have made their lives across the wider world – would, together, begin a fascinating journey into the question the Chinese have been asking since the beginning of their time: not just what it means to be Chinese, but what it means to be human in a complicated and constantly changing world.

For what it is worth, I also believe that if China's best dream came true – if the Chinese people were able to build a trust in the state and rebuild a trust in each other – China's measures of valuable achievement would rise. A greater security and human happiness, and a stronger and more balanced gdp; even Nobel prizes – for science as well as for literature and peace. I believe that foreigners would rush to its lands to observe the phenomenon of the rebirth of a state and its people – and that they would do this in such numbers that the ancient Nüwa who held up heaven would be struggling to stop the planet toppling off its axis. And I suspect that such a rebirth would give other states and other peoples, including but by no means limited to the West, the courage and the inspiration to make some much-needed changes of their own.

What if the dream does not come true? What if the Party and the people do not find a way to talk to each other?

When asked for my predictions on China as it stands today, I usually preface my reply with a question of my own. What will happen if the illusion of the world as a 'global economy' is not replaced with a clearer understanding that we are a planet of eight billion very different beings, with hopes and dreams that go well beyond economics, and with all of us subject to the changes of our cosmos? For while the phenomenon of the Party's single top-down mind may have distracted us from the country's wider fundamentals,

China is in many ways a microcosm of our planet. By size, it is one of the biggest masses of land in the world, with more terrestrial and sea borders than any other country. By population, it is so big that it accounts for nearly 20 percent of the people on earth, and so diverse that it includes almost all of the world's faiths and as many, if not more, minorities than any other part of the world. By production, China is the world's greatest producer of almost everything; by consumption it now rivals the West. China has almost every climatic and topographical variation in the world – and almost the full spectrum of environmental risk. And notwithstanding its reductions in poverty, it is a microcosm of much of the world's inequality: home to one of the world's biggest gaps between rich and poor and between the cities and the countryside, with a migrant population almost equal to the number of migrants in the world as a whole.

Indeed, China reflects so many features of our world at large that it might be the closest example we have of what the world might look like if it were a single state. Or, to put it all another way, some of what seem to be the epic peculiarities and risks of the Chinese world are in fact concentrations of the peculiarities and risks of the world at large. Countries of peasant fields are separated from states of sparkling cities by official passport-demanding walls – with the dirtiest, most dangerous and demanding occupations either located in the field or reserved for the men and women who leave the fields for the urban villages that offer them a possibility of touching the knowledge and wealth of the cities. Forests, rivers and lakes have been blackened by a planetary race to produce things faster and cheaper than anywhere else. Cancers have spread as chemicals of myriad descriptions are used to keep the inconvenient costs of objectively scientific economics if not at bay then at least invisible. Stressed by a race to keep themselves in the game of higher quality production and consumption, city people have fallen victim to a stress that cripples the lives of individuals and society alike. Education has been reduced to the improvement of production rather than the messy interrogation of what, in the greater scheme of things, the production is for, with university degrees testifying to nothing more than the unquestioning mastery of facts required for a higher quality job. Communities of different people defined by different histories, geographies or ideas have all been wrapped into the single top-down idea of a state, unified by little more than the purpose of efficiency. Individuals grapple with forces of a political and economic order that, one person one vote notwithstanding, seems to have lost all connection to the world of human beings.

Equally, while the Great Leap Forward was a disaster of such epic human proportions that it is difficult to compare to any single experience outside China, how many of us living in places where the state has become bigger and bigger (or working with large corporations) do not recognise the winds of commandism, chaotic directives and exaggeration? And although, unlike China, the West may have a large number of people who are still able to stand up and speak their individually 'messy' ideas of human truth, in a world where so many of the services on which we depend are locked up in technologies that can command but cannot listen, how many of us did not sadly smile with wry recognition at the story of the ancient Zhuanxu who decided that it would be easier to serve his people if they did not have a voice? The dangers inherent in the notion of unquestionable objectivity as an ideal – whether they come from a political Party, an economic system or a technology – should give us pause for thought about the future of the dream we are already living in.

In looking at China as a microcosm, I believe that it is important to remember that over the past three decades of embracing the Western idea of a science-driven economic development, China has become an amplifier and, indeed, an accelerator of many features inherent within the Western world. More human and material resources have been directed to the building of more cities and infrastructure, and to the taming of more nature and more people, than anywhere else in the world. Improvements in formal economic indicators seem, and are, enviable – poverty reduced, education expanded, wealth created at a speed and on a scale arguably never seen before. But, pursued without the limits of any inconvenient human subjectivity, not all of the gains proclaimed are as real as they seem. And in many cases, the human costs to those who have experienced these 'improvements' most directly have not only been great but have been clearly identifiable as the same human costs that have always followed the unbridled exercise of the single top-down mind.

Unschooled in China's longer and deeper story, most of China's gains have been attributed to the greater objectivity (efficiency) achievable by a single top-down mind, while the costs have mistakenly been assumed to be technical failures which could have been avoided if only the science of economics (or technology) had been better understood. In short, not only China but the world has come to be seen through a predominantly economic prism, even as the Chinese themselves have learnt, again and again, that the only prism that really matters is the question of whether and how heaven and its people are able to talk to each other.

With this context set, let us turn back to the question of what might happen if the dream that I have painted does *not* come true. What if the Party and the people do *not* find a way to talk to each other?

Like many in China (including some in the Party itself), I believe that China will continue to carry the costs of a state in which its people have little trust, and I believe that its people will bear more of the pain, the dangers and the risks which are found in any society where human beings do not trust each other, and where either those at the top are deaf to the voices on the ground, or the voices on the ground are muzzled before they can reach the top. China may (or may not) continue to experience a stronger gdp growth than many other countries (in its favour, it is a big country with a competitive instinct forged in the tooth and claw struggle for survival and self-strengthening of 1.4 billion people; and much of the rest of the world has problems of its own). As the Party and the people move further apart, however, the increasing political risk makes it unlikely that the economy will return to its earlier seeming stability unless and until the relationship between the Party's heaven and the people's earth changes. Certainly, any and all gdp growth will be matched with a rise in shocks: the small shocks that occur when truths are buried; the bigger shocks that occur when 'human portents' stand their ground.

Which shocks and where? To ask that question is to miss one of the greatest points that China's shamans ever made: order is a force far more complex than anything a single mind can master – and the more that a top-down mind considers that it has mastered everything, the greater the risk of shocks in all dimensions. Certainly, Party political campaigns notwithstanding, corruption – corruption of the kind that puts power above the rule of law – will continue to chew away at the fabric of everything, as everyone continues to look out for their own survival and self-strengthening, whatever the collective cost. Meanwhile, the cost of a Party-led corruption campaign conducted without a corresponding building of the people's trust, is likely to further erode the truth of any numbers.

I believe that, even as ever-greater efforts are made to erase inharmonious stories from public view, anger will continue to rise: the anger of those for whom the costs of the Party's harmonies have become too great to bear; the anger of those, particularly in Tibet and Xinjiang, who believe that if their voices are not heard in this generation, they may never be heard again; the rising rage and frustration of Chinese who find themselves in a garden whose walls are getting higher, even as the truth becomes more of a mirage.

I believe that more and more Chinese will look for the relative security of another world which will include, as always, the safer corners of private conversations and secret brotherhoods of men, and for those who can afford it, a foreign place to call home.

I believe that under such conditions China will not only become less safe from violence at home but, with the Party continuing to see a patriotic nationalism as the greatest guarantee of its own survival, less safe as a neighbour as well. I believe that the consequences of this will be felt across Asia: west across the Indian subcontinent; south across the South China Sea; east to Japan; north to Mongolia and Russia, with waves of insecurity flowing out across the wider world.

I believe that Taiwan and Hong Kong will become lightning rods for what will become the bitterly contested question of what it means to be Chinese. I also believe that it is highly likely that Hong Kong will, sooner or later, pay the price for its students' protests – and that its intellectual youth may well then become a blood brotherhood of their own. (To those who watched Hong Kong's 2014 questions, it may be worth noting that while the students' demands for free elections may have seemed unrealistically impatient to some, just as much at stake was the battle for the very Chinese idea that the name of a thing should be the same as its nature: that a shortlist of candidates approved by a single top-down mind should not be confused with a freedom to choose, and that the shadowy hand of a single top-down mind is not the same as an election. Just as much in question in 2014 Hong Kong was the ability of the West to distinguish between the idea of the rule *of* law, which places rulers *under* the law, and the idea of rule *by* law, whereby a single top-down mind declares rules that apply only to the people below. It was a test that some, more focused on order in the global economy, failed.)

Under these conditions, I also believe that it is quite possible that the question of what a human order means within a world of eight billion beings may ultimately come to be argued most compellingly by questioning minds from the Chinese, and Greater Chinese, lands – lands where the battling ideas about order are more easily recognised as critical questions of our human future.

*   *   *

If I am right that China is in many ways a microcosm of our planet, and that at the same time the objectivity of its single top-down mind has made it an amplifier and accelerator of risks already inherent in our human world, the consequences of China's failure to find a way in which heaven and earth can talk to each other augur poorly for us all. In this context, by 'heaven', I do not mean the Chinese Communist Party alone but the top-down ordering forces of our world, whether they be states, great corporations, or the systems of technology on which almost all of our economic activities, and so many of our human conversations, now depend. And by 'earth', I mean the subjectively human qualities of empathy, integrity and knowledge, including an ability to see our place within a world of a lot of other people.

Why would the consequences of China's failure augur poorly for us all? Aspiring for so long to the scale and speed of China's past economic growth, but with little understanding of the importance of China's inner battles for order, we have taken insufficient account of the fact that such growth has been predicated on a fundamentally different idea of order – one in which subjective human questions are overruled by 'objectivity'. To the extent that this *has* been taken into account, it has been assumed that the idea of democracy as 'one person, one vote' would be sufficient to enable us to achieve the goal of mass rapid economic growth without compromising our own dreams of human order for the wider world – even as we confuse a basic lack of familiarity with human lives led in very different climates and terrains, and with chasms of inequality, for an 'objectivity' of our own.

So many of our greatest minds have concentrated on mastering the mysteries of economic growth driven by systems of scientific efficiency that we have begun to believe that order is a matter of economic technocracy. With such an idea of order, we have dangerously reduced our ability to consider and value the human qualities of empathy, integrity and knowledge that not only remind us of the importance of looking beyond economics and technology but are an essential element of any truly stable order in and of themselves. Particularly the essential quality of empathy, upon which I believe all of our human lives depend.

Unlike China's intellectuals, we have given relatively little thought – and none of it with any urgency – to the fact that, unless we, as a world of people, are able not only to express but to insist upon the qualities of empathy, integrity and knowledge as qualities of citizenship, the present order of the Western world is likely to be as ephemeral as the order of China's past has so often been. Ironically, and albeit in voices and ideas that are hard to hear and understand (many invisible in the lower earth; others silenced), it is in China that the idea of order is battled over most.

My argument about the importance of being human is not an argument against either science or economics. Science itself, as Einstein and Fang Lizhi so powerfully demonstrated, is an extraordinary, and extraordinarily valuable, pursuit of knowledge. Economics, as a sub-set of science, can deliver tremendous insights into the ways in which we organise both the production of what we want and need and the distribution of the same. China's story reminds us, however, that the science of knowledge and the economics of life are dependent on human qualities, and that both are highly vulnerable to the risks of a single top-down mind.

From the beginning of time, it was Fuxi's subjectively human questions that unlocked the secrets of the cosmos. And from the earliest of the known shamans through to the present-day intellectuals who have inherited their questioning spirit, Chinese minds have argued that the pursuit of order without the qualities of being human is a dangerous risk for all. Confucius argued that where wealth and the efficiency of wealth-creation are valued over humanity, chaos will prevail. Zhuangzi poured scorn on the idea that a mind without humility could hold any knowledge at all. The poet prince Qu Yuan warned that it is our humanity that makes us fight for a better world and thus protects us from the terrors of tyranny. Wang Yangming, the Ming dynasty minister, argued that no investigation of things is worth its salt unless it is conducted with a human conscience – and that knowledge is only knowledge if the human qualities are consulted. As Kang Youwei crafted the big dream of a *Da Tong* Great Unity, Liang Qichao looked at all of the practical ways in which a people could come to think for themselves. The Hunanese Tan Sitong gave his life for the dream of an independently questioning mind. Li Dazhao urged a city youth to go and find their brothers in the fields. Peng Pai, the landlord's son, battled for peasants to have a voice. Wang Shiwei insisted that writing was an art of human truth. Fang Lizhi argued that no science can be science without the questions of the human mind.

Across China's time, in stories that were, I regret, too numerous to be told in the pages of this book, thousands of men and women have famously and bravely battled against the single top-down mind. They are familiar to readers who know the tale of how China came to think about order the way that it does; they are well known by the Chinese themselves. To these must be added the millions of people who became human portents across the ages: men and women whose miseries eventually became torrents of rage so powerful that they upset every top-down calculation of order, including those calculations concerned with the production and distribution of wealth.

To such stubborn humanists – among whose number are counted many who would, like Einstein and Fang Lizhi, be considered *true* scientists – the suspension of our human qualities is a real and present risk to the peace and security of the eight billion people on our planet, as it is to the planet itself. To describe such a suspension of human qualities as a temporary interruption necessary for the achievement of a greater utopian goal – say, the hundred years that Deng Xiaoping estimated it would take for China to finally realise the Marxist dream or the higher gdp, so coveted by the states of the world – is the greatest risk of all.

While China is so often associated with the triumphalism of the single top-down mind, my sense is that China's greatest heroes would weep not only at China today, but at the state of the world at large. From the ancient spirits of Fuxi, Qu Yuan and Zhuangzi, even Confucius (without the 'ism'), and the early Crouching Dragon, Zhuge Liang, to the later Tan Sitong, Kang Youwei, Liang Qichao, as well as the teachers and the students who laid the foundations of what they hoped would be a new China in the early twentieth century, including the foundations of the Communist Party, all would be shocked that the ancient question of human order remains as much a hostage to a single top-down mind as it was at the time of their lives. And my experience is that while the Party's promoted unity may have raised an official mist – a mist compounded by the fact that so few foreigners know the history, the geography and the language required to have a substantive conversation – many Chinese think as deeply, if not far more deeply, about this tragedy as anyone in the West. Indeed, given that, for the Chinese, the story of order has been both epic *and* human, the question of its present reality and its future possibilities is not dismissed as an abstract matter of politics, but is seen as the very personal experiences of oceans of human lives.

In looking at China as the story of the state with its single top-down mind, we miss the most obvious of its qualities: China is a land of beings who are as human as everyone else in the world. Over the last five thousand years, its people have asked some of the biggest questions known to man. And those people have included, and continue to include, some of the greatest hearts and minds on earth. And in concentrating our thoughts on the Party's ever-greater execution of economic productivity, rather than its ever-greater taming of human qualities not just to systems but to the idea of a global battle of the Chinese people against the rest of the world, we fail to look beyond the state to the people – including people within the Party as well as in the Chinese world at large. In so doing, we simply make it increasingly likely that we will all – the West, China and everyone else – end up in the ancient Zhou's catastrophic war of all against all: the war that so many of China's people have, across their history and so rightly, feared.

Are we really going to watch as the idea of the world as a realm of 'objective' states gets bigger and bigger? And as the realm of the objective state gets bigger, are we really going to look on as human beings are rolled into ever-bigger systems without a voice or identity beyond the powers of production and consumption? Are we really going to let our 'bigger' states battle it out until our world becomes a small group of competing regions, and then on until one – perhaps something like the state of Qin? – comes to rule all?

Most importantly, are we really not going to learn one of the most fundamental lessons that China has to teach us, and for which so many risked their lives to stand up so that we should hear the echo of their voices and not forget? The lesson that, for there to be any order in a state anywhere in the world, there needs to be a people with the human qualities on which all of our futures depend?

We continue to imagine that there is still a human world, even as it increasingly appears that the human world has been narrowed to the common denominator of economics. Indeed, we seem to have no name for our common 'state' of the wider world than the 'global economy'. And the Party's China stands before us, seemingly as evidence that the only way for a state to achieve any order at all is for the state to order more.

But, as so many Chinese have dreamed across the ages, a China that reconciles itself with its people on the basis of a conviction that human empathy is the foundation of civilisation could, of all states in the world, be the one to give us a model for finding a more human idea of order for a very big population of people, on a planet that is feeling increasingly small. Certainly, the story of its pursuit of order makes it the place through which we can see most clearly the difference that a dream might make.

Is the idea of a China where the Party and the people find a way to talk to each other, a naïve dream? Maybe.

Is it impossible? For all of our sakes, I hope not.

ALL UNDER HEAVEN?

I know that all good books are expected to end with a firm conclusion, and that any self-respecting book about China should provide the patient reader with a crystal clear prediction for what will come next, including a bet on whether or not China will 'collapse'. But this is not how this book will end. If one learns anything from the earliest of China's times, it is the wise recognition that nothing really ends: it just keeps changing. I have not written this book only to tell you that China changes. But I have written it to say that nothing, in China as anywhere else, is as black and white as it seems.

All Under Heaven began with a question: what are China's dreams of order? I set out to answer it through the story of the people who lived in the lands that we know today as China from the beginning of time to the present day. I found that the question of what order was, and what it was not, had been asked across those lands for five thousand years. And while the people of those lands have not yet got an answer that they can all agree upon, the fact that their story begins at the very point of man's earliest settlement gives them an unparalleled perspective. For some Chinese, the length of the story is a burden; for others, it is a triumph. Whichever view one takes, what is remarkable about it is what it tells us, through the trials and tribulations of so many thousands of years, about what it means to be a people, what it means to have a state, and what happens to human beings on the long journey to 'civilisation'.

At every point in writing this book, most of which was written in China, I was struck by how similar the events of the past were to those of the present. I was equally struck, at every point, by how similar were the questions faced by each of the changing Chinese dynasties over time, to questions that we all confront today. We can, and many do, devote our time to guessing where China will go next – up, down; richer, poorer; angrier, happier; together, apart; in peace, or at war. The stories in this book may well help us to think more carefully both about what we are asking and what the future might bring. But this would, in my small opinion, be to miss the point – and to miss the most remarkable thing that China's story reveals. Not the glittering train or how to get rich in five easy steps, or even how to rule the world, but the five thousand year old question of what it means to be Chinese. And in that question, what it means to be human: whether human as beings in a society of other beings, as beings within a state which does not approve of being subjectively human, or even as human beings who decide to try to leave the world behind. These are powerful questions within a question, which, seen through the best Chinese eyes, are answered in terms of putting ourselves in other people's shoes, of acknowledging the integrity of telling the truth as it is, of taking responsibility for our own actions, and of being responsible not only for our fellow man but for everything else that lives together with us on this earth.

By the time that I wrote the last words of this book, I had come to the conclusion that when the shamans began to observe the possibilities of nature's order all those thousands of years ago, we faced a choice: to settle into society, or not. Having made our choice, as time went on, the power of any individual to make that choice again diminished, even as society moved inexorably towards the strength of a state. We were then left with a question: not whether or not we want to live in a state (that choice is no longer ours to make), but what kind of a state we want to live in. To take Lu Xun's question: do we want to live in a counterfeit paradise or a good hell? And if we choose to live in a good hell can we, as human beings, make it any better by being the best humans that we can be?

From the beginning, and after twenty-five years of living in China, it was clear to me that this would be a book not just about China but about what China, as the microcosm of the world that it has for so long been, makes us think about our own world and ourselves: ourselves as other states, ourselves as other peoples, ourselves as other human beings. And in doing my own subjective thinking, as I wrote, I found that I could not forget a set of words that I had read right at the very beginning:

'There is a spirit which naturally is
Found within one's person.
Now it goes, now it comes.
None can conceive of it.
Lose it, inevitably there is disorder.
Obtain it, inevitably there is order.
If reverently you clear its dwelling
Place
The quintessential will
Spontaneously come.
If you achieve this state, you can govern the whole world.'

These words are attributed to the Duke of Zhou (and recorded in the seventh century BCE text of *The Guanzi*). That does not make them right, but it does mean they were probably written by a man with time on his hands to think, and with the first two and a half thousand years of China's story in his thoughts. Before states became so big that hermits would struggle to find the freedom to climb a mountain. Before the world separated into visible and invisible people. Before systems started to do the work of human minds and move us on into a world that we have not yet quite understood, but which is probably not, quite, the world that we think we live in.

If anyone were to ask me whether China (or any of us) will find its own dreams, I think those words would be my answer. And if anyone were to ask me to sum up the extraordinary journey that has been described in this book, I think my answer would be the same:

'If you try to possess it, you will destroy it: if you try to hold on to it – you will lose it.'

All Under Heaven? It is not just a question for China. It is a question for us all.

*We have created and composed these writings ... as a
means to knot the net of the Way and its Potency,
and weave the web of humankind and its affairs,
above, investigating them in heaven,
below, examining them on earth,
and in the middle, comprehending them through patterns.*

*Thus, numerous are the words we have composed
And extensive are the illustrations we have provided,
Yet we still fear that people will depart from the root and
follow the branches.*

The Huainanzi (second century BCE)

KEY SOURCES AND FURTHER READING:
A SHORT BIBLIOGRAPHIC NOTE

The story of China's dreams of order is told through a vast and varied literature. I have highlighted a very small selection of the many works that were consulted in the research on which *All Under Heaven* is based. Each has been chosen either because it illustrates an important point made, or because it offers a deeper perspective into times and issues described which may be of interest to the general reader. Some of the later works are novels: more than in many other parts of the world, much of China's truth is coded in its fiction. Most of the historical works are by academics, distilling decades of scholarship (and usually published by university presses, 'UP's); *All Under Heaven* would not have been possible without their work, and while I appreciate that this is a very different kind of book, I hope that it will bring many new readers to their extraordinary research.

The very last part of the book, the period from 1989 to 2014, draws on my own experience of the time, including much professional research and many conversations, as well as on published works.

General Reference
There are a number of histories of China: the greatest in size and scholarly insight is the 15 volume *Cambridge History of China* – with an additional volume on the ancient history of China (Cambridge UP, from 1978 onwards). Chronologically ordered, each of these volumes contains a series of essays addressing detailed aspects of life and thought across each period of China's history. Far shorter, and highly readable, is Patricia Ebrey's *Cambridge Illustrated History of China* (Cambridge UP, 1986).

The best detailed and readable history is Jonathan Spence's authoritative work which covers China from 1644 to the end of the twentieth century: *The Search for Modern China* (1990; 2nd edn, Norton, 1999).

Translations of the ancient texts can be found in the work of the Scottish missionary-scholar James Legge: *The Chinese Classics* (1861

– 1872; reprinted by Cosimo 2006), and in selected chapters of Max Muller's monumental *Sacred Books of the East* (which include works beyond China and are accessible at The Internet Sacred Text Archive, www.sacred-texts.com).

For a good geography with maps, see Caroline Blunden and Mark Elvins' *Cultural Atlas of China* (Equinox, 1983). For an excellent environmental history, see Mark Elvin's *Retreat of the Elephants* (Yale UP, 2006).

On mythology, see Anne Birrell's *Chinese Mythology: An Introduction* (John Hopkins UP, 1999) and her translation of the *Classic of Mountains and Seas* (Penguin Classics, 2000). On cosmology, see Wolfram Eberhard's *A Dictionary of Chinese Symbols* (Routledge and Kegan Paul, 1986). On beliefs, see *The Religion of the Chinese People*, Marcel Granet (Basil Blackwell Oxford, 1975).

On philosophy and political thought, see Benjamin Schwarz' *The World of Thought in Ancient China* (Harvard UP, 1985), and the much shorter *Political Philosophy of the Middle Kingdom* by Tongdong Bai (Zed Books, 2012). For a sense of China's political philosophy in the context of the wider world, see Francis Fukuyama's *The Origins of Political Order, From Prehuman Times to the French Revolution* (Profile Books, 2011). See also *An Intellectual History of Modern China*, Merle Goldman and Leo Ou-fan Lee (Cambridge UP, 2002).

On cities and walls at various points in China's history see Paul Wheatley's *The Pivot of the Four Quarters, A Preliminary Enquiry into the Origins and Character of the Ancient Chinese City* (Edinburgh UP, 1971), Mark Edward Lewis' *The Construction of Space in Early China* (State University of New York Press, 1999), and Arthur Cotterell's *Imperial Capitals of China, an Inside View* (Pimlico, 2008). On Beijing, see Jasper Becker's *City of Heavenly Tranquility: Beijing in the History of China* (Oxford UP, 2006). See also Geremie Barmé's *The Forbidden City* (Harvard UP, 2012). On the 'Long Wall', see Julia Lovell's *The Great Wall: China Against the World, 1000 BC – AD 2000* (Grove Press, 2007).

On modern China, Graham Hutchings' *Modern China, A Guide to a Century of Change* (Harvard UP, 2001) is a wonderful reference work. *The China Leadership Monitor* is an excellent source of contemporary insight on politics and policy. *Chinasmack* offers uncensored coverage of some of the stranger sides of life on the ground. Mao's works can be found online at the Marxists Internet Archive (www.marxists.org).

Book I

Part 1 A Heavenly Empire

Chapter 1 The Mists of Time

The story of China's earliest ancient past is well told by archaeologists, led by K. C. Chang (1931 – 2001). It is K. C. Chang who confirms what I had guessed, namely that China's ideas of order emerged from a world of shamans; see, for example, *The Archeology of Ancient China* (4th edn, Yale UP, 1987). See also K. C. Wu's *The Chinese Heritage, A New and Provocative View of the Origins of Chinese Society* (Crown Publishers, 1982). For a sense of the shamans' world, see the poet-prince Qu Yuan's Heavenly Questions (in *Songs of the South: An Ancient Chinese Anthology of Poems by Qu Yuan and other Poets*, transl. David Hawkes, Oxford: Clarendon Press, 1985).

The story of the Hall of Light is told by the long-time China resident and scholar William Edward Soothill (1861 – 1935) in his now-rare work *The Hall of Light: A Study of Early Chinese Kingship* (Philosophical Library, New York, 1952).

For descriptions of the early migrations and settlements and of life, see the works of K. C. Chang, particularly, *The Archeology of Ancient China* and *The formation of Chinese Civilisation* (4th edn Yale UP 1999 and 2005; also *Art, Myth and Ritual: the Path to Political Authority in China* (Harvard UP 1988).

For a description of the DNA links between the early Chinese and the earliest humans (those who walked out of Africa roughly 70,000 years ago), see Spencer Wells *The Journey of Man: A Genetic Odyssey* (Random House, 2004).

Chapter 2 A Heavenly People

The opening account of life in the fields of ancient China is drawn from the descriptions of Marcel Granet in *Chinese Civilisation* (Routledge, 1997).

For a sense of the mythological past (including a debate about whether the Shang were preceded by an earlier dynasty, known as the Xia), see Sarah Allan *The Shape of the Turtle: myth, art, and cosmos in early China* (SUNY Press, 1981) and *The Myth of the Xia Dynasty* (Journal of the Royal Asiatic Society, 1984). Roland Stoerckx's *The Animal and the Daemon in Early China* (SUNY Press, 2002) is a wonderful account of how nature provided the pattern for China's ideas of order.

K. C. Chang's *Shang Civilisation* (Yale UP, 1980) describes life under the Shang (including the flight of the black-haired people, a phenomenon seen from questions regularly engraved on the oracle bones). On the oracle bones and their meaning, see David Keightley's *Sources of Shang History: The Oracle Bone Inscriptions of Bronze Age China* (California UP, 1978). On Shang cities, Mark Elvin's *Retreat of the Elephants* (Yale UP, 2006) suggests that the Shang ruled over a population of 4 – 4 .5 million people divided between those who lived within walled cities and those who tilled the fields without). Elvin also describes the garrison-like nature of Shang cities, noting that it would have taken 3,500 men, working 200 days a year, over 10 years to build the early Shang capital of 'Aodu'. The story of the construction and mechanics of Shang cities (including the cosmological principles on which they were modelled (designed to reflect Heaven on earth) is told by Paul Wheatley's *Pivot of the Four Quarters* (Edinburgh UP, 1971).

The story of Zhuanxu's cutting of communications with heaven is told by K. C. Chang in *Art Myth and Ritual* (Harvard UP, 1988)

Chapter 3   Heaven on Earth?

The 'Martial' opera described in the opening paragraph of this chapter draws on Edward Shaughnessy's contribution to *Before Confucius*, in *From Liturgy to Literature: the Ritual Contexts of the Earliest Poems in the Book of Poetry* (SUNY Press, 1997). For an account of the importance of music in harmonising hearts and minds, see Lothar von Falkenhausen *Suspended Music: Chime Bells in the Culture of Bronze Age China* (University of California Press, 1994).

The idea of the Mandate of Heaven first appears in The Great Declaration, 1047 ('The iniquity of Shang is full, Heaven gives command to destroy it'). Seven hundred years later, during the time of the Warring States, one of Confucius' followers (Mencius) would observe that '(i)t was by humanity that the three dynasties gained the throne, and by not being human that they lost it.'

On Zhou cities, see Mark Lewis' chapter *The City State in Spring and Autumn China*, in Mogens Hansen's *A Comparative Study of Thirty City-State Cultures* (Royal Danish Academy of Sciences, 2000). For an illustration of the cities' detailed attention to correspondences between heaven and earth, see *The Annals of Lu Buwei* (transl. John Knoblock and Jeffrey Riegel, Stanford UP, 2000), which also describes the idea of yin and yang as a constant revolution. In *Retreat of the Elephants*, Mark Elvin notes that the climate of northern China changed considerably during the time of the Zhou – which may account for the extreme meticulousness. The Duke of Zhou's thoughts on meditation are set out in *The Zhou Li* (the Rites of Zhou, attributed to the Duke of Zhou). There are many versions of the *I Ching*. One of the most highly regarded is Richard Wilhelm's translation (with a foreword by Carl Jung) (Princeton UP, 1967).

What Confucius really thought is still being argued about. Key texts attributed to him are *The Analects, The Great Learning and The Cultivation of the Mean* (Penguin Classics). The clearest and most detailed descriptions of what he is thought to have said are found in the text of Mencius. The clearest insights into what he probably said and how that has been interpreted over the millennia can be found in Benjamin Schwarz' *The World of Thought in Ancient China* (see above). For a fascinating account of the story of writing and ideas (including the intellectual descendants of the shamans who became the Duke of Zhou's scholarly bureaucrats) see Mark Lewis' *Writing and Authority in Early China* (SUNY Press, 1999).

There are many translations of the *Dao De Jing*; my favourite is Martin Palmer's *The Illustrated Tao Te Ching* (Vega, 2003). For translations of the works of Zhuangzi, Mozi and the works of the most important 'legalists' (Xunzi, and Han Feizi), see Burton Watson's translations (Columbia UP, 2003). The competing ideas of the Confucians, the pursuers of the Dao and the legalists, are beautifully described by the early twentieth century English sinologist Arthur Waley in *Three Ways of Thought in Ancient China* (Stanford UP, 1939). For a deeper look at the intellectual battles that began at this time and have continued ever since, see A. C. Graham's *Disputers of the Tao* (Open Court, 1989).

Chapter 4   A Single Heart

The battle for Shangdang is known as the Battle of Changping (after the area to the south in which it was fought). The loss of Shangdang marked a crucial turning point in the Warring States. For an idea of what a Qin attack might have felt like, see Zhang Yimou's film *Hero* (2002).

The Qin dynasty is excellently described by Timothy Brook in *The Early Chinese Empires: Qin and Han* (Harvard UP, 2010). The ideas of Qin are powerfully illustrated by *The Book of Lord Shang* (transl. J.L.L. Duyvendak, The Lawbook Exchange, 2011), and well described by Derk Bodde in his now-rare work, *China's First Unifier: A Study of the Qin Dynasty as Seen in the Life of Li Si* (E. J. Brill, 1938). On the violence of the Qin (and earlier dynasties), see Mark Edward Lewis' *Sanctioned Violence in Early China* (SUNY Press, 1989). Arthur Cotterell provides a very readable account of the life of the First Qin Emperor (with illustrations), in *The First Emperor of China* (Macmillan, London, 1981).

For an account of the *chang cheng* long wall, (from the earliest times to the present day, including its American-inspired recasting as the 'Great Wall') see Julia Lovell's *The Great Wall, China Against The World, 1000 BC – AD 2000* (Atlantic Books, 2006).

Part 2   Heaven's Heart

Chapter 1   One Heaven, One Earth?

For a wonderful description of life in the Tang dynasty, see Edward Schafer's *The Golden Peaches of Samarkand* (California UP, 1963); see also Charles Benn, *Daily Life in Traditional China: The Tang Dynasty* (Greenwood Press, 2002).

China's battles against nomadic tribes are well described by Nicola di Cosmo in *Ancient China and its Enemies: The Rise of Nomadic Power in East Asian History* (Cambridge UP, 2004). For a description of the Xiongnu, see David Christian, *A History of Russia, Central Asia and Mongolia, Volume 1, Inner Eurasia from pre-history to the Mongol Empire* (Wiley-Blackwell, 1998). The story of Zhang Qian is told by Sima Qian in *The Records of the Grand Historian, Han Dynasty II* (transl. Burton Watson, Columbia UP, 1995).

For an idea of the arguments made in the 'conquest debates', see Mark Edward Lewis' *The Construction of Space in early China*. The arguments are not dissimilar to the present debates about Chinese foreign policy and militarisation. The supremacy of Confucianism over legalism was finally secured by the triumph of the Confucians in the debates known as the White Tiger Discussions (*bohu luntang*) which took place in 79 BCE.

There are many competing theories about the origin of the Mongols (who were not the only 'northern barbarians'). They first came to the attention of the Chinese as a tribe under the Shiwei clan of the Xianbei; some say that they were remnants of the old Xiongnu; others that they emerged from the Xianbei; given that both were confederations of tribes in an area that was constantly swirling with nomads, both or neither may be true.

Mark Edward Lewis tells the story of the Han Dynasty in *The Early Chinese Empires: Qin and Han* (Harvard UP, 2010); he goes on to cover the period from the Three Kingdoms to the end of the Sui in *China Between Empires: the Northern and Southern Dynasties* (Harvard UP, 2011), and then to tell the story of the Tang Dynasty in *China's Cosmopolitan Empire* (Harvard UP, 2009).

For a sense of the time of the Three Kingdoms in general, and Zhuge Liang in particular, see John Woo's film *Red Cliff* (2008).

For a discussion of the complications of race at this time, see Marc Abramson, *Ethnic Identity in Tang China* (Pennsylvania UP, 2011).

The ideas of Zhu Xi (Chu Hsi in Wade-Giles) can be seen in *Learning to be a Sage: Selections from the Conversations of Master Chu* (transl. Daniel K Gardner, University of California Press, 1990). For a fascinating account of dissent among Song dynasty intellectuals, see Alfreda Merck, *Poetry and Painting in Song China: The Subtle Art of Dissent* (Harvard University

Asia Centre, 2000). For a highly readable story of Chinngis Khan, see Jack Weatherford's *Genghis Khan and the Making of the Modern World* (Crown, 2004).

For thoughts on how the Chinese of the various times saw themselves and their land, see Richard Smith, *Chinese Maps* (Oxford UP, 1996).

Chapter 2   A Bright Idea

Geremie Barmé's *Forbidden City* (Harvard UP, 2012) is a succinct masterpiece. May Holdsworth & Caroline Courtauld offer a wonderfully visual account in *The Forbidden City: The Great Within* (Odyssey Publications, 1998). For those able to travel, there is little to compare with a combined visit to the Forbidden City in Beijing and the Palace Museum in Taibei (where many of the objects that once adorned the Forbidden City are displayed).

The story of the Ming dynasty (including the story of how a changing climate terrorised the Ming rulers, as well as the battle about the meaning of 'investigating things') is well told by Timothy Brook in *The Troubled Empire: China in the Yuan and Ming Dynasties* (Harvard UP, 2010). (The more detailed story of the weather and order is well told by Mark Elvin in *Who was Responsible for the Weather? Moral Meteorology in Late Imperial China* in *Beyond Joseph Needham* (University of Chicago Press, 1998)). Brook goes on to provide a wonderful description of wealth and its costs in daily life in *The Confusions of Pleasure, Commerce and Culture in Ming China* (University of California Press, 1998). See also Jonathan Spence's *Return to Dragon Mountain: Memories of a Late Ming man* (Norton, 2008). Craig Clunas' *Empire of Great Brightness: Visual and Material Cultures of Ming China, 1368 – 1644* (University of Hawai'i Press, 2007) is a visual delight as well as an interesting source on state intelligence and violence. For a fascinating account of the imperial examination system see Ichisada Miyazaki's *China's Examination Hell: Civil Service Examinations of Imperial China* (Yale UP, 1981).

For more detail on policy, economics and eunuchs, see Albert Chan's *The Glory and Fall of the Ming Dynasty* (University of Oaklahoma Press, 1982) and Ray Huang's *1587 A Year of No Significance: the Ming Dynasty in Decline* (Yale UP, 1981). For a deeper account of the emperors, see John W Dardess' *Ming China, 1368 – 1644: A Concise History of a Resilient Empire* (Rowman & Littlefield, 2011). The story of Zheng He is well told by Timothy Brook in *The Troubled Empire* (see above); a more detailed account can be found in Ma Huan's fascinating *Overall Survey of the Ocean's Shores, 1433* (transl. J. V. G. Mills, Cambridge University Press for the Hakluyt Society).

The story of Asian trade (interwoven with the story of silver) is important in understanding the latter fortunes and misfortunes of the Ming. Timothy Brook provides a wonderful perspective in *Mr. Selden's Map of China: The*

Spice Trade, a Lost Chart and the South China Sea (Rotterdam 2014); a shorter version of the story is told by the journalist Bill Hayton in his recent work *The South China Sea: The Struggle for Power in Asia* (Yale UP, 2014).

Chapter 3 This World and Beyond

The opening of this chapter was inspired by an eighth century (Tang dynasty) poem, by Wang Wei, called *Passing Xiangji Temple*; it can be accessed at Jean Ward's Wang Wei Remembered (Lulu.com).

Derk Bodde describes Chinese ideas of retreat in *The World of Nature*, in *China's Cultural Tradition, What and Whither? Source Problems in World Civilisations* (Holt Reinhart and Winston, Inc.,1957). The earliest recorded account of a flight from the world is by Qu Yuan in his epic poem *Li Sao* (*Encountering Trouble*, in *Songs of the South*, Penguin Classics, 1985). Early accounts of hermits are also given in the *Book of the Later Han* (6 – 189 AD); Laozi's *Daodejing* captures the appeal of retreat. More rational arguments for becoming a hermit are made by Zhuangzi. Bill Porter's *Road to Heaven: Encounters with Chinese Hermits* provides a wonderful contemporary account of China's hermits (Counterpoint Press, 1993).

The story of the arrival of Buddhism in China is told in two short but beautiful books: Daisaku Ikeda's *The Flower of Chinese Buddhism* (transl. Burton Watson, Middleway Press, 2009) and Arthur Wright's *Buddhism in Chinese History* (Stanford UP, 1959). On the battle between Buddhism, Daoism and Confucianism during the first millennium, see Mark Edward Lewis, *China Between the Empires*, and *China's Cosmopolitan Empire* (see above). Meir Shahar gives a fascinating account of the Shaolin monastery in *The Shaolin Monastery: History, Religion, and the Chinese Martial Arts*, (University of Hawai'i Press, 2008). For a wonderful account of Buddhism from the personal perspective on a 20th century life, see Sun Shuyun's *Ten Thousand Miles without a Cloud* (Harper Collins, 2003).

The story of Daoism is told by Holmes Welch in *Taoism: The Parting of the Way* (Beacon Press, 1971); Holmes Welch and Anna Seidel gather an interesting set of essays in *Facets of Taoism* (Yale UP, 1979) as do Livia Kohn and Harold D. Roth in *Daoist Identity: History, Lineage and Ritual* (University of Hawai'I Press, 2002). The influence of Daoism on the Tang Dynasty is told by Stephen R Bokenkampf in *Time After Time: Taoist Apocalyptic History and the Founding of the Tang Dynasty* (Academica Sinica, 1994).

Henri Maspero's *The Mythology of Modern China* in Asiatic Mythology (George G. Harrap & Co., 1932) provides a wonderful description of all beliefs, including the most popular. For an account of the battling fabric of Chinese beliefs, see *Unruly Gods: Divinity and Society in China*, ed. Meir Shahar and Robert P Weller (University of Hawai'i Press, 1996).

The most accessible (and shortest) version of the story of the Monkey King is the abridged 'Monkey' by Arthur Waley (Penguin Classics, 1942). By far and away the best translation of the story of the Monkey King is *The Journey to the West* by Anthony C. Yu (4 magical volumes; University of Chicago Press, 1977 – 1983).

Part 3 Whose Heaven?

Chapter 1 Someone Else's Sky

The events at Shanhai Guan are described in the wonderful work of Gertraude Roth Li, *State Building Before 1644* (Vol. 9, Part 1, Cambridge History of China. Cambridge UP, 2002).

For excellent descriptions of the Manju see Pamela Kyle Crossley's *The Manchus* (Wiley-Blackwell, 2002) and Mark Elliot's *The Manchu Way: The Eight Banners and Ethnic Identity in Late Imperial China* (Stanford UP, 2001). The Manju Qing's hunting grounds are beautifully described by Philippe Forêt's *Mapping Chengde* (University of Hawai'i Press, 2000).

The story of the Qing empire is very well told by William T. Rowe in *China's Last Empire: The Great Qing* (Harvard UP, 2009). The story of the Qing conquests is wonderfully told by Peter C Perdue's *China Marches West: The Qing Conquest of Central Eurasia* (Harvard UP, 2010). On the question of the Manju and their identity as the Qing dynasty, see Pamela Kyle Crossley's important *A Translucent Mirror* (California UP, 2002).

For excellent accounts of the reigns of Kangxi and Qianlong, see Jonathan Spence's *The K'ang-hsi Reign* and Alexander Woodside's *The Ch'ien-Lung Reign* (Vol. 9, Part 1, Cambridge History of China); see also Jonathan Spence's *Emperor of China: Self Portrait of Kang-hsi* (Knopf, 1974). The Hall of Mental Cultivation and of its Qing dynasty occupants is well described by Geremie Barmé's *Forbidden City* (see above).

The economics of the early Qing are told by Ramon H Myers and Yeh-chien Wang in *Economic Developments* (Vol. 9, Part 1, Cambridge History of China); see also Ramon Myers' wider *The Chinese Economy: Past and Present* (Wadsworth 1980).

The story of the Jesuits (and of the battle between Kangxi's ideas of an effective temporal order and the Pope's dream of an empire of souls that would come to be known as the 'Chinese Rites Controversy') is told by Jonathan Spence in *The Memory Palace of Matteo Ricci* (Viking Penguin, 1984). See also Spence's wonderful tale, *The Question of Hu* (Vintage, 1989), the thought-provoking story of a man who found himself caught between the two.

Chapter 2   Rivers of Fortune

This chapter owes much to Wiilliam T. Rowe's masterful account of late Qing dynasty Hankou, including its inhabitants and guilds: *Hankow: Commerce and Society in a Chinese City, 1796 – 1889* (Stanford UP, 1984); see also Rowe's parallel work, *Hankow: Conflict and Community in a Chinese City, 1796 – 1895* (Stanford UP, 1985).

For a wonderful description of life in Qing China during the 18th century, see Susan Naquin and Evelyn Rawski's *Chinese Society in the Eighteenth Century* (Yale UP, 1989). See also Benjamin Elman's *The Class of 1761: Examinations, State and Elite in Eighteenth Century China* (Stanford UP, 2004). For a rich description of the rise and fall of a Chinese family whose fortunes depended upon imperial favour, see Cao Xueqin's classic Qing dynasty novel *Dream of the Red Chamber* (transl. David Hawkes as *The Story of the Stone*, Penguin Classics, 1973). Cao's own family fortunes were made as Han loyalists to the Manju Qing with Cao's grandfather becoming a childhood friend of the Kangxi Emperor; they collapsed with the death of the Kangxi Emperor and the confiscation of their properties, the imprisonment of the family patriarch and the impoverishment of the family members, including a then very young Cao Xueqin. For a sense of the wealth created by China's rivers of fortunes and the challenges faced by their descendants, see Zhang Yimou's film *Raise the Red Lantern* (1991), set in the 1920s, and based on the true story of the Qiao family (scions of a Shanxi banker).

The world of rural China is masterfully described and analysed, region by region, by George W. Skinner in his classic work *Marketing and Social Structure in Rural China* (Journal of Asian Studies, 1964 – 1965). Skinner also provides an excellent account of the evolution of Chinese cities in his edition of essays *The City in Late Imperial China* (Stanford UP, 1977). The story of Shanghai is told by Linda Cooke Johnson in *Shanghai: From Market Town to Treaty Port, 1074 – 1858* (Stanford UP, 1995).

Arthur Waley provides a magnificent and succinct account of the opium wars (including a wonderful account of Lin Zexu and his letters to Queen Victoria) in *The Opium War Through Chinese Eyes* (Stanford UP, 1958). Peter Perdue's online course materials on *The First Opium War – The Anglo-Chinese War of 1839 – 1842* are a wonderful example of a fascinating and accessible academic work (ocw.mit.edu).

Stephen Platt provides an excellent account of the Taiping rebellion (including the way in which the Western 'opium warriors' got tangled up in the story) in *Autumn in the Heavenly Kingdom: China, The West and the Epic Story of the Taiping Civil War* (Atlantic Books, 2012). Jonathan Spence tells the story of Hong Xiuquan in *God's Chinese Son: The Taiping Heavenly Kingdom of Hong Xiuquan* (Norton, 1996).

Mary Clabaugh Wright's *The Last Stand of Chinese Conservatism*

(Stanford UP, 1962) provides a fascinating account of the rise and ideas of the self-strengtheners.

Chapter 3   Imagine a People

The inspiration for the title of this chapter, and a source of many thought-provoking insights, is a collection of essays: *Imagining the People: Chinese Intellectuals and the Concept of Citizenship, 1890 – 1920* (ed. Joshua Fogel and Peter Zarrow; East Gate, 1997). The story of the Hunanese is magnificently told by Stephen Platt in his *Provincial Patriots: The Hunanese and Modern China* (Harvard UP, 2007). The revolutionaries and their ideas are beautifully described by Jonathan Spence in *The Gate of Heavenly Peace: The Chinese and Their Revolution, 1895 – 1980* (Viking Press, 1982).

The story of the Battle of Weihaiwei was pieced together from many different historical sources.

The geopolitics of the Great Game are importantly described by Halford Mackinder in *The Geographical Pivot of History* (The Geographical Journal, 1904).

Joseph Esherick's *The Origins of the Boxer Uprising* (University of California Press, 1987) is an excellent account of the causes of the Boxer rebellion, which are far more important than the more popular stories of the Boxers' defeat.

On the impact of the ideas of West (many of which were brought to China through the translations of Yan Fu), on the rise of the self-strengtheners, and on the pursuit of *fuqiang* wealth and power, see Benjamin Schwarz *In Search of Wealth and Power: Yen Fu and the West* (Harvard UP, 1964). More recently, see Orville Schell and John Delury's *Wealth and Power, China's Long March to the Twenty-First Century* (Random House, 2013).

The ideas of Kang Youwei are set out in Kung-ch'uan Hsiao's *A Modern China and a New World: K'ang Yu-wei, Reformer and Utopian* (Washington UP, 1975). A more readable account is given by Young-Tsu Wong in *The Search for Material Civilisation: Kang Youwei's Journey to the West* (Taiwan Journal of East Asian Studies, Vol. 5, No. 1, 2008). Liang Qichao's story is told by Hao Chang in *Liang Ch'I-ch'ao and Intellectual Transition in China* (Harvard UP, 1971) and, more recently, by Pankaj Mishra in *From the Ruins of Empire* (Farrar, Strauss & Giroux, 2012). Liang Qichao set out his thoughts on America in *The Power and Threat of America* (1903; which can be found in *Land Without Ghosts: Chinese Impressions of America from the Mid-Nineteenth Century to the Present*, eds R. David Arkush, Leo O. Lee; University of California Press, 1993).

The story of Sun Yatsen is told by Orville Schell and John Delury in chapter 6 of *Wealth and Power* (see above). The story of Sun's kidnapping is told in *Kidnapped in London: being the story of my capture by, detention* at and release from the Chinese Legation, London (1897; reprinted by the Foreign Language Teaching and Research Press, 2012).

The story of the Dowager Empress Cixi is told by Orville Schell and John Delury in chapter 4 of *Wealth and Power* (see above). A more controversial account is given by Jung Chang in *The Concubine Who Launched Modern China: Empress Dowager Cixi* (Anchor, 2014).

By the mid nineteenth century, photographic images of the Qing dynasty begin to appear: see Liu Heung Shing's *China in Revolution* (Hong Kong UP, 2011).

Book II

The divergence between traditionally accepted China history and more recent 'revisionist' works is extreme in these two parts, with the Party's view of history directly challenged by many relatively recent authors. As highlighted in the Author's Note, where the stories are highly divergent, key revisionist works are referenced. The fact that such divergent views can exist, and that the past works of highly regarded China scholars accepted many 'facts' which are now contested, is an indication of the challenge of an order which places harmony above truth.

Part 4   Up in the City

Chapter 1   Midnight

Xu Zhimo's poems can be found in *Xu Zhimo, Selected Poems* (Oleander Press, 2012).

The opening to this chapter draws on the works of Chinese novels of the time.

For a beautiful description of the story of Republican Beijing, see Madeleine Yue Dong's book, *Republican Beijing, The City and Its Histories* (University of California Press, 2003). See also David Strand's *Rickshaw Beijing: City People and Politics in the 1920s* (University of California Press, 1989) and Stephen Haw's *Beijing, A Concise History* (Routledge, 2008). For a sense of the old and the new, see Jasper Becker's *City of Heavenly Tranquility: Beijing in the History of China* (Oxford UP, 2006). For a book on present-day Beijing that includes a perspective on the past, see *Beijing Time* by Michael Dutton, Hsiu-ju Stacy Lo and Dong Dong Wu (Harvard UP, 2010).

The story of the last emperor (including contemporary remarks on the last years of the Qing and the early Republic) is told by Reginald Fleming Johnston (the Scottish academic and British diplomat who became Puyi's tutor) in *Twilight in the Forbidden City* (Cambridge UP, 1934). It can also be seen in Bertolucci's film *The Last Emperor* (1987).

On the economics of Republican China, see Albert Feuerwerker's *Economic Trends in the Republic of China 1912 – 1949* (Center for Chinese Studies, University of Michigan, 1977).

The Republican era saw a flourishing of literature, as China's new generation of intellectuals turned their attention to describing the real life of the people. Of the many wonderful authors, see the works of the novelist and playwright, Lao She (1899 – 1966), whose *Camel Xiangzi* describes the life of a rickshaw driver (various translations, including *Rickshaw Boy* transl. Howard Goldblatt, Harper Perennial, 2010) and whose play, *Teahouse*, covers fifty years of change in the conversations of a teahouse, from 1898 – 1949 (transl. John Howard-Gibbon, China Books, 2013). See also Lu Xun's *Diary of a Madman* (transl. Julia Lovell, in *The Complete Fiction of Lu Xun*, Penguin Classics, 2009).

For a fascinating view of 1920s Beijing, see Sidney Gamble's *Peking, a Social Survey* (H. Milford, 1921), and the magical archive of his photographs available at Duke University's online library (www.library.duke.edu/digitalcollections/gamble).

For an account of the events of May 4, 1919, see Rana Mitter's *A Bitter Revolution: China's Struggle with the Modern World* (Oxford UP, 2005). See also Vera Schwarz' *The Chinese Enlightenment: Intellectuals and the Legacy of the May Fourth Movement* (University of California Press, 1986).

The story of Peking University and Cai Yuanpei was drawn together from many different sources, Chinese and Western. The original *honglou* red brick building of Peking University is now a museum and can be visited (29 Wusi Street, Dongcheng, Beijing).

The story of Liang Shuming is told by Guy S. Alitto in *The Last Confucian: Liang Shu-ming and the Chinese Dilemma of Modernity* (University of California Press, 1979). For an account of the impact of some of the foreign ideas that China was exploring, see David Kelly's *The Highest Chinadom: Nietzsche and the Chinese Mind, 1907 – 1989* in *Nietzche in Asia* (ed. G. Parkes, University of Chicago Press, 1991), and Tagore in China (eds Tan Chung and Amiya Dev, SAGE Publications, 2011).

The story of the 'science debates' is told by Zuoye Wang in *Saving China through Science: The Science Society of China, Scientific Nationalism, and Civil Society in Republican China* (Osiris, second Series, Vol. 17, Science and Civil Society (2002)), and by Wang Hui in *Scientific Worldview, Culture Debates, and the Reclassification of Knowledge in Twentieth-century China*, (Boundary 2, (2008)). China's science debates anticipated a later debate in 1930s Britain – described as a battle of 'cultures' (science versus humanism). The British battle was reprised 30 years later (in 1959) when it came to be known as the 'science wars', led by a battle between C. P. Snow and a

Cambridge Literary Critic F R Leavis, with Snow arguing for the superiority of science (see C P Snow, *The Two Cultures*, Rede Lecture, Cambridge May 7, 1959), and with Leavis arguing for the superiority of human values (and the study of the humanities).

For an account of the impact of the Japanese war on the civil war within China, see Rana Mitter's *China's War with Japan, 1937 – 1945: The Struggle for Survival* (Allen Lane, 2013).

Chapter 2   A Brave New World

The story of the Front Service Corp's 1938 journey (and the story of Ding Ling and the first part of her life) is told by Charles J. Alber in *Enduring the Revolution: Ding Ling and the Politics of Literature* (Praeger, 2001). Ding Ling's fictional account of He Yepin's execution was called *A Certain Night (Mouye)*; her loyal account of Communist reforms in 1930s China is set out in her novel, *The Sun Shines over the Sanggan River* (1948; Foreign Languages Press, 1984). For the story of the second part of Ding Ling's life, see Charles J. Alber, *Embracing the Lie: Ding Ling and the Politics of Literature in the Peoples Republic of China* (Praeger, 2004).

The story of Mao is told through many, now dramatically different, accounts. The classic work is Edgar Snow's still fascinating but now highly challenged *Red Star over China* (Penguin Books, 1972). The most dramatic of the revisionist works is Jung Chang and Jon Halliday's *Mao, the Unknown Story* (Vintage, 2007) which, based on the accounts of hundreds of those who were close to Mao, offers a compelling revision of the traditional story, albeit one which is challenged by many leading academics. Part of the controversy around the book results from the very different approaches taken by academics and non-academics, raising important and difficult questions about 'truth'. Jonathan Spence provides a very short and wonderfully readable account of Mao in *Mao Zedong: A Life* (Penguin Books, 1999).

The story of the evolution of the relationship between the Republican state and the secret societies (and of the road to the 1927 massacre of the Communists) is told by Joseph Fewsmith in *Party, State and Local Elites in Republican China: Merchant Organisations and Politics in Shanghai, 1890 – 1930* (University of Hawai'i Press, 1986). The role of China's secret societies, then and now, is important (and often overlooked).

The story of the Long March is heavily contested, with new works relying on first hand accounts and greater access to archives. The traditional account of the Long March is told by Harrison Salisbury in *The Long March: The Untold Story* (McGraw Hill, 1987). A far more credible account (drawing on first hand interviews and materials only recently made available) is given by Sun Shuyun in *The Long March* (Harper Perennial, 2007) who describes the Long March as the founding myth of the Party; see also Ed Jocelyn &

Andrew McEwan's *The Long March Remembered* (2006), and the accounts of the Long March in Jung Chang and Jon Halliday's *Mao, The Unknown Story (see above)*.

For an interesting account of the Russian choreography of the war between the Guomindang and the Communists, see Jung Chang and Jon Halliday's *Mao: The Unknown Story* (see above). For a fascinating account of China on the eve of the 1949 revolution, see A. Doak Barnett's *China on the Eve of Communist Takevoer* (Praeger, 1961).

For a first hand description of Yan'an, see Sidney Rittenberg's *The Man Who Stayed Behind* (with Amanda Bennett; Duke University Press, 2001). Rittenberg (born 1921) was an American journalist who went to China in 1944 and found his way to Yan'an; an occasional conduit for communications and an obvious target for suspicions of the West, he was imprisoned twice, once in 1949, for six years, and again, in 1968, for nearly 10 years.

For a description of Mao's art and literature campaign, see *Wild Lily, Prairie Fire: China's Road to Democracy, Yan'an to Tiananmen, 1942 – 1989* (ed. Gregor Benton & Alan Hunter; Princeton University Press, 1995). For a description of the techniques applied in thought reform, see Robert Lifton's *Thought Reform of Chinese Intellectuals: A Psychiatric Evaluation* (The Journal of Asian Studies, Vol. 16, 1956). Lifton's work was based on seventeen months of interviews with Chinese intellectuals who had managed to find their way to Hong Kong. For an understanding of the Party's idea of 'revolutionary' man and the impact of thought reform, see Theodore Hsi-En Chen, *The New Socialist Man* (Comparative Education Review, Vol. 13, No. 1, 1969).

On the ideas of those who wanted to build a bridge between the countryside and the cities, see Margherita Zanasi, *Far from the Treaty Ports: Fang Xianting and the Idea of Rural Modernity in 1930s China* (Modern China, Vol. 30, No. 1, 2004).

For a fascinating first-hand description of 1949 Beijing (including the search for books that would explain the new revolutionary order), see Derk Bodde's *Peking Diary – A Year of Revolution* (Henry Schuman Inc. New York, 1950).

Stuart Schram gives a wonderful account of Mao's ideas in *The Thought of Mao Tse-tung* (Cambridge UP, 1989). See also Roderick MacFarquhar, Timothy Cheek, Eugene Wu eds *The Secret Speeches of Chairman Mao: From the Hundred Flowers to the Great Leap Forward* (Council on East Asian Studies, Harvard UP, 1989). Mao's works (and speeches) can be found online at the Marxists Internet Archive (www.marxists.org/reference/archive/mao). On the 'withering away' of the state, see Solomon Bloom's *The "Withering Away" of the State* (Journal of the History of Ideas, Vol. 7, 1946).

On the Hundred Flowers campaign, see Roderick MacFarquhar's edition of essays *The Hundred Flowers Campaign and the Chinese Intellectuals*

(Octagon Books, 1974). See also Merle Goldman's *Literary Dissent in Communist China* (Harvard UP, 1967) and *China's Intellectuals and the State: In Search of a New Relationship* (eds Merle Goldman and Timothy Cheek, Harvard UP, 1987).

For an account of trade unions (and strikes) in the 1950s, see *Urban Spaces in Contemporary China: the potential for autonomy and community in post-Mao China,* (ed. Deborah S Davis, Cambridge University Press, 1995). For an account of life in a labour camp, written by an intellectual who spent 22 years – from 1957 to 1979 – in a camp in Ningxia, see Zhang Xianliang's novel *Half of Man is Woman* (transl. Martha Avery, Norton, 1986).

For a description of Liang Sicheng's architectural life, see Wilma Fairbank's *Liang and Lin: Partners in Exploring China's Architectural Past* (University of Pennsylvania Press, 2008); for a vision of the architecture that he loved, see Liang Ssu-ch'eng and Fairbank, *Chinese Architecture: A Pictorial History* (Dover, 2005). For a description of the 1959 National Day, see Sang Ye and Geremie R Barmé, *Thirteen National Days, a Retrospective* (China Heritage Quarterly, No. 17, 2009).

For contemporary descriptions of the revolutionary role and significance of the urban communes, see D. E. T. Luard, *The Urban Communes* (China Quarterly, No. 29, 1960), and Janet Saleff, *The Urban Communes and Anti-City Experiment in Communist China,* (China Quarterly, No. 29, 1967).

The story of Deng Tuo is told by Timothy Cheek in *Deng Tuo: Culture, Leninism and Alternative Marxism in the Chinese Communist Party* (Clarendon Press, 1997). The story of the Cultural Revolution is magisterially told by Roderick Macfarquhar in *Mao's Last Revolution* (Harvard University Press, 2008).

Chapter 3 Thinking Again

The poem describing the game of Go can be found in an article by Zu-yan Chen, *Great Chant on Observing Weiqi: An Archetype of Neo-Confucian Poetry* (Journal of the American Oriental Society, 2006). In the summer, it is still played in the street.

For a view of working life in 1970s China, see Michelangelo Antonioni's film *Chung Kuo Cina* (1972).

For an account of Fang Lizhi's work and life (including his 1972 article and the denunciations which followed), see James H Williams' *Fang Lizhi's Expanding Universe* (China Quarterly, 1990). See also Fang Lizhi's own words in the article *China's Despair and China's Hope* (transl. Perry Link, The New York Review of Books, 1989). For an account of the relationship between revolutionary China and Albert Einstein, see Danian Hu's *China and Albert Einstein: The Reception of the Physicist and His Theory in China, 1917 – 1979* (Harvard UP, 2005).

Life in post-Mao Beijing is well described by Martin King Whyte and William L Parish, *Urban Life in Contemporary China* (University of Chicago Press, 1984).

Life in post-Deng Beijing is well described in *Urban Spaces in Contemporary China: the potential for autonomy and community in post-Mao China* (ed. Deborah Davis, Cambridge UP, 1995).

The voices of the intellectuals are powerfully described in *Mao's Harvest: Voices from China's New Generation* (eds Helen Siu and Zelda Stern, Oxford UP, 1983). The political battles are described in *Sowing the Seeds of Democracy in China: Political Reform in the Deng Xiaopng Era* (ed. Merle Goodman, Harvard UP, 1994). The text of Wei Jinghsheng's 'Fifth Modernisation' can be found at www.weijingsheng.org. The changing role of Tiananmen is described by Wu Hung in *Remaking Beijing: Tiananmen Square and the Creation of a Political Space* (Reaktion Books, 2005).

Heshang, the documentary, can be accessed on YouTube. The series had such a powerful impact, and was so full of cultural references, that two exiled intellectuals, Su Xiaokang and Wang Luxiang, wrote *Deathsong of the River: a Readers' Guide to the Chinese TV Series Heshang* (transl. Richard Bodman and Pin Pin Wan, Cornell University East Asia Series, 1999).

The complex of economic and political challenges are described by Ken Lieberthal in *Governing China – From Revolution through Reform* (Norton, 1995). See also Maurice Meisner's *Mao's China and After, a History of the People's Republic* (The Free Press, 1999). Ezra Vogel's *Deng Xiaoping and the Transformation of China* (Harvard UP, 2013) offers important perspectives.

A first hand account of events from 1979 to 1989 can be found in Zhao Ziyang's personal recollections, published as *Prisoner of the State: The Secret Journal of Premier Zhao Ziyang* (ed. and transl. Bao Pu and Adi Ignatius, Simon & Schuster, 2010). The account was recorded by Zhao Ziyang in his courtyard prison, and hidden among his grandchildren's toys before being smuggled out of the country; banned in mainland China, it was published in Hong Kong, where it became a bestseller (with sales to visiting mainlanders as well as Hong Kong Chinese).

Part 5   Down in the Countryside
Many of the general works referred to in Part 4, including those on Mao, are also sources for Part 5.

Chapter 1   Snow in Summer

The story of the market was inspired by Sigrid Schmalzer's wonderful article *Breeding a Better China: Pigs, Practices and Place in a Chinese County, 1929 – 1937* (Geographical Review, Vol. 92, 2002).

The story of Ding Xian is told by Charles Hayford in *To The People,*

James Yen and Village China (Columbia University Press, 1990). See also Pearl Buck's interview with James Yen: *Tell the People, Talks with James Yen about the Mass Education Movement* (John Day & Co., 1945). Pearl Buck wrote *The Good Earth* (John Day & Co., 1931) a book about China's peasants which was a classic in its time but in the light of the new history, has become controversial. The story of medicine in the 'rural reconstruction' is told by Chen Zhiquan in *Medicine in Rural China: A Personal Account* (University of California Press, 1989).

The engagement of the intellectuals with the countryside is wonderfully described by Xiaorong Han in *Chinese Discourses on the Peasant, 1900 – 1949* (SUNY, 2005). See also Lu Xun's short story *Hometown* (1921). Chang-tai Hung's *Going to the People, Chinese Intellectuals and Folk Literature, 1918 – 1937* offers a fascinating insight into how the early students' journeys to the countryside shaped China's post-revolutionary culture. Sidney Gamble's photographs illuminate the countryside as well as the city (see above).

Fei Xiaotong's early works provide wonderful insights into the fabric of China's rural world, from *Peasant Life in China: A Field Study of Country Life in the Yangze Valley* (Routledge, 1939) to *Earthbound China* (University of Chicago Press, 1945) and *China's Gentry, Essays on Rural-Urban Relations* (rev. and ed. Margaret Park Redfield; University of Chicago Press, 1953). Morton Fried's *Fabric of Chinese Society* (Octagon, 1969) is a wonderful companion to the time. Liang Shuming's rural work is described by Guy Alitto in *The Last Confucian* (see above); it is also considered by Wu Shugang and Tong Binchang in *Liang Shuming's Rural Reconstruction Experiment and its Relevance for Building the New Socialist Countryside* (Contemporary Chinese Thought, Vol. 40, 2009). On the economics of the countryside, see G. William Skinner's thee-part work, *Marketing and Social Structure in Rural China* (see above).

Peng Pai's own story can be found in *Seeds of a Peasant Revolution: Report on the Haifeng Peasant Movement* (transl. Donald Holoch, Cornell University East Asia Papers, 1973). A very different story of Peng Pai is told by Jung Chang and Jon Halliday in *Mao: The Unknown Story* (see above) and by Fernando Galbiati in *Peng Pai and the Hailufeng Soviet* (Stanford UP, 1985). The contrasts are a reminder of how difficult it is to point to a historical 'truth'.

Chapter 2   Leaping Ahead

The account of Liu Lin village is based on Jan Myrdal's *Report from a Chinese Village* (Pantheon Books, 1965); Myrdal referred to it as 'Liu Ling' in his book. Like Edgar Snow's *Red Star Over China*, and Harrison Salisbury's *The Long March*, Myrdal's account is now seen more as an example of successful Party propaganda: the same propaganda heard and read by the Chinese of the time.

William Parish and Martin King Whyte provide a thorough account of the countryside under Mao in *Village and Family in Contemporary China* (University of Chicago Press, 1980). See also William Hinton's personal account of village life during this time in *Fanshen – A Documentary of Revolution in a Chinese Village* (1966; University of California Press, 1997). Hinton was an American farmer who was sent to China as a technician in 1948, and stayed on after the revolution, attaching himself to a land reform work team in Long Bow.

The story of the famine and the Party's reactions to it is best told by Yang Jisheng in *Tombstone: The Untold Story of Mao's Great Famine* (transl. Stacy Mosher and Guo Jian, Allen Lane, 2012); it is Yang who describes the 'five winds'. Sulamith Heins Potter and Jack Potter tell the post-Mao story of the peasants in *China's Peasants, The Anthropology of a Revolution*, (University of California, 1990).

Chapter 3   Winds, and More Winds

The account of Long Bow Village's power seizure is based on William Hinton's *Shenfan* (Random House, 1983).

William Hinton continues the story of the countryside with Shenfan. Having returned to the US in 1953 for a visit, he was swept up in the McCarthy investigations, and accused of anti-American behaviour; his passport confiscated, he remained in the US for fifteen years. Returning to China (and Long Bow Village), Hinton tells the story of the unravelling of the revolution. Hinton was a farmer and a revolutionary in his own right. Although I did not know that I would write *All Under Heaven*, Bill was one of the first people I met when I arrived in Beijing in 1989, and, when he wanted to use the early Joint Venture laws to help Long Bow Village find its feet in the new world, he became one of my first pro bono clients; his story was fascinating and he was one of the most straightforward people I have ever worked with.

The story of reform in the countryside is well told by Susan Whiting in *Power and Wealth in Rural China: The Political Economy of Institutional Change* (Cambridge UP, 2006).

The story of the sent-down students is well told by Thomas P Bernstein in *Up to the Mountains and Down to the Villages: The Transfer of Youth from Urban to Rural China* (Yale UP, 1977). For a description of the twists and turns of the Cultural Revolution (including the rise of the Red Guards and the counter-rise of the Rebel Red Guards), see Jonathan Unger's *Education Under Mao: Class and Competition in Canton Schools, 1960 – 1980* (Columbia UP, 1982). For the truth of a novel, see Dai Sijie's *Balzac and the Little Chinese Seamstress* (Vintage, 2001; also a film, written and directed by Dai Sijie). Dai spent four years in rural Sichuan in the early 1970s. The views of the students are captured in their own, very powerful, voices in *Mao's Harvest: Voices from China's New Generation* (see above).

The story of the transformation of the countryside from Mao through Deng is well told by Jonathan Unger's *The Transformation of Rural China* (M.E. Sharpe, 2002). The story of Wenzhou is wonderfully told both by Yia-Ling Liu in *The Private Economy and Local Politics in the Rural Industrialisation of Wenzhou* (China Quarterly, 1992), and by Anita Chan and Jonathan Unger in *Grey and Black: The Hidden Economy of Rural China* (Pacific Affairs, Vol. 85, 1982). The continuing post-Mao story of the peasants is well told by Sulamith Heins Potter and Jack Potter in *China's Peasants, The Anthropology of a Revolution* (see above). For a very human and thought-provoking account of what it was like to grow up in a small provincial town in the Cultural Revolution – and a wonderful insight into being Chinese, see Yu Hua's *Ten Words* (Gerald Duckworth & Co., 2012).

Book III

The chapters in this book draw as much on my personal experience (both professional and human) as on published works. Professionally, my work required a thorough understanding of the changes, including the evolving structure, politics and policies of the Party, the state and all kinds of business. I also ensured that it included an understanding of the impact on Chinese society and nature, and its implications for China in the wider world. From the early 2000s, this led to the preparation of detailed studies on both rural China and urban China; each was developed over a year of intense desk research and interviews. Humanly, I watched the news, saw the films, and listened to the stories that whispered across the city. Being directly affected by many of the changes, like every other Beijing resident, I explored them all at length with friends, both Chinese and foreign, and with the strangers one often meets in life. The popular and evolving commentary of the Party, of the intellectuals and of what the Party would call the workers (from taxi drivers to shop-keepers), was a strong influence on my writing.

Part 6   Great Man

Chapter 1   Full Speed Ahead

The opening description of Deng Xiaoping's journey to the south is based on details gathered from various books and articles.

Ezra Vogel's *Deng Xiaoping and the Transformation of China* and Zhao Ziyang's *Prisoner of the State: The Secret Journal of Premier Zhao Ziyang* (see above) are important sources.

The story of the special economic zones and of China's wider urbanisation is covered by many. Having spent years observing and analysing it for myself, I most enjoyed Thomas Campanella's *The Concrete Dragon: China's Urban Revolution and What It Means for the World* (Princeton Architectural Press, 2011).

The best description of the transformations of a village in southern China during this period is in the wonderful *Chen Village – Revolution to Globalisation,* by Anita Chan, Richard Madsen and Jonathan Unger (University of California Press, 2009). The story of the transformation of rural China is well told by Ezra Vogel in his biography of Deng Xiaoping. The work of the PLA is widely recorded; additional insights come from my own dialogues with Chinese property developers who had built their fortunes in Shenzhen (and become dedicated Buddhists). During my early years in China, I also spent a lot of time working with early Chinese financial institutions, and international development agencies, on projects spread across the country; I visited many towns and villages which were being swept up in the change, both exploring, in professional detail, the mechanisms of that change, and listening to many stories not only of the present but the past. I experienced, first hand through many conversations, the dream that snow might fall in summer.

He Qinglian's *The Pitfalls of Modernisation* was first published in Hong Kong (Mirror Books, 1997; China Today Publishing House, 1998) and then (in a revised text) in China, where it sold over 100,000 copies. The preface to *China's Descent into a Quagmire: The Political Economy of the Transition Era in China* has been translated into English (transl. Nancy Yang Liu and Lawrence R Sullivan, Chinese Economy, Vol. 34, 2001). Translations of some of He's articles can be found at www.hqlenglish.blogspot.com. The New York based *Epoch Times* (avowedly 'anti-Communist') also carries English language articles by He Qinglian (www.theepochtimes.com/n3/author/he-qinglian).

There is a vast literature about the economics of China's change. The best works are written by those who understand that the economics are inseparable from the politics on which everything is based. Important works include Barry Naughton's *The Chinese Economy: Transitions and Growth* (MIT Press, 2007), Minxin Pei's *China's Trapped Transition: The Limits of Developmental Autocracy* (Harvard UP, 2006), and Cheng Li's *China's Emerging Middle Class, Beyond Economic Transformation* (Brookings Institute, 2010). The book that I found most helpful in retracing the chronology of events and ideas of this period was Joe Fewsmith's *China Since Tiananmen: From Deng Xiaoping to Hu Jintao* (Cambridge UP, 2008). On the complexity of the human issues, see the excellent essays in *One China, Many Paths* (ed. Chaohua Wang; Verso, 2003).

The idea of *gao suzhi* is rooted in Confucius' belief in the importance of self-cultivation and in the importance of calling things by their proper name (known as the 'rectification of names'). It acquired a 20th century importance with questions of *minzu* minorities, and with the introduction of the one-child policy and a rising concern that attention should be given not just to the number of the people but their quality. There are many wonderful academic articles on gao suzhi; see, for example, Ann Anagnost's *The Corporeal Politics of Quality (Suzhi)* (Public Culture, Vol. 16, 2004) and Andrew Kipnis' *Suzhi: A Keyword Approach* (China Quarterly, 2006). Yinghong Cheng's *Creating the "New Man", From Enlightenment Ideals to Socialist Realities* (University of Hawai'i Press, 2009) provides a powerful perspective.

The story and significance of the Patriotic Education Campaign is well described by Zheng Wang in *Never Forget National Humiliation, Historical Memory in Chinese Politics and Foreign Relations* (Columbia UP, 2012).

The story of the Falun Gong is told by David Ownby in *Falun Gong and the Future of China* (Oxford UP, 2008).

The first years of Hu Jintao's rule (including the Party's management of SARS) are described by Willy Wo-Lap Lam in *Chinese Politics in the Hu Jintao Era: New Leaders, New Challenges* (M. E. Sharpe, 2006). Hu Jintao's reference to people at the root of any power is a reference to the writings of Mencius (329 – 289 BCE) in *Mencius* (transl. D C Lau, Penguin Classics, 2004).

Li Changping's letter to Zhu Rongji was first published by the brave Chinese newspaper *Southern Weekend* in 2000 (August 24); it then became the inspiration for his book *I Spoke the Truth to the Premier* (Chinese language, Guangming Daily Publishing House, 2002). *The Investigation into the Lives of Chinese Peasants* (the work of Chen Guidi and Wu Chuntao) was published in English as *Will the Boat Sink the Water? The Life of China's Peasants* (transl. Zhu Hong, Public Affairs, 2006).

There are many academic accounts of the technical changes to the cities. See, for example, the essays contained in *China's Emerging Cities* (ed. Wu Fulong, Routledge, 2007). For a fast paced account of the changes across city and countryside alike, see Jonathan Fenby's *Tiger Head, Snake Tails: China Today, How it Got There and Where It Is Heading* (Overlook, 2013). See also *Chinese Politics, State, Society and the Market* (eds Gries and Rosen; Routledge, 2010).

Chapter 2   Nature's Trails

Many different sources were consulted for the story of Banqiao's flood, including Dai Qing's Yangzi, Yangzi (see below).

The ancient story of China's environment is best told by Mark Elvin's *Retreat of the Elephants* (Yale UP, 2006).

Mao's battles are wonderfully described by Judith Shapiro in *Mao's War Against Nature, Politics and the Environment in Revolutionary China* (Cambridge UP, 2001).

On the Cold War story of the US, the USSR and China see Gordon Chang's *Friends and Enemies: The United States, China, and the Soviet Union, 1948 – 1972* (Stanford UP, 1990). An account of the Third Front is given by Barry Naughton in *The Third Front: Defence Industrialisation in the Chinese Interior* (China Quarterly, 1988).

The story of the one-child policy is well told in Susan Greenhalgh's *Planned Births, Unplanned Persons* (American Ethnologist, Vol. 30, 2003). An important account of the combination of population and environmental stress is provided by Qu Geping and Li Jinchang in *Population & the Environment in China* (ed. Robert Boardman, transl. Jiang Baozhong and Gu Ran, Lynne Rienner Publishers, 1994).

Early and important accounts of China's environmental crisis can be found in Vaclav Smil's *The Bad Earth: Environmental Degradation in China* (M.E. Sharpe, 1984) and Elizabeth Economy's *The River Runs Black: The Environmental Challenge to China's Future* (Cornell UP, 2004). The story of the industrial destruction of the countryside is very well told by Bryan Tilt in *The Struggle for Sustainability in Rural China: Environmental Values and Civil Society* (Columbia UP, 2010). It is also described by Bill Hinton in *The Great Reversal: The Privatisation of China, 1978 – 1989* (Monthly Review Press, 1990).

The human perspective is probably best recounted by China's novelists. For a sense of the extremes to which officials pushed their villages in efforts to keep up with the modernising winds from Beijing, see the fictional account of Liven village, in Yan Liangke's *Lenin's Kisses* (Grove Press, 2013). For an account of the human costs of the environmental devastation, see Yan Liangke's *Dream of Ding Village* (Grove Press, 2011). For an academic account based on field work, see Anna Lora-Wainwright's *Fighting for Breath: Living Morally and Dying of Cancer in a Chinese Village* (University of Hawai'i Press, 2013).

Dai Qing's 'homework' for the National People's Congress was initially bound and published in China; it was then banned in the mainland and subsequently published in Hong Kong and Taiwan with an English language edition entitled *Yangtze! Yangtze! Debate Over the Three Gorges Project* (transl. Nancy Liu et al, eds Patricia Adams and John Thibodeau, Earthscan, 1994). The subsequent story of the Three Gorges Dam, including a description of its risks, is told by Dai Qing in *The River Dragon Has Come!* (eds John Thibodeau and Philip Williams, transl. Ming Yi, M.E. Sharpe, 1998). For the story of a village that was resettled, see Jun Jing's excellent work, *The Temple of Memories, History, Power and Morality in a Chinese Village* (Stanford UP, 1996). See also Jia Zhangke's film *Still Life* (2006).

For a perspective on China's cities and the consumption of resources, see John Fernandez' *Resource Consumption of New Urban Construction in China* (Journal of Industrial Economy, Vol. 11, 2007). For a perspective on Beijing's present-day pollution, see Chai Jing's *Under the Dome* (February 28, 2015, watched over 150 million times in the first 3 days, then banned in China; it can still be found on YouTube through individual posts).

Overall, perhaps the most comprehensive and readable account of China's environmental devastation is Jonathan Watts' *When a Billion Chinese Jump* (Faber & Faber, 2010). For a picture book of China's natural world, see *Wild China, Natural Wonders of the World's Most Enigmatic Lands* (Yale UP, 2008).

Chapter 3   The Edges of Order

The protests described at the end of the opening paragraphs are those of March 2008.

The ideas of the civilised and the wild are well described in Roland Stoerckx's *The Animal and the Daemon in Early China* (see above).

The story of the Qing's expansion of China, and of their encounters with the tribes are well described by Pamela Crossley in *A Translucent Mirror: History and Identity in Qing Imperial Ideology* (University of California Press, 1999). See also *Empire at the Margins, Culture, Ethnicity, and Frontier in Early Modern China* (eds Pamela Crossley, Helen Siu, Donald Sutton; University of California Press, 2006). On the Manju embrace of the tribes, see Laura Hostetler's *Qing Colonial Enterprise, Ethnography and Cartography in Early Modern China* (University of Chicago Press, 2001). The story of earlier imperial encounters is told in *Cultural Encounters on China's Ethnic Frontiers* (ed. Stevan Harrell; University of Washington Press, 1995). The ancient and enduring impact of the northern nomads on China's worldview is well covered in Nicola Di Cosmo's *Ancient China and Its Enemies, The Rise of Nomadic Power in East Asian History* (Cambridge UP, 2002).

The very important story of how the Manju Qing forged an empire which became present-day China is told by Joseph Esherick in *How the Qing Became China* (eds Esherick, Kayali and Young; Rowman & Littlefield, 2006). For a description of the ancient unification of the Shu, the Ba and the Chu, whose lands became present-day Sichuan, see Steven F. Sage, *Ancient Sichuan and the Unification of China* (SUNY, 1992).

The racial complications of independence are fascinatingly described by Steven Platt in *Provincial Patriots: The Hunanese and Modern China* (see above). The most important work on the subject of race is Frank Dikotter's *The Discourse of Race in Modern China* (Hurst & Company, 1992).

The story of the Long March and its encounters with the wilder Chinese world is well told by Sun Shuyun *The Long March* and is included in Jung Chang and Jon Halliday's *Mao: The Unknown Story* (for both, see above).

The Party's attempts to sort out the question of the *minzu* minorities is well told by Thomas Mullaney in *Coming to Terms with the Nation: Ethnic Classification in Modern China* (University of California Press, 2011). For an example of an imperial picture book, see *The Art of Ethnography, A Chinese "Miao Album"* (transl. David Deal, Laura Hostetler and Charles McKhann, University of Washington Press, 2006). Colin Mackerras offers a good overview of the challenges (past and present) in *China's Ethinic Minorities and Globalisation* (RoutledgeCurzon, 2003).

The story of the Mongols' pursuit of independence (and its impact on Inner Mongolia) is told by Liu Xiaoyuan in *Reins of Liberation: An Entangled History of Mongolian Independence, Chinese Territoriality, and Great Power Hegemony, 1911 – 1950* (Stanford UP, 2006)

Every aspect of the story of Tibet (including Francis Younghusband's maxim guns) is masterfully recounted by Sam Shaik in *Tibet, A History* (Yale UP, 2013). Charles Bell's early 20th century account of Tibet is a classic (Oxford Clarendon Press, 1928). Xinran's moving novel *Sky Burial: An Epic Love Story of Tibet* (Vintage, 2005) is an attempt to find a path to peace.

The story of China's Muslim World is wonderfully described (and illustrated) by M.A. Aldrich and Lukas Nikol in *The Perfumed Palace, Islam's Journey from Mecca to Peking*, Garnet Publishing, 2010. The late 20th century story of the lands to the west is well told by A. Doak Barnett in *China's Far West: Four Decades of Change* (Westview Press, 1993). See also Jonathan Lipman's *Familiar Strangers: A History of Muslims in Northwest China* (University of Washington Press, 1998). The story of the Muslims' battle for independence is told by Dru Gladney in *Muslim Chinese, Ethnic Nationalism in the People's Republic* (Harvard UP, 1991).

The story of Inner Mongolia is told by Uradyn Bulag in *The Mongols at China's Edge: History and the Politics of National Unity* (Rowman and Littlefield, 2002). The story of Inner Mongolia's Cultural Revolution is told by Kerry Brown in *The Purge of the Inner Mongolian People's Party in the Chinese Cultural Revolution, 1967 – 69, A Function of Language, Power and Violence* (Global Oriental, 2006). The story of the grasslands is best told by Jiang Rong in the novel *Wolf Totem* (the pen-name of Lu Jiamin, who based the novel on his own personal experience; first published in China in 2004 where it became a best-seller; transl. Howard Goldblatt, Penguin, 2009).

There are a number of specialist books which tell the stories of the many southern minorities. See Erik Mueggler's *The Age of Wild Ghosts: Memory, Violence, and Place in Southwest China* (University of California Press, 2001), *Perspectives on the Yi of Southwest China* (ed. Stevan Harrell; University of California Press, 2001) and Nicholas Tapp's *The Hmong of*

China: Context, Agency, and the Imaginary (Brill, 2002). It is Tapp who tells the story of etchings on the Sichuan cliffs, and of the two brothers and their book. See also Louisa Schein's *Minority Rules: The Miao and the Feminine in China's Cultural Policies* (Duke University Press, 2000); it is Schein who tells the story of the Chinese Miao scholar who unearthed the origins of the Miao.

Rebiya Kadeer tells her story in *Dragon Fighter: One Woman's Epic Struggle for Peace with China* (with Alexandra Cavelius; Kales Press, 2009)

For an account of a journey through China and to the edges of its order, see Ma Jian's *Red Dust, A Path Through China* (transl. Flora Drew, Vintage Books, 2002).

For a powerful exploration of the relationship between China and Tibet, see the conversation between Wang Lixiong and Tsering Shakya in *The Struggle for Tibet* (Verso, 2009). Ian Johnson's interview with Wang Lixiong and his wife, the Tibetan poetess Woeser, can be found in The New York Review of Books, August 7 and 8, 2014.

Part 7   How Many Suns?

Chapter 1   The Heavenly Party

The opening account of the journey to the Great Hall of the People is based on whispers circulating in Beijing at the time, including an inner architectural insight shared by Richard Spencer.

The full text of the *Great Chant on Observing Weiqi* can be found in Zuyan Chen's article (see above).

The stories of Bo Xilai and Xi Jinping draw heavily on John Garnaut's *The Rise and Fall of the House of Bo* (Penguin, 2012) and the work of the South China Morning Post brought together in *The China Renaissance, The Rise of Xi Jinping and the 18th Communist Party Congress* (ed. Jonathan Sharp, South China Morning Post, 2013). More recently, see Evan Osnos' excellent *Born Red: How Xi Jinping, an unremarkable provincial administrator, became China's most authoritarian leader since Mao* (The New Yorker, April 6, 2015).

For an insight into Party scandals, see Chen Fang's novel *Wrath of Heaven: Scandal at the Top in China* (in Chinese, subtitled *The Anticorruption Bureau in Action*; Edko Publishing, 2000); the novel is based on the scandal which brought down Chen Xitong, one-time mayor of Beijing and head of a 'Beijing clique' who fell foul of Jiang Zemin and his 'Shanghai Clique'.

The Party is very well described in Richard McGregor's *The Party: The Secret World of China's Communist Rulers*. Frank Pieke provides excellent detail both generally and on the Party school in *The Good Communist: Elite Training and State Building in Today's China* (Cambridge UP, 2009).

David Shambaugh follows the challenges and rise of the Party in *China's Communist Party, Atrophy and Adaptation* (University of California Press, 2008).

The lead-up to the change of power in 2012 had a huge impact on life in Beijing, highly visible in the restaurants of the city and the frenzied schedules of those expecting promotions (or expected to support the bids for promotion). The speculation about the left or right outcome was the intense subject of everyone's conversations, and Wechat, for over a year. Wen Jiabao's observations on the risks facing the Party were publicly made, and publicly reported by the world's press (see for example Tania Branigan's *China needs political reform to avert historical tragedy, says Wen Jiabao*, The Guardian, March 14, 2012; and Jamil Anderlini's *Wen attacks party conservatives*, March 14, 2012, The Financial Times).

On the philosophy of the past as it influences the Party, see Tongdong Bai's wonderfully succinct *Political Philosophy of the Middle Kingdom* (see above).

The work of the Party's Propaganda Department (and the influence of Western ideas and technology) is well described by Anne-Marie Brady in *Marketing Dictatorship, Propaganda and Thought Work in Contemporary China* (Rowman & Littlefield, 2008). Yinghong Cheng's *Creating the "New Man"* (see above) is worth referring to again in this context. On *gao suzhi* high quality people, see the articles referred to above.

China's increasing attention to foreign policy and its rising nationalism are addressed in Zheng Wang's *Never Forget National Humiliation* (Columbia University Press, 2012) and William Callahan's *China, The Pessoptimist Nation* (Oxford UP, 2010). China's strategic choices are interestingly explored by Edward Luttwak in *The Rise of China vs. the Logic of Strategy* (Harvard UP, 2012). *Chinese Nationalism* (eds Jonathan Unger and Geremie Barmé; M.E. Sharpe, 1996) brings together a collection of essays which provide important context.

Chapter 2   Earth Below

Many sources were consulted for the account of the events in Wukan. These included contemporary news reports and documentary films; see *Wukan: After the Uprising* (AlJazeera, 2013).

On land disputes, see Eva Pils' excellent *Land Disputes, Rights Assertion, And Social Unrest in China: A Case from Sichuan* (Columbia Journal of Asian Law, 2006). On stability maintenance, see He Qinglian's *Stability Maintenance and China* www.hqlenglish.blogspot.com/2013/07/stability-maintenance-and-china. On village elections, see Kerry Brown's wonderful *Ballot Box China, Grassroots Democracy in the Final Major One-Party State* (Zed Books, 2011). The issue of a voice for the peasants goes back to the earliest days of the Party.

On the train journeys of peasant migrants, see Lixin Fan's documentary, *Last Train Home* (2009).The challenges of China's labourers are explored in *China's Peasants and Workers: Changing Class Identities* (ed. Beatriz Carrillo and David S.G. Goodman (Edward Elgar Publishing, 2012). Conditions in China's factories are described by many: see Leslie Chang's *Factory Girls: Voices from the Heart of Modern China* (Picador, 2008); also see *Factory Towns of South China: An Illustrated Guidebook* (Hong Kong UP, 2012). For an insight into China's great transformation, see Jia Zhangke's documentaries: *The Hometown Trilogy* (1997 – 2002).

There are many excellent academic articles about China's protest leaders, peasant lawyers and their battles for justice. These include Benjamin Liebman's *Class Action Litigation in China* (Harvard Law Review, Vol. 111, 1998), Ethan Michelson's *Climbing the Dispute Pagoda: Grievances and Appeals to the Official Justice System in Rural China* (American Sociological Review, Vol. 72, 2007), Liangjiang Li and Kevin O'Brian's *Protest Leadership in Rural China* (China Quarterly, Vol. 193, 2008), and Carl Minzner's *Riots and Cover-ups: Counterproductive Control of Local Agents in China* (University of Pennsylvania Journal of International Law, 2009).

The challenges facing 'low quality peasants' are well described by Rachel Murphy in *Turning Peasants into Modern Chinese Citizens: "Population Quality" Discourse, Demographic Transition and Primary Education* (China Quarterly, 2004). For an excellent account of the challenges facing China's rural migrants, see Hsiao-Hung Pai's *Scattered Sand: The Story of China's Rural Migrants* (Verso, 2012). For the daily extraordinary in rural (and urban) China, see ChinaSmack (www.chinasmack.com). On the question of *hukou* see Fei-ling Wang's *Conflict, resistance and the transformation of the hukou system* in *Chinese Society: change, conflict and resistance* (ed. Elizabeth Perry and Mark Selden; Routledge 2010)

On city education and *gao suzhi*, see Carolyn Hsu's *The city in the school and the school in the city: ideology, imagery, and institutions in Maoist and market socialist China* (Visual Studies, Vol. 23, 2008). Also see Amy Chua's *Battle Hymn of the Tiger Mother* (Bloomsbury, 2012) which offers a sense of the power of the best-selling Chinese language *Harvard Girl Liu Yiting: A Character in Training* (Writers Publishing House, 2000), a book that sold 1.5 m copies in its first 16 months. See also Gary Sigley's *Suzhi, the Body and the Fortunes of Technoscientific Reasoning in Contemporary China*, Luigi Tomba's *Of Quality, Harmony and Community: Civilisation and the Middle Class in Urban China*, and T. E. Woronov Governing *China's Children: Governmentality and "Education for Quality"* (all: Positions, Vol. 17, 2009) and Andrew Kipnis' *Subjectification and Education for Quality* (China, Economy and Society Vol. 40, 2011).

On life in the city, see Li Zhang's *Strangers in the City: Reconfigurations ^f Space, Power and Social Networks within China's Floating Population*

(Stanford UP, 2001), also see *In and Beyond the Headlines* (eds Timothy West and Lionel Jensen; Rowman & Littlefield, 2012). On change, see John Gittings' *The Changing Face of China: From Mao to Market* (Penguin, 2006) and *Chinese Characters: Profiles of Fast-Changing Lives in a Fast-Changing Land* (eds Angilee Shah and Jeffrey Wasserstrom; University of California Press, 2012). For a novel's perspective, see Xiaolu Guo's *Village of Stone* (Vintage, 2005). On the stresses of life in the city, see Emily Ng's *Heartache of the State, Enemy of the Self: Bipolar Disorder and Cultural Change in Urban China* (Culture Medicine and Psychiatry, Vol. 33, 2009) and note the reports of the China Sleep Research Society, which puts Beijing at the top of its sleeplessness ranking.

On urban civil society, see David Kelly's *Citizens' Movements and China's Public Intellectuals in the Hu-Wen Era* (Pacific Affairs, Vol. 79, 2006). On urban heroes, see Philip Pan's *Out of Mao's Shadow: The Struggle for the Soul of a New China* (Simon & Schuster, 2008).

On the idea of the global city, see Saskia Sassen's *The Global City: New York, London, Tokyo* (Princeton UP, 1991); see also Ian Cook's *Beijing as an internationalized metropolis* in *Globalisation and the Chinese City* (ed. Wu Fulong, Routledge, 2006).

My description of residents committees and village committees is based on personal experience as a resident of both a gated compound and a village, and on the experiences of friends, including friends who I have, as a lawyer, advised. Similarly, while many of the strolling (and other) protests were reported either in the media or over Wechat, a number of those in Beijing involved friends and colleagues, including friends who are also lawyers and journalists (as did the problems of the ngos). The cat and mouse game of the internet is familiar to almost everyone who lives in Beijing. Many articles have been written about it: see Rebecca Mackinnon's *Flatter World and Thicker Walls? Blogs, censorship and Civil Discourse in China* (Public Discourse, Vol. 134, 2008). One friend had the pleasure of living on the floor below an office of official cyber-surfers, where the lift offered interesting insights into another world.

There are many important works on the role of lawyers; see for example Jerome Cohen's *The Struggle for Autonomy of Beijing's Public Interest Lawyers,* in *Human Rights in China* (www.hrichina.org/en/content/3692). For an excellent description of China's legal system, including the socialist rule of law and model judges, see Carl Minzner's *China's Turn Against the Law* (American Journal of Comparative Law, 2011). On the challenges of being a journalist under Hu Jintao, see David Bandurski's *Jousting with Monsters: Journalists in a Rapidly Changing China* in *China In and Beyond the Headlines* (above). Being a journalist has become a lot more difficult since then. The rages of the people can be found at ChinaSmack (see above).

On the wider importance of Wukan's protests, the loss of trust and the rise of shadow brotherhoods, see John Lagerkvist, *The Wukan Uprising and Chinese State-Society Relations: Toward "Shadow Civil Society"?* (International Journal of China Studies, Vol. 3, 2012) and Kevin Hand's *Constitutionalising Wukan: The Value of the Constitution Outside the Courtroom* (China Brief, Vol. XII, 2012). See also Minxin Pei's *Trapped Transition* (see above).

Chapter 3   Being Chinese

An account of life in a Chinese prison can be found in Jiang Qisheng's *My Life in Prison, Memoirs of a Chinese Political Dissident* (transl. James Dew, Rowman & Littlefield, 2012) and Liao Yiwu's *For a Song and a Hundred Songs, A Poet's Journey Through A Chinese Prison* (transl. Wenguang Huang, Houghton Mifflin Harcourt, 2013). At the time of writing, Liu Xiaobo is in Jinzhou Prison, Liaoning.

There are many descriptions of the events of June Fourth. My account is based on discussions with journalists and diplomats who were there at the time and subsequently 'investigated things' on the ground. For a poet's truth (and a first hand recollection), see Liu Xiaobo's *June Fourth Elegies* (Jonathan Cape, 2012). For the declaration of the hunger-striking friends, see *Tiananmen Square Hunger Strike Declaration* (World Affairs, Vol. 152, 1989-1990). On Hou Dejian's story, see Linda Jaivin's *The Monkey and the Dragon: A True Story About Friendship, Music, Politics and Life on the Edge* (Text Publishing, 2001). On the impact of Tiananmen, see Louisa Lim's *The People's Republic of Amnesia* (Oxford UP, 2014).

Liao Yiwu's *Interviews with People from the Bottom of Society* can be found in an abridged form in *The Corpse Walker: Real Life Stories, China from the Bottom Up* (Anchor Books, 2009). On the challenges of being an author in China, see the acceptance speech of one of China's most widely read authors, Murong Xuecun (pen name) for the 2010 People's Literature Prize (11 November 2011; reported in the New York Times, 29 March 2012).

Yang Jisheng's *Tombstone* is available in English (see above). Heavily researched, it is the abridgement of an original 2 volume (1,208) page account. The most vocal of the parents looking for truth are the members of the group Tiananmen Mothers. Yuan Weishi's article was entitled *Modernisation and History Textbooks* (published by *Bingdian*, Freezing Point, January 11, 2006). On the world of China's intellectuals of the time, see Geremie Barmé's *In The Red: On the Contemporary Chinese Culture*, Columbia University Press, 1999.

Wang Lixiong founded China's first environmental ngo, Friends of Nature, with Liang Qichao's grandson (Liang Sicheng's son) Liang Congjie. His thoughts on Tibet (including the *Twelve Suggestions*) are set out in *The Struggle for Tibet* (see above); his thoughts on elections are set out in

Dissolving Power: A Successive Multi-Level Electoral System (published in China in 1994); his thoughts on Xinjiang were set out in *My West China, Your East Turkestan* (published in China, 2007).

For Liu Xiaobo's own voice, see the selection of essays and poems compiled by Perry Link and others in *No Enemies, No Hatred: Selected Essays and Poems* (Harvard UP, 2012). For an important biography of Liu Xiaobo, see Yu Jie's *Steel Gate to Freedom: The Life of Liu Xiaobo* (Rowman & Littlefield, September 1, 2015); Yu Jie is a Chengdu-born writer and activist who emigrated to the US in 2012 after years of threats, torture and a year of house arrest – he is well known for his 1998 essays *Fire and Ice*, which pointed to the calendars that celebrate May Fourth (1919) and asked people to look again at the banners of the day. On Charter 08, see Jean-Philippe Beja, Fu Hualing and Eva Pils' *Charter 08 and the Challenges of Political Reform in China* (Hong Kong UP, 2012) – and on the crime of state subversion, see Chapter 13 (*The Political Meaning of the Crime of "Subverting State Power"*) written by Teng Biao, one of China's most respected 'weiquan' ('rights protection') lawyers, a term used to describe lawyers committed to defending the civil rights of the people. At the time of writing, Teng Biao is in the US, a visiting fellow at the Harvard Law School.

On Ai Weiwei, see the documentary *Never Sorry* (Alison Klayman, 2012) and his own video clips. On Ai Weiwei's journey to Tan's hearing, including the under-the-blanket recording of the hotel beating, see Ai Weiwei, *Lao Ma Ti Hua* (www.youtube.com/watch?v=TUizD8WDDFI). The temple referred to by Tan Zuoren's lawyers is Wuhou Temple (Chengdu).

For Ai Weiwei's crab banquet, see Ai Weiwei / River Crab Feast @ Shanghai Studio on Vimeo (2010). On his internment, see Barnaby Martin's *Hanging Man: The Arrest of Ai Weiwei* (Faber & Faber, 2013) and Howard Brenton's play of the same name.

On censorship in China, see Perry Link's *The Anaconda in the Chandelier* (The New York Review of Books, April 11, 2002). On the rising arrests of China's intellectuals, see Evan Osnos' *Born Red* (see above). On the impact of the Party's controls, see Perry Link's *China After Tiananmen: Money, Yes; Ideas, No* (The New York Review of Books, March 31, 2014 On the Party's idea of 'the intellectual', see Eddy U's *Rectification of the Chinese Intellectual: On the Origins of the CCP Concept of Zhishifenzi* (Modern China, Vol. 35, 2009). On China's exiles, see Rowena Xiaoqing He's *Tiananmen Exiles, Voices of the Struggle for Democracy in China* (Palgrave Macmillan, 2014).

Chan Koonchung's *The Fat Years* (first published by Oxford UP Hong Kong and the Rye Field Publishing Company, both 2009; transl. Michael Duke and with an excellent preface by Julia Lovell, Doubleday, 2011). Chan describes his book in *Chinese Author: 'My Book Was Banned in My Home Country'*, www.huffingtonpost.com/chan-koonchung/book-banned-china).

On the importance of the rule of law, see Carl Minzners' *How China's*

Leaders Will Rule on the Law (Chinafile, October 15, 2014) and the subsequent conversation of some of the most experienced foreign China lawyers: *Rule of Law – Why Now?* Ira Belkin, Don Clarke, Jerry Cohen et al (Chinafile, October 17, 2014). For thoughtful reflections on why China continues to battle over the idea of order, see Wang Hui's *The End of the Revolution: China and the Limits of Modernity* (Verso, 2011) and Joseph Fewsmith's *The Logic and Limits of Political Reform in China* (Cambridge UP, 2013). On the problems of crossing the river by feeling for stones (also known as 'gradualism'), see Minxin Pei, *China's Trapped Transition*: the limits of developmental autocracy (see above). For an insight into the many different voices in China, see Evan Osnos' *Age of Ambition: Chasing Fortune, Truth and Faith in the New China* (Farrar, Strauss and Giroux, 2014).

Conclusion Dreaming

For a wonderfully thorough description of the *Da Tong* Great Unity ideal, see Albert Chen's *The Concept of 'Datong' in Chinese Philosophy as an Expression of the Idea of the Common Good* (Hong Kong University Faculty of Law Research Paper No. 2011/020; accessible at www.ssrn.com/link/U-Hong-Kong-LEG).

On the Dalai Lama's idea of Tibet as a Zone of Peace (part of a Five Point Peace Plan presented in an address to the US Congressional Human Rights Caucus, September 21, 1987), see www.dalailama.com/messages/tibet/five-point-peace-plan.

On 'Democracy is a good thing', see Yu Keping's *Democracy Is a Good Thing: Essays on Politics, Society, and Culture in Contemporary China* (Brookings Institution Press, 2011).